KINESICS:

The Power of Silent Command

KINESICS:

The Power of Silent Command

Merlyn Cundiff

Parker Publishing Company, Inc.
West Nyack, N. Y.

What This Book Can Do for You

In the next few minutes you are going to start to discover the secret of Silent Command — a secret so startling that it may change your life forever. You are about to learn how to unleash a titanic force that now sleeps within you — the force of KINESICS!

Actually, KINESICS is the oldest form of communication known to man. It is used by animals, birds, fish — even certain plants. And once you learn how it works, you can put this secret to work for you to achieve all the power, wealth, influence, and control over people you've ever wanted.

All of this is possible through a series of recent discoveries by America's greatest mind scientists. They have probed, tested, experimented, and studied this phenomenon for many years. Some have called it "body language" . . . others refer to it as "non-verbal communication" . . . "body communication" . . . "kinesics" . . . "persuasive communication" . . . and by many similar terms. All of these terms are identical, and I have used them interchangeably throughout this book.

The Secret of Silent Command

Once you have mastered the simple techniques of KINESICS . . . once you discover how to read people like a book, to know what they are thinking without their saying a word . . . you are ready for the next step: SILENT COMMAND.

Simply by standing or sitting in a certain way, by moving certain parts of your body in subtle ways, or by the other methods described in this book, you will find that you can project unspoken orders that must be obeyed.

"Does this power really exist?" you ask. And the answer is startling almost beyond belief. Not only does this power exist — but certain people are using it right now to win vast rewards and influence others. Perhaps someone is even using it to control YOU. Now the time has come to turn the tables!

This Book a Road Map to Your Goal

The purpose of this book is to show you the way . . . to give you a "psychic road map" that will guide you from where you are now to where you want to be . . . to bridge the gap between what you have and what you want.

In order to do this, you need only learn a few simple rules . . . some easily-mastered basic techniques . . . and find out when and how to apply them. There's no need to spend long hours doing this — if you are willing to spend just five minutes a day, the power of Silent Command can be yours.

Why Kinesics Must Work a Miracle for You

Kinesics is guaranteed to work for you — and so is Silent Command. Why? Because they have already worked for thousands of men and women in all walks of life. These men and women are no richer, no smarter, no better-educated than you are — but they all have one thing in common: a burning desire to better themselves. If — like them — you're not satisfied with just "half a loaf" . . . if — like them — you want the expensive clothes; the big, high-priced new cars; the fine mansion in the country; and scores of other luxuries you've been denied too long . . . then this book is for you.

Why should others enjoy the pleasures of life: the adventure of foreign travel, the thrill of leadership, the close friendship of attractive members of the opposite sex, the respect and admiration of everyone you meet, and all the other beautiful things you want . . . while you stand aside and eat your heart out? You deserve a full, heaping share of these golden blessings — and, if you follow the techniques I am shortly going to reveal, you will receive them ten times over!

The Simple . . . Easy . . . Fast Way to What You Want

Before I do, however, there are a few things you must understand. First, these techniques are simple to use. You do not need any special training or advanced education to use them. They have been tried by everyone from grade-school dropouts to college presidents, and have worked just as well for all.

Second, these techniques are easy to use. They require no equipment of any kind, except perhaps a pencil and paper, in some cases, to record your discoveries. Of course, if you have other equipment, you can certainly use it. A tape recorder may be handy for helping you pick up the techniques of Kinesics faster, for example. But I want to emphasize that you don't *need* such devices. All you need is a sincere desire to improve your life.

Third, these techniques work rapidly once you start to use them. In just a few minutes, you can see the innermost thoughts and desires of everyone you come in contact with, just as if they were written in indelible ink on their foreheads. You don't have to *guess* what others think about you, you *know*. You don't have to *wonder* what they really want from you, you *know*. And you don't have to *hope* you'll say the right thing every time, you *know*. You can't fail — because no one can have any secrets from you!

Some Amazing Results of "Silent Command"

In this book, you'll see how:

- A 73-year old woman used the secret of Silent Command to close a sale for $18,000,000.00.

- The movement of a spoon for two inches turned hostility between a man and a woman into a friendly, relaxed situation.
- A speaker took off his eyeglasses, and made his audience go wild with applause.
- A professor's "hot button" was pressed, and he immediately expressed his feelings with great passion.
- A doctor who "radiates" a certain attitude can become the leading doctor in his city.
- A man invites a beautiful woman to join him without saying a word.
  ... and many other instances of how KINESICS and the power of Silent Command worked miracles in the lives of executives, housewives, salesmen, teachers, secretaries, lovers, and other people in every rank of life.

Now — The Amazing Power of Silent Command Is Yours!

This has been the barest outline of what KINESICS and the power of Silent Command are, and how they can help you. In the pages that follow I am going to go into these things in detail, step by step, so that you will become master of these techniques from A to Z.

Some of these techniques may sound strange to you at first — but all I ask is that you read them and try them with an open mind. Once you see the wonderful results — how others do what you want them to, without your uttering a word — how loved ones come to you without your having to ask — how others start to do unexpected favors for you — and how you begin to command the esteem of friends, family, and fellow-workers almost overnight — then you will finally be convinced.

The Lifetime Plan for Silent Command Power Development

This book presents what is, in effect, a lifelong plan for the development of your Silent Command power — a plan that strengthens and increases your power over others year after year. It gives you what amounts to an invisible "leash" to lead others with ... a "psychic whip" that makes others obey you or suffer the consequences. Yet the methods you use are completely honest and ethical, and in no way violate anyone's religious or moral beliefs.

This new power is about to surge into your life. It will change things for the better for you, once and for all. It will shatter the walls that now hem you in, and guide you to some of the most exciting, pleasurable and rewarding experiences of your life.

There is but one word in the Book of Destiny. That word is "NOW!"

Merlyn Cundiff

Table of Contents

The Secret of Kinesics (cont.)

Kinesics Reveals Local Customs • Body Contact • Kinesics Is an Honest Revelation • What Pupil Widening Means • Painting the Face from the Inside • Pantomiming • Entire Scene in Body Communication • Masked Faces • Like an Old Shoe • A Costume Party • Dropping the Mask • Why Remove the Mask? • Table Positions and Silent Command • Kinesics of a Round Table • Who Picks Up the Tab? • Body Communication Speaks Constantly

How to Read People's Minds with Body Language • The Moment of Truth — How to Spot It • When to Use Silent Command • A Kinesics Technique worth $18,000,-000.00 • What Folded Arms Mean • He Wouldn't Ask Me • The King's Protector • What Eyes Reveal • Don't Ignore Shoulders • What Posture Tells You • How to Feel More Confident • How to Listen to Complex Body Language • Avoiding Offense • How to Notice the Small Body Whispers • Hands Over Eyes • Slapping One's Forehead • Fingers Together • Public Kinesics • Drumming Fingers • Foot Signals • Change of Position • Watch for Body Communication

The Territorial Need • Law Recognizes Its Sanctity • Sanctity of Space Transfer • Space Encroachment • The Spoon Episode • A Fascinating Experiment • The Mental Satisfaction of Space • The Deepest Human Need • Please Keep Your Distance • Mental Halitosis • The Privacy Zone • How Distance Communicates Respect • The Appearance of Intimacy • The Big-Top Table • Violating Zone Barriers

Reading Others' Minds • Visual Listening Reliable • Verbal Vs. Visual Communication • Convincing Actions • Less Say — More Do • Use This Tested Technique • Why Some People Get Hired and Others Don't • Lis-

How to Listen with Your Eyes (cont.)

tening with Your Subconscious • Your "Sixth Sense" and How to Use It • How to Turn On Your Magic Communicator • 20-20 Communication Vision • Employment Vision • How to Impress an Interviewer • Body Language Is a Two-Way Street • The Casual Friendly Approach • Getting Attention with Gimmicks • Three Miracles of Body Communication • The Invisible Barometer • How to Take Calculated Risks

Your Psychic Road Map • Secret of Structured Thinking • How to Move People to Action • Basic Formula for Action • The Crasher Technique • Basic Selling Technique • The Third Dimension Technique • Selecting the Right Method • The Cundiff 4-Ply System • The First Step • How to Make Others See Things Your Way • The Cloak and Dagger Technique • The Second Step • The Subjective Sale Technique • The Third Step • How to Offer Proof That Convinces • The "Q" Technique • The Fourth Step • How to Ask for Action • Refusal Is Not Rejection • Don't Fear Fear • Built-In Vince Lombardi • How to Overcome Objections Quickly • The Only Action That Counts • Step-by-Step Control Plan • Physical Interview • Mental Interview • Emotional Interview

Take Out Insurance on Good Communication • Case Study • Showing the Entire Picture • How to Increase Understanding • Diminishing Understanding • The Colonel's Command • Garnishing the Story • How to Get the Best Support from Others • Improving Efficiency • How to Add Value • Just a Fragment of the Picture

How to Build Up Others • Convincing Others Without Effort • The Cruelest Thing to Do • Discovery Applies to All Fields • Another Key Principal • How to Communicate Objectively — Not Subjectively • Five Words

The Vital Secret of Silent Command (cont.)

of Power • How to Get the Decision You Want • "Low Pressure" Influencing • Mental Television Broadcasting • How to Make People Pay Attention to You • Controlling the Communication Climate • The Message in the Eyes • The Ego Complex • How to Create Confidence in You

ITA VS. ICA • How a Doctor Becomes Rich • The Miracle That Takes Only a Few Seconds • The Remarkable Sign • This Sign Is Always There • Volcanic Spirits • The Great Idea • The Magic Key That Opens All Doors • A Rare Opportunity • The Masked Men Who Failed • The Ultimate Consumer • Searching the Soul • The Kinesics of the Reception Room • What Does Your Appearance Communicate? • How to Please a Woman • Ready and Willing • The Exalted Look

Secrets of Effective Company Meetings • When to Hold the Meeting • How to Plan the Meeting Strategy • How to Cover the Vital Points • Proper Direction of the Meeting • How to Open the Meeting • How to Maintain Control of the Meeting • Duty of the Chairman • Following Up • Incentive Policies • Training New People • How to Get Maximum Performance • Reviewing and Evaluating Work • What Is the Yardstick in Judging Me? • Making People Feel Involved • How to Fire People Without Bitterness • Giving Instruction Attractively • Examples of Good and Bad Communication • Overworked • Where to Put the Files • Old-Fashioned Method •Not My Responsibility • How Urgent? • I Don't Like the Program • The Six Most Useful Words for Supervisors

How to Introduce a Speaker • Importance of the Subject • Particularly Important to This Audience • Espe-

**How to Handle Specific Situations
with Silent Command (cont.)**

cially Qualified Speaker • A Model Introduction • Pros-
tituting an Introduction • The Rule of Brevity • The
Element of Surprise • Relationship Between Chairman
and Speaker • Platform Kinesics • How to Present a
Trophy or Plaque • Four Points of the Presentation •
Example of Presentation • How to Accept a Trophy or
Plaque • The Use of Exhibits • How to Reveal an Exhibit • Appearance and Disappearance • How to Build
Up the Exhibit's Importance • How to Use Notes • Handling Notes on the Platform • How to Give Prestige to
a Speech • Substitute Mental Notes

On Waking Up • Stoplights and Go-Lights • Starting with
the Right Attitude • Secret of Controlled Excitement •
Take This Simple Test • An Ancient Doctrine • The
Blind Spots • Radiation of Emotions • Understanding
Your Duties • How to Avoid Being a Victim • The Per-
fect "Out". • The Most Effective Tool • An Intriguing
Motivator • Benefits Not Features • The Great Differ-
ence • Appointment Vs. Interview • The Presentation •
Profitable Difficulty • The Blessings of Being Sensitive
• The Twin Factors You Need to Win • Insulation Against
Rejection • Restoration a Necessity • The Only Answer
• Continuous Motivation • The Master Secret

Courtship Signals in Animals and Men • Using the Power
of Sex Communication • Communication by Dress •
Color Communicating • Persuasion Through Odor • Using Eye Communication • The Come-Hither Look • The
"I Am Willing" Stare • The Extent of Intimacy • How
to Make an Appointment with Your Eyes • Communication by Voice Pitch • Body Position • The Language
of Sexual Communication

ONE

Kinesics and Persuasive Communication

Regardless of what else you derive from this book, please master the three primary rules of effective, persuasive communication:

1. Be *simple* in your presentation.
2. *Relate* your presentation to the other person's understanding.
3. Tell stories and give generous "for instance's."

We shall devote a whole chapter to each of these principles. In fact, throughout this entire book we shall refer again and again to these three cardinal rules that insure persuasion and understanding.

Simplicity Is Vital — The Complex and the Important Are Not the Same

Today, too often we confuse the complex with the important. We think that because something is important it also must be presented in a complex manner. We forget the divinity of simplicity.

I once heard someone say that if the safety pin had been invented in this generation no one would use it unless it had six moving parts, two transistors, and required servicing twice a year.

Anyone Can Learn to Communicate

Never forget this truth: Anyone who can talk or write can learn to communicate effectively if he will only follow certain basic principles.

The answer does not lie in any intricate formula; the solution is not contained in any hidden secret. In fact some might feel that the pattern is too obvious to need elaboration, too simple to need an explanation. I would agree completely, except for the fact that so few people follow this simple pattern.

Reduced to the lowest common denominator, persuasive communication is just this simple:

> First, you must know just what you want to say, and
> second, you must say it in a convincing way, which can
> be understood by others.

Because of the utter simplicity of the principle, people fail to realize that they must keep studying its applications. The idea is so simple it seems insignificant.

Many people feel that the art of persuasion can be mastered only by the person who sells a product or service, and that this art is only useful to salespeople. This is certainly not true. Everybody, regardless of what work he does, needs to be persuasive. Unless a person can sell himself through good communications, he will never advance or get ahead in life. No matter what your occupation is, you must learn to communicate in a persuasive way.

A noted industrialist recently made the remark that there is no phase of our economic life more neglected, in the light of its importance, than improving the ability of the average person in business to communicate. In business particularly, ability to communicate is extremely important in passing along the lessons of experience and in preventing mistakes. A teacher I once had would often say, "Don't keep mopping the floor; turn off the faucet!" He then would elaborate on the colossal insanity of spending so much time correcting mistakes that never should have occurred in the first place.

Today we have a whole new philosophy in the medical

field called preventive medicine. In the industrial safety field we have a similar philosophy known as accident prevention. Yes, in every field of endeavor today it is recognized that the only intelligent approach to our problems is found in preventive measures rather than expensive correction after the harm is done.

In no facet of our economic life is this principle more important than in the field of communication. A corporate president recently told me that if his company could only have prevented certain mistakes that never should have been made in the first place, the company's earnings during the past year would have been more than double. But then he went on to give the startling fact that these mistakes did not arise from a lack of company know-how but had their origin in lack of communication.

Good Communication Is the Vehicle of Success

The most valuable ore deposits of this world would lie worthless and unmined if there were no method of bringing them to the smelter. The richest forests would be of little industrial value unless there were facilities to bring the lumber to the mill.

The same principle holds true in communication. Regardless of how well informed you may be on any subject or in any field, unless you can transmit this information to others, it will remain, like the rich deposits of metal in the earth and the valuable lumber in the forest, of no value to anyone.

So let's start with the major premise that we can only bring our wares to market, yes, only cash in on our potentials, through persuasive communication.

How Much Time Do You Spend Communicating?

The average businessman today spends the greater part of his working hours engaged in communication. Salesmen and public relations people spend an even greater part of their time communicating with others. Consider for a moment your own case. Just how important is the art of communication to you?

Why are we so loath to spend the time necessary to prepare ourselves for this important endeavor? Think how much the productivity of our efforts would be increased if we could only improve our communication by ten per cent! The increased results added up over a whole year would be staggering.

Simple Communication Is a Never-Ending Study

Regardless of what line of endeavor a person follows he should always be studying and practicing to be a more persuasive communicator. School is never out for the person who wants to be a professional in making himself felt, heard and understood.

Constant study is important, not only because of the vast never-ending scope of this subject, but also because the meanings of words and phrases are constantly changing. No person can train himself in communicating and then simply stop studying.

A word which has a definite meaning today might suggest something else five years hence and have an entirely different meaning ten years from today. How much meaning do you think the words "jet-propelled," "ecology," "fall-out" or "computerized" would have had to the very best informed person of the twenties?

Communication Conditioning

It is important to realize that it is not enough to know the meaning of words or even to have an academic grasp of certain knowledge.

Until we so completely *condition* ourselves to these words and to this knowledge that we feel comfortable in their use, we cannot profit by such new acquisition to any extent.

A New Method of Conditioning

It is reported that the average salesman spends six years of his life today driving around in his automobile. He spends three years of his life dressing, shaving and preparing for work. He spends a comparable amount of time eating his meals. Wouldn't it be a great savings of time and also a great training experience if he could use some of this time to condition himself for better communication?

There are on the market today little cassette recorders which sell for as low as $20.00. These little recorders can be carried in our car or used while dressing and eating. They offer a wonderful opportunity for conditioning ourselves in any field of learning, and whether we are salespeople or not, they can help us condition ourselves for better communication.

I keep such a recorder on the seat of my car at all times. I have another in my home. Not only do I have tapes that constantly remind me of the principles of good communication, but I also have tapes that teach me the enunciation of commonly used words which are difficult to pronounce. Unless they could be quickly replaced, I would not sell these recorders and tapes at any price!

Kinesics and Silent Command

You must realize that you do not communicate through words alone. In this book we shall thoroughly cover the science of body communication known as *kinesics*. This is a most fascinating subject and one so important that it's one of the "hottest" things in psychology today.

Very few people realize that they communicate constantly without words. They communicate by the clothing they wear, by the general posture of their bodies, and even by the tone of their voice.

The person who learns to observe and interpret these body gestures has broadened his scope of understanding. The real expert even puts importance on the body whispers. In fact, he listens with his eyes as carefully as he does with his ears. This skill too must be developed through study and practice. It's the basis of all "Silent Command Power."

Don't Learn by Experience Alone

You may think that experience will teach you all you need to know about persuasive communication. Nothing is more misleading in the field of self-improvement than the state-ment that "experience is the best teacher." Experience is a teacher but the tuition is too high. We can't afford the many mistakes and loss of time that accompany trial and error.

In practically every field of endeavor the average person must be retrained four times in his lifetime. With the fast-moving changes and new adaptations of our economic system today it may soon be six times.

What if you had to retrain yourself four times through trial and error? Even if you lived long enough, you couldn't survive the emotional trauma it would cause.

The Secret of Synthetic Experience

The only time experience is the best teacher is when it is the other person's experience. Today we have the opportunity of learning by synthetic experience, also known as example.

A dog, chicken or horse only learns through its own experience. Man is the only animal that receives a message beyond the grave. We have books, records, cassette tapes, etc. which record the experience of others even in another generation.

I have known people engaged in a certain business for only two or three years who are far more experienced in their work than people who have been engaged in a similar business for thirty years.

Why? Because the person of only two or three years' experience took advantage of other people's experience by reading and studying.

What would you think of the engineering field if each new generation of engineers invented the wheel again? How much success do you think our generation would have had in inventing the computer if we had been restricted to only the knowledge accumulated during our lifetime? How popular would a surgeon be if he used only the knowledge he acquired through his own operations? How successful would a lawyer find himself if he did not take advantage of the knowledge accumulated over the years by other people?

The most expensive schooling anyone can get is from personal failures. This principle is not restricted to any particular endeavor.

If you are a salesman, remember that your customer's office was never intended to be a classroom for trial and error learning. Don't lose sales to get experience. It's not a fair exchange.

If you are a manufacturer, going broke in order to learn the relationship of income and outgo is a pretty expensive price for knowledge you could get from the experience of other manufacturers.

If you are a merchant, learn from the mistakes of other merchants to be sure that you establish proper purchase price and selling price before your inventory is dissipated.

The accumulation of knowledge today is a relay race and not a private event. Accept the baton of experience from the former runner before starting your race in life.

There is something too costly, reckless and devastating about trying to learn through one's own experience alone. It is like suicide, which I once heard someone describe as "the sincerest form of self-criticism." The trouble is that we get an opportunity to be sincere only once. The same person told of the man being hanged who said, "This is going to be a good lesson to me." The poor fellow never profited by his lesson.

Don't try to learn good communication the costly and unprofessional way.

In whatever line of endeavor you follow, you will find you must communicate with others persuasively. Unless you can transmit your ideas to others convincingly, they are about as useless as the proverbial sun dial in the shade.

You'll need to communicate effectively in your social life and in civic affairs just as much as in your business or profession. At a party or other social gathering, have you ever met a man or woman who deprived you of your solitude without furnishing you with company? This is typical of someone who has never learned the basic rules you'll learn in this book.

Don't let yourself fall into this category. Read this book again and again. Make its principles a part of you. Don't be handicapped by the inability to communicate!

TWO

How to Get Instant Cooperation from Others

Just as water cannot rise above its source, we cannot enlighten anyone beyond our own understanding. If we are honest with ourselves, we all shall admit that too often we start speaking without being sure what it is we want to say. I'm sure we all realize that this is a fatal error.

Know What You Want to Say

Form the habit of taking time to see in your mind's eye a clear and articulate picture of what you desire to communicate before speaking or writing. The importance of the information you desire to communicate and the urgency of the situation will determine how much time you can take for this "mental picture," of course.

This thinking and planning can vary from a casual conversation to hours or even days of outlining, writing and re-writing a speech or presentation of major importance. Remember, an advertising agency may take weeks preparing an important ad containing one picture and a few words to communicate a simple idea to the public. Preliminary thinking and planning is a *must* to avoid communication breakdowns.

25

Say It in a Way That Can Be Understood

In this book we will refer to the one with whom you are trying to communicate as the *respondent*. In various circumstances, your respondent may be an individual, a group, or even an entire audience of hundreds of people. However, this cardinal principle will always apply: Until you have put yourself in your respondent's shoes and adjusted your approach to *his* understanding, not yours, you are not communicating at all. You are only talking to yourself. Remember this corny old adage: Communication is a dance — and it takes two to tango. As you plan what you are going to say, never forget that your very purpose is to persuade and convince the other person. Concentrate on him rather than on yourself. Put yourself in his shoes.

People are not persuaded by what we say but rather by what they understand. In the art of persuasion, if we could only remember that principle, many of the misunderstandings in life could be avoided.

I am sure no one would take issue with the above statement. So let's look at some of the ways of insuring that what is said is related to the respondent's understanding.

First Consider the Respondent

You certainly would not think you could convey a message to a blind man through the sign language. I am sure you would not attempt to engage in oral conversation with a totally deaf person. The utter futility of talking to a person in a language foreign to his would certainly be obvious.

Yet, every day many of us make a communication mistake almost as unforgivable. We use words, phrases and sentences which are not understandable to the person with whom we are talking.

Something we understand today could easily have an entirely different meaning tomorrow because of change in customs or habits. For instance, I heard a girl say the other day that she had a hole in the seat of her stockings. Before the advent of the panty hose this statement would have had no meaning. But I assure you today it is a calculated hazard to any girl's wardrobe.

Watch Your Semantics

A friend of mine, Cavett Robert, recently told me that he took one of his twin daughters to the orthodontist to have her teeth examined.

The dentist took a look at her teeth, frowned, turned to my friend and said, "Your daughter has a traumatic malocclusion."

My friend said that he almost fainted. He thought he was going to lose his little girl.

Why couldn't the orthodontist have used laymen's language and merely said, "Your little girl has a slight over-bite"?

It is unfortunate that the more versed we become in the semantics of our own business or profession the more careful we must be in talking about our business or profession with outsiders. We forget that others are not as familiar with these terms as we are; consequently we are prone to use them in their presence.

Use His Yardstick of Understanding, Not Yours

I was recently waiting in a reception room for an appointment with a person who was engaged in an extensive farming operation.

To pass the time away I was thumbing through a government magazine on raising lettuce. I chanced to come across this statement, "Temperature is an important factor in the ecological optimum of crop development and the consequent exploitation of water and soil resources."

After reading the sentence several times — even writing it — I gave up on it. When the party I was to see finally came out, I handed him the magazine and asked what the mumbo-jumbo meant. He casually looked at it and said, "It means that if the weather is too hot or too cold the crops have a heck of a time."

I can't believe that the farmers, for whom the bulletin was written, would not have been just as confused by such a statement as I was.

Be sure you are on the same thought pattern with your listener.

We all remember the story of the little boy out on the school playground who said to his friend, "I ain't going."

The teacher, overhearing, walked over to him and said, "Don't say that, Johnny — it is 'I am not going, you are not going, she is not going, we are not going, they are not going'."

Johnny looked up and said, "Hey, Teacher, ain't nobody going?"

Any good communicator uses the yardstick of his respondent's understanding in framing his words, phrases and sentences.

Do Your Homework

When I am asked to speak before any group of people, what do you think is my first step? You are right; I must find out all I can about my audience.

A speech which might get a standing ovation from one audience may be destined to utter failure before another audience. This is a lesson which I have learned over the years from some sad experiences which I prefer to forget.

Recently I spoke to a group of telephone employees on a phase of communication. Naturally I could take certain liberties with such an audience that would be fatal in a speech to some other group.

So don't we all agree that first we must do our homework and study our audience to be sure just wherein lies the responsive note? This applies to both individuals and groups.

How to Be Flexible in Your Approach

Not long ago I jointly conducted a seminar on Human Engineering with an associate of mine. We were calling on people of varied professions and businesses to secure registrations.

My associate had over the years made such a habit of putting himself in the other person's shoes that without realizing it he would adapt the vernacular of the person on whom we were calling.

To a doctor he might say, "This course will certainly help to *heal* any communication faults you may have."

To a lawyer he would say, "John, the help you will get from this seminar will be a *sure verdict* in your favor."

Even to a garage man I remember he said, "Tom, I've got a real *puncture-proof* proposition for you."

Once I accompanied a real estate broker who called on a cotton farmer to sell him an apartment house. When the discussion of mortgage payments came around the broker said, "Bill, how many bales of cotton do you have stacked up outside? Do you know, Bill, three of those bales each year will make the mortgage payments?"

Now Bill understood the worth of that cotton and just how much land, expense and effort it took to produce each bale. The broker immediately received an enthusiastic and responsive reaction.

I sincerely believe that if this broker had been talking with a dairyman he would have quoted the mortgage payments in terms of the milk from a certain number of cows.

Relating to His Understanding Sets Up the Interview

Throughout this book we stress the difference between an appointment and an interview. When we are able to arrange a physical meeting with an individual we have secured an appointment. However, not until we have gotten into his mental and emotional presence do we have an interview. We shall repeat this principle over and over for emphasis.

Don't confine the application of this principle exclusively to the sales field. It applies in all cases where we deal with people. It is one of the cardinal principles in the art of persuasion.

I am sure that it is unnecessary to emphasize the fact that the surest way to move from the physical to the mental presence is by relating the conversation to matters which are in the field of the *listener's* understanding and interest.

How to Convince Rather Than Impress

I had occasion to speak to a state real estate association in a neighboring state. At the same convention and on the program was a vice-president of a bank in that state.

I don't doubt that the banker was well versed in financial matters. In fact his credentials were staggering. However, he made no effort to discuss problems from the real estate person's point of view. Everything he presented was from the approach of a banker and he even used the banker's vernacular. Except for the fact that I was sure I was at a real estate convention, his speech would have made me feel that I was at a bankers' seminar.

When the time came for questions the silence was deafening. The speaker had not only failed to give any solutions but he had not even stimulated or provoked any questions.

It was very obvious that this speaker was so concerned with preserving his banking image that there was no rapport whatsoever with his audience. I am sure you have had occasion to sit in an audience and observe a similar fiasco caused by a speaker.

How to Win Instant Acceptance

At this same convention was another banker. The difference in the reception of the two men was embarrassing. This second banker started out in a simple down-to-earth fashion, carefully relating to the real estate person's problem at the outset.

As I recall, he made an initial statement something like this: "Fellows, I realize you've got problems, serious problems, and I want you to know that we too are concerned over them. The fact is, your problems are our problems and we want to work with you in finding a solution to them."

So many questions evolved that there was time for only about half of them to be discussed.

Go Over to His Side

Talking in terms of the other person's position applies to every facet of life. Child psychologists tell us that nothing is more frustrating to a small child when he is afraid than to be told to "be a big man." In the first place he is not a big man; he is only a child. When we tell him to be a big man, we are trying to bring him over to our world, one which he is not yet prepared by nature to enter.

How much better it would be, psychologists tell us, if we would try to see *his* point of view and go over to *his* world. Why not try to relate to *his* understanding?

Wouldn't Johnny react much better if we said something like this: "Johnny, I know exactly how you feel because when I was your age I felt exactly the same way. But you know, Johnny, as you grow a little older you'll get over it as I did. In fact you'll look back someday and laugh about it."

Now isn't it obvious that we shall give Johnny more courage and that we shall establish better communication with him when we approach the problem from *his* point of view — not ours?

The Need for Understanding Continues

Johnny goes off to prep school and is homesick. Do you think Johnny would buy the approach; "You are now a man, Johnny, don't be a sissy. You don't want to be tied to your mother's apron strings all your life, do you?"

Actually Johnny is still not a man. He is still a boy, a homesick boy, going away from home for the first time.

Wouldn't an approach such as this be more effective:

"Johnny, it's tough when anyone who appreciates his home and loves his family has to go away for the first time. It would be sad indeed if your home meant so little to you that you wouldn't go through this experience. All of us go through it and it's bad — I remember. However, Johnny, you'll find that you will make new friends, find new interests, and after a week or two, while you'll not forget your home or love it any less, you'll find that this school will become a second home."

The Need for Understanding on the Job

Johnny has finished college and is in a big corporation which has many employees. At times he is bewildered by company policies and other matters that baffle him.

On one occasion Johnny failed to carry out a directive from his superintendent. The order seemed unnecessary to Johnny. He is now face to face with his superintendent and asks why the order was necessary anyway.

What if the superintendent had been concerned only with preserving his image? What if his major concern had been maintaining his authority? What if he had resorted to the old company policy routine, "Johnny, that is company policy and it's not for you, me or anyone else to question?" Would this have been persuasive communication or even good management? It would have solved nothing, only planted the seed for future trouble.

But let's suppose the superintendent communicates with Johnny by mentally going over to Johnny and mentally stepping into Johnny's shoes: "Johnny, it's very understandable that you should wonder about that order. When I first went with the company I felt just as you do now. In fact, it would be unnatural if every new man didn't feel a little bit as you feel. But you know, Johnny, as time went on and I learned more and more about the workings of the company, I realized that orders of this nature were necessary. Just be patient, Johnny, and go along with us and after a while, you, too, as

I did, will realize why it is so important that everyone follows the directives. I'll try to explain to you from time to time why these orders are so vital, although at times they may seem trivial to you."

It wasn't that Johnny really resisted the order, but he had resented the fact that no one had properly communicated with him regarding the purpose of the directives. Now he felt complimented that someone had approached the problem from his point of interest.

How to Bait the Hook

Will Rogers is credited with saying: "When you go fishing you bait the hook, not with what you like, but with what the fish likes. Did you ever taste a worm? Well, it tastes to you perhaps about like your favorite dish tastes to a fish."

A wonderful group of direct salesmen had a convention at Camelback Inn in Scottsdale, Arizona. I spoke at their opening banquet. These were enthusiastic, emotional people — complete extroverts.

My speech was light and entertaining. Purposely I avoided any heavy material. I didn't feel it was necessary to dwell too long on any subject. So I skipped lightly through, enjoying much playback from my audience. Never have I had a speech better received; never have I received more personal satisfaction from speaking.

A week later I spoke in the same room at Camelback, but this time for an engineers' convention. It was a very large convention and there were many people there who were important to my ambitions. In fact there were over 100 heads of companies that put on conventions for their individual companies. I felt sure that I would "wow" this group with the same speech, gaining the same results.

Did You Ever Feel Instant Failure?

Did you ever feel that you were the victim of instant failure? Did you ever suddenly tell yourself that perhaps you were in the wrong line of endeavor?

Those in the audience of engineers who were not looking at me like a tree full of owls had their mental slide-rules measuring my every statement. I felt that I was undergoing the paralysis of analysis.

Yes, I had made the great mistake of not doing my homework. It was the oratorical equivalent of a fumble on the one-yard line. I had neglected to give first consideration to the nature of my audience. I had violated one of the most important rules of good communication. I failed to approach my subject from my audience's point of view.

While a salesman is emotional and thrives on sentiment and generalizations, an engineer is conditioned in his training to analyze carefully, question every statement, and take nothing for granted. While a salesman is easily motivated an engineer fights against emotion because he feels that it warps his judgment.

Fortunately I had the presence of mind, after seeing my predicament, to reverse my approach. I became more analytical. I used comparisons, examples, testimonials, and offered proof of my position on certain matters.

Although this is not my favorite method of presenting my subject matter, to my relief I gradually saw a radical change in my audience. Before long I almost was convinced that they were rendering a verdict in my favor.

I assure you that this experience was very valuable to me. Never again shall I forget that with an audience as with an individual the communication approach must be made from the other person's point of view. Yes, all we say must be related to the other person's interest and understandings.

Face Saving Pays Dividends

Sometimes when we fail to relate our conversation to the other person's understanding we put him in a very embarrassing situation. The average person does not want to indicate that he fails to comprehend for fear he will appear stupid.

Whenever you find that you are attempting to communicate

by using words and examples foreign to your listener's understanding you should immediately accept the fact that you are
at fault. You should apologize for your inability to make yourself clear. You should convince your listeners that you, and not
they, are to blame. One of the worst offenses that you can commit is to attack another person's mental capacity. Whenever
you discover that you have directed the conversation into a
field where your listener is ill at ease you should save face for
him by immediately directing the conversation to another
field where he will find himself more comfortable.

If I had to single out any one chapter of this book and say
that it is of greatest importance, I believe I would have to say
that it is this chapter. Consider all matters contained herein.
Don't be satisfied to read this chapter only once. Read it many
times and use it as a reference.

THREE

The Amazing "FFF" Technique That Makes Others Agree

When I revealed to an elderly experienced speaker, who is a friend of mine, my decision to spend the rest of my life traveling the "chipped beef and mashed potato circuit," he replied with something I'll never forget:

"Well, Merlyn," he said, "knowing you as I do, I realize that nothing I say will change your plans. But I want you to remember this. To be successful in this rat race you must look like a girl, act like a lady, think like a man and work like a horse. Furthermore, you must have the wisdom of Solomon, the patience of Job, the strength and endurance of Hercules, and the skin of a rhinoceros."

I paid little attention to his statement, but after speaking over the country, running for airplanes and living out of a suitcase, I am convinced now that my friend was restrained in his observation.

The Play Is the Thing

Many people will buy the first two chapters of this book. They realize that good communication has its very beginning in the essence of simplicity and the approach from the other person's understanding. However, when we say that one must be dramatic, skepticism begins to creep in. Some people feel, "Here is where the dried pablum of academic theory starts. I knew that eventually we would get around to the psychological mumbo-jumbo."

Let's be fair in our approach and reserve our decision until we have completed this chapter.

Shakespeare said, "The play is the thing." In no field or endeavor is this more true than in the field of communication.

Everyone Loves a Story

People from five to 90 have always loved a story. Our introduction to the Bible was through Bible stories. Is there anyone whose early life was not thrilled by Grimm's fairy tales? Is there anyone whose childhood was so neglected that he was not introduced to "Little Red Riding Hood," or "Goldilocks and the Three Bears"?

So don't you see the magic of communication through stories? Any time we can tell a related story we are sure to hit a responsive note. We have guaranteed attention.

Any good story with a hero, a strong conflict, and at last a happy ending is a kind of little drama. Did it ever occur to you that in your effort to persuade others anytime you give an example or a "for instance" you are actually presenting a drama?

> Henry Smith was faced with this same decision. He felt the dilemma you must feel. However, he accepted this offer and look at the tremendous results he experienced.

Now let's analyze the parts of this little story. Henry Smith was the hero. He had a conflict in his mind — should he or should he not go along with this program? He had the foresight and courage to go along and the outcome was a happy ending.

How the FFF Principle Can Convince

For over two decades proponents of effective communication have urged, in both their writings and teachings, that we should generously use the FFF principle.

If I receive an objection or opposition to my position, it takes self-discipline on my part to refrain from impulsively defending myself. All of us know that in the courtroom of our conscience we have only witnesses for the defense. We have a compulsion to justify our stand, even if it means forgetting the other party's position.

Isn't the following a much more intelligent approach? "Mr. Pleasant, I know just how you feel" . . (first *F*). "Others have felt exactly that way also" . . (second *F*). "But Mr. Pleasant, this is what they have found" . . (third *F*).

Why FFF Is So Important

Now let's put the above under the microscope for examination. You *feel* — others *felt* also — but they *found*.

When I tell a person that I know how he feels I am showing him that I am interested in him — in his point of view. His position is recognized. He is not being ignored. People can tolerate being hated easier than being ignored.

Some people might think that the opposite of love is hate. It is not. It is the feeling of being ignored, of simply being treated as though they didn't exist. No one wants to be a non-person.

But when a person realizes that someone has made an effort to understand him, he is highly complimented. He is now conditioned to listen to the other side of the story. In fact he is likely to make a sincere effort to see the other person's point of view. Be sure to do yourself the favor of using these dynamic, highly charged words: "I know how you feel."

Second, when I say that others have felt that way also, I am eliminating any possibility that my prospect might think I consider his position as being stupid or unreasonable.

What reaction do you think I would get if I said something like this in reply to an objection? "If you were not a businessman I would think that you were kidding me." Or, "How you could ever seriously take a position like that simply defeats me."

Certainly you would get a different reaction than you

would get by some such statement as, "It's perfectly understandable why you should feel that way, Mr. Emerson. In
fact the last two people who benefited from this program
repeated almost your exact words."

Such an answer as this not only relaxes the prospect, but
also "saves face" for him.

The second part of the FFF principle can be inflammatory
and even explosive unless we treat it with care. Generously
use such expressions as "all of us agree"; "I suggest"; "As
you know"; "We all feel." Avoid such expressions as "Any-
body ought to know"; "Even a child would realize"; "A person with any sense could see."

Yes, I repeat that this second phase of the FFF principle
is designed to assure that the listener is not offended.

Now for the important third F. When I say that others
have *found* that certain results follow, I am not presenting
opinion or controversial matters to cause an argument. I am
only presenting a fact that influences. Just the mere fact
that others experienced certain results is highly persuasive
in itself. It suggests to the prospect the fear of loss. If he
does not do as others did, he runs the risk of losing the
advantages they enjoyed.

Imitator or Initiator — Thermometer or Thermostat

Ninety-five per cent of the people today are imitators and
only five per cent are initiators. The majority of people are
like thermometers that simply reflect the surrounding temperature — not like a thermostat that regulates its own
temperature.

We should never forget this great communication principle
which can be of unparalleled value to us:

> We shall never be able to give a more persuasive
> presentation than the fact that others did it and are glad
> they did it!

How to Read People's Minds

Many people delay buying an article or accepting a service simply because they are afraid that it is not the right thing to do.

These people mentally wear a big sign saying "Help me be right." Often they need assurance. They are completely sold on the object or idea, but they are afraid to take a definite stand. Always remember that nothing can eliminate their fear quicker or more certainly than the fact that others took a definite stand and experienced happy results.

Remember, the *feel, felt, found* approach is a great drama. It is insurance and persuasion of the very highest caliber. Avail yourself of this valuable method in every instance possible. Have stories and examples available for every point in your presentation. You may find an occasion to use them at any time. Never let the "cupboard be bare" as far as story illustrations are concerned.

Third Party Influence

In a court of law, if a party to a case testifies in his own behalf, the testimony is considered as a self-serving statement and has very little, if any, influence on the judge or jury. However, if a third party, one who is not in any way interested in either the plaintiff or defendant, gives the same testimony, such evidence is highly important and persuasive. The reason is, of course, that this third witness is considered an unprejudiced witness. It is naturally supposed that he is interested only in the facts and not in whether these facts may benefit one or the other party.

The same holds true with anyone trying to persuade another person. If a salesman tells a prospect how good his product is, this is a self-serving statement. Chances are that this will not be as persuasive as or carry the credibility of a story about a disinterested party who used the product and experienced good results.

Facts, Analogies and Comparisons Persuade

No judge will permit opinion, evidence, or conclusions of law by a witness to be entered into the court record.

The same principle holds true with someone you are trying to persuade. Don't think for a moment that he is carried away by your opinion or conclusions. He may be nice, may even appear to agree with you. But you have really offered him no persuasive material.

Get into the habit of using facts, analogies and comparisons to establish belief. If you can present these in story form they are even more persuasive. Don't forget that stories are communication's most treasured vehicles; stories have been the key that unlocks the mind ever since the first faint dawn of speech.

Get Into the Act

The persuasive communicator doesn't just confine himself to telling dramatic stories, but he gets into the act himself. He personally dramatizes the situation when the occasion calls for it. This requires a great deal of judgment, but nothing can be more impressive when the time is exactly right.

Because we hear it so often, we are tempted to put very little importance on the principle that actions speak louder than words. But don't forget that communication is not confined to written or spoken words.

The Ten-Minute Sand Glass Technique

I know a person who dramatically used a ten-minute sand glass effectively. The glass was a miniature hour glass.

When this person walked into anyone's office he would place the little glass on the desk with polite urgency and say, "You are a busy man, Mr. Jones, and so am I. When the sand runs to the bottom of the glass ten minutes will have elapsed. When that happens, if you are not convinced that I can help you, I shall leave quietly and politely. Is that fair enough?"

The glass worked like magic for this individual. Unless the other person spoke up immediately with some objection to the interview, the individual would continue, "The sand is running. In order to save time for us both I must show you this without delay."

The person assured me that very seldom was there even a question as to whether the one he was visiting was going to give him the ten minutes. The dramatic manner of going into the interview so intrigued the other person that he immediately agreed.

The Empty Envelope Technique

A salesman of accident insurance in my city gained many valuable interviews by simply sending an empty envelope to a prospect once a week for several weeks. The return address of the salesman was always on the envelope.

After a few weeks when the salesman made his call in person, the prospect was full of curiosity and naturally wanted to find out about the empty envelopes. This gave the salesman a dramatic lead into his presentation.

"Mr. Smith, those envelopes contained just exactly what you would receive each week in case of an accident, provided you do not have the protection I can give you." The salesman then followed this with a long pause.

Some people undoubtedly will say that they do not believe in gimmicks, gadgets and gismos — that this method of playing cloak and dagger or cat and mouse belongs to a by-gone age. If one feels this way, he should certainly not engage in such activities. But I have known very dedicated people who feel that if a prospect needs their product or service, they are justified in using any ethical means to cause him to accept the benefits and protection which they can offer.

How's Your Story Bank Account?

The persuasive communicator knows the power of a story, an example, a "for instance." He has one to meet every question or objection that might be brought up regarding his product or service. He knows that people will always listen to a story where opinion and statements might bore them. The natural curiosity as to how a story may end keeps a person's attention. Furthermore, it is very seldom that a story can lead to an argument. The third-party aspect gives insurance against such a danger.

Don't neglect this greatest of all vehicles of persuasion. Constantly collect stories that illustrate your points. Not only collect them but practice telling them until you can relate them in an interesting and dramatic way. And most important of all, *use* them. Seek occasions to tell them. They will work wonders for you.

FOUR

The Automatic Way to Get What You Want

The classic answer by the professional boxer, when asked the formula for winning, is "Always fight another round."

There is no better advice that can be given to a person who desires to persuade someone or bring someone to his way of thinking or close a sale than "Always ask another question."

Speakers, trainers, consultants and human engineers give lip service to this theory, but actually very few people place the importance on questioning which it deserves. Did it ever occur to you that the more professional a person is the more time he spends asking questions? This is the surest way of arriving at the truth. We have heard it said many times that it is more important to know the right questions than the right answers because if we ask the right questions, we are going to get the right answers.

An Ancient Greek Mind-Probing Technique

Socrates was one of the first great teachers. His greatness as a teacher was based primarily upon the fact that he led people to their conclusions through questions. In fact, the questioning method of teaching today is called Socratic because it is derived from the methods of this great man.

Starting the Two-Way Flow

The reasons for asking questions to assure good communication are almost too numerous to treat in this book. We shall, however, consider a few.

First of all, since true communication is a two-way flow of ideas and thoughts, asking questions is the only way to guarantee that there is a flow in both directions. This is the very basis of all communication. If we ever forget that there must be participation by both the sender and the receiver, by both the communicator and the respondent, then the whole communication process is born dead.

How to Pinpoint the Problem

Recently I accompanied a friend on a search in a quiet area for a small home to be converted into an art studio.

The first real estate agent we called upon seemed very alert and eager to discuss and show property. In fact, before my friend could tell her complete story, the salesman almost bodily dragged us into his car to show us "just exactly what she wanted."

It is true that we were shown a couple of houses that appeared to be a bargain in real estate investment. They were in quiet neighborhoods where sleep would be relatively undisturbed. We were told, without an opportunity to interrupt or explain our problem, that a mortgage over a long period of time could be arranged. In fact, we were given a 30-minute, rapid-fire lesson in financing.

My friend was so irritated that she completely closed her mind to any ideas of acceptance. She was not looking for an investment. She did not plan to sleep in the structure but only use it for a working studio. She was not concerned with any financing plan for she wanted to pay all cash and save interest.

From what my friend had told me earlier, I felt that either one of the properties would have been adequate to meet her needs. However, her attitude had been conditioned to refusal simply by that salesman's efforts to sell before he even considered my friend's problem.

A Technique That Saves Time

Think how different would have been the whole relationship in general and climate of acceptance in particular if the real estate salesman had observed the first great principle of communication.

What do you suppose would have been my friend's reaction if the salesman had made an approach such as this: "Mrs. Smith, in order that I can save you time and serve you better, do you mind if I ask you a few questions?"

Note that the salesman is even prefacing the questions with a question, a polite inquiry as to whether or not he may be permitted to ask questions. This is the ultimate in professional communication.

His questions should naturally have been in regard to purpose of the purchase, location, size, price, method of payment, etc. In my own mind I feel confident that if the salesman had followed the question route that day, he would have made a sale. My friend later bought a house, which, in my opinion, did not fill her need as adequately as either of the two properties shown us by the salesman.

How to Get What You Want Automatically

There is a law in our economic world as strong as the law of gravity itself. Most of the obstacles for those who offer a product or service could be reduced significantly if this law were fully accepted.

The law: If you spend enough time and effort helping other people get what they want, you will automatically get what you want. If you spend enough time and effort solving other people's problems, you will find that your problems are automatically solved or at least reduced to manageable proportions.

If you are offering a product or service, you have to communicate to the other person that your interest is primarily in solving his problem rather than disposing of your product, that your compulsion for service does actually exceed your passion for gain.

Of course, this means starting the interview with a series of questions to clarify and pinpoint the actual problem of that person.

Please never forget that until a person has agreed with you just exactly what his problem is, you are not communicating with that person. You are only talking to yourself, just pounding your own eardrums. I am sure no one would ever consider this to be communication.

A Two-Way Interest

Remember this cardinal principle of two-way communication when offering a service or product: the eagerness of your respondent to listen to your story can never be any greater than the enthusiasm you show in wanting to solve his problem. The depth of his interest in your product or service will depend on your interest in him.

Making the Initial Approach

While it is necessary to believe in your product or serivce, sometimes, if the most important aspect of communication is neglected, this great belief and enthusiasm can be a handicap.

I've known people who were so dedicated and enthusiastic over what they were offering that their initial approach was to communicate all the fine qualities of their product or service rather than first to inquire as to the problems and needs of the prospect.

Regardless of how sincere a person might be and regardless of his belief in his service or product, notwithstanding his loyalty to his company, his whole effort to communicate of no avail if he forgets this principle.

Measure of Value

People too often neglect a certain principle that is helpful in encouraging us to ask questions.

That principle is this: A bargain is measured only by the extent to which something solves our problem.

Then doesn't it follow as the night the day that we cannot put any value on a product or service until we ask enough questions to determine the value to the other party? Maybe there is a great value and maybe there is no value. In either event, communication is static until we have ascertained this fact.

A hunting lodge has a great value to a man who is an avid hunter. To others I am sure it would only be a liability.

A fine library is a fulfilled dream to one person. To another it's only so many red, green or blue feet of decoration in the living room.

A surgeon could not render service without his operating instruments. To a bricklayer they would only be articles of curiosity.

These examples are, of course, exaggerated instances, but we can relate the principle to all our activities.

Sincerity in Communication

One of the ABC's of communication is that people are persuaded more by the depth of our sincerity than by the height of our logic, more by our desire to solve their problem than by the brilliancy of describing our product or service.

How often have you heard the expression, "I'm not too sure about it, but he seems so sold on the idea that I am inclined to go along"?

There is the humorous example of the young man who wrote this letter to his sweetheart:

"My Darling, My Dear:

Never did a Romeo love his Juliet as I love thee. For you I would climb the Pyramids; for you I would descend the dangerous walls of the Grand Canyon. Just for a glimpse of you I'd brave the treacherous waves of the Bay of Fundy. For the touch of your hand I'd swim the Hellespont.

I can hardly live until again I can be in the sunshine of your presence.

As ever, your loving

John

P.S. I don't think I can come over tonight. It looks like rain."

The Technique the Professionals Use

One of the first principles that every sales organization teaches its young salesmen is that people love to buy but don't like to be sold. Furthermore, if a person can master the art of assisting people in buying, that is, in doing what they love to do, he has left the amateur ranks and joined the professionals.

There is no possible way for a person to communicate persuasively until he no longer "sells" people on what he wants but assists them in "buying" what they want and until he has adopted the habit of asking questions to find out what they want.

Questions do not have a separate place in any persuasive communication. They should permeate the entire presentation.

The very first sentence of any presentation should be in the form of a question. Analyze your own presentation and give yourself the professional test. Furthermore the second and the third and in most instances the entire first part of every presentation should be a series of questions.

The Question Approach

In the first place, if you start out your presentation asking me a series of questions, I am convinced from the very beginning that you are interested in my problems. Somehow

I get the feeling that you are "tailor-making" something for my particular needs — that perhaps somewhere down the line there is a solution to my problems. You have given me confidence from the very beginning.

When I go to my doctor what is the first thing that he does? Of course — he asks me questions. Immediately he has established the professional relationship. From the very beginning he has turned on little neon letters: *I am trying to find out your problem so I can help you.*

After he has asked sufficient questions and shown his interest in my problem by examining me, I am prepared to accept any reasonable solution he suggests. If he prescribes penicillin, I shall take penicillin. If he suggests rest and diet, I shall change my eating and sleeping habits. If he tells me he is putting me in the hospital for an operation, I simply will prepare myself for the event.

Now why do I buy his recommendations so completely? It is that he has been professional long enough to convince me that his sole purpose is to solve my problem. However, without questions he could never have taken this professional approach and never would he have won my confidence.

A Simple Test

Please, regardless of what may be your line of endeavor in this life, form the habit, in all of your human relations, of asking questions. You will lift communication to the very highest level.

The more professional a person is the more important to him is the process of questioning others. It is said that a doctor spends 80 per cent of his time asking questions and only 20 per cent of his time prescribing treatment. I believe this to be true in all of our sincere efforts to help people.

Give yourself the test: how much of *your* time do you spend trying to ascertain the needs of others and how much time do you spend trying to gain acceptance of your product and service or yourself?

What do you suppose my attitude would be if my doctor spent 80 per cent of his time prescribing a remedy and 20 per cent of his time studying my problem? I am sure I would say to myself, "I hope he is not pushing penicillin this week. I hope the pharmaceutical houses are not giving a trip to the doctor who can sell the greatest quantity of their product. I hope he is not in the last week of a contest to dispose of the largest amount of a certain drug, and needs just one more operation to meet his quota."

The Greatest Compliment

We are all finally accepting the principle today that the word *profession* has a new connotation.

Years ago it applied to a doctor, a lawyer, a professor and a few other areas of endeavor. Today the word "Pro" applies more to the quality than to the type of performance.

I heard someone in a speech not long ago say, "Any society that would scorn excellence in plumbing because plumbing might be considered a humble activity and that would, at the same time, tolerate mediocrity in philosophy because philosophy might be considered an exalted activity — that society never will have good plumbing nor good philosophy. Neither its pipes nor its theories will ever hold water."

One of the greatest compliments we can give to a person today is to say that he is certainly professional in all that he does. This can never be said about a person who offers a product or service unless that person follows the communication pattern of probing into people's problems through the question approach.

What You Have Vs. What You Want

Reduced to the lowest common denominator and stripped to the essence of simplicity, a problem is nothing more than the difference between what a person *has* and what he *wants*. Think about this for a moment. Can you think of any better illustration or definition?

Now this brings us to another consideration: if a problem is only the difference between what a person *has* and what he *wants,* then the extent of a person's problem is simply the distance between these two conditions.

So doesn't it stand to reason that the first two things that a professional problem solver is concerned with are, first, what a person has and what he wants; second, how far apart are these two conditions?

Most people could revolutionize their endeavors if they would only form the habit of finding out these two things before ever considering an offer of their services or product. How completely different would be the entire climate of the communication.

Defining the Problem

Often a person needs assistance in defining and clarifying his own problem. Many times a person calls upon another and finds that he must act in a dual capacity. First, he must help his prospect clarify his needs, and only secondarily, help satisfy these needs.

That is why people who sell furniture, drapes and the like often offer interior decorating services free of charge. Even our large utility companies offer engineering services to their prospective industrial, commercial and even domestic customers.

Bring this principle to your own endeavors. First, ask questions to determine needs. If your respondent is not sure of his needs, by all means proceed no further until, with your help, the needs are clearly agreed upon. Remember, as stated earlier, "Until the other person has definitely agreed with you concerning his exact needs you are not communicating with him, you are only talking to yourself."

Statement Vs. Admission

Which lays a better foundation or creates a finer climate for acceptance of your services or product: a statement by you or an admission by your respondent?

The answer is too simple to need elaboration. I repeat that if you make a statement regarding your service or product, regardless of how true or how brilliant it may be, it is still labeled in the communication vernacular as a self-serving statement. It is not persuasive. It is assumed to be a biased opinion because, if accepted, it benefits you.

This type of communication is given uncomplimentary names such as "hard sell" or "pressure approach."

But let's look at the other side of the picture. The most acceptable and highest form of evidence in law is called *admission against interest,* which means a statement that is ungarnished by prejudice in the witness' favor. This same principle applies in every day persuasion.

If your respondent makes a statement which identifies his problem, then you have already at least one-half convinced him. There is an admission of the need; the problem is out on the table.

Again we return to the method of gaining this admission — the *how* of good communication. It lies in generously asking questions.

I urge you to write the title of this chapter indelibly in your mind. Make it the directional compass of good communication — *Always ask another question.*

Controlling the Situation with Silent Command

We have heard it said many times that a skillful communicator directs the conversation. This is very true but often people are confused in thinking that this means they should dominate the situation.

Well-meaning but misguided communication consultants often urge an individual to keep a higher eye level than that of his prospect. They urge him to speak just a little louder than his prospect. They insist that he take the assumptive attitude at all times.

Always remember that a person's home or office is his castle and that he must be treated as king at all times. Too many people in an effort to be assumptuous actually become offensively presumptuous. This is one of the most basic secrets of Secret Command.

Forget the higher eye level. Don't try to shout your prospect down. You are playing with fire. Not only are such tactics inflammatory — they are explosive!

The best rudder to guide a conversation is the rudder of questions. If you constantly practice this, you will find that results are startling.

Shades of Difference in Communication

Questions offer the very best instrument for testing a person's disposition to accept your ideas, services or products.

In seeking to conclude a transaction, most people are fearful that they will "blow the deal" by moving too fast.

Only the skillful use of questions can prevent such a possibility.

If my respondent's reactions have been so positive that I am sure he is ready to accept my proposal, I would feel safe in such a final question as this:

> From what you have said and based on our conclusions,
> Mr. Smith, I am sure you are ready to go along on this
> recommendation right now, aren't you?

This is a bold question, but I don't feel that I am taking a chance because of my respondent's acceptance frame of mind.

However, let's suppose my respondent is interested but has not given me any good acceptance "signals." I would feel safe with a less bold question.

> Mr. Smith, from the information you have given me,
> I am confident that this is something you should consider
> seriously, isn't it?

Even though my respondent is not yet fully ready to accept my offer he would want to consider the advantages anyway.

Let's take a step even further. My respondent is only

slightly warm to the proposition I am offering. I want to be sure that my question is less challenging in its consequence.

> Mr. Smith, if you were sure that this service had helped others in your line of business, you would want to know about it, wouldn't you?

Here you are only getting the decision of the other person to open his mind so that he can consider your proposition.

Questions of this nature should be designed to get a *yes* reaction. Fortunately most questions are so flexible and elastic that they can be designed to receive a positive response from almost any attitude the other person might have.

Consider the last example. Would it be likely that a good businessman would not want the information which his competitors have? Would he take the attitude that even if others were helped by such services, he prefers to remain in the dark and not even know of the benefits? I am sure the situation is very obvious.

Getting Time to Think

While the benefits of questions are legion to a good communicator, don't forget that often a person is caught in a situation where he needs a few seconds to think, to organize a new approach. Many times you can "buy the time" by asking a question.

You may feel that a good listener should concentrate on listening and not be thinking of what he is to say next. As a general rule you are absolutely right. However, there are exceptions to the rule. Often an entirely new thought is brought into the conversation. Many times you will be caught by surprise. This may call for quick thinking or a new approach. A question often will give you this "life-saver." Don't overlook this possibility.

Again I urge you to write the theme of this chapter indelibly in your mind; make it the directional compass of persuasive communication. Remember — *Always ask another question!*

FIVE

The Psychic Compass That Reveals What Others Desire

How to Discover What Others Think

Chapter Four was devoted to the importance of asking questions. Unless, however, we listen to answers the questioning is of no importance. The very purpose of a question obviously is to elicit an answer, to find out a person's wants and needs.

Once we have received an expression of such, isn't it a waste of time and effort if we do not take advantage of the information by listening?

Studies made at the University of Minnesota show that the typical salesman spends 70 per cent of his working hours in communication. This is certainly not surprising because the average person today, in practically every line of endeavor, spends more than half of his time engaged in this activity.

The Minnesota study further showed that this communication activity breaks down into these proportions: nine per cent in writing, 16 per cent in reading, 30 per cent in talking, and 45 per cent in listening.

The amazing conclusion so apparent is that while most of a salesman's time is spent communicating, and although the greater part of communication consists of listening, despite this fact, little time is spent by him in training to be a good listener.

The Inaudible Sound

A friend of mine who teaches physics once told me something which at the time was difficult for me to believe.

He explained that if a dead tree fell in the forest and that if no person was within hearing distance, no sound was made by the falling tree. This of course is correct because it is based on the theory that sound is the reverberation of certain disturbance waves on eardrums. Thus, if no eardrums are within proximity of hearing distance, there can be no sound because the reverberation waves are dissipated into the air.

There is a parallel with communication. When one does not use the eardrums, even though he is in listening distance, there is no communication. While there technically might be a sound, the sound is not audible unless we are listening.

Creative Listening

There is a great difference between passive listening and active listening — between mere tolerance and definite interest. Unless our respondent is actively and energetically engaged in listening, we are not talking to him; we are only pounding our own eardrums. Of course this is a complete waste of time. No one has ever found a way to receive benefits from talking to one's self.

The Psychic Compass

An expert in the field of communication realizes that objections are the best guide to a person's thinking. He receives them as a directional compass that points out the path he should follow.

If we want to be certain that we do not leave any hidden objections the first part of our interview should be designed, with certain provocative statements, to cause the respondent to reveal his thinking. Usually a person gives us this revelation in the form of an objection.

When the objection comes the curtain is raised and the act begins. All has been prologue up to this moment.

At this point it is important for the communicator to listen carefully in order to receive full benefit from the objection. An objection is a signal to listen carefully — not a signal immediately to oppose the respondent's point of view.

Improving the Communication Climate

We all know that objections thrive on opposition but die on agreement.

How often have you heard a person say, "That's just not true, and I can prove it"?

Even if he proves that a person who voices an objection is wrong, he is in a worse position than if he had not. In any event there occurs an immediate breakdown in communication.

How much better it would have been to have been a good listener and heard him out.

Wouldn't the whole climate of communication have been better if he had said: "I am sure you have a good reason for feeling that way. I'd like to listen to you further."

Regardless of how strong a person may feel about something or how emotionally aroused he may be, if we encourage him to talk by indicating that we shall be a good listener, he gradually will let off steam and at the same time give us an indication of his thinking.

How to Get the Cue

If we can divorce ourselves from emotion, and listen as a doctor listens to our heart and lungs in a spirit of diagnosis, often we get the cue which may lead to effective persuasion even in the face of obstacles.

Regardless of what may be your business or profession try the experiment of being a good listener. Let's consider an illustration.

For instance, a supplier might hear from a purchasing agent: "Yes, I'll tell you why we stopped buying from your company. Your company unloaded a bunch of junk on us."

Now naturally the supplier's first impulse is to fight back, to defend his company in the same emotional tone. But remember that in communication we are often faced with this decision: do we want to give way to our immediate feelings or do we want to arrive at our goal?

Isn't it better to assume the role of a good listener? Suppose you were the supplier, and said, "Mr. Smith, I can certainly understand how upset you must have been. Do you mind telling me what happened?"

Now Mr. Smith has the opportunity to blow off steam. Also, while doing so, if you are a good listener, you might find your cue which might lead to correcting the whole situation.

After Mr. Smith's temper has dropped and after he has had his say, you might even hear him say, "In most cases I'll admit that you have given us a quality product but you certainly didn't in this case."

You now have a cue, one you would not have had if you had not encouraged Mr. Smith to talk, then listened sympathetically and let Mr. Smith know that you were truly concerned. He is now more than likely ready to listen to you with an open mind.

How to Follow Through on the Cue

"Mr. Smith, I am glad to hear you say that in most cases we have given you a quality product. This has certainly been our purpose in every instance, and I am distressed to find that in one instance we failed you. "I am sure that in your business you, too, are distressed whenever you find that you have failed in serving one of your customers. Please tell me how we can rectify the situation."

Now at this point shut up and be a good listener. Let him answer you fully. Encourage him to keep talking. The longer you can get him to talk now the better will be your position. He is telling you how the relationship can be glued back again. The more he talks the more he is committing himself to the former relationship. The suggestions are his and if followed he will co-operate. He has saved face. The ideas are his.

Problem Solving Through Listening

While there are many definitions of a problem, perhaps the best I have ever heard and the one we repeat over and over in this book is that it is the difference between what a person *wants* and what he's *got*. Furthermore, again we say that the extent of a person's problem is the distance between what he wants and what he already has.

Now wouldn't it be colossal insanity to tackle a problem before we actually know what the problem is and to what extent it exists?

Unless a person is a good listener he will never know this. The initial step in solving any problem is, through skillful questioning, to get the respondent to express his wants and also tell you what his present situation is. Again I say, however, that this is impossible unless we are good listeners.

Don't Be an Impulsive Respondent

Often a person's maturity is measured by the time which elapses between his stimulus and response.

If a person accosts me suddenly and criticizes some personal action of mine or takes issue with an opinion I have expressed, my first impulse is immediately to fight back.

How much more effective would be my results if I chose rather to be a patient listener and avoid an explosive response. After hesitating a few seconds what if I had said, "Mr. Jones, I am sure that you have given this matter careful consideration and I would appreciate it if you would enlighten me on your views."

A sincere response of this nature is a compliment to anyone. Even if Mr. Jones has a chip on his shoulder, he is inclined to make a mental bow and in so doing the chip will automatically fall off.

Again I say that the more I can encourage Mr. Jones to talk the more intent I should be in my listening. His emotions will inevitably subside. Finally he will not want to be outdone by my interest and politeness, and he will be ready to listen to my side of the story in a fair and open frame of mind.

Good Listening Pays Dividends

Sometimes through careful listening you will receive a gem of information that can pay off handsomely in dividends. Be sure, however, that this will never happen to you unless you are concentrating on what the communicator has to say. Sometimes you will find this through just a word or phrase.

John Thomas called on a wholesaler to sell typewriters. He received the same objection that other salesmen were getting: business was off and conditions were in a down swing.

But John was a careful listener. He remembered the statement by the purchasing agent, "Things would be different if the mills opened again."

When John read in the paper that the mills were opening, he was in the purchasing agent's office within hours and received a large order.

All of John's competitors had received virtually the same story, but John listened carefully and had made a mental note of what other salesmen had ignored.

Why People Don't Listen

Naturally we ask ourselves this question, "If listening is so very important to communication in general and to persuasion in particular, why is it that people resist listening?"

First, it is that so many people are suffering from the

disease most commonly known as laziness. To be a good listener is hard work — it takes real effort. Consequently, most people try to avoid it. They resist brainwork as earnestly as they resist manual labor.

Secondly, only a few people truly realize its importance. Most people erroneously think that they can better serve their own interests by pretending to listen while they are spending their time thinking about what they will say next. Actually, by not listening they have immediately become a party to fractured communication. The channels of mutual understanding have been closed.

And finally, many of us do not listen because we permit our emotions to enter the picture. Emotions cause an immediate hazard to understanding, a barrier to comprehension.

Emotions work in two different directions when it comes to listening. In some instances they can make us antagonistic to the speaker's position. Just as often they can make us over enthusiastic about his presentation.

Whenever emotions enter the picture, we must exercise self-discipline and avoid forming an opinion or making a decision until we can more intelligently and more calmly consider the facts.

How Can We Improve Our Listening Techniques?

The very first principle of improving our listening skill is to school ourselves in the habit of taking time actually to listen. Most of us have the mistaken idea that we are communicating only when we are talking. What could be more erroneous?

Most good persuasive communicators feel that the first part of any good interview should be designed, through provocative questioning, to cause the respondent to start talking. Then it is important for him to realize that he has entered the most important part of good communication — creative listening.

Certainly you must do a certain amount of talking in order to guide the conversation, but by all means remember this.

If the other person interrupts you, immediately stop talking and both politely and energetically begin to listen. If you don't you can be assured that anything you say will be falling on deaf ears. Your respondent is only interested in what he is waiting to say when you stop talking.

How Long Should You Wait Before Answering?

Even when the other person asks you a question, don't be too quick to answer. Don't be impulsive in your response. Regardless of how eager you may be to give an answer, if you hesitate slightly, you indicate that you are considering the question carefully and that you are anxious to use clear thinking and sound judgment.

Also, by waiting a couple of seconds or more before starting to answer, you are insuring that the respondent has finished his question.

Getting Complete Attention

The person speaking wants and has a right to expect more than just casual attention. He wants you to give complete and active attention to his question or position. It is very easy for a person through observing your expression and conduct to determine to what extent you are truly listening. If your mind is wandering, if you are bored or even if your attention is divided, this will be revealed by your manner. You cannot hide it.

Form the habit of giving your full attention. Not only do this but form the habit of letting the other person know through your gestures and expression that you are paying him the compliment of using your maximum listening powers.

Improving Your Concentration Span

The average person's concentration span is short. It is cut even shorter when there are distractions around him.

When listening, try not to notice things around your speaker that will prevent you from a full concentration on what is being said.

The Empathetic Listening Technique

Henry Ford once said, "If there is any one secret of success, it lies in the ability to get the other person's point of view and see things from his angle as well as your own."

When listening, try not to think of yourself as being across the desk or table from the speaker. Mentally go to his side and put your arm around him. Mentally make an effort to put yourself in his shoes. See the situation through his eyes. This is good listening.

How to Use the Psychic Compass to Help You

Regardless of how deeply and sincerely you believe in the art of creative listening, unless you adopt the principles contained in this chapter and in fact form the habit of using them, your roots will remain in sterile soil.

Take these principles and relate them to your particular business or profession. Commit as many as possible to memory. Form the habit of reviewing them periodically. Put them into practice. Make them your listening habits. Like a "psychic compass," they will point the way to Silent Command of others.

SIX

The Secret of Kinesics

That form of non-verbal communication known as body language has become popular here in America almost overnight. It is known as *kinesics*.

While this is hailed by many as a new and exciting science, actually it is the oldest form of communication known to man. Long before man learned to talk, his primary means of making his thoughts, demands, threats and fears known was through body communication. He has never given up this form of expression over the many centuries. He has only added other methods of communication to supplement it.

Even a casual reading of portions of the Old Testament gives examples of this body communication. Is there any doubt in anyone's mind what emotion Moses was showing or what message he was conveying when he threw down and broke the tablets at Mount Sinai after finding his people worshiping the golden calf?

The pages of history are full of examples of body communication.

Triumph or Surrender

Even during early civilizations certain body actions became symbolic of messages to be conveyed.

Kneeling or lying prostrate was a symbol of surrender or recognition of authority. The subject always knelt before the king or ruler. Even the vanquished armies would lie down in acknowledgment of surrender. Later the symbol became raised hands over the head. This was to show that there were no concealed weapons.

Victory in early days was accompanied by a triumphant entry into the city, with the victors riding horses or in chariots. The conquered walked on foot in front, or followed behind in chains. Our modern parade today is an outgrowth of this triumphant entry.

Later when new weapons were used, the surrender of the sword and the laying down of arms became the new symbol of surrender.

Hidden Meanings in Kinesics

Does it ever occur to us to wonder why a man who accompanies a lady down the sidewalk, walks on the street side keeping her next to the building? This is a symbol of protection.

In years past practically all streets were muddy and had pockets of water. Naturally the horses and carriages would splash this mud and water up on the sidewalk. By putting himself between the lady and the street a man was protecting the woman from the splashes of water and mud.

In walking down an aisle at church or elsewhere or in escorting a lady at a party the man has his escort on his left arm. This custom had its origin during the period when a man wore a sword for protection. By having his lady fair to his left, his right arm was free to reach for his sword as protection at a moment's notice.

Another interpretation is a little sentimental and one to which I personally would readily subscribe. A man's heart is on his left side. It is a display of chivalry and affection to carry a lady next to his heart. The Lord did not take a bone from Adam's foot in creating Eve so that she would be beneath him. He did not take a bone from his head so that she would be above him. He took a rib from Adam's left side so that her place would always be next to his heart

— and that is where man should keep her even in escorting her.

I once heard a very fine speech by a person who was not in harmony with the women's liberation movement. He felt that women would lose, if successful, more than they would gain. He titled his speech *Women's Lib or Adam's Rib*. I shall not take sides in this book, but I must say that this person presented a very moving argument in behalf of the theory that when God made Eve from Adam's rib he intended for her to remain at Adam's side, next to his heart and under his protection.

Is There a Founder of Kinesics?

Many people ask who was the first person to do an exhaustive study in the field of kinesics. Certainly no one in this century can make this claim.

One of the first was a Frenchman named Andrew Delsarte, who lived in the early part of the 19th century. He was a teacher of music and drama.

In 1892 one of Delsarte's former students wrote a book on the Delsarte system and entitled it *Gestures and Attitudes*.

Today's Kinesics

Not long ago when lecturing to one of my classes on the subject of kinesics, I asked the students to write on the board as many non-verbal body communications as possible which are used today.

Starting with such simple symbols as saluting, tipping one's hat, opening a door for another, pulling back a chair, shaking hands, throwing a kiss, waving good-by, bowing one's head, pointing one's finger, covering one's eyes, bowing from the waist, puckering up for a kiss, shaking a fist, stamping a foot, winking an eye, smiling, frowning, showing one's teeth and hunching one's shoulders, over 100 were written on the board in less than 20 minutes.

Kinesics Reveals Local Customs

I was invited to dinner while speaking in a Southern state. My host was the program chairman of the meeting I addressed.

He and his wife had five children. As we sat down for dinner each held the hand of the person next to him or her as they said the blessing. I, of course, entered into the ritual which impressed me very much.

When I said what a beautiful thing this was, the host told me that this hád been a custom in his family for many generations. He said that this spoke the language of thankfulness for their family circle. This was an impressive example of kinesics.

One of the youngsters assured me, however, that it had another purpose also. He said that this gave every member of the family an even break when hands were released to reach for the biscuits.

Body Contact

One form of kinesics can be either very effective or inflammatory or even explosive. That is body touch.

If it arises from a natural feeling and if it is genuine and sincere, it can carry a great message — far more effectively than words.

An older man may put his hand on the shoulder of a boy or young man as he counsels with him or gives him advice. A boy may gently take the hand of a girl as he pleads his affection for her. A person may take the arm of an elderly lady in a protective manner.

However, there is a sanctity of individuality and a barrier of privacy that no one has the right to invade in others. Unless there is a close intimacy between two people, not only should one not take the arm, hold the elbow or touch the other person, but he should maintain a respectful distance.

Often when I conclude a speech a number of people are nice enough to file by, shake my hand and thank me. Nothing pleases a speaker more. However, there are usually one or two people who want to stand for five minutes and tell me some old story or give me an example I can use in a speech or relate to me the long story of their lives. This is a calculated risk that every speaker must encounter.

In practically every case the person will hold your arm or sleeve in a gesture that communicates "You cannot get away until my story is finished." The moment a person grabs my arm I can identify him as one of those compulsive touchers. I've checked with other speakers and every one of them relates that he is assaulted by these people who can't resist the bodily contact.

Kinesics Is an Honest Revelation

Since our body language usually is stimulated by our sub-conscious it is usually more reliable than verbal communication. In fact, many times it contradicts what we say verbally. Since our subconscious is honest in the things it does, it is well to observe closely the actions of others regardless of what may be the words.

Those who deal in criminology claim that kinesics, if understood properly, is the best lie detector of all. If the body language and the verbal language are completely out of harmony, one can rest assured, according to the criminologist, that the person is hiding something. Later in this book we shall elaborate on the meaning of certain body language.

What Pupil Widening Means

A speaker at a food convention recently gave a report on a study which impressed me very much. He explained that in food chain stores there is never enough display space for items of food that the store owners want to offer. Consequently there is always great competition by food suppliers in wanting their particular brand to be given preference.

It is now a known and accepted fact that the pupils of a person's eyes enlarge, sometimes to twice their normal size, when the appearance of something delights them.

This speaker said that stores are installing hidden moving picture cameras with telescopic lenses that will record the dilation and contraction of the buyer's pupils as he or she looks at the packages on display. The lens is carefully concealed so that the buyer is not conscious of being filmed. The reaction must be under normal conditions.

This pupil reaction, according to the speaker, is far more reliable than any verbal survey that can be made from door to door or from verbal interviews at the store.

Painting the Face from the Inside

Expressions on others' faces convince us far more than words. If a person told me how happy he was and how much he enjoyed my company while he frowned and curled his lips in a snarling and sarcastic manner, I assure you I would not believe his words. By the same token if you smiled at me tenderly and gently with a sparkle of admiration in your eyes while telling me that you disliked me, I am afraid I would be neither offended nor convinced.

Now let's go a step further. All of us agree that we paint our faces from the inside. Our appearance is primarily the accumulation over the years of our past thoughts, impulses, desires, disappointments and emotions. Our present facial appearance and expression is the best recorded history of our past. Lincoln said that every person after 40 is responsible for his own looks.

Then doesn't it stand to reason that often our facial appearance is far more reliable than anything we can tell a person about ourselves? Why not form the habit of being observant in this regard and actually place real importance on character study which involves facial appearance and expression?

Pantomiming

The greatest of all comedians have been those who ex-
celled in body communication. Perhaps Charlie Chaplin
was the first of the greats in silent films. Buster Keaton,
Ben Turpin, Laurel and Hardy all depended upon non-
verbal entertainment for their popularity. Jimmy Durante
and Red Skelton are equally great today.

If I were asked to pick the greatest single piece of acting,
I would certainly consider among the first a pantomime
skit of Red Skelton imitating the old patriotic soldier watching a parade go by. No verbal rendition could ever approximate the revelation of emotions which was accomplished
through body communication. The last scene of the old
soldier, hardly able to walk, following the parade on his
cane, was enough to bring tears to the eyes of everyone.

Entire Scene in Body Communication

Just before the comedian Bert Lahr passed away I had
occasion to see him perform.

He went through an entire 20-minute scene with Nancy
Walker, and neither spoke a word. The audience was in a
state of frenzied hilarity throughout.

As I recall the pantomiming, it was as follows: Lahr,
dressed in a construction helmet and heavy shoes, walks
in carrying a lunch pail. He slams the door angrily but Nancy
ignores him. He slams it again, still gaining no attention.

He angrily opens his lunch pail, takes out a large sandwich with one bite out of it. Lahr glares at Nancy, takes
the sandwich over and throws it in the garbage pail, takes
a seat in a chair and begins reading the paper.

Nancy goes to the garbage can and gets the sandwich out.
She gets a knife, cuts off the piece of sandwich with the bite
out of it, wraps the rest of the sandwich in wax paper and
puts it back in the lunch pail.

Similar non-verbal scenes continued for the entire time.

It was almost unbelievable that an audience could be kept in convulsions for 20 minutes without a word spoken.

Masked Faces

Most people, fully realizing that they reveal their thoughts and feelings through their expressions, make an effort at times to hide their thoughts and feelings with a blank appearance. Did you ever ride the subway in New York City and look at the expressions on people's faces? On most public conveyances in large cities people wear a masked expression to hide what they are afraid they might otherwise reveal.

This practice is part of the protective armor of our society. We want to keep our inner lives to ourselves and at least not share this with strangers. In some countries of the East women actually wear real veils, not just imaginary ones, in order to hide their emotions from other people. Decency requires this.

One of the hardest things for some people to do is to remove this imaginary mask, relax and actually be themselves. They are in reality afraid to be natural. They do not realize that people are most attractive when they are themselves. If a person can't be attractive being himself, he certainly can't be acceptable trying to be something which he is not. People only exaggerate their faults and accentuate their shortcomings when they try to be something that they are not.

Like an Old Shoe

One of the nicest and most complimentary things that can be said about a person is that "he is like an old shoe." What is meant is that he is comfortable and relaxing to be with. We don't have to be on parade around him. He accepts the best in us and ignores the worst.

Above all else, we know that he is not wearing a mask. We accept him for what he is, and we don't feel that we must wear a mask either because we know that he accepts us in like spirit.

A person who does not reveal his thoughts and emotions around us by his expression causes us to clam up as a protective measure. Did you ever analyze your own reactions when you meet up with a "frozen-faced" person? You are immediately on guard. You find that you, too, retreat behind a mask.

A Costume Party

Did you ever wonder why a costume party generates so much gaiety and enthusiasm? It is because people know that their thoughts, feelings and emotions are not on parade. They can let their guard down. No longer do they feel inhibited. Since they are wearing a mask and hiding their emotions or since their costume diverts attention from their normal physical appearance, they have a feeling of escape from inspection.

The advice is so often given to "try being yourself." People who show an appearance of artificiality cause us to withdraw mentally and emotionally.

Dropping the Mask

People who under ordinary circumstances wear an imaginary mask will often, during times of tragedy or other unusual events, drop the mask and reveal their true feelings through non-verbal communication. Think back over your lifetime and ask yourself if at some time you have not been witness to just such an experience.

Many years ago I was taking a trip as part of a "packaged tour." About 30 people were on the tour. On the first day people only glanced at each other in a suspicious or curious fashion. No one wanted to make the first approach for fear that he would be refused and have his ego damaged. The same cold atmosphere prevailed that night. I was sure that we all were destined for a cold and impersonal four days.

During the middle of the second morning we had a blow-out, a thing which seldom happens to a bus. Everyone got off the bus. We were stranded out in the middle of nowhere. Unfortunately the jack would not function. Although cars stopped, an ordinary jack was not sufficient.

For four hours we waited for delivery of a message requesting a jack to be delivered and for the jack to reach us.

During this time people began to realize that they all had something in common; they all were hungry and stranded in the desert. They became very communicative. They took their masks off.

A little ranch house a half-mile away in the desert was sighted by one person. He went over, asked the owner to sell him a few groceries, then made several sandwiches which he brought back, along with some ice-cold pop.

By the time help finally arrived the entire group was hilariously laughing at their own plight. They talked freely, joked, and had completely dropped their guard. No one would believe such a transformation could come over a crowd in just a few hours.

The four-day trip turned out to be highly interesting and enjoyable to everyone. I am sure that friendships were started which perhaps last even to this day. All masks had been dropped and people communicated freely, non-verbally as well as otherwise.

Why Remove the Mask?

Some people might ask why they should drop the mask and let their non-verbal expression be communicated to others. They may feel that they have a right to privacy.

While it is true that we all want a certain amount of inviolable privacy at all times, it is a dangerous situation if we protect this privacy too far. No one is an island unto himself.

In the first place an exaggerated privacy stunts our emotional growth. We cannot learn to develop any meaningful relationships with others.

I once had two very dear friends, a husband and wife. Both were very brilliant people in the scholastic world. Each had a Ph.D. The wife had written a very fine book. The man was highly successful on the speaking circuit.

After about five years of separation back and forth, they finally were divorced. While both were attractive people and intelligent in many ways, neither was warm or expressive facially or in any other non-verbal means. Each, when speaking to me about the other, used the same expression, "I feel locked out and I don't seem to be able to break through."

Sometimes in our effort to protect the sanctity of individuality, we prevent an exquisite intimacy, without which no marriage can be totally successful. There is such a small shade of difference between privacy and loneliness. I've known people who finally take one step outside of themselves and arrive at happiness.

Sometimes it takes an unselfishness which a person does not have in order to drop the mask. One prefers the retreat to one's own privacy above the joy and companionship and affection of friendships and even marriage. Try a study of yourself. Don't be deprived of the great adventure of this world in an effort to preserve a so-called individuality which some people falsely feel they should keep by remaining locked up in a shell.

Table Positions and Silent Command

While we shall, in another chapter of this book, elaborate on the meaning of certain physical gestures, I would like to suggest that you start observing the position which people are inclined to take at a table. This is most revealing of the place in society which each person feels he occupies.

From time immemorial the leader of any group has always sat at the head of the table. We find this to be true whether he be king of his nation, leader of his group, or chief of his tribe. The place of authority is at the head. By sitting there, he is in Silent Command of the group.

This custom still exists today. At a banquet we honor

people by seating them at the head table. It is a courteous gesture; it is a non-verbal communication. We are in fact telling these people that they are important and that we want to give them the V.I.P. treatment.

The family position of authority has historically always gone to the father. That is why we always find him at the table's head. In rare instances we find the mother there. You can be sure that in such a case she has assumed the authoritative role in that family.

Not only does the chairman of the board of a company occupy the authoritative seat at the table, but usually those who are next highest in authority are closest to him in the order of their importance.

Kinesics of a Round Table

Since many nations are jealous of their prerogatives and will not take a secondary position at the conference table with other nations, the only way that some nations will sit together is at a round table. In this way there is no head or foot of the table.

One of the first recorded uses of the round table is found in stories of King Arthur and his knights. King Arthur wanted complete democracy in his court. He didn't want any one knight to be given preference over others. Consequently the custom of the round table was given birth. Those of us who have read literature of that day recall, however, that the plan didn't work too well. There arose great jealousy as to who would sit nearest the king.

Who Picks Up the Tab?

If you are at a dinner club and see a group of people at a table, who do you think will pay the tab? The host in practically every case is at the head of the table — he is in authority there. Everyone else is there only by invitation.

When a man takes his wife or a boy takes his best girl out to dinner, why is the woman seated on the inside of the booth and the man on the outside? It is because he is in the position of protection, in the authoritative position. He is the intermediary between the woman and the outside world. If she needs a second cup of coffee, he orders it for her. It is he who handles the situation and pays the bill.

Body Communication Speaks Constantly

From the time we wake up in the morning until we go to bed at night we are communicating constantly by our body actions — we never cease. We might even go beyond that and say that we communicate in our sleep.

If I overeat or if I am battling with some mental or emotional problem, I toss about at night in a very restless manner. If I have a sound night's sleep, then I am communicating with my body that all is well. I am not disturbed.

Then I think we can safely say that body communication takes place 24 hours throughout the day and night. It constitutes honest statements because it comes from our subconscious. Consciously a man may lie, but subconsciously he cannot. Since this type of communication is so important to us all, let's be a little more conscious of it. Also let's read this chapter again and study it carefully.

SEVEN

Kinesics and
Silent Command

It is said that words are the fingers that mold the mind of man. Others tell us that one picture is worth ten thousand words. Actually all of us realize that the more methods of communication we can put into effect the more articulate we can be. We must learn to be expressive in as many ways as possible.

How to Read People's Minds with
Body Language

During many of my seminars on persuasive communication people will ask the age-old question, "Merlyn, how can I be sure of the proper time to cause people to act?" In selling we call it the close.

Please remember this: when we attempt to persuade a person he is usually on his guard. He is very cautious about anything he says for fear he is committing himself. However, he is not cautious about his body language. Because of his efforts to conceal his feelings verbally he is often more articulate in his non-verbal communication than under ordinary circumstances.

This is why it is so important for us to be able to read the language of kinesics just as clearly as we can interpret words.

The Moment of Truth — How to Spot It

Have you ever attempted to persuade a person to commit himself, or give his consent to some line of action, and actually seen a positive decision given even though he didn't speak a word? It happens many times. Unfortunately, however, sometimes we miss the cue.

When to Use Silent Command

The most articulate communication, by a person, that he is no longer undecided but has made up his mind is the gentle stroking of his chin with his thumb and forefinger. Usually this is accompanied by a slight relaxed smile. Any indecision by a person is accompanied by a strain which usually is written on his face. When a decision is made, the tension is released, and usually a slight upward curling of the lips is evident.

When this occurs the period of persuasion is over — now is the time for action. Delay no longer!

I've seen the decision made and expressed definitely by actions and yet the communicator continue in an effort to persuade. I've even seen the communicator continue to the point where he causes the respondent to reverse his decision. A person who continues persuading after the respondent has non-verbally made a decision is similar to a hunter who kills his deer and stands there pumping shot into the dead buck.

A Kinesics Technique Worth $18,000,000.00

At a recent convention in Washington, D.C., I had occasion to meet a very interesting person. She was a 74-year-old real estate saleswoman from Oklahoma.

I asked her what her largest single sale had been. She told me that she celebrated her 73rd birthday with an 18 million dollar sale of oil land. She was one of these rare individuals who enjoy perpetual youth.

When I asked her if she intended to retire some day her answer was, "My blood is just as young as yours, Merlyn. Oh, it might be in an older container. Hardening of the arteries will never cause me to retire. I'll only retire if I get hardening of the attitudes." My guess is that she will never retire.

This very dynamic and very wise woman gave me a suggestion in kinesics which is worth passing on to you. She assured me that on many occasions she had realized a prospect had made up his mind to buy when he took a deep breath and released a big sigh. She said that this sigh of relief was the surest form of non-verbal communication that indecision was over and that the prospect was ready to take action.

Don't ignore this suggestion. Remember, it comes from a lady who made an 18 million dollar sale because she was sensitive to body communications!

What Folded Arms Mean

We have heard it said many times that folded arms mean, "I do not buy either you or what you sell." When I first started speaking on the circuit, I would often look out over my audience and feel almost panicky when I saw a number of folded arms.

Later on when I began studying kinesics I realized that it is the manner of folding one's arms that indicates resentment and signifies that "I am locking you out."

Remember this: If a person's arms are folded firmly and high upon his chest, this is a gesture of refusal. If he leans forward while in such a position it indicates even stronger resentment. If he goes further and has a frown or scowl on his face, the combination even might indicate to some degree an attitude of belligerence.

If a person folds his arms gently and loosely across the lower part of his body, this signifies relaxation and a good mood. Add to this a smile and you have your respondent or member of your audience in a jovial mood.

He Wouldn't Ask Me

I had occasion to talk with a salesman who was very upset and discouraged because a customer did not buy his
product. Since I knew both of them well, I asked the customer why he did not buy.

The customer assured me that the salesman needed some
sales instruction. He said, "I always buy from that company.
However, this new salesman never gave me a chance. He
kept talking and never presented me with the order to sign."

I delved into the matter further and asked the salesman
what the objection had been. He told me that the customer
had folded his arms and locked him out when he first sat
down. He explained to me that it would have been useless
even to try a close under such circumstances.

If one is to play the kinesics game, one must be an expert
at it. Here was a salesman who had lost a sale because he
misinterpreted body communication.

The King's Protector

We have all noted pictures of the palace guard or the king's
protector. He is always the big person standing erect with
folded arms and a stern expression on his face.

This communication has carried over into today's customs.
Note the person who stands guard at a hotel's private party
or one whose assignment is to see that some dignitary or
celebrity is not accosted by the public. Invariably he will
carry himself in a manner to discourage any trespass. His
body language says, "You are locked out; don't try to enter."

What Eyes Reveal

Above all else get the habit of watching the eyes of people
you are seeking to persuade.

If a person looks you straight in the eye in a pleasant
manner without trying to stare you down, you can rest assured

that this person is interested and perhaps will give you a fair consideration.

However, if the person is shifty-eyed and refuses to look at you directly, or if he drops his eyes — beware! This person will also be shifty in his verbal communication. Don't rely too strongly on what he says to you.

I've had occasion to see many respondents look up at the ceiling or cast their glance upward and rapidly blink their eyelids. This is a clear sign that they are considering your proposition seriously. In most cases this communicates the fact that they have already decided in your favor on the big issue. They are merely considering the details such as when, where, and how many. If you doubt this at all, study such a situation the next time it happens and you will find that among the dozen or more common methods of body communication this is one of the most reliable. Very seldom does it fail.

Raising one's eyebrow indicates disbelief while raising both eyebrows shows surprise. Winking one eye can be flirtatious, or if the person is too far away to communicate verbally, it can mean "I agree with you 100 per cent," especially if the wink is accompanied by a slight nod of the head and a smile.

Don't Ignore Shoulders

The use of one's shoulders is a very articulate and vivid form of body communication and yet very few people take time to consider this.

A person who "hunches" his shoulders or raises them casually communicates indifference. If this is accompanied by the raising of the eyebrows and even curling of the lips downward it communicates very strong indifference. He is definitely saying, "I couldn't care less."

A person who carries his shoulders in bent-forward or "hunched" position does not give us the impression of energy or determination. Don't always rely on this, however. If there is some physical defect that forces this posture, our diagnosis could be completely wrong.

It is particularly distasteful to see a young person in a slouched position. We immediately feel that we are in the presence of a person who has no ambition, who is not an organized person.

What Posture Tells You

By contrast, a person who stands erect with his shoulders upright radiates determination and energy. Merely by throwing his shoulders back and holding his head high he is communicating to us, "I love what I am doing, I know where I am going, and I intend to get there."

Did you ever wonder why a military school puts such great emphasis on correct posture with the shoulders thrown back? In fact, this is the first thing that is emphasized to new students. The reason is very simple. Authority, courage and determination are three things that must be learned if a man is to become a good soldier. Good posture radiates all three.

How would you feel if you saw a battalion of soldiers go by all bent over with their shoulders humped? Would you consider them a victorious group? Would they inspire confidence, or give you a feeling that you were protected? Our armed forces are concerned with building an image, a proud image. We even speak of the "military carriage" of one's person.

How to Feel More Confident

There are many reasons why a person should communicate confidence and ambition by good posture. Of no little importance is the fact that it has a great effect upon the person himself. Go to the mirror this moment and look at yourself. First hang your head, hunch your shoulders, and say, "I am a forceful individual. I am engineered for accomplishment, designed for success, and endowed with the seeds of greatness. There is absolutely nothing on the face of this earth that I cannot accomplish, if I so desire."

Do you sound very convincing to yourself? Did you buy the idea?

Now go back to that mirror. This time stride up to the mirror confidently with your head high and your shoulders thrown back. Now say the same thing. It makes a difference, doesn't it?

I don't intend to go into the controversial theory as to whether a person laughs because he is happy or is happy because he laughs, but I assure you that you cannot build an image in the eyes of another unless you first carry that same image in your own mind's eye.

How to Listen to Complex Body Language

Recently I took part in a management clinic in Dallas, Texas. After the clinic I was talking with one of the speakers, who told me that he and his family were moving to Denver. My first impression was to congratulate him and tell him that I thought it was a great idea.

Just behind him, however, I noticed that his wife was standing with one foot thrust forward, her head held high, and her chin thrust slightly upward. Her lips were pressed together tightly, her shoulders thrown back, and she had each of her hands on the shoulders of their two children who were very close to her side.

This picture told me much. Fortunately I checked myself before saying anything and passed over his statement with some casual remark.

I was very glad that I had followed this procedure because later that evening the wife told me very definitely that she was not about to take the children out of school and move to Denver. She even indicated that she did not know whether the family would ever move to Denver.

Don't you think you could improve your communication quotient if you formed the habit of "listening" to body language as well as verbal language? Why not try it for a week?

You will suddenly realize that there is a message which you have been ignoring all of your life. Don't use only a fragment of your listening ability. Be a "pro" and master kinesics.

Avoiding Offense

While giving a clinic on kinesics to a real estate firm not long ago, I asked those present to give any outstanding observations they had had in this field. One salesman in particular related a very sad incident, an experience, he assured me, that would never happen again.

This salesman had been showing a large ranch to a prospective buyer. He had spent about three days with the gentleman, who seemed very interested. In fact, the transaction was verbally agreed upon. All was accomplished except working out a few details and having the contract drawn up and executed.

While discussing a minor point, the salesman walked around the desk, put his arm around the gentleman, and patted him on the far shoulder. The gentleman stiffened, reddened, got up and walked out of the office and never came back.

The salesman asked me to analyze the situation for him. Not knowing all the facts and not having had the opportunity to observe the incident I could not be fully helpful. But please, *please* never take the liberty of bodily contact unless you are very sure of your ground. Not only do many people resent this, but they are actually offended and highly insulted by encroachment on their privacy. I emphatically discourage even the use of another's first name until the other person has made the initial approach. If you are a salesman, by all means let your prospect take the first step. Over the long haul you will find out that this is best.

How to Notice the Small Body Whispers

Not all body communications are to be taken too seriously, but it is at least well to be able to interpret them.

For instance, do you ever try to understand the emotion of

a person who rubs his nose while you are making an effort to get a decision from him? In most cases this is an indication of disapproval, disagreement, or even resentment. Of course the energy with which a person does this often tells us a great deal about the extent of his disapproval or resentment. When we observe such conduct it is well for us to consider carefully our next move. We have been told very clearly that the person is definitely not in the frame of mind to O.K. a contract or declare himself in favor of something.

Hands Over Eyes

Can you recall ever having seen a person suddenly throw his hand over his eyes? This, of course indicates that he is ashamed of something. It's a way of non-verbally apologizing to you for some thoughtlessness.

Slapping One's Forehead

You have forgotten something and you want to be demonstrative about it. What do you do to show the other party that you did not remember? Many of us slap our forehead and even close our eyes. This is in reality a combination of showing that we have forgotten and asking for forgiveness.

Fingers Together

If a person holds his hands in front of his chest with the fingers of each hand touching the same fingers of the other hand, it signifies confidence. This person is fortifying his remarks by saying in body language, "I know what I am talking about. I am something of an authority on what I am telling you."

This is a characteristic pose of my doctor. I have observed this on many occasions and I do not resent it at all. In fact, I have now begun to watch for it and am even a little disappointed if he does not do it at least once when I have an appointment.

The next time you have occasion to attend a conference where there are several panelists sitting at a table on the platform, please watch for this non-verbal means of communication. I give you a full guarantee that if you observe carefully you will see an exhibition of this more than once.

Public Kinesics

I once had a contest at a clinic to see who could name the greatest number of well-known statues that were created to give some body communication.

On this occasion there were over 30 such statues named. Among those named were The Thinker, Diana, Cupid, The End of the Trail and numerous others. The Thinker led in number of selections. Give yourself the test. Also note that every city of any size in the United States has one or more such statues. I was in Salt Lake City the other day and had occasion to observe four within five blocks of each other.

Drumming Fingers

Elsewhere in this book the point is stressed that an interview is not a true interview unless we are with a person both physically *and* mentally. Only then does true persuasion begin.

While a communicator may be with his respondent physically, you can be sure that he is not with him mentally if the respondent is drumming his fingers on the desk or table. Please note that in many cases where the respondent is tapping the desk or table with the fingers of one hand, his chin is resting on the other hand. These two gestures go together.

When you find yourself confronted with this situation, don't waste your time proceeding with the interview unless you can capture the person's interest. Any further presentation is like water on a duck's back.

Foot Signals

Many people like to sit in a position where they can observe the action of a person's feet.

If the respondent is moving his foot around nervously in a circle, he is portraying the same impatience that he would show by drumming his fingers.

However, if the shoe hangs loosely on the toe of the foot, this indicates relaxation; in fact it is a very encouraging gesture. Women in particular often are engaged in this gesture.

Change of Position

One of the most important facts to remember in the study of body communication is that change of physical position usually indicates a change of mental attitude. Sometimes this change is in favor of the persuader and sometimes it is against him. In any event, the moment that a person uncrosses his legs and leans forward, or folds his arms and leans back, or puts his hands behind his head and looks up, or makes any other obvious change in physical position, this is a cue that a *mental* shift has just taken place also.

Watch for Body Communication

It is impossible to discuss all of the physical gestures that tell us what the other person is thinking. Space does not permit it in this book.

I shall feel well repaid if I can only convince you of the importance of constantly watching for these gestures. You will be astounded when you realize how quickly you can master the art of interpreting the body language clearly.

Please form the habit of observation in the field of kinesics. When you do form this habit you will find that a new dimension in communication has opened to you.

EIGHT

Space Communication and Territorial Invasion

There is a most interesting phase of non-verbal communication, equally important with body communication, known as *space communication.*

Much is being written about this subject today. It has been given many different names by many people. Some have titled it "Zone Studies," others call it "Spaceology," still others have called it "Territorial Invasion." One even coined the name "Proxemics."

It is unimportant what we call it, but it is very important that we understand it, especially the important part it plays in today's communication.

The Territorial Need

Since the dawn of civilization everything that walks, crawls, flies or swims has had a territorial need. It is not enough to have space to live in. Whether for animal, fowl or fish, there must also be territorial identity.

The lion has always had his area that he dominates. It is clearly marked with boundaries just as definite as those boundaries a farmer might claim for his farm. The wolf pack has its definite run. Even fish and birds have habits of territorial occupancy.

So sacred is living space to people that it has been the basic cause of practically every war ever fought. It has been the moving factor that led to the discovery of new continents.

The settlers moved west because of the desire to acquire new territory.

Law Recognizes Its Sanctity

Man's very sanctity requires him to have geographical identity. We have always heard about the sanctity of the home. This is the one space that man can call his own. So sacred is it that the law recognizes the right of a man to protect it even if it requires the death of another.

Maybe some of you have read the book, *A Man Without a Country*. If so, you were impressed with the fact that a man has a great void in his life if he has no place where he can stand and say, "This is my own, my native land."

Sanctity of Space Transfer

While a home or other real estate can be transferred today merely by the delivery and recording of a deed, it was at one time far more difficult. There were no written deeds and no recordings. The method was as follows:

All of the people in the area were gathered together for an all-day festival. Food, drinks and entertainment were provided. Finally toward the end of the day the preacher gave a prayer. The person transferring the property would take a handful of the soil and hand it to the person receiving the transfer as symbolic of title transfer. Furthermore, the transferor would place his hand on a Bible and swear to defend the transferee's right to the property as long as he lived. Then after a prayer all of the people would walk together to all four corners of the property where the boundaries would be identified in the presence of all.

There was once a rather strange custom connected with a transfer. A boy from the neighborhood was chosen. At each corner of the property the boy was given a sound thrashing. This was to impress upon his memory just where the boundary lines were. If, in later years, there was a boundary dispute the boy so chosen was considered the expert. His testimony carried much weight. Besides the fact that he perhaps would live longer than the older people and be around more years to testify, his memory was thought to be more vivid since he had a good reason to remember each corner.

It was considered a great honor to be the chosen boy for the ceremony. However, I am not sure just how honored the boy himself felt, or whether he volunteered or whether he was given this honor against his will.

Space Encroachment

Everyone of us subconsciously feels a possessory right to a reasonable amount of space near ourselves. If we are sitting in a plane or bus next to someone, it is an unspoken law that each of us has a right to our particular territory which no one can invade.

Even if we are having lunch with an acquaintance this same rule holds true. We subconsciously divide the area of the table equally and are disturbed if there is an encroachment on our area. It is instinctive with us. Many times when an encroachment such as this occurs, we become upset and don't realize the cause of our emotional arousement.

The Spoon Episode

I was invited to speak at a banquet in Sarasota, Florida. At noon on the day of my engagement I was having lunch with the program chairman. After lunch we were talking and having coffee. For some strange reason I was conscious that my luncheon partner had leaned back from the table with his arms crossed indicating a body communication which said he was resentful of something I had said or done.

For a moment I was puzzled. Then I realized that I was playing with my spoon and that I had placed it over on his side of the table. He unconsciously felt an encroachment of his territory — I had invaded his space. After realizing this, in a relaxed manner, trying not to be obvious about it, I pulled the spoon two or three inches back from his territorial line.

The reaction was almost immediate. In less than one minute he was leaning forward in a friendly, relaxed manner, talking with me and smiling. I'm sure this person did not realize, and I of course did not tell him, that he had just been the guinea pig in a space encroachment experiment. I had, in effect, given him the Silent Command to be friendly.

A Fascinating Experiment

There is an old western song that says, "Don't fence me in."

Westerners are noted for their strong territorial consciousness. We see many movies today which have plots built around the fight between the cattlemen and farmers over the fences.

However, everyone of us has a fear of restriction of movement which applies to the foot or two of space that surrounds us.

On the day following the Sarasota incident I had been so intrigued that I made another experiment. I was sitting at the counter in the airport next to a very expressionless man. I gradually eased my knife and fork over close to his territorial area. I then casually sipped water and put the glass down slightly over in his space.

After a few nervous movements this man put his elbow down between us, thus staking his claim, rested his chin on it and pivoted around slightly, putting his back toward me. He obviously was fighting against the encroachment on his territory as strongly as possible without making a scene. I gradually withdrew my attack, but it was too late to get any change in his conduct. He did not trust me any longer. He kept his elbow and back as a defense wall and even ate with his left hand.

My experiment would have been a total success if I could only have been sure that he was right-handed. I wanted to ask him but I was not quite too sure where experimentation ended and aggressiveness began. So I rested my case without further effort.

The Mental Satisfaction of Space

I have a friend who owns a lovely home in the mountains only an hour and a half from Phoenix. She uses it fewer than a half-dozen times a year. She has refused several offers for it at figures which she admits are far beyond its worth. I have asked her on several occasions why she did not sell it. It is obvious that the limited use she makes of it doesn't even justify the expense of taxes and upkeep, much less the investment of money that is tied up.

My friend finally confided in me that the mountain home communicated a certain freedom of choice to her which had become very valuable. She said it meant a lot to her just to know that she could go up to her mountain home any time at the drop of a hat. She did not feel a territorial confinement because she was not limited to her home in Phoenix. I am confident that many people keep a second home for that reason and do not fully realize it.

The Deepest Human Need

After a speaking engagement in Chicago, an elderly couple came up to me and asked if they could talk with me for a few minutes. I agreed to meet them in the coffee shop within 15 minutes.

This couple first asked me about Arizona in general and then specifically about a certain subdivision of two-and-one-half-acre plots in northern Arizona. I gave them all the information I could but had to confess that I had not heard of the subdivision.

I was amazed when they told me that although they had owned the plot for seven years, they had never seen their land or even been in the state of Arizona.

However, they seemed happy over their purchase. They

assured me that they had already received a twofold return on their money just from the joy of knowing they were not forever confined to the limits of their place in Chicago.

Some day, they assured me, they would retire to their ranchero in Arizona. This was a dream of liberation from a restricted territory.

Psychologists tell us that the deepest human compulsion, next to the law of self-preservation and next to the sex urge, is the desire to own real estate. This compulsion arises from the fact that it is this real estate which gives us the space freedom which man must have.

Please Keep Your Distance

It is a generally accepted fact that the varying distance which we must keep between our body and that of another is determined by the degree of our intimacy. This is not only good taste, but relationships are also conditioned to this principle over a long period of time.

We have occasions to observe this every day. I was at a cocktail party the other day in a rather crowded room. A lady was sitting at a table in the presence of three men. A fourth man came up and sat down very close to her. He immediately patted her on the knee. She looked at him and smiled approvingly.

This was very articulate non-verbal communication. This little drama which took place in three seconds told me a great deal. This man was the husband. He had a right to occupy a space close to this woman. If any other man had sat that close, it would have been an invasion of her privacy, a violation of propriety and conventionality. The placing of his hand on her knee might even have been considered an insult. But a husband and wife enjoy an intimacy which does not extend outside the marital circle.

Mental Halitosis

During the years when I was receptionist, I had occasion to observe good taste and bad taste in the handling of space by people who called at our company.

The most irritating of all callers is the person who on his very first call practically crawls all over your desk trying to be a regular guy. Within minutes he wants to call you by your first name. Not only has he invaded your territorial privacy but your personal privacy as well. People such as this have mental halitosis; they simply brighten up the office when they leave.

The Privacy Zone

The person I liked and admired was the person who always stood a respectful distance away from the desk and politely and in a businesslike manner stated his business. This communicated courtesy and respect. Even though such a salesman and I may have eventually formed a friendship which permitted a first-name salutation, still I always desired to see that the intimacy of my desk zone was not invaded.

By standing at a respectful distance that person was communicating to me, "You are an important person in this company. You are even more important to me because you are the *only* person who can make it possible for me to see my prospect. Your desk is your office. Just as I would not bound into your office without being invited, I shall take no liberties with your desk or the close proximity therewith."

How Distance Communicates Respect

Have you ever been in court and noticed the position of the lawyer as he pleads his case?

Legal etiquette, my lawyer informs me, requires that he stand a full six to eight feet away from the judicial bench. Occasionally the judge may call the two lawyers involved up to the bench and speak to them in a tone of voice which cannot be heard by the jury or witnesses. The lawyer never penetrates the dignity of this zone unless it is by invitation of the judge.

The non-verbal communication on the part of the lawyer is very obvious. He is, by keeping his distance, proclaiming that he has utmost respect for the judicial system of our country and that he is not one to violate its canons.

The Appearance of Intimacy

There is another reason why lawyers are expected to keep a respectful distance from the judicial bench. If a lawyer and judge have been too closely associated in former practice of law or in any other way, that judge is required to disqualify himself in a case wherein that lawyer is involved. There should be no intimacy between the judge and any lawyers appearing before him.

Closeness of physical contact suggests intimacy, whether it be true or not. Therefore, the very appearance of intimacy should be avoided. A lawyer who tries to be too intimate with a judge is immediately suspected of ulterior motives, perhaps even of tampering with justice. For these reasons and for numerous others a lawyer is expected never to invade the judicial zone.

The Big-Top Table

To a lesser extent the chairman of the board and even the president of a corporation often have a large desk which is six or eight feet across. This means that they are protecting a large territory of intimacy. They can keep people at a distance.

This principle can be carried a step further by having an office for the private secretary or assistant through which one must pass before getting to the chairman or president. This extends their territorial control even farther.

A definite problem for many heads of corporations is the need to discourage a junior executive from trying to become too "palsy-walsy." A good chief executive can't even give the appearance of showing favorites. A large desk discourages this. If the junior executive is kept at a respectful distance, it is difficult for him to have anything but a respectful attitude.

Violating Zone Barriers

There is the type of person who, though well-meaning, has the unfortunate habit of letting his nose practically touch yours when he is speaking to you. You feel that this person, however innocent he may be, is invading your territory.

Most animals don't like their privacy invaded any more than man does. You can walk up to within a few feet of an animal at a zoo. If you go too close, he will move away.

There were a couple of little squirrels that would come up to our door at the last home where we lived. We often fed them nuts. About three feet was their territory of intimacy. If we came closer, they ran away.

Don't get the habit of violating zone barriers. It is not only bad manners, bad communication, but also it makes you personally become obnoxious.

NINE

How to Listen with Your Eyes

I once asked a very successful person to name the one quality which he considered most important to his success. Without a moment's hesitation he said, "I try to listen with my eyes as well as with my ears."

Reading Others' Minds

If this chapter accomplishes nothing else, I hope it can encourage you to form the habit of using your eyes to listen. Since we see a hundred times more than we hear, if we form the habit of using our eyes for listening as well as seeing our exposure is increased a hundred fold. Don't forget that listening is just as important as speaking in good communication. So if you can start listening with your eyes, you will start receiving messages which might make other people's minds an open book to you.

Visual Listening Reliable

"I know it is true because I saw it myself."
"Seeing is believing."
"Don't take his word. Go and see for yourself."
"Show me."

How many times have we heard the above expressions? In the spoken word there is a great margin for error and misunderstanding. Maybe the person who delivers the message is uninformed or perhaps he colors the statement through self-interest or prejudice. He might even use words that have one meaning to him but a different meaning to us. Noise interference might cause a complete misunderstanding.

This margin of error is greatly reduced when we draw our conclusions from personal observation.

I recently read an account of a trial in which there was a great variance and conflict of evidence. An accident had occurred on a bridge. No two witnesses described the bridge in the same way. Finally the judge instructed the jury, accompanied by the bailiff, to go out and inspect the bridge. The message given by observation, by *visual communication,* was more reliable than the testimony of all the witnesses.

Verbal Vs. Visual Communication

I heard a person humorously tell a long, wild story involving a personal experience. His wife, taking the story seriously, contradicted him, saying that she was there and the facts were not stated correctly.

The husband chuckled and said, "Another good story ruined by an eye-witness."

While the husband had purposely exaggerated the facts and had related the story with tongue in cheek, there is a good lesson in this story. Do we give to visual communication the credibility which is its due?

Convincing Actions

Have you ever heard the expression, "His actions speak so loudly that I cannot hear what he is saying"? This is just a way of saying that his visual communication is in conflict with his verbal communication since the first is so much more convincing, it drowns out his words.

As a ridiculous example, what would be your reaction to a man who spoke to a temperance organization while highly under the influence of whiskey? Even if the contents of his speech were brilliant, he certainly could not be persuasive. There would be a definite breakdown in communication.

An ardent suitor might proclaim his affections for his sweetheart to the high heavens. He might write her letters every day and compose poetry for her by the page. Soon, however, all of this would lose its persuasive power if he never made a proposal of marriage.

Less Say — More Do

The old slang expression, "Less say — more do," carries an important message. Verbal assurance soon loses its veracity unless it is backed up by action.

Last spring I took part in a five-day seminar, sponsored by a city in Iowa, on "How do we sell our city?" I was very much impressed with the motto of the city, "It's good to live in Keokuk." The whole climate of the week's seminar was built around the usual theme that business goes where it's invited and stays where it is well treated.

None of the city's propaganda, however, impressed me as much as what the citizens, through their Chamber of Commerce, actually did for new business. I am sure this great little city will continue to grow and enjoy new business as long as it continues to communicate through action as well as words.

Use This Tested Technique

All of us are prone to accept important principles mentally and yet fail to use them to our own advantage. Form the habit of better observation, of listening visually. If you concentrate on listening visually, you can soon form good observation habits.

Why Some People Get Hired and Others Don't

On one occasion I was engaged to recruit a number of women to do some survey work for a large national company.

Their job was to call on consumers and obtain reports on their buying habits.

On some occasions I would be aware of certain mental reservations when I employed a person. I could never quite put my finger on the exact reason for my hesitancy. Almost invariably, when I had these doubts the people turned out to be unsatisfactory. During the interview their answers to questions were satisfactory and past records of employment seemed O.K. Then what had prompted me to be skeptical?

On careful analysis I finally concluded that it had been the non-verbal communication which I had received at the time of the interview. Carelessness of dress and grooming on the part of some had been evident. I recalled a sloppiness of posture in one instance. Just the lack of assurance and confidence in the appearance of another had been observed.

Listening with Your Subconscious

I had been so anxious to be fair and unprejudiced in my selection of people for the assignment that I had based my selection almost entirely on the answers I received from the questionnaire and from their past record of employment which they themselves had submitted.

Our subconscious mind is not influenced by emotion and is not blinded by unimportant details. Furthermore, it bases its decision on credible evidence, visual observance being one of the most important. The subconscious is the best listening device we have. I am confident that none of us rely on its good judgment as we should.

Your "Sixth Sense" and How to Use It

Many of us vaguely refer to a sixth sense which we might possibly possess. Sometimes people are almost afraid to refer to this except in humor. If a businessman reported to his superiors that he had made an important decision based on this sixth sense, all eyebrows would be lifted.

Actually our sixth sense is one of the most, if not *the* most powerful and reliable mechanism for judgment and decision-making which we possess. It is our God-given subconscious mind. Through our subconscious alone can we comprehend reliably, uninfluenced by extraneous matters. Our subconscious knows no favorites. Its judgment cannot be warped by flattery, fear or undue influence.

How to Turn On Your Magic Communicator

Did you ever hear a person say, "I'd like to sleep on it. If I feel the same tomorrow as I do today about it, I shall go along on the idea"?

Now what is this person truly saying? Whether he knows it or not, this is what he feels:

"My subconscious is more reliable than my conscious. You may have influenced me unduly. I am not sure. Perhaps I have other things crowding my mind so that I cannot see the picture clearly. In any event I need reassurance. This comes to me only when I feel securely about it as well as think securely about it. I am putting this proposition completely in the hands of my subconscious mind. My subconscious is the supreme court in all my decisions. When I go to sleep my emotions will subside, my worries will cease, and I will not be subject to influence from unrelated matters. Tomorrow you will have your decision — a definite decision — and one that I shall have the courage to back up with action."

Please don't fail to avail yourself of this "Magic Communicator" — your subconscious. It is the most reliable listener you possess. Also, when it speaks to you, you be sure to listen. It is the one oracle which is yours.

20-20 Communication Vision

If you saw a certain fowl in the company of ducks and if it quacked like a duck, had feathers like a duck, and laid duck eggs, you wouldn't have to send for a veterinarian to find out that this was a duck. Just the simple power of observation would communicate that fact to you.

And yet in our everyday experiences we have things communicated just as forcefully to us, and we fail to use our 20-20 communication vision and accept these truths.

Employment Vision

The president of one of our nation's largest automotive industries once told me that the most costly mistake his company makes has to do with errors in employment of the wrong people for the wrong jobs. When I asked him the cause of these mistakes, he said without hesitation that it was because those who have the responsibility of employment too often take into consideration facts which should not be considered.

When I pressed him even further for information, this man of great experience said that in his considered judgment there were only two factors which should be given major importance in employment:

First, *the past record of the applicant.* The president assured me that the pattern of a man's conduct in the past is the best information on which to predict his future. People fight against change. Any change in their environment or in their conduct makes them feel insecure. Never can we find a more reliable prediction of a man's future conduct than his past record.

Second, *what is he doing now to prepare himself for greater opportunities in the future?* The president was very emphatic about this second criterion. He said that one should not take into consideration what the applicant plans to do about preparation in the future, and should not even give a great deal of consideration to courses he has taken in the too-distant past. The real test is what he is engaged in at present that will improve his capacity to do a better job.

How to Impress an Interviewer

One might wonder what communication has to do with employment.

When a person applies for a job, we can be sure that he wants to communicate the best impression possible. Consequently, we can be sure that all verbal communication is colored with personal interest. It would be very strange if it were any other way.

This is why an employer must resort to facts in order to make the best appraisement and best prediction of the applicant. An applicant naturally will want to impress the interviewer with his sincerity and his desire to do a good job. While this is all fine it cannot compare in importance with the sincerity and desire which the applicant showed in the past.

Body Language Is a Two-Way Street

We all hear the statement, which I repeat, that "Communication is a dance and it takes two to tango." This is just as true in body communication as in verbal communication. For instance, when I first started speaking on the circuit I concentrated intensely on the body language which I spoke to my audience. I practiced before a full-length mirror day after day and week after week. It was several years before I realized that the body language spoken by an *audience* to a *speaker* is just as important.

So let's take a look at non-verbal communication first by a speaker and then by an audience.

The Casual Friendly Approach

Unless my audience knows more about their particular business or profession than I, they have no right to attend the convention where I speak. And so the stiff, scholarly approach, as though I were a philosopher with a basket of sage knowledge, ready to hand out intellectual calories to all who can digest them, is out. Also, the use of gimmicks, gadgets and gismos is usually corny and leaves an audience cold. Even if one can keep complete attention, it doesn't mean that he is successful in his mission.

People attend a convention to get helpful information. If I can present this information in an entertaining way so that it can be remembered, then the audience will not have attended my session in vain.

If I want to be sure that I can accomplish this, I must have my subject matter so completely under control that I can think intensely while appearing physically to be relaxed. I must communicate the idea that I have a very important message to communicate, and that both the audience and I are going to have fun while I reveal this message.

This is why I always like a "roving mike" where possible. If I can move about and even walk among the members of the audience I can increase the informality and create a relaxed climate which I feel is important in my case.

Getting Attention with Gimmicks

Just as slang is an excuse and a poor substitute for good English, I feel very strongly that a speaker who uses an excessive number of gimmicks is offering a poor excuse for good body communication. While it is true that gimmicks can get attention, what a speaker really wants is favorable attention, attention to himself so that he can convey a helpful message. He can bring on the dancing girls, explode a firecracker, or have a bunny crawl out of the birthday cake, and eye-catching and surprising as these may be, they cannot capture the attention which can be created with good body communication.

Three Miracles of Body Communication

To be sure that he brings about the desired results, in a good convention presentation a speaker attempts to do three things. Body communication plays an important part in all three.

First, the speaker should see that the whole climate of his presentation is relaxed and informal. His facial expression, gestures, strolling among his audience and movements in

general are far more important in this respect than anything he has to say.

Second, since an audience wants not to be talked at but
rather communicated with, participation is vital. Frankly,
I have oratorical claustrophobia. I cannot stand planted
behind a podium. I want to cruise among my audience, ask
questions, and get complete involvement. Lately I have
added a new feature to this involvement. I call it "participation reward." Those who are attentive and participate are
given little prizes. Sometimes it is a record of one of my
speeches, sometimes just a 25 cent item, but this reward
keeps interest high.

Finally, don't take yourself seriously — concentrate on
your audience and your subject matter. I've seen speakers
who could be great platform artists if they could only learn
to take one step outside of themselves, look around at themselves and laugh.

If a speaker lays an egg, which every speaker will do sooner
or later, he should call his audience's attention to it and then
ask them to laugh with him at it.

Recently I was taking part in a seminar in Regina, Canada.
A speaker who preceded me got his tongue twisted three
consecutive times on a rather difficult word. I was embarrassed for him and I could feel the embarrassment of his
audience.

However, this speaker smiled, took his glasses off and
began cleaning them as he said, "I spent a thousand dollars
having my eyes fixed and now my mouth won't work."

His audience went wild with applause. Not only did he
break the tension but he made his audience love him. Any
time a speaker can exhibit a sense of humor at his own
expense, he is certain to win his audience.

Any speaker who can do these three things — create a
climate of informality, gain participation, and emphasize
the importance of his audience — will always be in demand.
However, he can never accomplish all this without a generous
use of body communication.

The minute I see more than two people in my audience
looking at their watches, staring into space, or folding their

arms high upon their chests, I know that one of two conditions prevails. Either my time is up and I should close, or
I must make a quick change of pace by getting immediate
participation or taking some steps to capture my audience's
attention.

The Invisible Barometer

Salesmen have an expression; when one sells a product to
a customer, then talks so much the customer changes his
mind, the salesman is said to "buy back his product." The
tragedy of tragedies in speech making is when a speaker
makes a good speech, then "buys himself back" by continuing to speak when he should shut up.

I make a point of picking out two or three people in my
audience who were the last to give me their attention.
These are the most important people to me. They constitute
my "invisible barometer." I watch them closely throughout
my speech. Usually they will be the first to become restless.
I then want to close my speech or change the pace before
the other, more patient members of my audience become
restless.

How to Take Calculated Risks

In many audiences a speaker has one or two people who
only "came for the ride," who just wanted to be with the
other people. They are bored with themselves and everyone
else. They not only pay no attention but they also communicate to the speaker that they can hardly wait for the
speaking ordeal to end. In this respect they are usually
very articulate.

This is the calculated risk of being a speaker. Nothing
can be done about it. While it annoys and distracts a new
speaker, one must learn to live with such a situation.

The only procedure for a speaker is to ignore them and
cling to the people who seem interested. As Mr. H. B. Swope

once said, "I cannot tell you the formula for success, but I can tell you the formula for failure: try to please everyone."

I might add that in some instances I have, when getting my audiences involved, corrected this situation by choosing an uninterested and bored person to do some role playing in front of the audience. It is rather amazing how many times such a person turns into a complete "ham" and seems to enjoy the limelight. My conscience usually hurts me when I resort to this, however, because participation should be a reward for attention. Most of the people actually love to be chosen for role playing before the group.

We have touched on just a few non-verbal forms of communication that have to do with listening, employment, platform speaking and dealing with people in general. Please read this chapter again and relate some of the principles found herein to your own experiences. Don't confine your understanding and participation in the great field of communication to mere writing and speaking. There are new horizons to observe and new worlds to conquer when we become experts in body and other non-verbal means of communication.

TEN

How to Project Unspoken Orders That Must Be Obeyed

A body of information given by someone to another person or to a group is a *presentation*. There will always be two philosophies of thinking on the subject of whether or not a presentation should be "canned."

One group insists the presentation should be completely prepared, that a straight line is the shortest distance between two points, and that this straight line can be followed only through a well-prepared presentation, followed meticulously.

The other group takes the stand that the completely prepared presentation is amateurish and unprofessional in every respect. They claim that any parrot-like presentation does not take into account unexpected events that might take place in the course of any interview.

Your Psychic Road Map

While I do not intend to champion either of these two theories totally, I am sure we all agree that communication in all facets and in all fields is far more effective if we follow certain basic patterns of procedure. For instance, I would not start out driving from Los Angeles to New York

115

without a road map. Just to head out in an eastward direction would be colossal insanity.

Regardless of how correct the road map might be, however, and notwithstanding how carefully I might have studied it, I could not follow it blindly. Maybe a bridge would be washed out, or a detour sign might appear. A highway department might close a mountain road due to a snow storm.

Secret of Structured Thinking

Then doesn't the intelligent approach seem to be something of a compromise between the two theories? Whether we make a speech, present a product or service, ask for a raise, hold a meeting or engage in any other form of important communication, we must have an outline of procedure or formula to follow. I like to think of this outline or formula as the steel girders of a building being constructed.

Regardless of whether we finish the building in brick, cement, glass or marble, this steel structure is necessary. If the color of the building be green, blue or black, still the basic frame must be there. If it be equipped with elevators, escalators or stairs, the steel structures must be there to support any of these.

How to Move People to Action

While it is true that much communication is designed only to educate or entertain, the real purpose of most of our communication in dealing with people every day is to cause them to act.

During this century there have appeared many different patterns of persuasion. All of them are effective when properly followed, and all are designed in their ultimate purpose to cause people to be moved to action.

Basic Formula for Action

Perhaps the first of the different formulae for persuading people to act became popular around the turn of the century.

It is found in all instructional books published by insurance companies and many other companies for their salesmen. It contains the three basic elements — pose the problem, offer the solution and ask for action.

The Crasher Technique

Just after the depression of 1929 a number of personal development schools sprung up everywhere. People were discouraged and were reaching for something. Out of these, the Dale Carnegie schools survived and became popular. They have been an important factor in sales and personal development over many years.

We find four elements in their pattern of persuasion. These were "Ho-Hum," "Why Bring That Up?", "For Instance" and "So What?"

In the Dale Carnegie classes a student was often given the assignment of standing before the class and presenting a speech. As the speaker faced his audience, the other students would say "Ho-hum" and indicate how completely bored they were at that moment and how unconcerned they were over anything they felt the speaker might have to say. This was a challenge to the speaker to open with a "ho-hum crasher" and get their attention. This might be done with a question, a provocative statement, or even by flashing an exhibit.

Then the audience would chant in unison, "Why bring that up?" It was now important for the speaker to explain to the audience why the subject brought up was important to their welfare — why they should listen.

Then the students would say, "For instance." This was a cue for the speaker to give an illustration or tell a story to prove his point.

Finally the audience would say together, "So what?" Now the speaker must tell the audience what he wanted them to do about it. He must appeal for action.

The Dale Carnegie formula is not limited to speaking or selling. It applies to every line of endeavor. This pattern reminds us that there is no excuse for effort except for action — no reason for action except for results.

Basic Selling Technique

Still later another formula took its place in most of our sales training sessions and development programs. We called it the "Attention, Interest, Desire and Action," or A.I.D.A., procedure.

The Third Dimension Technique

As human engineering becomes more popular, we have still another approach. It is sometimes spoken of as the third dimension approach.

The advocates of this theory maintain that while "what people do" and "why they do it" are important, these are important only to the extent that they can guide us in the most important phase of dealing with people, namely "how to cause them to do it." This theory is in reality an outgrowth of the "Attention, Interest, Desire and Action" pattern. It simply tells how one accomplishes the fourth facet of that program.

We must get a person's *attention.* How? By making him *like* us.

We must get his *interest.* How? By making him *understand* us.

We must get his *desire.* How? By making him *believe* us.

We finally must get *action.* How? By making him *trust* us.

So we can see in this pattern of persuasion the words *attention, interest, desire* and *action* have been replaced by the third dimensional human engineering words: he must *like* me; he must *understand* me; he must *believe* me; he must *trust* me.

Selecting the Right Method

I am confident that if a person went out and used any of these patterns enough and used them sincerely, he would be successful. But one of the great things about freedom of speech is that we have the blessings of choice.

Do yourself the favor of selecting any one of these or any

combination of these that will make you comfortable in your communication.

The Cundiff 4-Ply System

Over the years I have both taught and lived all of the above patterns of communication and have finally ended up with that which serves my purpose best. I feel comfortable with it. It is in harmony with all of the above but slightly different from them, because it uses "Silent Command" techniques, as well as the conventional ones.

I'd like to give it to you and elaborate on each part. The four steps which I suggest are these: present the problem, offer the solution, prove my case, and then ask for action.

The First Step

It is very important that in your initial effort to communicate in a way designed eventually to lead people to action, you must take the four steps in their logical sequence. Once you present any one of them out of proper order, the pattern will become chaotic.

The biggest mistake most of us make is that in our eagerness and enthusiasm to offer a solution and persuade other people to act as we desire, we fail to put due emphasis on the first step. This first step is the very essence of my whole formula. Unless you have a problem to solve, a need to fulfill, you have nothing to perform. It is similar to an effort to come back from a place you have never been.

How to Make Others See Things Your Way

You must agree with your respondent about the problem. Bear in mind that by "respondent" I may mean one other person, a group, or even a whole audience. In every case, that other person, group, or audience, must see the problem as you see it. It is not enough if you fully explain to the respondent just what you think his problem is. He must agree and commit himself to recognize the problem.

In fact, your first step is a sale within a sale. Until your respondent has bought the idea that he has a problem, and put himself on record that he has a problem and knows just what it is, you have no reason to consider going on to your next step.

As I have said earlier, a problem reduced to its simplest terms is nothing more than the difference between what a person has and what he wants. Sometimes your respondent needs your help in establishing these two conditions. Usually the first condition does not offer any great difficulty, but the second condition is much harder to establish.

In any event, don't let your enthusiasm for what you are proposing cause you to neglect this first step. Remember, pin it down definitely. Get the other person's unequivocal commitment on this point.

The Cloak and Dagger Technique

Many feel that you should not even approach this first step until your respondent's attention is fully gained. They favor gimmicks and gadgets to attract this attention even before discussing the problem.

I firmly believe that unless the problem can be presented and discussed so forcefully that in itself it receives complete attention and interest, we shall fail in this first step anyway. Be careful about playing cloak and dagger or cat and mouse in an effort to get another's attention. This is not the way to get favorable attention.

If attention were all I needed, I could burst into a person's office or home in a rude and insulting manner and get his attention every time. I might even get some quick action. But what I want is *favorable* attention.

Now let's suppose you have discussed your respondent's problem fully and that he has agreed with you just what it is. You are now ready for the next step.

The Second Step

Unless your proposal offers a solution to your respondent's problem, you have no excuse for even taking up his time. Your very presence there would constitute mental dishonesty.

In initially offering the solution, your manner must carry the enthusiasm which springs from your own conviction. Unless you are so sure your proposal satisfies his needs, unless you are positive that you have already solved his problem in your own mind, you cannot expect him to buy the idea.

The Subjective Sale Technique

In emphasizing this point at salesmen's seminars I always try to stress the "subjective sale." Unless the salesman himself completely buys the idea that he has the solution to the problem, he will never sell his prospect. Yes, this is the *important* sale. Fortify yourself with this conviction — arm yourself with sincerity. You are then prepared to discuss the fact that you have the solution to someone else's problem.

The Third Step

It is not enough merely to tell your prospect that you have the solution to his problem. Necessary as it is, even a deep conviction on your part that you can help him is not sufficient.

You must offer proof — convincing proof — that your proposal is his answer. This is done in many ways. You should always be prepared to offer plenty of evidence in this regard. Remember that mere statements and your opinions are self-serving and do not carry a great deal of weight. Offer quotes, give "for instance's," tell stories of other people's experiences and the happy results which resulted.

How to Offer Proof That Convinces

If you ever sat on a jury, you will recall that the judge in his instructions to you carefully told you that in considering evidence you must put more importance on facts, events and happenings than on mere statements by either party which might be to either's benefit.

I repeat that since time began stories and "for instance's" have been the greatest of all vehicles for persuasion. Everyone can relate himself to a story. Stories are understandable — they convince.

I again emphasize even more strongly that the most moving of all arguments is the fact that others "did it and are glad." Stories and for-instance's are our best method in this regard.

The "Q" Technique

Don't forget to use quotes where possible. The value of this type of persuasion is evidenced by the many, many testimonials we find in our national advertising today. Just the fact that some well-known athlete or other celebrity did something has a big impact. So valuable is this in causing people to accept a product or service that large fees are paid today for testimonials. I call this the "Q" technique.

The Fourth Step

Let's suppose that you have been successful in getting your respondent to agree on just exactly what his problem is. He listened carefully when you presented your proposal as a solution, fortified your position by giving an abundance of proof that your idea had solved many other similar problems for other people. This brings you to the fourth step. In fact, the first three steps are important only to the extent that they prepare your respondent for this fourth step. Yes, unless we get action the whole interview is merely a waste of time on everyone's part. But, by now, you have already planted your "unspoken orders" in his mind, so you're all set.

How to Ask for Action

It is almost unbelievable how many people are excellent in the art of persuasion until they get down to the point of causing the other person to act. Here they fail. If these people could only adopt the philosophy from the very beginning that there is no excuse for effort except to bring about action and no excuse for action except to bring about favorable results, they would be far more successful in good persuasion.

Refusal Is Not Rejection

All of us have a great compulsion to guard our own ego. One of the deepest human impulses is the desire to be accepted, to be a part of something. By contrast, when we are neglected or rejected we are hurt. The opposite of love is not hate, it is neglect and rejection.

Perhaps the principle reason that so many people are afraid to ask for action is that they fear the emotional trauma of being rejected. This puts our ego into a nose-dive. Since all of us are trying so hard to protect this ego, we have difficulty pursuing this fourth step just as strongly and sincerely as we handled the first three steps.

About the third time the average person receives a refusal of his proposal or idea, he accepts this refusal as a rejection of himself. This is something which a person must overcome if he ever expects to be professional in the art of persuasion. I have a friend, a great human engineer, who told me that whenever he gets a refusal he tells himself that what this person is really saying is, "I like you very much, but up to this point you have not given me enough evidence to cause me to act. Please see if there is not something else you can tell me which might persuade me."

Don't Fear Fear

I have never been one who subscribed to the feeling that one of our great freedoms should be freedom from fear. Fear is normal; it is part of nature's law of self-preservation; it is inoculation against laziness and complacency. However, fear can never lick us if we are not afraid of fear. Naturally we dislike refusals but let's never be afraid of them.

Many people mistakenly think that courage is freedom from fear. This is not true. Courage is proceeding in spite of fear. It is certainly no disgrace to be afraid. However, it is inexcusable to let fear overcome us.

The Built-In Vince Lombardi

Many stories have been circulated about the great Vince Lombardi. I heard one in particular just before he passed away which impressed me very much.

A first-year player had been working his heart out in practice for hours. Vince said to him, "Go into the showers. You're about the lousiest football player I ever had on the field."

About an hour later when the team went into the dressing room, there the rookie was crying like a baby. He was too tired and broken up even to take off his shoulder pads.

Vince went up to him, ruffled up his hair and said, "Son, I meant it when I said you were a lousy player. But I want you to listen carefully while I tell you something. I mean it. Someday you are going to be the greatest tackle the Green Bay Packers ever had. And the reason is that you are willing to work and, furthermore, I shall always be right here to guide you and encourage you and see that you are."

Immediately the kid brightened up and became a new person. He was ready to go out and practice another three hours.

Now the thing that impresses me most about that story is this: wouldn't it be wonderful if everyone of us who becomes discouraged could have a little built-in Vince Lombardi to pump us back up so we are ready to go right back out and exert the second effort?

The number of refusals we get is not as important as our reaction to them and our next step after receiving the refusals.

How to Overcome Objections Quickly

It is perfectly natural that a person who desires strongly to convince another will have, to some extent, an emotional trauma upon receiving a refusal. Yes, it will take a toll on him. He can be likened to a tire that gradually "goes down" as the refusals mount up. But his concern should be in formulating a method to pump himself back up to counteract the results of the refusals.

Throughout this book we suggest time and again the importance of tape recordings, books, records, clinics, seminars, schools and all methods of both increasing our knowledge and being motivated. Don't fail to take advantage of the opportunity.

The Only Action That Counts

Before leaving this fourth step in the art of persuasion, let's accept one principle absolutely: Action is not action at all unless it is *immediate action.* Persuasion takes place in one dimension of time and in only one. That is, of course, *now!*

Too many people buy the statement of a reluctant listener that he will give his consent in the future. Not only does this lead to a waste of time but the person seeking to convince is living in a world of *make-believe.*

A person is so far better off if he will be mentally honest with himself and accept the true fact, hard as it may be, that any decision to act which does not also carry the decision to act *now* is in reality a refusal. What else could it be?

Build your whole approach for action upon a request for immediate action. Stress the urgency of *now.*

Mr. Jones, if you could convince yourself that this will bring you the same profits that it has brought others, you would have no objection to okaying the contract so that we can get this program started now, would you?

Step-by-Step Control Plan

In taking the four important steps discussed in this chapter, let's be sure that we have good rapport at all times with our prospects.

Again I repeat that we must be orderly and completely organized as we proceed from one step to the next.

Physical Interview

It is obvious to us all that until we can get into the physical presence of a person our persuasion does not even begin. Of course we have telephone interviews, but that is not the point of discussion at this time. While I do not wish to dwell on the method of prospecting to secure a physical interview, I do want to suggest just two points to keep in mind:

First, always ask for the interview with polite urgency. It is the immediacy of the interview — the necessity of *now* — which is most convincing. A person always has time for anything which he considers important to him. If you can stress the importance of listening to you immediately, you are emphasizing the most important approach. Let your general conduct radiate this feeling of urgency. Unless you yourself communicate this feeling of importance, you certainly cannot expect the other person to consider the interview important.

Second, never, *never* try to sell anything but the appointment in your initial effort to gain this physical interview. Don't suggest anything except the importance of listening to what you have to say. If you refrain from letting the merits of your proposal become the subject of discussion at the time of seeking the appointment, you will find that the other person has very little or no reason for refusing the interview.

While a person may give other reasons for not wanting to

grant an interview, actually the real reason usually is that he feels that by granting an interview he is, in some measure, committing himself to accept your proposal or idea, or to buy your product or service. We can often dispel this fear with a preliminary remark such as this, "Mr. Jones, you may or may not have need for this. We can quickly find out. However, I feel that it is very important for you to have this information."

Again let me urge you never to attempt anything on the initial approach other than an acceptance of the physical interview.

Mental Interview

Many people have the mistaken idea that just because they are in the physical presence of a person they in reality have a true interview. I've seen a person sitting three feet away from another physically, yet he was ten thousand miles away mentally.

Have you ever seen an individual drum his fingers on his desk, squirm in his chair, and look up toward the ceiling in a manner which communicated the feeling "I wish I knew how to get rid of this joker"?

Please remember that you do not have an actual interview until you are in both the physical and the mental presence of a person. Do yourself a favor: don't take up another's time by even attempting the first three steps of persuasion unless the respondent gives you a mental as well as a physical interview.

Of course you would never be rude or insulting, but if you are convinced that the other party is not willing to give you the attention and interest which your call deserves, just politely excuse yourself with some such remark as, "Maybe some other time, Mr. Smith, when you are not so busy," or, "I am sorry Mr. Jones, I have information which is important to you, but I can see that this is not the time to present it to you." If you are polite and sincere in such remarks, often the whole climate of the interview will change immediately. If it doesn't, you have saved much wasted time for everyone.

Yes, until you are both physically and mentally in the presence of a person, you are not in a position to proceed with the steps in persuasion, namely, posing the problem, offering the solution, proving your case and asking for action.

Emotional Interview

In 85 per cent of the cases where a person is convinced and the decision made final it is while the prospect is emotionally aroused. It is part of human nature that people are moved to action only after they have been motivated. Consequently, everything we have said or done up to the point of emotional stimulus is mere prologue. This is by far the most important act in the drama we call persuasion.

Since people are different, that vehicle which arouses a person emotionally cannot be the same with all people. Pride may be the moving factor with some; profit may be the vulnerable spot with others; the responsive note with others might be need, love, or fear.

The responsibility of a good communicator seeking to persuade is to feel the emotional pulse of the other person and find out, through trial, to which of the above he will respond. This requires communication at its very finest.

I hope you will realize how many of the problems of life can be simplified and reduced to manageable proportions if one can only learn the pattern of persuasion. Go through the steps time and time again. Take certain hypothetical cases and practice these steps. You will receive dividends that you cannot afford to miss.

ELEVEN

Preventing Communication Breakdowns

One of the rewarding things about treating the subject of kinesics is that it is so broad it covers everything we say or do. There is very little danger of getting off our subject. It is like the sky itself. We can never get out from under it.

Take Out Insurance on Good Communication

The first three chapters of this book gave the three fundamentals of good communication: simplifying, relating the subject matter to the other person's understanding, and using stories generously to illustrate our point.

In Chapter Four we took out even more insurance against fractured communication. The proper method of asking questions is a real art. It accomplishes many purposes, but above all else it is the best guarantee that the communicator and the respondent are talking and listening about the same thing.

Chapter Five also gives us certain techniques to make sure that there is clarity of understanding at all times. Creative listening by the respondent not only enables him to get a better picture of the communicator's ideas but also encourages the communicator to keep this picture in focus.

Case Study

Years ago the teaching profession realized that one of the best ways to transmit knowledge on any subject to a person was through the case history method. Law schools began giving actual legal cases to even the first-year law students for study. This method was soon followed by the medical schools. Now the engineering schools and practically all specialized courses of study are built around the case method.

This method of teaching has its origin in the firm conviction that no knowledge or method is fully understood until we can apply this knowledge or method to some specific situation. When we can see thoughts and ideas in action, we have a new understanding and a new concept of what it is all about.

Not only are we able to see all parts in relation to the whole but when end results are in sight all steps seem to take on a special meaning.

Showing the Entire Picture

One of the great dangers of the assembly line in our system of modern mass production is that too often employees only see the small picture of their job performance. How much better understanding they would have of their own job if in their minds they could relate their activity to the completed product. Many companies that realize this fact try to give an employee at least a fair understanding of the other activities which combine with his to make the finished product.

One of the old revived Charlie Chaplin movies shows Charlie in an assembly line just tightening bolts as they go by. Long after he left work each day his arms would spasmodically jerk in the motion of turning that wrench. He didn't understand what he was building. All he knew was that he was to tighten those bolts as they went by.

How to Increase Understanding

There are many versions of the person who just puts together ingredients and one who creates end results. You remember, I am sure, the story of the person who walked up to two bricklayers and asked them what they were doing.

The first one said, "I am laying brick and getting a good wage for it — in fact, double for overtime."

When accosted, the second one said, "I am building a beautiful cathedral, one unsurpassed in beauty and one that will last forever."

No one can doubt that the second workman had a better communication and understanding, even with himself, regarding his endeavors.

Diminishing Understanding

As a child we played a game called "Gossip," in which several children would line up in a row and then an equal number in another row facing them. Someone would whisper a similar story into the ear of the two children who headed each line. Then the children would whisper the story into the ear of the child next to them. Finally, when the story reached the end of each line, the last person receiving it would tell the entire group what he heard. Laughter was always provoked by the entirely different story told by the last listener in each line.

Although this was only a child's game played for fun, it is amazing to note that this fractured communication takes place in so many facets of our business world today.

The Colonel's Command

Somewhere in the records of the army there is reported a story of a certain colonel who was an amateur astronomer.

Many years ago, it is alleged, he gave this order to his executive assistant:

Tomorrow evening at approximately 20 hundred hours Halley's Comet will be visible in this area, an event which occurs only once every 75 years. Have the men fall out in the battalion area in fatigues, and I will explain this rare phenomenon to them. In case of rain, we will not be able to see anything, so assemble the men in the theater and I will show them films of it.

Executive Officer to Company Commander:

By order of the Colonel, tomorrow at 20 hundred hours Halley's Comet will appear above the battalion area. If it rains, fall the men out in fatigues, then march to the theater where the rare phenomenon will take place, something which occurs only once every 75 years.

Company Commander to Lieutenant:

By order of the Colonel in fatigues at 20 hundred hours tomorrow evening, the phenomenal Halley's Comet will appear in the theater. In case of rain, in the battalion area, the Colonel will give another order, something which occurs once every 75 years.

Lieutenant to Sergeant:

Tomorrow at 20 hundred hours, the Colonel will appear in the theater with Halley's Comet, something which happens every 75 years; if it rains, the Colonel will order the comet into the battalion area.

Sergeant to Squad:

When it rains tomorrow at 20 hundred hours, the phenomenal 75-year-old General Halley, accompanied by the Colonel, will drive his Comet through the battalion area theater in fatigues.

This is often repeated as a comical story, but actually in our everyday conversation stories are varied just as greatly as they pass from person to person. I once heard a reliable source described as "the person we just met." An informed source is "the guy who told the fellow we just met." An unimpeachable source is "the guy who started the rumor in the first place."

Garnishing the Story

Often people delight in gossip so thoroughly that they almost deliberately hear a story in its mangled state.

A dear little old lady in my home town once slipped while wearing sneakers and broke her wrist. The story of the event traveled over the community and many different versions of the story were heard.

One lady was heard telling another, "It served her right! Anyone who would sneak up on another or slip up trying to overhear something should have an accident like that."

How to Get the Best Support from Others

Again I emphasize the fact that one of the best insurances we can take against breakdown in communication is to make an effort to get the respondent to see the entire picture. Do you think that an artist could make any major contribution to a masterpiece if he were only allowed to paint one fragment of the picture, never being permitted to see the entire work or even being told what it represented? How skillful do you think an assisting surgeon would be if the primary surgeon did not even let him know in advance what was to be the nature of the operation? Even the assisting nurses could not give the best support unless they were part of the team to bring about ultimate results.

Years ago I had a friend who worked in a large law firm in New York City. He often complained to me that a certain senior partner would give him points of law to research, but he never knew anything about the case to which the points of law applied. He assured me that he could have been far more helpful and thorough if the small fragment of law he researched could have been related in his own mind to the whole case.

In spite of the obvious diminished performance revealed by the above illustrations, we continue to see similar examples every day.

An acquaintance of mine works in a large electronics plant in Phoenix. She told me that she "wires a little gadget" over and over each day. She has no idea what purpose is served by this so-called gadget. She further stated that if she only knew what purpose it served she could guard much more carefully against defects in the wiring.

A personnel executive in General Motors stated that every person under his control, as part of his training, was permitted to follow his contribution (whether it be a section of a generator or a wheel) to its ultimate destination, even if a trip to another plant were necessary. He emphasized that this increased understanding on the employee's part paid off handsomely. It widened the scope of communication with that particular employee.

Improving Efficiency

Not only is greater efficiency encouraged by understanding of the ultimate product; morale of the employee is also enhanced. How long do you think you could remain interested in creating a product or performing a service if you were kept in the dark regarding its use or benefit to another? It would remain a "thing-a-ma-bob" or a "gismo" as far as you were concerned.

Just as we cannot impose responsibility upon a person without giving him authority to back up his responsibility, we cannot ask a person to take pride in his work unless he is given an opportunity to observe the fruits of his labor.

How to Add Value

As vital as communication is, just a very small variation in action can often make a huge difference.

There was a certain grammar school which had two candy stores located an equal distance from the school. These two stores sold the same candy at the same price. They each used the same kind of scales to weigh the candy. Yet a strange thing existed. One of the stores was always full of kids spending their allowance or lunch money. The other appeared on the verge of going broke. Someone made a study of the situation and this is what was discovered:

The proprietor of the busy store, upon receiving an order for a certain kind of candy, would put the little weights on his balance scales. At first he would put only a few pieces of candy on the scales — then a few more — and a few more. Each time he added candy the little purchaser would grin with delight. Finally when the sale was complete the youngster eagerly rushed out with his bargain, a happy customer.

Now let me remind you that the other store had the same candy at the same price. Yes, the proprietor even used the same kind of scales. However, his method of communicating the purchase was far different. This proprietor would put a large handful of candy on the scales. He would then start removing one or two pieces of candy at a time. Finally when the right amount was on the scales the proprietor would put it in a bag and hand it to the little disenchanted purchaser who had just gone through the emotional trauma of seeing what he first thought was a bargain dwindle in size.

Although each buyer actually received the same amount of candy, the two proprietors had communicated an entirely different story. One had been adding value; the other had been taking candy away from a child. Many of us, without realizing it, are guilty of a similar breakdown in communications.

Just a Fragment of the Picture

As children we read the story of the four blind men who visited a circus. They decided they wanted to visit the tent where the elephant was kept.

The first blind man went over and felt the side of the elephant and told the other two that an elephant resembled a wall. The second blind man took hold of a leg and said no, the elephant resembled a post. The third grasped the tail, and disagreed, saying the elephant was like a rope. The fourth took hold of the elephant's trunk, and shouted that the elephant was really like a snake. And they all began to quarrel, because each man got just a fragment of what an elephant is really like.

One of the greatest investments a company or a private employer can make is to invest in the understanding and morale of the employees by making sure that each employee not only understands his own work, but also is conscious of how it fits into the overall picture, into the ultimate results. Regardless of the cost, this is the cheapest insurance that can be taken out as a guard against communication breakdowns.

In your own communication with others, particularly when you wish to persuade them to do something, be sure that they see the total picture, the ultimate results of what you want them to do.

TWELVE

The Vital Secret of Silent Command

We have heard it said many times that all of life is nothing more than a crusade from the cradle to the grave in search of importance. In this trip we go through many emotional hungers and satisfactions. First, we want to be liked, then we want to be understood, then we want acceptance, then we crave to belong to something, and finally we want to be put on a pedestal and be recognized and bragged about.

The whole journey is one stimulated by the desire to feel important.

How to Build Up Others

Consequently, if we want to be sure that we keep the channels of communication open, if we want to be sure that people do not build walls of resistance to keep us out, let's learn to make people feel important. This is the vital secret of "Silent Command."

The world is made up of two kinds of conversationalists. We have those people who know how to build up the other person, guiding the conversation into fields of interest that can make an individual feel informed and at ease. Then we have the other group who only know how to talk about things that interest themselves. They ask no questions of the other person. They simply begin telling of events within the realm of their own experiences. One so-called conversation on their part constitutes over-exposure. They do not know how to engage in actual communication.

Convincing Others Without Effort

Let's consider a few ways that you can communicate this feeling of importance to me.

Give me the first opportunity to start a conversation if we should find ourselves in a situation where a conversation may ensue. If you do this and I begin talking, you can be sure that I shall start in a field that interests me. Even if it is on a subject of which you are uninformed, you will be surprised how well the conversation will progress if you only listen and occasionally let me know you are not bored by asking a few questions.

Maybe you find that I do not start a conversation voluntarily. Then why not ask me a few well-chosen questions to determine what my field of endeavor or my hobby is?

Recently I was in London and found myself sitting next to an English college professor at a dinner party. He seemed very reserved and I was almost embarrassed at the lack of communication between us. Every remark I made was answered, not rudely, but with a brisk and brief "no" or "yes."

Finally I made a real effort. I said, "I have had occasion to work with college students in both the United States and in Canada. I would be very interested in knowing if the college students of England are different in any major respect from those to whom I have been exposed. You teach them and I also understand that you have been a guest lecturer in the States. You have had an opportunity to make an excellent comparision. How do you feel about this?"

The professor immediately opened up. I found I had pressed his "hot button." After we discussed that subject, he volunteered other fields of interest and almost passionately gave a full expression of his views in each case.

At the end of the evening he assured me that he had never met a more enjoyable conversationlist or one more thoroughly

versed on so many subjects. Actually, I hardly had an opportunity to say anything and never once had I brought up
a new subject. I had only listened enthusiastically and occasionally had asked him to elaborate a little more in detail.

I assure you I was not making an effort to manipulate this
person. I was truly interested in the subject I suggested.
Through being put at ease in his own field of thought, he
felt a sense of importance and became a fountain-head of
conversation for the evening.

The Cruelest Thing to Do

One of the cruelest things we can do in the field of human
relations is to deprive another person of the right of
discovery.

Did you ever have a person tell you the ending of a sus-
pense picture you planned to see? Did anyone ever ruin the
reading of a "Who done it" for you by telling you it wasn't
the butler or the maid but a person you least expected?

The most lasting lessons of life are those where we are
permitted a certain degree of independence in our research
and where we finally realize certain truths through our own
unassisted discovery.

My chemistry teacher was not only a good science teacher
but also a great human engineer. He always kept the excitement of possible discovery before us. This gave us a feeling
of importance and an eagerness to pursue our studies.
Think how lacking he would have been in his communication
if he had removed the incentive of discovery by telling us in
advance what results we would find by mixing certain elements or compounds together.

Discovery Applies to All Fields

It has been my privilege over the years to do a considerable amount of training in the real estate profession —
especially in the specific field of persuasive communication.

I remember very vividly spending an afternoon with a salesman who was holding open house in a subdivision on the outskirts of Scottsdale, Arizona. A man and his wife were being shown through the house. In an excited tone of voice the lady, as she entered the living room, said to her husband, "Look, dear, the window frames Camelback Mountain. Isn't that fantastic?"

The salesman could have said, "Yes, that's what we have had in the ad all week. All houses in this subdivision are built so that Camelback Mountain can easily be seen from the living room window."

How deflating this would have been and how unkind to deprive the lady of feeling the importance of discovery.

The salesman was a good communicator. He acted surprised himself and said, "You are so right! It does look like a picture! And I'll bet as the light shadows fall and the colors change, one has a different picture every hour of the afternoon."

Our good communicator did not "up stage" his prospect. He did not move in and take over the conversation, but merely agreed and expanded. He was willing to let her win the Oscar — while he won the sale!

Try this method. It is extremely effective in the art of "Silent Command."

Another Key Principle

Throughout this entire book you will see repeated again and again an emphasis on the principle that people *love to buy* but *hate to be sold*.

Many reasons can be given to support this principle. One of the most important is that when a person is permitted to buy, he is not deprived of the joy of discovery. Furthermore, when a person reaches a conclusion voluntarily and through his own investigation, his decision is usually definite and not subject to easy change. Yes, the decision was his; no one influenced him — he made up his own mind.

How to Communicate Objectively — Not Subjectively

I repeat certain important sentences over and over throughout this book until they have the effect of a broken record. Believe me, it is consciously done and only done for emphasis.

Just a very few sentences carefully used can often make the difference between good and bad communication in the art of "Silent Command."

Five Words of Power

> Mr. Jones, if you could convince yourself that this would help your business, you would have no objection to okaying this purchase order so we can get delivery started at once, would you?

Why is this good communication?

It is communication of the very highest level of persuasion because you are permitting your prospect to act upon his own discovery. Note the magic words, which I urge you to eat, digest and make a part of your everyday vocabulary: *"If you could convince yourself."*

Just these few powerful words can often change what might be considered an effort to sell, yes, even pressure sell, into a polite assistance to one in his buying efforts. These words assure the prospect that he is important, that he is not deprived of the pleasure of acting upon his own good judgment. This is what "Silent Command" is all about.

How to Get the Decision You Want

> Mrs. Smith, based on what you have told me, don't we agree that this is the best thing to do?

Here again we are letting our prospect make the decision. She is kept in the picture and made to feel important. While we bring ourselves into the picture a little more strongly, any decision is based on the discovery the prospect made.

"Low-Pressure" Influencing

Many times when I have wanted to be sure that from the very beginning my respondents realized they would not be deprived of the enjoyment of acting upon their own discovery, I have tried to create the proper climate of communication with some such statement as this:

> Mr. and Mrs. Jones, I want to ask a favor of you. If I should inadvertently say anything that would influence you in the slightest, please call my attention to it, because I want any decision which you may make to be made on your own judgment uninfluenced by me. However, I want to be sure that I give you all the facts so that you can make the right decision.

Now let's analyze the above. How could I be clearer in my assurance that no one would try to high pressure them into anything, that no one would try to deprive them of the pleasure of discovery? However, I also try to make it clear that they will be assisted in their efforts to make a correct decision by being given all the facts.

Do yourself the favor of committing to memory the expressions contained in the last three subheadings of this chapter.

Mental Television Broadcasting

Whenever I face an audience, I am always conscious of the fact that my audience has a very great advantage over me. Each person has complete control over his or her mental television set. I can be tuned out at any time. Any person there can switch to another channel of interest. Maybe it's a consideration of their activities the night before. It might even be plans for the coming night. They can be leaning forward and looking at me as though they were listening. Yet they might be on another channel or even unplugged.

When I first began speaking on the circuit, this fact annoyed me. Finally I arrived at the realization that this is part of the protective armor of every audience. It is their standard equipment, their survival kit against the hazards of boring speakers.

Naturally I was concerned with the best method of being sure that I was not tuned out. All the textbooks on public speaking give many methods of capturing an audience's attention at the very start. They list numerous ways to crash that pre-occupational barrier. They assure us that good communication never leaves the starting gate unless we gain that initial attention.

How to Make People Pay Attention to You

Like all other speakers I have read such books and studied the various suggested techniques.

I know one speaker who always appears in a uniform, maybe an umpire's uniform or that of a prisoner. I am sure this is helpful to him in capturing good initial attention. He has a national reputation as an excellent speaker. Another of my friends does a juggler's act. This too must be effective in gaining that first interest because he is well accepted in all circles. I even once saw a speaker who, without saying a word, blew up a balloon and then burst it before a startled audience.

Research shows that our modern circuit speaker is an outgrowth of the medieval juggler, the king's jester and the traveling fiddler. Just to have a message is never enough. One must entertain and provoke attention in order to gain and sustain attention. However, I have found the only true attention getter for me.

Controlling the Communication Climate

After many years of facing an audience I finally learned that it is of little consequence whether my audience thinks that I am an important or a highly successful individual. The point of major concern is the importance with which I regard my audience.

The fact that I truly regard every person in my audience

as being of major importance seems to establish an initial climate of true communication far more effectively than any masquerade I could assume.

The Message in the Eyes

If a speaker on the platform or a person approaching an individual could only realize a certain important principle in communication, he would be much more effective in getting and holding attention.

Please consider this principle carefully. Written in the eyes of every person in my audience and also in the eyes of every respondent you approach, in large neon letters, is the question, "Are you trying to impress me or do you want to help me?"

The Ego Complex

Without being hypercritical of my fellow speakers, I've seen an excellent chairman of the day sell a speaker completely to the audience, only to see the speaker in the initial few minutes buy himself back through an effort to make his audience feel his importance. How different it is when the speaker spends those few minutes making his audience feel important. The ego complex has caused fractured communication for many of us.

How to Create Confidence in You

This principle of causing effective persuasion by making the other fellow feel important has many applications and many variations. A good leader or good executive today is more interested in getting his followers or employees to have confidence in themselves rather than in him. It takes a great deal of unselfishness and interest in other people, but such a quality is the very essence of greatness.

Ideas, however good they may be, are useless unless they

are put into use. For one week, in all your dealings with people let all you say and do communicate clearly the message *"You are important to me."* Don't be startled at the results. Just realize that miracles still do happen!

THIRTEEN

Unleashing the Ultimate Power of Silent Command

We have reached the ultimate in "Silent Command" when we can get people to do what we want them to do because they want to do it. The individuals who are paid most in our economic system are those who have learned the art of causing people to do things. Many people can educate and entertain others, but the real test of a leader is the ability to cause people to do things.

In this chapter I shall remind you of a few qualities that a leader must have. None of them are new to us, but again I say that we need reminding, even of the simplest and most elementary principles. Repetition, repetition, repetition — that's the greatest way of conditioning ourselves to deal with people problems.

ITA Vs. ICA

Have you ever dealt with a person who was smart, polite, and gifted with many good qualities, but you never could feel at ease around him? He appeared brilliant but lacked warmth. For lack of a better expression you labeled him as having the "ivory tower" attitude (ITA). You seemed locked out of his life. You could not get close to him however hard you tried.

On the other hand, have you known people who carried a self-generated warmth and sunshine around with them? You could see from the very beginning that they were interested in you. They simply radiated the "I care" attitude (ICA).

If we desire to learn the art of causing people to do things, to act, we must sincerely have this second attitude.

How a Doctor Becomes Rich

An associate of mine, who recently spoke at a medical convention, related the following story to me.

It appears that he arrived a little early for his speech. An older doctor was talking to a group of interns. According to my associate the older doctor made one of the most profound statements he had ever heard from the medical profession.

He said, "Young fellers, do you know who is the leading doctor in any city? He is not the doctor who is the best surgeon. He is not the doctor who knows the most about medicine. He is the doctor who carries around with him the best "I care" attitude.

Continuing, the doctor said, "Remember this: in 99 cases out of a hundred, regardless of how sick your patients may get, they are going to get well, provided you don't give them something to kill them. Nature is on your side.

"But if, during their sickness, the "I care" attitude is always showing, when they do get well they will swear on a stack of Bibles that through your genius you brought them back from death's door.

"Don't ever speak of a patient as *gall bladder in room 13.* Form the habit of being genuinely interested in your patients and let them know this."

Look at your own sign that you carry around with you. Do you see ITA or ICA?

The Miracle That Takes Only a Few Seconds

Much is said in this book about the art of "Silent Command" and the methods of causing people to obey our wishes, but I cannot emphasize too strongly the importance of that initial approach.

All sales trainers and consultants in the field of human engineering and all those seeking to improve the conduct of others concentrate on the principle that we have no second chance at a first impression. We can correct many mistakes in our interview, but we just can't soften up the cement once it has set.

Remember this: it is in the first few seconds of our interview with a respondent that we put a label on the purpose of our call. We communicate by our words, our actions, and our expression one of two things. We indicate either that we are only there to sell him our proposal, our product or service, or we are there to share valuable ideas and benefits.

The Remarkable Sign

Years ago when I was going from company to company offering a self-improvement course, I had occasion to call on a personnel director who was also purchasing agent for his company.

On his wall he had a sign that I'll never forget. In big bold letters was written "If you show me how your product or service will help me, I shall be even more eager to buy than you are to sell."

This is not just a little fancy sentence. It carries the very essence of good persuasion. If you can communicate to me from the very beginning that you have come to me with ideas to share, ideas that will help me, not just products to unload — "Shoes to get out of the factory" — I shall not even let you leave my office until I have heard your full story.

This Sign Is Always There

This is just as true in other occupations as it is in selling. Get into the habit of mentally seeing that sign just above the head of everyone you call upon, for whatever purpose. Try as hard as you will, you'll find that it is impossible to overwork the words "I have an idea to share with you," "Others have found a great benefit in this," or "This is how our services can increase your business."

Don't forget that the person you call upon is in business to make money. He is interested in your proposal, or your product or service, only to the extent that it will help him make more money. If it does this for him, he wants it, and if it doesn't, he couldn't care less. So shoot the arrow at the bullseye, not out into space.

If you start from the very beginning to talk about your respondent's company, his needs, his problems — not your proposal, your product or your service — you will find that you are oiling the hinges to the door which will quickly open to you.

Every person's favorite subject of discussion is himself and matters that will help him secure the things in life that he wants. Never fear that an initial approach on this subject will not get a responsive note.

Volcanic Spirits

One of the first jobs I ever had was as receptionist for a large food distributing company. Dozens of salesmen called on the company each day. It was interesting to observe the different approaches used, not only upon me to see the buyers, but also upon the buyers themselves.

I remember the method used by one salesman in particular who called upon the company several times a year. He always approached me in a volcanic spirit of excitement, telling me that he had an idea for my boss which couldn't wait. I recall the very words he used on several occasions. He said, "I don't mind waiting, but this idea *can't* wait."

The Great Idea

So aroused was my curiosity that I would always check with the buyer to find out what was the great idea that couldn't wait.

This salesman had made a habit of periodically picking up a plan or an idea which he felt would help his customers — something that had already proved beneficial to others. He was careful to choose an idea that would not help him or his company directly. His initial approach was always to present this plan or idea enthusiastically at the very beginning. The idea was usually good, but the thing that always impressed the buyer most was the fact that it was an unselfish idea — one that was designed to help the buyer, not himself.

To the best of my recollection this particular salesman, during the entire time I worked at that company, never failed to see the person he wanted to see.

The Magic Key That Opens all Doors

This plan of an altruistic approach is certainly not confined to salesmen. Regardless of what you do, you can adapt it. It's a great habit to form. Doors will open to you which you didn't even know existed.

Friends of mine who know that I speak all over the country often tell me of some great idea that I could use in a speech. I'm always interested — never too busy to listen.

Recently a friend of mine heard that I was to speak in Regina, Canada. He called me to tell me a little anecdote that Canadians might appreciate. I was grateful for the story was good and in perfect taste. I used it and it was highly acceptable.

Please never forget that an idea which will help the other person is the magic key that will open the door to any interview.

A Rare Opportunity

During the years as receptionist for the food company to which I referred, I had occasion to study the methods of countless salesmen. While waiting to see the buyers, many would unload their ambitions, aspirations, and even their problems on me. As a receptionist one must learn to be a good listener, a sincere listener, or resign from the job.

I had the rare opportunity to study the thinking and conduct of many of these salesmen who made numerous repeated calls. It was an education in human engineering in general and an education in sales techniques in particular. I'd like to share with you a few observations I made during these years.

The Masked Men Who Failed

I've known "hit-and-run" salesmen. Each time they called it was as though they were making a first call. They had written all over them: "My job is to get the food *out* of the factory — it's a relay race, brother! You take the ball at this point. My responsibility is over. It's up to you now."

While most people mask their faces, these people did an extreme job of it. They had an impersonal expression and manner about them. Their job was to unload a product and then hit the road to the next stop without ever looking back.

Somehow these people didn't seem to last too long. The mortality rate was high.

The Ultimate Consumer

By contrast, I remember vividly those salesmen who seemed even more interested in knowing how our people sold the last order than in making a new sale. They felt a responsibility for their product up to the time it reached the ultimate consumer.

These salesmen didn't feel that the sale was complete until their product had not only reached the retail market but also was in the shopping basket of the consumer.

My memory is much clearer regarding these people because they seemed to be around for years.

Searching the Soul

In looking back and studying salesmen who called at our plant, I must tax my memory to recall the product that some of them sold. I don't mean to imply that they were not good salesmen or were not loyal to their company. The food industry is so highly competitive that the amateurs are eliminated quickly. Also the "pie-in-the-sky, suede-shoe feller" is finished almost before he starts.

But there are some salesmen whom I can hardly separate in my mind from their product. There is old "Corn Flakes Charlie." I can't even remember his last name. He called at least once a week. Everybody loved him. We enjoyed seeing him make his appearance. If his products were not moving fast he hit the ceiling. He wanted to know *why*. If he couldn't get the answer at our office, he would call at the stores to study the situation.

No one in our company objected to the brusque methods of Corn Flakes Charlie. It is true that at times he upset things around our office with his emotional outbursts, but it was only because he loved his products. He wanted to see them sell, and he would help in any way to see that they did move.

Charlie had an expression that I dearly loved. I heard him say more than once, "There's only one thing bad about buying my product; when you buy it you get me too. Furthermore I insist on traveling with that box of cereal all the way to the consumer's breakfast table."

All of us could learn much from Charlie's attitude. Ask yourself, will you, just how much you are a part of your service or product. Does your interest in your product or service end the minute you are paid or do you feel a continuing responsibility? Are you so completely identified with your product or service that people think of you as one? Do a little soul searching at this point.

The Kinesics of the Reception Room

There are some salesmen who have a burning desire to have their product accepted. It is written all over them. They have controlled excitement gleaming in their eyes. Their depth of conviction and urgency of cause is communicated in their manner of conduct. Their very presence generates interest. Such salesmen are an example, not only to other salesmen, but also to those in non-selling occupations.

It was always easy for me to spot such a salesman when he walked up to the reception desk. Furthermore, I was confident that if I tried to slip him into a buyer's office between appointments, he was not going to abuse the privilege.

On the other hand we had our "commercial visitors," too. These people are also an example — an example to avoid.

"I just happened to be in the area and thought I'd drop around and chew the fat with Bill Jones. Is he in?"

Sometimes even when a salesman had an appointment, his entire conduct and demeanor communicated the idea, "I am here just to kill a little time with a buyer so that I can report to my company that I made a call."

It was my job to protect the buyers as best I could against these commercial visitors. Often I would amuse myself by trying to predict in advance whether a salesman was going to get an order or not. I became pretty good at it. Finally it wasn't necessary for me to check with the buyer. The expression on the salesman's face and his general conduct as he left usually communicated to me the information I wanted to know.

Before we go to another point give yourself a little examination. To what extent, whether you sell for a living or not, is your self-image that of a "productive salesman" and to what degree are you just a "commercial visitor"? When you approach a respondent, is it with an appearance of controlled excitement?

Does your manner say, "I can bring a profit to your company with my product. It's a great product. You cannot afford to lose this opportunity"?

Or is your role one of a commercial visitor who, by his complacent attitude, seems to say, "Well, I know I can't win 'em all. Maybe you have an order for me and maybe you don't. But anyway let's see what you might need today."

If you think this is exaggerating, please sit in a reception room where salesmen call on buyers. You will receive a liberal education.

What Does Your Appearance Communicate?

While I am not fastidious about a person's manner of dressing and while I realize that a salesman getting in and out of a car all day cannot forever appear as though he were modeling clothes, his appearance still communicates much about him. This is equally true in other occupations.

If a salesman is carefully groomed, shoes shined, suit pressed, clean shaven, he is in effect saying, "In all I do I am organized and careful over details. If you give me an opportunity to help you, I shall be just as careful and meticulous in handling your affairs."

On the other hand, if the salesman needs a shave and is wearing an unpressed suit, if his collar is frayed and his heels run down, he is communicating just as strongly that he will handle your affairs just as he handles himself. Please, never be licked before you start. At least give yourself a break and not let the interview be born dead because of your appearance.

At times I was horror stricken at the appearance of some salesmen. Their shabby appearance communicated to me that either their product was no good or that they were not good salesmen. In either event I had to protect the buyer from wasting his time with this "joker." If the fellow was worth talking to, he would at least be successful enough to buy a decent suit of clothes and keep himself properly groomed.

How to Please a Woman

Only a few salesmen fully realize how much a receptionist or secretary can help in arranging appointments, even at the last moment, if she really wants to do it.

It's impossible to deal with salesmen month after month and not have your favorites. Furthermore, I must confess that the big sign I mentally wore — *Make me feel important* — never shrank in size during my years as a receptionist.

Somehow I found that I could always be a little more successful in doing favors such as changing appointments and getting interviews for those salesmen who made me feel they considered my position as being important. This, of course, is equally true for persons within a company who wish to see their bosses.

Ready and Willing

No one is exempt from the desire to feel needed. If one feels that another person sincerely needs him and wants help, it is amazing what one is willing to do for that person.

On occasions I have been directly approached in somewhat this manner: "I am in trouble. I perhaps don't deserve your help. However, you are the only one who can help me. Carelessly I didn't make the appointment for this afternoon, but now I find I must fly out tonight. Do you suppose somehow you could help me see Mr. Smith?"

How would you feel if you had an honest approach in this manner? I'm sure you would be moved to help more than if a salesman tried some gimmick or started throwing his weight around.

The Exalted Look

No communication is as persuasive as the exalted look of a believer. It's strange how a person through his manner and expression can cause you to want to open doors for him. A person with a smile and with an attitude of belief in what he is offering radiates an atmosphere of acceptance.

As I say repeatedly throughout this book, "Enthusiasm is more persuasive than logic — excited dedication more moving than all the fancy language that can be concocted."

No statement was ever more true than that which claims that a man dies while he lives if he loses his enthusiasm. I suggest that we all include in our prayers each day, "Dear Lord, please don't let me ever die while I still live — let me die only when I'm dead."

FOURTEEN

Getting Cooperation in Business Through Silent Command

Charles Schwab, the great steel tycoon, once said, "The greatest single quality which contributes to success is the faculty of being able to cause people to cooperate." Many times, however, injustice is done to people. We accuse them of failure to cooperate, when in fact they are more than willing. The truth is that we have not properly communicated to them so that they can cooperate.

Let's examine a few situations where communication is important if we are to get the cooperation we desire.

Secrets of Effective Company Meetings

When people ask the question, "What do you think of company meetings?" it is similar to asking, "How high is up?" or "How deep is down?" It all depends upon the necessity of the meeting, how well we plan it, and the leadership in conducting it and the follow-up.

A meeting can be a costly way of conducting nothing or it can be a very inexpensive way of reaching an objective or solving a problem.

When to Hold the Meeting

Many times a problem concerns only two or three people, not even a whole department. To call a meeting of many employees in such a case as this is clearly as much a waste of time as burning down a house to roast a pig!

Committees which include too many people get less accomplished than single individuals. When the great engineer and executive Charles Kettering was told that Lindbergh had flown the Atlantic, he remarked, "I was always sure that it would never be done by a committee."

I know a certain department head who feels that it gives the employees a sense of importance to be involved in a department meeting. I've discussed these meetings with several of his employees. In many cases those who attend are not involved in the problem nor are they qualified to offer suggestions.

Actually these meetings produce just the opposite of the desired results. Many attending feel left out of the discussion. They feel their time is being wasted. I am sure much more would be accomplished both in problem solving and employee morale if the department head called together only the people involved in each individual problem.

Of course, if a policy matter is to be discussed which involves everyone, this is entirely different. People are more congenial in co-operating and adhering to a policy if they feel that they were taken into confidence and even given a hand in formulating the policy.

How to Plan the Meeting Strategy

If meetings are held too often and are permitted to get out of control "time-wise," they become boring and fail to get the enthusiastic participation which is necessary if they are to justify the time expended. This can be avoided if meetings are called only when necessary and if they are carefully planned in advance.

How to Cover the Vital Points

The effectiveness of many meetings is lost in the maze of incidental points. Meetings which take up the time of a number of people, I again remind you, are costly. Only important matters justify this cost.

If the meeting is scheduled to cover only one or two problems, those attending the meeting should be notified of the agenda in advance. They should be encouraged to give prior thought to the matters which are to come under discussion.

If one person is more involved than others in the matter to be discussed, he in particular should be alerted in time to make special preparation.

If any props are to be used such as slides, charts or flip charts, these should be carefully prepared in advance. They are a most important aid for projecting "Silent Commands."

Proper Direction of the Meeting

The one factor which determines the success of the meeting more than any other is the manner in which the chairman conducts the meeting. Above all else, unless the meeting was called simply to make an announcement — and this is a very expensive way to make an announcement — the chairman should encourage all attending to cooperate and express themselves fully. If one or two people are permitted to monopolize the time, the effectiveness of the meeting suffers.

How to Open the Meeting

A good chairman, regardless of whether those attending have been notified in advance of the objectives of the meeting, will open the meeting with a clear explanation of the purpose for which the members are there.

If certain problems of the company or a department are to be discussed, these should be explained simply. All present should be encouraged to give their ideas as to the best solution. In any group we have people who are reticent about volunteering their ideas. These should be asked to give their ideas, and, if necessary, asked specific questions to help them overcome their hesitancy.

How to Maintain Control of the Meeting

While a good chairman gets as much participation and involvement as seems necessary under the circumstances, he never loses control over the meeting. If a person takes up more time than is advisable, the effective chairman tactfully says something like, "Bill, you have contributed ideas generously. Now I'd like to get the ideas of others. John, how do you feel about the change in our schedule?"

Many people have great difficulty in expressing themselves clearly at a meeting. A good chairman will compliment the person and repeat the point in a more understandable way, saying, "John, I like your idea," and then rephrase the point in clearer terms, giving John the credit for the rephrased idea.

Never should a chairman use such wording as, "What John means is . . .," or "I am sure John is trying to say . . .." Such an approach is certain to discourage further participation by John.

One of the calculated risks of any meeting is the fact that after a period of time there is a tendency for those present to wander from the objectives of the meeting. It may be that much can be gained from a brief discussion of a few side issues. However, the chairman should always restate the objectives of the meeting after any such side excursion and bring the discussion back to the main points.

Duty of the Chairman

After there has been a full discussion and after decisions have been made, then steps must be taken to act on the decisions. It is the duty of the chairman to summarize the proceedings of the meeting and, where he has authority, delegate certain duties. Otherwise the whole meeting would be futile and a waste of time.

Follow-Up

Just as follow-up and report-back are necessary in any delegation of duties, they are also necessary after such a meeting. Any problem that is important enough to justify a meeting for its discussion is certainly important enough to require a follow-up to make sure that the decisions are carried out.

The next time you have a meeting in your company or department, try following the ideas expressed here. You will find that not only can much time be saved but also better results attained.

Incentive Policies

If a company is to follow the incentive policy in dealing with its employees, it must base both pay and promotion on performance rather than on the number of years worked. A company will have little trouble under such a policy *provided* it has good communication with its employees regarding the manner with which the policy is handled.

Training New People

Many times a supervisor fails to clarify with an employee just what is expected of him. Poor communication regarding job objectives causes breakdown in employee morale from the very beginning.

The most important single step with a new employee is to be sure that he understands completely what is expected of him. A conference should be arranged immediately upon his employment for the specific purpose of discussing his objectives. This should not be a casual conference and the employee should realize the specific purpose of the conference. In this way the employee will remember that his job objectives were clearly defined to him and he will also realize that his supervisor considers them to be important.

Just an explanation by the supervisor is not enough. There should be a thorough discussion with both employer and employee participating. The new employee should be urged to ask questions regarding anything he does not fully understand. He should be told that unless he is fully informed of what is expected of him he can not meet the requirements.

Many good supervisors, in order to take no chances with misunderstanding, will even say something like this: "Mr. Smith, just in order to help you be sure you understand your work objectives I'd like for you to relate to me what your understanding is of your duties."

How to Get Maximum Performance

In order to get the maximum performance from an employee, this employee must feel that his work is periodically analyzed. It is very difficult for an employee to take pride in the quality of his work over any prolonged period of time if he feels that shoddy work is overlooked and good performance is not recognized.

Reviewing and Evaluating Work

Any worthwhile employee not only wants his work evaluated but he also wants the supervisor to discuss his work with him. Every employee has a right to know where he stands with his company. If his work is satisfactory, he feels he should be told that it is. He feels entitled to a pat on the back. If his work is unsatisfactory, he also feels that he has a right to this report. He even feels that he should be told exactly in what way he did not measure up and coached on the manner in which he can improve his performance.

A good supervisor will keep a written report on each man for whom he is responsible. When evaluating an employee's work with him he should have this report in front of him. Not only is this the fair and accurate way of employee appraisals, but it also impresses the employee. He knows that any evaluation prepared over a period of time is more accurate than a mere discussion off the top of one's head.

What Is the Yardstick in Judging Me?

Just to be absolutely certain that there is full communication with the employee regarding his job analysis, it is well to discuss with him the yardstick with which he is to be judged.

Many companies use different factors in judging their employees and some put greater stress upon certain qualities than others. However, the following or some variation of these are found in most job analysis programs:

> How devoted is the employee in seeing that the general purposes of his company are carried out?
> What is the volume and quality of the work produced?
> How accurate is the employee in following company policies as well as specific instructions?
> Can this employee be depended upon to complete the job assigned on the schedule given?
> Is this employee a self-starter and always prompt or does he require constant supervision after the assignment has been made?
> Within the scope of his particular job is his thinking clear and his judgment sound?
> Are his relations with his fellow employees harmonious? In other words, is he a team worker or an individualist?
> If he deals with the public, what impression does he make? Does he communicate a good company image?

Making People Feel Involved

If my duties are accurately defined to me and if you periodically sit down with me and discuss my progress with the company, not only do I feel that my work is not being ignored but I feel involved in the company.

Please don't fail to criticize me constructively where criticism is due. If the only appraisal of my work is complimentary, I have no opportunity to improve myself. Furthermore, when you include both praise *and* criticism I feel that you are truly interested in seeing that I progress.

How to Fire People Without Bitterness

If I am called in suddenly and told that my work is unsatisfactory and that I am no longer with the company, I would resent such treatment.

However, if over a period of time I have been first reminded of shortcomings, then urged and finally warned about these faults, and furthermore if I had not corrected them, then my termination would certainly come as no surprise. I could not be bitter or feel that I had not been given ample opportunity to improve the quality of my work.

Giving Instruction Attractively

We have heard the old cliché, "It's not what you say but how you say it," so long that many of us consider it too "corny" to repeat. However, this is very true in the field of giving instructions. A supervisor who has the gift of having people do things because they want to do them is truly a magician; this power is magic.

I remember an instance which occurred when I was receptionist. It was Friday afternoon about closing time. I had experienced a strenuous week and I was eager to get home.

The president of our company rushed by my desk, dropped a file on it, and said, "I'm trying to catch a plane. This must be in the mail by midnight. I haven't time to explain. A letter of explanation is attached."

It is mild to say that I hit the ceiling. The week was up. I had worked hard. My plans for the evening had already been set. Why was it up to me to concern myself over this matter? Just how thoughtless could anyone be!

I started cleaning up my desk to leave for the weekend. I promised myself I was not going to touch the file even if it meant losing my job. Finally, as I was ready to go, I opened the file. I assure you it was out of curiosity and not with the slightest idea of doing anything about it.

There on top was a hurriedly scribbled note: "Merlyn, I am in real trouble. There is no excuse for what I did. How

I forgot this I'll never know. As you realize, this is our biggest account. It's a great imposition on you. Not only are you the only one I'd trust with this but you are the only one sweet and unselfish enough to help me out of this predicament. Please forgive me — I'll make it up to you in some way."

What would you have done? I'm sure — the same as I.

Yes, in the pleasure of feeling important and needed I lost any resentment. The important letter was in the mail by six-thirty and I kept my engagement. If necessary I would have worked all night, however.

Can you make your employees feel needed and important? It's unbelievable what a supervisor can get his employees to do and even do cheerfully, if only he uses the right approach.

Examples of Good and Bad Communication

Let's just look at a few examples of good and bad communication on the part of supervisors. When conducting clinics in the field of communication, I usually ask one lady to help in a little role playing. We name her Negative Nell. I then ask two men to volunteer. We call them the Positive Supervisor and the Negative Supervisor.

The three come to the platform. I hand each some material to read and ask them to "ham it up" and put real showmanship in their parts. Not only do these people usually turn out to be entertaining but they put over the message in a way that it's not forgotten.

Now let's review a few of these skits.

Overworked

Negative Nell: I can't get all this work done in just eight hours.
Negative Supervisor: The other girl did.

You can imagine what Nell's reaction would be to this statement by her supervisor. Now consider what a people-oriented supervisor would have said:

> *Positive Supervisor:* Which part of your work do you
> feel is the most urgent?

Now Nell begins to talk about the work. The Long Acre account can't be neglected. The Ford job is urgent. Maybe Nell will arrive, through her own reasoning, at the conclusion that nothing can be neglected. At least her judgment has been considered.

Where to Put the Files

> *Negative Nell:* Let's get rid of some of these files.
> *Negative Supervisor:* We can't. We use them daily.

What do you suppose a supervisor who is a human engineer would have said?

> *Positive Supervisor:* Where do you think would be a
> better location for them?

Now Nell begins to consider alternatives. They can't be put in the stock room; that's overcrowded. Certainly they can't be hauled to the basement. That's been flooded twice. Nell finally, upon her own volition, decides that perhaps there is no better place for them than where they are.

Old-Fashioned Method

> *Negative Nell:* This method is old-fashioned and out of
> date.
> *Negative Supervisor:* That's the way we have always
> done it.

How much better it would have been if the following answer had been given:

> *Positive Supervisor:* What method would you suggest?

Maybe Nell can suggest a better method. If so she will be helpful and happy as well. If not, it will finally occur to her that it's not a good policy to criticize unless you have first arrived at a better way of doing something.

Not My Responsibility

Negative Nell: It's not *my* responsibility.
Negative Supervisor: Well, somebody's got to do it.
Positive Supervisor: Who do you think should be responsible?

Now Nell brings her own reasoning into the picture. Mary can't do it; she's snowed under. Ethel is too new and inexperienced. Nell finally decides that perhaps, after all, she's the one to do it.

How Urgent?

Negative Nell: How soon do I have to have this done?
Negative Supervisor: It should have been done two hours ago.

How much cooperation do you think that answer is going to get from Nell?

Positive Supervisor: When would it be possible to have it completed?

Here the supervisor has given Nell an opportunity to take pride in her own performance. Nell can declare herself a fast worker or a slow worker. At least Nell feels that she has been given consideration.

I Don't Like the Program

Negative Nell: I don't think it's a good program and I don't have the time to get involved.
Negative Supervisor: I guess you'll just have to *take* the time.

What does our people-oriented supervisor say?

Positive Supervisor: Why do you think this would not be
a good program?

The Six Most Useful Words for Supervisors

Did you notice the common denominator of every answer
by the Positive Supervisor? He answered every time with a
question, the most powerful way to communicate if we want
to get cooperation.

Six of the most useful words for any supervisor to remember
are *who, what, when, which, where* and *why.* These are six
honest working words that will help him tremendously in his
communication with employees if he will only remember to
use them. The Positive Supervisor started every question
with one of these words. I am sure you noticed this.

I hope this chapter will convince you that good communication is the essence and nucleus of good cooperation. It is almost unbelievable, unless you have researched the matter, to
find how many people fail to cooperate, not because they lack
loyalty but because they lack understanding. Also we find that
many supervisors invite lack of cooperation because they are
not people-oriented in their communication. Please be careful in all your people transactions to communicate clearly.
Good communication breeds good cooperation; faulty communication generates lack of cooperation.

FIFTEEN

How to Handle
Specific Situations
with Silent Command

There are many transactions, performances and events in which we are involved that depend for their success upon good communication. To say that persuasive communication is simple but not easy appears to be a contradiction within itself. But actually this statement is very true. If a few basic principles of communication are thoroughly understood and followed meticulously, what might appear to be a difficult task often becomes the essence of simplicity.

This chapter might be considered a reference chapter. If you are called upon to do any of the things illustrated in this chapter and if you study the contents and follow the suggestions, you will find little difficulty in your task. In fact, you will take joy in the participation.

How to Introduce a Speaker

Please do not be concerned with the long lists given in many textbooks on the subject, of things to do and to remember when you introduce a speaker. Just the volume of information is enough to frighten many people from the task.

Actually there are only three important steps. If you forget all else and stick to these three, you will perform your task well and have the gratitude of your audience and *especially* of your speaker.

Importance of the Subject

Everyone enjoys taking part in an important event. It helps our ego and we attack the task with enthusiasm.

Especially is this true in the field of speech-making. If I am the speaker and I hear my chairman tell of the importance of my subject, I feel inspired to treat the important subject with care and excellence of performance. Also, such an approach sharpens the interest of the audience.

Yes, the first step in a good introduction is for the chairman to sell the audience initially on the fact that the subject is of utmost importance.

Particularly Important to This Audience

The next step brightens the opportunity of the speaker and lifts the event to an even greater level by telling why the subject is of great importance to this particular audience.

If the subject is sales and the audience consists of salesmen, this is very easy. If the audience is comprised of industrial workers and the subject is safety, again it is a simple matter. However, sometimes we must use our imagination and creative ability to take this second step.

Especially Qualified Speaker

The first two steps are, in reality, only preparation for the third step. In this third step we qualify the speaker for the task he is about to perform. We iterate his qualifications, experience, and training which make him an expert on his subject.

The method of presenting a speaker is elementary. Don't burden yourself with anything other than these three steps. They must follow in logical sequence, as listed. Each is related to the other and each has a particular task to be performed.If you follow this pattern, you cannot fail to be impressive in your introductions.

Now let's examine an example of the proper method of presenting a speaker.

A Model Introduction

Let's imagine that I am asked to introduce a speaker. The occasion is a banquet of safety engineers. The speaker is a specialist in the field of accident prevention.

> Members of our Safety Engineering Society and honored guests. The subject of safety is of great importance throughout the entire world.
>
> The fact is that the dignity of man, the freedom of life and the worship of God in all lands and in all times have never been any greater than the importance which the people of that particular nation put upon the safety and sanctity of life of the individual.
>
> This subject of safety is of particular interest to us here tonight, because in our profession we have dedicated our lives to accident prevention and to promoting standards of safety.
>
> There is no man in America today who is better qualified to bring us a message on safety than our guest speaker tonight.
>
> Jim Riley has been a professor of instruction and research on safety at M.I.T. for over 15 years. He has set up the safety program in many of our nation's largest industries. His great book *Life, Liberty and the Pursuit of Safety* is the bible in the safety department of practically every large company today.
>
> Those of you who have had the privilege of hearing Dr. Riley realize what a treat you have in store. To those of you who have not heard him I congratulate you on your good fortune here this evening.
>
> I now introduce Dr. Jim Riley, who will address you on the subject "Are Accidents Really Necessary?"

I cannot conceive of any circumstance which should call

for an introduction any longer than this one. All three bases were touched — the importance of the subject, the special importance to that particular audience, and finally the qualifications of the speaker.

Prostituting an Introduction

I've never heard a speaker complain about an introduction being too brief. However, nothing is more discouraging to a speaker than to be so unfortunate as to be inflicted with a chairman who prostitutes an introduction into an opportunity to render an oration.

Every speaker has had this unfortunate experience on at least one occasion. Mine came early in my speaking career. I was to address a convention banquet. The hour was late. The "Happy Hour" which preceded the banquet went about an hour overtime. Business and election of officers ran far over the time anticipated, and it was after ten o'clock when the program began.

The president apologized for the lateness of the hour and politely suggested that perhaps we should cut the program down in time. This suited me as I observed that the audience was almost in a coma.

Finally the chairman arose to introduce me. For exactly 23 minutes by my watch he told jokes, referred to remarks of other speakers over the years, and related the efforts that he and two pals of his had exerted eight years earlier in organizing the association. Eventually, when he was exhausted, he simply said, "And now it is my duty to introduce the speaker. Her qualifications and subject were contained in a bulletin sent you last week, and now here she is — let's bring her on with applause."

I carefully gave my name, spelled it, and then gave my subject and spoke for 18 minutes and sat down.

The wonderful audience gave me one of the most spontaneous standing ovations I have ever received. I am confident it was provoked through sympathy over my introduction and appreciation of my brevity.

The Rule of Brevity

Please don't think that I meant to imply that all or even most of the chairmen violate the rule of brevity in making introductions. However, we do have a few frustrated people who grasp the opportunity of chairmanship just to get before the public and expound their views.

Actually, if a person is a compulsive speaker, he should never accept the job of making an introduction. Some people simply can't restrain themselves while on the platform. Just as we have drug addicts and alcohol addicts, we have speaking addicts. If you are one, don't accept the job of introducing a speaker. One must be very unselfish to do the job well. The person introducing is merely the frame around the picture. He is there to make the speaker look good, not to up-stage him.

If he tells a joke or gives any matter of substance, he is taking away from the speaker. Of course, if the job is that of master of ceremonies, that is a different matter. I am referring here to the person whose sole job is to introduce the speaker. He should follow the three steps as outlined and restrict himself to just that role. Even if the master of ceremonies introduces the speaker, when he reaches that point, he, too, should reduce his activities to the pattern of the three steps.

In contrast to the 23-minute oration by the person who was to introduce me, I remember vividly an experience I had recently before the Greater Vancouver Real Estate Board in Canada. I was to give a two-hour seminar on communication as applied to real estate selling. I am sure I never had a nicer introduction and I say confidently it was the shortest.

In a crisp English accent, the chairman, to the best of my recollection, merely said,

> Lack of understanding and faulty communication is responsible for most of the world's troubles today. To those of us in real estate selling the subject of good communications is doubly important because without it we cannot survive. We have with us today America's

leading speaker on this subject. Mrs. Merlyn Cundiff has spoken in six foreign countries, written a book and made numerous records all in the field of communications. I now introduce Mrs. Merlyn Cundiff who will speak on the A.B.C. of selling — Always Be Communicating."

The Element of Surprise

Elsewhere in this book we elaborated on the destructive aspect of removing the element of surprise.

This principle applies in introduction of a speaker also. While we want to qualify a speaker in the third step of our introduction, we can often handicap his chances if we are too complimentary.

Give his qualifications but let him prove his own case. If the speaker is good, his audience is sure to find it out. If he is not, all the flamboyant compliments are not going to help his case.

Relationship Between Chairman and Speaker

I spoke to an organization on "Bosses' Night." At the time I was asked to speak I was told that the whole climate of the meeting should be one of levity and consequently I should not present any serious ideas but treat the occasion lightly. Though I do not consider myself a joke teller I agreed to speak with tongue in cheek and refrain from any heavy material.

Imagine my chagrin when a person I had never seen before, but who must have received his instructions somewhere, started introducing me in this vein: "This is a night for fun — not anything serious. Consequently we have invited a person to come here tonight and tell us a lot of jokes. If she is as funny as I hear she is she will have you rolling in the aisles. I now present your entertainer, Mrs. Cundiff."

Such a breakdown in communication as this can be disastrous to a speaker. If you are the chairman, take nothing for granted. Check your introduction with the speaker. It is a *must* if you want to avoid such experiences as the one stated above.

I am sure you are wondering if I escaped the ordeal mentioned above without battle scars. Though horrified at first over my predicament, I changed my subject to "Humorous Breakdowns in Communication." After 20 minutes of reciting impossible incidents of embarrassment arising out of fractured communication, I analyzed my own introduction as the breakdown of communication to end all breakdowns!

My audience was with me that night. I was thankful for my escape. However, I made a resolution which I have kept since that incident. If the chairman does not check with me regarding my introduction I always check with him, however clumsy may be the situation.

Platform Kinesics

When you introduce a speaker, never leave the podium until the speaker arrives at it. Then when he is only a few feet away, step back graciously and give the speaker your position. Never leave a podium unattended even for two seconds.

An unattended podium not only creates a bad impression with the audience but also puts the speaker at a disadvantage. The warmth of an introduction, however good, is lost and the spell broken when the podium is left unattended even momentarily.

If your speaker must walk up from the audience, stand by your guns and don't leave your post until he arrives. It is a courteous thing to do; your audience will like it and your speaker will be grateful.

Recently I had to walk up from the audience and the chairman and I had a two-person traffic jam on the steps to the stage. It was a clumsy situation and everyone was embarrassed unnecessarily.

You may never have occasion to introduce a speaker, but if the opportunity ever arises don't be afraid to accept it. You now know the fundamentals. You can't go wrong. Just as a matter of interest the next time you witness an introduction, note whether the chairman touches the three bases or whether he appropriates the occasion for the purpose of making a speech himself.

How to Present a Trophy or Plaque

If you are a member of any club, organization or association, chances are that you have many occasions to witness the presentation of a certificate, cup or trophy. You may even be called upon to make the presentation yourself. Good communication requires that this be done according to a simple and definite pattern. A straight line is the shortest distance between two points. So why race all around the world to arrive at the house next door?

As guest speaker at a sportsman's banquet I once heard a very interesting story concerning this question asked of Howard Hill, the great bow-and-arrow expert: "Mr. Hill, other people go hunting with high-powered rifles and the best equipment money can buy. Their percentage of success is very small. You, however, use only a bow and arrow, and yet, I understand, it is very rare that you return without your game. How is this possible?"

His answer was this: "I study my game's eating, sleeping and feeding habits. Then I plan my hunt with infinite care and follow these plans with utmost precision. If I did otherwise, I would not be hunting at all. I would only be walking in the woods."

Unfortunately too many people, in presenting a trophy, do not plan this important undertaking — they are merely "walking in the woods."

Now let's learn a little simple formula which will insure our being a master communicator in making such a presentation.

Four Points of the Presentation

Remember these four simple points that must be made clear if the presentation is to be professional in its nature. They should not be out of order:

1. The person responsible for the presentation.
2. The reason it is being given.
3. What the recipient did to earn it.
4. The actual presentation.

The actual presentation, which should occur only *after* the first three points are covered, should be made gracefully and as a concluding gesture. I'm sure all of us have seen the actual handing over of the trophy or cup before or during the speech of presentation. This destroys the dramatic effect.

If I drank a toast to an individual or to an occasion with a few well-chosen words, the incident would be clumsy and futile if I drank the toast before or during my words. No, I conclude my remarks and *then* drink the toast. Maybe you feel that this admonition is unnecessary. If you think so, just watch carefully the next few such presentations. I regret to predict that you will probably see many violations of this principle. A good presentation is thus spoiled unnecessarily.

Example of Presentation

Note the four points in the following presentation:

> Each year your Chamber of Commerce gives a plaque of honor to one of its members. *(Point #1.)*
>
> This plaque is given to the member who has, during the previous 12 months, been most active in chamber affairs. *(Point #2.)*
>
> Harry Smith, because of the many hours spent in chamber work and because of his outstanding work as head of the membership committee, has been selected by the awards committee to be the recipient of this plaque. *(Point #3.)*

It gives me pleasure to present this plaque to you, Mr. Smith, in behalf of your chamber, because of your outstanding work. *(Point #4.)*

The above is not complicated, is it? Please refer to it in the event you are to make a presentation some day. You can relate it to any occasion. It is simple and straight to the point.

How to Accept a Trophy or Plaque

If we picked the one platform occasion where more violations of good communication are made than any other, it would be the occasion of a trophy acceptance. We should not be critical but should be very forgiving in this instance.

In the first place in many cases the recipient is caught by surprise, and does not have time to ponder over the occasion or to arrange his thoughts or words. Very few people are at ease in delivering an impromptu speech.

Even if the recipient suspected that he would receive the award, in many cases he is so overcome by emotion that he cannot speak. This is not detrimental to him. A sincere display of unavoidable emotions is often far more impressive and communicates appreciation more articulately than anything that can be said.

But if you want to be able to say the proper thing in your acceptance of a trophy or certificate just analyze these three little points. It will insure a brilliant speech of acceptance every time.

1. Thank the person presenting the trophy.
2. Then thank the club, association or company responsible for the trophy.
3. Finally, as you fondle the trophy or cup affectionately, tell the group what you plan to do with it.

Now let's see how Harry Smith would accept the plaque presented to him at the Chamber of Commerce Banquet.

> Thank you, Ray Thomas. *(Point #1.)* My deepest appreciation to my chamber for this honor. *(Point #2.)* I shall hang this plaque on the wall of my office where I can see it every day and each time I look at it I shall remember my many friends who made this presentation possible. *(Point #3.)*

There is nothing complicated about the above. If you understand these three little points you can give an impromptu speech of acceptance any time. The fact is that it is bad taste to make such an acceptance speech too long.

Now that you understand this method of acceptance, I am sure that I could wake you up at three in the morning, make a presentation to you, and you could give a brilliant acceptance speech with only ten seconds of preparation.

It is good taste on the part of a recipient of an award to share the honors with any one or more people who may have assisted him. For instance, Harry Smith could have said, just after thanking Ray Thomas, who made the presentation:

> I accept this plaque in behalf of myself and the devoted members of the membership committee who are responsible for the membership increase of our chamber. *(Point #1.)*
>
> We all thank the chamber for this presentation. *(Point #2.)* I shall hang the plaque on the wall of my office where I can see it every day and each time I look at it, I shall remember the great cooperation on the part of the members of my committee and my many friends in the chamber who made this presentation possible. *(Point #3.)*

One of the unpardonable sins of trophy acceptance is to begin an acceptance speech by saying that you don't deserve the honor. You may have the best of intentions in such a remark, but it is "speech suicide," the oratorical equivalent to a blocked punt. It is almost as bad as starting a regular speech with an apology. The numerous reasons are too obvious to need explanation.

The Use of Exhibits

The proper use of an exhibit can add to practically every speech. Exhibits are dangerous, however, to an inexperienced speaker because exhibits if used improperly detract from a speech and in some cases can prove fatal.

Before demonstrating the proper use of an exhibit, let's analyze the reason an exhibit can be effective.

In the field of communication we are concerned with many factors which are involved in stimulus and response. No single one is more effective than sight. Consequently when we can add this factor to our oral presentation, we are increasing our communication considerably, using one of the most effective "Silent Command" techniques.

There is also a benefit to the speaker. When we can hold up an exhibit or present a picture on the screen, we are often more natural and more effective. We are never bothered with the handicap of self-consciousness. Consequently a person who is bothered by this self-consciousness will find great comfort in exhibits. Even his own attention is diverted from himself and directed toward the exhibit.

In the proper use of an exhibit there are a few principles which must be followed. If you don't use these principles, not only will you fail to get any benefit from the exhibits but also they will detract from any good communication you might have had without them.

Let's start with the major premise that exhibits are not very forgiving of improper use. You can't afford even to consider them unless you adhere to the principles communicated herein.

How to Reveal an Exhibit

Nothing is more distracting to an audience than to observe an exhibit which the speaker has half-hidden and half-revealed. Their curiosity is excited but not satisfied. We can be sure of only one thing. The audience is too interested in mystery to concentrate on anything the speaker might be saying.

The exhibit should be brought to the podium and put out of sight either before the speaking starts or during a coffee break or recess. Any elaborate exhibit brought to the podium while an audience is present, even if put out of sight after arriving, has done its destructive work. The audience will be on pins and needles wondering when it will be revealed.

An exhibit must be handled with the skill of a magician. At the time of its use, quickly and gracefully see that it makes its appearance.

Appearance and Disappearance

Unless you can see that the exhibit is capable of a disappearing act after its use, don't use it in the first place. If the exhibit lingers after it has served its purpose, it will only be a distracting factor to the audience. Don't compete with your exhibit for attention. It will be your friend and help you if you will let it, but it also can work to your detriment.

How to Build Up the Exhibit's Importance

In the event that the exhibit is one you can hold up, be sure to hold it delicately and respectfully out from you and only glance at it when you are calling attention to some feature of it. The proper use of an exhibit is not hard to perfect if you follow instructions and practice proper performance.

If you haven't noticed before, please observe carefully the next time you see a speaker use an exhibit. Unfortunately, in the majority of cases the speaker will direct his entire attention to the exhibit and ignore his audience. One would think he was making a speech to the exhibit.

Only one thing is worse than speaking to the exhibit and that is holding it in front of you and not out to the side. I've seen speakers hold a large card up in front of them so that they appeared to be "sandwich men." I've even seen them hold cards in front of their faces, thereby hiding themselves.

Regardless of what the exhibit is, treat it as though it were invaluable. Almost caress it — move it gently about. Your audience will not consider it of any greater importance than that which you give to it.

How to Use Notes

People are forever asking me at clinics and seminars on effective speaking whether or not the use of notes detracts from a speech.

The answer is the same as with so many things. It all depends on the manner in which you handle the situation. If you feel more comfortable with notes, I would urge you by all means to use them but to take the time to learn how to use them properly.

Have notes readily available. They should be kept on the podium in front of you where they can be seen at all times. If there is no podium, then have them in your hand.

When you refer to them, if they are on the podium just glance down; never bend over or duck your head to see them. If they are too far away, then pick them up and hold them out proudly with your head high as you refresh your memory or get your next cue.

Never give the impression that you are slyly trying to refresh your memory without letting your audience see you do it. Actually your audience has no objection to notes properly used, but if it feels you are not letting them in on the reference, then it seems "sneaky."

If ever you step away from the podium and then step back for the purpose of referring to your notes, you have made too big of a thing of it. You give the impression that you have forgotten your subject and are desperately trying to refresh your memory so that you can get back on the right track. Guard against this.

By the same token never try to hide your notes as a magician would, or make them disappear. Again, most audiences are fair provided you are fair with them.

Handling Notes on the Platform

When you do refer to notes which you are holding in your hand, bring your hand out and up, so that you can glance at them. Don't bend over or nod your head. Treat your notes respectfully and handle them gently. They are gems of wisdom you are carrying proudly to your audience — not a crutch to assist your memory.

How to Give Prestige to a Speech

I attended a conference which was addressed by a college president. He used notes but did so very skillfully.

On one occasion he said, "My next point I considered to be so important that I wrote it down to be sure I wouldn't overlook it."

He proudly held his notes out in front of him as he looked at them. In my own mind I felt that here was a man who considered his audience so important that he had prepared his subject matter. Furthermore, I could hardly wait to hear what the important point was to which he had referred.

At another point in his speech he quoted a certain person. As he glanced at his notes he said, "I considered this quotation a spark of genius and I wanted to be sure I quoted it exactly. So I wrote it down and I'll now read it to you."

I am sure no one could object to the use of notes in this manner. In fact, it gave authenticity and prestige to the entire speech.

Substitute Mental Notes

I am one of many speakers who, in their mind's eye, place imaginary words or figures on the walls of the auditorium to insure themselves of no breakdown in memory. It is a very easy thing to do. The more ridiculous the figure or little character, the less are your chances of forgetting. I sometimes go to the auditorium or other meeting place early in order that I can have time to fix the little figures indelibly in my memory. It may seem corny and overly simple, but it has the homely virtue of working.

Your ability to introduce a person, to present or accept a trophy, or even to use an exhibit properly will not alter the course of history or materially change your life. These are, however, useful skills to have, and can be easily mastered if you follow the elementary principles given in this chapter. Through continued practice of these principles you will find your ability to communicate is greatly increased.

SIXTEEN

The Lifetime Plan for Silent Command Power Development

Since we all agree that we are communicating all of our waking hours and since some of us even feel that by our body positions and movements we are communicating while asleep, doesn't it seem well to consider just how effectively we communicate during our 24 hours?

By relating yourself to a day's communication you can guard against the purely academic approach. Be sure to apply these principles to your everyday experience.

This chapter is going to explain a Lifetime Plan for Silent Command Power development. It will show you how you can start strengthening this power within you from the time you wake up in the morning, throughout your busy day at work, and for week after week, month after month, year after year, reaching and maintaining your powers at their full peak as long as you need them.

On Waking Up

It has been said that every person wakes up each morning to a world of his own making. What do we really mean by the old expression that we "got up on the wrong side of the bed today"?

A person upon awakening can communicate two things. He can get up eager to start the day. By his very manner he can say, "This is a great day — something wonderful is going to happen. In fact, I shall go out and make it happen." On the other hand, by his actions he can communicate, "I hope this day is no worse than yesterday."

I once heard a person relate that as we open our eyes each morning we silently say either "Good morning, God" or "Good God, it's morning."

It is very important to start out each day in a happy mood, figuratively standing tip-toe with expectation. If we feel this way, we communicate this feeling to all those around us. Just as an experiment, take an inventory of yourself tomorrow morning when you wake up. What image do you communicate?

Stoplights and Go-Lights

Are you relaxed as you drive to your work? If not, try relaxing. I promise you that a rigid, nervous person under a strain does not arrive at the office any sooner than one who takes everything in stride and rolls with the punches.

The intersection lights are put there to help speed up the traffic and get you to where you are going faster and with less congestion. In reality, we should speak of the traffic lights not as "stoplights" but as "go-lights."

Recently I stopped at a filling station in a large city and asked for directions to a certain auditorium. The attendant told me to go down to the third red light and turn to the left; two blocks from this red light would be the auditorium.

I was tempted to say, "Do you mean the third red light or the third green light?" But I was sure I would only congeal my own confusion still further.

Starting with the Right Attitude

The next time you observe a car waiting for the traffic light to change, notice how often you will see the driver glance up and down at the red light nervously. What do you think he is communicating? He is perhaps saying, "In this mad, wild, fitful, feverish life I can hardly afford to wait one minute for anything. If I keep looking up and down, maybe the light will change quicker."

Ponder a little on your own actions. Do you communicate to the person driving the car next to you that you have fallen into the "hurry, worry, bury" attitude of life?

Secret of Controlled Excitement

Now you are at your office and ready to face your day of work. What does your approach to your tasks express? Is it one of controlled excitement? Remember, I said that the richest person on this earth is the person who is having a love affair with his job. He is rich because he never drudges another day of his life. His activities constitute pleasure. His job is not just a source of income; it is a source of satisfaction and fulfillment. Lucky indeed is the person who finds excitement in what he is doing.

When is the last time you asked yourself just what it is that motivates you to follow your business, industry, or profession? If it's money alone that we are working for, we are underpaid. To feel chained to a job only for the sake of making a living is indeed a miserable situation. If you cannot find other satisfactions in your work besides just the income, you owe it to yourself to search for something else that *can* offer pleasure, excitement, and a challenge.

Take This Simple Test

Suppose that you are now busy at work with your fellow employees. The very success of your company's production depends on good communication. The art of communication is just as important to you whether you give or receive instructions. Remember, I emphasized from the very beginning that communication is a two-way street. Both the communicator and the respondent must be in complete harmony.

Think back over the last few weeks and try to remember if there has been a breakdown in communication where you were involved. If you can recall such an instance, try to analyze the situation and arrive at the cause of the misunderstanding. If you were part of the error, was the mistake made because of inarticulate speaking or because of careless listening?

An Ancient Doctrine

In law there is a doctrine called *contributory negligence*. One is not permitted to collect damages from a negligent person involved in an accident if the complaining party contributed to the accident by being negligent also. If I see a person driving carelessly toward me, and although I have plenty of time to avoid an accident by taking reasonable precautions I do not take them, then I cannot collect damages because in the sight of the law I contributed to the accident.

I feel that this same doctrine holds true in the field of communication.

The Blind Spots

Imagine that my supervisor calls me into his office and assigns to me a certain task to be performed. My supervisor at this time is under extreme pressure and radiates this nervousness to me. Observing how busy he is, I do not wish to take up any more of his time than necessary. Consequently I do not ask as many questions about the assignment as I would have asked if I had felt my supervisor had more time to spend with me.

When I approach the assigned task I now find many blind spots in my understanding of the job. I am faced with two alternatives. I can either take a chance on doing the job in a manner that may not comply with the way my supervisor wants it done or I can go back and ask for more instructions.

If I adopt the former, I am taking a chance which might turn out to be costly. It's strange that although a person often feels that he doesn't have time to do a job right he always has to find time to do it over if it is not done correctly.

If I proceed along the second course, then I can be sure that the sum total of time of the two meetings with my supervisor is more than would have been expended if I had asked many questions and insisted on clarification of those things I did not understand when first I was given instructions.

Radiation of Emotions

Now let's be honest about the communication by my supervisor and also by me. A person cannot afford to be too busy to give instruction clearly and understandably. If my supervisor was too busy to give instructions clearly, he should not have attempted to give them in the first place. He should have waited until he had more time. Again I say that if a person is under a strain, he radiates that emotion to his listener who also becomes nervous. Instructions, to be given correctly, must be given slowly and in a relaxed manner.

My supervisor should have taken the time to ask me questions to find out if I clearly understood the project. If there were a doubt in his mind, he could have even asked me to repeat to him my understanding of what I was to do.

Yes, my supervisor was clearly in error. He could have taken out insurance against misunderstanding by asking me questions and requesting that I repeat to him my understanding of my job. So I feel that we can safely say that in every case of lack of understanding the supervisor is not without blame.

Understanding Your Duties

The fact that my supervisor failed to make himself clear does not free me from blame. In no instance should I tackle a job assigned to me until I fully understand my duties. It might be embarrassing to me at times. I may not want to appear stupid. But it is not mentally honest for me to proceed until, in my own mind, I have a complete understanding of what I am to do.

From the point of view of what I owe to my company, it is not right for me to fail to stand my ground and insist on complete understanding, and furthermore, it will bring more embarrassment to me. And so I feel that we can safely say that in every case of lack of understanding the person receiving instructions is not without blame.

How to Avoid Being a Victim

On first impression you might feel that in the field of fractured communication it is unfair to indict both parties, but I disagree. I repeat that both parties have a method of taking out insurance against faulty understanding. This insurance lies in the activity of questioning.

All the supervisor in the above instance was required to do, if he wanted to take out insurance against lack of understanding, was to propound a series of questions. This would easily have revealed whether there was proper understanding or not. By the same token, if I do not fully understand instructions, I am only required to ask questions regarding things that are not fully clear to me.

Let's adopt the principle that no one is the innocent victim of errors because of faulty instructions given in the presence of a person who has the opportunity to ask questions. This may be a harsh indictment, but if we are to hold high standards in the field of communication we cannot in complete honesty take any other stand.

The Perfect "Out"

Suppose that my instructions from my supervisor were to call upon a certain person, a prospective client, to offer the services of our company. In this instance his instructions were clear; there was no breakdown in communication.

I call my prospective client for an appointment. Remember that in seeking the physical interview I only want to sell the importance of listening — not my services. This has been emphasized elsewhere in this book. I can't be too emphatic about it.

Again, one of the principal reasons for a person's failure

to give another an appointment is that he feels that in so doing he is in some small way committing himself to accept the product or service when offered. To guard against this I am very careful not even to mention the features or benefits of anything I have to offer when making the appointment. If necessary I even go further than this. I give the prospective client a perfect "out" without any embarrassment if he does not wish to accept our services.

> Mr. Jones, I have no idea at all whether you are interested in our services or not. You can decide very easily after hearing me. However, I do have some very valuable information about our services which might prove most important and beneficial to you. I'd like to know when it's most convenient for you to receive this information. May I come over at three this afternoon, or would an earlier time be more convenient for you?

The Most Effective Tool

Used correctly, the multiple choice of "yes" is one of the most effective tools in the art of communication and persuasion. However, if we are crude or too obvious about it, we can cause resentment in the other party. The whole theory of its effectiveness is based on the fact that "either or" is more palatable than "yes or no."

The danger of this tool is that if used without tact and finesse it seems like a gimmick and smacks of trickery. Common politeness demands that if I am asking you for an appointment, I should let you know that I am willing to see you at your convenience — not mine. And unless I suggest definite times, we do not arrive at any specific appointment.

An Intriguing Motivator

The ancient myth of Pandora and the box is an illustration of the effectiveness of curiosity as a motivator. Just as curiosity caused Pandora to open that box, this same curiosity has been opening doors ever since.

"Mr. Smith, other people in your line of work have found our product most beneficial. I'm sure you at least want to know how it has helped them."

"Our services brought an almost unbelievable savings to a company similar to yours. I can explain this great savings very easily and you can decide for yourself if you want this help also."

"The earnings of ABC company almost doubled when they took over this line. I can show this to you at your convenience and you can decide whether you are interested."

Benefits Not Features

There are two things that are particularly evident in the above remarks. Please note them both.

First, nothing is suggested about the details of the proposal (or product or service) itself. Without such information a prospect is not in a position either to accept or reject the idea. The communication is limited in scope. Only enough information is given to excite curiosity. This curiosity can only be satisfied through an appointment. This is very elementary, but too often we forget and tell too much about our product or service when seeking to sell the appointment.

Second, in the above efforts to set up an appointment, I offer only *benefits*. I am careful to steer away from *features*. This is done for several reasons.

Benefits excite curiosity much quicker and with greater certainty than features. The end results — the benefits — are always attractive. We can always relate ourselves to benefits, not always to features.

Also, if we speak only of benefits there is nothing for our respondent to reject. No one wants to refuse benefits to him. However, it would be different had I spoken of features in seeking to set up an appointment. Then there would have been something to consider in the line of comparisons. If I had said that I wanted an appointment to show a new type of inexpensive insulator, my respondent would now have information on which to decide against the appointment. He might say that his company had just laid in a big supply of insulators. He might say that they had already tested other brands and were satisfied with what they had. He might even question the inexpensive aspect of my approach and say that they had checked all prices and felt sure that their prices were right.

I am certain you see the value, when setting up an appointment, of arousing curiosity through only a brief communication of benefits.

The Great Difference

Many people do not realize that there is a great difference between an appointment and an interview. When we have gained an appointment, we have only received permission to go into the physical presence of our prospect — nothing more.

After we are in his physical presence, if we can then get into his presence mentally, that is, gain a reasonable amount of his attention and interest, we can say that we have an interview. We have emphasized this elsewhere in this book and we emphasize it again.

Please, *please* have the courage to walk away from an appointment if you can't get an interview. Be careful in your observation. If the body communication as well as the verbal communication by your respondent tells you that he has not given you a true interview, and if it becomes clear that you cannot at that time get the attention and interest you require for an interview, be professional enough to excuse yourself and leave.

Earlier in this book I have given you language that you can use. If you are tactful, your respondent will not be offended. After all, it is he who has refused the interview — not you. But don't waste your time!

Appointment Vs. Interview

A truly accomplished person in the field of communication always considers the appointment and interview as two entirely independent procedures. They are two distinct and different steps that must never be confused.

Some people never divorce or separate the two. These people are destined for great disenchantment in the field of dealing with others.

The Presentation

In the anatomy of persuasion it is, of course, unthinkable to consider the presentation until we have gotten through both the appointment and the interview. After we are in both the physical and mental presence of our respondent, we are ready to present the merits of our proposal. During this presentation we reach another plateau.

The appointment brought us into the physical presence of our respondent. The interview brought us into his mental presence through the attention and interest we gained. Now in our presentation we go from this mental presence into his emotional presence so that we can get action.

Since this chapter is primarily a review of principles we meet in a day's communication, I want to emphasize a few additional points on which we should concentrate.

Profitable Difficulty

I have had people differ with me violently when I have emphasized in my seminars, as I have emphasized and repeated throughout this book, that fear, apprehension and difficulty are to be welcomed by the ambitious person if he wants to continue in his growth.

Nature has a storehouse of riches for us all, but she only gives us those strengths which we need, when we need them, to meet and overcome the difficulties we meet in life. And so, since we only grow strong through adversity, there is a certain blessing we find in the obstacles we meet in our lives.

A very dear friend of mine who is truly a spiritual person seems to rise above any difficulty — and she has had many. I have known her for many years. At one time she complained a great deal After her husband died, leaving her with four children, she felt as though she were a martyr. So persistent was she in telling her troubles that she was avoided by most of her acquaintances.

However, as other difficulties faced her over the years, she began to get stronger and to grow with each disappointment and seemingly insurmountable obstacle. Now she is truly a great person. Her indomitable spirit is an inspiration to all who know her. She spends much of her time comforting other people who perhaps are materially more fortunate than she but not as strong spiritually. Her compassion and interest in others has constantly grown as she has overcome each obstacle. Each stumbling block has only turned out to be a stepping stone for this great person.

The Blessings of Being Sensitive

Many people who do research and who teach in the field of human engineering embrace the theory that unless a person is sensitive enough to experience a definite fear when he is approaching people who might refuse his proposal, product or service, he will never be successful in the art of persuading others. I definitely subscribe to this theory.

This belief is based on the fact that people are so complex that only a sensitive person can appreciate the many emotions, ambitions and aspirations that are harbored in the human brain. So please consider carefully this point of view. Weigh the facts carefully before you disagree.

I hope you go even further with me and subscribe to the fact that this sensitivity, even though it causes fear, is a blessing to be prized. Without it you will never be able to appreciate the feelings of other people; with it you have a great fear of refusal. ɪ repeat that about the third time we receive a refusal of our proposal product or service, we consider it a rejection of ourselves.

The Twin Factors You Need to Win

I would be mentally dishonest if I said that you could ever rid yourself of feeling the pangs of this fear of rejection without also losing the priceless sensitivity which I hope is yours. The two go hand in hand. You cannot enjoy the benefits of sensitivity without paying the price of fear.

Insulation Against Rejection

While we cannot completely get rid of this fear of rejection, and frankly if we did we would destroy our sensitiveness, we can reduce its acuteness to some extent without losing its benefits.

Man has always feared the unknown. Once he was petrified by thunder and lightning primarily because he did not understand their cause. Now that we understand these things, although we still have a certain respect and fear, we are not driven into a panic.

Similarly, if we realize why we have this healthy fear when we face the unknown response of a respondent, this knowledge helps us reduce this fear to manageable proportions. The mere fact that we realize nature gave us this fear of the unknown as part of self-preservation reduces the fear to some extent.

Restoration a Necessity

Yes, I hope you agree with me that as good sensitive persuasive communicators we do not desire completely to get rid of this fear of refusal. As these refusals of our product or service mount, I hope you agree with me still further that they become in our own mind rejections of ourselves. It's human nature to take this attitude. These rejections take a real toll upon us. The emotional trauma, however small, wears us down even as drops of water might wear down the hardest of rocks.

To be worn down and discouraged is no serious matter. I have said over and over, "Courage is not getting rid of fear — it is learning to cope with it."

If you have agreed with me this far, then there is only one thing left for us to do. Realizing that this inevitable fear will take a toll upon us, we must adopt a method to build ourselves up constantly just as rapidly or even faster than refusals can tear us down. This is the real test of our survival in the field of selling ideas, products or services.

The Only Answer

While some consulting and research firms might disagree on what specific tools are best for rekindling the fires of enthusiasm, all now agree upon two aspects of this necessary phase of training and conditioning.

First, if a company wishes to raise the enthusiasm of its employees no continuing program of motivation can successfully be given by an outsider. From time to time a person can be brought into an organization to raise temporarily the morale of that organization. The emotions may soar to great heights, but since emotions are transitory, this rise is only temporary. Consequently the problem is to get each individual to adopt his own program and habit of regenerating his spirits periodically.

Continuous Motivation

The second aspect of motivation agreed upon by all is that unless the program of recharging the enthusuasm of a person is permanent and pursued constantly, it is of no lasting value — if indeed it is of any value at all.

Thus our efforts should be directed at building within each person himself a self-motivation program to counteract the toll which refusals are bound to have upon him, and making every effort to convince that person that this is a never-ending task of rebuilding.

The Master Secret

One might feel that some of the matters covered in this chapter are foreign to communication. This is not true. The entire field of human engineering, every facet of the people business, is so interwoven with good persuasive communication, verbal and non-verbal, that one is blended with the other.

Put great importance on good communication in any and every field of your endeavors. You will never contribute to any great project, industry, business, or profession if you are not accomplished in communication. We cannot stress too strongly that the person who can't communicate his knowledge, regardless of the amount of knowledge or in what field it may lie, is no better off than the person who has no knowledge.

This is the Lifetime Plan I mentioned. It includes developing a positive mental attitude, sensitivity to the needs and wants of others, avoidance of being a victim, and self-motivation. These easily cultivated habits and attitudes can help you use *Kinesics* and the power of Silent Command many times more effectively. No matter what activity you're engaged in during the day, keep your eyes and ears open! Day by day, week by week, year by year, you will feel this incredible power build up in you!

SEVENTEEN

The Kinesics of Courtship and Romance

Nature intends to perpetuate each species of living thing, and uses courtship and sex as the instruments of this perpetuation. You can be sure, therefore, that all of us are generously provided with instinctive persuasive powers in this field. Almost unconsciously, men use their strongest powers of persuasive communication to attract women, and women use theirs to attract men. You can learn a lot about persuasive communication by observing the ways people use it to attract the opposite sex. The words people use in courtship, romance, and sex, and their non-verbal communications — using their bodies, color and style of clothing, jewelry and perfume — can tell you valuable things about how to be persuasive.

Men who are successful in wooing women often use many of the ways of persuasion described in the earlier chapters of this book. They also apply the lessons they learn in courtship to persuading their bosses and fellow-workers in business. Women in business know they must be attractive to others, not only to those in whom they might have a romantic interest. Both sexes must apply "courtship" to other types of relationships for persuasive communication.

One of the most successful career women I know is an officer in a large bank in the city where I live. This woman is handsome, charming, and immaculate in her dress. She is generously endowed by nature in her physical appearance.

Men enjoy transacting business with this woman, I am sure, as much because of her good looks as because of her business efficiency. She certainly capitalizes on her appearance, but never in a distasteful way. She has learned to apply persuasive communication in all relationships.

Courtship Signals in Animals and Men

The preening conduct of a bird, or the courtship dance of an animal, is designed to get the attention of the opposite sex. Human beings, too, have their own versions of a courtship dance for the same reason. It is a powerful attempt at persuasive communication, generally without words.

Such an attempt doesn't have to be an obvious approach or a noticeable demonstration. Suppose that several women are dining in a room alone. Several men come in and take a table nearby. Chances are more than likely that these women will take action that corresponds to the preening conduct of the birds. They will re-adjust their hair, fix their lipstick, and change the position of their bodies. One or two may excuse themselves to go to the powder room and primp there. In any event, "preening" steps will take place.

Likewise, let's suppose that four men are on the first tee of a golf course ready to tee off. Several very charming ladies who are strolling by stop to watch the performance. Do you think for a moment these men will conduct themselves in the same manner as they would if they were not being watched? The "strutting" and the "preening" will take place just as certainly as it did with the women except that it will express itself in a different manner. Each man is consciously on stage and puts forth special effort to make an impression.

Do you think that a small boy who pulls a little girl's long curls desires to hurt her? In reality he only wants to persuade her to notice him. It's his way of communicating the fact that he must not be ignored. At other times he'll hang by his knees or climb a tall tree because there are girls watching. This is simply his way of "preening." He attracts the attention of the opposite sex in the only way he knows how.

Using the Power of Sex Communication

On first impression it might appear that sex communication has only a limited function. Actually sexual attraction permeates practically every field of our private, our social, and our economic lives. It is widely used in advertising. The light-headed little girl on TV "with a body by Fisher and a brain by Tinkertoy" commands our attention for even the most uninteresting subjects. Have you noticed how many TV stations have employed such girls to telecast weather reports? And these types of sex communicators sell products. Many girls even try to imitate the Mae West "Come up and see me some time" style while giving the features and benefits of an automobile or house appliance.

Such use of sexy tones and manners to promote products annoys some people, but let's face it! Sex is here to stay. Love, as they say, may make the world go round, but sex keeps it populated. We must not ignore the power of sex when we study persuasive communication.

Communication by Dress

Just as the decor of a person's home reflects the personality of the owner, a person's dress and appearance communicate much to us about that person.

Consider these two extremes. A man is walking down the street in a black suit with a collar turned around. A moment later a young man, barefooted, long-haired, saunters down the same street. These two attires clearly communicate two different and distinct personalities, persuading us in different ways.

I am at a party and notice a young girl with a good figure. Her dress is cut low and seems even lower because the top button is unbuttoned. I don't have to tell you that the most carefully planned thing is a careless and accidental top button left open. I can't recall ever seeing this carelessness on the part of a woman who is not blessed with a full bosom. I suppose a flat-chested girl is by nature more careful and

meticulous in her dress. She doesn't forget this top button.
Nature gives her a better memory perhaps.

Does anyone doubt what the girl with the good figure is
communicating?

> Nature endowed me generously and I am proud of it.
> I want to show as much of myself as I can without
> appearing to be a floozy. The best way to do this is to
> pretend that I accidentally am revealing more of myself
> than I intend to do. You cannot hold me responsible
> for my mistake. When you stare at that portion of my
> body, I am complimented. But I look away when you
> do it for fear that you might know that I am conscious
> of what you are doing. Please continue to stare at me.

Just as a matter of interest to you, the next time you go
to a party carefully notice the attire of those who are there.
Based on your knowledge of the people there, ask yourself
if their dress is not designed to persuade in different ways.

Color Communicating

The personality of an individual is often revealed by the
colors adopted in his or her home and by the colors preferred in clothing. It has been said that bright colors are
worn by an extrovert and more conservative colors by an
introvert. To some extent this is true, but since brighter
colors have become more popular in all dress we might be
misled if we accepted this principle too literally.

In past years we have associated red, purple, and the
heavier colors with an invitation for sex participation. I am
sure that we cannot assume in our modern times that any
color, in and of itself, expresses this. However, we all certainly will agree that certain bright colors will encourage
the making of "advances" more than will subdued colors.

How would you feel if you went to a funeral and saw some
female relative of the deceased wearing a loud red coat and
a matching red dress? Certainly this color would not signify
sorrow and deep respect on the part of that person. Red is

a motivating color, one that brings stimulation and action, and is not suitable for the occasion.

A person wearing green on St. Patrick's day is communicating for sure. Likewise a red, white and blue dress worn on the Fourth of July certainly tells us something. The Christmas spirit is apparent in a person who wears red on December 25th. That person is communicating happiness, joy and good will to all mankind.

Persuasion Through Odor

No treatment of non-verbal communication is complete without at least a reference to odor.

Among animals the scent is perhaps the one most important factor in identity, invitation and response. We only have to observe animals to be convinced of this. It seems to be one of nature's miracles that a new-born calf and its mother can identify each other among a thousand cows and calves by mere scent.

An eligible young lady in many cases will go without food before she will deprive herself of a tantalizing perfume. If a man who is particularly attractive to a girl compliments her on a certain kind of perfume, what perfume do you think she will use when he next dates her? The persuasive effect of perfume in many cases brings a man to the emotional point of popping the question.

Most people claim that odor will bring back fond memories of things that happened years ago quicker and more vividly than anything else. I never smell roses without having my memory carry me back to my childhood days when I picked roses from our yard and carried them to my teacher. The communication is quick and vivid and sentimental.

I know a certain real estate person who always asks the owner of a house he is showing to put on the coffee pot before he brings the prospect out for inspection. He told me that nothing communicates comfort, relaxation and domestic atmosphere as vividly as the smell of coffee.

Using Eye Communication

Among the numerous ways that we communicate with our eyes none are more carefully planned than when we are trying to persuade the opposite sex. We use our eyes in different ways and in varying intensity.

It is true that many people have eyes which are more expressive than others. But I am sure that it would be difficult to find anyone who does not communicate to some degree with his eyes.

We have been told from childhood, "Don't stare." In most cases this is good advice. Staring is rude because it makes the object of our stare uncomfortable.

However, there are exceptions to this rule. For instance, a man stares admiringly as a beauty contestant walks by. His stare communicates, "You are a gorgeous creature. How wonderful it is to radiate such beauty. You make the world a nicer place in which to live because there are such people as you".

No woman resents a stare of admiration. If the stare, however, goes beyond admiration and has the leer of anticipation and desire for possession it makes many women uncomfortable.

The Come-Hither Look

A friendly glance by a person, accompanied by a smile, often communicates to either sex that he or she likes people and would enjoy a conversation. Such an attempt at persuasion is more likely to happen when one is on a plane, waiting in a reception room, at a social function or the like. Such occasions offer a natural climate for this type of experience.

Don't expect such a persuasive glance and smile to have this effect in a crowded elevator or walking down a busy street. If you attempt such a communication under the wrong circumstances you are certain to be embarrassed.

Remember that there are varying degrees of eye communication. A man often conveys the message to a girl, "May I join you?" simply by opening his eyes wider than usual and even slightly raising his eyebrows. I have seen this same inquiry made by simply squinting the eyes.

It depends a great deal on the circumstances and location. A wink has always been interpreted as an invitation. If a person looks into the eyes of a person beyond the usual second or two, he or she is usually inviting a response. This is in most instances considered the safest way to make an approach because it gives one a method of saving his ego if he doesn't get a favorable response.

The "I Am Willing" Stare

If the other party is congenial to a meeting, all he or she has to do is continue to stare back. This is articulate communication and implies that "I too, would like to make our relationship more intimate. You are permitted to accost me. I shall not be insulted. I shall not rebuff you or shatter your ego."

This staring back does not, however, communicate anything other than the preliminary meeting. In salesmanship, it is called "selling the appointment."

The Extent of Intimacy

If a man staring at a girl finds that she glances away before permitting enough time to elapse to commit herself, he can easily save his ego. He does not undergo the embarrassment of feeling that he was rejected. He too can glance away as though he never intended to send a message or offer an invitation.

The stare approach is complete insurance against a shattered ego. This is not true in many other methods of inviting a more intimate relationship. For instance, if a man asked a woman if he could join her and she raised her chin as though she were highly insulted and turned away, how could he save his ego by claiming that she misinterpreted his intent, that he never requested permission to join her?

It is amazing and almost unbelievable to find out the extent of intimacy which a man can reach with a woman as long as he constantly communicates to her "I still consider you to be a perfect lady." He may do this without speaking, as evidenced by the following reactions:

> "He looked at me so adoringly, how could I resist?"
> "I could tell by his expression that he was serious about me."
> "His big brown watery eyes, fixed on me so lovingly, convinced me that this was not just temporary with him. That's why I consented, if you must know why!"
> "He reached up with his arms in such a sincere pleading way, no woman could resist."

Everyone has a self-image which he or she must preserve. We can call it our self-respect or even our pride. It is important to us all that we maintain this. Actually what we think of ourselves is in reality more important than what other people think of us. The rule that you must persuade the other person you continue to respect him holds in other relations just as it does in courtship. Both men and women fear loss of respect, and will react coldly if your "look" indicates a lack of respect.

This principle of permitting the other party to save face is something we should remember in all facets of our dealings with other people.

A girl recently rushed up to me at an airport, thinking that I was someone else, and greeted me enthusiastically. When she realized that we had never met before she was greatly embarrassed. Seeing her plight, I said, "You look so familiar to me, too. I am *sure* we must have met somewhere."

Her embarrassment left her immediately and we laughed about the incident when it appeared to her that we both were mistaken.

Occasions are offered frequently where we can help the other party save face. All of us, I am sure, have read about the genial host, one of whose guests knocked over a glass of water and felt humiliated. The host made a point of doing the same thing twice before the evening was over. His guest soon gained his poise and even felt a little sorry for the host.

The most persuasive and successful "eye communicator" is one who conveys in his look that he is always willing to help the other person save face.

How to Make an Appointment with Your Eyes

One of the first lessons taught any new salesman is that the sale of the appointment should never be confused or mixed in with the sale of the product or service. His first task is to sell his prospect on just the importance of listening. Eye communication is mainly devoted to "selling the appointment."

The new salesman is even impressed with this fact: "It is easier to sell a person who isn't interested, if you can get the appointment, than to find a person who is interested."

Communication by Voice Pitch

Does anyone doubt that the low guttural voice of a Charles Boyer is a sex symbol? People today speak of a sexy voice just as they would speak of a sexy figure.

A high school teacher friend of mine was attending a teachers' conference. The first morning her eyes were caught by the intent and steady gaze of a handsome man, a tall and athletic fellow-teacher. My friend confessed that she had difficulty concentrating on her school work that day. Twice she found herself in a trance. She kept daydreaming of his stare.

"What shall I wear tonight to catch his attention?" she kept asking herself. She decided to wear a somewhat daring dress.

That night at the reception she appeared a little late, in her shortest and tightest dress, a rather low cut, black outfit. She wore her hair in an upswept style with her ears clearly showing and graced with long dangling earrings. I am sure that her appearance communicated in a loud voice, "I am delightful and available if you know how to make the right approach."

As she entered the reception hall, the first person she spotted was the handsome stranger, immaculately dressed and apparently waiting for her. At close range their eyes met again. Then she was shocked to hear a high, squeaky voice say, "May I sit with you for awhile?"

My friend told me she excused herself quickly. She was suddenly the victim of a headache, turned in early, and spent the evening with her books. Never in her life, she said, had she built her hopes up to such a disappointing let-down.

Actually, if my friend was really as anxious to meet the "right person" as she indicated she was, she should have waited to see if she could get him to drop his voice a half-octave or so. She put disproportionate importance on the pitch of his voice.

Nevertheless, this example shows how others may judge us, to our detriment, by the sound of our voices. As in courtship, so in other situations must we be sure our voices help us to persuade. We should all take inventory of our vocal personalities from time to time. What does the tone of your voice communicate to others?

I present a "voice clinic" once a year, and urge everyone who attends to purchase a small cassette tape recorder and bring it to the clinic. The first day we have those who are attending record a neutral message such as the alphabet or the multiplication table, in a tone that suggests either sex, pride, fear, surprise or other emotion. When each person has done this, others are asked to interpret the emotion when it is played back. Those who do not clearly communicate the emotion they intend are coached until they can do so. With the help of friends, you can develop this skill yourself.

Body Position

The position in which one stands and sits can give a persuasive message, according to all researchers and writers on this subject.

How does the strong, silent "sex symbol" of the movies

stand? Does he stand as though he were a soldier in the presence of an officer? No, he has a casual, sophisticated slouch. He throws out one hip as though it were almost out of joint. More weight is put on one leg than on the other, which is carelessly crossed over in front of him. A hand on one hip even helps to build the image.

This man is communicating, "I am a man of the world. I am sure of myself. I am relaxed and confident. It's not necessary for me to be eager or disturbed about the future — I don't have to be."

The average woman communicates more articulately with her standing position than a man. She has more to communicate with, and a woman's body is more flexible and lends itself to body language better.

The next time you see a group of women sitting together without any men near, just study their positions and manner of posture. Notice how the same women hold themselves and act while sitting in the presence of men. You can see that they neither sit in the same position nor act the same.

You might ask if this ability to distinguish the difference has any value. It has this value. If you wish to become experts in the field of persuasive communication, you must observe and study every facet of such expressions. We cannot be accomplished in one type of body communication without understanding such communication in its entirety.

You must remember that the meaning of a particular action depends upon time and place. If a woman is sitting in a bar alone at midnight and leans over to a man on the next stool and asks for a light, do you think she has a right to make this man feel that she has been insulted if he propositions her?

The time, place, and circumstances have much to do with interpreting the communication of certain acts or movements. If this same woman asks this same man for a match while they are both waiting in line for a plane ticket in a busy terminal, we have a right to draw entirely different conclusions from her actions.

The Language of Sexual Communication

It is well to understand the language of sexual communication, even though you may have no desire to send out sexual invitations, or interest in responding to such invitations. Your knowledge of persuasive communications, particularly non-verbal communications, will be increased if you observe the sexual communications of others, and to do this, you must truly learn to "listen with your eyes."

Look at the clothing people wear, their choice of colors and scents, the way in which they move their bodies and stare at others. People are becoming far more outspoken in bodily sexual communication than in the past. Study courtship and "preening" to learn which communications are persuasive and which are not. Maybe you yourself have been unconsciously sending out wrong messages to others.

EIGHTEEN

The Rewards of Silent Command

There are two balance sheets to every company. One is handled in the accounting department; the other, which might be called an "invisible balance sheet," is found in the personnel department. The first reflects the financial strength of the company. The second reflects the people strength of that company.

Which is more important is too obvious to need elaboration. If we wiped out all the physical assets of du Pont today, in perhaps a year's time these assets would be replaced and the company would be back in business. However, if all personnel were wiped out, there would likely be no du Pont Company ever again.

A Great Inventor's Secret

One of the most vital factors affecting this invisible balance sheet is the ability of a company to communicate. This communication within the company, as I stated before, is on a horizontal basis between employee and employee and on a vertical basis between supervisor and employee. Also we must consider communication with the public in building a public image.

This opportunity of building better communication is never ending. It can always be improved. As the great Thomas Edison said, "There is a better way to do it — find it."

An Action Plan for Daily Living

I once heard a third-day convention speaker utter a prayer: "Dear Lord, bless the speakers on the first day of a convention. Their listeners are fresh and full of intellectual curiosity. They have an opportunity to stir emotionally and stimulate mentally. Their opportunity is great — they are indeed fortunate.

"Also, dear Lord, bless and help the speakers on the second day. Their listeners are becoming tired and disinterested. These speakers need help; they are faced with a real problem.

"But as for any speaker on the third day of a convention, dear Lord, please have mercy on his soul."

I personally differ in this philosophy. I always prefer to be the last speaker at any convention. This is the time when those attending should pause, take inventory of what they have learned and resolve to do something about it. Nothing is more useless than knowledge which is not put into use; nothing is more powerful than knowledge put into action.

For the same reason I feel that the last chapter of this book is by far the most important.

I hope you will consider the communication ideas and principles covered in this book and give much thought and consideration to the manner in which you are going to adapt them to your work and everyday living.

How to Get Help When You Need It

One of the reasons why many people fail to use good ideas received from a book is that they try to absorb too many ideas on first exposure. This book is designed to be a reference book and also, hopefully, an enjoyable book.

After the first reading don't try to put into use more than one or two ideas. Don't try to remember too many things you read. Unless an idea is so good that it embraces you rather than being embraced by you, chances are that you will not remember it anyway. So on first reading pick out one or two ideas that reached out to you and then *start using them.*

Since this is a reference book, I hope you will refer to it many, many times. After one idea has become a part of you through constant use, go back and read again with the idea of taking another idea that appeals to you and putting that idea into use also.

Above all else please remember that to put one idea into use is far more beneficial than mentally to absorb a hundred ideas which you simply "pigeon-hole" away in your brain. I am sure you have realized while reading this book that my primary effort has been not to clutter your brain with numerous communication ideas but rather to encourage you in procedure which will enable you to use to best advantage the simple rules of good communication known to us all.

The one test of whether this book was worth my writing and worth your reading is found in this question, "Are you going to be better in your work for having read this book?" Unless you put at least one idea contained in this book into action, the answer to this question is "No."

In order to help you in your thinking as to whether this book will have any lasting effect upon you, I shall offer a few suggestions regarding your possible future action.

How to Prepare for the Future

First, do you have a strong desire to prepare yourself for more effective communication in the future? Do you really *want* to grow in strength so that you can compete in an increasingly competitive world? Do you have a compulsion to perfect your persuasive powers?

Don't be impulsive in your decision; don't consider this question lightly. Be honest with yourself. Not everyone has this desire. Many are satisfied to sit on life's sidelines and just watch the success parade go by. They not only lack any desire to lead the parade, but they don't even care to be in the parade. They are perfectly satisfied to be spectators and merely watch others march ahead.

Some people have built-in limitations; they prefer a life of quiet desperation; they are allergic to effort; they don't even burn the candle at one end. I've known people who started at the bottom of the ladder and simply found it more comfortable to remain there than to attempt to climb up rung by rung. They fall into that great category of people who prefer to endure the deprivations of failure rather than make the sacrifices of success. Of course, this is their privilege.

The Two-Edged Sword

We are all born free and equal in our right to fail as well as to succeed. Otherwise, we would not be living in a democracy.

Do you realize that the Constitution of the United States of America, the Bill of Rights, even the ancient Magna Charta, all guarantee to me that I have the right to fail as well as to succeed? This is the very essence of democracy. It is a two-edged sword, and it's up to me and me alone to choose which edge I shall use to carve out my future. I might tell you that I am a totally worthless individual, that I am absolutely unmotivated by anything, and furthermore, that I like it that way. My friend, this is no concern of yours. I am sure you would not admire me; I am positive you would not consider me a candidate for distinction; but disgusting as I might appear to you, you must respect my right to follow this formula for certain failure if I so desire.

I repeat the first question, do you have a strong desire to prepare yourself for the future?

The Second Question

The second question is of far greater importance. Even if you are sure you have the desire, is this desire strong enough and compulsive enough to cause you to do something about it? Are you sure you are willing to do certain things *now,* whether you enjoy doing them or not, which will lead with certainty to future happiness and success?

Man throughout all history, in all ages and in all lands, has been plagued with this great choice. Does he want to gratify his immediate impulse or does he want to accomplish

his ultimate purpose? This choice is yours at this time. Be
honest with yourself. If for some reason you cannot answer
these two questions in the affirmative, if for some reason your
thirst for success is not enough to make you willing to undergo
certain sacrifices, I say that you should abandon this book
at once. It has nothing of help for you. But if, on the other
hand, you desire your just share of the tasks and rewards of
this life, and furthermore, if you want them enough to make
some temporary sacrifices in order to obtain them, then this
book can be the road map to the great city of your dreams,
your ambitions, and your aspirations.

Every individual has within himself the seeds of his own
growth and the virus of his own destruction. Whether he
cultivates a condition for growth, or whether he creates a
climate for destruction depends upon his decision regarding
these two important questions. To answer the first question
is not enough; your decision must be made on both. For your
sake, I hope you make them both in the affirmative. I sincerely
believe that you have the strength, the ambition, and the self-
discipline to do so, or you would not have read this book to
its final chapter. I hope that I am right.

The Amazing Rewards of Silent Command

If you are willing to spend just five minutes a day to learn
the principles of Kinesics and Silent Command, as set forth
in this book, the doors of opportunity will swing open for
you. The good things of life will be yours for the asking,
whether you want money, power over others, devoted friends,
a respectful and obedient family, passionate romances with the
opposite sex, the admiration of your neighbors, community
leadership, or anything else. These are the rewards you can
expect — and win — if you master and use the techniques in
this book.

The Greatest Gift

And, while I don't want to sound like a "Johnny-one-note"
or a broken record, I repeat, "Unless you really want to

succeed in this life, unless you earnestly want to better yourselves, unless you sincerely want a greater share of the good things in this world, want them enough to do something about it now, you should forget about this book at this moment because nothing I can say, in fact nothing that anyone else can say, will help your tragic and hopeless situation in life."

Yes, we "gotta wanna." We must have the gift of dissatisfaction. We must want circumstances to be better than they now are. If we are completely satisfied with our present state of life, and with everything that surrounds us, the pilgrimage has ended for us and we have already settled in our little city of compromise. It is only through divine discontent that we keep moving forward.

Yes, we "gotta wanna." Needs are not enough; wants are the magic ingredients. Wants alone bring out the best within us, not needs.

We are not, and probably never will be, a needy people. Needs are too basic and logical, and they push us only while we are in the realm of desperation. Wants are emotional, inspirational, sentimental, and lift us to new levels of accomplishment.

The Magic Formula

If we want certain things in life badly enough, we automatically draw upon those resources within us and convert them to productivity. We might have needed certain things for a long time, but until we finally begin to want them, we shall certainly never get them, unless by accident. Many people who merely need things sit idly by and dream of the joys they will experience when their dreamship comes in. This is the only sure way of "missing the boat."

Some people reading this book might say, "Why shout the obvious? I realize that in a world of changing values, shifting methods, and increasing competition, I must constantly be improving myself by learning more effective communication and adjusting to meet these new challenges. Be specific, spell it out, don't deal in vague generalities; tell me exactly just what I can do. I feel that I am worth the investment and I am willing to invest whatever time, effort, and money necessary to keep pace with changing times."

If you belong to this group, I congratulate you, I salute you, I am happy for you. Furthermore, I will give you a directional compass in the form of a magic formula, which, if followed, will lead to the great city of your ambitions and aspirations. It is not complicated. And, it has the basic virtue of being certain in its results.

No Limits to Your Success

First, our preparation must be a constant process with no ending. It must be forever moving, never static. School is never out for the person who really wants to succeed. There is no saturation point. All economic research centers agree that because of the rapidly changing phases of our economy, the average person in any line of endeavor today, regardless of his particular field, must be retrained many times.

It is somewhat disenchanting, I know, to find that just as we learn one role in life we are suddenly called upon to play an entirely new part, unrehearsed, as the drama of life must go on either with us, or without us.

The Day of the Flying Clock

The constant demands of readjustment offer a challenge today that never existed before. No longer is preparation something that can be put in a drawer and forgotten about. Success itself has taken on a new definition. It might even be termed today the constant and continuing changes of our economic system. I must emphasize that success today is a journey, not a destination.

Furthermore, in making this trip the important thing is that we must be constantly moving forward — seeking the progressive realization of a predetermined goal. The speed of our progress is of minor importance. Of major importance is the direction in which we are moving and the fact that we are always moving forward. It takes patience, and patience is not an easy virtue. This is the day of the flying clock. The motto of many is "Hurry, worry, bury." We have instant coffee and instant tea, but there is no "quickie" in the field of human development. We don't explode into success; we grow into it. And our growth should never end. Any person who selects a goal in life which can be fully achieved, has already defined his own limitations. When we cease to grow, we begin to die.

Tennyson perhaps expressed the idea best in his description of Ulysses, wandering in search of knowledge, new places, and experience: "I am a part of all that I have met, yet all experience is an arch wherethrough gleams that untraveled world whose margin fades forever and forever as I move."

New Worlds to Conquer

Yes, I am sure you agree with me that regardless of how well-qualified a person may be to meet the rigors of life today, if he is lulled into a sense of false security that he needs no additional preparation for the future, that his journey can ever be ended, soon he will find that he is lost in the frustrations of medieval thinking. And so, first and foremost, we repeat over and over and over the principle that in order to keep pace with changing times, we must pursue a constant program of self-improvement, a never-ending journey into new fields of knowledge and communication.

How to Become a Leader

And now for the second principle in our formula for success, which I present in the form of a question: "Are we trying to change our circumstances in life without being willing to make the sacrifices to change ourselves? Are we looking for a better job without being willing to do a better job? Are we trying to build a future without being willing to build ourselves?"

When we have once embraced this great human law and have accepted it for all time, we will have simplified in some measure many of life's problems: *We cannot accomplish anything greater than that which we are.* The picture can be no greater than the artist, the statue than the sculptor, the book than the writer. Human laws, as we know, are just as certain as the laws of nature. Just as water cannot rise above its source, our accomplishments can be no greater than those qualities which have been instilled in us.

Since time began the world has been made up of two classes of people. There are those people who look for a position in life which is not too difficult for their capabilities. Then there are those ambitious, resourceful individuals who seek to improve and prepare themselves for greater positions and opportunities of life. Those who seek to find an easier way of life have always failed. Those who seek only to make themselves stronger to meet the difficulties of life are our leaders today. You can be one of them.

You Shall Be the Miracle

Two men were sent out with hacksaws to salvage the bottom of a boat for scrap iron. One returned dejectedly and said that the task was impossible. The iron was too hard for the saws. The other came back and requested a saw of stronger steel, saying that the saw was too soft.

Two ships went out into the oyster-bed area. One crew soon returned stating that the oysters which contained pearls were too deep for their diving gear. The other crew came back to port for new gear stating that the helmets were too weak for the depth they were required to go.

Henry Ford, the man who put America on wheels, finally decided in 1928 that he would abandon the Model T and come out with the Model A Ford. He produced a trial model and assigned the task of thorough study of the new model to two of his engineers. The first engineer reported that the engine was too strong for the body; the horsepower must be reduced. The second engineer reported that the body was too weak for the engine; the body must be strengthened. It is unnecessary to tell you which engineer became the head of the Engineering Department of Ford Motors.

Only the difficult offers a real challenge. Phillips Brooks crystallizes the principle in very beautiful language: "Do not pray for tasks equal to your powers; pray for powers equal to your tasks; then the doing of your work shall be no miracle, but you shall be the miracle."

The Secret of Lifelong Improvement

Yes, there is only one way to improve the work, and that is by improving the workman — only one way to insure a masterful production, and that is by inspiring the master. Edwin Markham, the great poet of our early century, expressed this truth beautifully when he said, "We are all blind until we see that in the human plan nothing is worth the making unless it makes the man. Why build these cities glorious, if man unbuilded goes? In vain we build the works unless the builder also grows."

And so doesn't it stand to reason that the only way a man can be sure of meeting the changing aspects of life today is to be willing to make sacrifices for this preparation? It is a sad commentary on our present society that many people are more concerned with what they *own* than with what they *are*. Don't you be one of them! Be willing to pay the price.

There is an old Chinese proverb that says; "Give a man a fish and he will eat for a day; teach him how to fish and you have satisfied his hunger for life."

Today Is Your Day!

And now for the third principle in our magic formula for success. Not only must we realize that preparation for life's tasks and opportunities is a continuing effort, not only must we be mindful that we can only build the future by building ourselves, but we must also accept the truth that unless we have the desire and the courage to start now, *today,* we have missed the boat. Opportunity has passed us by.

One of the unhappy circumstances of this life is that the world is full of well-meaning but misguided people who want to prepare for the future; in fact, they periodically vow emphatically that they want self-improvement enough to do something about it. Somehow they never get around to it. Unless we are willing to start this very moment, from this very room, we shall never do it.

There is no tomorrow; yesterday does not exist; today, this very moment, is the only theater in which we live. Now is our only existence; we only live in the present. I put this thought into a little poem. It made it easier for me to remember the importance of the present. Perhaps it will help you as well.

TODAY IS YOUR DAY

This is my day — I did not ask it,
But t'was given me — I'll surely grasp it.

Leap upon it with all my might,
Embrace it, love it, hold it tight.

Yesterday is but a cancelled check,
It'll not return at call or beck.

Tomorrow is just a promissory note.
On this I will not dream and gloat.

Today alone is legal tender,
To this I pledge my best to render.

Now is the only time we live,
To this I pledge my best to give.

How valuable is your time to you? Can you afford to wait to start this preparation? What are you doing to make time more valuable to you? Have you evaluated it in terms of the human equation?

Our time is too valuable to waste. Furthermore, we know there is no tomorrow. So unless we resolve with all the sincerity which we possess that we shall start this very moment to build for the future, I am afraid that tomorrow, next week, next year, ten years from now, honest as may be our intentions, we will still find ourselves in the wilderness of procrastination, still responding to the siren songs of complacency. Why can't we realize that there is no other way except by starting *now*?

The Supreme Challenge

How satisfied are we with our lives up to this point? If we could live that part over again, would we do it differently? Do you plan to continue in the same pattern? I believe that most people who claim to be self-made men, if they had the opportunity to do it over, would welcome outside help.

It is the duty of every person to search humbly, sincerely — yes, and even prayerfully — for his place in the divine pattern of things, the place where he can contribute and give his best. The world owes us nothing, but we owe ourselves and our family the duty to develop our God-given qualities to the ultimate. It is a great challenge, and not an easy one to meet. But it is up to us and to us alone to make our dreams come true, our plans come alive.

But some of us would rather settle into a rut called complacency than find our own rainbow. The temptation of procrastination can be a cancerous sore, infested with destruction of the future; a jailer of progress, the chains and shackles that hold us back from our dreams and ambitions.

But if you believe in yourself enough, and value the future enough to start a program of self-improvement now, I salute you. One of the characteristics of a successful man is that he is never too busy chopping wood to take time out to sharpen the axe. I hope you will realize that this self-improvement is not complete until you learn good communication.

Opportunity Is Everywhere

My friends, I urge you to enter the great, the challenging, and the exciting world of persuasive communication. Don't let life pass you by. It is a tragedy to see unfulfilled dreams, unrealized ambitions, doors of opportunity which have remained unopened so long that the hinges are actually rusty. The great sorrow of this life is no longer a man without an opportunity; it is opportunity begging to be embraced by man.

You Cannot Fail

Yes, if you are willing to start a continuous self-improvement program, if you realize that you can only improve future conditions by improving yourself, and most important of all, if you have the ambitions, the ability, and the courage to make an immediate decision to start now, I say that you already are a success although you may have to wait a short time for the fruits of success. I say that you are already wealthy, and some day you will have money to prove it. Fortified thus, you cannot, and I know you will not, fail.

What you can do you ought to do. What you ought to do, I am sure you can do. And what you can do and ought to do, by the grace of God, I know you will do.

Good luck, God bless you; I hope you decide to prepare for the future, because believe me, *you are worth the investment!*

The World Food Problem 1950–1980

For Jill, Susan, Catherine and Stephen, with much love

The World Food Problem 1950–1980

David Grigg

Basil Blackwell

First published 1985

Basil Blackwell Ltd
108 Cowley Road, Oxford OX4 1JF, UK

Basil Blackwell Inc.
432 Park Avenue South, Suite 1505,
New York, NY 10016, USA

British Library Cataloguing in Publication Data
Grigg, David, *1934–*
   The world food problem 1950–1980.
   1. Food supply–History–20th century
   I. Title
   338.1′9′0904   HD9000.5

   ISBN 0–631–13481–6

Library of Congress Cataloging in Publication Data
Grigg, David B.
   The world food problem, 1950–1980.

   Bibliography: p.
   Includes index.
   1. Food supply.   I. Title.
   HD9000.5.G74   1985   363.8   84–28376
   ISBN 0–631–13481–6

Typeset by System 4 Associates, Gerrards Cross, Buckinghamshire.
Printed in Great Britain by Page Bros (Norwich) Ltd.

Contents

Acknowledgements

My interest in the problems discussed in this book was first stimulated by Vic Dennison; it was encouraged by Benny Farmer in the 1950s and since, and by the late Charles Fisher in the 1960s. I hope this book may encourage and stimulate others, as their teaching and example did – and does – encourage me.

I am grateful to Mrs Claire Davidson, Miss Anita Fletcher and Mrs Penny Shamma for typing the manuscript of this book with their usual efficiency and – when allowed – great dispatch. I am similarly beholden to Mr Graham Dyson, Mr Paul Coles and Miss Sheila Ottewell for drawing the maps and graphs.

I am grateful for permission to reproduce and redraw illustrations from *Ceres*, the FAO review on agriculture and development (figures 2.5, 8.3 and 11.4); A. and E. Weber and the *European Review of Agricultural Economics* (figures 3.1 and 3.2); HMSO (figure 7.1); George Philip & Son Limited (figure 8.2): Methuen & Co. (figure 8.4); Armand Colin Éditeur (figure 9.1); Holt-Saunders Ltd (figure 10.1).

David Grigg

1

Introduction

For much of human history the majority of mankind has been under-nourished, and for much of human history this, it would seem, has been stoically accepted; there are few records left to tell us. But from the eighteenth century, writers began to argue that hunger could be overcome, sought explanations of its continued existence and proposed solutions to the problem. Hunger and malnutrition survived in Europe into the nineteenth century, but by the 1930s were greatly diminished. But, for the most part, when Europeans discussed this problem they confined their attention to their own continent and the people of European origin settled overseas. Thus when Sir William Crookes predicted in 1899 that the world's wheat supply would soon prove insufficient he was thinking mainly of the food supplies of Europeans, as was Yves Guyot in 1904 and G. B. Roorbach in 1917. Even the League of Nations, which in 1928 declared that two-thirds of the world's population was inadequately fed, in its subsequent three volume report concerned itself largely with Europe.[1]

Indeed it was not until the Second World War that Europeans and Americans began to concern themselves with the *world* food problem. In a meeting at Hot Springs in Colorado in 1943, a conference looked forward to a *world* free from hunger.[2]

Thus since the end of the Second World War there has been much discussion of the world food problem. Indeed it might sometimes seem

[1] Sir William Crookes, *The Wheat Problem*, London, 1917; Yves Guyot, 'The bread and meat of the world', *American Statistical Association*, **67–8**, 1904, pp. 79–119; G. P. Roorbach, 'The world's food supply', *Annals of the American Academy of Political and Social Science*, **74**, 1917, pp. 1–13; League of Nations, *The Problem of Nutrition*, three volumes, Geneva, 1936.
[2] G. C. L. Bertram, 'Population trends and the world's resources', *Geographical Journal*, **107**, 1946, pp. 191–210.

that a shortage of food and a prevalence of hunger had only existed since 1945. This is obviously not so. It is more that changes since 1945 have brought the problem to the world's attention far more forcibly than before, for a number of reasons.

The first was the foundation in 1945 of the United Nations and its subsidiary, the Food and Agriculture Organization (FAO). The latter was formed to try and improve agricultural output and solve the problem of hunger. Later international organizations such as the World Bank and voluntary associations like Oxfam have promoted knowledge about the world food problem and attempted practical solutions.

Second, more people have written and spoken about the problem than at any time in the past. The spread of literacy in the developing world, the growth of newspapers and the extension of radio and television have made most people in Europe and North America aware of the problem, and, of course, the remarkable increase in travel has allowed more Europeans to visit Africa, Asia and Latin America. All these changes have also made Africans, Asians and Latin Americans – or at least some of them – aware of their condition in comparison with the West, an awareness heightened by the struggle for and achievement of independence in the period since 1945.

Third, the problem of hunger – the world food problem – has received far more attention from the academic world. Since 1945 universities have multiplied in all parts of the world, and both traditional and new disciplines have turned their attention to the economic problems of the developing world and in particular to the problems of food supplies. In all subjects the proliferation of knowledge since 1945 has been remarkable, and not least in the study of the world food problem.

Fourth, the causes and solutions of the world food problem have been a matter of ideological controversy, and this alone would have been enough to attract attention. In both the popular view, and in the opinion of many academic writers, the world food problem since 1945 has been due to the population explosion in the developing countries, and if this is so then something should be done to restrain population growth. But attempts to introduce family planning methods into Africa, Asia and Latin America met much opposition in the 1950s and 1960s. Catholics and other religious groups were opposed to the use of contraceptives; they were joined, in a curious alliance, by socialists who believed that it was not population growth that caused hunger, but the imperfections of capitalist society. [3] In the 1970s this verbal conflict has subsided, to

[3] K. McQuillan, 'Common themes in Catholic and Marxist thought on population and development', *Population and Development Review*, 5, 1979, pp. 689–99.

be replaced by another. If hunger is a result of poverty – and it assuredly is – then the way to solve the world food problem is to transform the economies of the developing world, for it is there that the problem of lack of food is largely confined. How the (in 1950) largely agrarian and economically backward countries of Africa, Asia and Latin America were to be transformed has been a matter of endless dispute between those who advocate socialist central planning and those who believe in the virtues of the market economies of the West. Although this battle has been fought on paper between academics in Western countries, it has of course also taken place in practice in many of the newly independent countries of the developing world since 1945.

For these and other reasons the world food problem has become a familiar topic in the last 35 years, and of books and articles upon the subject there is no end. Best known are those which have prophesied doom. The idea that population growth will at some time in the future outrun food supplies, and universal starvation arrive, has been much publicized, from W. Vogt's *The Road to Survival*, published in 1949, through *Famine 1975*, by W. and P. Paddock, to the more scholarly but equally gloomy publications of the Club of Rome.[4] But of course, much else has been written. The hunger of much of the world has been seen as due to a bewildering variety of causes; excessive population growth remains the most popular, but there is no shortage of other explanations. These include the greed of Europeans and their addiction to meat, the evils of colonial and neocolonial exploitation, the incompetence of socialist collective agriculture, the backwardness of traditional farmers, the spread of deserts, and the heating up, as well as the cooling down, of the earth's atmosphere.

This book deals with what *has* happened: it does not predict, nor does it claim that there is one overriding cause of hunger. Instead an attempt is made to trace the changes in food production and food consumption which have taken place since the end of the Second World War, or more exactly, because the first statistics became available then, since 1950. The period discussed ends in 1980 because that is the most recent date for which most statistics are available.

The world food problem since 1950 is that a large proportion of the population of Africa, Asia and Latin America is either undernourished or malnourished or both. This is a chronic condition. Famines, (acute food shortages) that afflict local areas for relatively short periods are

---

[4] W. Vogt, *Road to Survival*, London, 1949; W. Paddock and P. Paddock, *Famine 1975*, London, 1967; D. H. Meadows and D. I. Meadows, *The Limits to Growth: A Report for the Club of Rome on the Predicament of Mankind*, London, 1972.

not discussed, although it is often outbreaks of famine that draw attention in the West to the problems of the developing countries. Although few deny that there are problems of hunger in the developing world, estimates of the numbers of people undernourished in the late 1970s varied from 62 million to 3000 million (see pp. 6–28). Obviously, the definition and measurement of hunger is far from easy, and this is discussed in chapter 2. The world food problem has not emerged in the post-war period simply as a result of rapid population growth in the developing countries. Indeed, as is shown in chapter 3, the proportion of the world's population with inadequate diets has probably diminished since 1950; prior to the end of the nineteenth century, malnutrition if not under-nutrition was as widespread in Europe as in many parts of the developing world today.

Hunger has been attributed to both population growth – the idea that numbers have grown more rapidly than food output – and to poverty. The changes in population and the extent of poverty are outlined in chapter 4, and in chapter 5 the relationship between food output and population growth is examined more closely.

Most of the rest of the book attempts to trace the growth of food output since 1950. The expansion of the world's arable land is considered in chapter 6, and then each of the major regions is discussed – the developed countries, Africa, Latin America and Asia. These chapters try to trace precisely how food output has been increased and to consider some of the difficulties that have been faced and, in some countries, overcome. The penultimate chapter deals with the trade in foodstuffs, for few developing countries are self-sufficient.

This book is not an essay in prophecy; nor does it offer any easy solution to the problems of hunger. It tries to show what has happened in the immediate past. Some lessons can be learnt from this and may be of help in facing the future.

2

The Extent of Hunger

There has been no shortage of attempts to estimate the numbers suffering from hunger. In 1950 Sir John Boyd Orr, the first Director of the Food and Agriculture Organization, claimed that 'a lifetime of malnutrition and actual hunger is the lot of at least two-thirds of mankind'; the same proportion had been suggested by a League of Nations committee in 1928.[1] In the 1970s there were several attempts to estimate the number undernourished or malnourished; these varied greatly (table 2.1) owing to the different bases for measurement. T. T. Poleman, for example, argued that undernutrition was confined to children under five years of age and to pregnant and lactating women; in contrast J. Katzmann classified countries on the basis of the available food supplies per caput. His estimate thus included the total population of all countries with a daily per caput supply of less than 2900 calories and 40 grams of animal protein. But before examining the ways of estimating the extent of hunger it is necessary to consider some aspects of human needs for food.

UNDERNUTRITION AND MALNUTRITION

Nutrition experts have conventionally distinguished between under-nutrition and malnutrition, although the two conditions are interrelated.

The human body needs energy for two purposes. A human being who is at rest and performs no activities at all still needs energy for the brain, heart, lungs and other organs to function. This is the *basal metabolic rate*. Energy for this and other functions is obtained from eating food

[1] Sir John Boyd Orr, 'The food problem', *Scientific American*, **183**, pp. 11–15; J. de Castro, *The Geography of Hunger*, London, 1952, p. 16.

Table 2.1   Estimates of the numbers undernourished in the 1970s

Numbers undernourished (millions)	Year	Notes	Source
62 to 309	1975	Number of children under five and pregnant women	Poleman, 1981
455[a]	1972–4	Number having available less than 1.2 basal metabolic rate	FAO, 1977
1000	1973	'suffering from overt hunger'	Borgstrom, 1973
1000	1970	'serious hunger or malnutrition'	Brown, 1975
1373	1975	—	Reutlinger and Selowsky, 1976
1200 to 1500[a]	1977	—	Ensminger and Bomani, 1980
1500	1970	—	Berg, 1973
3000	1975–7	—	Katzmann, 1980

[a] Developing market economies only.
Sources: A. Berg, *The Nutrition Factor: Its Role in National Development*, 1973, p. 5; G. Borgstrom, *The Food and People Dilemma*, North Scituate, Mass., 1973, p. 53; L. R. Brown with E. P. Eckholm, *By Bread Alone*, Oxford, 1975, p. 32; D. Ensminger and P. Bomani, *Conquest of World Hunger and Poverty*, Ames, Iowa, 1980, p. 35; FAO, *The Fourth World Food Survey*, Rome, 1977, p. 53; International Food Policy Research Institute, *Recent and Prospective Developments in Food Consumption: Some Policy Issues*, Research Report no. 2, Washington DC, 1977, p. 14; J. Katzmann, 'Besoins alimentaires et potentialités des pays en voie de développement', *Mondes Développées*, **29–30**, 1980, pp. 53–6; T. T. Poleman, *Quantifying the Nutrition Situation in Developing Countries*, Cornell Agricultural Economics Staff Paper no. 79–33, 1979; T. T. Poleman, 'A reappraisal of the extent of world hunger', *Food Policy*, **6**, *1981*, 236–52; S. Reutlinger and M. Selowsky, *Malnutrition and Poverty: Magnitude and Policy Options*, World Bank Staff Occasional Papers, no. 25, Johns Hopkins University Press, 1976

that is converted into energy in the body. Most foods have some energy value, measured in calories, but this varies greatly from food to food. Thus one ounce of cheese provides 120 calories, but one ounce of lettuce only 3 calories.[2] Estimates of the calorie intake needed to maintain the basal metabolic rate have been made, and averages for men and women of different weights and ages have been published. Thus the *average* daily intake necessary for a man weighing 56 kg is 1580 calories.[3] Unfortunately for those who wish to estimate the minimum

[2]   Ministry of Agriculture, *Manual of Nutrition*, HMSO, London, 1970, p. 13. The term 'calorie' is used in this book, as is conventional, although strictly speaking the units are kilocalories.

[3]   Food and Agriculture Organization/World Health Organization, *Energy and Protein Requirements; Report of a Joint FAO/WHO Ad Hoc Expert Committee*, WHO, Geneva, 1973, p. 107.

calorific requirements there is evidence of considerable individual variation in the metabolic rate and in addition there is some evidence that the metabolic rate of adults on a low calorie intake adjusts without any change in health or work ability.[4]

But human beings obviously need a calorific intake above the basal metabolic rate to go about their daily lives. Food is needed for work, but the amount needed varies according to the type of work done. Thus men of a given body weight involved in sedentary activities such as office work expend only 1.8 calories per minute, but a man labouring in the building industry expends 6 calories per minute and a man felling trees expends over 8 calories per minute. An FAO committee has estimated that adult males – of the same weight – require per day 2700 calories where only light activity is undertaken, 3000 calories for moderate activity, 3500 calories for a very active occupation and 4000 calories for exceptional activity.[5] But there are further problems in estimating the average daily calorific needs. The needs of the average woman are less than those of the average man, except during pregnancy and breast feeding; the daily needs of children and adolescents are less than those of adults, except during the spurt of growth before adolescence. With increasing age people work less hard and the metabolic rate declines, and so energy needs are less. Furthermore food is needed to heat the body, and so calorific needs are greater in cold than in hot climates. To complicate the picture still further there are studies that show that men with a very low calorific intake can carry out the same work as efficiently as men on much higher calorific intakes without any adverse effects on health.[6]

It is clearly difficult to prescribe the precise calorific intake that is necessary to avoid *undernutrition*. A man who is initially healthy and working satisfactorily can be said to become undernourished if subsequently either his body weight falls, or his capacity to work diminishes, or both occur together. A human being deprived of all food will starve to death; this occurs after about 40 days without food and when the original body weight has fallen by 40 per cent.[7]

[4] T. N. Srinivasan, 'Measuring malnutrition', *Ceres*, **16** (2), 1983, pp. 23–7; P. V. Sukhatme and S. Margen, 'Autoregulatory homeostatic nature of energy balance', *American Journal of Clinical Nutrition*, **35**, 1982, pp. 355–65; W. Edmundson, 'Individual variations in basal metabolic rate and mechanical work efficiency in East Java', *Ecology of Food and Nutrition*, **8**, 1979, pp. 189–95.
[5] FAO/WHO, *op. cit.*, p. 29.
[6] Sukhatme and Margen, *op. cit.*; Edmundson, *op. cit.*; Srinivasan, *op. cit.*
[7] Ministry of Agriculture, *op. cit.*, p. 18.

PROTEINS AND VITAMINS

Human beings can be chronically undernourished; their body weight and height will be less than those who are adequately fed, and their ability to work will also be less. But the diet may also be deficient not only in quantity but also in quality. This is described as *malnutrition*. The human body needs not only calories for energy purposes but also protein and vitamins; the absence or insufficiency of these nutrients gives rise to specific diseases.

The role of protein in human nutrition has been a matter of much controversy.[8] Protein is needed during growth, and is necessary to replace body tissue. Most plant and animal foods contain protein, but in differing amounts and of different biological values. Protein is made up of a number of amino acids; twelve of these are essential, that is they cannot be synthesized in the human body but have to be acquired from foods. Eggs and some other animal foods contain all the essential amino acids; no single plant food, in contrast, contains all the essential amino acids. It was once thought that plant foods contained too little protein to satisfy human needs and that only animal protein would provide the essential amino acids. However it is now believed that a purely vegetable diet, if eaten in sufficient quantity and variety, will provide the minimum amount of protein necessary for health; and that although no single plant food will provide all the essential amino acids, these can be provided by eating a mixture of vegetable foods.[9] Most traditional diets do contain the appropriate combination. There are however some exceptions. First, the tropical roots such as manioc and sago have a very low protein content and diets dependent upon these crops may well not provide sufficient protein.[10] Second, as the protein content of most food crops is only about 10 per cent, they have to be eaten in considerable bulk if the minimum protein requirements are to be met; this is no problem for adults, but it may be difficult for infants and young children. Third, animal foods are not only a source of protein but also the major source of some of the vitamins. Consequently some nutritionists believe that at least 5 per cent of the total protein intake should be of animal origin.[11]

[8] D. M. Hegsted, 'Protein calorie malnutrition', *American Scientist*, **66**, 1978, pp. 61–5.

[9] D. S. McLaren, 'The great protein fiasco', *The Lancet*, **ii**, 1974, pp. 93–6.

[10] P. R. Payne, 'Proteins in human nutrition; nutritional requirement and social needs', *Folia Veterinaria Latina*, **6**, 1976, pp. 23–33.

[11] P. V. Sukhatme, 'Human calorie and protein needs and how far they are satisfied today', in B. Benjamin, P. R. Cox and J. Peel (eds), *Resources and Population*, London,

These changed views on the role of protein in the diet have led to changes in policy on nutrition and medical diagnosis. In the 1960s many agencies such as FAO believed that the fundamental cause of malnutrition was the lack of animal protein, and developing countries were urged to increase their output of animal foods. Now FAO argues that if sufficient calories are provided, the diet will contain enough protein, and indeed enough vitamins. In the 1960s it was thought that protein deficiency diseases such as kwashiorkor were due to an inadequate amount of protein in the food eaten. Subsequent research has shown that in many cases children with kwashiorkor apparently had been receiving an adequate protein intake, but too few calories. Their bodies then used protein stored in muscles and elsewhere as a source of energy. Thus the characteristic symptoms of protein deficiency were due not to a low protein intake in the food supply, but to an inadequate energy intake. [12]

The importance of minor elements in the diet has been slowly discovered over the last 70 years, as it has been shown how the absence of vitamins can lead to specific deficiency diseases. An inadequate intake of vitamin A (or retinol) leads to poor sight and eventually may cause blindness. Vitamin D deficiencies cause poor bone formation; rickets, common in Britain and the United States in the 1930s, is one consequence. A lack of iodine causes goitre. Vitamin C deficiency is a cause of scurvy, which however is now rare. The lack of vitamin B_1 (or thiamine) gave rise to beriberi, a disease found in much of East and South East Asia – but not India – in the late nineteenth and early twentieth centuries. Most of the B_1 in rice was contained in the husk, which was removed in milling after the introduction of steel rolling mills in the 1870s. It is a disease now rarely found. Pellagra is more widespread, but on the decline. It is due to a shortage of niacin, one of the vitamin B group, and was found in people living mainly upon maize; once this was realized the incidence of the disease declined, and it is now only common in Africa. [13]

Although vitamin deficiency diseases – together with others such as that caused by lack of iron – are still widespread they have nearly

---

1973, pp. 25–43; F. Aylward and M. Jul, *Protein and Nutrition Policy in Low Income Countries*, London, 1975, p. 32; 'The food situation and the child: an overview', *Food and Nutrition*, 5, 1979, pp. 4–8.

[12] McLaren, *op. cit.*; J. C. Waterlow and P. R. Payne, 'The protein gap', *Nature*, 258, 1975, pp. 113–17.

[13] R. Passmore, B. Nicol and M. Rao, *Handbook on Human Nutritional Requirements*, World Health Organization, Geneva, 1974.

everywhere declined over the last half century. [14] The principal reasons for this are that the amounts of vitamin needed to eliminate the diseases are very small in physical quantities and that they can all be synthesized in the laboratory. In contrast the provision of energy and protein still requires considerable quantities of foodstuffs.

MALNUTRITION AND INFECTIOUS DISEASE

Although it might seem self-evident that a malnourished person should be more susceptible to infectious disease, in the immediate post-war period this was not thought to be so. Studies of the Dutch population in the famine of 1944 showed that there was no increase in the prevalence of infectious disease, and similar conclusions were drawn from other work on starvation and disease. [15] However, views on the relationship between infectious disease and malnutrition have changed. [16] It is now believed that malnutrition damages the body's immune systems, and that malnourished people are more likely to catch certain infectious diseases and are less likely to survive them than a well fed person. Furthermore the prevalence of infectious disease is thought to increase malnutrition. Malnutrition is found in areas of poverty, which are also areas of poor hygiene and sanitation. In such areas diseases of the stomach and intestines are common: infants and young children are particularly susceptible to these diseases. Such diseases cause loss of appetite and vomiting and impair the ability of the gut to absorb nutrients. Thus children who are offered sufficient food, or indeed eat it, none the less may suffer from malnutrition because of their poor health. Thus it is now agreed that the improvement of public and private sanitation and hygiene would reduce the prevalence of malnutrition among children,

[14] J. M. Bengoa, 'Prevention of protein-calorie malnutrition', in R. E. Olsen (ed.), *Protein-Calorie Malnutrition*, Academic Press, London, 1975; J. Mayer, 'The dimensions of human hunger', *Scientific American*, 235, 1976, pp. 40–9; J. Yudkin, 'Some basic principles of nutrition', in D. S. Miller and D. J. Oddy (eds), *The Making of the Modern British Diet*, London, 1976, pp. 196–203.
[15] M. C. Latham, 'Nutrition and infection in national development', *Science*, 188, 1975, pp. 561–5.
[16] R. Martorell, 'Interrelationships between diet, infectious disease and nutritional status', in L. S. Greene and F. E. Johnston (eds), *Social and Biological Predictors of Nutritional Status, Physical Growth, and Neurological Development*, London, 1980, pp. 81–106; N. S. Scrimshaw, 'Interactions of malnutrition and infection: advances in understanding', in Olsen, *op. cit.*, pp. 353–67.

and that malnutrition is by no means always simply a consequence of inadequate food supplies.[17]

ESTIMATING THE NUMBERS MALNOURISHED AND UNDERNOURISHED

There are three ways in which the numbers suffering from hunger can be estimated: through the symptoms of deficiency diseases; through the amount of food consumed; and through the amount of food available.

The symptoms of malnutrition and undernutrition

Undernutrition and malnutrition give rise to diseases which can be recognized by the clinical diagnosis of symptoms; by the measurement of body weight, height and other indicators and their comparison with healthy growth; and by changes in the chemical composition of the body. The only accurate way to measure the extent of hunger is by counting the numbers with such symptoms. This is unfortunately difficult for several reasons.

First, much of the population of the developing world lacks medical care and nutritional experts or teams capable of undertaking such inquiries. Although there are numerous published accounts of the diagnosis and treatment of nutritional diseases, or measurements of changes in weight and height, they cover a very small proportion of the world's population. Furthermore many such surveys have been undertaken during periods of food crisis, and their results may not be representative of the population under normal conditions.

Second, most of the diseases due to poor nutrition may occur in both extreme and mild forms. Protein calorie malnutrition, which afflicts principally young children, may occur as kwashiorkor, which can lead to death if not treated, or it may mean that a child is slightly less in height and body weight than well fed children of his age. The magnitude of the problem depends upon the diagnostic criteria adopted. Thus a survey of the health of children in a number of countries in Central America found that between 0.1 and 0.9 per cent were suffering from severe forms of protein energy malnutrition, but between 50 and 73 per cent had reduced weight for their age. Similarly, in India it was

[17] Hegsted, *op. cit.*, pp. 61–5; R. W. Wenlock, 'Endemic malaria, malnutrition and child deaths', *Food Policy*, **6** (2), 1981, pp. 105–12; L. J. Mata, R. A. Kranial, J. T. Urrutia and B. Garcia, 'Effect of infection on food intake and the nutritional state: perspectives as viewed from the village', *American Journal of Clinical Nutrition*, **30**, 1977, pp. 1215–27.

estimated 1.2 per cent of children had kwashiorkor, but 80 per cent showed signs of reduced growth due to an inadequate diet. [18]

Thus information upon the prevalence of deficiency diseases is sporadic and it is not possible to estimate the numbers suffering from hunger in this way. Such information that is available is summarized here.

Of the vitamin deficiency diseases, scurvy, due to a shortage of vitamin C and once common in parts of Europe, is now rare in either the developed or the developing world. Rickets, still widespread in Western Europe and the United States in the 1930s, has greatly declined, although it is still found in parts of the tropics. [19] Pellagra has also declined, but is still found. Pellagra is due to a lack of niacin, one of the vitamin B group, and was found in those who obtained a high proportion of their diet from maize. However, pellagra has never been common in Central and South America, where maize was domesticated and is widely grown. Here it was invariably eaten with beans, and the corns were treated with alkali before grinding. Pellagra was first reported in southern and eastern Europe after the introduction of maize and its widespread adoption as a food crop in the eighteenth century. It is still found in Romania, but elsewhere in Europe is unknown. The major incidence of the disease is now in Africa, where it has also been found among those dependent upon sorghum. [20] Beriberi has greatly diminished since its cause was discovered (see p. 9). Two diseases have not declined. In 1958 it was estimated that there were 200 million cases of endemic goitre in the world, due to lack of iodine. Xeropthalmia, due to an inadequate amount of vitamin A, was said to be causing 10,000 children a year to go blind in the Far East. [21]

Of greater significance than the preceding diseases are the illnesses and deaths that arise among children who are lacking in calorie or protein supply. Children who are breast fed do not suffer from malnutrition, but once they are weaned they are very much at risk. First of all,

---

[18] G. H. Beaton and J. M. Bengoa, 'Nutrition and health in perspective: an intro-duction', in G. H. Beaton and J. M. Bengoa, *Nutrition in Preventive Medicine: The Major Deficiency Syndromes, Epidemiology and Approaches to Control*, World Health Organization, Geneva, 1971, p. 45; C. Gopalan, 'Protein versus calories in the treat-ment of protein calorie malnutrition: metabolic and population studies in India', in Olsen, *op. cit.*, pp. 329–41.

[19] J. M. Bengoa, 'The state of world nutrition', in M. Rechcigl, Jr., *Man, Food and Nutrition*, Cleveland, Ohio, 1973, pp. 1–13; Mayer, *op. cit.*

[20] Bengoa, *op. cit.*, 1973; Passmore *et al.*, *op. cit.*; J. D. Haas and G. G. Harrison, 'Nutritional anthropology and biological adaptation', *Annual Review of Anthropology*, **6**, 1977, pp. 69–101.

[21] Food and Agriculture Organization, *The Fourth World Food Survey*, Rome, 1977, p. 110.

infants in impoverished areas are highly susceptible to disease. In a study of children in a Mexican village it was found that on average each child had 35 illnesses in the first two years of life, and was ill for one-third of the time; this would reduce the efficiency of food intake considerably. [22] Second, although the absolute amounts of calories and protein needed by young children are less than those of adults, the needs per unit of body weight are high. Studies of food consumption within households are rare, but suggest that women and children get not only less than adult males but also less than their needs. Poorly fed children are often permanently affected by inadequate food. Their height and body weight is retarded, and as adults they are shorter and lighter than the well fed; some have suggested that malnutrition in childhood permanently retards mental development. [23]

The acute forms of disease resulting from hunger are nutritional marasmus and kwashiorkor. In the former, muscles waste, there is a loss of subcutaneous fat, the buttocks diminish, the skin is loose, and there are eye lesions and skin rashes. The child is weak, apathetic and tires very easily. [24] This is due to a lack of calories. In contrast, protein deficiency causes kwashiorkor, where hair reddens and straightens, the body is typically swollen, the face is moonlike in shape, and skin rashes and ulcers occur. [25] Many children exhibit symptoms of both diseases, and it is now usual to refer to *protein calorie malnutrition*. As noted earlier, this can vary from the acute stage of kwashiorkor or marasmus to mild retardation of growth. J. M. Bengoa has reviewed the results of surveys of protein calorie malnutrition in 46 countries between 1963 and 1972 (table 2.2) and has also estimated the absolute numbers of children under five years of age suffering from malnutrition (table 2.3), apparently by assuming that the *median* figure for each continent in table 2.2 can be used as a *mean* to calculate the percentage of the numbers under five in 1970. As the population of less developed countries – excluding China – increased by 28 per cent between 1970 and 1980, and the percentage of the population under five also increased, a similar incidence of malnutrition in 1980 would yield about 130 million children under five suffering from malnutrition.

[22] M. Murioz de Chavez, 'Malnutrition: socioeconomic effects and policies in developing countries', in P. B. Pearson and J. R. Greenwell, *Nutrition, Food and Man*, Tucson, Arizona, 1980, pp. 38–45.

[23] E. M. Demaeyer, 'Clinical manifestations of malnutrition', in D. N. Walcher, N. Kretchmer and H. L. Barnett, *Food, Man and Society*, New York, 1976.

[24] K. M. Cahill, 'The clinical face of famine in Somalia', in K. M. Cahill (ed.) *Famine*, New York, 1982.

[25] Cahill, *op. cit.*; Demaeyer, *op. cit.*

Table 2.2   Range and median of percentage prevalence of protein calorie malnutrition in community surveys, 1963–72

Area	Number of of surveys[a]	Number of children examined	Severe forms		Moderate forms	
			Range (%)	Median (%)	Range (%)	Median (%)
Latin America	11	108,715	0.5–6.3	1.6	3.5–32.0	18.9
Africa	7	24,759	1.7–9.8	4.4	5.4–44.9	26.5
Asia[b]	7	39,494	1.1–20.0	3.2	16.0–46.4	31.2
Total	25	172,948	0.5–20.0	2.6	3.5–46.4	18.9

[a] Surveys were all of at least 1000 children, mainly under five years old.
[b] Excluding China and Japan.
Source: J. M. Bengoa, 'The state of world nutrition', in M. Rechcigl, Jr. (ed.), *Man, Food and Nutrition*, Cleveland, 1973, p. 6

Table 2.3   Estimates of total numbers of children under five years of age suffering from severe or moderate protein calorie malnutrition, *c*. 1970

	Severe (thousands)	Moderate (thousands)	Total (thousands)
Latin America	700	9,000	9,700
Africa	2,700	16,000	18,700
Asia[a]	6,600	64,000	70,600
Total	10,000	89,000	99,000

[a] Excluding China and Japan.
Source: J. M. Bengoa, 'The state of world nutrition', in M. Rechcigl, Jr. (ed.), *Man, Food and Nutrition*, Cleveland, 1973, p. 7

Bengoa has also made an estimate of the number of children under 14 years of age suffering from protein calorie malnutrition. In 1966, 269 million of the 667 – 40 per cent of children under 14 – were suffering from undernourishment. There are no comparable figures for more recent years, but in 1978–80 approximately 1200 million of the population of the developing world were under 15. If the incidence of protein malnutrition was the same as in 1966 then 480 million would have been affected by this disease.[26]

The consequences of malnutrition among preschool children are stunting in growth, low body weight and listlessness, which is reflected in adulthood in a reduced capacity to work. But malnutrition may also be directly or indirectly responsible for the deaths of children under

[26] J. M. Bengoa, 'Recent trends in the public health aspects of protein calorie malnutrition', *WHO Chronicle*, **24**, 1970, pp. 552–61.

five. The fact that a high proportion of children under five in areas of malnutrition are also victims of numerous respiratory and intestinal infections makes the cause of death difficult to determine. However, an analysis of some 11,000 deaths of children under five in Latin America in the 1960s found that malnutrition was the underlying cause of death of 7 per cent and an associated cause for 46.2 per cent. [27]

Household surveys and income distribution studies

The only accurate way to measure hunger is to count the numbers with symptoms of nutritional deficiency diseases and, as has been seen, this is difficult. Another, but indirect approach, is to measure the amount of food consumed by individuals, by households or by groups, and to compare this with some estimate of the minimum requirements needed to avoid malnutrition and undernutrition. Both these approaches have limitations.

Studies of food intake necessarily deal only with comparatively small groups. The most accurate way to estimate the nutrients received is to measure the food before it is digested and convert this to nutrients received. Most such surveys are based upon answers to questions about the food consumed by households in the preceding day or in the preceding week. Such surveys are difficult to organize, rarely cover the whole of a year and may not be representative of the total population of a country. An alternative approach is not to measure calorific intake but to record the amount of money spent on food, to determine the cost of a minimum diet, and then to estimate the numbers who cannot afford the minimum diet. [28]

Both these methods require the measured intake to be compared with a norm, a safety level, or the minimum requirements. Over these there has been much controversy. Various FAO and World Health Organization committees have published recommended levels in terms of calories and protein. They have begun by recommending the minimum needs for an adult male aged 20–39 with a given body weight and a given level of activity. Tables are also prepared to show the reductions or increases necessary for age, sex, body weight and different levels of activity. The FAO recommendations, the most recent of which were published in 1973 and are currently being revised, have been much criticized, principally on the grounds that the average requirements will conceal a great range in individual needs. [29] P. V. Sukhatme has pointed

[27] Bengoa, *op. cit.*, 1975.
[28] D. S. Miller, 'Nutrition surveys', in Miller and Oddy, *op. cit.*, pp. 202–13.
[29] FAO/WHO, *op. cit.*

out that the FAO average for an adult male in India is 2550 calories, but individual minimum needs may range from 1750 to 3350 calories. It seems generally agreed that the FAO figures overstate minimum needs, and thus any estimates based on these data will overestimate the extent of hunger. Certainly some household surveys demonstrate that some groups live healthy, hard working lives on calorie intakes much lower than FAO requirements. Thus tribes in New Guinea led healthy lives on 1700 calories per day, and in Central Java apparently healthy villagers only received 1392 calories per day. On the other hand labourers in Panama, to whom food was made freely available, ate an average of 3355 calories per day without any sign of gaining weight.[30]

However, quite apart from the methodological problems of interpreting such surveys, they are not sufficiently representative of national populations to allow any national or world estimates of hunger to be made. Much the same may be said of income surveys: however, surveys of income and food consumption in various countries do reveal facts of major importance about the consumption of food. Sample surveys of households in India in 1973–4, in rural Kenya in 1975, in southern Nigeria in 1970, and in Brazil in 1970 (figure 2.1) show that there is a great range in average consumption per caput, and that this consumption is closely related to income. Such data support the assumption that poverty is the main cause of hunger, although it should be remembered that in many developing countries much of the food for farm families is produced on the farm and income levels may be irrelevant. Such surveys also indicate a way of measuring the number of people who have less than the minimum requirements.

Thus in India 58 per cent of the sample population had less than the national mean of 2217 calories, and 79 per cent had less than the FAO adult male's minimum requirement for India (table 2.4).

A further problem in interpreting household consumption surveys is that calorie intake is normally measured as per caput for the household. Yet there is evidence that there is maldistribution within most households, with men getting more than women; children – except in early adolescence – used fewer calories than adults. But a study of peasant households in Nigeria showed that although adults were getting more than FAO requirements, children were getting considerably less than the estimated needs of their age group.[31]

[30] Edmundson, *op. cit.*; Sukhatme and Margen, *op. cit.*; N. S. Scrimshaw and L. Taylor, 'Food', *Scientific American*, **243**, 1980, pp. 74–84.
[31] B. M. Nicol, 'Causes of famine in the past and in the future', in G. Blix, Y. Hofvander and B. Vahlquist, *Famine: A Symposium*, Uppsala, Swedish Nutrition Foundation, 1971.

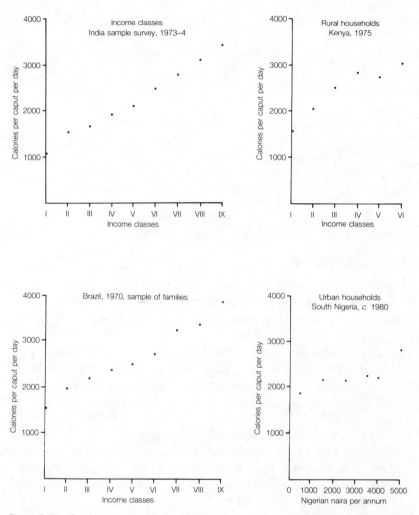

Figure 2.1   Food consumption by income class, India, Kenya, Brazil and southern Nigeria

Sources: J. Uyganga, 'Food habits and nutritional status in southern Nigeria', *Journal of Tropical Geography*, **49**, 1979, pp. 86–91; E. R. A. Alves, A. R. Teixeora Filho and H. Tollini, 'Brazil', in D. Ensminger (ed.), *Food Enough or Starvation for Millions*, New Delhi, 1977; K. Parikh and F. Rabar (eds), *Food for All in a Sustainable World: The IIASA Food and Agriculture Program*, Laxenburg, Austria, 1981

Table 2.4   Sample survey, India, 1973–4

Income class	% of total population	Daily calorie consumption per caput	Daily calorie deficiency per person
I	5	1102	1108
II	5	1528	682
III	10	1647	563
IV	18	1904	306
V	20	2115	—
VI	21	2495	—
VII	11	2805	—
VIII	7	3140	—
IX	3	3440	—
Mean	100	2217	—

Source: K. Parikh and F. Rabar (eds), *Food for All in a Sustainable World: the IIASA Food and Agriculture Program*, International Institute for Applied Systems Analysis, Laxenburg, Austria, 1981

Food availability data

A third way in which the extent of hunger can be measured is to estimate the amount of food available in a country in a given year, and to express this in terms of calories per caput per day. FAO has published the results of such food balance sheets annually for all countries since 1960, for a selection of countries in the 1930s, and for the period 1948–52. Most estimates of the extent of world hunger are based upon these figures. [32]

A figure for an individual country is arrived at in the following way. The total food output in a year is estimated and converted into calories. There is deducted from this all exports of food crops, crops fed to livestock, the food used for industrial purposes, and seed for the following year's crop. Added on to this figure is the calorific value of food imports and any food in stocks from previous years. It is assumed that there is a loss due to pests and diseases between field and retail outlet, and so the total output is reduced by 10 per cent.

These estimates have been much criticized. [33] Few developing countries

[32] FAO, *Production Yearbooks*, since 1961; FAO, *World Food Survey*, Washington DC, 1946; FAO, *The Second World Food Survey*, Rome, 1952; FAO, *op. cit.*, 1977.
[33] M. K. Bennett, 'Longer and shorter views of the Malthusian prospect', *Food Research Institute Studies*, 4, 1963, pp. 3–12; W. H. Calloway, 'World calorie/protein needs', in Pearson and Greenwell, *op. cit.*, pp. 82–7; C. Clark and J. Boyd Turner, 'World population growth and future food trends', in Rechcigl, *op. cit.*, pp. 55–77; R. W. Hay, 'The statistics of hunger', *Food Policy*, 3, 1978, pp. 243–55; T. T. Poleman, *Quantifying the Nutrition Situation in Developing Countries*, Cornell Agricultural Economics Staff Paper no. 79–33, 1979; T. T. Poleman, 'World food: myth and reality', in R. Sinha (ed.), *The World Food Problem: Consensus and Conflict*, Oxford, 1978, pp. 383–94.

have annual agricultural censuses, and so for many of these countries annual food output is estimated by FAO statisticians. Even where censuses are carried out farmers are notoriously reluctant to report their output accurately for fear of taxation, and yields tend to be underestimated. Output of meat is difficult to measure unless there are figures from slaughterhouses. The estimates exclude alcoholic drinks, game, human milk, and the gathering of fruits and berries, and do not allow for any loss in preparation in the kitchen or in waste. Thus even as an estimate of total calories available per caput per day these figures have their defects. In 1978–80 the figures ranged from 3766 calories in Ireland to only 1729 calories in Ethiopia. The average daily supply in the developed countries in 1975–7 was 3373 calories, in the developing only 2282 calories.

That there is a difference in food availability between the developed and the developing countries is not in question. However, the contrast is not quite as simple as averages for the two blocs would suggest. Although only Japan of the developed countries has a figure of less than 3000 calories per caput per day (figure 2.2), there are several countries in the developing world with available food supplies little short of the developed countries, particularly in the Middle East and South America. There is indeed a continuum between those with high and those with low supplies, as can be seen when countries are arranged in order (figure 2.3).

The available food supply data has been used by many writers on the assumption that it is identical to consumption. This is not so, for it includes stocks, which are available but not necessarily consumed. In some developed countries annual records of food consumption are kept. The United Kingdom annual food survey illustrates some of the problems of interpreting food availability data. Each year the United Kingdom government collects data on quantities of food purchased for consumption in a sample of households. It can be seen (table 2.5) that average per caput consumption by households reached a peak in 1954–6 and has since declined to only 2240 calories per caput per day, whereas the FAO available food supply estimate in 1978–80 was 3525 calories; this discrepancy is partly explained by the fact that household consumption excludes sweets, soft drinks and alcohol, which in 1979 would have provided 334 calories per day, and also meals eaten outside the household, which increased in the 1970s. On the other hand, no estimate is allowed in the household consumption figure for waste in the home. The annual report on consumption does however also include an estimate of the amount of food moving into consumption, which includes foodstuffs going to retailers, institutions, restaurants and manufacturers

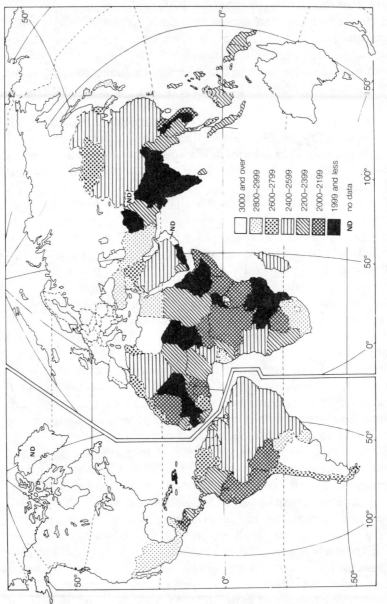

3000 and over

2800–2999

2600–2799

2400–2599

2200–2399

2000–2199

1999 and less

ND no data

Figure 2.2   Total food supply, available calories per caput per day, average 1978–80.

Source: FAO, *Production Yearbook 1981*, vol. 35, Rome, 1982

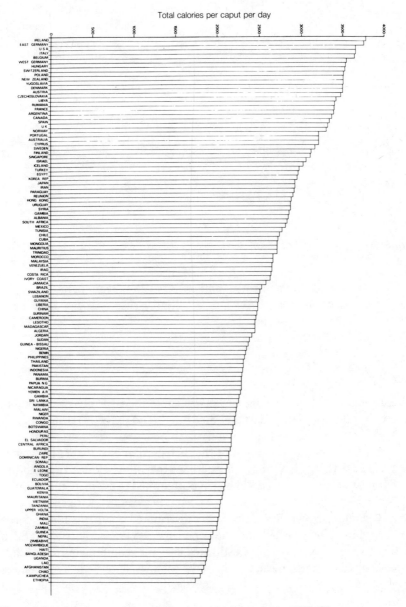

Total calories per caput per day

Figure 2.3   Calories per caput per day by countries, average 1978–80
Source: FAO, *Production Yearbook 1981*, vol. 35, Rome, 1982

Table 2.5   Estimates of consumption and available food supplies, UK, 1948–80

	Foodstuffs moving into consumption	FAO available food supplies	Household consumption survey
1948–50	—	3130	2474[b]
1951–3	—	3110	2479
1954–6	3130[a]	3220	2660
1957–9	3153	3230	2623
1960–2	3170	3270	2633
1963–5	3156	3260	2613
1966–8	3096	3180	2570
1970–1	3072	3170	2525
1972–4	3020	3376	2383
1975–7	2923	3305	2276
1978–80	2906	3525	2246

[a] 1956 only.
[b] 1950 only.
Sources: *Domestic Food Consumption and Expenditure, Annual Reports, 1950 to 1980*, HMSO; FAO, *Production Yearbooks 1966 to 1981*, Rome

of soft and alcoholic drinks and sweets. But even here there are discrepancies with the FAO figures. Similar discrepancies have been noted for other countries.[34]

NATIONAL NEEDS

Although the very low figures of available food supply per caput in much of Africa, South East and South Asia and parts of Latin America suggest that food *consumption* must also be low in these areas, as they stand they give no indication of the distribution of hunger. However, FAO statisticians have made calculations that allow the food availability figures to be further used. They have attempted to estimate the number of calories needed to provide every person in a country with an adequate diet, assuming that the calories were distributed according to the needs of each individual, which depends upon age, sex and activity level. Such a calculation begins with the estimated calorific requirements of an adult male of the assumed mean weight of the country concerned.[35] Allowances are then made for the lower intakes needed by children, women, and

[34]   C. Geissler and D. Miller, 'Nutrition and GNP: a comparison of problems in Thailand and the Philippines', *Food Policy*, 7, 1982, pp. 191–206; J. Katzmann, 'Besoins alimentaires et potentialités des pays en voie de développement', *Mondes Développeés*, **29–30**, 1980, pp. 53–6.
[35]   FAO/WHO, *op cit.*, p. 78.

older people, a correction that can be made if there are demographic data on the sex ratio and age structure of each country. The activity level is assumed to be moderate. These estimates were published for every country, developed and developing, in the *Fourth World Food Survey*[36] and ranged from 2000 calories per day for Afghanistan to 2710 calories per day in Finland. The range for developing countries was between 2000 and 2501 calories. Their national requirements were lower than those of the developed countries, which ranged from 2410 to 2710 calories, because of lower body weights and the higher proportion of children in the population. In 1970 26.7 per cent of the population of the developed regions were less than 15 years old, compared with 40.5 per cent of the population in the developing region.[37]

Food availability can then be expressed as a percentage of minimum requirements (figure 2.4). This shows that if food supplies were distributed according to individual needs there would be no undernutrition anywhere in North America, Europe, the USSR, Australasia or Japan. This is much as expected. But there are also many developing countries where available supplies exceeded needs in 1978–80, however slightly – China, Korea, Indonesia, Malaysia, Thailand, Pakistan, Sri Lanka, most of North Africa and the Middle East, Mexico, Venezuela, Brazil, and temperate South America.

On the other hand there are areas where even if food was evenly distributed – and the figure, it should be recalled, includes food imports – the minimum needs would not be met. This includes the Andean republics of South America, parts of Central America, most of Africa south of the Sahara, much of the Indian subcontinent, Vietnam, Kampuchea and Laos.

INCOME DISTRIBUTION AND CONSUMPTION

But there are undoubtedly problems of malnutrition in many of the developing countries that have supplies which are above requirements. The reason for this is, of course, that food supplies are not allocated according to individual need, and it is unlikely that there is any country where this is so. In the 1970s Western visitors to China – and of course the Chinese government itself – stated that malnutrition had been eliminated by rationing. More recently there have been admissions by

[36] FAO, *op. cit.*, 1977, pp. 77–80.
[37] United Nations, *Concise Report on the World Population Situation in 1970–75 and its Long Range Implications*, New York, 1974, p. 25.

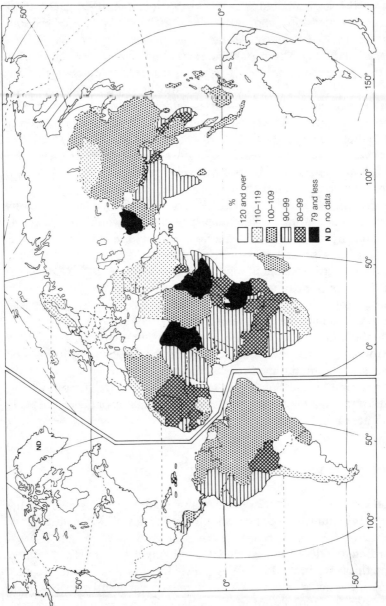

Figure 2.4   Available food supplies per caput per day as a percentage of national minimum requirements, 1978–80
Sources: FAO, *Production Yearbook 1981,* vol. 35, Rome, 1982; *The Fourth World Food Survey,* Rome, 1977

Chinese officials that at least 10 per cent of the Chinese population had inadequate diets; furthermore, rations of rice in the towns are thought to be 25–30 per cent above those in rural areas, so that equality of food intake has not been achieved.[38]

The main reason for the great differences in calorific intakes between different groups in the developing countries is income, as it is indeed in the developed countries. The difference is that in the developed countries the lowest income groups have, generally, sufficient money to buy an adequate diet. In the United Kingdom there are only minor differences in calorie and animal protein consumption between income groups. In the developing countries this is not so, as can be seen from figure 2.1 and table 2.4. In India 5 per cent of the sample population had an average daily consumption of only 1102 calories and 20 per cent less than 1700 calories, neither of which could have produced an adequate diet.

ESTIMATES OF THE NUMBERS UNDERNOURISHED

Unfortunately such income distribution figures are not available for many developing countries, and so estimates of those having inadequate diets cannot be made in this way for the world. However, in the *Fourth World Food Survey* an attempt was made to estimate both the absolute numbers undernourished and the percentage of the population of developing countries that were undernourished. It was assumed that individual daily consumption in any country would range from about 600–1000 calories to 4500 calories. The average daily consumption was taken to be the available food supply per caput in 1972–4. A beta type distribution of the Pearson group was then fitted to the range, standard deviation and mean of each country. This allowed the proportion of the population having a given consumption of calories per day to be estimated. The next step was to establish the minimum requirements. It was decided to set these at the number of calories needed for maintenance without activity, which was, because of the loss of energy in heating the body, the calorie requirement not for the basal metabolic rate (BMR), but for 1.5 BMR. However, because of variations in individual BMR which are neglected in averages, the minimum requirements were set at 1.2 BMR. This ranged for developing countries from 1487 calories to 1631 calories. It was then possible to estimate from the beta type distributions the proportion of the population having less than this minimum and, by FAO's definition, undernourished.

[38] L. M. Li, 'Feeding China's one billion: perspectives from history', in Cahill, *op. cit.*

As the minimum requirement allowed no energy intake for activity during the waking day, this minimum must surely have been set too low. As J. C. Waterlow has observed, if people are existing at this level – and clearly not totally inactive all day – then they must have made a remarkable metabolic adaptation to such low calorific intakes. [39] On the other hand, because the criteria are consistent for each country, such a calculation, if not accurately indicating the extent of undernutrition, should indicate where the problem is most acute. S. Mazumdar[40] has shown that there is a linear relationship between the proportions undernourished in a country, as calculated by FAO, and food availability as a percentage of requirements (figure 2.5). It is thus possible to apply the technique which FAO used with food supply data for 1972–4 to more recent information. This suggests that in 1978–80 the proportion of the population undernourished ranged from over 40 per cent in Bolivia, Afghanistan and several African states, to less than 10 per cent in much of the Middle East and North Africa (figure 2.6).

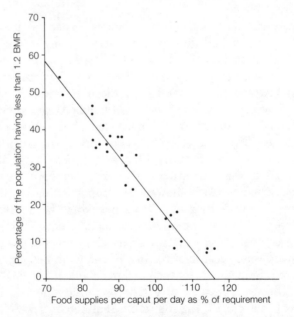

Figure 2.5   Relationship between food availability as a percentage of requirements and the percentage of the population undernourished in Africa

Source: S. Mazumdar, 'Realistic food goals for Africa', *Ceres*, **13**, 1980, pp. 36–41

[39] J. C. Waterlow, 'Childhood malnutrition – the global problem', *Proceedings of the Nutrition Society*, **38**, 1979, pp. 1–9.
[40] S. Mazumdar, 'Realistic food goals for Africa', *Ceres*, **13**, 1980, pp. 36–40.

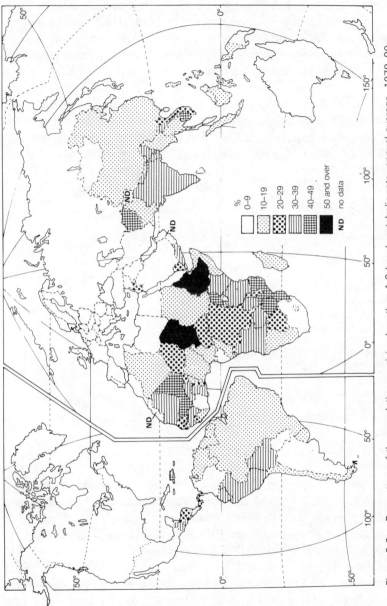

Figure 2.6 Percentage of the population receiving less than 1.2 basal metabolic rate, annual average, 1978–80

Sources: FAO, *Production Yearbook 1981*, vol. 35, Rome, 1982; *The Fourth World Food Survey*, Rome, 1977

The most severely affected regions were the Andean republics of South America, much of sub-Saharan Africa, and the Indian subcontinent. FAO did not include the Asian centrally planned economies in their calculations. But as the calculation estimated 10 per cent of the Chinese population to be undernourished in 1978–80, and this is compatible with recent Chinese estimates, there seems no reason to exclude them.

Thus in 1978–80 535 million received less than 1.2 BMR – nearly 12 per cent of the world's population, and 17 per cent of the population of the developing world. The proportion undernourished was greatest in Africa and least in Latin America, but the bulk of the numbers were to be found in South, South East and East Asia (table 2.6 and figure 2.7).

Table 2.6   Proportion and numbers of the population receiving less than 1.2 basal metabolic rate, 1980

	Millions	% of population
Africa	72	19.6
Latin America	41	11.3
Near East	19	8.9
Far East, excluding China	303	23.1
All developing, excluding China	436	19.3
China	99	10.0
All developing	535	17.0

Source: FAO, The State of Food and Agriculture 1981, Rome, 1982

WORLD BANK ESTIMATES OF HUNGER

Estimates of the extent of hunger made by S. Reutlinger and M. Selowsky have been widely quoted in recent years. Like the FAO estimates produced in the Fourth World Food Survey, they have attempted to allow for differences in consumption between classes. They began with FAO data on food availability per caput at the country level, but excluding the Asian centrally planned economies, for 1965. They assumed that FAO estimates of national requirements per caput were the minimum level needed to avoid undernutrition; this level is of course much higher than the 1.2 BMR level used in the Fourth World Food Survey. They then calculated the average income per caput for eight income classes in each country, and from this estimated the average calorie consumption per caput for each income group. As the population

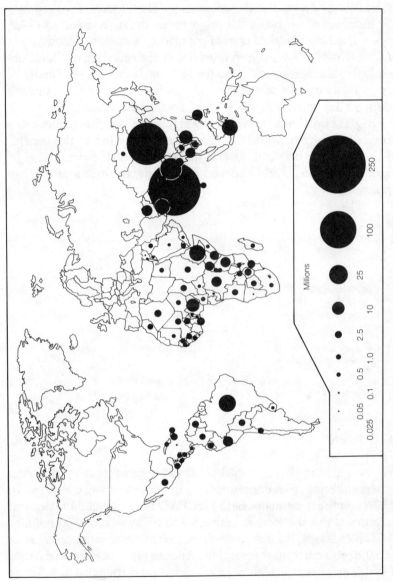

Figure 2.7 Numbers receiving less than 1.2 basal metabolic rate, 1978–80
Sources: FAO, *Production Yearbook 1981*, vol. 35, Rome, 1982; *The Fourth World Food Survey*, Rome, 1977

of each income group was known, it was possible to estimate the total number falling below national requirements. They then made an estimate of the numbers which would fall below minimum requirements in 1975 using assumed but plausible rates of population, income and food output growth (table 2.7). These figures, even with the exclusion of China, are much higher than those estimated for 1978–80 using the FAO method. They certainly overestimate the numbers, for the calculations include all those in any income group with an average food availability below the FAO national requirements. Clearly some will have above the average. Attempts to allow for this in later work led to the conclusion that in 1975 between 40 and 60 per cent of the population of the underdeveloped world suffered from undernutrition, rather than 71 per cent.[41]

Table 2.7   Numbers and proportion undernourished, 1975

	Millions	% of population
Latin America	112	36
Asia[a]	924	82
Middle East	94	51
Africa	243	77
Developing countries	1373	71

[a] Excluding China.
Source: S. Reutlinger and M. Selowsky, *Malnutrition and Poverty: Magnitude and Policy Options*, World Bank Staff Occasional Papers no. 23, 1976, p. 31

CONCLUSIONS

It will be apparent that it is difficult if not impossible to estimate the numbers suffering from undernutrition in the developing countries. In the 1970s indirect estimates based on FAO food availability data and requirements put the total at between 450 millions and 1300 millions if China is excluded. All that can be hoped is that these estimates indicate where the problem is most severe; the Andean republics, parts of Africa and South Asia have the highest proportions of their population suffering from undernutrition, but in absolute terms South Asia has the largest numbers.

[41] S. Reutlinger and H. Alderman, 'The prevalence of calorie deficient diets in developing countries', *World Development*, **8**, 1980, pp. 399–411.

3

A Short History of Hunger

Few of the recent estimates of the extent of world hunger have attempted to measure change over time; even fewer have considered the extent of hunger in the *developed* world. Yet half a century ago most discussions of the problem of world hunger were concerned with the problems of malnutrition as much in Europe and North America as in Africa, Asia or Latin America. Indeed it is only since the end of the Second World War that malnutrition has ceased to be a major problem in Europe and the United States. In this chapter the decline of undernutrition and malnutrition in Europe is described; and then an attempt is made to trace the changes in the extent of hunger in the developing world since the 1930s.

THE ELIMINATION OF HUNGER IN EUROPE

Pre-industrial Europe

Most historians would agree with Carlo Cipolla that before 1800 the poor of Europe – most of the population – were in a chronic state of undernourishment.[1] Those who relied upon wages had to spend most of their income on food. Moreover, because bread was the cheapest source of energy, it and other vegetable foods were the bulk of the diet, with little meat, milk or cheese being eaten. Nor were farmers – at least those with little land – much better off. Wilhelm Abel has calculated that a twelfth century farmer with 6 hectares would have to give half his grain to Church or lord, leaving a family of five with only half a kilogram of grain per head per day – too little by modern

[1] Carlo M. Cipolla, *Before the Industrial Revolution: European Society and Economy 1000–1700*, London, 1976, p. 31.

standards. Braudel has surmised that pre-industrial Europeans got about 2000 calories per day, much the same as Chinese agriculture produced before the eighteenth century, and similar to India today.[2]

But more attention has been paid to the fluctuations in food consumption in pre-industrial Europe than to average conditions, for it was the extremes that attracted contemporary writers and, later, historians. Long and short term fluctuations can be distinguished.

The long term has been outlined by Braudel and Abel. The bubonic plague of 1348–50 drastically reduced the population of Europe, which did not recover until the late fifteenth century. However, for the surviving farmer there was more land, and, for the labourer and artisan, higher real wages. The population of Europe was better fed in the fourteenth and fifteenth centuries than in the sixteenth, seventeenth or eighteenth centuries. There is little evidence on food consumption to support this; it is inferred from the trends in the purchasing power of wages, which fell in the late sixteenth century and did not recover to their medieval level until the mid nineteenth century. Some fragmentary data on meat consumption suggest that meat was a common part of the diet in the fourteenth century and then declined, not recovering to the medieval level in Germany until the mid nineteenth century.[3]

Rather more attention has been paid by historians to short term fluctuations in food consumption. They were of two types. First were famines, where food shortages occurred for one or more years over a wide area. Second were the more localized food shortages which occurred only in one parish or a group of parishes, led perhaps to a few deaths, and were treated by contemporaries as part of the normal course of events. Indeed these subsistence crises received little attention from historians until work by historical demographers on parish registers revealed their existence.

Famines are a much discussed part of European history. Thus few parts of Western Europe escaped the great crisis of 1314–16, and they are well attested from then until the 1840s. Although it was Ireland that suffered most from the failure of the potato crop in the 1840s, other parts of Europe also had acute food shortages at that time. But this may be decribed as the last major famine in Western Europe. The frequency

---

[2] Wilhelm Abel, *Agricultural Fluctuations in Europe from the Thirteenth to the Twentieth Centuries*, London, 1980, p. 32; F. Braudel, *Capitalism and Material Life 1400–1850*, London, 1974, p. 87; D. Perkins, *Agricultural Development in China, 1368–1968*, Edinburgh, 1969.

[3] Abel, *op. cit.*, pp. 71, 255; Braudel, *op. cit.*, pp. 67, 128–30; B. Bennassar and J. Goy, 'Contribution à l'histoire de la consommation alimentaire du XIVe siècle', *Annales ESC*, **30**, 1975, pp. 402–30.

and extent of famine had been in decline in Western Europe long before the mid nineteenth century. The last major famines occurred in England in the 1620s, in Scotland in the 1690s, in Germany, Switzerland and Scandinavia in 1732, and in France in 1795, although many parts of Europe were afflicted with harvest failure and high prices in 1816.[4] These major outbreaks, covering large areas, declined in impact in the eighteenth century. Not only were better farming methods increasing crop yields, but new crops like the potato were providing more secure supplies, and a wider range of crops was freeing the population from the hazards of depending upon one grain. Equally important, transport improvement both internally and internationally was reducing isolation, and governments both local and national were paying more attention to what would nowadays be called famine relief.[5]

These major crises have of course received much attention from historians. But there were other less dramatic but more frequent and localized demographic crises which have been revealed by the work of historical demographers studying the registers of individual parishes, particularly in France. From the late sixteenth to the early eighteenth century, crises were common. Harvest failure led to a rise in the death rate, a fall in the birth rate and fewer marriages. Once the crisis was past, marriages and births recovered. Initially these events were described as *subsistence crises*, and deaths were attributed to starvation. But others have argued that this was rare, and the malnourished were simply more susceptible to infectious disease. As in the developing countries today, poverty, malnutrition and infectious disease were interlocked and inter-related. But even these local crises were diminishing in the eighteenth century: thus although the English rioted over food prices in the later eighteenth century, few died from hunger.[6]

[4] H. S. Lucas, 'The great European famine of 1315, 1316 and 1317', *Speculum*, 5, 1930, pp. 343–77; M. Bergman, 'The potato blight in the Netherlands and its social consequences 1845–1847', *International Review of Social History*, 12, 1967, pp. 390–431; A. B. Appleby, 'Epidemics and famine in the Little Ice Age', *Journal of Interdisciplinary History*, 10, 1979, pp. 643–63; J. D. Post, *The Last Great Subsistence Crisis in the Western World*, London, 1977.
[5] M. W. Flinn, 'The stabilisation of mortality in pre-industrial Western Europe', *Journal of European Economic History*, 32, 1974, pp. 1289–1328.
[6] J. Meuvret, 'Demographic crisis in France from the sixteenth to the eighteenth century', in D. V. Glass and D. E. C. Eversley (eds), *Population in History: Essays in Historical Demography*, London, 1965, pp. 507–22; J. Stevenson, 'Food riots in England, 1792–1818', in R. Quinault and J. Stevenson (eds), *Popular Protest and Public Order: Six Studies in British History 1790–1920*, London, 1974, pp. 33–74; C. Walford, 'On the famines of the world, past and present', *Journal of the Statistical Society*, 41, 1878, pp. 433–526.

There are no estimates of national consumption levels or available food supplies before the nineteenth century, and the level of food consumption has been inferred from trends in real wages or contemporary descriptions of meals consumed by the very rich or the very poor. In the last two decades historians have attempted to establish the history of European nutrition upon a more scientific basis using the records of food bought for institutions such as monasteries, workhouses, schools and military establishments. [7] However, the national food supplies of various countries have been calculated from the early nineteenth century and converted into their nutritional equivalents. It is thus possible to trace changes in the level and composition of national diets from the early nineteenth century to the present. [8]

Trends in national food supplies after 1800

Estimates have been made for Norway from the eighteenth century to the second half of the nineteenth century (table 3.1), and for France and Germany from 1800 to the present and for Italy, the United States and Japan from the later nineteenth century (figure 3.1). Together with more detailed estimates for France, they allow the major trends in available food supplies – but not actual consumption – to be discerned.

Table 3.1   Estimated food supplies in Norway (calories per caput per day)

1723	1400	1835	2250
1809	1800	1855–65	3300

Source: M. Drake, 'Norway', in W. R. Lee (ed.), European Demography and Economic Growth, 1979, p. 293.

In the early nineteenth century, Norway (table 3.1) and France and Germany (figure 3.1) had daily food supplies below 2000 calories per caput. They were thus similar to many countries in Africa and South Asia in 1978–80, and had supplies well *below* most of modern Latin America, North Africa, the Near East and East Asia. France's supply of total protein in the early nineteenth century – just over 50 grams per caput per day – was also below that of many countries in Africa and Asia today, as was the supply of animal protein. In France and Germany the latter was below 20 grams, again similar to many

[7] J. Hemardinquer, Pour une Histoire de l'alimentation, Paris, 1970.
[8] J. C. Toutain, La Consommation Alimentaire en France de 1789 à 1964, Économies et Sociétés, vol. 5, Paris, 1971.

developing countries at present (figure 3.2). Not all Western Europe was so poorly provided; in the southern Netherlands the daily supply was 2200 calories, but with alcohol included this exceeded 2500 calories; 73 grams of protein were available.[9]

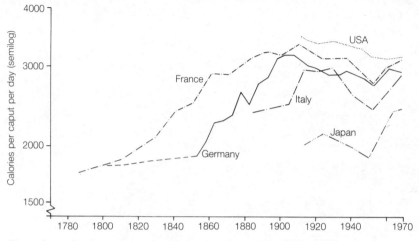

Figure 3.1　Food supply in selected developed countries, 1780–1960
Source: A. Weber and E. Weber, 'The structure of world protein consumption and future nitrogen requirements', *European Review of Agricultural Economics*, 2 1974–5, pp. 169–92

However, after 1800 there was a continuous increase in the calorie supply per caput in France and Germany (figure 3.1). It exceeded 3000 calories per caput in Norway by the 1850s, in Britain possibly by the 1850s and certainly by the 1880s, in France by the 1870s and in Italy by the early twentieth century. At the beginning of the nineteenth century not only were national supplies per caput very low, but most of the calories were derived from vegetable foods; three-quarters of the French food supply was provided by bread and potatoes. After the 1820s calorie supply increased rapidly. The amount of animal food also increased, but relatively slowly (table 3.2); as late as the 1870s 70 per cent of French calories were still derived from bread and potatoes.[10]

[9] C. Lis and H. Soly, 'Food consumption in Antwerp between 1807 and 1859; a contribution to the standard of living debate', *Economic History Review*, **30**, 1977, pp. 460–81.
[10] Lis and Soly, *op. cit.*; Toutain, *op. cit.*, pp. 1979–83; M. Drake, 'Norway', in W. R. Lee (ed.), *European Demography and Economic Growth*, London, 1979, p. 293; D. J. Oddy, 'The health of the people', in T. Barker and M. Drake (eds), *Population and Society in Britain 1850–1980*, London, 1982, pp. 121–32; W. A. McKenzie, 'Changes in the standard of living in the United Kingdom, 1860–1914', *Economica*, **1**, 1921, pp. 211–30.

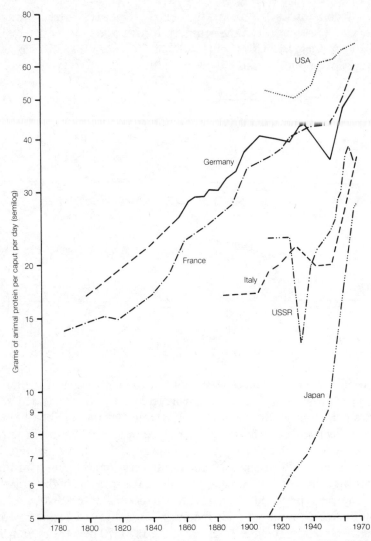

Figure 3.2   Supply of animal protein, selected developed countries, 1780–1960
Source: A. Weber and E. Weber, 'The structure of world protein consumption and future nitrogen requirements', *European Review of Agricultural Economics*, **2**, 1974–5, pp. 169–92

Table 3.2   Meat consumption in the German Empire in the nineteenth century (kilograms per head per year)

1816	13.6	1892	32.5
1840	21.6	1904–5	46.8
1873	29.5		

Source: W. Abel, *Agricultural Fluctuations in Europe. From the Thirteenth to the Twentieth Centuries*, London, 1980, p. 267

At the end of the nineteenth century there began a fundamental change in the diet of Western Europe. Once national food supplies had reached 3000 calories per caput there was comparatively little further increase in total calorie supply, or for that matter in total protein supply. Instead there were major changes in the composition of the diet. Animal foods began to provide an increasing proportion of calorie intake. Thus in France animals foods provided one-fifth of all calories in 1900, but this had risen by the 1960s to one-third. In 1900 75 per cent of all protein intake was derived from vegetable foods, but by the 1960s two-thirds of all protein came from animal foods. Not only have vegetable foods provided a declining percentage of calorific intake this century, but the absolute quantities of bread and potatoes consumed has declined. There has also been an increase in fat and sugar consumption. [11]

Since 1800 there have been fundamental changes in food supplies in Western Europe. Paul Bairoch has calculated, using FAO estimates of nutritional requirements and the age and sex structures of the French population in 1830, that the minimum national requirements were 2300 calories per caput per day. In the early nineteenth century France, Norway and Germany all had supplies below this level. Hence, even if national supplies had been equitably distributed, they would have been insufficient. From the 1820s there were rapid increases in national food supplies, such that by the mid nineteenth century most countries had available food supplies sufficient to eliminate hunger. The increase in calorie supplies came mainly from increases in supplies of bread and potatoes. But from the 1890s there was a steady increase in the proportion of food supplies derived from animal foods. [12]

Hence at various times in the nineteenth century the national food supplies of most West European countries reached a level sufficient to eliminate undernutrition and malnutrition. But as has already been seen, national food supplies are not a sufficient guide to the extent of hunger.

Household consumption

That the food supplies of West European countries were not equally distributed in the nineteenth century, in the first half of this century,

[11] M. Aymard, 'Towards the history of nutrition: some methological remarks', in R. Forster and O. Ranum (eds), *Food and Drink in History: Selections from the Annales*, Baltimore, 1979, pp. 1–16; H. J. Teuteberg, 'The general relationships between diet and industrialization', in E. and R. Forster (eds), *European Diet from Pre-industrial to Modern Times*, London, 1975, pp. 61–110; Toutain, *op. cit.*
[12] P. Bairoch, 'Écarts internationaux des niveaux de vie avant la révolution industrielle', *Annales ESC*, **34**, 1979, pp. 145–71.

or indeed today, is undoubted; nor is there any doubt that low incomes were the prime cause of low food intake. D. J. Oddy has shown, from a number of household budgets of the late nineteenth century, how calorific intake varied with income in England (table 3.3).

Table 3.3   Income and nutritional value of household budgets, England, 1887–1901

	Income class (shillings per week)	Calories per caput per day	Grams of protein per caput per day
A	Under 18	1578	42
B	18 to 21	1964	51
C	21 to 30	2113	58
D	30 and over	2537	72
E	Families with servants	3256	96

Source: D. J. Oddy, 'Working class diets in late nineteenth century Britain', *Economic History Review*, **23**, 1970, pp. 314–23

There is little doubt that elsewhere in Europe the nutritional intake of poor families was inadequate in the later nineteenth century. Budgets of poor households in France collected by Le Play and his followers between 1856 and 1901 gave a mean of 2791 calories, but the range was from 1638 to 4678. One peasant household had a daily supply of 4161 calories, but 86 per cent of this was derived from bread.[13]

Most historians seem agreed that, although national food supplies were sufficient for much of the second half of the nineteenth century in Britain, there must have been widespread malnutrition because of the very marked inequalities in income distribution and the low level of wages of the poorest, although there is no reliable way of measuring the extent of malnutrition or (less common) undernutrition.[14] The Edwardian period saw considerable concern about the extent of malnutrition. The health and nutrition of the working class became a matter of government enquiry, prompted initially by the discovery that many

[13] C. Dauphin and P. Pézerat, 'Les consommations populaires dans la seconde moitié du XIXe siècle à travers les monographies de l'école de Le Play', *Annales ESC*, **30**, 1975, pp. 537–52.

[14] T. C. Barker, D. J. Oddy and J. Yudkin, *The Dietary Surveys of Dr Edward Smith, 1862–3: A New Assessment*, Department of Nutrition, Queen Elizabeth College, University of London, Occasional Paper no. 1, Staples Press, London, 1970; J. C. McKenzie, 'The composition and nutritional value of diets in Manchester and Dukinfield, 1841', *Lancashire and Cheshire Antiquarian Society Transactions*, **72**, 1962, pp. 126–39; B. E. Supple, 'Income and demand, 1860–1913', in R. Floud and D. McCloskey (eds), *The Economic History of Britain since 1700. Volume 2: 1860 to the 1970s*, Cambridge, 1981, p. 132; D. J. Oddy, 'Food in nineteenth century England: nutrition in the first urban society', *Proceedings of the Nutrition Society*, **29**, 1970, pp. 150–7.

volunteers for the Boer War were rejected on medical grounds, and that part of the cause of this was malnutrition. The reports of the school inspectors also revealed much evidence of malnutrition among children. On the eve of the First World War the Board of Education stated that 11 per cent of English children had defective nutrition. [15]

Malnutrition persisted into the inter-war period. By then more was known of the causes of malnutrition, more data were available on nutrition and more scientific surveys could be carried out. The depression of the 1930s and the large number of unemployed drew attention to this problem. Sir John Boyd Orr estimated that half the population of Britain had incomes too small to provide a diet sufficient for optimum growth and health. The League of Nations was much concerned with the extent of malnutrition in Europe, and had laid down minimum nutritional requirements for health. The British Medical Association calculated that one-third of the population of Britain lacked the incomes to acquire this diet. Nor was malnutrition confined to Britain. A later League of Nations report stated that there was no country in Europe where all the population reached the minimum diet and that scurvy, anaemia and rickets were widespread. Government reports in the United States also revealed an alarming level of malnutrition. [16]

Changes in health, nutrition and mortality

Modern inquiries into undernutrition in the developing countries have compared the growth of children in height and body weight with a healthy norm to obtain some measure of the extent of hunger. Long term changes in the height of children, adolescents and young men can also indicate how the nutritional status of a population has changed over time, although of course other factors may influence height. Similarly, the age of menarche in girls is influenced by a variety of factors, but long term changes are thought to reflect changes in nutrition.

There is evidence to suggest that there have been significant increases in average height in Europe over the last 100 years and probably over even longer periods. Thus adult males in Europe are now 6 to 9 cm

---

[15] John Burnett, *Plenty and Want: A Social History of Diet in England from 1815 to the Present Day*, Harmondsworth, 1968, pp. 271, 301, 303, 307; D. J. Oddy, *op. cit.*, 1982; F. Le Gros Clark and R. M. Titmus, *Our Food Problem and its Relation to our National Defences*, Penguin, 1939.

[16] Sir John Boyd Orr, *Food, Health and Income*, London, 1937; Le Gros Clark and Titmus, *op. cit.*, p. 125; League of Nations, *The Problem of Nutrition. Volume 1: Interim Report of the Mixed Committee on the Problem of Nutrition. Volume 3: Nutrition in Various Countries*, Geneva, 1936; J. de Castro, *The Geography of Hunger*, London, 1952.

taller than they were in the 1870s. In Norway, for example, although there was little increase in the average height of adults between 1760 and 1830, it rose by 3 mm per decade over the next 45 years and by 6 mm per decade from 1875 to 1935. Records of conscripts in Holland show a similar rate of increase, although height actually fell between 1820 and 1860. Studies of children also show that average height for particular ages has risen. Thus the height and weight of schoolchildren in Oslo rose between 1920 and 1940, fell during the War, and increased thereafter. In Sweden the average height of 18 year old boys rose from 168.5 cm in 1883 to 178.4 cm in 1969–71. Rather more dramatic evidence is available on children in London. The records of the Marine Society, who placed poor children in the navy, suggest that the average height of boys born after 1815 was 7.5 to 12.5 cm greater than those born in the 1770s. Thirteen year olds born 1753–80 averaged 130 cm; a sample of 13 year old boys in the London County Council area in 1965 averaged 155.5 cm. [17]

Differences in nutrition are also a major factor in the age of menarche among girls. At any one time there are differences according to income, those in richer families reaching menarche earlier than those in poorer. There are also changes over time; a study of working class women in Norway suggests that the average age of menarche fell from 15 years in the 1840s to 13 in 1950. Comparable declines have been recorded in England. [18]

Although nutrition may not be the only cause of changes in height, body weight and menarche over time – genetic factors may help explain long term increases in height – it is undoubtedly important, and these changes reflect improved nutrition in Europe over the last 150 years. It is noteworthy that recent studies suggest that native born whites in the United States were not far short of modern heights as early as the late eighteenth century and were taller than Europeans at the time. The difference in height between adult males in Europe and those in the United States has markedly diminished in this century, as have differences in average height between children and

---

[17] J. M. Tanner, 'Earlier maturation in man', *Scientific American*, 218, 1968, pp. 21–7; G. H. Bruntland, K. Liestøllesdal and L. Walløe, 'Height, weight and menarcheal age of Oslo schoolchildren during the last 60 years', *Annals of Human Biology*, 7, 1980, pp. 307–22; B. Ljung, A. Bergsteen-Brucefors and G. Lindgren, 'The secular trend in physical growth in Sweden', *Annals of Human Biology*, 1, 1974, pp. 245–56; R. Floud and K. W. Wachter, 'Poverty and physical stature: evidence on the standard of living of London boys, 1770–1870', *Social Science History*, 6, 1982, pp. 422–52.
[18] Tanner, *op. cit.*; K. Liestøl, 'Social conditions and menarcheal age: the importance of early years of life', *Annals of Human Biology*, 9, 1982, pp. 521–37.

adults of different income groups within developed countries.[19]

Child nutrition and mortality

Modern nutritional experts believe that protein calorie deficiency is a major cause of child mortality, that is the death rate of children aged one to five. However, the close interrelationship between infection and malnutrition makes authoritative pronouncements on this difficult, and certainly a decline in the child mortality rate may reflect improvements in sanitation and water supplies as much as improvements in nutritional status.

There is little evidence of *acute* protein calorie malnutrition in Britain or the United States in the nineteenth century, although symptoms that appear to resemble kwashiorkor were described in Germany, Switzerland and Italy. Moderate and mild forms, however, are thought to have been widespread. In those countries for which records of child mortality exist there was a decline in the nineteenth century that has continued to the present; in most countries the decline in infant and child mortality preceded that of the older age groups.[20]

The longest available series of child mortality rates is for Sweden. In the late eighteenth century rates exceeded 40 per thousand but began a continuous decline from the second decade of the nineteenth century, reaching 25 per thousand in the 1830s, 16 per thousand in 1899–1902 and 4.1 per thousand in 1929–32. The rate now stands at 0.4 per thousand. The decline in Denmark followed a very similar course. In England the rate was higher than in Sweden in the mid nineteenth century – at about 35 per thousand – and did not begin a permanent decline until the 1860s; it remained above the Scandinavian rates until after the Second World War. France and the Netherlands also showed improvement in expectation of life at younger ages from the mid nineteenth century.[21] There remains considerable controversy about the

[19] Tanner, *op. cit.*; R. W. Fogel, S. L. Engerman and J. Trussell, 'Exploring the uses of data in height: the analysis of long term trends in nutrition, labour welfare and labour productivity', *Social Science History*, 6, 1982, pp. 401–21.

[20] W. R. Aykroyd, 'Nutrition and mortality in infancy and early childhood: past and present relationships', *American Journal of Clinical Nutrition*, 24, 1971, pp. 480–7; S. H. Preston and E. van de Walle, 'Urban French mortality in the nineteenth century', *Population Studies*, 32, 1978, pp. 275–97.

[21] G. Fridlizius, 'Sweden', in W. R. Lee (ed.), *European Demography and Economic Growth*, London, 1979, pp. 284–318; O. Andersen, 'Denmark', in Lee, *op. cit.*, p. 112; R. I. Woods, 'The structure of mortality in mid-nineteenth-century England and Wales', *Journal of Historical Geography*, 8, 1982, pp. 373–94; P. Deprez, 'The Low Countries', in Lee, *op. cit.*, p. 281; Preston and van de Walle, *op. cit.*

evidence of child mortality rates as a guide to improved nutritional status. Some authorities believe that falling mortality in the nineteenth century was due to better food supplies, a reduced rate of malnutrition and hence greater resistance to infectious disease. Others have doubted the significance of nutrition and have attributed most of the decline to improvements in public health, noting that the life expectancy of well fed American families in the mid nineteenth century was not very different from the supposedly malnourished West Europeans. It can be said, however, that in the early nineteenth century child mortality rates were comparable with those in the poorer developing countries in the 1940s – over 40 per thousand – and have fallen to levels below 1 per thousand today. [22]

The combined evidence of national food supplies, household budgets, heights and falling child mortality rates suggests an overwhelming improvement in the nutritional status of the population of Western Europe from the eighteenth century to the present. In the late eighteenth century and early nineteenth century national food supplies were as low as those in the poorer parts of Africa and South Asia at present. The nineteenth century saw rapid growth in calorie supplies, this century the growing importance of animal foods. But malnutrition persisted until the 1930s because significant proportions of the population had incomes too low to provide an adequate diet. By the 1930s Portugal was the only country in Europe with a national food supply below national requirements.

THE DEVELOPING COUNTRIES, 1930–80

Litle is known of the nutritional status of the populations of Africa, Asia and Latin America before the twentieth century. The first estimates of calorie supplies were made by FAO in the first *World Food Survey*, published in 1946 but relying upon data collected in the 1930s. It is clear that the great difference between the developing and developed countries already existed (figure 3.3) although calorie availability per caput was lower than at present in both regions. Clearly the comparatively low supplies of developing countries today cannot be due, as is sometimes suggested, solely to the rapid population growth of the last 40 years.

[22] T. McKeown, 'Food, infection and population', *Journal of Interdisciplinary History*, **14**, 1983, pp. 227–47; A. G Carmichael, 'Infection, hidden hunger and history', *Journal of Interdisciplinary History*, **14**, 1983, pp. 249–64; M. Livi-Bacci, 'The nutrition-mortality link in past times: a comment', *Journal of Interdisciplinary History*, **14**, 1983, pp. 293–6.

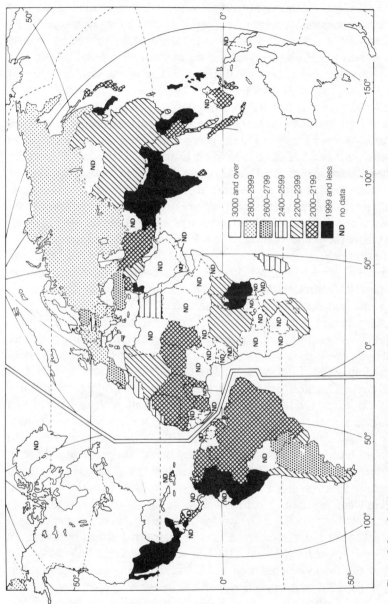

Figure 3.3   Calorie supply per caput per day, 1934–8
Source: FAO, *World Food Survey,* Washington DC, 1946

If calories per caput were inadequate in the 1930s in much of Africa, Asia and Latin America, so too was the quality of the diet. There are no national records of protein per caput in the 1930s. However M. K. Bennet estimated the proportion of total calorie intake derived from cereal and root crops. He argued that if the proportion exceeded 80 per cent the population would be malnourished. [23] The whole of Asia – except Japan – and most of Africa fell into this category, whereas parts of Eastern Europe and North Africa had between 70 and 80 per cent, comparable with France in the early nineteenth century (figure 3.4). Nowhere in Latin America however did the proportion exceed 70 per cent. North America, Australasia and North West Europe had less than 40 per cent of their calories from cereals and roots. By the 1960s (figure 3.5) there had been marked changes in both the developed and the developing countries; in only a handful of countries did the proportion still exceed 80 per cent, and most of the population of Latin America lived in countries where the proportion was below 50 per cent. The difference, within the developed region, between Western Europe on the one hand and southern Europe, Eastern Europe and the Soviet Union on the other still persists, although the proportion of calories derived from cereals and roots had declined in the latter areas.

Since the end of the Second World War more detailed and more reliable evidence on national food supplies has become available. Furthermore the Food and Agriculture Organization of the United Nations has published four world food surveys. These should give some indication of the trend in the numbers malnourished in the developing world (table 3.4). The first *World Food Survey* (1946) dealt with the 1930s and estimated that then one-half of the world's population had inadequate diets. The *Second World Food Survey* (1952) made no estimate of the extent of hunger, but noted that 59.5 per cent of the population lived in countries where daily food supplies were less than 2200 calories, and a similar proportion lived in countries where daily supplies of animal protein were less than 15 grams; it must be assumed that it is this information that Sir John Boyd Orr used to make his statement that two-thirds of the world's population lived lives of malnutrition and hunger. [24] In the *Third World Food Survey* (1963) it was argued that only 10–15 per cent of the world's population had an insufficient calorie supply, but that 60 per cent of the population of the developing countries suffered from malnutrition. By the time of the *Fourth World Food Survey*, it had

---

[23] M. K. Bennet, 'International contrasts in food consumption', *Geographical Review*, **31**, 1941, 365–76.

[24] Sir John Boyd Orr, 'The food problem', *Scientific American*, **183**, 1950, pp. 11–15.

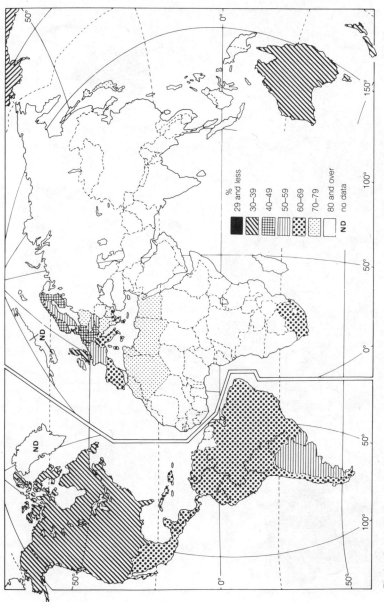

Figure 3.4   Percentage of calorie supply per caput per day derived from cereals and roots, 1934–8
Source: M. K. Bennett, 'International contrasts in food consumption', *Geographical Review*, **31**, 1941, pp. 365–76

%
■ 29 and less
▨ 30–39
▦ 40–49
▤ 50–59
▨ 60–69
▨ 70–79
■ 80 and over
ND no data

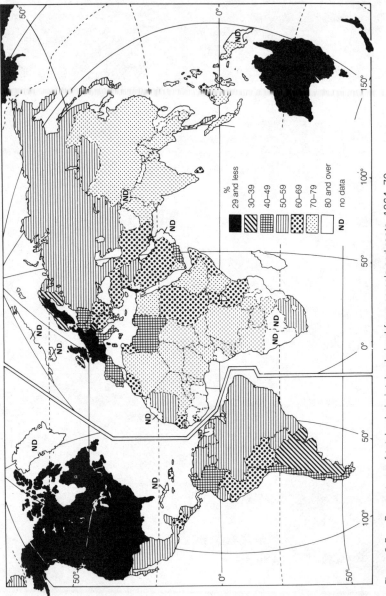

%

29 and less

30–39

40–49

50–59

60–69

70–79

80 and over

ND   no data

Figure 3.5   Percentage of total calorie intake derived from cereals and roots, 1964–70

Source: FAO, *Production Yearbook 1970*, vol. 24, Rome, 1971

Table 3.4   Estimates of the extent of world hunger made by FAO

| Date of survey | Size of sample | Extent of hunger | Number or proportion | | Total number undernourished or malnourished (millions) | As a % of world | World population (millions) |
			Undernourished	Malnourished			
1934–8	70 countries with 90% of world population	'Half the world's population... (live)... at a level of food consumption which was not high enough to maintain health'					
1934–8	80% of the world's population	Not stated	38.6% of the population lived in countries with daily food supplies less than 2200 calories	59% of the population lation lived in countries where daily supply of animal protein is less than 15 grams	1050	50	2100
1949–50	80% of the world's population	Not stated	59.5% of the population lived in countries with daily food supplies less than 2200 calories	58% of the population lived in countries where daily supply of animal protein is less than 15 grams	1240	59	2100
1957–9	80 countries with 95% of world population	10–15% of the world's population are under-nourished and up to half suffer from hunger or malnutrition	10–15% of the world population	'The incidence of malnutrition in the less developed countries is estimated at 60%'	1490 'up to half ...' = 1430 'the incidence of mal-nutrition. ...' = 1160	59.9 / 50	2500
1972–4	58 less developed countries containing 56% of the population. Asian Communist countries excluded	455 million have a food intake below 1.2 basal metabolic rate	455			40	2870
					455	11,8	3830

Sources: FAO, World Food Survey, Washington DC, 1946; The Second World Food Survey, Rome, 1952; The Third World Food Survey, Rome, 1963; The Fourth World Food Survey, Rome, 1977.

been decided that animal protein was not essential for health and that a diet which provided a sufficient supply of calories would also provide sufficient protein and vitamins. This survey found that only 455 millions in the non-Communist developing countries suffered from undernutrition. Estimates for the Communist countries would make the total 630 million, about 15 per cent of the world's population. World Bank estimates for the same period however put the number undernourished much higher, at 1500 million.

The apparent decline in the proportion and the absolute numbers suffering from undernutrition and malnutrition in the FAO surveys is a result of the very different ways in which each survey defined and measured hunger; hence the fall from 1950 to 1972–4 cannot be used to show that the problem of hunger has diminished. It is however possible to use the figures on available food supplies published by FAO, if not to provide an accurate estimate of the extent of hunger, at least to indicate some trends between 1950 and 1980. There are three ways of doing this.

Trends in available food supplies per caput. Between 1950 and 1980 available food supply per caput rose in the world as a whole, in the developed world, in the developing world, and in all the major regions (table 3.5). Indeed in only ten countries for which data were available in both 1978–80 and 1950 were food supplies per caput lower in the former than in the latter. There is no information on how these supplies were distributed among the population in either year, but in 1950 available supplies in Africa and Asia were very low, and even if supplies had been equally distributed would probably not have provided an adequate diet. However, it is very clear that the dramatic decline in food supplies per caput predicted by many in 1950 has not occurred.

Numbers living in countries with less than 2200 calories per caput per day. In the *Second World Food Survey* attention was drawn to the numbers living in countries with less than 2200 calories, and it was assumed that a large proportion of the population of these countries would be undernourished. This seems reasonable, for when in the *Fourth World Food Survey* national minimum requirements were estimated for each developing country, in most cases they were more than 2200 calories. There was little change in the proportion of the world's population living in such countries between 1950 and 1961–5, while the absolute numbers greatly increased (table 3.6). However, since 1961–5 both the proportion and the absolute numbers have declined. None the less, by 1978–80 one-third of the population of the developing world still lived in countries with daily food supplies less than 2200 calories and 27 per cent in countries with supplies less than 2000 calories.

Table 3.5   Average available food supply per caput per day, 1950–80

	1950	*1961–5*	*1969–71*	*1978–80*	*1950–80* *% change*
Developed					
Europe	2689[a]	3420	3339	3477	29.3
North America	3131	3492	3467	3624	15.7
Oceania[b]	3176	3432	3360	3257	2.5
USSR	3020	3542	3388	3486	12.2
Total developed	2878	3471	3382	3486	21.1
Developing					
Asia[c]	1924	2068	2192	2326	20.9
Africa[d]	2020[e]	2165	2276	2311	14.4
Latin America	2376	2413	2531	2591	9.0
Total developing	1977	2115	2239	2350	18.9
World	2253	2494	2537	2617	16.2

[a] No data for Eastern Europe: assumed to be same as Western Europe for aggregated figures.
[b] Australia and New Zealand only.
[c] Includes China, Japan, Israel.
[d] All Africa, including South Africa.
[e] Data for 44 per cent of population only; other countries assumed to have same average.
Sources: FAO, *The Second World Food Survey*, Rome, 1952; *Production Yearbook 1976*, vol. 30, Rome, 1977; *Production Yearbook 1982*, vol. 36, Rome, 1983

Table 3.6   World population in three intake classes (calories per caput per day), 1950, 1961–5 and 1978–80

Percentage of total population

Intake class	*1950*	*1961–5*	*1978–80*
Less than 2200	59.8	57.6	25.6
2200–2599	9.7	11.5	38.8
2600 and over	30.5	30.9	35.6
Total	100.0	100.0	100.0

Numbers (millions)

Intake class	*1950*	*1961–5*	*1978–80*
Less than 2200	1251.1	1822.7	1103.5
2200–2599	205.7	365.1	1665.4
2600 and over	633.1	979.2	1532.0
Total	2089.9	3167.0	4300.9

Sources: FAO, *The Second World Food Survey*, Rome, 1952; *Production Yearbook 1976*, vol. 30, Rome, 1977; *Production Yearbook 1982*, vol. 36, Rome, 1983; *Production Yearbook 1957*, vol. 8, Rome, 1958; United Nations, *Demographic Yearbook 1950*, New York, 1951

Changes in the numbers receiving less than 1.2 BMR. In the preceding chapter the FAO method for estimating the proportion of a population receiving less than 1.2 basal metabolic rate was described and applied to food supplies per head in 1978–80. The same can be done for countries in 1950 and 1961–5. It will be seen (table 3.7) that the proportion of the world's population receiving less than this number of calories has declined from 23 per cent in 1950 to 12 per cent in 1978–80. The population of the developing world nearly doubled in this period and, although the proportion has fallen, the absolute numbers have decreased only very slightly since 1950.

Table 3.7　Population receiving less than the minimum requirements of 1.2 basal metabolic rate, 1950–80

	1948–50	1961–5	1972–4	1978–80
Numbers (millions)				
Africa	60	94	83	72
Latin America	46	54	46	41
Asia (inc. China)	444	502	397	421
Total	550	650	526	534
Percentage of population				
Developing countries	34	29	20	17
All countries	23	21	13	12

Sources: FAO, *The Fourth World Food Survey*, Rome, 1977; *The State of Food and Agriculture, 1981*, Rome, 1982; *Production Yearbooks*, Rome, 1948 onwards.

Declines in child mortality

As seen earlier there was a continuous fall in child mortality in Western Europe from the middle of the nineteenth century. This must have reflected a decline not simply in malnutrition but also in infectious diseases.[25] In the period since the end of the Second World War there has also been a marked decline in child mortality in those few countries in the developing world for which age specific mortality rates are available (tables 3.8 and 3.9). Although in the few African countries for which estimates are available, such as Togo and Benin, child mortality is over 40 per thousand (comparable with Sweden in the late eighteenth century), in many developing countries it has fallen below 10 per thousand, a rate not achieved in England and Wales until 1920. The important point however is that in every country for which data are

[25] G. H. Beaton and J. M. Bengoa, 'Practical population indicators of health and nutrition', in G. H. Beaton and J. M. Bengoa (eds), *Nutrition in Preventive Medicine*, World Health Organization, Geneva, 1971.

available the trend has been downwards. Thus, in so far as child mortality rates are an indicator of the prevalence of acute protein calorie malnutrition, the rate has declined, although of course in some cases the absolute number of deaths may have risen because of the much greater populations.

Table 3.8   Mortality rate in children aged one to four years (per 1000 children)

	1950–2	*1960–2*	*1966*	*1975*[a]
Sweden	1.3[b]	0.9	0.7[c]	0.4
United Kingdom	1.4[b]	0.9	0.8[c]	0.6[d]
Uruguay	2.2	1.3	1.3	1.6
Trinidad and Tobago	5.8	2.5	2.0	1.9
Argentina	5.0	4.3	2.4	0.7
Jamaica	10.5	6.8	4.7	—
Venezuela	11.9	5.7	4.9	1.6
Chile	12.9	8.2	5.0	2.2
Costa Rica	14.6	7.5	6.0	3.1
Panama	9.5	7.9	8.0	3.4
Peru	19.8	15.7	10.5	8.3
Mexico	28.6	13.8	10.9	—
El Salvador	31.1	17.1	13.5	8.8[e]
Guatemala	46.3	32.4	29.5	—

[a] Male child mortality only.
[b] 1950.
[c] 1965.
[d] England and Wales.
[e] 1971.
Sources: J. M. Bengoa, 'Recent trends in the public health aspects of protein-calorie malnutrition', *WHO Chronicle*, **24**, 1970, pp. 552–61; United Nations, *Demographic Yearbook 1979*, New York.

Table 3.9   Child mortality rates in selected countries

	1950s	*1970s*
Thailand	14.4 (1956)	5.6 (1970)
Sri Lanka	14.8 (1955)	10.3 (1963)
Philippines	11.8 (1958)	7.2 (1970)
Malaya	11.4 (1957)	2.5 (1976)
Colombia	23.0 (1951)	7.8 (1973)

Sources: United Nations, *Demographic Yearbooks*, New York

CONCLUSIONS

Although it is not possible to make any firm statements about the extent of hunger over the last 200 hundred years, some conclusions can be drawn.

First, in the early nineteenth century many countries in Western

Europe had available food supplies which were below the national minimum requirements, and from this it can be inferred that a considerable but unknown proportion of the population was both undernourished and malnourished.

Second, by the later nineteenth century most countries in Western Europe had national food supplies that would have provided an adequate diet for all if distributed according to needs. But contemporary descriptions suggest that malnutrition was still widespread. The evidence of contemporary working class household budgets, the reports of school inspectors, and the rejection rates of army volunteers all suggest widespread malnutrition in England. [26] Malnutrition was still widespread in the 1930s, not only in Britain but also in Europe and the United States. Indeed it was not until the period since the end of the Second World War that malnutrition declined to a very small proportion of the population of the developed world. The principal reason for the earlier widespread malnutrition was poverty; substantial proportions of the population had incomes too small to buy an adequate diet. Thus it was not until the remarkable economic growth in the 1950s and 1960s that the incomes of the least well paid rose above the levels necessary to provide an adequate diet. There were other factors that contributed to the decline of malnutrition. The first was the improved knowledge of nutrition; it was not until the early part of this century that the significance of vitamins was known. The second was the decline in infectious disease from the late nineteenth century; as cleaner water supplies and more effective sanitation were provided, so the incidence of gastric diseases declined, and this may have reduced the influence of malnutrition. Third, in much of Europe and the United States legislation to prevent the sale of diseased and adulterated food must have not only reduced poisoning but also increased the nutritional value of foods sold in shops. Finally, in some countries the state made efforts to improve the diet of children; thus for example in Britain the provision of school meals and milk may have helped reduce the extent of malnutrition.

Thus it is clear that the provision of adequate national food supplies is not sufficient to ensure the elimination of undernutrition and malnutrition. The poor must have enough money to purchase the minimum diet. It is disturbing to note that there was a lag of up to a century between some European countries' achievement of an adequate national food supply and the elimination of malnutrition. But equally clearly

---

[26] Le Gros Clark and Titmus, *op. cit.*; F. B. Smith, *The People's Health 1830–1910*, London, 1979, pp. 17, 178–83; D. J. Oddy, 'Working class diets in late nineteenth century Britain', *Economic History Review*, **23**, 1970, pp. 314–23.

in the early nineteenth century much of Europe had insufficient food supplies for its population quite regardless of income differences; this was attributable to the very low level of agricultural productivity, the high cost of transporting food, the difficulties of preserving perishable foods, and the losses of foods in storage. Nor are all countries in the developing world today capable of providing an adequate food supply even when imports are taken into account (see figure 2.5).

In the post-war period malnutrition has been largely confined to the developing countries; paradoxically, at the time it became fashionable to speak of the *world* food problem, malnutrition became a problem almost exclusively of Africa, Asia and Latin America. It would seem likely that during this period the proportion of the population of the developing countries suffering from undernutrition has declined; even with the great increase in population, the absolute numbers have slightly declined. This is *a fortiori* true of the world as a whole over the last 200 years. In the developed world malnutrition has been slowly eliminated; it remains now confined to the developing world.

4

Population and Poverty

In the 1930s malnutrition was thought to be due to poverty; few attributed the problems in Europe or the United States to excessive population growth. Indeed the prime concern of demographers at the time was why European population growth was so low. The *World Food Survey* (1946) also argued that the extent of hunger was due to poverty and had little to say about population growth, but by the time of the *Second World Food Survey* (1952) there were fears that the rapidity of population growth in the developing countries, which was becoming apparent as the first censuses taken for some time became available, might prevent the elimination of hunger.[1] Throughout the 1950s and 1960s it came to be assumed that the major cause of hunger in the developing countries was population growth: quite simply the numbers in Africa, Asia and Latin America were growing faster than the capacity of agriculture to supply food.

By the 1970s, however, this point of view was under challenge. It could be shown first that per caput food supplies were very low in the developing countries in the 1930s (see p. 43), so that although post-war population growth may have prevented the improvement of post-war consumption levels, it could hardly be said to have caused their lowness. Second, after all the gloomy predictions of the 1950s and 1960s, it seemed clear that at the world level food production had kept up with population growth, and that world food supplies per caput were somewhat above the level of the 1930s or early 1950s. It became common to attribute hunger in the developing countries to poverty, and efforts were made to measure the numbers without the resources to acquire enough food.

[1] FAO, *World Food Survey*, Washington DC, 1946; *The Second World Food Survey*, Rome, 1952.

Unfortunately these conflicting views of the problem have been connected with opposing ideological views of the world. There has been a tendency for those who believe that inequality of income distribution is the only cause of hunger to ignore the consequences of population growth, and for those who believe that poverty is solely a result of too rapid population growth to neglect the inequities of land tenure. There seems no need to take such entrenched positions. At any one time the existence of undernutrition or malnutrition is surely due to poverty – to the lack of income, employment opportunities or sufficient land. But, over time, population growth is equally surely one cause of poverty.

The aim of this chapter is to outline the growth of population in the world since 1950, with some reflections on earlier growth, as a background for the discussion of the growth of food output per caput in chapter 5. Some of the main features of poverty are then discussed.

THE POST-WAR GROWTH OF POPULATION

The rapid growth of population since 1950 has increased the number of consumers of food, and the changing geographical distribution has influenced levels of consumption. Increasing numbers have also, of course, increased the number of producers of food. Both aspects must be noted.

There is no doubting the rapidity of population growth in the developing countries between 1950 and 1980; not only did the population of Africa, Asia and Latin America increase far more rapidly than the developed countries in the same period, but far more rapidly than in any part of the world before 1950. [2]

Between 1950 and 1980 the population of the developing world nearly doubled (table 4.1). In only one quinquennium did the rate of increase in any of the three continents fall below 2.0 per cent (table 4.2). However, the rate reached a peak in the early 1960s and has since fallen slightly. The exception to this trend is Africa, whose rate of increase has risen throughout the period. Although the rate of increase in the developed world has been less than half that in the developing world, there have been considerable absolute increases in the population of these countries in the last 30 years, a fact that is sometimes overlooked. The rate of increase in the developed world reached a peak in the late 1950s and has since steadily declined (table 4.2).

[2] D. Grigg, 'Modern population growth in historical perspective', *Geography*, 67, 1982, pp. 97–108.

Table 4.1   Population: major regions, 1950–80

	1950	1960	1970	1980	Increase 1950–80	
		(millions)			(millions)	(%)
Developing						
Africa	219	275	354	469	250	114
Latin America	164	215	283	368	204	124
Asia	1296	1589	1987	2442	1146	88
Total developing	1679	2079	2624	3279	1600	95
Developed						
Europe	392	425	460	484	92	24
North America	166	199	226	246	80	48
USSR	180	211	244	267	87	48
Australasia	10	13	15	18	8	76
Japan	84	94	104	116	32	38
Total developed	832	942	1049	1131	300	36
World	2513	3021	3673	4410	1900	76

Source: United Nations, *Demographic Yearbook 1980*, New York, 1982, p. 133

There are however quite significant regional differences within the two spheres. Within the developed countries the increase 1950–80 has been least in Western Europe and most in North America and Australia. Within the developing world the increase has been greatest in central America, northern South America, parts of Africa, South West Asia and parts of South East Asia. However, in China and India, by far the most populous countries in the world, post-war population increase has been comparatively modest; indeed parts of the developed world have increased as rapidly. Thus China's population rose by 72 per cent between 1950 and 1980, India's by 85 per cent. In the same period, the population of Canada rose by 74 per cent. The difference lies of course in the absolute numbers. India's population in 1980 was 305 million more than in 1950, China's 400 million and Canada's only 10 million.[3]

TRENDS IN MORTALITY AND FERTILITY

Although some parts of the developing world experienced an increase in fertility in the 1950s and 1960s, there is no doubt that the main cause of the great upsurge in population has been a decline in mortality

[3] United Nations, *Demographic Yearbook 1980*, New York, 1982.

Table 4.2 World and major regions; rates of population increase, 1950–80 (average rate of increase per cent per annum)

	1950–4	1955–9	1960–4	1965–9	1970–4	1975–80	1950–80
Developing							
Africa	2.2	2.4	2.5	2.6	2.8	2.9	2.6
Latin America	2.7	2.8	2.8	2.8	2.7	2.7	2.7
Asia	1.9	2.2	2.3	2.2	2.1	2.0	2.1
Total developing	2.0	2.3	2.4	2.3	2.3	2.2	2.3
Developed							
North America	1.8	1.8	1.5	1.1	0.9	0.8	1.3
Europe	0.8	0.8	0.9	0.7	0.6	0.4	0.7
USSR	1.7	1.8	1.5	1.1	0.8	0.9	1.3
Australia and New Zealand	2.5	2.2	2.0	1.9	1.6	1.2	1.9
Japan	1.4	0.9	1.0	1.0	1.3	0.9	1.1
Total developed	1.3	1.3	1.2	0.9	0.8	0.6	1.0
World	1.8	2.0	2.0	1.9	1.8	1.8	1.9

Sources: United Nations, *Demographic Yearbook 1978*, New York, 1979; *Demographic Yearbook 1980*, New York, 1982

combined with, until recently, little or no change in fertility. In most developing countries the crude death rate is now half what is was just after the Second World War, and there have also been dramatic declines in infant and child mortality. The reasons for this decline are not entirely clear, although a number of possible explanations have been put forward. First the improvements in chemical therapy in the 1930s and 1940s have been extended from the developed to the developing countries. Antibiotics have cured bacterial illnesses, and vaccines have increased immunity to a variety of contagious diseases. Second, advances in preventive health have reduced the prevalence of certain contagious diseases. The improvement of water supplies and sewage disposal has reduced the incidence of gastrinal diseases, and immediately after the Second World War the spraying of badly drained areas with DDT destroyed mosquitoes and thus reduced malaria. However, malaria has reappeared as a major disease in recent years as mosquitoes have developed immunity to DDT and its successors. Third, the increase in income per caput in the less developed countries may also have contributed to the decline in the death rate, by improving nutrition, increasing the provision of medical services and raising standards of literacy and general education. The better education of women has been particularly important in the reduction of infant and child mortality. Although crude death rates are still declining in the developing world, in most countries the rate of decline was greater before the mid 1960s than since.[4]

The decline in mortality that was so rapid in the 1950s was not at first accompanied by any change in the crude birth rate, which was high, particularly in Africa and Latin America. This was because marriage was almost universal in the developing countries, most women married when very young, and there was little attempt to control births within marriage. However, by the mid 1960s signs of a decline in fertility were becoming apparent in countries with a Chinese population such as Taiwan, Malaya and Singapore, and also in China itself. Later there was fertility decline in other parts of Asia and in Latin America, but (table 4.3) not as yet in Africa. This fall in fertility seems to have been due not only to the spread of family planning methods, but also to a rise

[4] S. H. Preston, 'The changing relationship between mortality and level of economic development', *Population Studies*, **29**, 1978, pp. 231–48; S. H. Preston, 'Causes and consequences of mortality declines in less developed countries during the twentieth century', in R. A. Easterlin (ed.), *Population and Economic Change in Developing Countries*, Chicago, 1980, pp. 289–360; W. Parker Maudlin, 'Population trends and prospects', *Science*, **209**, 1980, pp. 148–57; D. R. Gwatkins, 'Indications of change in developing country mortality trends: the end of an era', *Population and Development Review*, **6**, 1980, pp. 615–44.

Table 4.3 Crude birth and death rates, 1958–80

	Crude birth rates (per thousand)		Crude death rates (per thousand)	
	1953–7	*1975–80*	*1953–7*	*1975–80*
Africa	45	46	27	17
Asia	39	31	18	12
Latin America	40	35	16	8
Europe	19	15	11	11
Oceania	25	22	9	9
North America	25	15	9	9
USSR	26	18	8	9
World	34	29	18	12

Sources: United Nations, *Demographic Yearbook 1958*, New York, 1958, p. 104; *Demographic Yearbook 1980*, New York, 1982, p. 133

in the age of marriage of women and some decline in the proportion of women ever married.[5] The most dramatic reduction in fertility appears to have been achieved in China, where since the early 1960s the government has encouraged the adoption of birth control methods, discouraged early marriage and penalized the parents of large families. In the last few years there has been a campaign to promote one child families. The crude birth rate is thought to have fallen from 33 per thousand in 1970 to 17 per thousand in 1977. But although there has been a substantial decline in crude birth rates in the developing world, and although mortality has been falling more slowly since 1970, the rate of natural increase continues to be high, and by 1980 only a slight reduction in the rate of population increase had been achieved. In the period 1975–80 the average rate of increase exceeded 3.0 per cent per annum in most of Central America and northern South America, much of Africa and South West Asia. However, in both China and India the rate of increase was below 2.0 per cent per annum and below 2.5 per cent in much of South East Asia.[6]

[5] S. Kuznets, *Population, Capital and Growth; Selected Essays*, 1973, pp. 95–102; D. Kirk, 'World population and birth rates: agreements and disagreements', *Population and Development Review*, 5, 1979, pp. 387–404; R. H. Cassen, 'Current trends in population change and their causes', *Population and Development Review*, 4, 1978, pp. 331–53; Y. Blayo and J. Verron, 'La fecondité dans quelques pays d'Asie orientali', *Population*, 32, 1977, pp. 945–7; D. F. S. Fernando, 'Recent fertility decline in Ceylon', *Population Studies*, 26, 1973, pp. 445–54; 'Changing nuptiality patterns in Sri Lanka 1901–1971', *Population Studies*, 29, 1975, pp. 179–90.
[6] A. J. Coale, 'Population trends, population policy and population studies in China', *Population and Development Review*, 7, 1981, pp. 85–7; United Nations, *op. cit.*

Population growth in the developed countries merits less attention for there are comparatively few problems of undernutrition or malnutrition. Yet the population of this area has risen by one-third since 1950; there were 300 million more people to be fed in 1980 than there were in 1950. This is small compared with the 1600 million people added to the developing countries, but none the less this has required an increase in food output. By 1950 crude death rates were already low in the developed countries, having been declining for at least a century; although the mortality rates of most age groups have declined between 1950 and 1980, the ageing of the population has ensured that crude death rates have not greatly fallen. Thus in most parts of the developed world it has been trends in fertility that have determined the rate of population increase. By the 1930s fertility had fallen very low in most of the Western World – although not in the Soviet Union or in Eastern Europe – but there was a rise in fertility after the end of the Second World War in Western Europe and the European settlements overseas. This was halted in the mid 1960s, and by the 1970s fertility had fallen so low that annual deaths were exceeding births in some West European states.[7]

POPULATION GROWTH IN A LARGER PERSPECTIVE

In the 1950s much emphasis was put upon the dramatic decline in the death rate in the developing countries. Some historians had contrasted the rapid growth of European populations in the nineteenth and twentieth centuries with the apparently slow increases in Africa, Asia and Latin America. It was assumed that economic growth in the developed world had reduced mortality in Europe and North America, but that there was little progress in mortality reduction in the developing countries until after 1945. The population explosion in the less developed countries was thought to have no precedent.

This is not now thought to be so. Although the rates of increase of 2 per cent per annum or more in the developing world were higher than those found before 1950, rates of increase were then already comparatively high. Paul Bairoch believes that the developing countries were increasing at 0.5 per cent per annum in the first two decades of this century, at over 1 per cent in each decade until 1950 and since

---

[7] J. Bourgeois Pichat, 'Recent demographic changes in Western Europe', *Population and Development Review*, 7, 1981, pp. 19–42.

then at over 2 per cent.[8] Reliable information on population increase in the developing countries is hard to come by before the 1940s, but certainly many countries appear to have experienced quite rapid increases in the first half of the twentieth century. Egypt's population increased more than 1 per cent per annum in every decade after 1900, as did Brazil's, and Thailand's population was increasing at over 2 per cent per annum in both the 1920s and the 1930s. The reason for this quite brisk increase in population was apparently a decline in mortality, although this is well documented only for Latin America, where mortality has been declining since 1900 and probably before then. Thus expectation of life at birth in Brazil rose from 29 years in 1900 to 45 years in 1950, and in Mexico from 25 years to 47 years.[9]

Indeed over the last 200 years the rate of population increase in the countries now defined as developed and developing has not been greatly different (table 4.4). The upturn in Europe's population, which occurred in the eighteenth century, was once thought to be unique. But modern estimates of population elsewhere in the world suggest that the increase was almost universal.[10] The difference between the rate of population growth in the developed and the developing countries was most marked

Table 4.4   Population growth in the developed and developing worlds, 1750–1980

Average rate of increase (per cent per annum)

	1750–99	1800–49	1850–99	1900–49	1950–80	1750–1980
Developed[a]	0.4	0.7	1.0	0.8	1.0	0.75
Developing	0.4	0.5	0.3	0.9	2.3	0.7

Percentage of world population in developed and developing countries

	1750	1800	1850	1900	1950	1980
Developing	75	75	73	66	67	74
Developed[a]	25	25	27	34	33	26

[a] Europe, USSR, North America, Japan, Australia and New Zealand.
Sources: United Nations, *The Determinants and Consequences of World Population Growth*, vol. 1, New York, 1973; J. D. Durand, 'Historical estimates of world population: an evaluation', *Population and Development Review*, **3**, 1977, pp. 253–96; United Nations, *Demographic Yearbook 1980*, New York, 1982

[8] P. Bairoch, *The Economic Development of the Third World since 1900*, London, 1975, p. 6.
[9] D. Grigg, *Population Growth and Agrarian Change; An Historical Perspective*, Cambridge, 1980, p. 238; J. Ho, 'La évolution de la mortalité en Amérique Latine', *Population*, **25**, 1970, pp. 103–6.
[10] J. D. Durand, 'Historical estimates of world population; an evaluation', *Population and Development Review*, **3**, 1977, pp. 253–96.

between 1850 and 1899 (table 4.4). The population of the developing countries was heavily weighted by that of China, and in the second half of the nineteenth century the population of China fell during the Taiping rebellion and recovered slowly thereafter. In some parts of the developing world population increase was very rapid. Thus Java's population tripled between 1800 and 1900, whereas Egypt's quadrupled, as did Central America's between 1825 and 1980.[11] Thus in 1980 the developing countries contained much the same proportion of the world's population as they did in 1750 (table 4.4). The present high densities and rapid growth are not a sudden event, but the acceleration of a long term trend.

URBANIZATION AND POPULATION GROWTH

In 1950 the bulk of the population of the developing countries lived in rural areas and were dependent upon agriculture for their livelihood. Since then there has been a radical change in distribution, for cities have grown rapidly both in absolute numbers and as a proportion of the population, the numbers living in towns increasing over three times and the proportion rising from 16 to 30 per cent (table 4.5).

Table 4.5   Urban populations, 1950–80

	1950		1980	
	(millions)	*(% of total)*	*(millions)*	*(% of total)*
Developing				
Africa	31.8	14.5	132.9	28.9
Latin America	67.5	41.2	240.6	64.7
East Asia	70.8	16.7	267.9	33.1
South Asia	104.9	15.6	329.8	23.9
Total developing	275.0	16.7	971.2	30.5
Developed				
North America	106.0	63.8	183.0	73.7
Europe	222.6	53.7	369.3	68.8
Oceania	7.7	61.2	17.8	75.9
USSR	70.7	39.3	173.6	64.8
Japan	41.9	50.2	91.9	78.2
Total developed	448.9	52.5	835.6	70.2
World	723.9	28.9	1806.8	41.3

Source: United Nations, *Patterns of Urban and Rural Population Growth*, New York, 1980

[11] D. Grigg, *op. cit.*, 1980, p. 238.

This rapid growth in the urban population has been due both to a rise in the natural increase in towns, where medical facilities and preventive health are superior to those in the rural areas, and to migration from the rural areas. The rapid growth of rural population in many parts of the developing world has reduced the size of farms, increased the number without land, and accelerated out-migration, and the towns have generally offered higher wages and better social facilities. Unfortunately the growth of employment opportunities in the towns has not matched the increase in urban population, so that poverty is widespread in the cities.

This changing distribution of the population has, however, had some significance for the food supply. In the first place, urban incomes in all parts of the developing world – including China – are higher than those in the rural areas. Not only do the towns contain most of the manufacturing industry (with its higher wage rates) and a substantial white collar population, but many developing countries, aware that political power is concentrated in the cities, have attempted to placate the urban population by limiting the increases in food prices. Higher incomes in the towns means that these are the sources of increased demand for animal foodstuffs, and the changes in diet have caused imports of wheat and livestock products even in the poorer developing countries.

Second, the concentration of population in the towns has increased the proportion of food that has to be moved and, because of the high cost of transport in many developing countries, has increased the difficulties of supplying food at reasonable prices.

CHANGES IN THE RURAL POPULATION

But perhaps the most significant contribution of urbanization to agriculture has been to reduce, by migration, the growth of the rural and agricultural populations. In the nineteenth century the process of industrialization was accompanied by rural–urban migration, but for much of the nineteenth century the agricultural populations of Europe and the United States continued to increase. At the beginning of this century they began a slow decline as out-migration exceeded natural increase. This process has accelerated since the end of the Second World War and agricultural populations in the developed world have halved (table 4.6; see also pp. 120–2). In the developing countries, in contrast, the agricultural population has increased by 45 per cent, much lower, of course, than the natural increase of the rural areas. The agricultural

Table 4.6　Changes in the agricultural populations of the developing regions, 1950–80

	1950		1980		1950–80	
	Agricultural population[a]	Agricultural labour force[b]	Agricultural population	Agricultural labour force	Agricultural population	Agricultural labour force
	(millions)		(millions)		(% change)	
All developed	255	147	123	66	−52	−55
All developing	1324	529	1920	748	45	41
Africa	173	66	298	101	72	53
Latin America	87	30	125	39	44	30
Asia	1064	433	1497	608	41	40

[a] Those economically active in agriculture and their dependents.
[b] Those economically active in agriculture.

Sources: FAO, The state of Food and Agriculture 1973, Rome, 1973, p. 88; Production Yearbook 1971, vol. 25, 1972; Production Yearbook 1981, vol. 35, 1982.

labour force has increased most in Africa, least in Latin America. Some of this increased labour force has been absorbed in the expansion of the cultivated area (see pp. 90–116), or by more labour intensive methods. But in many areas there has been difficulty in absorbing these extra numbers, and in many parts of the developing world the subdivision of farms and a rise in the number of landless has resulted. Without the migration to the towns these problems would have been even more acute.

INCOME CHANGES AND FOOD CONSUMPTION

If poverty is the major cause of hunger then changes in income and income distribution are at the root of the problems of the developing countries. Thus the progress of economic growth over the last 30 years is of fundamental importance in explaining the persistence and distribution of hunger.

In the 1950s it was thought that population growth would not only reduce food supplies per caput but also prevent any increase in income per caput. Many argued that increases in population would prevent the accumulation of the capital that was necessary for economic growth. In the event this was not so. Gross domestic product (GDP), the value of all goods and services produced in a year, has risen per caput in virtually all of both the industrial countries and those defined by the World Bank as middle income and low income (table 4.7). In the 1950s the rate of increase was greatest in the industrial countries and least in the low income countries, but between 1960 and 1980 the middle income countries were increasing more rapidly than the developed countries. In terms of the major regions, growth has been most rapid in the Middle East, where oil exports have bolstered national incomes, and least in South Asia. By 1980 (figure 4.1) the world pattern of incomes had not radically changed from the pattern of 1950; Japan had, of course, joined the industrial nations, and incomes in the Middle East had greatly risen. But the contrast between the developed countries – North America, Europe, the USSR and Australasia – and the developing countries persists, and indeed, some would argue, the gap between them has widened. But perhaps the most notable change has been increasing divergence between the income levels of the various developing countries. Latin American GDP per caput has always been above that of Africa and Asia, but the growth of oil exports, the successful development of manufacturing in countries such as Mexico, Brazil, Korea, Taiwan, Hong Kong and Singapore has widened the gap in income levels between various countries in the developing world.

Table 4.7   Changes in gross domestic product

World (excluding centrally planned economies) 1950–80

	GDP per caput (1980 US $)			Average annual rate of growth (%)	
	1950	1960	1980	1950–60	1960–80
Industrialized countries	3841	5197	9684	3.1	3.2
Middle income countries	625	802	1521	2.5	3.3
Low income countries	164	174	245	0.6	1.7

Source: World Bank, *World Development Report 1980*, Washington DC, 1980, p. 35

Regions 1950–75

	GDP per caput (1974 US $)		Annual growth rate 1950–75 (% p.a.)
	1950	1975	
South Asia	85	132	1.7
Africa	170	308	2.4
Latin America	495	944	2.6
East Asia	130	341	3.9
China	113	320	4.2
Middle East	460	1660	5.2
All developing	160	375	3.4

Source: D. Morawetz, *Twenty Five Years of Economic Development 1950 to 1975*, Baltimore, 1977, p. 13

However, although all parts of the developing world have experienced growth in national income per caput, poverty remains. Since the early 1970s much attention has been paid to income distribution and absolute poverty. [12] There is little doubt that incomes are inequitably distributed not merely in the developing countries, but also in the developed. Thus in 1970 it was estimated that the poorest 40 per cent of the population received in the centrally planned industrial economies 25 per cent of the total income, in the industrial market economies 16 per cent and in the developing countries 12.5 per cent. [13] Some writers have argued that increasing inequality is an inevitable feature of economic growth – at least in the early stages. Thus much attention has been paid to the introduction of new farming methods in South Asia since 1965 (see

[12] I. Adelman and C. T. Morris, *Economic Growth and Social Equality in Developing Countries*, Stanford, 1973; H. Chenery, M. S. Ahluwalia, C. L. G. Bell, J. H. Duby and R. Jolly, *Redistribution with Growth*, Oxford, 1974.

[13] World Bank, *World Development Report 1981*, Washington DC, 1981, pp. 134–5.

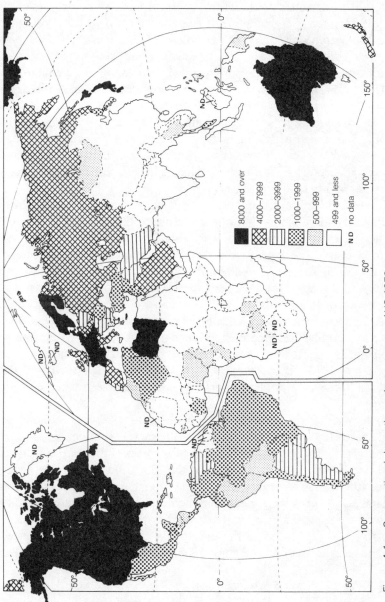

8000 and over
4000–7999
2000–3999
1000–1999
500–999
499 and less
ND no data

Figure 4.1 Gross national domestic product per caput, $US 1979
Source: World Bank, World Bank Development Report 1981, Washington DC, 1981

pp. 222–4). It has been argued that only the larger farmers can afford fertilizers and tractors, and that they have increased their incomes more rapidly than small farmers, while some small farmers have lost their land and become labourers. In their turn, landless labourers have their incomes reduced as machinery makes them redundant. Similar arguments have been put forward to account for continuing rural poverty in Latin America, where the adoption of modern farming methods on large farms has increased aggregate incomes and productivity but also increased inequality. Some have argued that the lowest income groups have had an absolute decline in incomes. Similar arguments have been put forward to account for growing inequality in urban populations, where manufacturing industry is dominated by large capitalist enterprises that use labour saving machinery. [14]

Some would argue that the evidence on increasing income inequalities is unsatisfactory, others that it is irrelevant to the problem of hunger. If the real incomes of the poor are rising then food consumption will increase even if the gap between the poorest and the richest is increasing. Hence there have been attempts to measure the extent of absolute poverty. Such attempts have tried to measure either the numbers and proportion of the population with less than a defined income or, more recently, those lacking an adequate diet and minimum levels of housing, education and health. One such estimate (table 4.8) suggests that about 1100 million people were without basic needs in the developing countries in the late 1970s; this compares with a World Bank estimate of 780 million living in absolute poverty in 1980. Both estimates exclude China. [15]

As to whether the numbers living in absolute poverty or without the basic needs has increased over the last 30 years, it is impossible to say. Nmerous studies have suggested that the incomes of the poorest sections of society were in absolute decline in the 1960s and early 1970s; many other studies, however, claim that the proportion of the population in the lowest category were increasing their real incomes. These extremes may be highlighted by noting that according to one authority only one-third of the population of the developing countries has experienced any increase in real income since 1960, whereas according to another

[14] K. Griffin, *The Political Economy of Agrarian Change*, Oxford, 1974; A. de Janvry, *The Agrarian Question and Reformism in Latin America*, Baltimore, 1981; International Labour Office, *Poverty and Landlessness in Rural Asia*, Geneva, 1977.

[15] World Bank, *World Development Report 1980*, Washington DC, 1980, pp. 33–62; M. S. Ahluwalia, N. G. Carter and H. B. Chenery, 'Growth and poverty in developing countries', *Journal of Development Economics*, 6, 1979, pp. 299–345; P. Streeten, *First Things First: Meeting Basic Human Needs in Developing Countries*, Oxford, 1980.

two-thirds have benefitted. [16] An attempt has been made to estimate the numbers of the developing world with an income of less than $200 per annum; these data include China. The figures based on gross domestic product suggest a decline in the numbers in poverty since 1960 (table 4.9), but those using consumption expenditure data show an increase of 300 million between 1950 and 1977. In both cases the proportion has declined.

Table 4.8   Population lacking basic needs

	1974		1982[c]	
	(millions)	*(% of total population)*	*(millions)*	*(% of total population)*
Latin America	94	30.6	86	23.2
Near East[a]	40	26.0	36	18.0
Asia[b]	759	53.0	788	60.0
Tropical Africa	205	67.6	210	54.0
All developing	1098	56.0	1120	47.0

[a] Middle East and African oil exporters.
[b] Excluding China.
[c] Figures are a projection from 1974 data.
Source: M. J. D. Hopkins, 'A global forecast of absolute poverty and employment', *International Labour Review*, **119**, 1980, pp. 565–79

Table 4.9   Numbers (millions) with an income of less than US $200

	1950	1960	1970	1972	1977
Gross domestic product data					
	1178	1249	1226	1177	1043
Consumption expenditure data					
	1297	1478	—	—	1666

Source: A. Berry, F. Bourguignon and C. Morrison, 'Changes in the world distribution of income between 1950 and 1977', *Economic Journal*, **93**, 1983, pp. 331–50

CONCLUSIONS

The great increase in population between 1950 and 1980 has not prevented an increase in world food output per caput; nor has it

[16] C. H. Wood and J. A. M. de Carvaltio, 'Population growth and the distribution of household income: the case of Brazil', *Sociological Quarterly*, **23**, 1982, pp. 49–65; D. Morawetz, *Twenty Five Years of Economic Development, 1950–1975*, Baltimore, 1977.

prevented a substantial increase in per caput national incomes, since 1950, in nearly all the developing nations. But economic growth has not, of course, eliminated poverty, although it has probably reduced the proportion of the world's population (but not the numbers) with very low incomes. There is no doubt that at any one time the principal reason for hunger is poverty, although the extent of poverty, like the extent of hunger, is difficult to define, and changes over time are equally difficult to determine.

5

The Growth of World Food Output

In the immediate aftermath of the Second World War many writers believed not only that there would be very rapid population growth in the forthcoming decades but also that there was little prospect of any substantial increase in agricultural output. It was argued that most of the world's good land was already in cultivation, and any further colonization of new land would only be at prohibitive cost; that crop yields in Western Europe were already high and could not be greatly increased; and that farmers in the developing countries were primarily subsistence farmers, unresponsive to market forces and unlikely to increase their very low crop yields.[1] Much the same gloomy prophecies about world agriculture had been made in earlier times and indeed are currently being made.[2] Before considering how food production has increased in the last 40 years it may be useful to look briefly at food production in the past.

THE TREND IN FOOD PRODUCTION BEFORE 1950

Little is known of the trends in agricultural production before the eighteenth century; the evidence from tithe returns in Europe suggests that food production followed the course of population growth, with

[1] G. B. Cressey, 'Land for 2.4 billion neighbours', *Economic Geography*, **29**, 1953, pp. 1–9; R. M. Salter, 'World soil and fertilizer needs in relation to food needs', *Science*, **105**, 1947, pp. 533–8.
[2] Sir W. Crookes, *The Wheat Problem*, London, 1899; G. C. Anderson, 'An agricultural view of the world population – food crisis', *Journal of Soil and Water Conservation*, **27**, 1972, pp. 52–6; L. R. Brown and E. P. Eckholm, *By Bread Alone*, London, 1975.

output per head rising for brief periods and for other periods falling.[3] In the eighteenth century food output began a steady and continuous increase, and it is this period that has been described as one of agricultural revolution. Even so estimates of the rate of increase suggest that growth was slow; in England and France agricultural output rose at about 0.5 per cent per annum, and so did little more than keep pace with population growth.[4]

In the nineteenth century output grew more rapidly. England and France had rates of growth over the whole century which exceeded 1 per cent per annum, but output rose more rapidly in the first half of the century than in the second half; this contrast was particularly marked in Britain, where output rose very little between the 1860s and the 1930s. In Germany output rose at 1.3 per cent per annum between 1800 and 1883. In parts of Eastern Europe the end of feudalism and the extinction of open field and common land did not occur until the mid nineteenth century and was followed by rapid growth – between 1 and 2 per cent in Silesia and Hungary. In the European settled areas overseas the rates of increase were greater than in Western Europe, for much fertile land was brought rapidly into cultivation. In the United States the rate of increase fell below 2 per cent per annum in only two decades, and exceeded 4 per cent in the 1870s. The first half of the twentieth century saw varying rates of growth in agricultural output; in Britain in the 1920s and 1930s output fell, and the depression of the inter-war period retarded the growth of output in other countries.[5]

There are few estimates of the growth of food output in Africa, Asia and Latin America before 1950, for there were few agricultural censuses. There was undoubtedly a rapid development of agricultural output

[3] E. Le Roy Ladurie and J. Goy, *Tithe and Agrarian History from the Fourteenth to the Nineteenth Century*, Cambridge, 1982.

[4] B. H. Slicher van Bath, 'Agriculture in the vital revolution', in C. H. Wilson and E. E. Rich (eds), *Cambridge Economic History of Europe. Volume 4: The Economic Organization of Early Modern Europe*, Cambridge, 1977; P. Deane and W. A. Cole, *British Economic Growth, 1688–1959*, Cambridge, 1962, pp. 65, 78; J. C. Toutain, *Le Produit de l'Agriculture Français*, vol. 1, Paris, 1961, pp. 213–15.

[5] Toutain, *op. cit.*, vol. 2, pp. 127–9; Deane and Cole, *op. cit.*, p. 170; T. W. Fletcher, 'Drescher's index: a comment', *Manchester School of Economic and Social Studies*, **23**, 1955, p. 181; W. R. Lee, 'Primary sector output and mortality changes in early XIXth century Bavaria', *Journal of European Economic History*, **6**, 1977, pp. 155–62; M. R. Haines, 'Agriculture and development in Prussian Upper Silesia, 1846–1913', *Journal of Economic History*, **42**, 1982, pp. 355–84; M. Towne and W. D. Rasmussen, 'Farm gross product and gross investment in the nineteenth century', in National Bureau of Economic Research, *Trends in the American Economy in the Nineteenth Century. Studies in Income and Wealth, volume 24*, Princeton, New Jersey, 1960, p. 260.

in Latin America, Africa and parts of South East Asia between the 1870s and the 1930s, but most of this was of crops for export to Europe and the United States. Paul Bairoch has estimated that the output of export crops grew at 2.6 per cent per annum in the late nineteenth century and at over 3.5 per cent between 1900 and 1940. The few estimates of food output suggest much slower growth – notably in India and China – and in the developing countries as a whole food output probably grew more slowly than population.[6]

MEASURING FOOD OUTPUT SINCE 1950

There are two ways of estimating the growth in the volume of food output since 1950. First, estimates of the area in arable land and in the major food crops have been collected and published by the Food and Agriculture Organization of the United Nations both for the major regions and for individual countries. Combined with estimates of crop yields these can give some indication of changes in crop production. Second, indices of agricultural and food output have been prepared and published by FAO since the early 1950s.

Changes in land use and crop yields

Between 1950 and 1980 the world's arable area increased by 16 per cent, and at much the same rate in the developed and developing regions (table 5.1). Within the developed regions, however, the area in arable declined in Europe and showed only a small addition in North America; most of the increase was attributable to the expansion of cultivation in the USSR in the 1950s and to a continuous but smaller growth in Australia. In the developing countries there were substantial absolute and proportional increases in Latin America and Asia, but an apparent decline in Africa. But this demonstrates the limitations of the statistics. Arable land includes not only annual crops such as wheat and permanent crops such as tea or cocoa, but also grass sown for five years or less and fallow. Fallow land is defined as land used for crops but not necessarily in crops every year. It can thus include a variety of different types of fallow. In many semi-arid regions cereals are only sown in alternate years to conserve moisture. In cool temperate areas a cold, late

[6] Paul Bairoch, *The Economic Development of the Third World since 1900*, London, 1975; G. Blyn, *Agricultural Trends in India, 1891–1957: Output, Availability, and Productivity*, Philadelphia, 1966; D. H. Perkins, *Agricultural Development in China, 1368–1968*, Edinburgh, 1969.

Table 5.1 Arable land, 1950–80 (million hectares)

	1950	1955	1961–5	1969–71	1975	1980	Change 1950–80 (million hectares)	(%)
Developed								
Europe	148	151	152	145	143	140	−8	−0.05
USSR	175	220	229	232	232	231	56	32
North America	220	229	222	232	253	234	14	6
Oceania	17	25	35	42	47	46	29	171
Total developed	560	625	638	651	675	651	91	16
Developing								
Latin America	86	102	116	146	154	162	76	88
Asia	348	426	447	443	452	455	107	31
Africa	228	232	190	171	143	145	−83	−36
Total developing	662	760	753	760	749	762	100	15
World	1222	1385	1391	1411	1424	1413	191	16

Sources: FAO, *Production Yearbook 1981*, vol. 35, Rome, 1982, pp. 45–56; *Production Yearbook 1976*, vol. 30, Rome 1977, pp. 45–56; *Production Yearbook 1957*, vol. 11, Rome 1958, pp. 3–7

autumn may prevent sowing, and land is recorded as bare fallow. In some countries such as the United States land may be withdrawn from crops to prevent overproduction, but this idle land is still recorded as arable. Most significant in many parts of the tropics, land is sown to crops for two or three years, then abandoned and colonized by the natural vegetation. This period of natural fallow may last only two or three years or as long as 25 years. In the 1950s and 1960s it was the practice to include such fallow land in statistics of arable, but in the last fifteen years many African countries have ceased to include it in their returns of arable. Hence the apparent decline in the area in arable in that continent (table 5.1).

A more accurate measure of the extension of the land in crops may be obtained from FAO estimates of the land in the major *food* crops; this excludes fallow and the non-food crops which are part of arable land. But there are other problems. Some countries return the area *sown* to crops, others the area *harvested*. More seriously, in some countries land that is double cropped is returned twice, in others only once. The data reveal that the world area in the major food crops increased by 23 per cent between 1950 and 1980 (table 5.2). In the developed world there was decline in Europe and a small increase in North America; most of the developed world's increase came in the Soviet Union in the 1950s. Increases in the developing countries in both absolute and pro-portional terms were much greater, and included a substantial increase, not a decline, in Africa and the area doubled in Latin America.

Information on crop yields is much less reliable; however, estimates of the yield of all cereals, which make up 70–80 per cent of the area of all food crops, are available (table 5.3). These show that the average world yield rose by 82 per cent in the post-war period: somewhat surprisingly yields in the developing countries increased more than in the developed, and most of this increase came after 1965–6.

An indication of the trend in food production since 1950 can be obtained by multiplying the area in the major food crops by yield and comparing 1950 and 1980. Total output rose by 124 per cent, but the increase in the volume of output was greater in the developing countries than in the developed countries (table 5.4).

Independent estimates of cereal area and yields have been made by T. N. Barr (table 5.4b). His figures give a greater increase in the volume of world output 1950–80 – 149 per cent – and, as with the FAO figures, a greater increase in the developing countries than the developed.

Thus the volume of output of the major food crops rose by some 124 per cent 1950–80, and the volume of output of cereals, the main source of food for much of the world, by 149 per cent. Neither figure is an

Table 5.2   Area in major food crops,[a] 1950–80 (million hectares)

	1948–52	1961–5	1969–71	1979–80	Change 1950–80 (million hectares)	(%)
Developed						
North America	124.3	98.1	101.2	126.9	2.6	2.0
Europe	92.2	92.5	88.7	86.3	−5.9	−6.8
USSR	108.5	145.0	137.3	141.8	33.3	30.7
Oceania	6.6	9.9	12.7	17.2	10.6	160.6
Total developed	331.6	345.5	339.9	372.2	40.6	12.2
Developing						
Latin America	43.5	57.5	69.5	86.7	43.2	99.3
Asia	337.7	385.0	375.0	393.0	55.6	16.4
Africa	57.8	80.2	89.9	98.9	41.1	71.1
Total developing	439.0	522.7	534.4	578.6	139.9	31.9
World	770.6	868.2	874.3	950.8	180.5	23.4

[a] Includes all grain crops, potatoes, sweet potatoes, yams, pulses and oilseeds.

Sources: FAO, *Production Yearbook 1981*, vol. 35, Rome, 1982, pp. 93–137; *Production Yearbook 1976*, vol. 30, Rome, 1977, pp. 89–134; *Production Yearbook 1957*, vol. 11, Rome, 1958, pp. 31–2

declara-

on Forum, 220 I Street, NE,
or or The Hunger Project.

Table 5.4   Estimates of the increase in the volume of output, 1948–52 to 1978–80

(a) Total area in major food crops × average yield of cereals[a]

	1948–52			1978–80			Increase 1948–52 to 1978–80 (%)		
	Area (million ha)	Yield (tonnes per ha)	Production (tonnes)	Area (million ha)	Yield (tonnes per ha)	Production (tonnes)	Area	Yield	Production
World	771	1.21	933	951	2.2	2092	23	82	124
Developed	332	1.53	507	372	2.6	967	12	70	91
Developing	439	0.97	425	578	1.9	1086	32	96	155

[a] Food crops other than cereals are assumed to have increased their yields at the same rate as cereals.
Sources: FAO, Production Yearbook 1957, vol. 11, Rome, 1958; Production Yearbook 1967, vol. 21, Rome, 1968; Production Yearbook 1976, vol. 30, Rome, 1977; Production Yearbook 1981, vol. 35, Rome, 1982

(b) Cereal crops only

	1948–52			1979–80			Increase 1948–52 to 1979–80 (%)		
	Area (million ha)	Yield (tonnes per ha)	Production (tonnes)	Area (million ha)	Yield (tonnes per ha)	Production (tonnes)	Area	Yield	Production
World	511	1.13	578	715	2.01	1444	40	78	149
Developed	293	1.29	378	304	2.61	794	4	102	110
Developing	218	0.92	200	411	1.53	650	88	66	225

Sources: T. N. Barr, 'The world food situation and global grain prospects', Science 214, 1981, pp. 1087–95.

Table 5.3   Yield of all cereals, 1950–80 (kilograms per hectare)

	1948–52	1956	1961–2	1965–6	1969–71	1975–6	1979–80	% increase 1950–80
World	1210	1354	1428	1550	1806	1892	2200	82
Developed	1526	1770	2231	2426	2464	3002	2618	71
Developing	967	1162	1080	1091	1463	1375	1883	95
Developing as % of developed	63	66	49	45	60	46	72	—

Sources: FAO, Production Yearbook 1957, vol. 11, Rome, 1958, p. 31; Production Yearbook 1967, vol. 21, Rome, 1968, p. 33; Production Yearbook 1976, vol. 30, Rome, 1977, pp. 89–91; Production Yearbook 1981, vol. 35, Rome, 1982, pp. 93–5

Rates of increase by major regions down to 1976 are shown in table 5.5. These data confirm that output has increased more rapidly in the developing regions, and also that the decline in the rate of increase in output in the 1970s mainly took place in the developed world. Of the developing regions, only Africa had a rate of increase lower in 1971–80 than in 1961–70.

It is clear from the data presented so far in this chapter that food production has not stagnated in the last 30 or 40 years. On the contrary it has increased at far greater rates than in the past. Nor has this increase been confined to the developed countries, where there has been a technological revolution since 1945. Indeed in the developing region as a whole output has increased more rapidly than in the developed world.

CHANGES IN FOOD PRODUCTION PER CAPUT

World food output has at the least doubled since 1950; and only in Africa has there been any serious fall in the rate of increase in output. But of course this praiseworthy achievement by farmers must be set against the very rapid growth in population since 1950. Between 1950 and 1980 the population of the world increased by 76 per cent, significantly *less* than the increase in world food output. J. L. Simon has calculated that world food output per capita in 1976 was 28 per cent above 1950.[9] There is thus no question, at the global scale, of population having outrun food production since 1950.

But of course there has been a fundamental regional difference in the rate of population growth. In the developed world 1950–80 the population increased by only 36 per cent. In contrast, in the same period the population of the developing regions rose by 95 per cent; Latin America increased its population by 124 per cent, Africa by 114 per cent and Asia by 88 per cent (table 4.1). The consequences of this differential population growth are clear. Food output per caput has risen considerably in the developed world, where dramatic food increases have been combined with modest population increases; but in the developing world dramatic increases in food production have been matched by equally dramatic increases in population (figure 5.1). None the less, food production has kept ahead of population growth in the major regions, and in the Near East, the Far East and Latin America food output per caput is some 10–15 per cent above the level of the 1950s (figure 5.2). This has not been so in Africa, however, where the rate of population

[9] J. L. Simon, 'Resources, population, environment: an oversupply of false bad news', *Science*, **208**, 1980, pp. 1431–7.

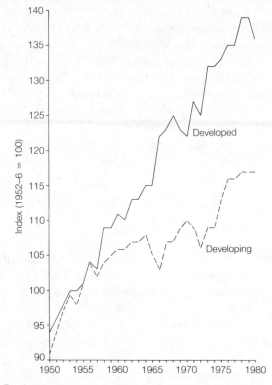

Figure 5.1   Food output per caput, developed and developing regions, 1950–80
Source: FAO, *Production Yearbook 1981*, vol. 35, Rome, 1982; *Production Yearbook 1976*, vol. 30, Rome, 1977; *Production Yearbook 1970*, vol. 24, Rome, 1971

increase in the 1970s was above that of the 1950s and 1960s, but the rate of increase in food production fell considerably. Hence output per caput has been falling since the early 1960s (table 5.5).

The use of indices for major regions may conceal important differences in food production within these regions. Data on food output per caput is available for countries since 1960–5. In a considerable number of countries food output per caput fell in both the 1960s and the 1970s (figure 5.3). Most of these countries are in Africa, but include Bangladesh, Nepal, Afghanistan, Mongolia and Cambodia in Asia, and Haiti, Ecuador and Guyana in Latin America.

Serious as this is, the great bulk of the population of the developing world live in countries where food production has kept ahead of population growth. The countries shown to have had a decline in food output per caput from 1960 to 1980 contained only 13 per cent of the population of Africa, Asia and Latin America in 1980. Rather more – 18 per cent – live in countries where food production per caput fell between 1970 and 1980.

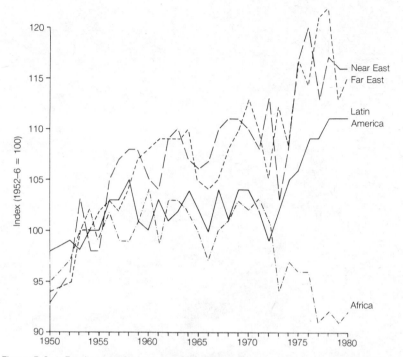

Figure 5.2   Food output per caput, 1950–80, developing regions (excluding China)
Sources: FAO, *Production Yearbook 1970*, vol. 24, Rome, 1971; *Production Yearbook 1981*, vol. 35, Rome, 1982

THE STRUCTURE OF FOOD OUTPUT

In the last 40 years nearly all of Europe's extra food output has come from increased yield per hectare; the area in arable declined in every country in Europe between 1950 and 1980. In contrast most of Latin America's increased output has come from extending the area in cultivation, and yield increases have been less important. Historically the relative importance of yield and area has varied considerably.

There is little reliable information upon trends in land use, yields or output before the nineteenth century, but most of the increase in output probably came from bringing new land into cultivation, for yields were low and showed little increase over time. Thus in most of Europe crop yields increased by no more than 10 per cent between 1500 and 1800. The exception was in England and the Low Countries, where yields increased by one-third or more, mostly after 1600.[10]

[10]   Slicher van Bath, *op. cit.*, p. 81; M. Overton, 'Estimating crop yields from probate inventories; an example from East Anglia, 1585–1735', *Journal of Economic History*, **39**, 1975, pp. 363–78; D. B. Grigg, *The Dynamics of Agricultural Change: The Historical Experience*, London, 1982, pp. 130, 172–5, 184–9.

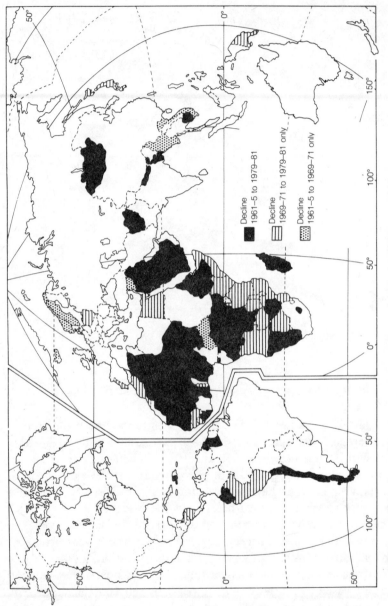

Decline
1961–5 to 1979–81

Decline
1969–71 to 1979–81 only

Decline
1961–5 to 1969–71 only

Figure 5.3   Decline in food output per caput total population in the 1960s and 1970s
Sources: FAO, Production Yearbook 1981, vol. 35, Rome, 1982; Production Yearbook 1976, vol. 30, Rome, 1977

Most historians believe that the later eighteenth and nineteenth centuries saw a marked increase in crop yields, and this period has been described as one of agricultural revolution. Higher yields were obtained by more intensive cultivation to rid the land of weeds, growing legumes such as clover to increase the nitrogen content of the soils, and feeding livestock on roots, hay and oilseeds to increase both their weight and the manure supply. Higher yields were also obtained by growing new crops with a higher calorific output per hectare such as potatoes, sugarbeet and maize.[11] Thus output per hectare in Western Europe rose steadily if not dramatically in the nineteenth century, and continued to increase down to the 1930s (figure 5.4). But this period also saw a continued increase in the area sown to crops. After 1750 rising cereal prices prompted farmers to reclaim land not previously cultivated.

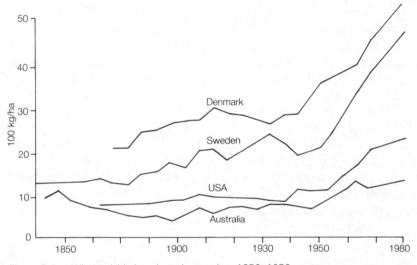

Figure 5.4   Wheat yields in selected countries, 1850–1950
Source: D. B. Grigg, *The Dynamics of Agricultural Change: The Historical Experience*, London, 1982, p. 130

But equally important farmers throughout Western Europe began to sow crops on the fallow. In 1700 about half the arable land in England was in fallow each year, and similar or even larger proportions were to be found elsewhere in Western Europe. By 1900 the fallow had been largely eliminated. Thus although the nineteenth century is normally seen as one of rising yields, the increased area in crops made a major contribution to extra food output. In the heyday of the 'agricultural

[11] G. P. H. Chorley, 'The agricultural revolution in northern Europe, 1750–1880: nitrogen, legumes and crop productivity', *Economic History Review*, **34**, 1981, pp. 71–93.

revolution' in England, between 1750 and 1850, higher yields accounted for only one-third of the increased output, extra area two-thirds. [12] By the end of the nineteenth century most countries in Western Europe had reached their maximum arable area, and there was little change until 1950. Since the 1950s there has been a decline in arable area, but grain yields have doubled. Thus, in Western Europe there has been a progressive increase in the contribution of crop yields to the raising of food production. Before the eighteenth century increased yields made very little contribution, and until the mid nineteenth century colonizing new land and reducing the fallow accounted for a majority of output increase. By the 1980s yield increases were accounting for all but a small proportion of output increases.

The European settlements overseas – Canada, Australia, the United States – together with the Soviet Union have had a very different history, owing largely to their lower population densities. In 1800 Western Europe had a long history of settlement and high population densities, as did parts of northern Russia; but southern Russia, and the west of North America and Australasia, were sparsely populated although containing large areas of fertile land. These lands were settled in the nineteenth century, and it was this addition of new land that accounted for most of their increase in food output. Crop yields showed very little sign of increase in the nineteenth century or indeed in the first 30 or 40 years of this century (figure 5.4), and wheat yields remained well below those in Western Europe. Since the 1930s however crop yields in North America have increased dramatically, and have accounted for most of the increase in food output since 1950. Only in the Soviet Union and Australia have increases in the area sown to crops accounted for much of the increase in output.

YIELD AND AREA EXPANSION IN FOOD OUTPUT
INCREASES SINCE 1950

Numerous statements – often contradictory – have been made about the relative importance of the increases in yield and area in contributing to the growth of food output since 1950. This is partly due to the unreliability of figures in area and yield in the 1950s, and the absence of accurate data on most food crops other than cereals in the developing countries. Yet root crops form an important part of food output in

[12] G. E. Mingay, *The Agricultural Revolution: Changes in Agriculture 1650–1880*, London, 1977; D. Grigg, *op. cit.*, p. 187.

Africa and, to a lesser extent, in Latin America and Asia. Table 5.6 shows the relative importance of yields and area in contributing to the increased output of cereals between 1950 and 1980. Although cereal crops contribute a substantial part of the world's crop output, these figures probably understate the importance of area increase. First, they do not include other food crops; second, cereal crops have had greater increases in yield than other food crops since 1950. None the less they provide an approximate guide to events between 1950 and 1980.

Table 5.6   Relative contribution of yield and area to increases in world cereal output, 1950–80 (percentages)

	1950–60		1960–70		1970–80		1950–80	
	Area	Yield	Area	Yield	Area	Yield	Area	Yield
Developed	−2	102	−5	105	42	58	3	97
Developing	82	18	25	75	16	84	40	60
World	56	44	12	88	25	75	15	85

Source: T. N. Barr, 'The world food situation and global grain prospects', *Science*, **214**, 1981, pp. 1087–95

First, it can be seen that increases in yield have accounted for more than four-fifths of the world increase in cereal production since 1950. In the 1950s the contribution of area expansion was greater, and has since declined. Second, in the developed countries yield increases have been of overwhelming importance, although in the 1970s some of the additional output did come from area increases, mainly in the United States (see p. 120). In the developing countries, on the other hand, some 40 per cent of all increased cereal output 1950–80 came from bringing new land into cultivation; yield increases, however, have grown progressively more important since 1950.

There have been important regional variations in the contributions of area expansion to the growth of cereal output over the last 20 years (table 5.7). In the developing world increases in the cultivated area have been of most importance in Latin America and Africa, both comparatively sparsely populated and said to contain large reserves of cultivable land. In contrast in South Asia and the Middle East most production increases have come from yield increases. But, as noted earlier, these figures probably understate the importance of area expansion. Thus it has been estimated that area expansion accounted for two-thirds of the increase in agricultural output in Latin America between 1950 and 1980;

Table 5.7   Cereal production increases due to area expansion and yield increase, 1961–2 to 1979–80, by major regions (percentages)

	Area	Yield
Developing		
Latin America	54	46
Africa	52	48
East Asia	48	52
South Asia	27	73
Middle East	20	80
Total developing	23	77
Developed		
United States	19	81
Oceania	13	87
Soviet Union	4	96
Western Europe	0	100
Eastern Europe	−21	121
Total developed	14	86
World	19	81

Source: T. N. Barr, 'The world food situation and global grain prospects', *Science*, **214**, 1981, pp.1087–95

most authorities believe that there has been little increase in crop yields in Africa and that the expansion of the cultivated area has accounted for most of the extra food output over the last 30 years.[13]

CONCLUSIONS

It has been shown in this chapter that there have been considerable increases in food output in the world since 1950 – output at least doubled – and that the rate of increase has been higher in the developing than the developed countries. However, the much higher rates of population growth in the developing world have meant that there has been comparatively little increase in output per caput; food production has just kept ahead of population growth. In some countries – mainly in Africa – there has been a decline in output per head over the last

[13] World Bank, *Accelerated Development in Sub-Saharan Africa: An Agenda for Action*, Washington DC, 1981; C. Christensen, *et al.*, *Food Problems and Prospects in Sub-Saharan Africa: The Decade of the 1980s*, International Economics Division, Economic Research Service, United States Department of Agriculture, Washington DC, 1981; FAO, *The State of Food and Agriculture 1978*, Rome, 1979, pp. 2–32.

20 years. Hence the great regional differences in per caput consumption already apparent in the 1930s and 1948–52 (see pp. 45, 49) have been perpetuated.

Until the middle of the nineteenth century much of the increased food output required by slow population growth came from colonizing new land or, particularly after 1600, by reducing the fallow area. From the middle of the nineteenth century, however, crop yields began to increase more rapidly and in Western Europe have accounted for nearly all the increased food output since 1950. In the developing countries area expansion has continued to be an important source of extra food production, particularly in Africa and Latin America, but since the mid 1960s much of the extra food in these regions has come from higher yields.

The following five chapters examine in more detail how food output has been increased 1950–80. Chapter 6 reviews the expansion of the cultivated area in different parts of the world; chapters 7 to 10 look at the expansion of food production in the developed world and in Africa, Latin America and Asia.

6

The Expansion of the World's Arable Land

It was not until the middle of the nineteenth century that increases in crop yields began to contribute a significant proportion of the increases in food production. Before then in Europe and Asia the expansion of the arable area was the prime response to the slow rise in the population. The more rapid increases in population in the nineteenth century led to not only higher crop yields but also the need for food imports. Europe's arable area stagnated from the late nineteenth century until the 1940s and then began to decline. Most of the food imports into Europe came from the European settled areas overseas and from southern Russia. Between the middle of the nineteenth century and the Second World War there was a remarkable increase in the area in cropland in these countries, particularly in the United States and Russia. Over 200 million hectares of cropland came into cultivation between 1860 and the 1930s (table 6.1).

Estimates of the area in arable in the developing world before this century, or indeed before the 1950s, are unreliable. Nevertheless those estimates that are available suggest a steady expansion of the area in crops in Japan, China, India and Java; furthermore arable expansion probably kept up with population growth until the late nineteenth century, since when there has been a decline in arable per caput in all but India (table 6.2).

The world's arable area may have increased by two-thirds or more in the period between 1870 and 1950.[1] By the latter date most of the world's good land seemed to be in cultivation, and few writers believed there were large areas left for farmer to colonize. Yet since 1950 the

[1] D. Grigg, 'The growth and distribution of the world's arable land, 1870–1970', *Geography*, **59**, 1974, 104–10.

arable area has increased by 16 per cent and the area in the major food crops by 23 per cent (tables 5.1 and 5.2), some 220 million hectares, equivalent to the area added in the overseas European settlements between 1870 and 1940 (table 6.1).

Table 6.1   The expansion of cropland in areas of recent settlement

	1860	1880	1900	1920	1930	1960
United States	65.8	75.9	128.8	162.4	166.8	158.3
Russia	49.2	102.6	113.3	—	109.4	195.9
Canada	—	6.06	8.4	20.2	23.4	25.0
Argentina	—	—	5.6	—	24.2	22.0
Australia	0.4	1.6	3.2	6.0	10.1	11.7

Source: D. B. Grigg, *The Agricultural Systems of the World: An Evolutionary Approach*, Cambridge, 1974, p. 262

THE POTENTIAL ARABLE AREA

Much of the new land settled after 1860 was very fertile, particularly in the United States corn belt and the Russian chernozem zone. Once these areas had been brought into cultivation it was thought that there was little good land left. However it has always proved remarkably difficult to predict the supplies of potential arable land. Unused land can be classified on the basis of its physical characteristics. Some land, such as the permafrost areas of North America or northern Eurasia, is unlikely ever to be used for crops; nor are desert areas without access to irrigation water, or the steep slopes of much of the world's mountains. The cultivation of the rest depends upon factors that are difficult to predict, such as future technology, food prices and production costs.

Not surprisingly, estimates of the potential arable area vary greatly (table 6.3). Thus Pearson and Harper estimated in 1945 that the area suitable for food crops was only 1048 million hectares, which was less than the area then under arable. At the other extreme C. B. Fawcett and L. D. Stamp put the potential arable at over 4000 million hectares, three times the present arable area. Most estimates of the potential arable have been made by calculating the areas too dry, too cold, too steep and with infertile soils and by assuming that the residual could be cultivated. Two recent estimates, however – those of the President's Advisory Committee and of P. Buringh and a group of Dutch agronomists – have built up their world estimates from a consideration of small regions based on soil and climatic characteristics. Their estimates are remarkably similar: they argue that about 3200 million hectares could

Table 6.2   The arable area and arable land per caput of the total population, selected Asian countries

	Japan		China		All India		Java	
	Arable area (ha)	Arable per caput (ha)	Arable (million ha)	Arable per caput (ha)	Arable (million ha)	Arable per caput (ha)	Arable (million ha)	Arable per caput (ha)
1600	2.1	0.12	33.5	0.21	46.4	0.37	—	—
1800	3.0	0.12	63.4	0.23	—	—	1.5	0.3
1870	3.5	0.12	81.6	0.23	—	—	—	—
1900	5.4	0.12	91.7	0.21	79.5	0.28	6.6	0.23
1920	5.9	0.11	—	—	—	—	8.0	0.23
1930	6.0	0.09	98.9	0.19	83.2	0.21	8.4	0.2
1960	5.7	0.06	113.1	0.17	151.5	0.26	8.8	0.14

Source: D. B. Grigg, The Agricultural Systems of the World: An Evolutionary Approach, Cambridge, 1974, pp. 84, 92, 96, 100, 261.

Table 6.3   Estimates of the potential arable area (million hectares)

	(a) Total land	(b) Potential arable	(c) Arable in use	(d) Additional arable	(e) (b) as % of (a)	(f) (d) as % of (c)
Fawcett, 1930	14,510	4404	—	—	29	—
Alsberg, 1937	14,510	2591	1424–1554	1037–1167	18	67–80
Pearson and Harper, 1945[a]	14,450	1048	619	429	7	69
Baker, 1947	13,470[b]	1554	1036	518	12	50
Salter, 1947	14,500	1994	1015–1450[c]	526	14	36–52
Kellog, 1951	—	1615	1012	603	—	59
Stamp, 1952	14,454	4084	1214–1619	2465–2870	28	152–236
Prasslov and Rasov, 1950	14,500	3700	1384[d]	2316	26	167
Orvedal, 1958	14,812	4027	1384	2643	27	190
President's Committee, 1967	13,150[b]	3187	1386	1801	24	130
Buringh et al., 1974	13,530[b]	3220	1413	1807	24	128
Gerasimov, 1983	13,339	2678	1427	1251	20	88

[a] Food crops only.

[b] Excluding polar regions.

[c] Salter's figure for land in arable is 7–10 per cent of land surface, for which he gives no estimate but appears to follow Prasslov and Rasov.

[d] Prasslov and Rasov's estimate of arable land was 783 million hectares; 1384 million ha is the FAO estimate for 1950.

Sources: C. B. Fawcett, 'The extent of the cultivable land', Geographical Journal, 76, 1930, pp. 504–9; C. Alsberg, 'The food supply in the migration process', in I. Bowman (ed.), Limits of Land Settlement, Washington DC, 1937, pp. 25–6; F. A. Pearson and F. A. Harper, The World's Hunger, New York, 1945; O. E. Baker, 'The population prospect in relation to the world's agricultural resources' Journal of Geography, 46, 1947, pp. 203–20; R. M. Salter, 'World soil and fertiliser resources in relation to food needs', Science, 105, 1947, pp. 533–8; C. Kellog, Food, Soil and People, 1951; L. D. Stamp, Land for Tomorrow, 1952; Prasslov and Rasov quoted in L. D. Stamp, Our Developing World, 1960, pp. 63–4; A. C. Orvedal quoted in United States Department of Agriculture, Yearbook for 1964, Farmers World, Washington DC, 1965, pp. 62–3; President's Science Advisory Committee, The World Food Problem, vol. 2, Washington DC, 1967, p. 433; P. Buringh, H. D. J. Van Heemst and G. J. Staring, Computation of the Absolute Maximum Food Production of the World, Wageningen, 1975; P. Gerasimov, 'Land resources of the world, their use and reserves', Geoforum, 14, 1983, pp. 427–39

be used to grow crops, one-quarter of the world's land area; as some 1400 million hectares are in use, 1800 million hectares remain to be cultivated.

Of the 1800 million hectares that remain to be brought into cultivation according to the Pesident's Science Advisory Committee (table 6.4), just over one-quarter are in the developed world and 71 per cent in the developing countries. Of the former, Europe has very little potential, North America the most. In the developing regions Asia has little potential, indeed only one-fifth more than the present arable area. Thus nine-tenths of the potential arable in the developing regions – and two-thirds of the world's total – lie in the tropical regions of Africa and South America, in the rain forest and savannah zones of those two continents.

Table 6.4   Arable land and potential arable land, 1967

	(a) Total area	(b) Potential arable area	(c) Arable in use	(d) Additional arable (b) − (c)	(e) Potential arable as % of total area	(f) Additional land as % of arable in use (d) as % of (c)
Developing						
Africa	3,019	732	158	574	24.2	363
Asia	2,735	627	518	109	22.9	21
South America	1,752	679	77	602	38.8	781
Total developing	7,506	2038	753	1285	27.2	170
Developed						
Europe	478	174	153	21	36.4	14
Australia	822	154	16	138	18.7	862
North America	2,110	456	238	227	22.0	95
USSR	2,234	356	226	130	15.9	58
Total developed	5,644	1149	633	516	20.4	82
Total	13,150	3187	1386	1801	24.2	130

Source: President's Science Advisory Committee, *The World Food Problem*, vol. 2, Washington DC, 1967, p. 434

Although the world – in particular the tropical regions of Africa and Latin America – apparently has large reserves of future cropland, two caveats must be made. First, although only 11 per cent of the land area of the earth is used for crops, some 24 per cent is used for grazing livestock; the latter area corresponds very closely to the areas of potential but unused arable land. The conversion of these areas to crops would of course result in a net gain in food output, but not quite as large a gain as might be initially supposed. Second, although considerable parts of the rain forest and the savannah areas of Latin America and, especially, Africa are already in cultivation, these regions do present technical problems not yet resolved.[2]

THE DISTRIBUTION OF ARABLE LAND, 1980

In view of the great concern over world food supplies, it is somewhat surprising to find that only 11.2 per cent of the world's land area is used for arable, and not all that is used for crops every year. Although some arable land is found in nearly all parts of the globe, there are four great zones which contain 70 per cent of the world total (table 6.5). The first is in North America, mainly west of the Appalachians, and reaching north into the Canadian prairies (figure 6.1). The northward extension of this zone is limited by the shortness of the growing season,

Table 6.5   Arable land, 1980

	Million hectares	As a % of land area	As a % of world arable	Hectares per caput total population
Developed				
North America	235	12.8	16.1	0.94
Western Europe	95	25.4	6.5	0.26
Australasia	45	5.7	3.1	2.5
USSR and Eastern Europe	278	11.9	19.0	0.74
Japan	5	13.5	0.3	0.04
Total developed	658	12.3	45.0	0.6
Developing				
Africa	164	6.7	11.2	0.4
Latin America	162	8.0	11.1	0.45
Near East	87	7.3	5.9	0.41
Far East	268	33.1	18.3	0.22
Asian CPE[a]	112	9.7	7.7	0.10
Other developing	12	13.6	0.8	2.3
Total developing	805	10.4	55	0.24
World	1463	11.2	100	0.33

[a] CPE: centrally planned economies.
Source: FAO, *Production Yearbook 1981*, vol. 35, Rome, 1982

[2] D. H. Jansen, 'Tropical agroecosystems', *Science*, **183**, 1212–19; Jen-Hu Chang, 'The agricultural potential of the humid tropics', *Geographical Review*, **58**, 1968, 33–61.

Figure 6.1   The world distribution of arable land
Source: The Times Atlas of the World, London, 1968, pp. xxvi–xxvii

westwards by low and variable rainfall, although the extension of irrigation in the west in the last 40 years has been important. Most of this area has been settled only since 1800; crop yields are low when compared with Western Europe but output per head of the workforce is high.

Second is the great zone stretching from Ireland to the Urals and beyond; it includes nearly one-quarter of the world's arable land compared with 16 per cent in North America, but supports a far greater population. To the north cold winters and short growing seasons preclude cultivation, and the considerable upland areas are used mainly for grass rather than crops. Most of the region has a long history of agricultural settlement; the great frontier area of the chernozem soils of southern Russia has been occupied from the late eighteenth century onwards, and the semi-arid region east of the Urals has been brought into cultivation in the 1950s. There is a marked difference between west and east. In Eastern Europe and the Soviet Union there is three-quarters of a hectare of arable per head of the total population, not far short of the one hectare in North America, but in Western Europe there is only one-quarter of a hectare, little more than that available in the Far East.

In the developing world the two great zones are the Indian subcontinent and China; both areas have very long histories of settlement and both have high population densities, so that there is very little arable land per caput. In Africa and Latin America there are no great continuous zones of cropland as in the four regions described, but they are both apparently well endowed with arable land, containing together one-fifth of the world's arable land and with nearly one-half of a hectare per caput. But as will be seen, much of this arable land is infrequently cropped (see pp. 98–9).

Although Western Europe and Japan have very low supplies of arable land per caput, the developed world as a whole has 45 per cent of the world's arable land but only one-quarter of the population. This is a major, obvious, but neglected factor in accounting for the world distribution of food supplies.

THE EXPANSION OF THE ARABLE AREA, 1950–80

Earlier it was noted that the world's arable area had increased by 16 per cent between 1950 and 1980 and the area in the major food crops by 23 per cent; and that this increase had been greatest in Latin America, where the area in food crops had doubled, and least in Asia, where it rose by only 16 per cent (table 5.2). These figures almost certainly understate the actual expansion of the area in crops.

There are three ways in which the area in crops can be increased. The first is the *reduction of the fallow*. As noted earlier, many farming systems, notably in Africa and Latin America, have a period of natural fallow in which soil fertility is restored under the natural vegetation. In the last 30 or 40 years the length of the fallow period has been shortened and the period in crops has increased, much as it was in Western Europe between 1650 and 1900. Second, in most European farming systems only one crop can be grown in a year; the growing season is generally too short for more than one staple food crop. However, in much of the tropics it is possible to grow two major crops one after the other in one year. The increase of *multiple cropping* has probably been of considerable importance in increasing the area sown to crops in Asia since 1950. Third, land hitherto unused, *new land*, has been colonized in many parts of the world since 1950, although often at the expense of grazing land. Last, it should be noted that these considerable increases in the area sown to crops have not been a complete net gain, for there has been a loss of cropland to urban expansion, soil erosion and salinity.

The reduction of fallow

In the eighteenth and nineteenth centuries the fallow in Europe was drastically reduced. Sown with potatoes and sugar beet it directly increased food output; sown with clover and fodder roots it increased the weight and number of livestock and the supply of manure. But in the developing world much of the arable area is still in fallow. In the 1960s it was estimated that only 56 per cent of the arable land in North Africa and the Middle East was sown to crops in any one year: rainfed cereals need a fallow between crops to conserve soil moisture, and in much of the irrigated area salinity and waterlogging requires land to be temporarily withdrawn from cultivation.[3] In tropical Africa much of the arable is still farmed by shifting agriculture and bush fallowing: land is sown to crops for two or three years and then abandoned to the natural vegetation for periods from three to 30 years. If the period of regeneration is long enough – it varies according to the climate and type of vegetation – soil fertility is restored and the land may be cropped again. Throughout tropical Africa rising population densities have caused

---

[3] FAO, *Provisional Indicative World Plan for Agricultural Development*, vol. 1, 1970, p. 45.

the reduction of the fallow and an increase in the area in crops. However, if no alternative means of maintaining soil fertility – such as growing leguminous crops or the use of manure or chemical fertilizers – is adopted, soil fertility will decline, and eventually soil erosion may cause the land to be abandoned. There is no doubt that this process of fallow reduction has occurred, has increased the area in crops, and in some cases has led to the degradation and destruction of land, but there are no reliable comprehensive statistics (see pp. 143–7). In the 1960s, however, only 42 per cent of the arable of tropical Africa was thought to be in crops.[4] In Latin America considerable areas are to be found in natural fallow and much the same process of fallow reduction and later degradation has occurred. There are also areas of grain production in semi-arid zones where fallowing is practised, and the irrigated areas, as in the Middle East, are underutilized. Only half Mexico's considerable irrigated area is cropped in any one year. In the 1960s it was estimated that only 54 per cent of Latin America's arable was sown to crops. In Asia, in contrast, 100 per cent of the cropland was sown each year. But this was an average reflecting very great regional variations. In the sparsely settled forest areas of Borneo or the interior of South East Asia shifting cultivation is still to be found, where fallows may last for 25 years. In contrast, in many parts of China, the Indian deltas and plains, and Java and the Philippines, much of the land carries two grain crops in a year.[5]

Much of the world's arable still lies in fallow each year – one-third in the 1970s according to P. Buringh[6] – but the fallow has been continuously reduced in the post-war period as population and the need for extra food has grown. Unfortunately there is no way of estimating the extra area sown to crops, or lost through soil erosion.

Multiple cropping

In most cool, temperate regions the length of the winter precludes the growth of more than one staple food crop, although several vegetable crops may be possible. However, in the subtropics and tropics temperatures are high enough for crop growth throughout the year provided moisture, from rainfall or irrigation, is available; hence two or even three cereal crops can be sown and harvested in a year. Multiple cropping

---

[4] FAO, *op. cit.*, p. 44.
[5] D. J. Fox, 'Mexico', in H. Blakemore and C. T. Smith (eds), *Latin America: Geographical Perspectives*, London, 1983, p. 41; FAO, *op. cit.*, pp. 44–5.
[6] P. Buringh, 'Food production potential of the world', in R. Sinha (ed.), *The World Food Problem*, London, 1978, pp. 477–85.

has been practised in Egypt and parts of Asia for a very long period, and its extension is an important method of increasing the harvested area and total food output. It is however difficult to establish with any accuracy the proportion of the world's arable that is multicropped or the extent to which it increased between 1950 and 1980. D. G. Dalrymple's survey suggests that about 93 million hectares were multicropped in c. 1965, 6.7 per cent of the world area then under arable (table 6.6). Most of the area multicropped was in Asia and China and India had by far the largest areas. In Latin America some multiple cropping is found in the densely populated areas in the uplands of central America and the Andes; it was practised on some of the irrigated areas of Mexico (but only 3 per cent of the total arable), the oases of the Peruvian coast and the interior of Argentina. In Africa multiple cropping is rare except in the irrigated areas of Egypt and the Sudan and some of the irrigation schemes of the savannah areas of West Africa.[7]

Table 6.6   Estimates of arable area multiple cropped, c. 1965

	Million hectares	Index of cropping
China	51.4	147
India	20.2	115
Bangladesh	3.4	139
Philippines	2.0	136
Egypt	1.8	173
Java	1.6	120
Japan	1.5	126
Pakistan	1.2	108
South Korea	1.2	153
North Vietnam	0.8	147
Burma	0.8	111

Source: D. Dalrymple, *Survey of Multiple Cropping in Less Developed Nations*, Foreign Economic Development Service, US Department of Agriculture, Washington DC, 1971

It is in Asia that multiple cropping is most common, although there are great variations in the intensity. This is normally measured by expressing the area harvested in a year as a percentage of the arable area, or of the net sown area (table 6.6). In Thailand only 1 per cent of the arable area is sown twice to crops in a year; in contrast the index

[7] D. G. Dalrymple, *Survey of Multiple Cropping in Less Developed Nations*, Foreign Economic Development Service, US Department of Agriculture, Washington DC, 1971; D. J. Andrews and A. H. Kassav, 'The importance of multiple cropping in increasing world food supplies', in R. I. Papendick, P. A. Sanchez, G. B. Triplett (eds), *Multiple Cropping*, American Society of Agronomy Special Publication no. 27, Madison, Wisconsin, 1976, pp. 1–10; Fox, *op. cit.*

of multiple cropping had reached 188 in Egypt in 1970–2 and 232 in parts of southern China, where three cereal crops can be grown in a year.[8]

Multiple cropping appears to have increased in Asia since 1950, although there are few reliable statistics. In India the index of cropping was 111 in 1947, but this had risen to 118.6 in 1970–1. In China there has been little increase in the net area in food crops since 1952, but the index of cropping rose from 131 in 1952 to 165 in 1980; increases in the index have also been recorded in Indonesia and Egypt. The intensity of multiple cropping is closely related to the density of population, and the expansion has been related to the growth of population and the need for extra food. However, its increase had been facilitated by the introduction of new varieties of wheat and rice that mature more rapidly than traditional varieties, thus making it possible to grow two cereal crops in a year. Although multiple cropping is possible in areas that rely upon rainfall alone, and is found in Java and the Philippines, it is generally closely associated with irrigated land, for whereas much of Asia has temperatures high enough for crop growth throughout the year, rather fewer areas have enough wet months to sustain two cereal crops.[9]

Irrigation and its expansion. Irrigation is by no means easy to define. It can encompass on the one hand massive reservoirs such as the Aswan dam in Egypt which stores the Nile's waters and releases them during the low season, and on the other simple earth dams in Sri Lanka that hold water from the monsoon rains which can be used in the dry season. Sometimes the term is used to describe the system of canals and ditches that carry the flood waters of a river to the distant parts of a flood plain.

The purpose of irrigation is not, of course, only to allow multiple cropping. Irrigation can be used to extend cultivation into areas where rainfall is too low for any crops to be grown, or to supplement rainfall, overcome variability and increase yields. In many humid areas such as England or the eastern United States high value crops may be irrigated during dry spells. None the less, efficient irrigation systems do enable multiple cropping to be practised.

[8] H. G. Nasr, 'Multiple cropping in some countries of the Middle East', in Papendick *et al.*, *op. cit.*, pp. 117–27; Dalrymple, *op. cit.*

[9] E. Dayal, 'Impact of irrigation expansion on multiple cropping in India', *Tijdschrift voor Economische en Sociale Geografie*, **68**, 1971, pp. 100–9; Dalrymple, *op. cit.*; S. Ishikama, 'China's economic growth since 1949 – an assessment', *China Quarterly*, **94**, 1983, pp. 242–81.

Although irrigation has been practised in Asia for several thousand years, much of the present irrigated area has been established in the last 80 years.[10] The world irrigated area was only 8 million hectares in 1800, but reached 40 million in 1900, 120 million in 1950 and has since risen to 211 million; 14 per cent of the world's arable land is now irrigated.[11] However, the significance of the irrigated areas is greater than this would suggest, for not only is multiple cropping possible, but also yields are higher and less variable than in rainfed farming and high value crops are grown. Irrigated areas thus account for a greater proportion of food output than the small area would suggest.

Asia has two-thirds of the world's irrigated area, and 29 per cent of its arable is irrigated (table 6.7). India and China have by far the largest areas of irrigation; they are followed by the United States and the Soviet Union, both of which have nearly 20 million hectares. In the developing world, however, most of the irrigated land lies in Asia. If Egypt and Sudan are excluded, Africa has an insignificant area. In Latin America one-third of the total irrigated area is in Mexico, and nearly all of the

Table 6.7   Irrigated areas of the world, 1950–80

	1950 (million hectares)	1980 (million hectares)	Increase 1950–80		Irrigated 1980 as % of arable 1980
			(million hectares)	(%)	
Developing					
Asia	83.5	134.3	50.8	61	29
Africa	5.8	8.4	2.6	45	5
Latin America	6.5	14.2	7.7	118	9
Total developing	95.8	156.9	61.1	64	19
Developed					
North America	10.9	21.0	10.1	93	4
USSR	6.5	17.5	11.0	169	8
Australasia	0.7	1.7	1.0	143	2
Europe	6.4	14.5	8.1	127	10
Total developed	24.5	54.7	30.2	123	8
World	120.4	211.7	91.3	76	14

Source: N. D. Gulhati, *Irrigation in the World: A Global Review*, New Delhi, 1955; FAO, *Production Yearbook 1980*, vol. 34, Rome, 1981, p. 57

[10] N. D. Gulhati, *Irrigation in the World: A Global Review*, New Delhi, 1955, p. vii.
[11] L. R. Brown and E. Eckholm, *By Bread Alone*, London, 1975, p. 94; Gulhati, *op. cit.*; FAO, *Production Yearbook 1980*, vol. 34, Rome, 1981, p. 57.

rest is in Brazil, Argentina and Peru; the last has one-third of its total farmland under irrigation. Not only has Asia the largest area in irrigation but, of the developing regions, it has had by far the biggest absolute increase since 1950 (table 6.7).

Mixed cropping. The term multiple cropping is normally used to describe the sequential growth of two or more crops in the same field in the same year. However, the growth of one crop alone in a field or plot, although typical of Europe, North America and most parts of Asia, is less common in Africa and Asia. In the *milpa* systems of Latin America and the bush fallowing of Africa plots of land are left fallow for several years between periods of cropping. But when the plots are cropped they are not necessarily sown to one crop; more commonly a mixture of crops is sown. The prime purpose of this is to protect the soil from the impact of raindrops and the direct rays of the sun and, if crops which require different periods to mature are grown, to space out the harvest period. Most agronomists ignored mixed cropping until recently, or assumed it was a primitive practice. But it has been shown that an area under several crops not only provides protection but also gives a higher output per unit area than the same area under one crop alone. First, if a variety of crops with different maturing periods is grown, then the whole year's available photosynthesis is utilized, not simply that of the period occupied by one crop. Second, different crops use different soil nutrients. Third, a mixture of crops prevents plant diseases establishing themselves.

Mixed cropping is widely practised in Latin America and Africa; thus 60 per cent of Latin America's maize is grown with another crop, often beans. In northern Nigeria 83 per cent of the arable area is in mixed crops. However, the extent to which mixed cropping has increased since 1950, and thus raised the calorific output of arable land, is unknown. [12]

The colonization of new land

Although there are no accurate figures on the increase in cropland due to the reduction of fallow or the spread of multiple cropping, some indication of the new land brought into cultivation since 1950 can be obtained by comparing the area in arable in 1950 and 1980 (table 5.1). In Latin America arable land increased by 76 million hectares or 88 per cent; in Asia by 107 million hectares or 30 per cent. The data for

[12] W. C. Beets, *Multiple Cropping and Tropical Farming Systems*, Boulder, Colorado, 1982, pp. 7, 8, 10, 43, 63.

Africa are unfortunately unreliable, but it seems unlikely that there was an actual decline (see pp. 150–4). In the 1970s new land in the world was being settled at the rate of 4–5 million hectares per annum, an addition to the arable area of only 0.3 per cent per annum.[13]

The reasons for land settlement have been various; increasing the food supply has not always been the prime motive. Thus in the aftermath of partition in 1947 the Indian government established colonies on waste land in India. Initially this was to settle refugees from Pakistan; since then the aim has been to settle landless labourers. This has been the purpose of land settlement schemes elsewhere, notably in Kenya and Java, both countries with very rapid rural population increase. In some countries the landless were provided with land by expropriating part or all of larger holdings, as in Iran, Taiwan, North Vietnam and China. Elsewhere land settlement has been seen as an alternative to land reform. In Latin America few governments have been prepared to change the inequitable distribution of land ownership, and the colonization of new land has been seen as a way of providing land for the landless without the problems of reform.

There are other reasons for land settlement. In South America the Amazon basin is divided among 11 countries; in each it is remote from the major centres of population, rural or urban, and sparsely populated. In the past settlements have been made for military reasons, to defend the land against the encroachments of neighbouring states. More recently the Amazon has been seen as an untapped area of major resources – not only food but also timber, oil and minerals – and nearly all the states have attempted, with varying degrees of success, to integrate the Amazon basin into their national economies. Military reasons led the Thai government to establish agricultural settlements on their borders with Laos, and in the Philippines the Huk rebels who surrendered to the government were settled on land in Mindanao.[14]

Nor have all land settlement schemes been primarily aimed at providing extra food. In Malaya, where schemes have been properly planned and efficiently executed compared with much of the rest of

[13] T. J. Goering, *Agricultural Land Settlement*, a World Bank Issues Paper, Washington DC, 1978.
[14] Tunku Shamsul Bahrein, 'Development planning: land settlement policies and practices in South East Asia', in R. J. Pryor (ed.), *Migration and Development in South East Asia; a Demographic Perspective*, Kuala Lumpur, 1979, pp. 295–304; R. Ng. 'Land settlement projects in Thailand', *Geography*, 53, 1968, pp. 179–82; B. H. Farmer, *Agricultural Colonization in India since Independence*, London, 1974; R. C. Eidt, 'Pioneer settlement in Eastern Peru', *Annals of the Association of American Geographers*, 52, 1962, pp. 255–78.

the world, much new land has been used for planting rubber and oil palms. Indeed the aim of many governments has been to prevent settlers reverting to subsistence; cash crops have been prescribed as part of the settlement policy. [15]

Land colonization schemes sponsored by governments and other organizations have had very mixed success. In India, although there has been a substantial increase in the area under crops, the cost to the state has been great and the return on investment very low. In terms of increasing the food supply the government of India would probably have been better advised to have invested in improving crop yields on the existing arable area. In Egypt 445,000 hectares have been reclaimed since 1952, and most of this was laid out in state farms. Yet crop yields on this land are only half those on the old lands, and on only one-third of the farms have incomes exceeded variable costs; that is, two-thirds of the farms made a loss even before the cost of reclamation is considered. Nor have land settlement schemes made much impact upon landlessness. Thus in ten years Kenya settled 250,000 people, but this was no more than one year's rural natural increase. In 20 years 1 million people left Java under government spnsorship to settle in the outer provinces; in the same period Java's rural population increased by 20 million. [16]

New land in Latin America. In Latin America the expansion of the cropland has made a major contribution to the increase in food output; the harvested area rose by 70 per cent between 1950 and 1975, and two-thirds of the extra output came from increasing the area in crops. In Brazil in the same period four-fifths of the increased output came from extra cropland. This emphasis on increasing area rather than yields reflects not only the comparatively low population densities in much of the continent but also a long historical tradition. [17]

When the Spanish arrived in the Americas in the early sixteenth century they found that most of the lowland areas were sparsely populated by Amerindians who practised shifting agriculture or *milpa*. However, in the uplands of Central America and the Andes there were more densely populated areas with sophisticated and intensive farming, although lacking the plough, the horse, cattle or sheep; the civilizations

[15] R. D. Hill, *Agriculture in the Malaysian Region*, Budapest, 1982, pp. 116–17.
[16] Farmer, *op. cit.*, p. 292; C. H. Gotsch and W. M. Dyer, 'Rhetoric and reason in the Egyptian New Lands debate', *Food Research Institute Studies*, **18**, pp. 129–49; Goering, *op. cit.*
[17] FAO, *The State of Food and Agriculture 1978*, Rome, 1979, pp. 2–32.

of the Incas and the Aztecs were the richest of these areas. The Spanish settled these areas, for the control of labour was essential to mine silver or grow crops for export. The Portuguese settled the coasts of Brazil and imported African slaves to work sugar-cane plantations, and the Spanish later settled the land around the estuary of the Plata. But in the mid nineteenth century much of the continent was very sparsely populated and it lacked mass immigration from Europe. Nor had any class of independent farmers sprung up, and most of the land was held by a small minority. In the later nineteenth century, however, there was an expansion of the cultivated area, particularly in Argentina and to a lesser extent in Uruguay; Italian and other immigrants expanded the area in wheat and maize. In Brazil the coffee frontier expanded inland from São Paulo, and in the Caribbean and later the Pacific lowlands of Central America bananas or other tropical crops were raised on plantations for export.

The rapid population growth of this century has led to considerable demographic pressure in the upland areas, and there has been a slow move downwards from the uplands to the Caribbean and Pacific lowlands helped by the building of roads and the eradication of malaria. In Mexico not only was there a major land reform in the 1930s but also the state invested in irrigation schemes particularly in the arid north west. The area irrigated rose from 1 million hectares in 1926 to 4.3 million hectares in the 1960s, half of this on land not previously farmed.[18] But more dramatic has been the expansion of farmland in southern Brazil, south and west from São Paulo towards Paraguay and Uruguay, and northwards towards and beyond the new capital Brasilia. In 1930 Brazil's cultivated area was only 6.6 million hectares, but by 1970 it exceeded 30 million hectares; indeed by the 1970s Brazil had become the world's second food exporter after the USA. Much of this northward push was into the *cerrado*, an area similar in soils and climate to the African savannah, and used until the 1970s only for extensive cattle raising.[19] But it is the Amazon basin, where comparatively little land has been brought into cultivation, to which most attention has been paid.

[18] Fox, *op. cit.*, p. 41.

[19] J. H. Galloway, 'Brazil', in Blakemore and Smith, *op. cit.*, pp. 358–68; S. Cunningham, 'Recent development in the Centre-West region', *Bank of London and South America Review*, 14, pp. 44–52; R. Andrew Nickson, 'Brazilian colonization of the eastern border region of Paraguay', *Journal of Latin America Studies*, 13, 1981, pp. 111–37; J. D. Henshall and R. P. Momsen, Jr, *A Geography of Brazilian Development*, London, 1974; J. Foweraker, *The Struggle for Land: A Political Economy of the Pioneer Frontier in Brazil from 1930 to the Present Day*, Cambridge, 1981.

The Amazon basin. Until after the Second World War the Amazon basin was sparsely populated; it was lacking in roads and railways, and river transport was poorly developed. In the late nineteenth century rubber collecting led to a boom around Manaus, and missionaries and soldiers had made their way down from the Andes to the *oriente* or *montana*, the forested slopes and lowlands to the east in the upper tributaries of the Amazon. This movement east from the Andes has been prompted by a number of factors. First has been the rapid growth of population in the upland areas of Colombia, Bolivia, Ecuador and Peru, which has led to both spontaneous and government sponsored settlements in the upper Amazon basin. Second has been the discovery of oil – which attracted workmen who stayed to farm – and the building of roads. Third has been the military need to settle the land, for Ecuador, Colombia and Peru have all been in conflict over their boundaries. Between 1950 and 1975 85,000 people moved from the Bolivian *altiplano* to the *oriente*, 250,000 from the Ecuadorian uplands and some 100,000 from Peru.[20] In Brazil the building of roads – beginning with the Belém–Brasilia road in 1960, and accelerating in the 1970s with the construction of the TransAmazon highway – has led to a considerable movement into the Amazon. The population along the Belém–Brasilia highway rose from 200,000 to 2 million between 1960 and 1970.[21] Initially the government of Brazil hoped the opening up of the Amazon would provide farms for the many landless from the drought ridden north east; but this has been far from successful. Hopes were of settling 100,000 in the 1970s. By 1977 only 6000 had moved from the north east into the Amazon basin. In 1975 the Brazilian government abandoned the welfare aspects of its Amazon programme and turned to development for profit, in alliance with large corporations, often foreign, to exploit not only the land but also timber and minerals.[22]

Since the 1960s much concern has been expressed about the future of the Amazon environment and the fate of the Amerindian population. Comparatively little rain forest remains in Africa or Asia, and the area in Amazonia constitutes one-half of the total. But on this and many other matters it is hard to find accurate information for the basin

[20] E. Allen, 'New settlement in the Upper Amazon basin', *Bank of London and South America Review*, **9**, 1975, pp. 622–8.

[21] W. Denevan, 'Development and the imminent demise of the Amazon rainforest', *Professional Geographer*, **25**, 1973, pp. 130–5.

[22] M. Hiracka, 'The development of Amazonia', *Geographical Review*, **72**, 1982, pp. 94–8; E. F. Moran, *Developing the Amazon*, Bloomington, Indiana, 1981; E. F. Moran, 'Ecological, anthropological and agronomic research in the Amazon basin', *Latin American Research Review*, **171**, 1982, pp. 3–41; C. Weil, 'Amazon update; developments since 1970', *Focus*, **33**, 1983.

as a whole. There is no reliable estimate of the proportion of the forest cleared, but it has been put as low as 5 per cent and as high as 15 per cent.[23] Although the use of remote sensing techniques in Brazil has increased knowledge of the basin, too little is still known of the soils and climate, although it is clear that there is far greater variety than once was thought. It used to be argued that only the *varzea* or alluvial soils of the river valleys were potential arable land, and they constitute only 5 per cent of the total area, and four-fifths are seasonally flooded. The *terra firme* or upland soils were once said to be uniformly poor, leached of their nutrients and liable to soil exhaustion once the forest had been cleared. That these soils are far more varied is undoubted, but there is as yet little knowledge of their value for long term agriculture. Nor is there any proven system of permanent cultivation, other than growing tree crops or the extensive shifting cultivation and gathering practised by the indigenous peoples. However, experimental work suggests that sustained continuous cropping of annual crops is possible with the right combination of chemical fertilizers.[24]

The process of settlement has followed a similar course in both the Brazilian and the Andean Amazon. Although governments have encouraged the cultivation of cash crops, most settlers, whether spontaneous or in government schemes, have practised slash and burn, growing food crops such as rice, maize and yucca. Their holdings are generally small – less than 50 hectares – and many, after a few years of slash and burn agriculture, seed the land to grass and raise beef cattle, for which there is a market among the rich in both south east Brazil and in the Andean cities. But the holdings of the original settlers are too small for extensive cattle raising, and they are frequently absorbed by large corporate ranches which sow improved grasses, raise improved breeds of cattle and control plant and animal disease with pesticides. Some 80 per cent of the cultivated land in the Ecuadorian *oriente* is in grass, and crops elsewhere seem to be a small proportion of the cleared area.[25]

[23] Denevan, *op. cit.*
[24] Moran, *op. cit.*, 1982; M. J. Eden, 'Ecology and land development: the case of the Amazonian rainforest', *Transactions of the Institute of British Geographers*, 3, (new series), 1978, pp. 444–63; J. Kirkby, 'Agricultural land use and the settlement of Amazonia', *Pacific Viewpoint*, 17, 1976, pp. 105–32; P. A. Sanchez and S. G. Salinas, 'Low input technology for managing oxisols and ultisols in tropical America', *Advances in Agronomy*, 34, 1981, pp. 279–406.
[25] R. Bromley, 'The colonization of humid tropical areas in Ecuador', *Singapore Journal of Tropical Geography*, 2, 1981, pp. 15–26; J. M. Kirby, 'Colombian land use change and the development of the oriente', *Pacific Viewpoint*, 19, 1978, pp. 1–25; J. M. Kleinpenning, 'A further evaluation of the policy for the integration of the Amazon basin', *Tijdschrift voor Economische en Sociale Geografie*, 69, 1978, pp. 78–85.

Although there is no denying that there has been substantial settlement in the Amazon basin in the last 30 years, there is little reliable evidence on the areas cleared and settled, the area in crops or the quantities of food produced. Much that has been written on the subject has dealt with the threat to the Indian way of life or the problems that arise when the rain forest is destroyed. Yet it would seem that although some colonization has made a significant contribution to national food supplies – notably in Bolivia – on the whole the Amazon has not yet given a significant increase to Latin America's food supplies.

New land in Asia. Asia, like Europe, has a long history of settlement and by 1950 had very high population densities. Unlike Europe, most of the population were still employed in agriculture, and the density of the agricultural population was higher than elsewhere. Further, more of the total area was devoted to arable land – 16 per cent – than in Latin America or Africa. Much of the arable was in the deltas and lower alluvial plains of the great rivers, where wet rice cultivation has sustained high densities for two millenia or more. Before 1950 there had been a steady increase in the area in arable land over a long period, particularly in South East Asia, where not only were more food crops grown but the development of plantations for the production of export crops became significant from the late nineteenth century. [26]

In the post-war period there has been both state organized and spontaneous colonization of land in nearly every country in Asia, in many cases prompted by the need to provide land for a rapidly growing landless population. In India there have been substantial additions to the cultivated area in a variety of regions, much of it by adding to the irrigated area which doubled between 1947 and 1973, particularly as the result of canal building and the construction of tube wells in the Punjab and Rajasthan. [27] In the north of the Ganges plain the *terai* or foothill area has been brought into cultivation since the eradication of malaria; that part of the *terai* which is in Nepal has seen a particularly rapid expansion of cropland since 1960. [28] In Assam, which was sparsely populated in the mid nineteenth century, migration and rapid population growth have converted the lowlands to a densely populated zone

[26] D. B. Grigg, *The Agricultural Systems of the World: An Evolutionary Approach*, Cambridge, 1974, pp. 88, 92, 93, 96–108, 230–5.
[27] R. Wade, 'India's changing strategy of irrigation development', in E. W. Coward, Jr (ed.), *Irrigation and Agricultural Development in Asia; Perspectives from the Social Sciences*, Ithaca, 1980, pp. 345–64.
[28] B. H. Farmer, *Agricultural Colonization in South and South East Asia*, Hull University Press, 1969; P. Blaikie, J. Cameron and D. Seddon, *Nepal in Crisis: Growth and Stagnation at the Periphery*, Oxford, 1980, p. 18.

in the last half century. In Ceylon colonization schemes to settle the dry zone were begun at independence, and required the extension of irrigation. Some 70,000 hectares of paddy land were created in this manner between 1948 and 1964, and the total area of cropland has increased by 40 per cent since 1948. [29]

China, after India, has the largest area of arable land in Asia; in 1950 this was far more densely populated than the Indian subcontinent. More of the land was double cropped and irrigated, and yields were already high compared with much of the rest of Asia. Statistics of Chinese agriculture were published in the 1950s, and then little was known until the recent release by the Chinese government of statistics for the late 1970s. The old 18 provinces of Han China were very densely populated, and there was little prospect of substantial expansion in this zone; some steep slopes in the south were terraced and attempts were made to convert cemeteries to cropland, and land on the coast north of the Yangtze and near the Hwangh-Ho delta were embanked and used for cropland. However, the Chinese looked to the north for their new lands. Manchuria had been closed to Han settlement by the Manchu dynasty until late in the nineteenth century; thereafter it became a classic zone of agricultural colonization until the Japanese invasion in the 1930s. The Chinese have certainly expanded cropland in this area, mainly by the establishment of state farms in unsettled areas. But the extent of this expansion is unknown. [30] Recent statistics suggest that although the sown area has increased since the 1950s, the arable area has declined. This may be due to soil erosion in the south, but it may also be a result of underreporting of arable land by provinces in order to avoid taxation and the compulsory deliveries of food to the towns. [31]

In the archipelago of South East Asia the settlement of some new land has required movement from island to island. At the beginning of this century the Philippines came under American rule: there was a marked contrast between the density of population on most of Luzon and some of the smaller Visayan islands, and the sparsely populated island of Mindanao and the north east of Luzon. Attempts to expand

[29] G. H. Peiris, 'Land reform and agrarian change in Sri Lanka', *Modern Asian Studies*, 12, 1978, pp. 611–28; B. H. Farmer, *Peasant Colonization in Ceylon*, London, 1957; T. F. Rasmussen, 'Population and land utilization in the Assam Valley', *Journal of Tropical Geography*, 141, 1960, 51–76.

[30] T. R. Tregear, *China: A Geographical Survey*, London, 1976, p. 108; R. Welch, H. C. Lo and C. W. Pannel, 'Mapping China's new agricultural lands', *Photogrammetric Engineering and Remote Sensing*, 45, 1979, pp. 1221–8.

[31] K. R. Walker, 'China's grain production, 1978–80 and 1952–57; some basic statistics', *China Quarterly*, no. 86, 1981, pp. 215–47.

the area of settlement were begun by introducing legislation comparable to the American Homestead Acts, allowing the occupation of up to 24 hectares of public land. Movement to Mindanao became substantial in the late 1930s, with spontaneous movement exceeding assisted colonization. But by the 1960s population densities in Mindanao were approaching those in Luzon, and the very problems that colonization was supposed to overcome – fragmentation, tenancy and rural indebtedness – were appearing. [32]

In Indonesia a contrast between Java, with its very high population density, and the outer provinces of Borneo, Sumatra and the Celebes, with very low density, was and is very marked. In the nineteenth century Java under Dutch rule had experienced rapid population growth and by 1900 the centre and east of the island had very high rural population densities. The drainage of the northern plains had added to the arable area and elaborate systems of water control, multiple cropping and intensive cultivation had raised rice yields, and in the east the adoption of cassava as a food crop had increased food output. However there seemed little prospect of further increasing the cultivated area or of population growth slowing down.

In 1905 the Dutch introduced the policy of transmigration; Javanese were to be moved to the outer provinces, Sumatra in particular, both to relieve population density and to provide labour for the plantations on that island. Between 1905 and 1941 190,000 Javanese migrated, principally to Sumatra and mainly to the southern province of Lampung. Most of the migrants grew rice, as they had in their homeland. After independence the government continued the policy of transmigration, and between 1952 and 1974 600,000 left Java. Further movements were planned in the late 1970s. This policy has no doubt increased Indonesia's cultivated area; whereas Java's arable area has remained stagnant since 1950, that in the outer provinces has increased considerably, but this has not increased the prosperity of the settlers or Indonesia's rice supplies. Nor have the numbers leaving Java been sufficient to improve the lot of the Javanese. The total number leaving Java in 20 years was no more than one year's natural increase in that island. [33]

---

[32] G. W. Jones, 'Population growth, empty land and economic development in Indonesia, the Philippines and Malaysia', *Kajtan Ekonomi Malaysia*, 5, 1968, pp. 1–18; P. Krinks, 'Old wine in a new bottle: land settlement and agrarian problems in the Philippines', *Journal of South East Asian Studies*, 5, 1974, pp. 1–17.

[33] J. M. Hardjono, *Transmigration in Indonesia*, Kuala Lumpur, 1977; Jones, *op. cit.*; G. W. Jones, 'Indonesia: the transmigration programme and development planning', in R. J. Pryor, *op. cit.*, pp. 212–21.

Africa. Although African food output has increased since 1950, the rate of increase has been lower than in any other major region; it fell between the late 1960s and the 1970s, and in much of the continent has been below the rate of population increase for over a decade. Although data on yields and land use are unreliable, most recent writers seem agreed that food crop yields have increased very little, and indeed may have declined. The bulk of increased output has thus been due to an increase in the area sown to crops. Between 1961–5 and 1976 the greatest increase in arable land was in East Africa, where it rose by one-third; the least was in the Sahel, where the increase was only 2.5 per cent and has since declined. [34]

In Africa multiple cropping has made little contribution to extra cropland, in contrast to Asia. Little of the continent's arable land is irrigated, and on that double cropping is rare, although the length of the growing season does not preclude it. Thus there are 70,000 hectares of irrigated land in the inland delta of Mali but only one seventh is double cropped. This lack of double cropping does need some qualification. Multiple cropping is a term normally used to describe the sequential raising of one crop in a field. However, in much of Africa it is common to grow several crops on a plot; evidence suggests that this gives a higher dry matter yield per hectare than monoculture. [35]

The area under crops has thus been increased primarily by reducing the fallow periods and the colonization of new land, either spontaneously or by government sponsored schemes. In the last 30 years there have been substantial increases in population density in nearly all parts of Africa, and this has led to changes in the type of farming. When densities were low, shifting agriculture could be practised. In this system forest or savannah land was cleared in small plots and a mixture of crops sown for two or three years. The plots were then abandoned and trees and grass colonized the land; 20 years or more in natural fallow was sufficient to restore soil fertility. Such a system was accompanied by periodic movement of the village to be near the plots in cultivation. The growth of population density has made such farming impossible and it is now rare. Bush fallowing, with shorter periods of fallow, remains predominant. The reduction of fallow has however increased the frequency with which crops are grown and hence the area in crops. But

[34] World Bank, *Accelerated Development in Sub-Saharan Africa: An Agenda for Action*, Washington DC, 1981; C. Christensen, *et al.*, *Food Problems and Prospects in Sub-Saharan Africa: The Decade of the 1980s*, International Economics Division, Economic Research Service, United States Department of Agriculture, Washington DC, 1981.
[35] Christensen *et al.*, *op. cit.*; Beets, *op. cit.*

unless some means of maintaining soil fertility is introduced this reduction leads to a fall in soil fertility and yields and in extreme cases to soil erosion, and the land may have to be abandoned. Yields have fallen, for example, in the west highlands of Kenya and the Mossi plateau of Upper Volta. [36]

The spontaneous occupation of uncultivated areas has also occurred in parts of Africa. This has been possible where the tsetse fly has been eliminated and in such cases good land has been brought into cultivation. Elsewhere – as in parts of the Sahel, in Tanzania and Ethiopia – settlement has moved into semi-arid areas which have been liable to crop failure from droughts and to soil erosion due to inadequate fallowing. There have been numerous land settlement schemes in Africa both before and after independence. Increasing the food supply has not been the only motive, they have not all led to an increase in cropping, and most of the large schemes have been judged to be failures.

The first and still the largest settlement scheme in Africa began in the Gezira in the Sudan before the First World War. At independence in 1955, 180,000 hectares were irrigated by the Nile; over half, however, were in cotton. Since then further irrigation has extended the area to over 330,000 hectares. Other significant irrigation schemes were begun by the French in Mali, Senegal and Mauritania and by the British in northern Nigeria. The irrigation schemes in the West African savannah, together with irrigation on European farms in Zimbabwe, made up nearly all the African irrigated area outside Egypt, the Sudan and Madagascar. [37]

Elsewhere in Africa land settlement schemes have had a variety of motives. In Ghana and Zambia the building of dams for hydroelectricity works required the resettlement of large numbers living in the flooded areas; in Kenya, Zambia and Zimbabwe Africans have been settled on lands formerly owned by Europeans. In Zambia and Kenya there have been schemes to resettle those living in densely populated and eroded lands. Clearly not all land settlement schemes involved a net increase in the arable area; it seems likely that in most parts of Africa fallow reduction and spontaneous colonization – as in the mechanized rainfed agriculture of central Sudan – has contributed more to the increase in food output than settlement schemes. [38]

[36] Christensen *et al.*, *op. cit.*
[37] K. M. Barbour, 'The Sudan since independence', *Journal of Modern African Studies*, **18**, 1980, pp. 73–97; World Bank, *op. cit.*, pp. 14, 73, 76; M. B. K. Darkoh, 'Desertification in Tanzania', *Geography*, **67**, 1982, pp. 320–33; R. J. Harrison Church, 'Problems and development of the dry zone of West Africa', *Geographical Journal*, **127**, 1961, pp. 187–204; G. M. Higgins, A. H. Kassam, L. Naiken and M. M. Shah, 'Africa's agricultural potential', *Ceres*, **14**, 1981, pp. 13–21.
[38] B. Floyd and M. Adinde, 'Farm settlements in Eastern Nigeria: a geographical

THE LOSS OF LAND

There has been a substantial gain in the area sown to crops since 1950, although the precise figure is in doubt. There is no doubt again that some arable land has been lost, and in recent years much attention has been drawn to the loss of arable land in both the developed and the developing countries.

This is not new. In the 1930s the soil erosion in the west of the United States received much publicity and revived interest in soil conservation techniques. R. V. Jacks and R. O. Whyte pointed out that the loss of land through soil erosion and the fall in soil fertility threatened future agricultural output not only in the United States but in many other parts of the world, a theme that was taken up, in a more dramatic manner, by several writers in the late 1940s and early 1950s.[39] The fear that good agricultural land is being lost has been revived in the 1970s. In Britain there has been a long dispute about the loss of farmland to urban expansion and afforestation, and in the United States there have been similar controversies.[40] In the developing countries the loss of land to urban expansion has not been of great importance, except in countries such as Egypt. Two events have drawn attention again to the loss of farmland. The first has been the growing awareness that much of the world's tropical forests are being destroyed. The second was the drought in the Sahel in the years 1969–74; there was much debate about the causes of the famine at this time, and some argued that the Sahara was spreading southwards. Whatever the truth of this statement there has been a revived interest in the loss of farmland due to human mismanagement of the environment. Although much has been written upon this, there is a singular lack of reliable data on the subject. Nor is this surprising, for the phenomenon is very difficult to define. There are, for example, parts of Africa where the reduction of fallow has led to gullying and the land has had to be abandoned: on the other hand over much larger areas fallow reduction has reduced the plant nutrient

approach', *Economic Geography*, **43**, 1967, pp. 189–230; T. E. Hilton, 'The Volta resettlement project', *Journal of Tropical Geography*, **24**, 1967, pp. 12–21; G. Kay, 'Resettlement and land use planning in Zambia: the Chipangali scheme', *Scottish Geographical Magazine*, **81**, 1965, pp. 163–77; R. Chambers, *Settlement Schemes in Tropical Africa: A Study of Organization and Development*, London, 1969.
[39] G. V. Jacks and R. O. Whyte, *The Rape of the Earth*, London, 1939; W. Vogt, *Road to Survival*, London, 1949; M. Roberts, *The Estate of Man*, London, 1952; F. Osborn, *Our Plundered Planet*, London, 1948.
[40] R. Best, *Land Use and Living Space*, London, 1981; R. H. Jackson, *Land Use in America*, London, 1981.

content of the soil and hence crop yields have fallen, but the land has not been abandoned. Thus there is a wide range of conditions contained within the terms *land degradation* or *desertification*. There has been a reduction of soil fertility and some land has been abandoned in many parts of the world, although there is no way of measuring the extent. Irrigated areas have presented particular problems. When large quantities of water are spread over farmland, much of the water is not used by crops but sinks downward, and eventually the permanent water table rises, causing waterlogging. Irrigated areas in hot regions are also prone to salinity. Water rises by capillary action to the surface and salts toxic to plants are deposited in the soil profile or on the surface. It has been claimed that one-fifth of the world's irrigated area is subject to either salinity or waterlogging and this has led to some land being abandoned and yields being reduced. The Near East is particularly susceptible to these problems. Half of the irrigated land in Syria is said to be affected by salinity or waterlogging, 30 per cent in Egypt, and 15 per cent in Iran and, in the 1960s, three-quarters in Pakistan. These conditions are not irreversible. Indeed in Pakistan tube wells have been used to lower the level of the water table. [41]

Soil is constantly being lost owing to natural processes. It is when loss exceeds the formation of new soil that problems arise. Once natural vegetation is removed and farming undertaken, soil loss is likely to occur in all regions. The risk of erosion is greatest in areas of low rainfall, very high temperatures and on steep slopes. Most traditional farmers have devised techniques to avoid soil erosion, but these may be ignored; in some cases their problems may be due to others' rather than their own activities. Thus in the Indus region of Pakistan flooding has been caused by the deforestation of the Himalayan foothills where the tributaries rise; this has accelerated runoff and caused flooding lower down. In Java recent deforestation of upland areas has caused the silting of irrigation systems in the lower parts of catchment areas. Where population pressure has increased the cultivation of very steep slopes, soil erosion has occurred, as in El Salvador and parts of Mexico. In Africa, particularly in parts of Kenya, Ethiopia and the western Sahel, population growth has prompted arable expansion into dry areas which are particularly prone to wind erosion. Nor is it cropping alone that causes soil erosion. The growth of cattle numbers in parts of tropical Africa and

[41] L. R. Brown, 'Soil and civilisation: the decline of food security', *Third World Quarterly*, 5, 1983, pp. 103–17; FAO, *The State of Food and Agriculture 1977*, Rome, 1978, pp. 3–13; E. P. Eckholm, *Losing Ground: Environmental Stress and World Food Prospects*, New York, 1976.

also in the arid regions of north west Africa has caused overgrazing; as the number of palatable species declines, so have cattle numbers been increased, so that not only is the fodder supply reduced but land becomes progressively degraded.[42]

Examples of land degradation are legion, but figures on actual loss few; those that exist are often contradictory. It has been suggested that one-fifth of the current world arable area is subject to land degradation; and it has been argued that since the beginning of farming some 10,000 years ago an area equivalent to the present arable area has been lost to agriculture through soil erosion. The basis of this latter estimate is less than clear. None the less the loss of land is obviously significant; the growth of world food output since 1950 could have been greater without such losses.[43]

CONCLUSIONS

Although increases in crop yields have accounted for a high proportion of total world food output since 1950, increases in the area sown to crops have been important in the developing countries, particularly in Latin America and Africa. Increases in area have not come from the cultivation of new land alone. In Asia the increase in multiple cropping has been significant; in Africa the reduction of fallow has increased the area sown. The colonization of new land has also provided employment for the landless in the older established areas, although rarely more than a small minority.

---

[42] Eckholom, *op. cit.*, pp. 41, 62, 94–5, 119–20, 167; D. J. Fox, *op. cit.*, pp. 33, 39, 44; P. Blaikie *et al.*, *op. cit.*, pp. 11–19.
[43] Brown, *op. cit.*; United Nations, *Desertification: Its Causes and Consequences*, Oxford, 1977, p. 6.

7

Agricultural Development in the Developed Countries since 1945

Few discussions of the world food problem deal with the growth of food output in the developed countries, for there malnutrition is uncommon and the agricultural problems are those of surplus not shortage. Yet there are good reasons for discussing food output in these countries.

First, malnutrition was far more common in the 1930s than it is now. In North America and Western Europe national food supplies were adequate, and malnutrition was due to poverty and ignorance. On the other hand, in the Soviet Union and some countries in Eastern Europe, food supplies were low and there was need for greater output to provide an adequate diet, particularly of animal foods. Food supplies declined in the Second World War in the Soviet Union and most of Europe; during the war labour and other resources were taken out of agriculture, fighting disrupted food production, and lack of transport made the movement of food difficult. Shortages continued for five or six years after the end of the war. In the late 1940s there were still fears about the future food supplies of Europe and Russia, although in the event recovery was rapid.

Second, although food output in Western Europe was restored to pre-war levels by 1950, somewhat later in Eastern Europe, there has been need for an increase in food output since 1945 on two counts. One is that population increased by over 300 million in the developed countries between 1950 and 1980. The other is that rising incomes in the 1950s and 1960s increased demand for more livestock products. But with the exception of the Soviet Union, consumption needs were largely satisfied by the early 1960s. Since then, however, not only has population increased slowly, but rising incomes have been spent not on extra food but on other goods. Output, however, continued to rise and outpaced demand, so that for much of the late 1960s and the 1970s agriculture in Western Europe and North America was plagued with food surpluses.

A third reason for considering production in the developed countries is the role of trade in the food supply of the developing countries. Many developing countries have become dependent upon food imports in the last 15 years, in the form of either trade or aid. Although the cost of food surpluses in Western agriculture has been the subject of much criticism, the developed countries, and in particular the United States, have become the source of most of the world's grain exports. Without the production increases of the last 30 years this would not have been possible.

THE GROWTH OF FOOD OUTPUT

Food output in Europe grew slowly in the first half of this century, but since 1950 has grown at unprecedented rates. Total food output in the developed countries approximately doubled between 1950 and 1980, but output per caput, because of comparatively slow population growth, has risen far more rapidly (see p. 81). There have, however, been considerable variations in the rate of increase between countries within the developed world. Some of the highest rates have been achieved in Eastern Europe and the USSR. Although productivity in Russian agriculture remains much lower than in the West, output increased very rapidly between 1950 and 1980; one estimate puts it at 3.5 per cent per annum, over twice the rate in the United States.[1] In West Germany and the United Kingdom gross output doubled between 1950 and the 1970s; and this was matched in several other countries in Western Europe. On the other hand, a few countries have had very little increase. Between 1952 and 1976 Norwegian agricultural output increased by only 5 per cent, and in Sweden, where government policy has been to restrict home output to 80 per cent of calorific needs, output actually declined in this period.[2]

---

[1] FAO, *Agricultural Adjustment in Developed Countries*, Rome, 1972, pp. 124–5; K. R. Gray, 'Soviet agricultural specialization and efficiency', *Soviet Studies*, 31, 1979, pp. 542–8, footnote 1, p. 546.

[2] D. Andrews, M. Mitchell and A. Weber, *The Development of Agriculture in Germany and the UK: Three Comparative Time Series, 1870–1975*, Wye College, Ashford, Kent, Centre for European Agricultural Studies, Miscellaneous Studies no. 4, 1979, pp. 11, 60–2; E. P. Cunningham, 'The revolution in Irish agriculture, with particular reference to animal production', *Journal of the Royal Agricultural Society of England*, 141, 1980, pp. 88–98; A. Maris and J. de Veer, 'Dutch agriculture in the period 1950–1970 and a look ahead', *European Review of Agricultural*

THE EXPANSION OF THE ARABLE AREA

Traditionally the major means of raising food output has been to increase the area in cultivation, but, as has been seen (p. 87), this has become less important as the capacity to increase crop yields has risen. In the post-war period most of the food output in the developed countries has come from higher yields; the arable area has shown little advance and indeed in many countries has fallen (see p. 74).

The area used for crops and grass has declined in nearly every country in Europe since 1950, although these *net* figures conceal more complex changes. In every country there have been losses due to urban expansion and, in some, to afforestation. This has been most serious in small and densely populated countries. In Belgium the agricultural area was two-thirds of the total land area in 1929, but in 1977 was only half. In The Netherlands reclamation of polders in the Zuider Zee has added to the agricultural area, but losses due to urban expansion have reduced the total cropland. In the 1950s, for example, some 3400 hectares were reclaimed, but 4000 were lost to urban expansion. [3] In some countries losses in one region have been compensated for by gains elsewhere; thus in Canada marginal land has been abandoned in the east, particularly in Nova Scotia and New Brunswick, but there have been gains in the prairies. [4] In most of the developed world there have been few substantial additions to the arable area since 1950. There are, however, three exceptions to this.

First, in the Soviet Union, a remarkable expansion of the cultivated area was achieved in the 1950s. Some 36 million hectares of land were ploughed up in the semi-arid areas of Kazakhstan, the northern Caucasus and Siberia between 1954 and 1960, and Russian grain output was raised by 50 per cent. Since then, however, there has been little increase in the sown area, which was 202 million hectares in 1960 and 216 million in 1980. A large proportion of the present grain area is in these dry regions, and climatic fluctuations have led to great variations in Russian output over the last 25 years. [5]

Economics, 1, 1973, pp. 63–78; J. P. O'Hagan, *Growth and Adjustment in National Agricultures*, London, 1978, p. 51; Central Statistical Office, *Economic Trends, Annual Supplement*, no. 7, 1982, table 84.
[3] C. Christians, 'Les resultats de 25 années de modernisation d'une agriculture avancée; l'exemple Belge', *Hommes et Terres du Nord*, 4, 1980, pp. 23–40; P. Lamartine Yates, *Food, Land and Manpower in Western Europe*, London, 1960, p. 118.
[4] M. J. Troughton, *Canadian Agriculture*, Budapest, 1982, p. 43.
[5] F. Durgin, 'The Virgin Lands programme, 1954–60', *Soviet Studies*, 13, 1961–2, pp. 255–80; K. Wadekin, 'Soviet agriculture's dependence on the West', *Foreign Affairs*, 60, 1982, pp. 882–903.

Second, in the United States the *arable* area has not greatly changed. Losses of cropland from urban expansion in the north east have been made up by the reclamation of wet lands in the Mississippi valley and the irrigation of dry lands in the south west. The area actually sown to crops has, however, fluctuated with variations in United States government policy. At various times farmers have been paid not to sow land to crops and so the cropland has diminished; arable land has been left idle or summer fallowing has been increased. At other times there have been incentives to increase output and land withdrawn from cultivation at government behest has been sown again, and fallows in the semi-arid grain regions have been reduced to increase the sown area. Between 1945 and 1970 most of the increase in United States food output came from higher yields. Between 1970 and 1980, however, output rose by 20 per cent, yield by very little; much of this additional output came from an expansion of the sown area.[6]

A third region where area expansion has been important is Australia, where wheat accounts for a high proportion of the cropland. In the immediate post-war period increases in both the area in crops and in yields helped raise food output. But in the 1960s wheat cropping expanded into marginal lands where yields were lower than in the more humid regions. Since the mid 1960s the national wheat yield has stagnated, and area expansion accounts for the continued increase in crop output.[7]

Although increased area has played an important role in increasing food output in some regions of the developed world, its importance has been dwarfed by increases in the yield of crops and animals. Before considering these improvements, however, some structural changes in agriculture must be touched upon.

STRUCTURAL CHANGE IN THE DEVELOPED COUNTRIES

In Africa, Asia and Latin America the agricultural labour force rose by 50 per cent between 1950 and 1980 and thus has contributed, by more intensive cultivation, to increased food output. Quite different circumstances obtain in the developed world. The agricultural labour

    [6] W. W. Cochrane, *The Development of American Agriculture: A Historical Analysis*, Minneapolis, 1979, p. 162; E. O. Heady, 'The agriculture of the United States', *Scientific American*, **235**, 1976, pp. 107–27.
    [7] C. M. Donald, 'Innovation in Australian agriculture', in D. B. Williams (ed.), *Agriculture in the Australian Economy*, Sydney, 1982, p. 64; D. P. Vincent, A. A. Powell and P. B. Dixon, 'Changes in the supply of agricultural products', in D. B. Williams, *op. cit.*, pp. 215–16.

force was in slow decline in the United States and north west Europe before 1945, but was still increasing in Russia, Australasia, Eastern and southern Europe. Since 1950 there has been an unprecedented decline in the workforce in the developed countries, which is now less than half what it was in 1950 (table 7.1). There are various reasons for this decline, but of greatest importance has been the attraction of much higher wages in the urban economy, so that in the period of remarkable economic expansion between 1945 and 1973 many millions left the land for the towns. This has led to the substitution of labour by machinery and power, which has occurred, at varying rates, throughout the developed world. In every country the tractor has replaced the horse, and tractors have become bigger and faster; the combine harvester, hardly known in Europe before 1945, now harvests nearly all grain. A variety of machines unknown or in the experimental stage before the war now harvest crops which were once hand picked, such as tomatoes, tobacco, cotton, potatoes and sugar-beet. Livestock production has been similarly transformed. In 1950 only 3 per cent of the cows in the EEC region were milked by machine, whereas now only 3 per cent are milked by hand; in addition, haymaking has been mechanized.[8] Not only has the horse been replaced as a source of power, but so too has man.

Table 7.1 Labour force in agriculture, developed countries, 1950–80

	United States	Western Europe	Eastern Europe and USSR
1950	23,048	42,096	76,842
1960	15,635	33,146	67,616
1970	9,712	22,626	49,362
1980	6,051	16,445	38,622

Sources: United Nations, *Economic Bulletin for Europe*, **35** (2), 1983, p. 172; G. C. Fite, *American Farmers: The New Minority*, Bloomington, Indiana, 1981, p. 101

In the 1930s few farms in the USA or Western Europe had electricity supplies. Now the main tasks in the farmyard and farm buildings, once done by hand, are performed with the aid of electricity. The growth in the use of machinery and the dramatic decline in the labour force has led to remarkable increases in labour productivity. In 1950 in Western Europe it took 100 man-hours to cultivate 1 ha of cereals; now

[8] G. Thiede, 'L'agriculture Européenne et la révolution technique', in M. Tracy and I. Hodac (eds), *Prospects for Agriculture in the European Economic Community*, Bruges, 1979, pp. 110–138; G. C. Fite, *American Farmers: The New Minority*, Bloomington, Indiana, 1981, pp. 109–11.

it takes only 10 man-hours. In the United States agricultural output rose by 55 per cent between 1950 and 1972, but in the same period the number of million man-hours worked in a year on the land fell from 15,137 to 6172.[9]

Not only farm labourers but farmers have left the land in North America and Europe, particularly the occupiers of very small farms (table 7.2). This has allowed other farms to get bigger and made the use of machines economically possible. In the United States the average size of farm rose from 80 ha in 1950 to 100 ha in 1980. In Europe average sizes were, and remain, much smaller, but have still shown considerable increases. In Belgium, for example, the average size in 1950 was 5 ha but is now 11 ha, and in Sweden the average arable holding rose from 12.5 ha in 1951 to 20.1 ha in 1971, and in Denmark from 16 ha to 24 ha between 1960 and 1977.[10]

Table 7.2   Number of farms and farmers, 1950–80

	Thousand farms		Thousand farmers		
	USA	France	Netherlands	UK	West Germany
1950	5648	—	232	440	1285
1955	—	2134	—	429	1245
1960	3963	—	203	418	1158
1967	3162	1604	—	341	886
1970	2949	—	156	316	767
1975	2521	1225	—	266	645
1980	2428	—	100[a]	—	—

[a] Projected.

Sources: G. C. Fite, *American Farmers: The New Minority*, Bloomington, Indiana, 1981, p. 101; D. Andrews, M. Mitchell and A. Weber, *The Development of Agriculture in Germany and the UK: Three Comparative Time Series, 1870–1975*, Wye College, Ashford, Kent, Centre for European Agricultural Studies, Miscellaneous Study no. 4, 1979, pp. 21–2; G. P. Hirsch and A. H. Maunder, *Farm Amalgamation in Western Europe*, Farnborough, 1978, p. 92; A. Maris and J. de Veer, 'Dutch agriculture in the period 1950–1970 and a look ahead', *European Review of Agricultural Economics*, 1, 1973, pp. 63–78

SCIENCE, TECHNOLOGY AND GOVERNMENT SUPPORT

The primary consequence of mechanization has been to greatly increase labour productivity and cut increases in the cost of production. It has

[9] Thiede, *op. cit.*; W. D. Rasmussen, 'A post-script: twenty five years of change in farm productivity', *Agricultural History*, **49**, 1975, pp. 84–6.
[10] S. S. Batie and R. G. Healey, 'The future of American agriculture', *Scientific American*, **248**, 1983, pp. 27–35; Christians, *op. cit.*, pp. 23–40; O'Hagan, *op. cit.*; G. Brown, 'Agriculture in the EEC. 6: Denmark', *Span*, **23**, 1980, pp. 29–31.

also allowed better and faster cultivation and more timely sowing and harvesting, thus increasing yields. But the increases in yields have been mainly due to other causes.

During the first half of this century crop yields rose slowly in Western Europe and even more slowly in North America and Australia, where there was an abundance of land, and farmers aimed at maximizing output per caput rather than output per hectare (see figure 5.4). In the 1930s most farmers in Europe still relied upon growing crops in rotation and the use of farmyard manure to maintain soil fertility and to increase crop yields, although some chemical fertilizers were applied, particularly in the Low Countries and West Germany. In Britain only potatoes and sugar-beet received any significant amounts. Plant breeding institutions were established in several countries after the rediscovery of Mendel's theory in 1900; the exchange of new varieties led to some increases in yields. The Danish barley Kenia, for example, was adopted in England and France. Perhaps the most significant plant breeding advance at this time was the development of hybrid corn in the United States. First bred in 1914, it began to be grown commercially in the early 1930s. Weeds were controlled by rotations and by deep cultivation with a mouldboard plough and by hand hoeing. Some inorganic pesticides were known but were little used, and effective selective herbicides or fungicides were not available. Improvements in livestock breeding and feeding were also known. Artificial insemination was first used in Denmark in the 1930s; ideas on balanced feeds for livestock had been developed in Germany and were being adopted elsewhere; and in Britain, The Netherlands and New Zealand there was much research on grass varieties and grassland management. But in the 1920s and 1930s farming in most of the developed world was depressed and few farmers could afford to innovate, either in yield increasing improvements or in purchasing machines such as tractors, combine harvesters or milkers.[11]

However, the emergencies of the Second World War and the continued food shortages immediately afterwards led nearly all governments

---

[11] P. Lamartine Yates, *Food Production in Western Europe: An Economic Survey of Agriculture in Six Countries*, London, 1960; J. P. Johnson and D. J. Halliday, 'The development of fertiliser use in the UK since 1945', in A. H. Bunting (ed.), *Change in Agriculture*, London, 1970, pp. 265–73; Z. Griliches, 'Hybrid corn and the economics of innovation', *Science*, **132**, 1960, pp. 275–80; J. G. Elliot, 'Weed control: past, present and future – a historical perspective', in R. G. Hurd, P. V. Biscoe and C. Dennis (eds), *Opportunities for Increasing Crop Yields*, 1980, London, pp. 285–95; W. F. Raymond, 'Grassland research', in G. W. Cooke (ed.), *Agricultural Research 1931–1980; A History of the Agricultural Research Council and a Review of Development in Agricultural Science During the Last Fifty Years*, London, 1981.

to encourage production, and a variety of guaranteed prices, deficiency payments, subsidies and tariffs brought prosperity back to farming. In most countries farmers began to adopt the improved technologies made available in the 1920s and 1930s. Since then most states have encouraged research in all branches of agriculture, and a continuous flow of new machines, crop varieties, fertilizers and pesticides has provided farmers with the means of yet further increasing yields and output.

HIGHER CROP YIELDS

The application of new techniques in farming has raised yields at unprecedented rates since the end of the Second World War. Thus it has been estimated that in Western Europe wheat yields increased at 0.8 per cent per annum between 1850 and 1913 and at 0.6 per cent between 1913 and 1938, but between 1939 and 1970 at 2.2 per cent, reaching 2.6 per cent in the 1960s. Wheat yields have doubled in 30 years in many countries (table 7.3); even in those countries where yields were already high in 1950, such as The Netherlands and Belgium, there have been considerable gains, although the land abundant countries such as the United States and Australia still have much lower yields than north west Europe. Most arable crops have had substantial increases in yields, but generally increases have been greatest in the cereals; increases in sugar-beet in Britain (table 7.4), for example, have been much less than those in wheat, potatoes and barley, and in the United States soybeans

Table 7.3   Wheat and milk yields in Western Europe

	Milk			Wheat		
	1948–50 (kg/cow)	1978–80 (kg/cow)	Increase (%)	1948–50 (kg/ha)	1978–80 (kg/ha)	Increase (%)
Netherlands	3657	5008	37	3530	6236	77
Belgium	3367	3849	14	3143	4999	59
Denmark	3117	4861	56	3587	5039	40
Sweden	2703	5186	92	2223	4292	93
United Kingdom	2673	4795	79	2687	5456	103
Switzerland	2843	4103	44	2647	4591	73
West Germany	2173	3986	83	2470	4810	95
Ireland	1933	3105	61	2243	4994	122
France	1730	3183	84	1830	4993	172
Norway	1963	5074	158	2190	4133	89
USA	—	5232	—	1120	2220	91
Australia	—	2963	—	1120	1370	22
USSR	—	2150	—	840	1691	101

Sources: United Nations, *Economic Bulletin for Europe*, **35** (2), 1983, pp. 167, 168; FAO, *Production Yearbook 1980*, vol. 34, Rome, 1981; *Production Yearbook 1964*, vol. 18, Rome, 1965

Table 7.4   Crop yields in the USA and the UK (tonnes per hectare)

	United States				United Kingdom		
	1950	1977	% increase		1950	1980	% increase
Wheat	1.05	2.05	95	Wheat	2.7	5.9	118
Maize	2.5	6.04	141	Barley	2.5	4.4	76
Potatoes	19.2	32.8	71	Potatoes	18.2	35.8	97
Soybeans	1.6	1.9	18	Sugar-beet	26.6	34.9	31

Sources: Ministry of Agriculture, *Agricultural Statistics for the United Kingdom, 1980 and 1981*, London, 1982; *Century of Agricultural Statistics in Great Britain, 1866–1966*, London, 1968

and potatoes have lagged behind maize and wheat (table 7.4).[12]

The precise reasons for the increase in yields are difficult to determine because there have been so many changes in technology in the last 30 years. New varieties have been adopted, more chemical fertilizers have been used, pesticides and herbicides have reduced crop damage and the competition of weeds, irrigation and underdrainage have improved environmental conditions, and the use of machinery has allowed sowing and harvesting to take place at optimum times. However, research in both Britain and the United States suggests that the breeding of new cereal varieties has been the single most important cause of increased yields, accounting for approximately half the recorded gains.[13]

Plant breeders have been able to improve cereals in a variety of ways. The breeding of varieties with a high response to fertilizer has been important, and the introduction of short stemmed varieties, able to carry an increased head of grain, has been crucial. Immunity to specific diseases has been significant, and the traditional breeders' art of producing varieties for different environments has continued. In the United States hybrid corn varieties were originally grown in the corn belt. Local varieties were necessary when the hybrid was extended north into Ontario, south west into Texas and south east into the old cotton belt. In Britain Scandinavian barleys have been crossed with indigenous varieties to produce a variety that can be grown in wetter and cooler

[12] FAO *op. cit.*, p. 62.
[13] T. J. Riggs *et al.*, 'Comparison of spring barley varieties grown in England and Wales between 1880 and 1980', *Journal of Agricultural Science*, **97**, 1981, pp. 599–610; R. Riley, 'Plant breeding', in Cooke, *op. cit.*; R. B. Austin, 'Actual and potential yields of wheat and barley in the United Kingdom', *ADAS Quarterly Review*, **29**, 1978, pp. 76–87; V. Silvey, 'The contribution of new varieties to increasing cereal yield in England and Wales', *Journal of the National Institute of Agricultural Botany*, **14**, 1978, pp. 367–84; N. F. Jensen, 'Limits to growth in world food production', *Science*, **201**, 1978, pp. 317–20.

regions, helping to explain the remarkable expansion of barley growing in Britain since the 1930s. [14]

Plant breeders have produced a succession of improvements. Farmers have adopted new varieties rapidly, not only within countries but across international borders. Thus the French wheat Capelle-Desprez was introduced into Britain in 1954; by 1965 88 per cent of the winter wheat area was sown with it. But the subsequent introduction of better varieties led to its equally rapid demise; by 1975 only 3 per cent was sown with the variety. The Maris family of winter wheats, which replaced Capelle-Desprez, was equally rapidly adopted in France. The speed with which new varieties are introduced must not, however, be exaggerated. In Britain there is a lag of some 12 years between the planning of a new variety and the distribution of new seed to farmers. [15]

The majority of discussions of yield increases place most emphasis upon the rapid growth of fertilizer consumption since 1950. Certainly the growth cannot be denied; the consumption of fertilizers tripled in the United States between 1950 and 1972, rose ten fold in Canada between 1939 and 1975, and increased five fold in the countries of the EEC between 1950 and the 1970s. This, however, possibly overstates the gain in plant nutrients in the soil; prior to the Second World War chemical fertilizers were comparatively expensive and large applications of farmyard manure, which contains nitrogen, phosphorus and potash, the essential nutrients, were made by the better farmers. Chemical fertilizers were also applied in the intensive farming areas of north west Europe. Since then chemical fertilizers have greatly increased in consumption but in parts of Europe and the United States less farmyard manure is now applied. [16]

In the 1950s and 1960s the use of nitrogen, phosphorus and potash fertilizers increased at much the same rate, but by the 1960s the phosphorus and potassium content of soils in the more advanced

[14] I. R. Bowler, 'The agricultural pattern', in R. J. Johnston and J. C. Dornkamp (eds), *The Changing Geography of the United Kingdom*, London, 1982, pp. 75–104; A. H. Dawson, 'The great increase in barley growing in Scotland', *Geography*, 65, 1980, pp. 213–17; J. D. Palmer, 'Plant breeding today', *Journal of the Royal Agricultural Society of England and Wales*, 131, 1970, pp. 7–17; J. F. Shepherd, 'The development of new wheat varieties in the Pacific north west', *Agricultural History*, 54, 1980, pp. 52–63; G. Doussinault, A. Berbigier and M. Pollacksek, 'Trends in cereal breeding in France', *Outlook on Agriculture*, 7, 1973, pp. 222–6.
[15] P. W. Russell Eggitt, 'Choosing between crops; aspects that effect the user', *Philosophical Transactions of the Royal Society of London*, series B, 28, 1977, pp. 93–106; Riley, *op. cit.*; K. Dexter, 'The impact of technology on the political economy of agriculture', *Journal of Agricultural Economics*, 28, 1977, pp. 211–19.
[16] Heady, *op. cit.*; Troughton, *op. cit.*, pp. 211–19; Thiede, *op. cit.*

countries of Western Europe could be maintained with relatively light applications of these nutrients. Hence much of the subsequent increase has been in straight nitrogen, which is the most common limiting factor in increasing crop yields (figure 7.1). By the 1970s fertilizer consumption in Belgium, Norway, The Netherlands and West Germany was thought to be near the optimum, as it was on much of the cereal crop in England. But comparatively little was used on grassland; whereas leys receive fertilizer, permanent grass receives little. [17] There are, however, still considerable variations in fertilizer consumption within the developed world (table 7.5).

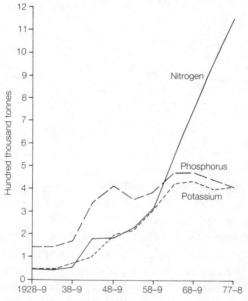

Figure 7.1   Use of nitrogen, phosphorus and potassium fertilizers in the United Kingdom, 1950–80
Source: Sir Hans Kornberg, *Agriculture and Pollution*, Royal Commission on Environmental Pollution, Seventh Report, London, HMSO Cmnd 7644, 1979, Figure 2.3

Although new varieties and the increase in the supply of plant nutrients have been of critical importance in raising crop yields, the adoption of chemical herbicides, pesticides, and fungicides has also made a valuable contribution. Before 1945 weeds – any plants which compete with the crop for plant nutrients in the soil – were kept down mainly by

[17] 'European agriculture towards the end of the 20th century', *Economic Bulletin for Europe*, **25**, 1983, pp. 164–5, 175, p. 73; Christians, *op. cit.*, p. 40; U. Varjo, *Finnish Farming: Typology and Economics*, Budapest, 1977; P. J. Gersmehl, 'No-till farming: the regional applicability of a revolutionary agricultural technology', *Geographical Review*, **68**, 1978, pp. 66–75; A. H. Kampp, *An Agricultural Geography of Denmark*, Budapest, 1975, p. 73.

Table 7.5   Consumption of mineral fertilizers, 1948–50, 1961–5, 1979 (kilograms of N, P₂O₅ and K₂O per hectare of agricultural land)

	1948–50	1961–5	1979	% increase 1950–79	% increase 1961–5 to 1979
Netherlands	315	232	341	8	47
West Germany	99	185	292	195	58
Belgium	161	244	293	82	20
Norway	108	154	284	162	54
Denmark	82	146	239	191	64
France	31	82	185	496	125
Sweden	39	83	142	264	71
UK	88	74	103	17	39
Switzerland	25	56	79	216	41
Italy	—	45	133	—	195
USA	8	21	48	500	128
USSR	2	6	28	1300	366
Canada	—	8	26	—	225

Sources: FAO, *Production Yearbook 1957*, vol. 11, Rome, 1958; *Fertilizer Yearbook 1981*, vol. 31, Rome, 1982; *Annual Fertilizer Review 1977*, Rome, 1978

cultivation with a mouldboard plough, which inverts the soil and destroys weeds, and by hoeing during the growth of the crop. The invention of selective herbicides that destroyed weeds before or during growth has reduced labour needs, and has both allowed cultivation with tines and some direct drilling and helped to increase crop yields. Chemical pesticides and fungicides were known before 1945, but were not efficient and were little used. Discoveries during and since the war of a number of efficient pesticides have been followed by much research in the chemical industries. In Britain some 800 different chemical sprays have been marketed, and the appropriate machinery has been developed and is now widely used. The importance of chemical spraying should not be underestimated. The total loss to world food output from pests, diseases and weeds has been put at one-third of the standing crop, and a further 15 per cent is lost in store after the harvest. Even in Great Britain, where chemical spraying has been widely adopted, some 10 per cent of the value of the 1976 crop was lost to disease, and in 1970 15 per cent of the United States corn crop was lost to a fungal infection. Not surprisingly pesticides, once available, have been rapidly adopted. The real monetary value of pesticides applied rose by 15 times in the non-Communist world between 1953 and 1978, and most of this was consumed in the developed countries.[18]

[18] D. W. Robinson, 'The impact of herbicides on crop production', in R. Hurd, P. V. Biscoe and C. Dennis, *op. cit.*, pp. 297–312; W. Graham-Bryce, 'Crop protection: a consideration of the effectiveness and disadvantages of current methods and scope

Crop yields in the developed countries have thus been increased because farmers have purchased extra inputs developed and made off the farm. New plant varieties have been bred by state breeding institutes and seed merchants, and fertilizers, pesticides and herbicides produced by the chemical industries. Changes on the farm have also improved the crop's environment. Irrigation is not of major importance in the developed countries, but its extension has helped increase crop yields as well as allowing dry lands to be cultivated. In the United States the irrigated area has tripled since 1940 and now produces one-quarter of the value of agricultural output. In much of northern Europe poor drainage has limited crop yields. The underdrainage of heavy soils reduces waterlogging and helps increase yields.[19]

LIVESTOCK PRODUCTION

Although most discussions of post-war agriculture deal with advances in the productivity of arable land, livestock production makes up a majority of agricultural output; it accounts for at least half the total value of agricultural output in every country in the developed world, varying from 55 per cent in France and the USSR to over 85 per cent in Denmark. Over the last 30 years animal production has generally increased more rapidly than crop production, the acceleration of a process that began about a century ago in some Western countries, more recently in others.[20]

In nearly all Western countries the total output of animal products has increased substantially since 1950; Canada and the United Kingdom illustrate widespread tendencies (tables 7.6 and 7.7).

These increases in output have been achieved partly by increases in the number of animals kept, partly by increases in their productivity.

---

for improvement', *Philosophical Transactions of the Royal Society of London*, series B, **281**, 1977, pp. 163–79; Batie and Healey, *op. cit.*, pp. 27–35; E. R. Bullen, 'How much cultivation?', *Philosophical Transactions of the Royal Society of London*, series B, **281**, 1977, pp. 83–92.
[19] F. H. W. Green, 'Recent changes in land use and treatment', *Geographical Journal*, **142**, 1976, pp. 12–26; Batie and Healey, *op. cit.*, pp. 27–35.
[20] Wadekin, *op. cit.*; Jean Chombert de Lauve, *L'Aventure Agricole de la France de 1945 à nos jours*, Paris, 1979, p. 41; P. H. Knudsen, *Agriculture in Denmark*, Agricultural Research Council of Denmark, Copenhagen, 1977, p. 32; Kampp, *op. cit.*, p. 74; J. B. Viallion, 'Croissance agricole en France et en Bourgogne de 1852–1970, *Revue d'Histoire Economique et Sociale*, **55**, 1977, pp. 464–98; E. J. Ojala, *Agriculture and Economic Progress*, London, 1952.

Table 7.6   Livestock output in the United Kingdom

	1930s	1978
	(thousand tonnes)	
Beef and veal	550	1048
Mutton and lamb	190	238
Pork	210	634
Poultry meat	89	726
	(million litres)	
Milk	8.4	14.9

Source: W. Holmes, 'Animal husbandry, 1931–1980', in G. W. Cooke (ed.), *Agricultural Research 1931–1981: A History of the Agricultural Research Council and a Review of Development in Agricultural Science during the Last Fifty Years*, Agricultural Research Council, London, 1981

Table 7.7   Livestock slaughtered in Canada (thousands)

	Cattle	Pigs	Sheep and lambs
1951	1734	4488	438
1961	2731	5850	633
1971	3251	9743	205
1976	4331	7493	188

Source: M. Troughton, *Canadian Agriculture*, Budapest, 1982, p. 166

All livestock numbers have increased in the major regions of the developed world since 1950, with the exception of a decline in sheep – and, apparently, of chickens – in North America (table. 7.8). As there has been little change in the agricultural area over this period, the density of livestock has risen considerably. This has only been possible as a result of changes in the methods of feeding livestock. Animals can be fed in a variety of ways, but the fundamental contrast is exemplified by the differences between Ireland and Denmark or the United States and Australia. In Denmark 90 per cent of the farmland is in crops and most of this is fed to cows and pigs. In Ireland 90 per cent of the farmland is in grass and this provides much of the diet of livestock. In the United States 90 per cent of arable output is fed to livestock, in Australia only 10 per cent. Thus in Ireland and Australia ruminants – cattle and sheep – rely primarily on grass for their fodder, in Denmark they rely upon arable crops.[21]

In the 1930s there was a greater reliance upon grass in all developed countries; but in several countries in Western Europe considerable

[21] Donald, *op. cit.*, 1982, p. 77; Knudsen, *op. cit.*, p. 16; Cunningham, *op. cit.*

Table 7.8   Increase in livestock numbers in the developed countries, 1950–80 (thousands)

		1948–52	1978–80	% change 1950–80
Cattle				
	Western Europe	66,335	88,460	33
	North America	88,369	123,814	40
	Australia	19,458	36,254	86
	USSR	55,780	113,958	104
Sheep				
	Western Europe	46,510	59,133	27
	North America	32,000	16,700	− 48
	Australia	145,000	198,000	37
	USSR	76,800	143,000	66
Pigs				
	Western Europe	34,778	86,180	149
	North America	63,626	69,832	9
	Australia	1,702	2,840	66
	USSR	19,720	72,631	268
Chickens				
	Western Europe	369,519	727,879	97
	North America	508,044	475,000	‐6
	Australia	19,188	50,200	161
	USSR	452,000[a]	898,000	86

[a] (1958–9).
Sources: FAO, *Production Yearbook 1963*, vol. 18, Rome, 1964; *Production Yearbook 1980*, vol. 34, Rome, 1981

areas were devoted to fodder crops of which potatoes and fodder roots were among the most important. Some grain was fed to cattle, and concentrates, made from imported oilseeds, were also used. Pigs and poultry, which are non-ruminants and cannot easily digest grass and therefore have to be fed with crops that can also be directly fed to man, were fed with a variety of feeds including grain, potatoes, fodder roots and skimmed milk.

In the last 30 years there have been substantial changes in the nature of livestock feeding and the efficiency of fodder production. Grass remains a major source of feed in some countries, notably Ireland, Britain, New Zealand and The Netherlands, but the output per hectare has increased substantially. Research on grass varieties has led to the introduction of higher yielding varieties; in Britain, for example, Belgian and Dutch varieties have been adopted. There have been considerable increases in the application of fertilizers, particularly nitrogen fertilizers, and the use of lime – notably in Ireland – has reduced soil acidity and increased yields. The introduction of electric fencing has improved the management of grazing lands, and the cutting of hay has been mechanized. [22]

Perhaps greater changes have taken place in the use of arable crops as fodder. Root crops, which were an important part of the fodder supply in the 1930s, needed much labour to weed and harvest, and in most countries have declined as labour has become scarcer. Some new fodder crops have been introduced; soybeans and hybrid grain sorghum have been most important in the United States, and in western Europe maize, a high yielding fodder, has advanced northwards. But the principal change has been the increased use of cereals, and particularly barley, as a feed for cattle, pigs and poultry. Fewer crops grown on the farm – with the exception of grass – are now fed *directly* to livestock. Knowledge of the dietary needs of animals at different stages of their growth has led to the idea of balanced rations, and much fodder supply is now bought from firms who produce compounds made up of grain and high protein foods; the latter were formerly provided in Europe by imported African oilseeds or fishmeal, but these have been increasingly replaced in the last ten years by soybeans imported from the United States and Brazil. [23]

There has thus been a considerable increase in the supply of fodder for livestock, partly from higher yields and partly, in Europe and the USSR, by increased imports of feed. But improvements in livestock and their environment have improved the efficiency with which fodder is converted into milk, meat and eggs.

Since the 1930s advances in the knowledge of livestock diseases, and the development of vaccines and antibiotics, has greatly reduced the impact of disease. Among cattle the elimination of bovine tuberculosis and the great reduction of brucellosis have been of critical importance, and there have been parallel advances in the reduction of disease among pigs and poultry. Indeed, the confinement of large numbers of pigs and poultry in small areas would have been impossible without control of disease. Cattle have been bred to improve the efficiency with which feed is converted into meat. In Britain milk formerly came mainly from

[22] Raymond, *op. cit.*; T. H. Davies, 'The evolution of modern dairy cow grazing systems', *ADAS Quarterly Review*, 22, 1976, pp. 275–82; D. A. Gillmore, 'Agriculture', in D. A. Gillmore (ed.), *Irish Resources and Land Use*, Dublin, 1979, p. 126.
[23] J. P. Berlan, J. P. Bertrand and L. Lebas, 'The growth of the American soybean complex', *European Review of Agricultural Economics*, 4, 1977, pp. 395–416; Knudsen, *op. cit.*, pp. 27, 30, 37; R. E. H. Mellor, *The Two Germanies; A Modern Geography*, London, 1978, p. 291; J. T. Coppock, 'Agricultural changes in Britain', *Geography*, 49, 1964, pp. 322–7; FAO, *op. cit.*, pp. 50–2.

Friesians. West European breeds such as the Charollais, Simmental and Limousin have become established in North America and Britain. Modern pigs and poultry are largely hybrids, replacing the local varieties. Indeed modern broiler hens in Western Europe are mainly of American origin. The control of the productive capacity of livestock has been increased by the spread of artificial insemination, which began in Denmark, Britain and the United States in the 1930s but is now a more widespread practice. [24]

Better quality animals, which are now better fed and better housed, has greatly increased livestock productivity. The increase of milk yields is one index of this (table 7.3); but there are other measures. The output of eggs per hen has doubled in Britain in the last two decades. The number of piglets per sow per annum has risen from 11 in 1946 to 17 in 1976, and the average number of lambs per ewe has risen. For these and other reasons, the efficiency with which fodder is converted into meat or milk has increased, most noticeably among pigs and poultry. In 1946 in Britain, it took 5 kg of feed to produce 1 kg of pig meat; in the 1970s this had fallen to 3.5 kg. For poultry the feed needed to produce 1 kg of meat had fallen from 3 kg to 1 kg over the same period. [25]

There have been other changes in the efficiency of livestock production in the last 30 years. It is perhaps necessary to note some important trends in the organization of livestock raising. In the 1930s there were some important regional differences in the means of producing meat and milk, but in Europe pigs and poultry were generally produced on mixed farms, which also raised crops and other livestock. Indeed poultry were a very subsidiary part of mixed farming, and only in Denmark and the corn belt of the United States was pig production specialized and intensive. Since 1945 pig production and poultry rearing have in many countries become separated from general farming; special buildings and controlled lighting, ventilation systems and the purchase of all feed – so that little land is needed – has produced a system of meat production which is very different from traditional farming practices and, although efficient, has alarmed many critics of factory farming. These systems have been part of a general tendency for much larger herds and flocks in livestock

[24] Knudsen, *op. cit.*, p. 34; K. N. Burns, 'Diseases of farm animals', in Cooke, *op. cit.*, pp. 255–76; A. S. Foot, 'Changes in milk production, 1930–1970', *Journal of the Royal Agricultural Society of England*, **131**, 1971, pp. 30–42; J. W. B. King, 'Animal breeding research in Britain 1931–1981', in G. Cooke, *op. cit.*, pp. 277–88; A. C. L. Brown 'Animal health: present and future', *Philosophical Transactions of the Royal Society of London*, series B, **281**, 1977, pp. 181–91; Sir Keith Baxter, 'Animal nutrition', in G. Cooke, *op. cit.*, pp. 247–54.
[25] A. C. L. Brown, *op. cit.*

production. Indeed the changes in livestock produced since 1945 have been as radical as those in arable output, and the advances in output per man as dramatic as those in arable production.[26]

CONCLUSIONS

During the last 40 years agriculture has undergone a revolution more profound than anything experienced in the past. Although there remain marked differences in productivity between countries within the developed world, there have been marked increases in output and productivity over time in all countries, whether in the East or the West. By the late 1950s agriculture in the developed countries had fully recovered from the War and was providing a diet which met the demands of an increasingly affluent public. Since then output has continued to rise, owing to further increases in productivity. Scientific advances made in government and some private research institutes have provided new ways of reducing the time spent on farm operations, increasing crop yields and output per animal. But by the 1960s most of the population of the developed countries were able to buy a satisfactory diet, with a large proportion of livestock products. Further increases in incomes did not lead to yet further increases in the consumption of foodstuffs, and problems of surplus emerged in many countries in Western Europe and North America.

Throughout the period most countries, for political and strategic reasons, have protected their farmers against imports by tariffs, by guaranteed prices or by subsidized inputs. Methods of protection have varied, but they have generally been such as to provide small and inefficient farmers with a reasonable living. But technological advance has had serious consequences. Pre-war farmers bought relatively few inputs; most were produced on the farm. Over much of the last 30 years input prices have risen more than agricultural prices, so that costs have risen more than incomes; farm real incomes and farm incomes, compared with non-farm incomes, have declined. Thus, in spite of the great increases in food output, neither consumer nor farmer have been satisfied.

[26] D. B. Bellis, 'Pig farming in the United Kingdom – its development and future trends', *Journal of the Royal Agricultural Society of England*, **129**, 1968, pp. 24–42; Fite, *op. cit.*, p. 128.

8

Tropical Africa

Since the end of the Second World War no part of the developing world has had such a sad agricultural history as the countries of tropical Africa. In 1945 all but Ethiopia and Liberia were European colonies. Ghana was the first country to become independent, in 1957, and the other British and the French colonies soon received their freedom; colonial power finally ended when Mozambique became independent in 1974. Economic changes have been less fortunate. Between 1945 and 1960 most parts of Africa prospered. The economic recovery of Europe provided a rising market for Africa's agricultural products, and for much of this period the terms of trade favoured primary exporters. Food output at least kept pace with population growth, and indeed may have exceeded it; food imports in the 1950s were very small. [1] But since 1960 the situation has deteriorated. Food output has of course increased; but the *rate* of increase in the 1960s was 2.7 per cent per annum, compared with 2.1 per cent in the 1950s, and in the 1970s had fallen to 1.8 per cent, well below that in other developing regions (table 5.5).

This has been compounded by changes in population growth. Whereas in every other region the rate of increase in the 1970s was lower than in the 1960s, in Africa it has risen continuously since 1945 and in 1978–80 was, in many countries in Africa, growing at rates rarely experienced elsewhere in the world. The population of Kenya, for example, was increasing at 3.9 per cent per annum in the 1970s. As a result food output per head has declined in most countries in tropical Africa in the 1960s and 1970s. In 1962–4 Africa's food self-sufficiency ratio was 98 per cent; by 1972–4 it had fallen to 90 per cent. The volume of food imports trebled between 1962–4 and 1972–4 and doubled in

[1] FAO, *The State of Food and Agriculture 1958*, Rome, 1958, p. 97.

the 1970s. [2] The burden of imports is greater than these figures suggest: from 1960 to 1970 the price of cereals, the major part of food imports, rose by 50 per cent, but between 1970 and 1980 increased sixfold. In 1980 the cost of food imports was equal to tropical Africa's agricultural export earnings (table 11.7). [3] In spite of these imports most African countries had food supplies which were less than national requirements in 1978–80 (figure 2.4). Africa's problems were not confined to difficulties with food supplies. In the 1970s gross national product per caput – if Nigeria is excluded – fell 0.5 per cent per annum, and current account deficits rose from $1.5 billion in 1970 to $8 billion in 1980. [4]

POPULATION AND LAND

Africa is frequently described as sparsely populated. It is also often described as a continent with an abundance of farming land. This view requires qualification, on a number of grounds.

First, if total population is related to the land area, then Africa is certainly sparsely populated, although no more so than North America, Russia or Australia (figure 8.1a). It is also true that if agricultural area is related to the total population then Africa appears to be well endowed (figure 8.1b). Further enquiry suggests, however, that the situation is not so favourable. The urban and non-agricultural populations of Africa are a much smaller proportion of total population than in other major regions, so that if the agricultural population is related to the agricultural area then Africa's density is only exceeded by Asia (figure 8.1c). Much of the total agricultural area is poor grazing land – the semi-arid regions of the Sahel and East Africa. If only arable land is considered, then the density of the agricultural population to arable land is seen to be higher than in Latin America although well below the densities of Asia (figure 8.1d). But figures for arable land exaggerate Africa's position, for a high proportion of this area is in natural fallow, and not producing crops. If agricultural population is related to the total harvested area

[2] FAO, *The State of Food and Agriculture 1978*, Rome, 1979, pp. 2–3; E. H. Hartmans, 'African food production: research against time', *Outlook on Agriculture*, 12 (4), 1983, pp. 165–71.

[3] But see estimates in C. Christensen *et al.*, *Food Problems and Prospects in Sub-Saharan Africa: The Decade of the 1980s*, International Economics Division, Economic Research Service, United States Department of Agriculture, Washington DC, 1981.

[4] C. Harvey, 'The economy of sub-Saharan Africa: a critique of the World Bank's report', *African Contemporary Record: Annual Survey and Documents*, 14, (2), 1981–2, pp. A114–A119.

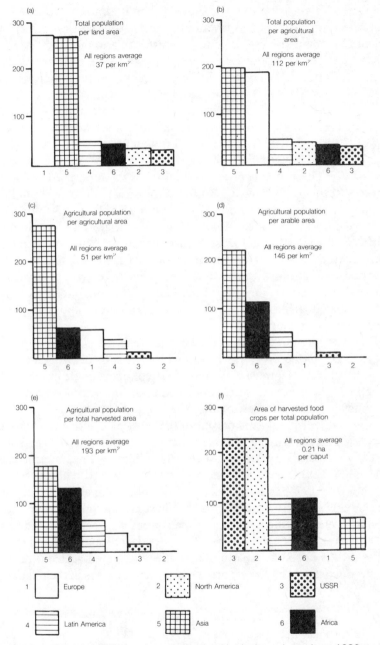

Figure 8.1   Total and agricultural population densities in the major regions, 1980
(index: all regions = 100)
Source: FAO, *Production Yearbook 1981*, vol. 35, Rome, 1982

– and FAO figures on this unfortunately omit a number of crops – then Africa again gives a less favourable impression (figure 8.1e). If the agricultural population is related to the harvested area of *food* crops then Africa has less land under food crops per head of the total population than Asia, but much the same as Latin America (figure 8.1f).

Second, the *distribution* of population must be considered. Whereas there may well be considerable areas in Africa that are underpopulated, there are certainly regions of high density, and a considerable proportion of the population is concentrated in a small area. In about 1970 one-third of Africa's population lived on only 2 per cent of the total land area.[5] The major centres of population in tropical Africa were (figure 8.2) the coastal areas of Benin and Nigeria with some 50 million people, Hausaland in northern Nigeria with 25 million, 25 million in Rwanda-Burundi and areas around Lake Victoria, and 15 million in central Ethiopia, all living at high rural densities. The concentration of population is particularly marked in East Africa where half the total population of Tanzania, Uganda and Kenya live in the Kenya highlands or near Lake Victoria on only 13 per cent of the total area.[6] Clearly, although much of Africa has very low densities it is not without problems of population pressure.[7]

Third, population density must be related to the carrying capacity of the land. It would be widely agreed that it is difficult to measure carrying capacity. However, a group of agricultural experts has recently attempted to relate the existing population to the potential food output.[8] They have done this by estimating the length of the growing season, and calculating the calorific output of the most productive food crops. They then calculated the numbers that could be supported for some 10,000 unit areas in Africa, at three levels of input – low, intermediate and high. These carry capacities were then compared with the actual population in 1975. In two areas the 1975 population already exceeded the carrying capacity (figure 8.3). The first are the relatively sparsely populated areas of the Sahel and Sudan zones of West Africa and the lowland areas of East Africa, where the potential output is low and much of the area is devoted to pastoral activities or rainfed agriculture of a low productivity. The second are the high density areas in the relatively

[5] A. T. Grove, *Africa*, London, 1978, p. 61.

[6] W. T. Morgan, *East Africa*, London, 1973, pp. 130–3.

[7] R. W. Steel, 'Problems of population pressure in tropical Africa', *Transactions of the Institute of British Geographers*, **49**, 1970, pp. 1–14.

[8] G. M. Higgins et al., 'Africa's agricultural potential', *Ceres*, **14** (5), 1981, pp. 13–21.

Inhabitants per km²

☐ under 6
▥ 6–50
▦ 50–200
■ over 200

Figure 8.2   World population densities
Source: The University Atlas, London, 1983, pp. 8–9

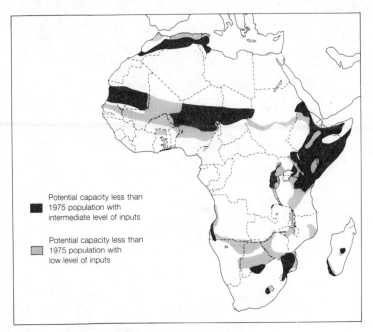

Figure 8.3   Carrying capacity and population density in Africa
Source: G. M. Higgins *et al*, 'Africa's agricultural potential', *Ceres*, **14**, 181, pp. 13–21

fertile districts of Rwanda-Burundi, the eastern shores of Lake Victoria, and the Kenyan highlands.

It is not argued here that Africa is overpopulated or that high densities are a primary obstacle to agricultural development. It is clear, however, that the rapid population growth of the last 50 years has led to problems of population pressure in parts of Africa, that not all Africa has abundant land supplies, and that not all African farming systems have low labour inputs.

THE AFRICAN ENVIRONMENT

European views of the African environment have ranged from the excessively optimistic to the unnecessarily pessimistic; some brief account of its salient features is necessary.

Low temperatures are not a limiting factor in the distribution of crops or livestock in tropical Africa. Only in some of the upland regions of East Africa does cold limit cultivation; this makes up 0.3 per cent of the land area of the continent.[9] In most parts of Africa temperatures provide a growing season long enough for a wide range of tropical and

[9] Higgins *et al.*, *op. cit.*

subtropical crops, although it is not easy to grow the major temperate zone crops. Wheat, for example, is confined to the upland areas of East Africa. It is differences in rainfall, not temperature, that determine variations in the agricultural geography of the continent. In the coastal areas of West Africa and the Congo basin annual rainfall is high, generally over 1400 mm. This region has two seasonal peaks of rainfall, as the intertropical convergence zone moves north and then south in the northern summer, and there are few months which are dry. Away from this zone, where the original vegetation was rain forest, annual rainfall diminishes and the dry season lengthens. In West Africa there are corresponding changes in the vegetation.

The rain forest is followed northwards by the Guinea zone, or humid savannahs; then the Sudan zone, where grass rather than woodland predominates and there are five to seven dry months; and then the Sahel, where grass and thorn bush predominate and the dry season may be as long as ten months of the year.[10] Beyond lies the Sahara. In East Africa the arid zone occupies much of the Horn and the lowland areas of Kenya and Tanzania. South of the Congo basin savannah areas of varying types occur and, although annual rainfall may be high, dry seasons of varying intensity predominate.

It is the length of the dry season that is critical for farming in much of Africa; nor is this merely a matter of the rainfall received. The high temperatures that prevail over much of tropical Africa throughout the year give very high rates of evaporation – four times those in the British Isles – and reduce the moisture available for crops.[11] The length of the growing season varies considerably. In the humid tropics there is little or no dry season and perennial crops can be grown; the length diminishes as annual rainfall declines and only annual crops are possible. With diminishing rainfall variability increases; the amount of rainfall received varies considerably from year to year, as does the timing of the onset of the rainy season, and this, in the savannah regions, has a profound influence upon crop yields. Only half of Africa has sufficient rainfall for rainfed agriculture and, in much of this zone, yields fluctuate considerably from year to year.[12]

African soils have been a matter of much debate and are still not

[10] P. Burnham, 'Changing agricultural and pastoral ecologies in the West African Savanna region', in D. R. Harris (ed.), *Human Ecology in Savanna Environments*, London, 1980, pp. 148–50.
[11] Grove, *op. cit.*, p. 16.
[12] Higgins *et al.*, *op. cit.*; S. Gregory, 'Rainfall reliability', in M. F. Thomas and G. W. Whittington (eds), *Environment and Land Use in Africa*, London, 1969, pp. 57–82.

properly understood. Compared with other parts of the world Africa has disadvantages. Much of the continent has been without earth movements for very long geological periods. Because of this there are few recent deposits to form the parent material of soils. The recent earth movements have given volcanic activity only in limited areas in Cameroon and East Africa. There are no large deposits of boulder clay, as in North America or parts of Europe. Furthermore the long periods of stability mean that the upper layers of deposits have been subject to chemical decomposition and leaching for very long periods. Finally, for a combination of physical and cultural reasons the deltas and lower reaches of African rivers – with the exception of the Nile – have not proved suitable for agriculture, in marked contrast with Asia.[13] The very high temperatures and, in the forest regions, the high rainfall have created problems for farmers. Under a forest cover soil temperatures rarely exceed 26°C, but when the vegetation is removed temperatures on the soil surface may reach 42°C. This accelerates the rate of plant decomposition and of leaching. Most of the plant nutrients in the forest ecosystem are stored in the vegetation and its removal for cultivation leads to a rapid decline in nutrients and humus in the soil, adverse changes in soil porosity and an increase in acidity. The most successful farming systems in the forest are those that simulate the forest cover, either by planting perennial shrubs and trees or by growing an intermixture of cereals, roots and shrubs that provide protection from the high temperatures and the impact of rain drops. It does not follow that African soils are inherently infertile or that they cannot be farmed successfully; it is simply that the traditional methods of farming, with long fallows of natural vegetation to restore fertility, have been undermined by the growth of population, and no entirely satisfactory replacement has yet been devised.[14]

MAJOR TYPES OF FARMING IN AFRICA

African farming shows a great deal of diversity. Some of its characteristics are outlined briefly in the following section.

Crops and livestock

A wide range of crops is grown in Africa. In the forest regions perennial crops such as coffee and rubber can be grown; food crops include

[13] Grove, *op. cit.*, pp. 7, 11.
[14] Hartmans, *op. cit.*

maize and bananas, but the distinctive features of these regions are the root crops – yams, taro and manioc, the last also being found in drier regions. West and central Africa is the only part of the world where root crops, with their low protein content, form a large part of the calorie intake. Rice is not of importance except in Madagascar, in Sierra Leone, where it has long been grown as an upland crop, and in small areas of irrigation in the West African savannah. In the savannah regions perennial crops cannot be grown without irrigation. The dominant food crops are a variety of millets and sorghum in both West Africa and eastern and southern Africa, where, however, maize is dominant. Groundnuts and cotton are the characteristic cash crops of the savannah areas. [15]

Most African farmers produce only crops; livestock are kept by pastoralists. Few farmers use ox drawn ploughs (see pp. 160–1) and the integration of crop and livestock production is rare. Much of Africa is infested with the tsetse fly, which transfers trypanosomiasis, a disease endemic in African game, from the game to cattle. Cattle other than the indigenous dwarf varieties are not numerous in most of humid tropical Africa; they are found mainly in the drier regions which lack the thick bush which provide the tsetse fly with its natural habitat. Approximately one-third of Africa is affected by the tsetse fly. Its eradication, it has been calculated, would allow an increase of some 125 million cattle. [16]

Population, soils and fallowing

Perhaps the most distinctive features of African farming are the methods of maintaining soil fertility, and the relationship between population density and land use.

At the beginning of this century population densities throughout most of Africa were low and the most common form of farming was shifting cultivation. When land was to be planted with crops the natural or secondary vegetation, whether forest or savannah, was cleared with the aid of an axe or machete; the larger trees were left and the stumps of others often not cleared. The vegetation was burnt. Crops were then planted with the aid of a digging stick; there was little or no preparation of a seed bed, although some root crops were planted in mounds of soil in

[15] G. P. Murdock, 'Staple subsistence crops in Africa', *Geographical Review*, **50**, 1960, pp. 523–40.
[16] C. K. Eicher, 'Facing up to Africa's food crisis', *Foreign Affairs*, **61** (1), 1982, pp. 151–74; A. Blair Rains, 'African pastoralism', *Outlook on Agriculture*, **11** (3), 1982, pp. 96–103.

the forest regions. Unlike in Europe or Asia, the plot was planted not to one crop but to a mixture, which might include roots, cereals and perhaps shrubs. Little or no weeding was practised, no fertilizer or cattle manure was applied, and after two or three years the land was abandoned and the natural vegetation allowed to recolonize the plot. Other plots were cleared for cultivation, and in some cases the village huts moved to the new site. Twenty or 30 years in natural fallow restored plant nutrients to the soil and the land could be sown to crops again. Such a farming system was almost universally condemned by Europeans. However, by the 1930s it began to be believed that this farming system, in Lord Hailey's words, was 'less a device of barbarism than a concession to the character of the soil'.[17] Later, Allan argued that the length of the fallow and the techniques employed were a function of inherent fertility: the poorer the soil, the longer the fallow needed. Agronomists showed that fallows, if of sufficient length, were capable of maintaining soil fertility in the long run.[18] and that many of the features of the system were an excellent adjustment to the tropical environment. Thus, leaving stumps in the cleared plots accelerated later colonization of the fallow. Burning the vegetation made the soil friable and the ash added some plant nutrients to the soil. Growing a mixture of crops, particularly a combination of roots, cereals and shrubs, provided cover for the soil, reduced soil temperatures and protected it from the impact of rain drops. More recent research suggests that the growth of a combination of crops can give a higher output per unit area than single stands.[19] As noted earlier, a fallow of adequate length does restore soil fertility. Many would argue that shifting agriculture, or bush fallowing as this method is now generally called, although giving low yields gives quite high outputs per head, for, in the absence of much soil preparation or weeding, labour inputs are low. A further advantage is that growing a combination of crops with different periods of maturing staggers the harvest dates.

More recently a different interpretation has been put upon the development of bush fallowing. Shifting cultivation requires a very long fallow, and thus needs abundant land. As population increases, less land is available and the fallow period is reduced. This requires some altermative

[17] Lord Hailey, *An African Survey: A Study of Problems Arising in Africa South of the Sahara*, London, 1938, p. 879.
[18] W. Allan, *The African Husbandman*, Edinburgh, 1965; P. H. Nye and J. D. Greenland, *The Soil under Shifting Cultivation*, Technical Communication no. 51, Commonwealth Agricultural Bureau, Harpenden, 1960.
[19] R. Tourte and J. C. Moomaw, 'Traditional African systems of agriculture and their improvement', in C. L. A. Leakey and J. B. Wills (eds), *Food Crops of the Lowland Tropics*, Oxford, 1977, pp. 295–311.

means of maintaining crop yields such as weeding, the use of manures, and the planting of fallows with rapid growing grasses or leguminous plants, all requiring extra labour. [20] Thus the major variations in farming in tropical Africa have been related to increasing population density; as density rises so the fallow is reduced, practices that help maintain crop yields are adopted, and farming moves from extensive to intensive methods. [21] If, however, alternative means of maintaining soil fertility are not adopted then yields fall and soil erosion occurs. [22]

African farming then can be differentiated upon the basis of the length of fallow, which in turn may be related to population density (figure 8.4). Shifting cultivation, where the site of the village is moved and fallows exceed 20 years, is now less common. In West Africa it is confined

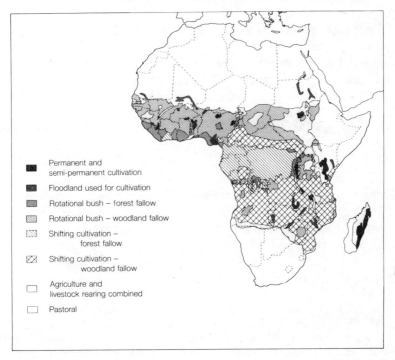

Figure 8.4   Types of farming in Africa
Source: W. B. Morgan, 'Peasant agriculture in tropical Africa', in M. F. Thomas and G. W. Whittington (eds), *Environment and Land Use in Africa*, London, 1967, pp. 242–73

[20] E. Boserup, *The Conditions of Agricultural Growth*, London, 1965.
[21] M. B. Gleave and H. P. White, 'Population density and agricultural systems in West Africa', in Thomas and Whittington, *op. cit.*, pp. 273–300.
[22] J. M. Hunter and G. K. Ntiri, 'Speculations on the future of shifting agriculture in Africa', *Journal of the Developing Areas*, **12**, 1978, pp. 183–208.

to a few parts of the forest. In central Africa – the Congo basin – and in much of southern Africa it is still the dominant mode, owing partly to the lower population densities, but also to the relative absence of towns compared with West Africa. But the growth of population density has reduced its extent. In Kenya, for example, it was common in the 1930s but is now rare. Bush fallowing, where the fallows are shorter and neither forest nor woodland become re-established, occupies most of West Africa and the Sudan zone that stretches into Ethiopia. Probably three quarters of Africa's cultivated land is in either shifting cultivation or bush fallowing. Permanent agriculture, where fallows are non-existent or very short, occupies little area but includes much of the population. It exists over most of the Kenyan highlands, eastern Madagascar where wet rice is grown, the Hausa area of northern Nigeria, south eastern Nigeria and parts of Burundi and Rwanda.[23]

The problems of bush fallowing are two fold. First, where adequate measures to maintain soil fertility are not taken, soil fertility is not restored, crop yields decline and soil erosion may occur. The first signs of this problem came in the 1930s. Not only was population beginning to increase after a long period of stability, but European occupation of land, notably in Kenya and Southern Rhodesia, had limited the fallow area available to African farmers. In the 1930s and 1940s colonial governments attempted to introduce conservation methods, with limited success. Since 1950 the population of Africa has increased by 114 per cent, the rural population by 73 per cent. Throughout Africa the length of the fallow has been reduced and this was frequently followed by declining yields and in some cases soil erosion. Although yields of food crops in Africa are not known with confidence there is evidence of decline in areas where fallows have been reduced – in the groundnut zone of Senegal, in Niger, in the Mossi plateau of upper Volta, the highlands of west Kenya and in Mali, Sudan and Ghana.[24]

[23] Judith Heyer, J. K. Maitha and W. M. Senga, *Agricultural Development in Kenya: An Economic Assessment*, Nairobi, 1976, p. 198; W. B. Morgan, 'Peasant agriculture in tropical Africa', in Thomas and Whittington, *op. cit.*, pp. 241–73; M. J. Mortimore, 'Land and population pressure in the Kano close settled zone, northern Nigeria', *Advancement of Science*, 23, 1967, pp. 677–86.
[24] Eicher, *op. cit.*; C. T. Agnew, 'Water availability and the development of rainfed agriculture in south-west Niger, West Africa', *Transactions of the Institute of British Geographers*, 7, 1982, pp. 419–57; Christensen *et al.*, *op. cit.*; U. Lele, 'Rural Africa: modernization, equity and long term development', *Science*, 211, 1981, pp. 547–53; R. M. Lawson, *The Changing Economy of the Lower Volta, 1954–67: A Study in the Dynamics of Rural Economic Growth*, London, 1972, pp. 40–4; P. Roberts, 'Rural development and the rural economy in Niger, 1900–75', in J. Heyer, P. Roberts and G. Williams (eds), *Rural Development in Tropical Africa*, London, 1981, pp. 1–15.

Second, most recent technical advances in agriculture have been made in temperate areas and are adapted to the climatic and technological conditions of permanent agriculture; their introduction into Africa requires considerable modifications of bush fallowing. Thus the use of the plough or tractor to increase the area in cultivation requires the complete clearance of vegetation and makes natural fallows difficult to restore. Although African soils are low in plant nutrients, particularly phosphorus, the use of chemical fertilizers is difficult, for high temperatures and heavy rainfall in the forest zone leach them out of the soil, and in the drier areas they cannot be absorbed by the soil. The cultivation of a variety of crops in cleared plots precludes the use of pesticides, which are specific to a single crop, and harvesting machinery cannot be used except on single stands. The introduction of large scale farming using the plough and other heavy machinery has led to some notable disasters in colonial times and since.

Small farms and commercialization

Large farms exist in Africa. Thus in Zimbabwe and Zambia European farmers with large holdings still exist, although in dwindling numbers. In Kenya many European farms passed to Kenyans did not change in size after independence. Plantations are to be found although few in both numbers and as a proportion of total farmland. In some African countries large scale farming on the Soviet model has been tried, notably in Ghana, and in the Sudan large scale mechanized farming of grain has developed in the last 20 years. But the great majority of farms in Africa are small. Thus in Ethiopia the average size of farm is less than 5 hectares; in Tanzania 83 per cent of farms are less than 3 hectares, in Malawi 80 per cent. In the Kano close settled zone the average family holding is over 3 ha, but only 1.2–1.5 ha are in crops; the rest is in fallow. Farms in southern Nigeria are also overwhelmingly small.[25]

But these small farms provide most of Africa's food output and a substantial proportion of its export crops. Thirty years ago African farming was described as predominantly subsistence; it is still true that a majority of African farmers produce food primarily for their own consumption. It has been estimated that only half African total agricultural

[25] G. Hyden, *Beyond Ujamaa in Tanzania: Underdevelopment and an Uncaptured Peasantry*, 1980, p. 10; A. Getahrun, 'Agricultural systems in Ethiopia', *Agricultural Systems*, 3, 1975, pp. 281–93; B. H. Kinsey and I. Ahmed, 'Mechanical innovations on small African farms: problems of development and diffusion', *International Labour Review*, 122 (2), 1983, p. 222; Mortimore, *op. cit.*; W. B. Morgan, 'Farming practice, settlement patterns and population density in south-eastern Nigeria', *Geographical Journal*, 121, 1955, pp. 320–33.

output is marketed; of this, half is export crops, half food crops. The growth of a large urban market, combined with the existence of a substantial rural population without land – 8–10 million rural Africans are estimated to have no land – has led to an increase in the production of food crops for cash rather than simply farm consumption. However, most African farmers still produce their own food first, and crops for sale are a secondary matter. Only in a few areas have farmers given up food farming to concentrate upon export crops, as in the groundnut areas of Senegal, in some of the cocoa areas of Nigeria and the cotton areas of the Gezira in the Sudan.[26]

Few economists now argue that African farmers are unresponsive to price changes, or that their farming behaviour is determined primarily by cultural rather than economic norms. None the less, African governments have had much difficulty in controlling peasant farm output, and in securing food supplies from the countryside for the towns.

THE GROWTH OF AGRICULTURAL OUTPUT

Export crops

In the second half of the nineteenth century the growth of incomes and industry in Europe provided Africa with the opportunity to export a variety of agricultural commodities, notably oilseeds. Initially European involvement was solely through traders, but by the early twentieth century most of tropical Africa had become French, British, German or Portuguese colonies. The rapid growth of agricultural exports since 1900 came from three types of farms. First, Europeans settled in Kenya, Southern and Northern Rhodesia and the Portuguese colonies of Mozambique and Angola. Exports from European farms included tobacco, tea and coffee. In some colonies Africans were forbidden to grow these cash crops in order to maintain prices for European settlers. In Northern Rhodesia much of the maize for consumption in the copper belt was produced on European farms. Second, land was leased to foreign companies to produce crops on plantations. Thus in the Congo land was leased to Unilever to produce palm oil, sisal was grown in Tanganyika, rubber in Liberia and sugar in Mozambique. In West Africa, however, both the British and French colonial governments were reluctant to allow either plantation companies or European settlement.

[26] K. R. M. Anthony, *et al.*, *Agricultural Change in Tropical Africa*, London, 1979, pp. 33, 88, 138; J. H. Cleave, *African Farmers: Labour Use in the Development of Smallholder Agriculture*, London, 1974, p. 16.

Third, African small holders adopted cash crops which were sold to European traders in the major ports. The most notable examples of indigenous production were cocoa in Ghana and southern Nigeria, groundnuts in Senegal and northern Nigeria, and cotton in Uganda.[27]

The growth of these exports crops was very rapid between 1900 and 1930. Nigerian exports, for example, rose fivefold, declined during the depression of the 1930s and during the Second World War, and then boomed again in the immediate post-war period.[28] The extent of the area under cash crops at about 1950 is not known with any accuracy, but it has been argued that it occupied 15 per cent of the area cultivated by the indigenous population,[29] and in the first half of the century the area under export crops grew more rapidly than the area in food crops.[30] Since the 1950s there have been changes in both the organization and the production of export crops. In Kenya African small holders have rapidly adopted crops that they were formerly forbidden to grow, such as tea. Coffee has emerged as a major export crop, particularly in the Ivory Coast and Kenya. In some areas plantations have been nationalized – notably in Tanzania and the former Portuguese colonies – and the number of European settlers has declined in Kenya, Zambia, Angola and Mozambique. Elsewhere, on the other hand, state plantations have been encouraged by independent countries. More to the point, the great boom in the volume of agricultural exports levelled off in the mid 1960s, and in the 1970s earnings declined in many countries. There have been a number of reasons for this. First, the prolonged drought of the 1960s and 1970s reduced output in the savannah zones. Second, the rise in petroleum prices in the 1970s meant that imports from the developed countries became expensive relative to African exports. Third, the recession of the 1970s has reduced demand for African exports, and fourth, other developing countries have emerged as competitors, notably in palm oil, but in other commodities as well. In the 1970s some well established exports declined substantially, such as cocoa from Ghana, and in the late 1970s Nigeria was *importing* groundnuts and palm oil.[31]

[27] J. Levi and M. Havinden, *Economics of African Agriculture*, London, 1982, pp. 32–43; Anthony *et al.*, *op. cit.*, pp. 38–42.
[28] G. K. Helleiner, *Peasant Agriculture, Government and Economic Growth in Nigeria*, Homewood, Illinois, 1966, p. 5.
[29] FAO, *op. cit.*, 1958, p. 59.
[30] FAO, *African Survey*, Rome, 1962, p. 34.
[31] B. Beckman, 'Ghana, 1951–78: the agrarian basis of the post-colonial state', in Heyer, Roberts and Williams, *op. cit.*, pp. 143–67; R. A. Joseph, 'Affluence and under-development: the Nigerian experience', *Journal of Modern African Studies*, 16 (2), 1978, pp. 221–39; Anthony *et al.*, *op. cit.*, pp. 38–57.

The role of exports in African economic development has been subject to much debate. Twenty years ago René Dumont commented on the absurdity of groundnuts being exported from countries where humans had too little protein, to be fed to cattle in Europe. [32] Others have argued that the substantial area devoted to export crops – possibly 10–15 per cent of the harvested area in tropical Africa [33] – should be used to grow food crops for home consumption. But African states are here in a difficult position, for exports of agricultural products account for a high proportion of foreign earnings in all except Nigeria and Zambia, where oil and copper provide most export earnings. Loss of these earnings would greatly retard African countries' attempts to modernize their economies and improve their standards of living.

Food crops

Little is known of the growth of food production prior to 1950. Since then food output has certainly increased substantially, but at a declining rate (see table 5.5). There are however important variations. Between 1960 and 1976 food output increased by more than 50 per cent in only a handful of nations in tropical Africa; in Zambia, Zimbabwe, Malawi, Tanzania, the Sudan, and the Ivory Coast (figure 8.5). But in the same period the population of tropical Africa increased by 75 per cent. Thus in most countries population outpaced the growth of food, and output per caput fell; the only exceptions were Malawi, Tanzania, the Sudan, Gabon, Liberia, Cameroon, Congo, Sierra Leone and the Ivory Coast (figure 8.6).

The lack of reliable statistics on food crops and the confusion between fallow and cultivated area make it difficult to estimate the relative importance of area increase and higher yields in the growth of food output in Africa. Most authorities believe that yields have increased little and extra output has come mainly from increasing the area in crops. Thus the area in crops is thought to have increased by 12 per cent between 1960 and 1975, with the greatest increases in East Africa but an actual decline in the Sahel. During the same period 90 per cent of the increased cereal output came from area expansion, only 10 per cent from yield increases. Increases in area have come not only from the expansion of settlement into unoccupied areas, particularly in the Sudan, but from the reduction of fallow and an increase in the period for which crops are grown between fallows. Expansion into new areas has often been into marginal areas, as in the Sahel during the rainier periods of the

[32] R. Dumont, *False Start in Africa*, London, 1966, p. 115.
[33] FAO, *Production Yearbook 1980*, vol. 34, Rome, 1981.

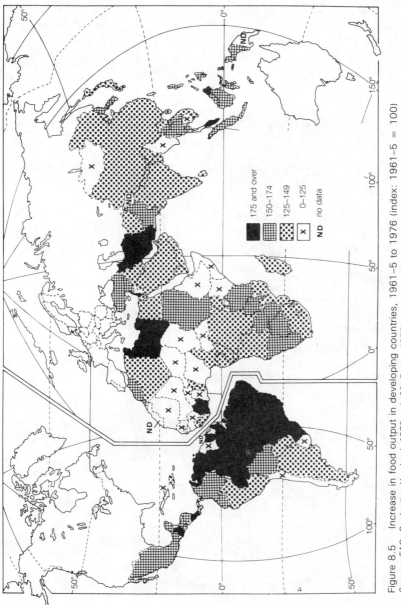

Figure 8.5   Increase in food output in developing countries, 1961–5 to 1976 (index: 1961–5 = 100)
Source: FAO, *Production Yearbook 1976*, vol. 30, Rome, 1977

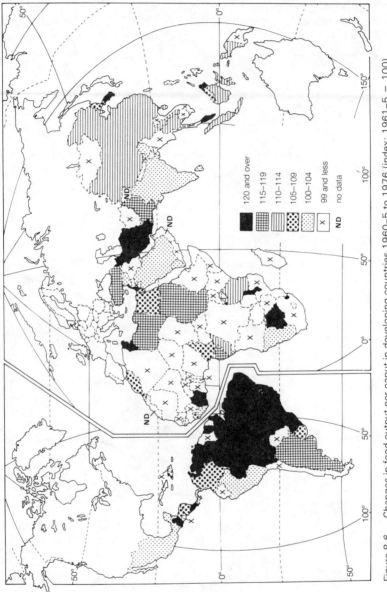

Figure 8.6   Changes in food output per caput in developing countries 1960–5 to 1976 (index: 1961–5 = 100)
Source: FAO, *Production Yearbook 1976*, vol. 30, Rome, 1977

1960s, or into the drier regions of northern Buganda in the 1950s. [34]

Data on the area in the major food crops confirm the belief that the area in crops has increased while yields have stagnated or even declined (figure 8.7). Decline has occurred where poor land has been cultivated, or fallows reduced, as in southern Niger. [35] In the Kano close settled zone the fallow period has been steadily reduced over the last half century; although intensive farming practices have been adopted, crop yields have stagnated for the last 30 years. [36]

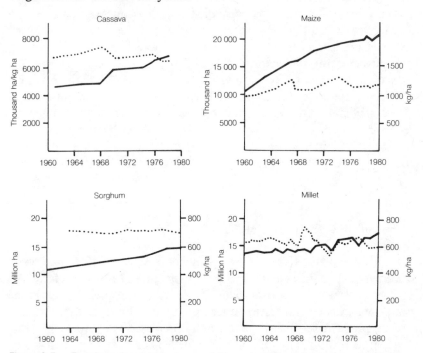

Figure 8.7   Trends in the yield and area of the major African food crops, 1960–80
Sources: FAO, *Production Yearbook 1976*, vol. 30, Rome, 1977; *Production Yearbook 1981*, vol. 35, Rome, 1982

[34] Anthony *et al.*, *op. cit.*, p. 37; Christensen, *et al.*, *op. cit.*; Lele, *op. cit.*; World Bank, *Accelerated Development in Sub-Saharan Africa: An Agenda for Action*, Washington DC, 1981, p. 47; J. M. Cohen, 'Land tenure and rural development in Africa', in R. H. Bates and M. F. Lofchie (eds), *Agricultural Development in Africa: Issues of Public Policy*, New York, 1980, pp. 349–400; B. Aklilu, 'The diffusion of fertilizer in Ethiopia: patterns, determinants and implications', *Journal of Developing Areas*, **14**, 1980, pp. 387–94; A. T. Grove, 'Geographical introduction to the Sahel', *Geographical Journal*, **144**, 1978, pp. 407–15; G. B. Masefield, 'Agricultural change in Uganda, 1945–1960', *Food Research Institute Studies*, **3** (2), 1962.
[35] Agnew, *op. cit.*; Roberts, *op. cit.*
[36] A. H. Kassam *et al.*, 'Improving food crop production in the Sudan savanna zone of Northern Nigeria', *Outlook on Agriculture*, **8** (6), 1983, pp. 341–7.

Not only have the yields of the food crops increased comparatively little in the last 30 years, but African yields are for the most part well below those in the developed regions (figure 8.8), as might be expected, but also below those in Latin America and Asia. This is to some extent inherent in the traditional farming system, where natural fallowing aimed only to maintain yields, and where labour inputs were minimized so that although yields were low, output per head was high. Once fallow was reduced, some means of maintaining – let alone increasing – yields was necessary. The traditional separation of crop production and livestock keeping precluded the use of animal manure, and the absence of tropical legumes as effective as those of temperate regions has excluded another way of increasing nitrogen in the soil.

In the developed countries and in parts of Asia and Latin America traditional methods of farming had been developed by this century that gave crop yields above those found in Africa; they have since been further increased by the application of modern methods of farming. In Africa this has not happened. Inputs are lower in Africa than in either Latin America or Asia (figure 8.9); not surprisingly, crop yields remain low (figure 8.8).

THE USE OF CHEMICAL FERTILIZERS

Chemical fertilizers were almost unknown in Africa in 1950, and were confined to plantations and some of the cash crops of European farmers, such as tobacco in Southern Rhodesia. [37] But the use of chemical fertilizers was equally limited in Latin America and Asia 30 years ago. African consumption of fertilizers has certainly increased since then, but the level of utilization is much lower than in Asia or Latin America (table 8.1). Furthermore, the use of fertilizers has remained concentrated on relatively few farms and generally upon cash crops. Thus in Kenya, one of the more succesful African states in post-independent times, nearly half of all fertilizer consumption is for three cash crops, coffee, tea and sugar-cane; only 3 per cent is used by small holders for food crops. [38] There are numerous reasons for the limited increase in fertilizer consumption. Although African soils are deficient in plant nutrients, and crops might be expected to show good responses to fertilizer, there

[37] W. V. Blewett, 'The farming picture in tropical Africa', *World Crops*, 2, 1950.
[38] P. Wyeth, 'Economic development in Kenyan agriculture', in Tony Killick (ed.), *Papers on the Kenyan Economy: Performance, Problems and Policies*, Nairobi, 1983, pp. 299–310.

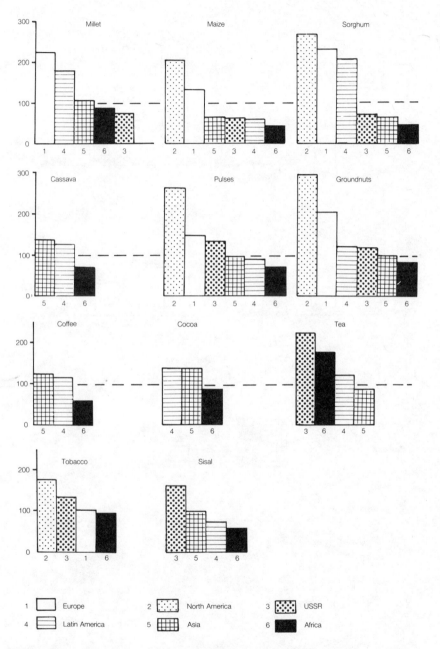

Figure 8.8   Yields of the major food crops by regions, 1980 (world average = 100)
Source: FAO, *Production Yearbook 1981*, vol. 35, Rome, 1982

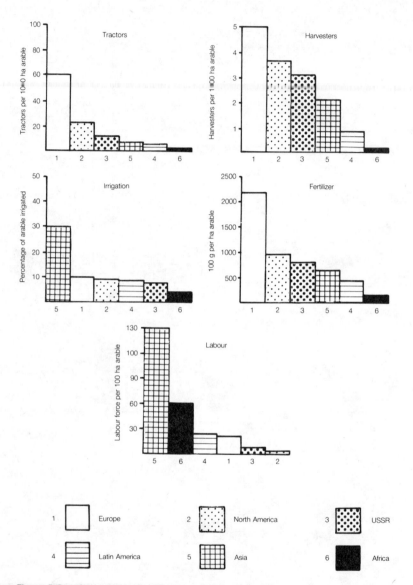

Figure 8.9   Agricultural inputs per hectare and per caput, 1980: major regions
Source: FAO, *Production Yearbook 1981*, vol. 35, Rome, 1982

Table 8.1   Fertilizer consumption, 1949–51 to 1980–1 (kilograms per hectare of arable, all nutrients)

	1949–51	*1980–1*	*Increase factor*
Latin America	3.1	46	14.8
Far East[a]	1.6	38	23.8
Near East[b]	2.4	34	14.2
Africa[c]	0.4	10	25.0
Asian CPE[d]	—	146	—
Developing	1.4	49	35.0
Developed	22.3	116	5.2
World	12.4	80	6.5

[a] Excluding China and Japan.
[b] Excluding Israel.
[c] Excluding South Africa.
[d] CPE: centrally planned economies.
Sources: FAO, *The State of Food and Agriculture 1970*, Rome, 1971; *The State of Food and Agriculture 1982*, Rome, 1983

are agronomic problems in optimizing its use. In the forest regions where the forest is cleared the combination of very high temperatures and heavy rainfall leaches the nutrients down into the soil and away from the roots of crops. In the drier savannah regions the unreliability of rainfall and, in much of the savannah, the lower amounts mean fertilizers may not be taken into solution and into the soil but may be oxidized on the surface. The successful use of fertilizer in these regions requires the use of irrigation, which is rare (see p. 159). Moreover, most African crop varieties have been selected not to respond to fertilizer but rather to survive drought or disease.[39]

Economic problems have also delayed the adoption of fertilizers. Where land remains abundant, there is little economic point in using fertilizers; where densities are higher, and only fertilizers can increase yields, farmers find the price too high in relation to the extra yield gained from their use. The chemical fertilizers used in Africa are nearly all produced in Europe or North America; the cost of moving them inland from the ports adds greatly to their cost and, in a country where tractors are still few, distributing fertilizers around the scattered plots of the typical African farm is time consuming. Modern transport routes in Africa were built to link cash crop zones to ports, and many food farmers are still

[39] Anthony *et al.*, *op. cit.*, p. 276; A. C. Coulson, 'Tanzania's fertilizer factory', *Journal of Modern African Studies*, **15**, 1977, pp. 119–25.

dependent upon head loading to market their crops and to acquire inputs. Thus, in Ghana and Sierra Leone some 70 per cent of produce is still moved to market by head load. For most, if not a majority, of African food producers the use of fertilizer is economically impossible.[40]

CROP VARIETIES

Much of the increase in crop yields in Europe and Asia since 1950 has been attributable to the breeding of crop varieties that are immune to disease and responsive to fertilizer use. However, the breeding of new varieties is specific to the climate and soils of a region, and although the technique of breeding can be adopted in other climates, the seeds themselves can only rarely be directly transferred. In Africa the little research on agriculture in colonial times was directed to improvements in export crops. Since 1950 great advances have been made in the Americas and Asia in breeding new high yielding varieties of maize, wheat and rice. But for the most part these advances have not been adopted in Africa. Rice is little grown in Africa; methods of rice growing comparable to those in Asia are found in eastern Madagascar, but otherwise rice growing was confined to Sierra Leone where indigenous rices were grown using shifting cultivation. Since the 1930s wet rice has been produced there and also in some irrigated schemes in the West African savannah. But the successful cultivation of high yielding rices needs careful water control and irrigation which is uncommon in Africa. New wheat varieties have been successfully adopted in Latin America and Asia, but wheat can only be grown in the upland areas of East Africa; new varieties have been adopted with success in parts of Ethiopia.[41] Hybrid maize, originally bred in the USA and then successfully adopted in Mexico, has proved more successful in Africa, where, unlike wheat or rice, it is a major food crop. Maize varieties bred in Kenya and issued in 1964 were rapidly adopted by small holders; by 1973 half Kenya's maize was sown to hybrid seed, giving yields considerably above that of traditional seed. Successful adoption has also occurred in Zambia and parts of Ethiopia, but only a small minority of all African farmers have so far adopted new seed, not least because its successful growth requires heavy fertilizer application. Unfortunately comparatively little progress

[40] R. E. Clute, 'The role of agriculture in African development', *African Studies Review*, **25** (4), 1982, pp. 1–20; Christensen *et al.*, *op. cit.*
[41] U. Lele, *The Design of Rural Development: Lessons from Africa*, London, 1975, p. 46; Wyeth, *op. cit.*

has been made in improving the other African staples of roots, millets and sorghum. [42]

IRRIGATION

In much of the African savannahs rainfall is not only low but is concentrated in a short period, limiting the types of crop that can be grown. The onset of the rainy season, to which period cultivation is confined, is variable, and the lower the rainfall the greater the variability. There are thus large parts of Africa where crop cultivation is impossible, and considerable areas where crops are grown but yields are low and variable. In Asia and North Africa irrigation has been a long established solution to this problem, but irrigation and water control techniques played little part in the traditional farming systems of tropical Africa with the exception of eastern Madagascar, although some riverine soils were used after seasonal flooding in Senegal, the Niger valley and Lake Chad. Indeed in 1980 only 1.8 per cent of tropical Africa's arable land was irrigated; full water control occurred on only 2.5 million hectares, 65 per cent of which were in the Gezira region of the Sudan and 15 per cent in Madagascar. [43] Irrigation has largely come as a result of external forces. Madagascar was settled by Indonesian migrants some 2000 years ago, and most other irrigation schemes either were a result of colonial government initiative or were undertaken by European settlers. The Gezira scheme in the Sudan was begun in 1925 during British rule, although the area irrigated has increased substantially since independence; in Senegal the French established rice growing on the Richard Toll scheme, and also began the irrigation of the inland delta of the Niger in Mali; in Zimbabwe some 30,000 hectares are irrigated in the Chiredzi-Hippo valley triangle, a European farmed area. Some 28 per cent of the value of Zimbabwe's agricultural output comes from irrigated land. But although the area irrigated in tropical Africa has increased more rapidly than the expansion of the arable area since 1950, it remains an unimportant part of African farming. [44]

[42] K. R. M. Anthony and V. C. Uchendu, 'Agricultural change in Mazabuku district, Zambia', *Food Research Institute Studies*, **9**, 1970, pp. 215–67; Eicher, *op. cit.*; B. F. Johnston, 'Agricultural production potentials and small farmer strategies in sub-Saharan Africa', in Bates and Lofchie, *op. cit.*, pp. 67–97.

[43] World Bank, *op. cit.*, p. 76; M. G. Adams and J. Howell, 'Developing the traditional sector in the Sudan', *Economic Development and Cultural Change*, **27**, 1979, pp. 505–18.

[44] Christensen *et al.*, *op. cit.*, 1981, p. 29; A. M. O'Connor, *The Geography of Tropical African Development*, London, 1978, pp. 34–8.

IMPLEMENTS, MACHINES AND LABOUR

Most African farmers still use relatively simple implements to farm the land. Land is cleared with axes and machetes and the vegetation burnt. In the more extensive systems planting is undertaken with a digging stick, in the more intensive systems with broad blade hoes with short handles. Weeding is done with hoes, which are also used to harvest root crops, and the sickle or hands are used for the cereals. The use of machinery is rare, and tractors or harvesting machines are uncommon outside European farmed areas or on some large scale settlement schemes (figure 8.9). The plough was unknown or unadopted in Africa south of the Sahara before 1900, and there was no tradition of using draught animals for ploughs or for pulling carts. Although the numbers of both ox drawn ploughs and tractors have increased in the last 30 years, most of the farm work is still done by human muscle, and draught animals make a far smaller contribution to farm work than elsewhere in the developing world (table 8.2). The early European settlers introduced ox drawn ploughs and in some regions in the 1920s and 1930s they were adopted by Africans, notably in Uganda, where it was associated with the spread of cotton after 1910, and in parts of Northern Rhodesia and Kenya. [45] In the West African savannah both British and French colonial governments advocated not only the adoption of ox drawn ploughs but also the integration of livestock and crops, but with limited success. Thus in the Kusai district of north east Ghana bullocks and ploughs were introduced in the 1930s; by 1960 only 12 per cent of the households had them. In Senegal the number of ploughs has risen rapidly and in 1972 there were 21,000; but this was on only 1–2 per cent of all holdings. [46]

The slow progress of the ox drawn plough is not surprising, for its adoption requires fundamental changes in bush fallowing and presents problems to peasants. The use of the plough requires removal of all the vegetation before use, unlike bush fallowing, and makes the

[45] Anthony *et al.*, *op. cit.*, pp. 140, 271; L. H. Brown, 'Agricultural change in Kenya, 1945–1960', *Food Research Institute Studies*, 8, 1968, pp. 33–90; D. J. Dodge, *Agricultural Policy and Performance in Zambia; History, Prospects and Proposals for Change*, Institute of International Studies, Berkeley Research Series no. 32, 1977, p. 8.

[46] A. Shepherd, 'Agrarian change in northern Ghana: public investment, capitalist farming and famine', in Heyer, Roberts and Williams, *op. cit.*; C. Uzureau, 'Animal draught in West Africa', *World Crops*, **26**, 1974, pp. 112–14; Y. Orev, 'Animal draught in Africa', *World Crops*, **24**, 1972, pp. 236–7.

Table 8.2   Percentage share of different power sources in total power input for crop production, 1980

	Labour	Draught	Machines
Africa	81	16	3
Far East	64	34	2
Latin America	56	25	19
Near East	63	25	12
All low income	63	35	2

Source: B. H. Kinsey and I. Ahmed, 'Mechanical innovations on small African farms; problems of development and diffusion', *International Labour Review*, **122**, 1983, p. 227

establishment of a natural fallow slow. This in turn requires the development of some alternative means of maintaining soil fertility if yields are not to decline. The oxen do not provide enough manure for even a very small holding. Oxen need fodder, particularly in the period before the beginning of the rainy season when ploughing takes place; in this dry period fodder is in short supply. In Kenya it needs 4 hectares of land to feed two oxen; few peasant holdings have such an area available or the credit to buy and feed the oxen throughout the year. In the humid tropical areas the prevalence of the tsetse fly and the lack of suitable fodder crops have hampered the spread of the ox.[47]

The advantage of the ox drawn plough is threefold. First, it enables farmers to cultivate a larger area; thus in Mali families with only the hoe can crop no more than 3 ha, those with a plough 5–10 ha. Second, by removing more weeds it may increase crop yields. Third, it may reduce the amount of labour necessary. But these are not always advantages. In the drier parts of Africa there is little agricultural activity for much of the dry season. Much labour is then needed when the rains begin, and the land must be cultivated and sown as rapidly as possible. Later there is a further labour peak when weeding becomes necessary. Increasing the area sown by using the plough may lead to labour shortages during the weeding period. Given the cost of acquiring and feeding oxen, and given the abundance of labour in some parts of Africa, the economic advantages of ox drawn ploughs over hand labour are not clear cut.

The role of labour in African agricultural production is of course paramount, machinery and oxen providing no more than one-fifth of the power used on farms. It would seem that there are few labour shortages if the figures for agricultural population densities are to be believed (figure 8.1); furthermore, the agricultural population of Africa has increased rapidly since 1950, by 72 per cent compared with 41 per

[47] Brown, *op. cit.*

cent in Asia and 44 per cent in Latin America (table 4.6). However this is not necessarily a guide to labour availability and it has been suggested that labour shortages have restrained the growth of food output. First, in many parts of Africa, and particularly in the east and south, large proportions of the male population are temporarily absent in the cities or in mining areas. Thus some 60–80 per cent of the labour in African agriculture is undertaken by women.[48] Second, surveys of activities in African rural areas suggest that Africans work about 1000 hours a year compared with 2000 hours a year in European agriculture and 3000 hours in Asia. In African communities much time is spent on associated activities such as processing and marketing crops.[49] Thus the labour input is less than the agricultural densities might suggest. Third, there are, of course, major spatial variations in population density, so that in some of the sparsely populated areas labour is insufficient to allow increases in output. Fourth, and perhaps most important, in most of savannah Africa there are seasonal bottlenecks in work, so that lack of labour does preclude the expansion of the area in crops and the amount of weeding that can be done. This presents considerable problems when both food and cash crops are grown. Thus in Chad the sowings of sorghum and cotton occur at the same time.[50]

It has often been believed that mechanization can overcome the problems of both spatial and seasonal labour shortages and fundamentally increase African food output. Under both colonial and independent regimes, there have been a series of land settlement schemes, particularly in the savannah zones, where the state has tried to develop mechanization, and in particular the use of tractors. For a variety of reasons, agronomic, economic and social, few of these schemes have been successful; the cost of providing spare parts, petrol and maintenance has too often been prohibitive. Thus in the Office of the Niger settlement scheme in Mali ox drawn ploughs have largely replaced the original tractors, and in the Tanganyika groundnut scheme in the late 1940s the cost of servicing machinery and the problems of maintaining soil fertility once the bush had been cleared led to the early abandonment of the scheme.[51]

---

[48] Lele, *op. cit.*, 1975, p. 26.
[49] Cleave, *op. cit.*
[50] Burnham, *op. cit.*; J. Tosh, 'The cash-crop revolution in tropical Africa: an agricultural re-appraisal', *African Affairs*, **79**, 1980, pp. 79–94.
[51] Uzureau, *op. cit.*

THE GROWTH OF FOOD OUTPUT: LIVESTOCK

Livestock products are a very small part of African food consumption; calories derived from animal foods make up only 7 per cent of all calories compared with 9 per cent in Asia, 19 per cent in Latin America and 32 per cent in Europe. Livestock products are a small proportion of the value of total agricultural output in most African countries, although there are some obvious exceptions. A large proportion of the population of Mali, Mauritania, Botswana and Somalia are nomadic pastoralists. In the last country some two-thirds of total agricultural output comes from animals. Compared with Asia or Latin America, cattle densities are low (table 8.3). This is partly explained by the distribution of livestock. The presence of the tsetse fly excludes cattle – except the indigenous dwarf cattle – from much of the humid tropical regions, and parts of the savannah areas. Thus in Kenya half the total area is infested with tsetse, one-third of Uganda, and one-quarter of Kenya. [52]

In contrast to Europe, or many parts of the developing world, the bulk of the livestock are kept not on farms where crops are grown, but by pastoralists who grow little or no crops and of whom many are nomadic. Nor are crops grown for their fodder. African cattle, sheep and goats are for the most part dependent upon the natural vegetation, and particularly savannah grasses, for their food. Fodder supplies are thus limited not just to the rainy season but to the earlier parts of that season, for much dry matter growth after the first flush of the season is indigestible. [53] During the dry season not only are the herds short of fodder, which they can partly overcome by migrating to distant areas or seeking pasture in seasonally flooded plains; there is also a lack of drinking water. Not surprisingly cattle put on weight very slowly. For most African pastoralists the major product of cattle is milk, but in the absence of good pastures yields are very low. Thus among the Masai and the other pastoral peoples of eastern Kenya milk yields average only 150 litres a year compared with 3000 litres obtained on European managed farms in the uplands. [54] It has often been argued that African

---

[52] V. Jamal, 'Nomads and farmers: incomes and poverty in rural Somalia', in D. Ghai and S. Radwan (eds), *Agrarian Policies and Rural Poverty in Africa*, International Labour Office, Geneva, 1983, pp. 281–311; W. Deshler, 'Livestock trypanosomiasis and human settlement in north eastern Uganda', *Geographical Review*, **50**, 1960, pp. 541–54.

[53] Rains, *op. cit.*, pp. 96–103.

[54] C. Stein and C. Schultze, 'Land use and development potential in the arid regions of Kenya', *Applied Sciences and Development*, **12**, 1978, pp. 47–64.

Table 8.3   Livestock in the developing regions

| | Numbers per hectare agricultural land | | % change 1961–5 to 1980 |
	1961–5	1980	
Cattle[a]			
Asia	0.44	0.11	0
Africa	0.13	0.18	38
Latin America	0.31	0.31	0
Sheep and goats			
Asia	0.45	0.56	24
Africa	0.15	0.34	126
Latin America	0.11	0.20	81
Pigs			
Asia	0.24	0.36	50
Africa	0.005	0.06	110
Latin America	0.08	0.12	50
Total livestock units[b]			
Asia	0.7	0.8	14
Africa	0.17	0.29	71
Latin America	0.39	0.45	15

[a] Including water buffalo.
[b] Including poultry. Livestock units are total numbers × 1 for cattle, × 0.1 for sheep and goats, × 0.5 for pigs and × 0.05 for poultry.
Source: FAO, *Production Yearbook 1976*, vol. 30, Rome, 1977; *Production Yearbook 1981*, vol. 35, Rome, 1982

pastoralists regard their livestock as a prestige symbol rather than a means of income. This may be so; they are certainly regarded, both by pastoralists and by sedentary farmers who own cattle, as a source of income to be sold only in times of extreme poverty. More cattle are sold for meat than might be thought, but the slaughter rate is still low – about 9 per cent in eastern Kenya.[55]

In spite of the low productivity of livestock in Africa, the numbers kept have increased substantially in the last 20 years, even though there have been substantial losses during drought years. Thus one-third of Botswana's cattle were lost in the droughts of 1961–6, and in the prolonged droughts of the early 1970s there were severe losses in the Sahel zone. In Mauritania the number of cattle fell from 2.5 million head in 1968 to just over 1 million in 1973.[56] This long run increase

[55] Heyer, Mathia, and Senga, *op. cit.*, p. 190.
[56] D. E. Vermeer, 'Collision of climate, cattle and culture in Mauritania during the 1970s', *Geographical Review*, 71, 1981, pp. 281–97; C. Colclough and P. Fallon, 'Rural poverty in Botswana: dimensions, causes and constraints', in Ghai and Radwan, *op. cit.*, pp. 129–54.

in livestock densities (table 8.3) has led to widespread overgrazing. In most pastoral areas livestock are individually owned, but the land is held in common. Thus there is little or no incentive for individuals to keep their numbers at the carrying capacity of the range. In Kenya attempts have been made to overcome this by grouping pastoralists into co-operatives, where the cattle are collectively owned, or by marking the range out in individual ranches.[57]

Although the numbers of cattle have increased substantially since the early 1960s, the amount of meat and milk produced has increased more slowly, partly reflecting the limited market for meat outside the towns where incomes have grown more rapidly than in rural areas. Little progress has been made in raising productivity, either by promoting ranches with controlled grazing and supplementary feeding, or in integrating crops and livestock on the same farm; most of the progress has been achieved on European owned farms in Kenya, Zimbabwe and Zambia.

GOVERNMENT AND INSTITUTIONS

In about 1950 African farming systems produced a poor but adequate diet largely through bush fallowing systems, although in some densely populated areas more intensive methods were practised. Crop yields were low and, outside the European areas, maintained by natural fallowing; output per head, however, was reasonably high. Since 1950 population has more than doubled. Increases in food output have been achieved by reducing the fallow and increasing the area in crops. Crop yields have not risen very much and, indeed, in some areas have declined. To attain the higher yields necessary to feed the population adequately it is necessary either to improve yields in the traditional systems or to import the technologies that have transformed European agriculture; the preceding sections have outlined how limited the adoption of new technologies has been. It is necessary now to turn to the reasons beyond those of agronomy, population and environment that have inhibited the increase of food output.

Agriculture and economic development

In the immediate post-war period economists and governments in both Europe and the developing countries believed that the standard of living

---

[57] Jamal, *op. cit.*; Stein and Schultze, *op. cit.*

could only be raised by economic growth, and that this was most easily achieved by encouraging the development of manufacturing industry. It is not surprising then that after independence many African states tried to encourage industrial growth, although they all had an acute shortage of capital, skilled labour, managerial talent and, often, raw materials. Many countries produced national plans, in which the improvement of industry and transport took priority and the creation of health and educational facilities was also important. This left very little planned investment to be allocated to agriculture, in spite of the fact that the majority of the population lived in rural areas and a high proportion of export earnings came from agriculture. It has been estimated that less than 10 per cent of capital expenditure in Africa is in agriculture compared with 20 per cent in India. Of individual countries, Tanzania allocated 12.5 per cent to agriculture in the 1970s, the first national plan in Zambia 12 per cent, Sierra Leone only 3–4 per cent, and even Kenya, with a comparatively successful agricultural performance, only 12.6 per cent. Malawi and the Ivory Coast were rare exceptions, the latter having allocated 28–30 per cent of public expenditure to agriculture, Malawi 19 per cent.[58] The food crisis of the early 1970s and the consequent steep rise in the price of food imports has led some states to change their policies, in theory if not always in practice. Both Nigeria and Ghana have adopted plans aiming at self-sufficiency in food, and in Zambia the new national plan announced in 1980 allocated 30 per cent of the capital budget to agriculture.[59]

Export crops and government policy

In both Nigeria and Ghana the British government introduced marketing boards to control the prices and flow of the major export crops. The boards paid fixed prices to the peasant for cocoa or groundnuts, and

---

[58] Lele, *op. cit.*, 1975; D. Ghai and S. Radwan, 'Agrarian change, differentiation and rural poverty in Africa: a general survey', in Ghai and Radwan, *op. cit.*, pp. 1–29; B. Dunham and C. Hines, *Agribusiness in Africa*, London, 1983, p. 120; Dodge, *op. cit.*, p. 51; J. Levi, 'African agriculture misunderstood; policy in Sierra Leone', *Food Research Institute Studies*, 13, 1974, pp. 239–62; Wyeth, *op. cit.*; J. Hinderink and J. J. Sterkenburg, 'Agricultural policy and production in Africa; the aims, the methods and the means', *Journal of Modern African Studies*, 21, 1983, pp. 1–23.

[59] B. N. Floyd, 'Agricultural planning in Nigeria', *Geography*, 67, 1982, pp. 345–8; T. Forrest, 'Agricultural policies in Nigeria 1900–78', in Heyer, Roberts and Williams, *op. cit.*, pp. 222–58; W. Smith, 'Crisis and response: agricultural development and Zambia's third National Development Plan', *Geography*, 66, 1981, pp. 134–6.

then sold the produce at the prevailing world price. It was hoped to supplement earnings in years of low world prices with the profits made in good years so that the peasant would be insulated from the fluctuation in world prices. First introduced in the 1930s, marketing boards dealt with individual export crops; the idea very rapidly spread to other British colonies and later was adopted in most French colonies. The marketing boards have been retained since independence, and indeed nearly all African export crops are now controlled by marketing boards; attempts have also been made to extend the system to food crops. [60] The marketing boards have been subject to fierce criticism. It has been argued that, by retaining a high proportion of foreign earnings, and paying peasants a much lower price, governments have heavily taxed peasants and reduced the incentive to increase output or improve productivity. In only a few countries – such as the Ivory Coast – have the marketing boards put earnings back into agriculture. The main beneficiaries have been not the farmers but a large white collar population living in the cities and employed by the marketing boards. Some have argued that the marketing boards have no useful function and should be abolished, allowing the price mechanism full play. [61]

Food crops and the government

In many African countries attempts have been made to control food prices in much the way that marketing boards have controlled export prices. In Africa since independence the major cities have seen what little industrial development there has been, and also a remarkable growth of administrators employed by the government. Political power has also been concentrated in the major cities, and governments have been eager to placate the urban populations. Thus attempts have been made to limit the increases in food prices, to the disadvantage of the farmers, and urban wages have been subject to less restraint. There is thus a greater gap between urban and rural incomes than in other parts of the developing world. Whereas in Asia the ratio is 1:2 or 1:2.5, in Africa it is estimated to be 1:4 to 1:9. African agriculture has had the 'role of a milch-cow...to support a dubiously productive urban elite in both public and private sectors'. [62]

[60] Johnston, *op. cit.*; M. Roemer, 'Economic development in Africa: performance since independence and a strategy for the future', *Daedalus*, 111, 1982, pp. 125–48.
[61] Levi and Havinden, *op. cit.*; Hinderink and Sterkenberg, *op. cit.*; R. M. Hecht, 'The Ivory Coast economic "Miracle"': what benefits for peasant farmers?' *Journal of Modern African Studies*, 21 (1), 1983, pp. 25–53.
[62] Lele, *op. cit.*, 1981; M. Lipton, 'African agricultural development: the EEC's new role', *Development Policy Review*, 1, 1983, pp. 1–21.

Furthermore, import substitution policies that protect home industries and workers in industry have meant that the prices of farmers' purchases have risen far more than the prices farmers receive. Hence although African states have suffered from unfavourable terms of trade for their primary exports in the last decade or so, within the states the rural sector has suffered *vis-à-vis* the urban areas. This has greatly reduced the incentive for farmers to increase output or productivity. Indeed many economists believe that increases in food prices would lead to an increase in food production and resolve many of Africa's food problems.[63]

Research and extension

Much of the advance in output and productivity in the developed countries in the last 40 years can be attributed to research in agronomy and the provision of extension services that have instructed farmers in the use of new methods, crops, fertilizers and pesticides. Such services are not widely available in Africa. Colonial governments established agricultural research stations in some African colonies early in the century; they were staffed almost entirely by Europeans, and dealt mainly with the problems of export crops. Valuable work was done on the adoption of American cotton varieties in Uganda, on the cross-breeding of oil palm varieties, in the 1950s on the diseases of cocoa plants, and in Sierra Leone on new varieties of rice.[64] Interest in African farming was limited until the 1930s; problems of soil erosion then attracted attention in the British colonies. In East Africa attempts were made to introduce conservation methods such as terracing, although with limited success. A more fundamental effort at change was made in northern Nigeria and north east Ghana where attempts were made to promote the use of ox drawn ploughs, the integration of livestock and crop production, and the use of manures and rotations.[65]

Since the 1950s more attention has been paid to indigenous food crops, and research in this field has had better results than is sometimes allowed. Hybrid maize suitable for the conditions of eastern and southern Africa have been bred and, in Kenya, widely adopted, and new varieties for the more humid conditions of southern Nigeria have been successfully tested.[66] But research in agriculture in Africa has been limited by lack of funds and by an acute shortage of African research workers. There is a further dilemma. The very high cost of imported technologies

[63] Johnston, *op. cit.*; Harvey, *op. cit.*
[64] Anthony *et al.*, *op. cit.*, pp. 249–52.
[65] Lord Hailey, *op. cit.*
[66] Hartmans, *op. cit.*

using fertilizers and pesticides and high yielding crop varieties suggests that research should be aimed at improving the indigenous farming systems, for they are adapted to the local ecological conditions. The need for replacing natural fallows with suitable rapid growing legumes is here paramount. But even if such traditional techniques were developed it is perhaps doubtful if they could provide yield increases large enough to keep up with likely future population growth. It is this which leads many to argue that the new technologies must be adopted in Africa if undernutrition and malnutrition are to be overcome.

The adoption of new technologies in Europe and America has been greatly assisted by the provision of extension services, and in particular of agents who can advise farmers about how to improve their methods. Attempts to provide similar services in Africa have foundered upon the lack of trained extension workers, who are often said to be of poor quality. With a shortage of extension workers to reach a large number of very small holdings, there have been considerable debates about the strategy of extension. Focusing on the bigger and better farmers in the hope that others will imitate their successes has not always worked and has often created a gap between the progressive farmers and the rest. Most of the extension work has been addressed to the male heads of households; yet women do a large proportion of the work on farms.[67] The problems of reaching a large population of small holders has doubtless prompted many African countries to create state directed farms where, in theory, it is easier to introduce farming improvements. This has often diverted funds away from the small farmers who produce the bulk of the food. Thus in Tanzania in the early 1970s an attempt was made to relocate the dispersed rural population in villages, on the grounds that it was cheaper to provide health and other welfare services to nucleated settlements; at the same time communal farming was encouraged for ideological reasons. It was felt that this would allow *all* farmers to be reached rather than a minority. But at the same time 80 per cent of all planned investment in agriculture went on large government projects, only 3 per cent to small holders in villages.[68]

Government instability

African independence led to the creation of states based on the boundary lines drawn by European governments in the late nineteenth century. This has led to at least two severe disadvantages for the independent

---

[67] Lele, *op. cit.*, 1975, pp. 67,76; Anthony *et al.*, *op. cit.*, p. 234.
[68] Dunham and Hines, *op. cit.*, p. 120.

states. First, many of them have remarkably small populations. Tropical Africa's population of nearly 350 million in 1980 was split into 49 political units, of which 22 had individual populations of less than 5 million and a total population of 40 million (table 8.4). This clearly provides many of these states with an inadequate market, and duplicates the needs for research and agricultural services. Furthermore many of the boundaries cut tribal groupings and, perhaps more dangerous, contain feuding ethnic groups.

Table 8.4.   Population size of African states

Population classes (millions)	Number of states	Population (millions)
0–0.9	9	4.5
1–1.9	5	7.0
2–2.9	2	4.9
3–3.9	3	10.5
4–4.9	3	13.7
5–9.9	18	80.3
10–19.9	6	87.9
20–29.9	2	60.8
30.0 and over	1	77.5
Total	49	347.1

In the last 20 years African states have suffered from acute political instability; there have been over 20 internal coups, and 14 wars. Not only has this led to a quadrupling of real military spending, but it has prevented consistent economic policies being followed and has also led to physical destruction in rural areas.[69]

TENURE AND SOCIAL CONDITIONS

Thirty-five years ago most colonial authorities thought there were two primary obstacles to the increase of African food output: land tenure and the social attitudes of the population. Currently few writers put much stress upon these factors.

The principal feature of land tenure in traditional African life was the lack of individual freehold. Land was held communally by the tribe or village group, and land was allocated to individuals within the tribe by the tribal leader or village chief; those who cultivated a piece of land

[69] C. Leys, 'African economic development in theory and practice', *Daedalus*, 111, 1982, pp. 99–124.

had the right to the products of that land, but not to sell it. Rent was not paid for the use of land and tenancy was unknown, except in Ethiopia where share cropping survived until 1974. Land that reverted to bush for fallow returned to communal ownership. Inheritance was not practised. There were doubtless greater variations in systems of land tenure than Europeans realized, but these essential features were widespread. This system had considerable advantages in a simple, sparsely populated society where there was little commercial production of crops and few things to buy. Above all it ensured that everyone had some land, and there were no great inequalities in the size of holdings, for land was allocated according to need.

But with European intervention in the twentieth century tenurial conditions became subject to stress. As population grew so the availability of land declined. This was compounded by the fact that in Kenya, Mozambique and Southern and Northern Rhodesia substantial areas were appropriated for the exclusive use of European settlers. The spread of cash crops, the use of money and the commercialization of agriculture also led to changes. But it was believed by most Europeans that the system of tenure inhibited improvements in agricultural productivity. The lack of freehold prevented farmers borrowing to improve their land; the fact that farmers did not farm the same plots of land over time inhibited permanent improvements to the land; and the allocation of land according to needs prevented the more efficient farmers increasing the area they could cultivate. In addition most African farms consisted of several separate plots of land, and this reduced efficiency.

In Kenya the British colonial government consolidated holdings and introduced freehold in the former Kikuyu areas in the 1950s. Elsewhere overt changes in land tenure have been fewer, except where former European held lands have been subdivided among Africans, as in parts of Zambia, Kenya or Zimbabwe, or nationalized as in Mozambique. In practice communal tenure has not inhibited progress. Thus the remarkable increase in the area in crops in Ivory Coast was possible because it was allowed that the first person to clear new land had the right to its use. Elsewhere inheritance has become more common, particularly in the cash crop areas, or near towns. Few authorities now believe that tenurial conditions are a major obstacle to progress.[70]

Although African farms remain predominantly small some differentiation has emerged in the last 30 years. Ironically, although this was once thought to be a measure of progress, it is now said to be a cause of social inequality and poverty. But differences in farm size are small

[70] Hecht, *op. cit.*; Anthony *et al.*, *op. cit.*, p. 291.

compared with those in much of Asia and especially in Latin America. The number of large farms has probably increased, as has the use of hired labour; at the same time the other farms have been subdivided as population has grown. But the progress of capitalist farming – if this is to be characterized by the emergence of large farms and a large landless labour force – has been relatively slow. [71]

While Africa remained under European rule many believed that the social conditions of the African people, and particularly in their tribal context, would hamper any improvement in agricultural output and productivity. Africans, it was argued, were not economic men in the way that European farmers were; profit maximization was not their primary aim and social obligations came before economic motives in determining behaviour; African farmers were thought not to respond to the incentives of price changes. Such views are no longer emphasized as obstacles to increases in output. It is not that African food producers do not respond to prices so much as that food prices have been held down by urban governments. Farmers do not ignore innovations for cultural reasons, but because they do not appear to give any substantial increase in output or are too costly to buy. [72]

DEPENDENCY AND EXPLOITATION

So far Africa's failure to raise food output sufficiently has been attributed to the inadequacies of the traditional farming systems under rapid population growth and the failure to adopt new technologies, and these have been compounded by unsound economic policies. But there are those who believe that Africa's plight is a result primarily of colonial exploitation. Not only, it is argued, did Europeans seize African land in the south and east of Africa, but also, by introducing taxation and other means, they compelled Africans to work on European estates and in European mines. Further, Africans themselves became dependent upon the export of cash crops to Europe, for which there are no other markets. This policy has been supported in the post-independent period by local

[71] J. Carlsen, *Economic and Social Transformation in Rural Kenya*, Scandinavian Institute of African Studies, Uppsala, 1980, p. 192; Ghai and Radwan, *op. cit.*, pp. 1–29.
[72] J. Sadie, 'The social anthropology of economic underdevelopment', *Economic Journal*, **70**, 1960, pp. 294–303; W. O. Jones, 'Economic man in Africa', *Food Research Institute Studies*, **1**, 1960, pp. 107–34.

elites who benefit from connections, not with European governments, but with mining and agricultural marketing companies. [73]

The implication of such themes is not explored here, save in that they relate to food production. Cash crops do occupy a substantial proportion of African cultivated area (between 10 and 15 per cent), although not all of the output is exported. It has also been argued that they occupy a disproportionate amount of the better land. [74] It would seem reasonable to suggest that the area devoted to export crops should be diverted to food production; this would enable food imports to be reduced as well as improving the inadequate consumption. But African states have a dilemma. Agricultural exports, in spite of their lack of buoyancy in the last decade, still provide a large proportion of foreign earnings, which are required for a wide range of goods other than food imports. A return to a policy of self-sufficiency may make matters worse.

CONCLUSIONS

Africa has the least successful record of any of the developing regions in the post-war period. In 1950 available supplies of food were low – below, for the most part, estimated requirements – and malnutrition if not undernutrition was widespread. Since 1950 the population of tropical Africa has increased far more rapidly than any other region and there has been no sign of any reduction in the rate of increase. Food production in the immediate post-war period kept up with population growth, but since the 1960s the rate of increase has fallen, and output per caput has fallen dramatically. Hence in 1978–80 only a handful of African countries had food supplies – including imports – that met needs even if supplies had been distributed according to requirements rather than by income or by possession of land.

Most of the increased food output has come from increasing the area in crops, principally by reducing the fallow rather than by occupying uncultivated areas. Crop yields have increased very little, and in some areas have fallen. Bush fallowing is still the prevailing agricultural system; this is a system that will maintain yields if the fallow is sufficient, but not one capable of dramatic increases in yield with traditional methods.

[73] S. Amin, 'Underdevelopment and dependence in Black Africa – origins and contemporary forms', *Journal of Modern African Studies*, **10**, 1972, pp. 503–24; M. F. Lofchie and S. K. Commins, 'Food deficits and agricultural policies in tropical Africa', *Journal of Modern African Studies*, **20**, 1982, pp. 1–25.
[74] FAO, *op. cit.*, 1979, pp. 2–5.

In other parts of the world – and in a few parts of Africa – good increases in yields have been obtained through the use of chemical fertilizers, better water control and new crop varieties. Few of these inputs are used in Africa.

Behind these agronomic problems lie difficulties in government policies, a dependence upon export crops and a history of government instability, war and civil war. It is, perhaps, surprising not that Africa's food output has increased so slowly but that it has increased at all.

9

Latin America

Latin America's food problems are very different from those of Africa, yet there are a number of important similarities between the two continents. First, Latin America has a comparatively low population density, 18 per square kilometre compared with 16 for Africa. Indeed the density of the agricultural population to the arable area (figure 8.1d) is noticeably lower than in Africa or Asia. As in Africa, however, population is concentrated in relatively few areas and there are large expanses with very low densities, and hence an apparent abundance of agricultural land. The geographical distribution of population today reflects conditions found at the time of European arrival, when the Amerindian population was concentrated in the upland basins of Mexico, Central America and parts of the Andes; the Pacific coastlands were neglected except for the oases of the Peruvian desert. There were few Indians in the rain forests of the Caribbean coast or the Amazon. The Spanish and Portuguese who conquered the continent in the sixteenth century needed labour as well as land and hence settled initially in the densely populated areas. The Portuguese, who settled the coast of Brazil, brought slaves from Africa to work their sugar-cane plantations, but until the nineteenth century migration from Europe was comparatively slow and mainly from Iberia. In the late nineteenth century there was a substantial immigration from both Iberia and other parts of Europe into Argentina, Uruguay and the southern states of Brazil.

In spite of the frontier movements of the last 200 years into the interior of Latin America, the present distribution still reflects that in 1500. The highest rural densities are found in the southern uplands of Mexico, western Guatemala, El Salvador and the volcanic meseta of Costa Rica; in the Andes there are major settlements in the intermontane uplands – the *altiplano* – from Colombia south to Bolivia. In Brazil rural settlement in this century has advanced away from the coast into

São Paulo state, Parana and south towards Paraguay and Uruguay, but the major pattern remains unchanged. Half Latin America's population lies within 300 km of the coast, and in few places are there densities comparable with those of rural Asia, except in parts of southern Mexico. The major change, apart from the Brazilian frontier, is the movement down from the uplands to the Pacific coast or to the Amazonian *selva*. Thus in Peru the sierra had 76 per cent of the national population in 1876, but this had fallen to 42 per cent in 1972, by when the coast had more than half the population. In Ecuador the coast has also replaced the sierra, having 12 per cent of the population in 1856, and in 1972 54 per cent. Bolivia has no coastal region, and so it is the land to the east of the Andes that has gained at the expense of the *altiplano*; the *oriente* had 29 per cent of the population in 1976, compared with 20 per cent in 1950.[1] The low population densities throughout much of Latin America have meant that, as in Africa, many farming systems have periods of fallow in the cropping sequence. Continuous cropping is unusual and multiple cropping rare except in the irrigated areas. However, the area in fallow has steadily declined; in the peasant farming areas population growth has reduced the land available and fallows have had to be reduced, whereas in the more advanced farming areas the use of fertilizers and irrigation has allowed continuous cropping. In the early 1960s 54 per cent of Latin America's arable land was in fallow, in the 1970s only one-third. In Mexico half the country's arable land was in fallow in the 1930s, but by 1960 this had fallen to 35 per cent; however, even in the densely populated rural areas of south central Mexico, 25 per cent of the arable was still in fallow. In such areas a year or two in crops is followed by one or two years in fallow, without any restoration of the natural vegetation; but in the more sparsely populated rain forest areas of Amazonia where isolated Indian communities survive, patches of land are cleared by slash and burn only once in 20 years or more. Such is the abundance of land – or more accurately the belief that land is abundant – that, as the Brazilian frontier penetrated into São Paulo and Parana in the first half of this century, land was sown to coffee and other crops and abandoned when yields declined. Farmers then moved onwards to reclaim new land, leaving eroded and thinly settled land behind them which generally became pasture. Only recently has this practice, which gave rise to the

---

[1] H. Blakemore and C. T. Smith, 'Introduction', in H. Blakemore and C. T. Smith (eds), *Latin America: Geographical Perspectives*, London, 1983, p. 12; C. T. Smith, 'The central Andes', in Blakemore and Smith, *op. cit.*, pp. 278, 295.

'hollow frontier', given way to more intensive practices. [2]

A third characteristic that Latin America shares with Africa, and indeed with all the developing regions, is a dependence upon agricultural exports (figure 11.7). In 1977 agricultural exports formed 44 per cent of all Latin America's exports by value – a decline from 53 per cent in 1950 – and three-quarters of all these went to Western Europe and the United States. In only three countries were agricultural exports less than 30 per cent of all exports (table 9.1); in Bolivia and Venezuela tin and petroleum made up the majority. In Honduras and Cuba, in contrast, over 90 per cent of all exports were agricultural. Even in Brazil and Mexico, which have well developed industrial sectors and important exports of manufactured goods, agricultural exports were 55 and 31 per cent respectively. [3]

ECONOMIC DEVELOPMENT AND URBANIZATION

The contrasts between Latin America and Africa are, however, more important than the similarities, for Latin America has a higher level of economic development than Africa or most of Asia, and a very different farm structure.

The gross domestic product per caput of most Latin American states was higher than those in Africa or Asia in 1950, and remains so today (figure 4.1). Only Haiti falls into the low income bracket as defined by the World Bank. The richer countries – Mexico, Brazil, Uruguay, Argentina and Venezuela – have many features in common with the developed countries; indeed, 30 years ago Argentina and Uruguay were so classified in United Nations publications. Venezuela owes its high income per caput primarily to petroleum exports, but Mexico and Brazil have developed a substantial industrial sector in the last 30 years. In all these countries agriculture contributes less than 15 per cent of the gross domestic product, and in Chile, Argentina, Brazil and Venezuela the agricultural population is one-fifth or less of the labour force. In Argentina, Uruguay and Cuba crude birth rates have fallen towards

[2] P. Lamartine Yates, *Mexico's Agricultural Dilemma*, Tucson, Arizona, 1981, pp. 41, 60; FAO, *Prospects for Agricultural Development in Latin America*, Rome, 1954, p. 69; Inter-American Development Bank, *Economic and Social Progress in Latin America; Natural Resources*, Washington DC, 1982, p. 21; FAO, *Provisional Indicative World Plan for Agricultural Development*, vol. 1, Rome, 1970, p. 44.

[3] 'Agriculture in Latin America: problems and prospects', *Economic Bulletin of Latin America*, 8, 1963, pp. 147–94; N. Gligo, 'The environmental dimension in agricultural development', *Cepal Review*, 12, 1980, pp. 129–43.

Table 9.1 Economic and social characteristics of Latin American countries

	GDP per caput (US$ 1979)	% of GDP from agriculture	Agricultural exports as a % of all exports	Annual growth of population 1970–9 (%)	Crude birth rate per thousand 1979	% of labour force in agriculture	Urban population as a % of total
Haiti	260	–	40	1.7	41	74	16
Honduras	530	32	90	3.3	46	63	23
Bolivia	550	17	10	2.5	43	50	24
Nicaragua	660	29	82	3.3	45	40	41
El Salvador	670	28	63	2.9	39	51	38
Peru	730	10	43	2.7	38	38	46
Dominican Rep.	990	19	75	2.9	36	50	30
Colombia	1010	29	78	2.3	30	27	48
Guatemala	1020	–	78	2.9	40	56	33
Ecuador	1040	15	57	3.3	40	52	34
Paraguay	1057	31	89	2.9	38	52	36
Panama	1400	–	64	2.3	31	34	41
Cuba	1410	–	94	1.4	18	24	65
Mexico	1640	16	31	2.9	36	37	51
Chile	1690	11	21	1.7	23	20	68
Brazil	1780	11	55	2.2	29	40.	46
Costa Rica	1820	19	71	2.5	29	30	37
Uruguay	2100	13	56	0.3	20	11	80
Argentina	2230	13	72	1.6	21	13	74
Venezuela	3120	6	1	3.3	35	19	67

Source: World Bank, World Development Report 1981, Washington DC, 1981

European levels, although in most of Latin America fertility remains high and the rate of population growth is very high, nearer to that of Africa than of Europe (table 9.1).

Much of the early Spanish settlement was in towns, and a higher proportion of the population was living in towns in 1950 than in Africa and Asia. This contrast persists: in 1980 65 per cent of Latin America's population lived in urban places compared with 29 per cent in Africa, 33 per cent in East Asia and 24 per cent in South Asia. The level of urbanization in Argentina and Uruguay is comparable with Western Europe, that in Cuba, Chile and Venezuela not far short. Only Haiti, Honduras and Bolivia remain predominantly rural societies (table 9.1). The rapid growth of the urban population in the last 30 years – it has risen fourfold – is partly due to high fertility and falling mortality rates. But this has been combined with much migration from the countryside, especially into the very large towns. It has been estimated that some 40 million people left the country between 1950 and 1975, attracted by the higher wages and better public services. In the country not only are employment opportunities fewer, incomes lower and public services such as education, public health and welfare poorer, but in some regions the landlord class can still exert great and repressive power over the peasantry.[4]

Because so many of the rural immigrants are young, and have married and had children in the towns, the towns have gained by their natural increase, and the rural areas have lost a substantial part of their population in the child bearing ages. Consequently by the 1970s the urban population of Latin America was increasing by 7 million a year, the rural population by only 1.5 million. Thus the rate of increase of the rural population in Latin America has been less than that in Asia or Africa. Indeed in parts of Latin America the rural and agricultural population has stagnated or even declined. In most Latin American countries the national rural populations have increased since 1950; but when populations are studied at local level rural depopulation can be seen to be occurring in – among others – Peru, Ecuador and Colombia. In the last country the urban population rose fivefold between 1938 and 1973, and from 31 per cent of the total population to 61 per cent. The rural population increased absolutely in the country as a whole, from 7 million in 1951 to nearly 9 million in 1973. But numerous administrative districts in the older densely settled areas suffered absolute declines in their

[4] E. V. Iglesias, 'The ambivalence of Latin American agriculture', *Cepal Review*, **6**, 1978, pp. 7–18; F. C. Turner, 'The rush to the cities in Latin America', *Science*, **192**, 1976, pp. 955–62.

populations in the 1960s and 1970s. This was primarily due to migration to the towns, but there was also movement to settle in the foothills of the Andes. This movement away from the older upland rural areas to either the *selva* east of the Andes or to the Pacific coastlands is found from Colombia south to Bolivia and also in Central America. Combined with the flow to the towns it has led to local rural depopulation in parts of Latin America, a phenomenon not yet found in Africa or Asia.[5]

Most of the rural population are dependent upon agriculture for their livelihood, and the trends in the rural population have effected changes in the agricultural population. The latter is particularly difficult to define in Latin America (see p. 183), but the numbers employed have increased less rapidly than in Africa, where the agricultural population increased by 72 per cent between 1950 and 1980 (see table 4.6). In Latin America the agricultural population increased by only 33 per cent in the same period (table 9.2). This comparatively slow growth in the agricultural labour force in the post-war period has been the result of two contrasting tendencies. Most of those working in agriculture in Latin America possess very small plots of land, although they may supplement their incomes by working temporarily on larger farms. Between 1950 and 1970 this group, 76 per cent of the total, increased at 0.69 per cent per annum. This was achieved by the subdivision of farms and by the establishment of small farms in pioneer zones (table 9.3). One-quarter of the agricultural population were dependent upon wages earned working on plantations and other large farms; their numbers increased much more slowly between 1950 and 1970, and probably more slowly in the 1970s, for on the large farms of Latin America mechanization has been rapid since the 1960s and many labourers have been displaced or become temporary rather than permanent employees. Indeed in some countries the total number employed in agriculture has been declining at the national level as machines have replaced labour. This has been the case in Argentina and Uruguay since the 1950s, and in Venezuela, Chile and the Brazilian state of São Paulo the agricultural labour force has been stagnant for some time.[6]

[5] D. A. Preston, 'Rural emigration and the future of agriculture in Ecuador', in D. A. Preston (ed.), *Environment, Society and Rural Change in Latin America*, Chichester, 1980, pp. 195–208; L. S. Williams and E. C. Griffin, 'Rural and small town depopulation in Colombia', *Geographical Review*, **68**, 1978, pp. 13–30; C. T. Smith, *op. cit.*, pp. 279–90.

[6] K. C. Abercrombie, 'Agricultural mechanisation and employment in Latin America', *International Labour Review*, **106**, 1972, pp. 11–45; L. L. Cordovez, 'Trends and recent changes in the Latin American food and agriculture situation', *Cepal Review*, **16**, 1982, pp. 7–14; B. Sorj, 'Agrarian structures and policies in present day Brazil', *Latin American Perspectives*, **7** (11), 1980.

Table 9.2   The agricultural and non-agricultural population in Latin America, 1950-80 (millions)

	1950	1970	1980
Agricultural population	94	116	126
Non-agricultural population	68	167	242
Total population	162	283	368

Source: FAO, *Production Yearbook 1967*, vol. 11, Rome, 1958; *Production Yearbook 1976*, vol. 30, Rome, 1977; *Production Yearbook 1980*, vol. 34, Rome, 1981

Table 9.3   The agricultural work force in 13 Latin American countries

	1950 (millions)	1970 (millions)	% increase per annum	% all
Agricultural wage earners	7.6	8.3	0.4	24
Agricultural non wage earners	14.7	17.0	0.69	76
Total agricultural work force	22.3	25.3	—	100

Source: P. Peek, *Agrarian Change and Rural Emigration in Latin America*, International Labour Organization, Geneva, 1978

Thus the two sectors of the rural population have quite different problems. In the peasant sector of very small farms incomes are low, farms are subdivided, steep slopes are cultivated with subsequent soil erosion, and families have to seek employment off the farm, often by migratory labour. Thus in the uplands of Guatemala farmers get about half their total income by working on the large farms of the Caribbean and Pacific lowlands during harvest time, and even since the land reforms of the 1970s Indian farmers from the Peruvian sierra still move to the oases of the coast to work on the sugar and cotton plantations – now co-operatives. The peasant sector has absorbed much of the rural population growth since the 1950s; the subdivision of the farms has meant that a considerable proportion of the agricultural work force is under-employed, in 1970 between one-fifth and one-third. The smaller number of landless labourers, perhaps one-quarter of the total rural workforce, have had different problems. As land reform measures ended the servile conditions that existed in the 1950s, where *colonos*, *peons* and others received small plots of land in return for working on hacienda, so many landlords ended the provision of land and substituted wages, and as minimum wage legislation was slowly passed so landlords replaced labour with machines. One noticeable trend has been for the permanent labour force to be pared to the minimum, temporary labour being hired in the periods of heavy labour needs. So rapid has been the growth of the urban population in the last 30 years that there are few opportunities for employment left in the cities for the impoverished rural populations. Not surprisingly it has been calculated that two-thirds of the rural population of Latin America live in poverty compared with one-quarter of the urban population, and that average urban incomes in 1970 were three to four times those in the rural areas.[7]

LAND DISTRIBUTION AND LAND REFORM

The industrialization of parts of Latin America and the large scale flight to the cities have meant that the increase of the agricultural population has not been at such a rapid rate as in Africa or involved such large numbers as in Asia, although of course it has given rise to grave difficulties. But underlying many of the agricultural problems of Latin America today is the distribution of land and the farm size structure, which is very different from any other part of the world.

In the sixteenth century the Spanish and Portuguese conquerors allocated very large grants of land to individuals; Indians who lived on these holdings were required to work the land and often to undertake other services such as domestic work; in return they were allowed to use small plots of land. In some areas Indian communities retained much of their land but this was often expropriated in the nineteenth century. In Brazil the Portuguese imported slaves from Africa to work the sugar plantations, and slaves were also taken to other parts of Latin America. The hacienda, where very large units of land were operated by *peons*, *colonos*, *inquilinos* or *huasipungos* in return for land in small amounts upon the estate, became the typical Latin American system of land ownership and operation, although there were many variations. Thus in the Peruvian *altiplano* nearly all of a landlord's estate would be divided among the Indian population, and income came in the form of rent. More commonly *peons* worked the land under the supervision of the landlord or a manager, while supporting themselves on small plots of land either on or near the hacienda. After the end of slavery in Brazil

[7] P. Dorner and R. Quiros, 'Institutional dualism in Central America's agricultural development', *Journal of Latin American Studies*, 5, 1973, pp. 217–32; E. Feder, *The Rape of the Peasantry; Latin America's Landholding System*, New York, 1971, pp. 29, 33; S. Barraclough, 'Rural development and employment prospects in Latin America', in A. J. Field (ed.), *City and Country in the Third World: Issues in the Modernization of Latin America*, Cambridge, Massachusetts, 1970, pp. 97–135; G. Gomez and A. Perez, 'The process of modernization in Latin American agriculture', *Cepal Review*, 8, 1979, pp. 55–74.

share cropping became a typical form of land holding in the north east, and in the south coffee *fazendas* were often worked by share croppers. What was conspicuously absent was the medium sized family farm that characterized much of North America or Western Europe. There were some exceptions. Medium sized owner occupied farms were found in the upland area of Costa Rica, although they have diminished in importance in this century, and the colonization of Antioquia in Columbia was partly by such farmers. In Haiti slavery and the plantation gave way to small owner occupied farms after the revolution of 1798. In Argentina and more so in southern Brazil many of the European immigrants of the late nineteenth century eventually gained title to small and medium sized farms, and the states of Rio Grande do Sul and Santa Catarina have many family farms. But in most of Latin America there remains a great difference between the very large number of small farms occupying a small proportion of the farmland, and the very few holdings occupying a large proportion of the area.[8]

Statistics on the ownership of land, the size of farms and the number of landless labourers are notoriously unreliable in Latin America, and comparisons between countries are difficult to undertake. There is often a confusion between the size of units of ownership and that of units of operation; in some countries the labourers with small plots of land they receive for working the hacienda are recorded as labourers, in other as farmers. Most of the data available refer to the 1950s or 1960s.[9] But there is no denying the remarkable concentration of land in a few hands. In about 1960 two-thirds of the agricultural land in Latin America was occupied by holdings of 1000 ha of more, which made up only 1.4 per cent of all holdings (table 9.4). Conversely three-quarters of all holdings were less than 20 ha but occupied only 3.7 per cent of the agricultural area. Such inequality is not to be found elsewhere. Thus in Africa (table 9.5) small holdings of less than 2 ha were two-thirds of all farms, but they occupied one-fifth of the farmland, in the Far East they were 71 per cent of holdings but also occupied one-fifth of the farmland. Large holdings nowhere occupy such a large proportion of the total farmland as in Latin America, and their average size in Africa and Asia is much smaller (table 9.5). Because of the inconsistencies in the way that workers

[8] S. Barraclough, *Agrarian Structure in Latin America*, Lexington, Massachusetts, 1973.
[9] Feder, *op. cit.*, pp. 17–18; Alain de Janvry, *The Agrarian Question and Reformism in Latin America*, Baltimore, 1981, p. 111; S. Barraclough and A. L. Domike, 'Agrarian structure in seven Latin American countries', *Land Economics*, **42**, 1960, pp. 391–424.

with small plots of land are recorded, it is difficult to establish what proportion of the Latin American rural population is without land; it has been put variously as 25, 33, 40 and 63 per cent. However, a comparison of landlessness made by FAO suggests that 34 per cent of Latin America's agricultural population is without land, compared with 31 per cent in the Far East, 25 per cent in the Near East and 10 per cent in Africa.[10]

Table 9.4   Farm structure in Latin America, *c.* 1960

Farm size	Number of holdings		Area	
	(thousands)	*(%)*	*(million ha)*	*(%)*
Under 20 ha	5445	72.6	27.0	3.7
20–100 ha	1350	18.0	60.6	8.4
100–1000 ha	600	8.0	166.0	22.9
1000 ha and over	105	1.4	470.0	65.0
Total	7500	100.0	723.6	100.0

Source: J. Chonchol, 'Land tenure and development in Latin America', in C. Veliz (ed.), *Obstacles to Change in Latin America*, Oxford, 1965, pp. 79–90

Table 9.5   Small and large holdings in the developing countries

	Small holdings			Large holdings		
	Numbers *(%)*	Area *(%)*	Average size *(ha)*	Numbers *(%)*	Area *(%)*	Average size *(ha)*
Latin America	66.0	3.7	2.7	7.9	80.3	514
Africa	66.0	22.4	1.0	3.6	34.0	28
Near East	50.0	11.2	1.6	10.3	54.7	50
Far East	71.1	21.7	0.7	4.0	31.1	17

Definitions:

	Small	Large
Latin America	Below 10 ha	Above 100 ha
Africa, Far East	Below 2 ha	Above 10 ha
Near East	Below 5 ha	Above 20 ha

Source: P. Harrison, 'The inequities that curb potential', *Ceres*, **81**, 1981, pp. 22–6

In the past the landowners of Latin America had not only land but great financial and political power, and the prospects of altering the distribution of land were remote. In this century there have been many

[10] De Janvry, *op. cit.*, p. 131; Feder, *op. cit.*, p. 54; P. Harrison, 'The inequities that curb potential', *Ceres*, 8, 1981, pp. 22–6; P. Peek, *Agrarian Change and Rural Emigration in Latin America*, International Labour Organization, Geneva, 1978.

attempts to redistribute land, some successful. The Mexican revolution was followed by legislation in 1917 that gave the rural population entitlement to claim land, and also specified the sort of land that would be expropriated. It was not until the 1930s that expropriation and allocation took place, but by 1980 some 77 million hectares had been distributed. Most of this was given not to individuals but to communities called *ejidos*. Although land was generally worked by individuals – only a few *ejidos* were collectively operated – *ejido* land could not be sold or rented out. About one-half of the agricultural area of Mexico is *ejido* land and one-half privately owned. In Bolivia the revolution of 1952 was followed by peasant invasions of hacienda land, and the legislation of 1953 followed rather than caused expropriation. The Cuban revolution ended private ownership of the sugar plantations, but did not lead to land redistribution although the status of the labourers on the state farms was improved. In the 1970s the military government of Peru nationalized the foreign owned plantations of the coast and expropriated hacienda land in the sierra; nearly 8 million hectares had been allocated to peasants by 1976, and only 16 per cent of the Peruvian agricultural population remained landless. More recently land has been expropriated in El Salvador and Nicaragua, but there have been few significant changes elsewhere; in Chile the reforms carried out under Allende have been reversed. Although there has been little significant land redistribution elsewhere, the servile status of tenancies – such as that of the *huasipungo* in Ecuador – has nearly everywhere been abolished. In most countries – particularly those where land redistribution has not taken place – governments have encouraged the colonization of new land, perhaps as an easy alternative to the problems of expropriation.[11] Although land reform has reduced the importance of large farms in a few countries, they remain the dominant unit of production in Latin America, but dependent now upon wage labour rather than *colonos*. The principal change in farm size has been the great increase in the number of small farms, and the reduction of their average size. Thus for example in the

[11] D. J. Fox, 'Mexico', in Blakemore and Smith, *op. cit.*, p. 47; C. T. Smith, 'Land reform as a precondition for Green Revolution in Latin America', in T. P. Bayliss-Smith and Sudhir Wanmali (eds), *Understanding Green Revolutions: Agrarian Change and Development Planning in South Asia*, Cambridge, 1984, pp. 18–36; C. Kay, 'Achievements and contradictions of the Peruvian agrarian reform', *Journal of Development Studies*, 18, 1981, pp. 141–70; C. S. Blankstein and C. Zuvekas, Jr., 'Agrarian reform in Ecuador: an evaluation of past efforts and the development of a new approach', *Economic Development and Cultural Change*, 22, 1973, pp. 73–94; D. Browning, 'Agrarian reform in El Salvador', *Journal of Latin American Studies*, 15, 1983, pp. 399–426.

sierra of Peru the number of holdings less than 5 ha rose from 500,000 to 884,000 between 1961 and 1972, and in Guatemala farms of less than 0.7 ha were only one-fifth of all holdings in 1950, but 41 per cent by 1979. In Brazil the average size of holdings less than 5 ha fell from 4.25 in 1960 to 3.6 in 1970, and in Ecuador from 1.7 ha to 1.5 ha. This increase has had various causes. Existing holdings have been subdivided by population growth; many of the farms allocated in reform have been small, and similarly much of the settlement in pioneer zones has been on a small scale. Indeed in many areas of colonization the latifundia–minifundia pattern has reappeared.[12]

LAND USE IN LATIN AMERICA

It is over 5000 miles from the United States border with Mexico to Cape Horn. Not surprisingly Latin America includes a diversity of environments and types of farming, although neither are as well described as might be wished. The core of Latin America is the Amazon basin where high temperatures throughout the year and heavy rainfall with only locally a significant dry season sustains the *selva*, or rain forest, the most luxuriant vegetation type on earth. In spite of the recent attempts to exploit the rainforest, it remains sparsely populated. Rain forest or tropical forest also occurs on the Caribbean coast, south of Vera Cruz, and the original vegetation of the Brazilian coast from Recife to Rio de Janeiro was tropical forest, although far less luxuriant than the rain forest and with a significant dry season. Between the Amazon and the Brazilian coast lie crystalline plateaux with a marked dry season, and a vegetation adapted to seasonal drought, a combination of grass and trees; in the north east interior of Brazil the *caatinga* is drought resistant; southwards towards Paraguay grass is the dominant vegetation, as it was in much of Argentina and Uruguay where a subtropical climate and good soils sustain the most productive farming systems of the continent. Southwards into Patagonia aridity precludes crop production, and the extreme south, in Argentina and Chile, are the only lowland cool temperate climates of Latin America.[13]

The most distinctive feature of the continent is the upland area which

[12] Smith, *op. cit.*, 1983, p. 292; V. Bulmer-Thomas, 'Economic development in the long run – Central America since 1920', *Journal of Latin American Studies*, 15, 1983, pp. 269–94; de Janvry, *op. cit.*, pp. 121–2.
[13] M. M. Cole, '*Cerrado, caatinga and pantanal*; the distribution and origin of the savanna vegetation of Brazil', *Geographical Journal*, 126, 1960, pp. 168–79.

stretches from Mexico to Chile. This region has two important characteristics. First, the numerous volcanoes provide fertile soils. Second,
the altitude reduces temperatures and thus gives rise to distinctive zones
where crops of very different climatic regions are grown quite close –
horizontally – to each other. For the most part, however, the upland
areas suitable for agriculture, although locally giving rise to high rural
densities, are small in extent and separated by terrain difficult to traverse.
In some parts of the Andes settlement occurs at heights where temperatures are so low as to only allow the growth of the more hardy temperate
crops such as the potato or barley, and south from northern Peru the
intermontane basins suffer not only from frost but also from drought,
particularly in southern Bolivia, where the only possible form of
agriculture is sheep rearing.

The Pacific coastlands of Latin America, generally very narrow,
although for the most part hot, all experience a marked dry season. From
Ecuador southwards this becomes an arid zone, where agriculture is
only possible using the water of streams descending from the Andes,
most noticeably in northern Peru. Southwards, central Chile has a climate
and agriculture comparable with that of the Mediterranean basin.

Classifications of Latin American agriculture are apt to be based upon
its farm structure; there are few typologies based on land use, and even
fewer attempts to map the distribution of farm types. Aggregate figures
for Latin America can be deceptive for, although there are 39 independent states (if the Caribbean countries are included), Brazil, Argentina
and Mexico account for two-thirds of the total land area, three-quarters
of the arable land and 60 per cent of the population. Some of the essential features of land use are displayed in table 9.6. Although much
emphasis is usually placed upon the importance of export crops, it is
the food crops that occupy most of the cropped area. Maize is widely
grown, and by far the most important single crop. Wheat, although the
second cereal crop, is largely grown in Argentina and southern Brazil.
In the latter wheat is increasingly grown in rotation with soybean. This
crop has expanded remarkably in the last 20 years and Brazil is now
the second most important world source of soybeans and soybean
products. Rice has also expanded considerably. It is widely grown in
Latin America, not as an irrigated crop – only 30 per cent of the total
rice area – but as an upland, dry crop; the bulk is grown in central
and southern Brazil.

Root crops, although occupying a comparatively small area, are
regionally significant; potatoes are important in the Andean *altiplano*,
and manioc (cassava) in many lowland shifting cultivation regions.
Fruit and vegetables occupy a considerable area, but particularly in the

environs of the major cities. The traditional export crops of cocoa, sugar-cane and coffee (and bananas and cotton, for which output but not area data are available) occupy rather less of the total arable than might be expected, although locally – particularly in Central America – they are often dominant in the land use pattern.

Table 9.6　Land use in Latin America, 1961–5 and 1980 (million hectares)

	1961–5	1980
Arable area	116	161
Pasture	493	539
Forest	1061	1019
Irrigated land	10	14
All cereals	40	50
Wheat	8	10
Rice	5	8
Barley	1	1
Maize	22	26
Sorghum	2	4
All root crops	3.5	4.5
Potatoes	1	1.1
Sweet potatoes	0.4	0.4
Cassava	2	2.8
Pulses	6.3	8.5
Soybeans	0.4	11.4
Vegetables	9.6	16.9
Sugar-cane	4.5	6.3
Bananas	n.d.	n.d.
Coffee	4.3	5.5
Cotton	n.d.	n.d.
Cocoa	1	1.1

Sources: FAO, *Production Yearbook 1981*, vol. 35, Rome, 1982; *Production Yearbook 1976*, vol. 30, Rome, 1977

Latin America has more livestock per caput of the total population than any of the major regions, although the density is low; pasture occupies nearly five times the area of crops, and the tradition of extensive livestock raising is long established. The Spanish and Portuguese brought long horned cattle to the Americas in the sixteenth century, and also the Spanish methods of livestock raising – the open range, the annual round-up and branding and the mounted herdsmen. Ranching became a major form of land use in northern Mexico in the seventeenth and eighteenth centuries, as it did in the *cerrado* of Brazil, whereas in the late nineteenth century a more progressive system of livestock production developed in Argentina and Uruguay. In much of Latin America the quality of the cattle is low, European breeds having been adopted only in Argentina and Uruguay and on a few ranches in northern Mexico. Not only are densities low, but feeds other than the natural vegetation are uncommon, cattle take six years to reach slaughtering, and losses from disease and drought are high. Dairying is a recent development outside the temperate south, and is mainly found near the cities, particularly in southern Brazil. Indeed in São Paulo state the value of livestock products now exceeds that of coffee. [14]

There have been few attempts to establish maps of types of farming in Latin America; indeed there are few systematic accounts of the agricultural geography of the continent. However, the most useful typological distinction is probably between the Indian and *mestizo* small scale farms, producing mainly food crops, that are to be found in the plateaux of Mexico, Central America and the Andes, and the large scale hacienda and plantations, often producing one crop only and oriented to export. But in southern Brazil and parts of Argentina European immigrants have established farms producing a variety of products, some for home consumption, some for export, on a much smaller scale than the traditional hacienda, but efficient and often highly mechanized. [15]

THE GROWTH OF FOOD OUTPUT

In the 1950s Latin American agriculture was widely described as backward, and it is not without its critics today. Yet food output has increased rapidly since the end of the Second World War, at 3.1 per cent per annum in the 1950s, 3.5 per cent in the 1960s and 3.8 per cent in the 1970s (table 5.5). Over the period 1950–77 output rose at 3.2 per cent per annum, and between 1961–5 and 1976 it increased by over 50 per cent in most countries; only in a few countries – including Peru – was the growth of output sluggish (figure 8.5). There is no sign of the sad decline found in Africa. But Latin America, like Africa, has had a very high rate of population increase: 2.8 per cent per annum in the 1960s and 2.7 per cent in the 1970s (table 4.2). Consequently the rate of food output growth per caput has been less impressive; indeed in a number of countries, including El Salvador and Ecuador, it declined between 1961–5 and 1976. These countries held a population of 52 million in 1980, only 14 per cent of the population of Latin America. However, only in ten countries (figure 2.4) was national food supply

[14] R. C. West and J. P. Augelli, *Middle America: Its Lands and People*, New York, 1966, pp. 336–7.
[15] A. S. Morris, *South America*, London, 1979, pp. 27–29.

below estimated requirements in 1978–80, and in several countries there were very considerable increases in food output per caput 1960–80 (figure 8.6). The situation in Latin America is thus very different from that in Africa. [16]

Although there have been increases in crop yields in many parts of Latin America since 1950, most of the increased food output has come from the expansion of the area in crops. The arable area increased from 86 million hectares in 1950 to 162 million in 1980, although the reservations on the definition of arable land should be recalled (see p. 73) But the area in the major food crops recorded by FAO also indicates a doubling of the area between 1950 and 1980 (table 5.1), a figure confirmed by other estimates. Some two-thirds of the extra food produced in Latin America since 1950 has come from the expansion of area; the increase due to higher yields has however slowly increased with time. Thus between the mid 1930s and the mid 1950s crop yields accounted for only 20 per cent of the extra food, in the 1960s 30 per cent and in the 1970s 40 per cent. The way in which the area has been expanded has been quite different from either Africa or Asia. Multiple cropping is rare in Latin America except in some irrigated areas, but only 9 per cent of the arable is irrigated and one-third of this is in Mexico. The area double cropped in Mexico has risen from 40,000 hectares in 1950 to 800,000 hectares in 1980 but this was only 15 per cent of Mexico's irrigated land. Indeed a substantial part of this is left fallow each year owing to problems of salinity. Nor has the reduction of fallow been a major contributor to the increased area in crops as it has been in Africa, although it is true that the fallow has been much reduced in parts of southern Mexico, Central America and the Andean *altiplano*. Of most importance has been the colonization of new land, a matter touched upon in an earlier chapter but of so much importance in Latin America that it merits further consideration. [17]

THE COLONIZATION OF NEW LAND IN LATIN AMERICA

It will be recalled that the Indian and early Iberian settlement of Latin America was confined to the uplands of Central America and the Andes, and the coasts of Brazil. The lowland rain forest of Central America and the Amazon basin had a thin population, practising a combination of shifting agriculture and gathering and hunting, whereas the drier

[16]   L. L. Cordovez, *op. cit.*
[17]   Gomez and Perez, *op. cit.*; Yates, *op. cit.*, p. 60.

cerrado and pampa areas of Brazil, Uruguay and Argentina were occupied by extensive ranching, as was much of northern Mexico and the *llanos* of Venezuela. Three events have led to the integration of these regions into the economic life of Latin America and their denser settlement. The first was the development of export commodities for Western Europe and the United States, notably bananas from the Caribbean coast of Central America, coffee from São Paulo, and meat and later wheat from Argentina. These were not of course the first exports from Latin America, but in the late nineteenth century capital from the former regions became increasingly important, and there was also considerable emigration from Europe to southern Brazil and Argentina. Second, a beginning was made early in this century in the conquest of the diseases endemic to the tropical lowlands, although it was not until after the Second World War that malaria was eradicated, removing an obstacle to permanent settlement. The third was the slow extension of transport, without which it was difficult to get people in or goods out. The most extensive railway building was in Argentina, but railways were built elsewhere; indeed the banana boom in the 1890s was a consequence of the railway built by Minor Keith from the Caribbean coast to the inland and upland capital of Costa Rica, San José. In the last 30 years railways and, more important, highways have been built to link the Andean *altiplano* with the Amazon territories in Brazil, Peru, Ecuador and Colombia, prompted by military needs and the exploitation of oil, but allowing agricultural settlement. In the 1970s the Brazilian government undertook an extensive programme of road building in the Amazon.

Development of the remoter regions was on the whole slow until the 1930s and 1940s, but since then new land has been added in marginal environments at a prodigious rate. In Mexico the government invested heavily in irrigation in the north west; the tropical lowlands on the Caribbean coast, largely undeveloped before 1940, have been the scene of considerable settlement, spontaneous and government backed, large scale and small scale, partly subsistence, partly export oriented. Indeed the Gulf states now provide one-quarter of Mexican agricultural output. The arable area of Mexico rose from 32 million ha in 1932 to 47 million in 1970. The Andean and Central American republics have seen settlement of their Pacific lowlands, prompted in both cases by the eradication of malaria and the building of the Pan-American highway; this has been particularly notable in Ecuador, where the Pacific lowland is more humid than that to the north and south. Settlement here was prompted initially by the banana boom in the 1940s and 1950s but other crops, including rice, have become important; between 1954 and 1974 three-quarters of a million hectares were cleared for cultivation and the coast has replaced the sierra as the economic centre of the country. In Peru and Bolivia the movement has been essentially eastwards; the Peruvian coast is arid and the prospects of extending the irrigated area are limited, and Bolivia has no Pacific coastland. The Bolivian *altiplano* was densely populated in the north and at the time of the 1953 revolution there was little development in either the eastern Andean hills – the *yungas* – or the lowland *selva* region. However, this area has been rapidly developed by both small scale Indian settlement and capitalist production, so that the province of Cochabamba now has one-third of Bolivia's cultivated land; between 1950 and 1973 80 per cent of the increase in agricultural production was accounted for by Santa Cruz and the *yungas*.[18]

The most dramatic frontier developments have come however in Brazil and Argentina; the remarkable expansion of beef and wheat production in Argentina paralleled the development of Canada and Australia earlier in this century, but in the 1950s expansion halted. Not so in Brazil. From 1900 onwards the state of São Paulo was occupied by coffee production, the frontier moving rapidly westwards and into northern Parana in the 1930s. Occupation of the southern states of Santa Catarina and Rio Grande do Sul, partly by European immigrants, partly by Brazilians, began in the late nineteenth century, but the rapid growth of the arable area, including the cultivation of rice, wheat and soybeans, has been mainly since the 1950s. Nor has the expansion of the cultivated area been confined to the progressive south. The area of food crops in the north east, poverty stricken, drought ridden and apparently undynamic, doubled between 1950 and 1968. More dramatically the movement of the capital to Brasilia in the *cerrado* has prompted the movement of crop cultivation into this once exclusively livestock region in Goiás southern Mato Grosso and Minas Gerais. Lastly has come the much heralded frontier in the Amazon rain forest, as yet not very productive of crops. The addition to the Brazilian cropland has been formidable. In 1920 6.6 million ha were cultivated, but in the 1970s 30 million. However, it is perhaps easy to exaggerate the significance of this. In fact it is only in the south of Brazil that more than 40 per cent of

[18]   C. Dozier, 'Agriculture and development in Mexico's Tabasco lowlands: planning and potential', *Journal of Developing Areas*, 5, 1970, pp. 61–72; J. Revel-Mouroz, 'Mexican colonization experience in the humid tropics', in Preston, *op. cit.*, pp. 83–102; Yates, *op. cit.*, p. 47; C. Weil, 'Migration among landholdings by Bolivian campesinos', *Geographical Review*, 73, 1983, pp. 182–97; A. Delavaud, 'From colonization to agricultural development: the case of coastal Ecuador', in Preston, *op. cit.*, pp. 67–81; M. Nelson, *The Development of Tropical Lands: Policy Issues in Latin America*, Baltimore, 1973, p. 22.

the land is in crops; most of the country remains unexploited (figure 9.1).[19]

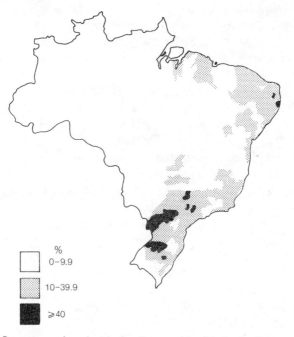

%

☐ 0–9.9

▨ 10–39.9

■ ≥40

Figure 9.1   Percentage of total agricultural area cultivated, Brazil, 1970
Source: B. Bret, 'Données et réflexions sur l'agriculture Brésilienne', *Annales de Géographie*, **84**, 1975, pp. 557–88

TECHNOLOGICAL CHANGE

In 1950 the technological level of farming in much of Latin America was low. Rotations were rare – although on peasant farms inter-cropping was practised (see p. 103) and monoculture characterized many areas of export crops, the land being cultivated until exhausted, the farmers then moving on to new areas. Although the continent has a large population of cattle and sheep, livestock and crop production were rarely combined and livestock manure was not an important source of plant nutrients; few chemical fertilizers were in use. Farm implements were

[19] J. H. Galloway, 'Brazil', in Blakemore and Smith, *op. cit.*, p. 359; D. E. Goodman, 'Rural structure, surplus mobilisation, and modes of production in a peripheral region: the Brazilian north-east', *Journal of Peasant Studies*, 5, 1977, pp. 3–32; B. Bret, 'Données et réflexions sur l'agriculture Brésilienne', *Annales de Géographie*, **84**, 1975, pp. 557–88.

for the most part simple. Only 15 per cent of Latin America's cropland was worked with tractors; more than half the tractors were to be found in Argentina, Uruguay and southern Brazil; elsewhere oxen and simple wooden ploughs were in use, but most of Latin America's land was worked only with a hoe, machete, digging stick or foot plough. In 1950 only one-quarter of Brazil's farms had ploughs. Human labour was still the major source of power. [20]

There seemed to be straightforward explanations for this low productivity. On the hacienda only very small proportions of the land were actually used for crops, most being idle, and large amounts were fallow. The landowner could derive from this a more than adequate income, for the labour force was captive, tied to the land by servile tenancies. Labour costs were low, and land untaxed or grossly undertaxed. Many landlords were absentee, and profits either went in conspicuous consumption or were invested elsewhere than in agriculture. On the other hand the bulk of the population was on small farms, frequently fragmented, often on steep slopes, with no access to capital and few resources other than their labour. Although their crop yields were higher than those on the larger farms, there was little prospect of increasing them. For all this, although the yield of food crops in Latin America was well below those in Europe in 1950, they were very similar to those in Asia and significantly above those of Africa (table 9.7).

Table 9.7   Yields of food crops, 1948–52 (100 kilograms per hectare)

	Latin America	Asia	Africa	Europe
Maize	10.7	10.2	7.4	15.5
Wheat	10.6	7.6	6.0	15.8
Rice	16.9	15.8	9.6	42.3
Barley	10.6	10.2	6.7	21.5
Potatoes	52.4	68.9	54.4	163.0

Source: FAO, *Production Yearbook 1957*, vol. 11, Rome, 1958, pp. 31-2

THE ADOPTION OF NEW CROP VARIETIES

Although the expansion of area in crops has been the major cause of increased food output since 1950, yields have increased; one authority claims that the general level of yields rose 40 per cent between 1950

[20] FAO, *op. cit.*, 1954; 'Agriculture in Latin America; problems and prospects', *op. cit.*; J. D. Henshall and R. P. Momsen, Jr., *A Geography of Brazilian Development*, London, 1974, p. 76.

and 1976. This seems a little high, but there has certainly been a significant increase in the use of modern inputs. The breeding and diffusion of high yield varieties is most normally associated with Asia, but the early advances in such breeding were made in the Americas. Before the Second World War hybrid maize was bred in the USA. Combined with liberal use of fertilizer, but not irrigation water, hybrids largely replaced open pollinated varieties in the USA by the 1950s, giving good increases in yields. Hybrids adapted to the climatic conditions of parts of Latin America were bred after the Second World War, but the extent to which they have replaced indigenous open pollinated varieties is not clear. Maize yields certainly increased between the 1930s and 1970s in Mexico, but only one-quarter of the area in maize was planted with hybrid in the 1970s. In Mexico maize, as in most other Latin American countries, is grown primarily in the traditional small scale sector. Hybrid maize was not universally approved by peasants. Hybrid seed, unlike traditional varieties, has to be bought annually from seed merchants and is thus costly, and many peasants preferred the taste of the traditional strains. Hybrid maize has made progress elsewhere: 30 per cent of all farmers in El Salvador were using it in the early 1970s. FAO estimates suggest maize yield in Latin America rose by about one-third between 1960 and 1980.[21]

Better known are the semi-dwarf wheat varieties developed by the Ford Foundation in Mexico and released to farmers there in 1961. These varieties need irrigation and fertilizer for optimum yield, and have been very widely adopted in Asia. But wheat is not grown by irrigation in most of Latin America – north west Mexico being a notable exception – and is not suited to the climate of most of the continent. Much of the area sown with high yielding varieties is found in Argentina, where neither is it irrigated nor does it receive much fertilizer. Its virtue there is its short growing season, which allows a soybean crop to follow. Although a comparatively high proportion of Latin America's wheat is in new high yield varieties (table 9.8), wheat occupies only a small proportion of the area in food crops. In Mexico, however, it did have a spectacular success. Virtually all wheat was semi-dwarf by 1970, and yield quadrupled between 1950 and 1975. Rice is not a traditional crop

[21] Gomez and Perez, *op. cit.*; Fox, *op. cit.*, p. 46; C. Hewitt de Alcantara, *Modernizing Mexican Agriculture: Socioeconomic Implications of Technological Changes, 1940–1970*, Geneva, 1976; C. Hewitt de Alcantara, 'The Green Revolution as history: the Mexican experience', *Development and Change*, 5, 1973–74, pp. 25–44; L. Harlan Davis, 'Foreign aid to the small farmer: the El Salvador experience', *Latin American Economic Affairs*, **29**, 1975, pp. 81–91; FAO, *Production Yearbook 1981*, vol. 35, Rome, 1982.

in Latin America, and three-quarters of that grain is not paddy but upland rice. The area under rice has however increased considerably in the last 30 years, from about 3 million hectares in 1950 to 8 million in 1980. The introduction of the Philippine variety in the mid 1960s into Colombia had a spectacular success; local modifications of IR-8 have replaced the indigenous varieties, and irrigated rice the once dominant upland varieties. Rice has become the country's leading food crop. Even so traditional upland varieties remain the main source of rice (table 9.8), particularly in Brazil, the major producer, where it is mainly grown as a mechanized dry crop. [22]

Table 9.8   Percentage of Latin American crops sown with new high yielding varieties, 1977

	Wheat	Rice	Total
Asia	72.4	30.4	41.1
Near East	17.0	3.6	16.5
Africa	22.5	2.7	6.5
Latin America	41.0[a]	13.0	30.8

[a] Unreliable, probably an overestimate.
Source: D. Dalrymple, *Development and Spread of High Yielding Varieties of Wheat and Rice in the Less Developed Nations*, Washington DC, 1978

Although in places the adoption of new varieties has led to prodigious increases in crop yields, the adoption rate has been very variable. Less than one-fifth of the rice and at the very most 40 per cent of the wheat is sown with the new varieties, not always with the benefit of irrigation or fertilizer. This substantial innovation, although more important in Latin America than in Africa or the Near East, has bypassed the majority of Latin America's farmers, a theme which will be returned to later. It must also be recalled that although the adoption of new inputs has occurred in some areas, giving increased yields, in others the reduction of fallowing or overcropping has led to a decline in yields.

FERTILIZERS

In 1950 little chemical fertilizer was used in crop production in Latin America; but then nor was it much in use in Africa or Asia at that time.

[22] D. G. Dalrymple, *Development and Spread of High Yielding Varieties of Wheat and Rice in the Less Developed Nations*, Washington, 1978; G. M. Scobie and R. Posada, 'The impact of technical change on income distribution: the case of rice in Columbia', *American Journal of Agricultural Economics*, **60**, 1978, pp. 85–92;

The most liberal usage was on the sugar plantations of Cuba and the Peruvian oases; it was rarely used in Argentina, technically the most advanced country at that time, and in Brazil 75 per cent of all the small quantity of fertilizer was used in the southern states of São Paulo and Rio Grande do Sul. Since 1950 the consumption of fertilizer per hectare has increased at a considerable rate – as it has in all the developing regions (table 8.1) – and Latin American consumption levels are well above Africa and much the same as in the Near East and Far East, although well below Europe, China and North America. However, the progress of fertilizer consumption per hectare may be gauged by the fact that Latin American levels are comparable with those of North America in 1960. Although Latin America has to import much of its fertilizer, unlike Africa it has a substantial home industry, producing 64 per cent of its nitrogen fertilizer, two-thirds of its phosphates but less than one-fifth of its potash. But the home production is for the most part at high cost, so that fertilizers are much more expensive per unit of output than in the United States or Western Europe. To buy 1 kg of nitrogen fertilizer the US farmer has to sell 2.4 kg of corn, the Chilean farmer 5, the Brazilian 8 and the Uruguayan 10.[23]

MECHANIZATION

There is no doubt that there has been a substantial adoption of new inputs that raise crop yields in Latin America since 1950, in contrast to much of Africa. There has also been a notable adoption of machinery, whose consequences have not always been happy.

In 1950 most of Latin America's arable land was worked with the hoe. Oxen and the plough – in Mexico the horse and the plough – cultivated an unknown but comparatively small area, and tractors were rare, working perhaps 15 per cent of the continent's cultivated area. Most of the tractors in use were to be found in Argentina, Uruguay, southern Brazil and Mexico, but the number of hectares of arable worked with the tractor was low compared with the developed countries (table 9.9), although substantially above Africa or Asia. Since 1950 there has been a remarkable increase in the number of tractors in use in Latin

W. C. Thiesenhusen, 'Green Revolution in Latin America: income effects, policy decisions', *Monthly Labour Review*, **95**, 1972, pp. 20–7; E. J. Wellhausen, 'The agriculture of Mexico', *Scientific American*, **235**, 1976, pp. 129–50.

[23] FAO, *op. cit.*, 1954; FAO, *Annual Fertilizer Review*, Rome, 1982, vol. 32, 1983; de Janvry, *op. cit.*, p. 164.

America, from about 128,000 in 1950 to 880,000 in 1980. In the same period the arable area has possibly doubled, so the number of hectares worked by each tractor has risen considerably, although at no greater rate in Latin America than in Africa, Asia or China. None the less the area worked by tractor has increased to approximately one-third of the cultivated area in 1980. This means, of course, that two-thirds is still worked by hand or by oxen. One recent and problematic estimate suggests that approximately one-fifth of the work done on Latin American farms was undertaken by machinery, one-quarter by draught animals, but over one-half by hand (table 8.2); this indicates a greater degree of mechanization than elsewhere in the developing countries. [24]

Table 9.9   Arable land per tractor, 1950–80

	1950 (ha)	1980 (ha)	1980 as % of 1950
North America	54	41	76
Oceania	140	108	77
Europe	143	15	10
USSR	226	91	43
Latin America	783	183	23
Africa	2,209	408	18
Asia	7,609	282	3
China	109,000	134	0.1

Sources: FAO, *Production Yearbook 1957*, vol. 11, Rome, 1958; *Production Yearbook 1980*, vol. 34, Rome, 1981

Although the level of mechanization in Latin America is above that in Africa or Asia (other than apparently China), it is still well below that of the developed countries, or indeed Europe or North America in the 1950s (table 9.9), There are several reasons for this. Although a number of Latin American countries produce tractors and other implements, they are for the most part expensive, whether imported or produced at home. In about 1970 a tractor cost the Brazilian farmer – in real purchasing power – about ten times what it cost the United States farmer. Nor is the tractor economic or appropriate in much of Latin America; on the small farms of much of the uplands of Central America or the Andes, not only has population pressure led to the acute subdivision of farms, hardly justifying the use of machinery, but many slopes are too steep for the use of machinery without the risk of soil erosion. Indeed it was argued that the highly eroded nature of much of

[24] E. Ortega, 'Peasant agriculture in Latin America, *Cepal Review*, **16**, 1982, pp. 75–111.

Mexico's farmland 30 years ago was due to the replacement of the hoe by the ox and plough. Elsewhere it has been argued that there are too many machines in use. In much of Brazil there is still a rural labour surplus; in the 1960s and 1970s subsidized credit for the purchase of agricultural machinery and rapid inflation made it cheap to acquire machinery, and the labour force was much reduced, at considerable social cost. [25]

PEASANT AND CAPITALIST

It has been argued that Latin American agriculture has split into two distinct sectors in the last 30 years. Whereas in 1950 most of the hacienda were backward, many of these have been converted into capitalist enterprises which have aimed at maximizing profits. They have adopted new inputs, greatly increased their output, taken on labour saving machinery, ended the servile tenancy and the allocation of land in return for labour, replaced the tenant with wage labour and made every effort to reduce the labour force. Further, these farms have concentrated upon export crops.

In contrast is the somewhat loosely defined peasant sector. According to E. Ortega this sector employs half the rural population of Latin America, over two-thirds in the Andean republics; they farm 45 million of the 105 million hectares sown to crops in 1979, although they have only one-third of the total agricultural area. Their farms are small, averaging 11 hectares of which only 3.3 hectares are in crops; the bulk of these holdings are very small, 39 per cent being less than 2 hectares. Most of these peasants still try to produce their own food. But they are not subsistence farmers, for not only do they sell much of their output, but they provide a substantial part of total agricultural output, and particularly food crops for the domestic market. They are not, however, exclusively food producers. Thus it has been estimated that in Central America the output of the small scale intensive sector is 80 per cent food for the home market and 20 per cent crops for export, whereas the large scale producers export 75 per cent of their output. In Ecuador small farms produce much of the banana production and 60 per cent of the cocoa, and in Mexico, where the large private holdings have come

[25] J. H. Saunders and V. W. Ruttan, 'Biased choice of technology in Brazilian agriculture', in H. P. Binswanger and V. W. Ruttan (eds), *Induced Innovation: Technology, Institutions and Development*, Baltimore, 1978, pp. 276–96; J. Saunders, 'The modernization of Brazilian society', in J. Saunders (ed.), *Modern Brazil: New Patterns and Development*, Gainesville, Florida, 1971, pp. 1–28.

to dominate the market, nearly half the cotton output is produced by peasants.[26]

The transformation of the former hacienda sector – or part of it – into modern capitalist agriculture is by no means easy to trace, much of its history being buried in polemics. The sources of the new entrepreneurial class are various. In countries where substantial parts of large haciendas were expropriated, those remaining have been converted into efficient estates. This class has been particularly important in Mexico. In some of the Andean republics land reform proposals have promised protection to efficiently operated haciendas, and this has encouraged improvement. Foreign owned plantations, such as the banana companies of Central America and the sugar plantations of the Peruvian coast, have been in the vanguard of technical change. In some Latin American countries rapid growth of incomes in the towns has provided good markets. In the environs of cities in southern Brazil small farmers have become small capitalist producers of vegetables, milk and fruit, and urban capital has flowed into many farms. The rise of food processing industries, both home and foreign owned, increased the efficiency of farming in certain commodities – in southern Brazil, for example, barley for breweries and tobacco.[27]

The attitude of the state to the agriculture in Latin America has been ambivalent. In the post-war period most Latin American governments believed prosperity would only come through industrialization and therefore erected tariff walls to protect the infant consumer goods industries. However, foreign earnings were needed to purchase capital goods for these industries, and the only source of earnings was agricultural exports. The fall in demand for these in the 1930s and 1940s had encouraged many economists to believe that they had little future. In the event they have remained buoyant in the long run, particularly where some countries – such as Brazil – have been able to switch to new products, notably soybeans. Home production also presented a dilemma, for rapid population growth needed rapid food output; if these were not forthcoming, rising food prices would have led to rapid wage inflation and halted industrial expansion.

Government policies have varied considerably. In Mexico before 1942 the state land reform encouraged the growth of the *ejido* and was opposed to large scale farming. After 1942 attention was directed to industrialization. It was believed that the *ejidos* were unable to provide a sufficient

---

[26] Ortega, *op. cit.*; Bulmer-Thomas, *op. cit.*
[27] R. Pebayle, 'Rural innovation and the organization of space in southern Brazil', in Preston, *op. cit.*, pp. 103–19; de Alcantara, *op. cit.*, 1976.

growth of food or exports for industrialization. The government therefore encouraged the growth of private farming, investing heavily in irrigation in the north west where land was sold to private owners. The provision of credit, the new seeds and extension work were all oriented to the large farmer rather than the peasant. In Brazil agriculture was largely neglected until 1964, since when there has been credit for the purchase of machinery and an attempt to stabilize producer prices and encourage export crops. [28]

Whatever the vagaries of government policies, the adoption of new inputs has tended to be concentrated upon particular crops, upon larger farms and in specific areas, and the peasant areas, it is claimed, have largely been bypassed. Thus in Brazil the first tractors were used by European immigrants in Rio Grando do Sul; they spread slowly into São Paulo and Minas Gerais. The total number of tractors in Brazil has risen phenomenally from less than 2000 in 1920 to 8327 in 1950 and 156,000 in 1970, and doubled between 1970 and 1980; yet 86 per cent of all are to be found in the south. Although Mexico has had chemical plants producing insecticides since the 1940s, most of those in use in Latin America are confined largely to cotton, a major export crop in several countries. In Mexico the use of high yielding seeds has been limited to the larger farms, and in particular the irrigated farms. Although seeds and fertilizers can be bought in small amounts by peasants, irrigation in Mexico is largely found in the large farm areas of the north west. According to Cynthia Hewitt de Alcantara, because the new high yielding varieties only flourish with irrigation, 80 per cent of Mexico's farmers have been bypassed by Mexico's green revolution. Certainly agricultural output in Mexico is remarkably concentrated, particularly in the irrigated areas. In the early 1970s, 7 per cent of Mexico's farmers produced 45 per cent of the value of output on only 2 per cent of the cropland; in the 1950s 80 per cent of all the increase in output came in the irrigated north west. In Bolivia, where small holders are still a dominant part of the rural population, new inputs have been largely confined to sugar-cane and cotton; in Brazil two-thirds of the fertilizers are used on cotton, sugar-cane and soybeans, and in Ecuador the same proportion goes on sugar-cane, coffee and bananas. [29]

[28] D. W. Adams, 'Agricultural credit in Latin America', *American Journal of Agricultural Economics*, 53, 1971, pp. 163–72; D. Goodman and M. Redclift, *From Peasant to Proletarian: Capitalist Development and Agrarian Transitions*, Oxford, pp. 145–8; de Janvry, *op. cit.*, pp. 158–60; de Alcantara, *op. cit.*, 1973–4.
[29] Henshall and Momsen, *op. cit.*, p. 99; FAO, *Production Yearbook 1981*, vol. 35, Rome, 1982; Cordovez, *op. cit.*; de Alcantara, *op. cit.*, 1973–4; Wellhausen, *op. cit.*; Gomez and Perez, *op. cit.*; E. Boyd Wennergren and M. D. Whitaker, *The Status of Bolivian Agriculture*, New York, 1975, p. 111; de Janvry, *op. cit.*, p. 160.

The size of the peasant sector is a matter of debate, depending on what size of farm is defined as peasant or small scale. Undoubtedly it constitutes a substantial proportion of the population and a large proportion of the cultivated area, although not of total agricultural area, for much of the larger estates are still either idle, in fallow or in grass (table 9.10). Thus in Colombia, Argentina and Ecuador the small holders produced over half the value of agricultural output in the 1960s, although with less than half the agricultural area. This was because small farmers cultivated a high proportion of their land, and farmed it more intensively.[30] But the significance of the small holders is that they produce a high proportion of domestic food consumption. Thus in Brazil family farms – those without hired labour – produce 80 per cent of the staple foods; half the manioc and beans, the diet of the poor, comes from holdings with less than 20 hectares. In Mexico small farms produce two-thirds of the maize and beans. In Peru small farms, with only 15 per cent of the total agricultural area, produce half the cereals and three-quarters of the root crop. This split is most marked in El Salvador, where the larger farms produce coffee, and farms of less than 5 ha grow 60 per cent of the maize and beans.[31]

It has been argued that the peasant sector, unable to purchase the new inputs that have increased yields in the capitalist sector, has stagnated. This may be true, but it would be wrong to suppose that all small scale farming has been undynamic. In Ecuador the peasant sector increased output more rapidly than the agricultural economy as a whole between 1965 and 1977, and in Bolivia the peasant sector, which would appear to be the most backward on the continent, increased output at 4.4 per cent per annum between 1950 and 1976. Nor have all small farmers been unenterprising; in Brazil 60 per cent of the soybean crop is produced on family farms. It is true, however, that the peasant sector has made little contribution to livestock output, which in Latin America is carried out predominantly on large units. It is also true that labour productivity is far greater on the large farms than the small; in Colombia the value of output per hectare is 10 per cent greater on small than large holdings, but output per caput on the large farms is ten times greater than on small holdings.[32]

[30] R. A. Berry, 'Land distribution, income distribution and the productive efficiency of Columbian agriculture', *Food Research Institute Studies*, 72, 1973, pp. 199–232.
[31] Ortega, *op. cit.*; de Janvry, *op. cit.*, pp. 132–3; 160; L. H. Davis and D. E. Weisenhausen, 'Small farmer market development: the El Salvador experience', *Journal of Developing Areas*, 15, 1981, pp. 407–16.
[32] Ortega, *op. cit.*; Berry, *op. cit.*

Table 9.10   Size of the small holding sector in the 1960s

	% of agricultural families			% of land used		% of value of agricultural output	
	Estates	Landless	Small holders	Estates	Small holders	Estates	Small holders
Argentina	5.2	36.3	58.5	51.9	48.1	42.4	57.1
Brazil	14.6	61.9	23.5	93.5	6.5	78.7	21.3
Chile	9.5	49.7	40.8	92.6	7.4	80.0	20.0
Colombia	5.0	24.7	70.3	72.8	27.2	47.8	52.2
Ecuador	2.4	34.5	63.1	64.4	35.6	40.7	59.3
Guatemala	1.6	27.0	71.4	22.3	27.7	56.4	43.6

Source: A. Pearse, 'Subsistence farming is far from dead', Ceres, 2, 1969, pp. 38–43.

AGRIBUSINESS, EXPORTS AND FOOD SUPPLY

The remarkable increase in population since 1950 has made it difficult for Latin American farmers to maintain the per caput output of food crops, particularly as much of the undoubted improvement in farming has been confined to the capitalist sector that has emerged in the last 25 years. Many have argued that this problem has been compounded by the fact that many of the larger farms have concentrated upon export crops, and that export crops have increased at the expense of the food crops. This has been attributed by some not simply to the preference for the more profitable nature of export crops, but also to the increasing control by foreign companies over Latin American farming.

The presence of foreign companies in Latin American agriculture is far from new. British investment in the Argentine beef industry, the Guyanese and other Caribbean sugar plantations was long established. American companies developed the banana plantations of Costa Rica, Honduras and Guatemala, and the sugar plantations of the Peruvian coast. Since the nationalization of sugar plantations in Cuba, Guyana and more recently Peru, foreign companies have been loath to own land and have concentrated more on the processing of food crops, bought from local growers, and the trading of these commodities on the international market. In addition American companies have been important in the establishment of input industries in Mexico and Brazil, making fertilizers, machinery and pesticides. American corporations have also leased or bought areas in the Amazon basin in the last ten years.

Whether export crops – controlled by foreign companies or not – have grown more rapidly than food crops over the last 30 years is difficult to substantiate. Not all apparent export crops are exported; thus one-third of Peru's sugar output is consumed at home. None the less, exports account for a substantial part of Latin American agricultural output; in 1980 17 per cent of the total value was exported. In individual countries exports appear to have increased at the expense of food production. In El Salvador, for example, food output per caput has declined since the 1950s, but agricultural output has kept up with population growth. On the good volcanic soils food crops have been displaced by coffee, and in the coastal areas new land has been devoted not to food crops but to cotton. In Central America as a whole there has been increasing polarization between the small scale sector producing food crops for home consumption, and the larger farms concentrating upon export crops; in some countries exports account for over 70 per cent of total agricultural output. In the drier lower areas of Central America, particularly on the Pacific coastlands, there has been development of cattle ranching, aimed at exports for the United States, often at the expense of food production. Elsewhere in Latin America there has been rapid development of export crops; in the 1970s the area under export crops rose at 5.4 per cent per annum, that under food crops by only 2.9 per cent, much of this accounted for by the rise of soybeans as a major export crop. [33]

It would be somewhat more difficult to show that there has been a major swing to export crops at the expense of food crops in Latin America as a whole (table 9.6). What is certainly true is that in the 1970s food imports began to increase rapidly – six fold, to be compared with a trebling of exports – and by 1980 food imports were 12 per cent of all Latin America's food supply. [34]

CONCLUSIONS

Latin America differs from Asia in that much of its increase in food output has come from the expansion of the area in crops. Furthermore, unlike most of the rest of the developing world it has a large scale capitalist agriculture, utilizing a wide range of manufacturing inputs, increasing yields and often shedding labour as a result of the use of machinery. This was possible because of the existing distribution of land. Large farms have not had to be built up by amalgamation; they already existed. Not all hacienda have of course been transformed in this way. Third, few countries in Latin America, in spite of the growth of food imports, have food supplies below national requirements.

In Latin America the problem of hunger is not that agriculture has failed to produce sufficient food, but that large sections of the rural population have insufficient income to buy enough food or land to produce it, and that the extraordinary growth of population in the cities has also left many without jobs. In the rural areas the redistribution of land may provide some solution to this problem, although it should be recalled that in some areas, notably in the *altiplano* of Peru and Bolivia, redistribution has not solved the problem; there was not enough land to go round.

[33] C. T. Smith, 'Aspects of agriculture and settlement in Peru', *Geographical Journal*, **126**, 1960, pp. 297–412; Cordovez, *op. cit.*; W. H. Durham, *Scarcity and Survival in Central America: Ecological Origins of the Soccer War*, Stanford, 1979, pp. 30–3, 34; Dorner and Quiros, *op. cit.*; Bulmer-Thomas, *op. cit.*; R. Burbach and P. Flynn, *Agribusiness in the Americas*, New York, 1980, p. 105.
[34] Cordovez, *op. cit.*; Inter-American Development Bank, *op. cit.*, p. 119.

10

Asia

The area of Asia is smaller than that of Africa, and only a quarter larger than America, but its population – 2578 million in 1980 – greatly exceeds that of the two other continents. Indeed China alone (1000 million) exceeds the combined population of Latin America (363 million) and Africa (377 million), as does South Asia, the former British India (855 million). The land mass and its huge population show a remarkable internal diversity.

Asia, unlike South America and Africa, lies largely north of the equator. The area with high temperatures, rainfall throughout the year and a natural vegetation of rain forest – rapidly being reduced – lies in the south in Indonesia, and parts of mainland South East Asia. The bulk of South, South East and East Asia has a climate dominated by the monsoon. Indrafts of hot, maritime air bring heavy rainfall to most areas for a few months in the summer. During the winter high pressures establish themselves over the Eurasian land mass, and southward moving air is cool and dry, although only the north of China, the Tibetan plateau and some northern upland areas have winters where low temperatures preclude crop growth. The variability of the monsoon, both in amount and the timing of its onset, means that farming in much of the continent depends upon irrigation to a much greater extent than elsewhere. This is true even of South West Asia, where the monsoon has little influence and rain falls mainly in the winter.

The topography of Asia is dominated by the mountains that run from Turkey through Iran and in northern India become the Himalayas and northwards the Tibetan plateau. Much of the interior of mainland South East Asia is mountainous, and southern China is an upland region with many steep slopes. The major areas of settlement are, in contrast to Africa or Latin America, the deltas and flat alluvial plains, notably the Hwang-Ho in northern China, the Ganges-Brahmaputra in northern

India, Pakistan and Bangladesh, and the deltas of the Mekong, the Red River, the Chao Phraya and the Irrawady in South East Asia. In all these areas, except north west India and northern China, rice is the major crop, partly because in the flooded deltas of Bangladesh, lower Burma and Thailand few other crops can be grown, but also because the flat land provides an ideal site for the crop, which gives comparatively high yields even with traditional methods. Rice probably provides half the calorific intake of the Asian population.

Economically and politically Asia shows great contrasts. China, Vietnam, North Korea and Mongolia all have centrally planned socialist economies, and Burma has a socialist regime although its farming has yet to be collectivized. India alone in Asia has established a form of parliamentary government, and has a mixed economy. Elsewhere market economies predominate, although state direction is often strong. Over the last 30 years most Asian countries have had marked economic growth. But in only two areas has this growth lifted net national income per caput above the lowest rungs (table 10.1). First, in South West Asia petroleum exports have given several countries above average national incomes per caput, notably Saudi Arabia. Second, a number of countries have had a marked development of manufacturing industry. However, these countries – Taiwan, North and South Korea, Hong Kong and Singapore – contain a small fragment of Asia's population. China, India, Bangladesh and Pakistan all remain very poor, and Indonesia owes its present slightly greater income per caput to oil exports over the last decade (table 10.1). Although in South West Asia and in limited parts of East Asia the agricultural population has fallen to less than half the labour force, and in spite of the rapid urban growth in many countries, Asia remains essentially rural and agricultural. In China only 13 per cent of the population lives in towns and over 70 per cent of the labour force works in agriculture; although towns hold rather more of the population in South Asia, over 70 per cent of the labour force is still dependent upon agriculture for a livelihood (table 10.1).

POPULATION GROWTH AND POPULATION DENSITY

Asia, like Latin America and Africa, has experienced a remarkable population growth since 1950, and rates of increase remain high (table 10.1). However, in contrast to these continents Asia in 1950 already had very high densities, and its rate of increase since has been somewhat slower. Indeed in some countries there has been a marked decline in the rate of increase, notably in China. Because the proportion employed

Table 10.1   Economic aspects of Asia

	GNP per caput ($ US)	% of labour in agriculture	% of population in towns	Agriculture as a % of all exports	Rate of population growth 1970–9 (% p.a.)
Saudi Arabia	7820	62	67	0	4.5
Iraq	2410	43	72	1	3.3
Iran	1648	40	50	2	2.9
Korea, Rep.	1480	36	55	10	1.9
Malaysia	1370	51	29	52	2.2
Turkey	1330	54	47	72	2.5
Jordan	1180	21	56	30	3.4
Korea, DPR	1130	50	60	29	2.5
Syria	1030	32	50	26	3.6
Mongolia	780	56	51	81	2.9
Philippines	600	47	36	52	2.6
Thailand	590	77	14	64	2.4
Indonesia	370	59	20	26	2.3
Pakistan	260	57	28	38	3.1
China	260	71	13	38	1.9
Sri Lanka	230	54	27	81	1.7
India	190	71	22	30	2.1
Vietnam	—	71	19	32	2.9
Afghanistan	170	79	15	70	2.6
Burma	160	67	27	77	2.2
Nepal	130	93	5	87	2.2
Bangladesh	90	74	11	36	3.0
Laos	—	76	14	64	1.4
Kampuchea	—	—	—	83	—

Source: World Bank, *World Development Report 1981*, Washington DC, 1981

in agriculture remains high, the density of the agricultural population to the arable area is much higher in Asia than in Latin America or Africa (see figure 8.1). This does not mean of course that all parts of Asia have high densities. Much of the arid South West is sparsely populated, as is the cold and dry Tibetan plateau and north west China. The interior of mainland South East Asia is unoccupied, and densities are low on some of the islands of the South East Asian archipelago, notably Kalimantan and New Guinea.

There are also marked regional variations in density between the settled areas of Asia. Most notable is the contrast between the agricultural density of East Asia and the rest of the continent. Agricultural densities are very high in China, Korea and North Vietnam and were equally high, before the post-war industrialization, in Japan. Elsewhere densities are much lower except in Bangladesh and Java (table 10.2).

Table 10.2 Some characteristics of modern Asian agriculture, c. 1980

	Arable as a % of total area	Irrigated as a % of arable	Agricultural population per hectare of arable	Tractors per thousand ha of arable	Fertilizer per ha of arable (kg)	Rice yield (kg/ha)	Wheat yield (kg/ha)	HYV[a] as a % of rice	HYV[a] as a % of wheat	Multiple cropping index
Korea, DPR	19	47	3.7	13	326	6000	2452	—	—	—
Japan	13	67	2.6	224	372	5128	3051	—	—	—
Korea, Republic	22	52	6.8	1	376	4353	3300	47	—	150
China	11	46	5.9	7	150	4200	1878	80	25	—
Indonesia	11	28	4.5	1	63	3301	—	41	—	—
Malaysia	13	9	1.5	2	105	2841	—	37	—	—
Burma	15	10	1.8	1	10	2601	903	7	—	111
Sri Lanka	33	24	3.7	11	77	2590	—	63	—	—
Pakistan	26	70	2.3	2	50	2418	1563	40	76	121
Philippines	33	13	2.3	2	34	2238	—	68	—	136
Vietnam	19	28	6.3	4	41	2106	—	—	—	—
Afghanistan	12	33	1.5	—	6	2095	1125	—	—	—
Bangladesh	68	18	8.1	—	46	2020	1899	14	73	148
India	57	23	2.6	2	31	2010	1436	36	72	120
Nepal	17	10	5.7	—	10	1940	1222	18	73	117
Thailand	33	15	2.0	2	16	1899	—	11	—	—
Laos	4	13	3.1	1	8	1439	—	—	—	1
Kampuchea	17	3	1.6	—	3	833	—	—	—	0

[a] HYV = high yielding varieties.

Sources: FAO, The State of Food and Agriculture 1982, Rome, 1983; Production Yearbook 1981, vol. 35, Rome, 1982; D. Dalrymple, Development and Spread of High-Yielding Varieties of Wheat and Rice in the Less Developed Nations, United States, Department of Agriculture, Washington DC 1978; Survey of Multiple Cropping in Less Developed Nations, United States Department of Agriculture, Washington DC, 1971

SOME ASPECTS OF ASIAN AGRICULTURE: CROPS
AND LIVESTOCK

Asian agriculture has more in common with the traditional agriculture
of Europe than that of modern Africa or Latin America. The typical
farm is small, operated by the farmer and his family. Much of the produce
is consumed on the farms; 80 per cent of Chinese food grain never leaves
the farms and even in Thailand, a rice exporter, two-thirds of all rice
is consumed on the farms.[1] The land is cultivated with a plough drawn
by oxen or water buffalo, although in some very densely populated areas
only the hoe is used. Most of the seed is broadcast, although in some
rice areas, particularly in East Asia, rice is transplanted from nursery
fields to the paddies (table 10.8). The sickle is the usual implement for
harvesting, although in Java and Thailand a hand knife is used. A great
variety of food crops is grown, but the dominant crop is rice, which
takes second place to wheat only in northern South Asia and northern
China. Maize is important in China and parts of South East Asia. Millets
and sorghum are grown in the drier areas which lack irrigation, in
northern China and the interior of the Indian subcontinent. Minor food
crops such as cassava, peanuts and sweet potatoes are locally important
(table 10.3).

Table 10.3   Land use in Asia, 1961–5 and 1980 (million hectares)

	1961–5	*1980*
Cereals	294	304
Rice	114.4	129.1
Wheat	61.9	80.4
Maize	22.4	36.9
Millet and sorghum	68.5	44.4
Roots and tubers	18.4	17.9
Pulses	37.8	33.8
Oilseeds	31.1	50.1
Sugar-cane and sugar-beet	4.5	6.5
Coffee	0.48	0.8
Tea	1.1	2.1
Jute	2.5	2.6
Rubber	4.25	—
Cotton	11.7	—
Tobacco	1.9	2.2

Sources: FAO, *Production Yearbook 1981*, vol. 35, Rome, 1982; *Production Yearbook 1976*, vol. 30,
Rome, 1977; *Production Yearbook 1965*, vol. 19, Rome, 1966

[1] A. Doak Barnett, *China and the World Food System*, London, 1979, p. 65; R. C. Y.
Ng, 'Development and change in rural Thailand', *Asian Affairs*, **10**, 1979, pp. 62–8.

Oilseeds and pulses make up the bulk of the remaining cropland. Non-food crops constitute a small proportion of the total arable, which is surprising considering the importance of plantation crops in the economies of some countries. Agricultural products account for half or more of the exports of Malaysia, the Philippines, Thailand, Sri Lanka and Burma (table 10.1). In the nineteenth century the development of jute, coffee, tea and rubber in Bangladesh, India, Ceylon and Malaya, was almost entirely for export to Europe; in Indonesia sugar-cane, rubber and coffee were grown for the same market, and from the deltas of Burma, Thailand and southern Vietnam rice was exported to other Asian countries and to Europe. Agricultural exports remain an important part of the exports of many Asian countries (table 10.1), but a dual system of a peasant sector and a commercial exporting sector occurs only in Sri Lanka and Malaya, perhaps in Sumatra. Elsewhere food crops dominate. Thus even in Bangladesh, where jute provided nine-tenths of all agricultural exports by value, the crop occupies only 7 per cent of the arable area, and in Java the estates occupy much the same proportion.

Livestock are found throughout Asia and their densities are often surprisingly high, considering the competition for land between man and animal. Two livestock enterprises are unimportant in Asia. The extensive rearing of cattle and sheep, widely found in Latin America and Africa, is confined in Asia to northern China and Mongolia. Nor is dairying, a major part of the output of developed countries, of any significance. Dairy products are not consumed by the Chinese and certain other peoples, such as the Thai, possibly because of their difficulties in absorbing lactose in the intestine. In India and the Indian influenced areas of South East Asia milking is practised, but the poor quality of the cows and fodder and the low incomes of the population make it an incidental feature of livestock keeping. Although India has the largest cattle population in the world, it produces less than 1 per cent of the annual world beef output. Little land is available for feeding livestock in India; they live largely from the straw of food grains and waste land. Cattle thus use most of their feed to fuel their exertions pulling ploughs and wagons, and put on weight very slowly. The Hindu reluctance to slaughter cattle prevents the development of a livestock industry, and cattle are valued for their draught power and as a source of manure both for the fields and for fuel. This reluctance to slaughter livestock also prevails among the Buddhist populations of South East Asia, and the poverty of tropical grasses also hampers development. In much of East Asia and Java the very high density of population excludes the keeping of cattle except – along with water buffaloes – as draught animals, and in China poultry and particularly pigs provide all of the very little meat that is eaten; both poultry and pigs are non-ruminants and compete with man for grain and roots, but can utilize food wastes. Over much of Asia – the South West, Pakistan, Bangladesh, Malaya and Indonesia – pigs are not kept because the populations are predominantly Muslim in origin.[2]

FARM SIZE AND LAND OWNERSHIP

In Africa the dominant production unit is small, and large farms occupy little of the farmland; in Latin America, although the occupiers of very small holdings dominate farm structure, large and very large farms make up most of the farmland. But in Asia farms are very small, *and* they occupy most of the cropland. Nor has there been any tradition of large farms. There has been no European settlement or land appropriation even though much of the continent was part of European empires until 1948. Plantations were established by the British, Dutch and French, but most of these have been nationalized since independence, and in some cases subdivided; however, even when not subdivided they occupied – and occupy – a small fraction of the agricultural land (table 10.4).

Thus most farms in Asia are very small. Between one-half and nine-tenths are less than 2 hectares. In Indonesia 70 per cent are less than 1 hectare (table 10.5). Indeed it is debatable where the line is to be drawn between the rural household which is landless and that which has land and is recorded as a farm; certainly in Java and many other parts of Asia farm families gain a significant part of their income from activities off the farm. The large farm in Asia is normally defined as over 10 hectares; they are a small proportion of all farms, but in some countries, notably in India, Pakistan and the Philippines, they occupy one-third or more of the farmland (table 10.4). Elsewhere – particularly in Korea, Taiwan, Thailand, Bangladesh and Indonesia – the small farms occupy most of the farmland. In contrast to Latin America, where the most rapid agricultural growth has occurred on large farms, and that on the small farms has stagnated, in Asia some of the most rapid growth rates have occurred in countries – Taiwan, Malaya, and Korea – where the average size of the farm is below 2 hectares and there are few large farms.

Until 1948 China was a country of small farms, much of it rented to tenants. Between 1948 and 1952 the land of landlords and some of

[2] D. Grigg, *An Introduction to Agricultural Geography*, 1984, pp. 186–92.

Table 10.4   Farm size in Asian countries, 1970s

	Number of farms (%)				Area of farmland (%)			
	0–2 ha	2–5 ha	5–10 ha	10 ha and over	0–2 ha	2–5 ha	5–10 ha	10 ha and over
Bangladesh	88	10	—	2	58	32	—	10
India	70	18	8	4	21	26	23	30
South Korea	94	—	—	—	80	—	—	—
Malaya	72	27	—	—	48	47	—	—
Pakistan	50	27	15	8	9	23	26	43
Philippines	41	40	13	6	11	31	24	33
Thailand	50	30	16	4	20	32	32	16
Nepal	87	10	2	1	46	31	12	11

Sources: Asian Development Bank, *Rural Asia: Challenge and Opportunity*, 1977, p. 98; *Economic Bulletin for Asia and the Pacific*, **30** (1), 1979, pp. 24–53

Table 10.5   Farm size in selected Asian countries (number of farms in each size group, as a percentage of all farms)

	0–0.5 ha	0.5–1.0 ha	1–5 ha	5–10 ha	10 ha +	Average size (ha)
Sri Lanka	35.3	30.0	30.2	3.2	1.2	1.38
India	19.4	—	43.5	18.9	18.2	2.3
Philippines	4.1	7.4	69.5	13.4	5.6	2.58
Thailand	10.3	8.3	56.9	19.2	5.4	2.95
South Korea	35.0	32.0	32.0	1.0	0.0	0.91
Indonesia	45.6	24.7	27.5	1.6	0.6	0.99

Source: R. Montgomery and Toto Sugito, 'Changes in the structure of farms and farming in Indonesia between censuses, 1963–1973: the issues of inequality and near landlessness', *Journal of South East Asian Studies*, **11**, 1980, pp. 348–65

the richer peasants was seized and distributed to the landless and those with smaller holdings. China thus became a country of small owner occupied farms, similar to much of the rest of Asia, although with less tenancy (table 10.6). However, in the period 1952–8 the small family holdings of the Chinese peasant were grouped into successively larger units; first were the mutual aid teams, then the agricultural production co-operatives, the advanced agricultural co-operatives and in 1958 the communes. Private ownership of land was abolished in 1956–7. The level of decision making and accounting has varied; at times decisions have been made at commune level, which may consist of 5000 house-holds, at other times decisions have been made at village level. Since 1977 the introduction of the production responsibility system has meant that the accounting unit has shifted back towards the village and even household level. It is impossible to produce data on the size of farms comparable with the non-Communist parts of Asia.[3]

Table 10.6   Farm size in China after the land reforms, 1948–52

Class	% of families	% of total area	Average area owned (ha)
Poor peasant	57.1	46.8	0.8
Middle peasant	35.8	44.8	1.3
Rich peasant	3.6	6.4	1.75
Landlord	2.6	2.1	0.8

Source: Azizur Rahman Khan, 'The distribution of income in rural China', in International Labour Office, *Poverty and Landlessness in Rural Asia*, Geneva, 1977

In the socialist countries of Asia land is not owned by individuals. Elsewhere the bulk of the agricultural land is farmed by owner occupiers, but tenancy does persist and is regarded as a problem. Tenant farmers rarely have the security that they possess in most European countries, and may be evicted at short notice. However, landlords in most parts of Asia are not like those of Latin America, owning vast estates; more commonly landlords have comparatively small amounts of land divided among tenants – often share croppers – in one or a few adjacent villages. Information on the extent of tenancy is often out of date, and difficult to interpret. For those countries for which data exist, however, owner

[3] J. G. Gurley, 'Rural development in China 1949–75, and the lessons to be learned from it', in N. Maxwell (ed.), *China's Road to Development*, London, 1979, pp. 5–26; Reeitsu Kojima, 'China's new agricultural policy', *Developing Economies*, **20**, 1982, pp. 390–413; J. Gray, 'China's new agricultural revolution', *IDS Bulletin*, **13**, 1982, pp. 36–43.

occupiers are a majority everywhere except in the Philippines and Pakistan (table 10.7). About 43 per cent of the farmland in Pakistan is farmed by tenants, 20 per cent in India and 23 per cent in Bangladesh.[4]

Table 10.7   Tenants and owner occupiers in selected Asian countries (% of holdings)

	Fully owned by operator	Partly owned by operator	Tenant (cash and share crop)
Sri Lanka (1947)	67.0	—	33.0
India (1960)	60.2	22.9	16.9
Philippines (1960)	44.7	14.4	39.9
Thailand (1963)	81.9	14.0	4.1
South Korea (1969)	73.5	19.6	7.0
Indonesia (1973)	74.8	22.0	3.2
Pakistan (1960)	41.0	17.0	42.0

Sources: R. Montgomery and Toto Sugito, 'Changes in the structure of farms and farming in Indonesia between censuses, 1963–1973: the issues of inequality and near landlessness', *Journal of South East Asian Studies*, 11, 1980, pp. 348–65; Azizur Rahman Khan, 'Poverty and inequality in rural Bangladesh', in International Labour Office, *Poverty and landlessness in Rural Asia*, Geneva, 1977, pp. 137–60

Land reform has been urged in Asia on grounds of both equity and efficiency, but outside East Asia much has been proposed but little done. In Taiwan and South Korea reforms first controlled rents, then transferred ownership to the occupier and placed ceilings upon the amount that could be owned or farmed. There is thus a remarkable equality in farm size and little tenancy.[5] The transfer of land in China to the poorer peasants involved 46 per cent of the arable, and was thus the most comprehensive reform in Asia, although all peasants subsequently lost ownership in the collectivization of 1956–8. Several states have attempted to redistribute land by putting a ceiling upon the amount an individual could own, and some land has been expropriated and redistributed. The amounts, however, have generally been small, for the laws on redistribution have proved all too easy to evade.[6] However in some countries land redistribution, even if fully accomplished, could do little to solve the problems of landlessness and near landlessness. In Java in 1960, in an attempt to redistribute land declared surplus,

[4] B. L. C. Johnson, *India: Resources and Development*, London, 1979, p. 20; 'Prospects for the economic development of Bangladesh in the 1980s', *Economic Bulletin for Asia and the Pacific*, **31**, 1980, pp. 94–105.
[5] Cheng-Hung Liao and M. Yand, 'Socio-economic change in rural Taiwan, 1950–78', *South East Asian Studies*, **18**, 1981, pp. 539–45.
[6] B. H. Farmer, *An Introduction to South Asia*, London, 1984, pp. 188, 210, 212; A. Bhaduri, 'A comparative study of land reform in South Asia', *Economic Bulletin for Asia and the Pacific*, **30**, 1979, pp. 1–13.

350,000 hectares were put above the ceiling of permissible ownership. However, there were at the time 3 million families seeking land.[7]

Although it has been claimed that in many parts of Asia tenants are being evicted and larger holdings are formed under the spur of commercialization and mechanization, reliable figures on farm size are few and far between, and suggest that it is the increase in the number of small farms that is most noticeable. This is not surprising, given the formidable increase in the farm populations over the last 30 years, and the custom of dividing land among all the sons – and often daughters as well – at inheritance.

ASIAN AGRICULTURE IN 1950

Long before the post-war decline in mortality and the subsequent rapid growth of population, much of Asia had very high population densities; there was a notable difference in densities between East Asia and the rest of Asia. Agricultural technologies were largely traditional and farm work depended almost exclusively upon human and animal labour; few if any inputs were bought. East Asia and the Indian subcontinent had possessed high agricultural densities for centuries, and had adapted to the slow growth of population by increasing labour inputs. This intensity was greatest in south China, Japan, Korea and north Vietnam, and was markedly lower in South East Asia, where the rice exports of the deltas of Burma, Thailand and Vietnam are a comparatively recent development. Thus over long periods, and because of the lack of easily cultivable land, the populations of East Asia had increased rice yields by using more and more intensive practices. Wet rice needs very large inputs of labour. The crop is grown with the stalk partially submerged for much of the growing season, and thus has to be grown in small, flat fields surrounded by bunds, together with some means of withdrawing water before the crop ripens and is harvested. Most rice is *not* irrigated; two-thirds of the rice grown in South and South East Asia relies upon the monsoon rainfall, either directly or by flooding from rivers.[8] If the land is irrigated, further water control measures are needed, requiring a considerable expenditure of labour and capital. Rice can be broadcast in the paddy fields, or the seed can be sown in nursery plots and transplanted into the main fields after several weeks' growth. As in the

---

[7] P. Krinks, 'Rural changes in Java: an end to involution?', *Geography*, **63**, 1978, pp. 31–6.

[8] FAO, *The State of Food and Agriculture 1978*, Rome, 1979, p. 22.

provision of irrigation, this increases yields. The frequency of weeding also can be increased to raise yields. Rice benefits from the blue-green algae that live in the flooded paddy fields and add nitrogen to the soil. Livestock manure is scarce in much of Asia, because of the shortage of fodder, but in China and certain other East Asian countries night soil was applied to the rice crop. If the land was irrigated – or if the monsoon was particularly heavy – the rice harvest could be followed by another cereal crop, exceptionally by a second crop of rice (table 10.8).

Thus by 1950 – indeed by a much earlier date – there was a marked difference in rice yields between East Asia and the rest of the continent, reflecting greater labour intensity, which in turn roughly reflected differences in agricultural population density.

In the 1890s most of Japan's rice was already irrigated. Careful selection of indigenous varieties of rice produced one – the *ponlai* – that responded well to chemical fertilizers, and the combination of an improved variety, irrigation and increased fertilizer application increased yields between 1890 and 1910. Japan acquired Korea and Taiwan as colonies in 1900, and used these countries as a source of rice. In both countries the Japanese increased the area under irrigation, began extension schemes, arranged credit schemes for farmers and provided chemical fertilizers. Rice output increased markedly between 1920 and 1940, partly due to higher yields but also due to an increase in the area double cropped, which the extension of irrigation made possible. Thus by 1950 there was a pronounced difference in rice yields between Japan, Taiwan and Korea and the rest of Asia; in south China comparable yields were due to the great amounts of pig, draught animal and human excreta used as organic manure, a practice uncommon elsewhere in Asia.[9]

THE GROWTH OF FOOD OUTPUT, 1950-80

Little is known of the rate at which agricultural production increased in Asia before 1950. It has been suggested, however, that in China food

[9] Japan FAO Association, *A Century of Technical Development in Japanese Agriculture*, Tokyo, 1959; Sung Hwan Ban, 'Agricultural growth in Korea 1918-1971', in Y. Hayami, V. W. Ruttan and H. M. Southworth, *Agricultural Growth in Japan, Taiwan, Korea and the Philippines*, Honolulu, Hawaii, 1979, pp. 90-116; S. Pao-San Ho, 'Agricultural transformation under colonialism: the case of Taiwan', *Journal of Economic History*, 28, 1965, pp. 313-40; D. J. Puchala and J. Stavely, 'The political economy of Taiwanese agricultural development', in R. E. Hopkins, D. J. Puchala and R. B. Talbot, *Food, Politics and Agricultural Development: Case Studies in the Public Policy of Rural Modernization*, Boulder, Colorado, 1979, pp. 112-17; S. McCune, *Korea's Heritage: A Regional and Social*

Table 10.8   Rice production in Asia, c. 1950

	Yield (tonnes per ha)	% of rice area irrigated	% of rice transplanted	% of land double cropped	% of land double cropped with rice	Chemical fertilizer kg per hectare of arable)
Japan	5.1	96	95	35	0.3	146
South China	4.5	62	–	66	13–15	4[a]
Taiwan	3.2	79	–	93	42	88
South Korea	3.3	58	100	28	–	53
Tongking Delta	2.5	46	–	–	50	–
Mekong Delta	2.1	20	80	low	10	–
Thailand	1.5	24	80	low	–	0.3
Cambodia	1.2	–	–	–	–	–
Lower Burma	1.6	11	90	low	–	0.02
Malaya	2.4	11	94	low	6	0.4
Java	1.7	49	79	25	15–20	1.0[b]
Philippines	1.2	30	80	–	16	0.5
Bangladesh	1.7	12	74	24	–	0.2[c]
Sri Lanka	1.7	60	6	–	32	–
India	1.5	20	–	13	–	0.5

[a] All China.
[b] Indonesia.
[c] All Pakistan.

Source: D. B. Grigg, The Agricultural Systems of the World: An Evolutionary Approach, Cambridge, 1974. p. 78

output just about kept pace with population growth from the 1880s to the 1930s; in India it did not, and food production per caput fell from 1900 to 1947.[10] In contrast many countries in South East Asia had rapid rates of increase in agricultural output from the late nineteenth century until the 1930s, but this was not of food for home consumption but crops grown for export – rubber, rice and sugar-cane.

Since 1950 the rate of increase in food output has greatly increased and compares favourably with that of Africa and Latin America (see table 5.5). Some regions have grown at very high rates. Thus Mexico's agricultural output rose at 6.3 per cent per annum in 1952–65, the Punjab reached 5.5 per cent, and while Brazil increased at 4.2 per cent in the same period, Taiwan rose at 4.5 per cent. In the 1950s and 1960s agricultural output rose at 4 per cent per annum in both the Philippines and Thailand. Although the food grain statistics of the two most populous countries, India and China, are open to various interpretations, both have achieved very substantial increases (table 10.9).[11]

Table 10.9   Food grain output, India and China (million tonnes)

	India	China
c. 1950	60	163
1964–9	90	194
1969–71	118	243
1981–2	134	318

Sources: B. H. Farmer, *An Introduction to South Asia*, London, 1984, pp. 174–5; A. Doak Barnett, *China and the World Food System*, London, 1979, p. 37; S. Ishikawa, 'China's economic growth since 1949: an assessment', *China Quarterly*, no. 94, 1983, pp. 217–18

Clearly there have been marked variations between countries in the rate of increase and also, for the same country, between decades. Burma and Indonesia, for example, after a long period of slow growth made considerable increases in the 1970s. Between 1961–5 and 1976 food

Geography, Tokyo, 1957, pp. 85–6; Y. Hayami, 'Elements of induced innovation: a historical perspective for the Green Revolution', *Explorations in Economic History*, 8, 1971, pp. 445–72.

[10] R. H. Myers, 'Land, property rights and agriculture in modern China', in R. Barker and R. Sinha (eds), *The Chinese Agricultural Economy*, London, 1982, pp. 37–47; G. Blyn, *Agricultural Trends in India, 1891–1947*, New York, 1966.

[11] R. H. Day and Inderjit Singh, *Economic Development as an Adaptive Process: The Green Revolution in the Indian Punjab*, Cambridge, 1977, p. 51; C. C. David and R. Barker, 'Agricultural growth in the Philippines, 1948–1971', in Hayami, Ruttan and Southworth, *op. cit.*, pp. 117–42; D. Feeny, *The Political Economy of productivity: Thai Agricultural Development 1880–1975*, Vancouver, 1982, p. 44.

output grew most rapidly in Indonesia, Thailand, Syria, Korea, Turkey, Taiwan, Malaysia, Iran and the Philippines, very slowly in Kampuchea and Burma. India and China, which account for such a large proportion of the population and output, had a modest intermediate position (figure 8.5). [12]

However, food and agricultural output has to be related to the increase in population, and then the performance of Asian agriculture seems less impressive. Of the two most populous countries, China's performance (according to FAO estimates) is the better, for food output per caput rose 21 per cent between 1961–5 and 1976 (figure 8.6). However, statistics issued by the Chinese government since 1977 suggest that food output per caput hardly changed between 1957 and 1977, although it may have risen in the late 1970s and early 1980s. In India food output has kept ahead of population growth but, until the late 1970s, by only a small margin. [13] More spectacular improvements in food supply have been sustained in Korea, Iran, Malaysia and Pakistan, but food supply per caput has declined in the 1960s and 1970s in Afghanistan, Mongolia, Nepal, Iraq, Burma, Bangladesh, Kampuchea and Vietnam. Thus the impressive increases in food output for Asia as a whole clearly need to be qualified. In 1978–80 food supplies per caput were below national requirements in Jordan, Yemen, Afghanistan, India, Nepal, Bangladesh, Laos and Vietnam. Only in South West Asia, Malaysia and Korea did the supply substantially exceed requirements, and in these countries food *imports* were important (figure 2.4).

YIELD AND AREA

The long history of settlement in much of Asia meant that by 1950 there was little cultivable land left unoccupied, and most of the arable land supported dense agricultural populations. Some land colonization has taken place in Asia since the War (see pp. 109–11), and in some countries

[12] Khin Maung Kyi, 'Modernization of Burmese agriculture: problems and prospects', *South East Asian Affairs*, 1982, pp. 115–31; FAO, *The State of Food and Agriculture 1970*, Rome, 1971, p. 128; FAO, *Production Yearbook 1981*, vol. 35, Rome, 1982.

[13] R. Barker, D. G. Sisler and B. Rose, 'Prospects for growth in grain production', in Barker and Sinha, *op. cit.*, pp. 163–81; K. R. Walker, 'China's grain production 1975–80 and 1952–7: some basic statistics', *China Quarterly*, no. 86, 1981, pp. 215–47; V. Smil, 'Food in China', *Current History*, 75, 1978, pp. 69–72; J. S. Sarma, 'India – a drive towards self-sufficiency in food grains', *American Journal of Agricultural Economics*, **60**, 1978, pp. 859–64.

extra food output has come primarily from area expansion rather than yield increases, notably in Thailand. But, as in Latin America, the proportion of increased output attributable to extra area has declined since 1950. In India approximately half the increase in grain output 1950–60 was due to area expansion, but since then 80 per cent of the increase has been due to higher yields. In China the arable area is less than in 1950, although the sown area has increased substantially because of the spread of double cropping; none the less it has been estimated that 90 per cent of the increased food output since 1950 has been due to higher yields (table 10.10).[14]

Table 10.10   Percentage of cereal output increase due to higher yields

	1961–5 to 1970	1970–9
South and SE Asia	66	72
East Asia	73	42[a]
SW Asia	37	65
Africa	31	18
Latin America	37	54

[a] Low figure probably due to increase in double cropping.
Source: FAO, *The State of Food and Agriculture 1979*, Rome, 1980, pp. 6–16

In the 1960s and 1970s yield increases were the most important source of increased output in all parts of Asia, and were far more important than in Latin America or Africa. This is not surprising. Most estimates of the potential arable area in Asia suggest that the land remaining uncultivated which could be used for crops is no more than one-fifth of the present arable area, whereas in Latin America and Africa the available land greatly exceeds that in use (see table 6.4).[15] Area expansion can be achieved by colonizing new land, by reducing the fallow or by multiple cropping. The last will be dealt with later; land colonization has already been touched upon (see pp. 109–11). Something must be said of fallow reduction.

In Africa and Latin America large areas of arable land were in fallow in the 1960s, and in Africa the reduction of this fallow has been an important source of increased food output. In Asia virtually all the arable is sown each year. However, this figure is a composite; in most Asian countries some of the arable is sown more than once each year, and a

[14] Sarma, *op. cit.*; Walker, *op. cit.*
[15] P. Buringh, H. D. J. van Heemst and G. J. Staring, *Computation of the Absolute Maximum Food Production of the World*, Wageningen, 1975; President's Science Advisory Committee, *The World Food Problem*, vol. 2, Washington DC, 1967, p. 434.

much smaller amount is farmed by shifting cultivation and sown only once in several years. Most of the shifting cultivation remaining in Asia is to be found in the interior of mainland South East Asia, or in Sumatra, Kalimantan or Papua New Guinea. In Indonesia both food and cash crops are grown in *ladang*; rubber is particularly easy to integrate into *ladang*. But shifting cultivation supports a comparatively small proportion of Asia's population, and what reduction of fallow has taken place has added little to food output in Asia in the last 30 years. [16]

CROP YIELDS IN ASIA, 1950–80: THE GREEN REVOLUTION

In the mid 1960s high yielding varieties of wheat were introduced into Asia from Mexico, and a high yielding rice, 1R-8, was developed at the International Rice Research Institute in the Philippines and made available in the rest of Asia. Together with the use of chemical fertilizers, pesticides and irrigation, these crops gave yields well above those of traditional varieties. The adoption of these new varieties was rapid; the consequences of these changes (unfortunately dubbed the green revolution) have given rise to a large and often polemical literature. The yields obtained by farmers have been lower than those obtained on experimental farms, a fact that would not surprise most agronomists. The use of the 'miracle' seeds has not solved the problem of hunger in Asia, if for no other reason than that the population of Asia increased by 750 million between 1965 and 1980. The new seeds have been widely adopted by those growing wheat, less so by those growing rice; but wheat and rice, although the major food grains, are not all the food supplies of Asia. Thus in 1980 only about one-quarter of the seed used for food grains in S and SE Asia consisted of new high yielding varieties. [17] As a revolution the changes are clearly less than a total transformation of rural Asia. But the rapid growth of output produced on these farms where the new technology has been adopted has helped to maintain the rate of increase of food output and has prevented price rises that would have occurred in the absence of increased output. Some critics, who have reluctantly agreed that there have been improvements in food output and crop yields, have argued that the adoption of the new technologies has benefited large farmers and not small, increased the number of landless and lowered their incomes, caused the eviction of tenants and increased the gap in incomes between the landless and the small farmers on the one hand,

[16] J. E. Spencer, *Shifting Cultivation in Southeastern Asia*, Berkeley, 1966.
[17] FAO, *The State of Food and Agriculture 1982*, Rome, 1983, p. 65.

and the large farmer on the other. The literature on these subjects is confusing and controversial, and varies from the broad generalization applied to the whole of Asia, with little reference to any substantial facts, to the careful study of two or three villages over two or three years. The problems are compounded by the difficulty of obtaining reliable information on incomes, farm size and landlessness; further, even where it can be shown that farms are getting larger, landlessness increasing or agricultural wages falling, these can often be plausibly explained by causes other than the spread of a new technology. The growth of population, for example, can surely be a possible cause of both increasing numbers without land and falling agricultural wages. These matters have been much discussed.[18] The purpose of the following sections is to assess the impact of the new farming methods upon food output.

There have been great variations in the increase in crop yields in Asia. Thus in Pakistan the adoption of Mexican wheats led to a doubling of yields between 1965 and 1976. On the other hand rice yields have increased very slowly in Burma and Thailand over 30 years.[19] Furthermore, so much attention has been paid to the period after 1965 when the first new varieties were introduced that it has been forgotten that yield increases were being obtained before 1965 without the use of the high yielding varieties. Indeed, in Taiwan, Korean and Japan rapid increases in yield were obtained before 1950 by using more fertilizer, better but not high yielding varieties, and more careful cultivation (see p. 217).

A comparison of the average yields of the major food grains in Asia for 1950–9, 1960–9 and 1970–9 allows a more realistic appreciation of

[18] A. Pearse, *Seeds of Plenty, Seeds of Want: Social and Economic Implications of the Green Revolution*, Oxford, 1980; K. Griffin, *The Political Economy of Agrarian Change: An Essay on the Green Revolution: Economic Gains and Political Costs*, Princeton, 1971; B. Sen, *The Green Revolution in India: A Perspective*, New Delhi, 1974; B. H. Farmer, *Green Revolution? Technology and Change in Rice Growing Areas of Tamil Nadu and Sri Lanka*, London, 1977; M. Ghaffar Chaudhury, 'Green Revolution and rural incomes: Pakistan's experience', *Pakistan Development Review*, 21, 1982, pp. 173–205; M. Prahladachar, 'Income distribution effects of the Green Revolution in India: a review of empirical evidence', *World Development*, 11, 1983, pp. 927–44; D. G. Dalrymple, 'The adoption of high yielding grain varieties in developing nations', *Agricultural History*, 53, 1979, pp. 704–26; C. E. Pray, 'The Green Revolution as a case study in transfer of technology', *Annals of the American Academy of Political and Social Science*, no. 458, 1981, pp. 68–80; V. W. Ruttan and H. P. Binswanger, 'Induced innovation and the Green Revolution', in H. P. Binswanger and V. W. Ruttan (eds), *Induced Innovation: Technology, Institutions and Development*, Baltimore, 1978, pp. 358–408.

[19] B. H. Farmer, *op. cit.*, 1984, p. 177.

crop yield increases (table 10.11). The greatest increases came in wheat, which is the second ranking grain in Asia, and the least in millets. Data for China, which probably exaggerates yields and their increase, suggest a similar pattern in that country (table 10.12).[20]

Table 10.11   Average crop yields in Asia, excluding China and Japan (tonnes per hectare)

	1950–9	1960–9	1970–9	% increase
Wheat	0.83	0.94	1.28	54
Rice	1.39	1.66	1.99	43
Maize	0.92	1.12	1.28	39
Millets and sorghum	0.44	0.48	0.57	30

Source: FAO, *The State of Food and Agriculture 1980*, Rome, 1981, p. 17

Table 10.12   Crop yields in China, 1952–80 (tonnes per hectare)

	1952–7	1976–8	% change
Rice	2.5	3.7	47
Wheat	0.83	1.75	112
Maize	1.34	2.68	100
Millet	1.1	1.6	46
Gaoliang	1.2	2.4	100

Source: K. R. Walker, 'China's grain production 1975–80 and 1952–57: some basic statistics', *China Quarterly*, no. 86, 1981, p. 223

NEW CROP VARIETIES

In India some 40,000 varieties of rice are grown;[21] other food grains also have numerous varieties. These have been selected by farmers over very long periods to adapt to local microenvironments. Thus in the flooded deltas of the Irrawady and Chao Phraya floating rice varieties are used, long stalked rice that can survive the rapid rise in the water level. In the more northerly locations, such as Japan and Korea, there is a premium on rapid maturity; the indigenous varieties of Japan also have short stalks that prevent lodging. Varieties also have to be adapted to changes in day length, which varies with latitude. Local varieties often have a built-in immunity to local disease. There are also varieties suited to rainfed conditions and others to the more regular water supply of irrigated areas. Most traditional varieties are adapted to give reasonable

[20] Walker, *op. cit.*
[21] B. H. Farmer, 'The Green Revolution in South Asian ricefields: environment and production', *Journal of Development Studies*, **15**, 1978, pp. 304–19.

yields under poor or uncertain ecological conditions rather than to give high yields under optimum conditions. Up to the post-war period improved varieties were selected either by farmers from observation of their better yielding crops or, more exceptionally, by agricultural scientists from observation of many varieties grown for comparison on experimental farms; this was the case of *ponlai* rice in Japan, later taken to Taiwan and Korea. They gave yields 20–30 per cent above the indigenous varieties in the 1930s.[22]

This type of selection proceeded in many parts of Asia, especially in India, after 1950. However, the most notable advances came in the 1960s in China and the Philippines. Advances in plant breeding had allowed the selection of specific qualities in seed. In the early 1960s a rice variety IR-8 was bred at the International Rice Research Institute in the Philippines which had a number of characteristics. First, it was not sensitive to changes in day length, and could be grown at any latitude. Second, it had a short stalk and did not lodge with a large grain. Third, it was more responsive to chemical fertilizer than any traditional variety then grown. This – and later rice varieties developed from IR-8 – gave much higher yields than any traditional varieties. However, they needed a controlled water supply, which meant irrigation; a far greater dosage of fertilizer than was being used anywhere in Asia except Taiwan, Japan and South Korea (table 10.15); and, because they lacked the immunity to disease that the indigenous varieties possessed, the use of pesticides. In 1965 Mexican semi-dwarf varieties of wheat were introduced into India and Pakistan; they also gave much higher yields than traditional varieties if provided with an adequate moisture supply, chemical fertilizers and pest control. In the 1960s the Chinese produced, independently of the research in the Philippines, a dwarf indica rice that required chemical fertilizers and a controlled water supply; it gave yield increases comparable with IR-8 but matured more rapidly. Mexican wheats were imported into China in 1969 and cross bred with local varieties.[23] Since the introduction of the first IRRI varieties in 1965–6, the original varieties have been improved and, most important, adapted by cross breeding to local environments. In addition progress has been made in breeding

[22] Yhi-Min Ho, *Agricultural Development of Taiwan, 1903–60*, Kingsport, Tennessee, 1966, p. 87.
[23] T. B. Wiens, 'Technological change', in Barker and Sinha, *op. cit.*, pp. 99–120: D. G. Dalrymple, *Development and Spread of High Yielding Varieties of Wheat and Rice in the Less Developed Nations*, United States Department of Agriculture, Washington DC, 1978; C. J. Baker, 'Frogs and farmers: the Green Revolution in India and its murky past', in T. P. Bayliss-Smith and S. Wanmali (eds), *Understanding Green Revolutions*, Cambridge, 1984, pp. 37–52.

high yielding varieties that prosper both without irrigation and in flooded delta conditions. [24]

The new varieties have been rapidly adopted by farmers. By 1976–7 nearly half the wheat and rice in Asia was sown with high yielding varieties or the improved Chinese varieties (table 10.13). But there was a great difference between China and the rest of Asia. Approximately 80 per cent of the rice in China was sown with improved high yielding varieties, but in the rest of Asia only 30 per cent was sown with IRRI rices. Conversely, whereas only 25 per cent of the wheat was sown with new varieties in China, some 72 per cent of the wheat area in the rest of Asia was sown with Mexican wheats. This is explained by state policies and the existence of irrigation facilities. Prior to the introduction of the IRRI rice varieties in India the government was aiming to concentrate improvement in the areas with good irrigation by providing improved – but not high yielding – varieties, fertilizers and credit. Not surprisingly, when the new wheat and rice was available attention was turned first to the irrigated areas, for both the wheat and rice high yielding varieties only give good yields under irrigated conditions. But only 36 per cent of the wet rice in Asia (excluding China) is irrigated. [25] Elsewhere, the crop relies upon the monsoon rains, which can be very variable in both quantity and timing. Furthermore the short stalked IRRI varieties cannot be grown in rice areas that are flooded during the monsoon.

Table 10.13   High yielding varieties (HYVs) and improved Chinese varieties: area sown to rice and wheat, 1976–7

	Rice		Wheat	
	Area in HYVs (million ha)	HYVs as % of all rice	Area in HYVs (million ha)	HYVs as % of all wheat
China	28.96	80	7.03	25
Rest of Asia	24.2	30.4	19.67	72.4
All Asia	53.16	45.7	26.70	48.4

Sources: D. G. Dalrymple, *Development and Spread of High Yielding Varieties of Wheat and Rice in the Less Developed Nations*, Washington DC, 1978; R. C. Hsu, *Food for One Billion: China's Agriculture since 1949*, Boulder, Colorado, 1982, p. 65; R. Barker, D. G. Sisler and B. Rose, 'Prospects for growth in grain production', in R. Barker and R. Sinha (eds), *The Chinese Agricultural Economy*, London, 1982, pp. 163–81

[24] E. Dayal, 'Regional responses to high yield varieties of rice in India', *Singapore Journal of Tropical Geography*, **4**, 1983, pp. 87–98.
[25] FAO, *op. cit.*, 1979, p. 22.

Thus they could not be easily grown in the delta of the Ganges-Brahmaputra (except under irrigation in the dry season), the Irrawady or the Chao Phraya. Indeed the wide differences in the adoption rate of HYV rice can be directly related to the proportion of the area of rice that can be irrigated (figure 10.1 and table 10.14). Very little of the rice area of Burma, Thailand, or Bangladesh is sown with the new varieties. Most of the wheat sown in Asia outside China was grown in northern South Asia in relatively dry areas with, however, well developed irrigation systems. This zone includes the Punjab region in Pakistan and India, Haryana and western Uttar Pradesh, and here there has been a very rapid and successful adoption of HYV wheat .

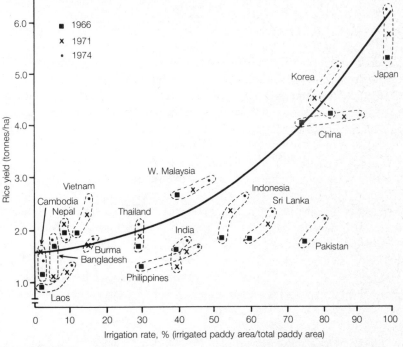

Figure 10.1   Rice yields and the area irrigated, Asia, 1960s and 1970s
Source: Asian Development Bank, *Rural Asia, Challenge and Opportunities*, New York, 1978, p. 157

In China the situation was quite the opposite. In the late 1950s, before the introduction of the new Chinese high yielding varieties, most of the irrigated land lay in the south. Wheat, although grown as a second crop, was primarily grown in the north China plain where only 20 per cent of it was irrigated. In the early 1960s, when rapid recovery from the fall in food output 1959–61 was necessary, the Chinese government concentrated resources and new inputs in the areas of 'high and stable

Table 10.14　High yielding variety (HYV) rice and irrigation, 1975

	Rice irrigated (%)	Rice in HYVs (%)
Pakistan	100	40
Malaya	77	37
Sri Lanka	61	63
Indonesia	47	41
Philippines	41	68
India	40	36
Burma	17	7
Bangladesh	16	14
Nepal	16	18
Vietnam	15	n.d.
Thailand	11	11

Source: FAO, *The State of Food and Agriculture 1977*, Rome, 1978, pp. 2–16

yields', which meant the irrigated southern rice areas, where by 1977 80 per cent of the rice was sown with new varieties.

In the 1960s and early 1970s little attention was paid to the north, because of the lack of irrigation. But in the 1970s the great increase in tube wells led to the adoption of Chinese-Mexican wheats; by 1980 80 per cent of the wheat grown in the north China plain was irrigated.[26]

Although the new high yielding wheats and rices have received most attention, there have been other improvements in the varieties grown. Thus in Thailand very little IRRI rice is grown; none the less 30–40 per cent of Thailand's rice area is sown with improved varieties. Similarly improved varieties of other crops have been adopted. In India high yielding varieties of *jowra*, *bajra* and maize have been developed, and by 1972–3 28 per cent of the land in these crops was sown with high yielding varieties. In China a hybrid maize, a cross between varieties from the United States and indigenous seed, occupied 60 per cent of the sown area by the late 1970s.[27]

[26] Barker, Sisler and Rose, *op. cit.*, pp. 163–82; H. J. Groen and J. A. Kilpatrick, 'Chinese agricultural production', in Joint Economic Committee, *Chinese Economy Post Mao: A Compendium of Papers Submitted to the Joint Economic Committee Congress of the United States, Vol. 1: Policy and Performance*, Washington DC, 1978, pp. 607–52; R. M. Field and J. A. Kilpatrick, 'Chinese grain production: an interpretation of the data', *China Quarterly*, no. 74, 1978, pp. 369–84; R. C. Hsu, *Food for One Billion: China's Agriculture since 1949*, Boulder, Colorado, 1982, p. 65.
[27] F. D. O'Reilly and P. I. McDonald, *Thailand's Agriculture*, Budapest, 1983, p. 54; T. B. Wiens, 'Agriculture in the Four Modernizations', in C. W. Pannell and C. L. Salter (eds), *China Geographer*, *11*, *Agriculture*, Boulder, Colorado, 1981, pp. 57–72; K. Chakravarti, 'The impact of high yielding grain varieties on food grain production in India', *Canadian Geographer*, **20**, 1976, pp. 199–223.

Although the distribution of irrigation seems to have been the major determinant of the rate of adoption by region, there are certainly other factors influencing differences between areas and farmers. The adoption of the HYV package of seeds, fertilizers and pesticides costs a great deal more per hectare than the use of traditional varieties – in Bangladesh, for example, 60 per cent more. It was thought in the early years of the introduction of the new varieties that large farmers, with greater access to credit and more able to run risks, were adopting the HYVs but not small farmers. But as data from the mid 1970s has become available it is clear that occupiers of small holdings have adopted the new seeds, although often with a time lag. Nor has the HYV rice always been confined to the irrigated areas. In the Philippines in 1975 78 per cent of irrigated rice was sown with IRRI rice; but so was 50 per cent of the rainfed rice. Of considerable importance in determining the rate of adoption has been the rice–fertilizer price ratio. There are considerable variations in the price of rice and also the local price of fertilizer, owing either to market forces or to state intervention. The more favourable the ratio, the more likely it is that the new seeds and fertilizer will be adopted. Thus in Burma there was little incentive to increase costs by using new seeds and fertilizers, for the price of rice remained fixed by the government from 1952 to 1975, and farmers found that even the low cost traditional rices made a loss. In contrast in Pakistan fertilizer is cheap relative to rice prices.[28]

THE USE OF FERTILIZERS AND MANURE

In 1950 the supply of plant nutrients to crops was provided in a number of ways. Wet rice received nitrogen from blue-green algae; it is estimated that these free living bacteria can fix up to 78 kg of nitrogen per hectare. In parts of East Asia a green crop was ploughed in, and in China soybeans and elsewhere beans and peas had bacteria associated with nodules on their roots that added nitrogen. In the lower rivers and deltas flooding added some nutrients in suspension and solution. Chemical fertilizers

[28] Y. Hayami, 'Induced innovation, Green Revolution and income distribution: comment', *Economic Development and Cultural Change*, 30, 1981, pp. 169–76; M. Prahladachar, *op. cit.*; P. Flores-Moya, R. E. Evenson, Y. Hayami, 'Social returns to rice research in the Philippines: domestic benefits and foreign spillover', *Economic Development and Cultural Change*, 26, 1978, pp. 591–607; C. P. Timmer and W. P. Falcon, 'The political economy of rice production and trade in Asia', in L. Reynolds (ed.), *Agriculture in Development Theory*, Princeton, 1975, pp. 373–408; M. Rezaul Karim, *The Food-Population Dilemma in Bangladesh*, Comilla, 1980, p. 63.

were not of any importance except, of course, in Japan, Korea and Taiwan. Elsewhere animal manure was the principal source of plant nutrients, but the supply was almost certainly low (there is no satisfactory data) except in China. In China pig dung and human excreta were used as organic manures in the 1950s, as they had been of course before 1950. In 1957 chemical fertilizers were hardly used in China, providing only 4 kg per hectare of arable; but organic manures provided between 36 and 110 kg of plant nutrients, a level far exceeding that obtained from this source elsewhere in Asia. Indeed the amount of organic manure produced doubled between 1952| and 1977, largely through an increase in the number of pigs kept, many of them on private plots; organic manures still provided two-thirds of all the plant nutrients. But this was not without its cost. The acute lack of fodder meant that in 1957 about 20 per cent of China's unprocessed grain was being used for feeding livestock. Further, the collection of pig manure, its fermentation and its distribution to the fields takes a remarkable amount of labour. It has been estimated that the production and application occupies 20 to 40 per cent of the working year. [29]

Between 1950 and 1965 there was a considerable increase in the consumption of chemical fertilizers in most countries in Asia, but the level was still low in 1965 except in Japan, Korea and Taiwan (table 10.15). In the Philippines, for example, chemical fertilizers were used on only 5 per cent of the cultivated area before 1965, and in Thailand in 1963 only 9 per cent of farmers used any chemicals; indeed only one-third applied even farmyard manure. Since the early 1960s, with the spread of HYVs and their need for heavy fertilizer applications, the consumption of fertilizer has risen dramatically in nearly all the Asian countries. The average rose more than fivefold between 1961–5 and 1980 (table 10.15) and at a prodigious rate in some countries which had low levels; in Pakistan, for example, the level rose by a factor of 15. But there is still a marked gap between East Asia and the rest of the continent. [30]

[29] Kuan-I Chen and R. T. Tsuchigane, 'An assessment of China's food grain supplies in 1980', *Asian Survey*, **16**, 1976, pp. 931–47; S. Ishikawa, 'Prospects for the Chinese economy in the 1980s', *Economic Bulletin for Asia and the Pacific*, **31**, 1980, pp. 1–30; Gurley, *op. cit.*; T. B. Wiens, 'The evolution of policy and capabilities in China's agricultural technology', in Joint Economic Committee, *op. cit.*, pp. 671–703; T. G. Rawski, 'Agricultural employment and technology', in Barker and Sinha, *op. cit.*, pp. 121–36; C. W. Pannell and L. J. C. Ma, *China: The Geography of Development and Modernization*, 1983, p. 130.

[30] David and Barker, *op. cit.*, pp. 127–42; O'Reilly and McDonald, *op. cit.*, pp. 16, 32–3.

Table 10.15   Chemical fertilizers in Asia, 1950–79 (kg per hectare of cropland)

	1950	1961–5	1972	1979
Japan	146.2	305.2	389.5	477.1
South Korea	52.5	157.0	288.9	383.6
North Korea	—	78.3	176.2	336.0
Taiwan	87.8	201.8	150.3	261.1
China	4.0	13.3	45.5	109.2
Malaysia	0.4	9.4	35.5	103.2
Pakistan	0.2	3.4	22.8	51.9
Bangladesh		4.4	20.0	44.6
Indonesia	1.0	8.4	28.9	44.1
Philippines	0.5	13.3	25.6	34.6
India	0.5	3.7	16.7	29.6
Thailand	0.3	2.2	10.8	17.4
Burma	0.02	0.7	4.6	10.5
Asian average[a]	1.6	11.8	31.0	61.5
World average	12.4	27.9	54.3	77.1

[a] Excluding China and Japan.
Sources: FAO, *Production Yearbook 1957*, vol. 11, Rome, 1958; *Production Yearbook 1962*, vol. 16, Rome, 1963; *The State of Food and Agriculture 1970*, Rome, 1971; R. C. Hsu, *Food for One Billion: China's Agriculture since 1949*, Boulder, Colorado, 1982, p. 57

Initially most Asian countries relied upon imports of fertilizer; but India now produces half her needs. In China the 1960s saw the rapid growth of fertilizer consumption. This was initially either imported or made in small factories in the communes. In 1972 the Chinese government purchased 13 urea plants. Because the heavy application of organic manures provides enough potassium and phosphorus, most of the chemical fertilizer applied is straight nitrogen. There are, as noted, still very wide variations in the use of fertilizer per hectare (table 10.15). Few HYVs receive the recommended dosage, and it is often of reduced value because it is applied at the wrong time. Furthermore many farmers have found that greater financial returns are obtained by using suboptimal applications.[31]

IRRIGATION

Irrigation has been part of Asian agriculture for several millenia, and a much higher proportion of the arable land (29 per cent) is irrigated

[31] J. D. Gavan and J. A. Dixon, 'India; a perspective on the food situation', *Science*, **188**, 1975, pp. 541–9; Hsu, *op. cit.*, pp. 53,58; Wiens, *op. cit.*, 1978; Barnett, *op. cit.*, p. 50; R. W. Herdt and T. H. Wickham, 'Exploring the gap between potential and actual rice yield in the Philippines', *Food Research Institute Studies*, **14**, 1975, pp. 163–81.

than in Africa or Latin America. There are also very marked regional differences in the amount of land irrigated. Pakistan has the highest proportion but with this exception the ratio roughly reflects population density. China, Korea, Japan and Taiwan have more than half their arable irrigated, Nepal, Kampuchea, Thailand, the Philippines, Bangladesh, Laos and Malaysia have less than one-fifth. It is salutary to remember that over two-thirds of Asia's arable is not irrigated and that much of the irrigation is recent; in Pakistan and the Indian Punjab it was begun by the British at the beginning of this century.

The function of most irrigation systems in Asia is to secure the water supply for the main crop during the monsoon because of the unreliability of that rainfall. Storage played a small part in Asian irrigation systems; their main function was to impound river flow during the period of high flow and divert river water by canals to the farmers' fields. In the last 30 years more emphasis has been put upon storage reservoirs and multipurpose water control. Thus the Chinese have, since 1949, been attempting to control the floods of the Yellow River by a series of dams in its upper reaches, to produce hydroelectricity, reduce silting and salinity and provide irrigation water. A principal problem of irrigation systems is their inefficiency. In India 60–70 per cent of the water entering the system is lost through evaporation in storage and transit and by seepage through the canal bottoms, and a figure of 50 per cent has been cited for China. Indeed the 'high and stable yielding' areas of China – those with both efficient irrigation and underdrainage – seem to cover only 22 million hectares, that is about one-half of the area irrigated. Without some means of removing irrigation water land can easily become waterlogged and salts are deposited on the surface, initially reducing yields and eventually causing abandonment. Substantial areas in Pakistan were suffering from salinization in the 1960s although the spread of tube wells has reduced the problem. Salinity is a major problem in north China; in addition the Yellow River runs through the loess region in its upper reaches, and silting in the lower reaches clogs irrigation canals. [32]

The advantages of irrigation are considerable. It helps reduce the

[32] V. Smil, 'Controlling the Yellow River', *Geographical Review*, **69**, 1979, pp. 253–72; Gavan and Dixon, *op. cit.*; R. Wade, 'India's changing strategy of irrigation development', in E. W. Coward, Jr. (ed.), *Irrigation and Agricultural Development in Asia*, Ithaca, 1980, pp. 345–64; J. Gray, 'China's new agricultural revolution', *IDS Bulletin*, **13**, 1982, pp. 36–43; Groen and Kilpatrick, *op. cit.*; B. Stone, 'The use of agricultural statistics', in Barker and Sinha, *op. cit.*, pp. 205–45; W. R. Gasse, *Survey of Irrigation in Eight Asian Nations*, United States Department of Agriculture, Washington DC, 1981; R. F. Dernberger, 'Agriculture in Communist development strategy', in Barker and Sinha, *op. cit.*, pp. 65–79.

variations in yield caused by fluctuations in rainfall; efficient irrigation systems allow a second crop; a controlled supply of water is necessary for the high yields of the new varieties, for without adequate moisture the value of fertilizers is much reduced; and further, in some areas irrigation allows crop growth in areas formerly too dry. The benefits of irrigation are clear. Thus in Asia excluding China only one-third of the rice area is irrigated, but produced 60 per cent of the output. It is not surprising that in both India and China government policy has directed new inputs – seed, fertilizer and machinery – to these areas, and great attempts have been made to extend the irrigated area. [33]

It is difficult to trace accurately the expansion of the irrigated area. Some data record the arable area irrigated, others the gross sown area, thus including the multiple cropping that data for the net sown area exclude. There is also a distinction to be made between the area for which irrigation water can be made available, and that on which it is actually used. The extension of the area in China and India is generally agreed to have been considerable (table 10.16). In China in the 1950s and 1960s the communes organized labour in the slack season to undertake not only local water control works, but also large scale works on the Yellow River. In both countries there has been a significant change in the means of obtaining water. In India and Pakistan canals have been the major means of distributing water from major rivers. In the Deccan, and in parts of Tamil Nadu and Sri Lanka, dams across small streams were important. In the last 30 years tube wells have greatly increased in numbers, tapping groundwater and also acting as a means of reducing waterlogging. They have spread at a prodigious rate: in Tamil Nadu tubewells increased from 14,000 in 1951 to 743,000 in 1976, in north China 1 million were dug in ten years, and in Pakistan and India they have become of major importance (table 10.17). [34] Water in wells can of course be lifted by human or animal labour. But in China, India and Pakistan wells have been increasingly fuelled by diesel or electricity. In India some 45 per cent of villages now have electricity, in China half the production teams. [35]

The expansion of irrigation in Asia has had a major effect upon crop yields, helped the extension of double cropping, and is the centre of much of the rapid advance in the last 30 years. It is likely that future expansion of food output will depend upon their increasing efficiency.

---

[33] FAO, *op. cit.*, 1979, p. 22.

[34] Dayal, *op. cit.*; Wiens, *op. cit.*, 1982.

[35] Hsu, *op. cit.*, p. 82; G. Etienne, *India's Changing Rural Scene 1963–1979*, Delhi, 1982, p. 180.

Table 10.16   Irrigation in Asia, 1950–80

	1950		1980	
	Area (million ha)	% of arable	Area (million ha)	% of arable
China	26.1	26.7	47.3	47.5
India	20.8	19.0	31.3	22.0
Pakistan	} 8.9	} 36.4	14.3	70.9
Bangladesh			1.62	17.8
Indonesia	5.0	28.2	5.4	27.8
Korea, South	0.57	28.5	1.15	52.7
Thailand	0.88	11.4	2.65	6.75
Malaya	0.11	5.0	0.37	8.6

Sources: R. C. Hsu, *Food for One Billion: China's Agriculture since 1949*, Boulder, Colorado, 1982, p. 72; E. Dayal, 'Impact of irrigation expansion on multiple cropping in India', *Tijdschrift voor Economische en Sociale Geografie*, **68**, 1977, pp. 100–9; FAO, *Production Yearbook 1957*, vol. 11, Rome, 1958; FAO, *Production Yearbook 1981*, vol. 35, Rome, 1982

Table 10.17   Irrigation in Pakistan and India

Source of irrigation water, Pakistan (thousand cubic metres)

	Canals	Tube wells	Total
1965–6	68	12	80
1976–7	72	36	107

India, area commanded by (million hectares)

	Canals	Tanks	Wells
1950	8.2	3.6	5.9
1975–6	13.7	3.9	14.3

Source: B. H. Farmer, *An Introduction to South Asia*, London 1984, p. 182; Mahmood Hasan Khan, *Underdevelopment and Agrarian Structure*, Boulder, Colorado, 1981, p. 43

MULTIPLE CROPPING

One of the distinctive features of Asian agriculture is, and always has been, multiple cropping. But, as with other intensive features, it was best developed in the densely populated areas of East Asia, and was and is less common in the less densely populated areas. Thus the *multiple cropping index* – the ratio of the gross sown area to the arable area – is 150 in China, considerably higher in Taiwan, but 101 or less in Kampuchea and Thailand (see table 10.18).

Table 10.18   Changes in the intensity of cropping in Asia, 1950–80

	c. 1950	*c. 1980*
India	110	118
Bangladesh	134	141
Pakistan	111	121
Nepal	125	117
Malaya[a]	101	160
China	130	150
Taiwan	151	180[b]
Burma	107	111[c]
Philippines	126	136[d]
Thailand	—	101[e]

[a] Rice only.
[b] 1956–60.
[c] 1965–6.
[d] 1960.
[e] 1966.
Sources: B. L. C. Johnson, *Development in South Asia*, Harmondsworth, 1983, p. 62; D. S. Gibbons, R. de Koninck and Ibrahim Hasan, *Agricultural Modernization, Poverty and Inequality: The Distributional Impact of the Green Revolution in Regions of Malaysia and Indonesia*, London, 1980, p. 6; D. Dalrymple, *Survey of Multiple Cropping in Less Developed Nations*, United States Department of Agriculture, Washington DC, 1971

The primary determinant of double cropping is temperature; but the length of the growing season only precludes the sowing of a second cereal crop in the more northerly parts of China, Korea and Japan. In most of Asia it is the seasonal distribution of rainfall that limits the growth of a second crop. It follows that irrigation would seem to be a major factor in the extent and expansion of double cropping. This needs some qualification. Much of the irrigation in Asia has only limited storage facilities, and there may be insufficient water for a second crop. Nor may it always be possible to grow a second crop. Thus in some irrigated areas in Tamil Nadu cotton and sugar-cane are grown and occupy the land for most of the year. Even where irrigation has been provided specifically to introduce double cropping it may not occur. Thus in the recently irrigated areas of north east Thailand only 1.6 per cent of the land is used for a second crop. This is because farmers have traditionally done other jobs in the dry season, and the income from these jobs is greater than that which can be obtained from growing a second crop.[36]

In many parts of Asia double cropping is not confined to the irrigated areas. A good summer monsoon leaves enough soil moisture for a second crop — although not generally for rice. Indeed in India 72 per cent of the

[36] R. H. Brannon, C. T. Alton and J. T. Davis, 'Irrigated dry season crop production in north east Thailand; a case study', *Journal of Developing Areas*, **14**, 1980, pp. 191–200.

of the land sown twice is not irrigated. However, the increase in double cropping since 1950 has generally been associated with the irrigated areas in India and elsewhere. The introduction of high yielding varieties has increased the possibilities of double cropping, for the IRRI rice varieties mature more rapidly than most traditional varieties. The Chinese have preferred their indigenous high yielding rices to the IRRI varieties because they have an even shorter growing season, allowing not only double cropping but even triple cropping in parts of south China.[37]

Although 50 million hectares are double cropped in India, the cropping index has only advanced a few points since 1950, as is true in Bangladesh and Pakistan (table 10.18). The most spectacular increase has been in Malaya. Only a low proportion of Malaya's cropland is double cropped because oil palm and rubber occupy a large part of the farmland. In the 1950s Malaya relied upon rice imports to feed its population. Since then vigorous state schemes have greatly increased the proportion of rice cultivation that is irrigated, and associated with this has been a prodigious increase in the double cropping of rice. Combined with some increase in yields, Malaya's rice imports have fallen from 43 per cent of consumption in the 1950s to 10 per cent in the late 1970s.[38]

In China there has also been a substantial increase in double cropping. The cropping index has always been high in the south where a high proportion of the rice area was irrigated and rice was followed by wheat or barley. Much less of the north China plain was irrigated, but since the late 1960s the spread of tube wells has increased the irrigation and the double cropping index. In the south second crops have been further extended, and triple cropping has been encouraged. In 1948 triple cropping was found only in Hai-nan island in the extreme south. In the late 1960s and early 1970s the Chinese government encouraged the spread of triple cropping, often into areas to which it was unsuited. Since 1976 triple cropping has declined in certain areas, such as Szechwan; peasants found that the net output was less than that obtained under double cropping. None the less cropping intensity has increased significantly in China, from 130 in 1950 to 150 in 1980; the index is well over

[37] E. Dayal, 'Impact of irrigation expansion on multiple cropping in India', *Tijdschrift voor Economische en Sociale Geografie*, **68**, 1977, pp. 100–9; B. Dasgupta, *Agrarian Change and the New Technology in India*, Geneva, 1977, p. 90; F. Leeming, 'Progress towards triple cropping in China', *Asian Survey*, **19**, 1979, pp. 450–67.
[38] D. G. Dalrymple, *Survey of Multiple Cropping in Less Developed Nations*, United States, Department of Agriculture, Washington DC, 1971; D. S. Gibbons, R. de Koninck and Ibrahim Hasan, *Agricultural Modernization, Poverty and Inequality: The Distributional Impact of the Green Revolution in Regions of Malaysia and Indonesia*, London, 1981, p. 7.

200 in parts of the south, and this increase is though to have accounted for 40 per cent of the increase in rice output between 1949 and 1975. It is to be doubted if the extension of multiple cropping has been as significant elsewhere, except in Malaya. However, the increase in the sown area has been of importance in raising food output in Asia, and is an important future source of increased output.[39]

LABOUR SUPPLY AND MECHANIZATION

Between 1965 and 1980 the agricultural population of Asia increased by 256 million, Africa by 76 million and Latin America by 15 million, the increase being respectively 21, 34 and 14 per cent. The growth of the agricultural populations of Asia since 1950 (see table 4.6) has been a function of the rate of rural natural increase and the rate of migration to the towns. In Asia the rate of rural increase has been less than that in much of Latin America or Africa; but in few parts of Asia has the flight to the cities been so marked as in Latin America. Thus Asia's agricultural populations have increased more slowly than Africa's, but more rapidly than in Latin America. The absolute numbers are formidable. The agricultural labour force in China in 1950 was about 170 million, in 1980 not far short of 300 million; in India it was 102 million in 1951, 165 million in 1980. Only in two places in Asia has the agricultural population declined – Taiwan and South Korea. Here the growth of manufacturing industry has attracted labour out of agriculture.[40]

The growth of the agricultural population has of course presented agriculture with considerable problems, for population densities were already high in 1950 and the colonization of new land has not been sufficient to provide land for the increasing numbers. Thus it is not surprising to find that the numbers without land have increased substantially, although it should be noted that the definition of landless varies a great deal and the figures are not easy to interpret (table 10.19). Thus in Indonesia in the 1960s the number of very small holdings increased substantially. Whether someone with 0.1 ha is to be counted as landless

[39] Leeming, *op. cit.*; Walker, *op. cit.*; G. T. Trewartha and Shou-Jen Yang, 'Notes on rice growing in China', *Annals of the Association of American Geographers*, **38**, 1948, pp. 277–81; Wu Chuan-chun, 'The transformation of the agricultural landscape in China', L. J. C. Ma and A. G. Noble (eds), *The Environment: Chinese and American Views*, London, 1981, pp. 35–43.
[40] Stone, *op. cit.*, pp. 210–11.

or a farmer is a matter of debate. Consequently there are very different estimates of the extent of landlessness in Asia (note the various estimates for Bangladesh in table 10.19), although there is little doubt that in absolute terms it has increased since 1950, and that in some countries landlessness has increased faster than population growth (table 10.19).

Table 10.19   Percentage of rural households without land in Asia

	c. 1954–5	c. 1961–2	c. 1971–2	c. 1978
India	30.8[a]	27.5	25.6	—
India	—	—	10.0	—
Pakistan	—	—	34.0	—
Bangladesh	14	17	—	28.8
Bangladesh	—	—	31	—
Bangladesh	—	—	17.5	—
Bangladesh	—	—	—	33.0
Bangladesh	—	—	—	11.07
Bangladesh	—	2	38	—
Indonesia	—	—	12.1	—
Thailand	—	—	—	4.7
China	10[a]	—	—	—
Taiwan	—	—	—	very low

[a] 1948.

Sources: A. Bhaduri, 'A comparative study of land reform in South Asia', *Economic Bulletin for Asia and the Pacific*, **30**, 1979, pp. 1–13; M. Cain, 'Landlessness in India and Bangladesh: a critical review of national data sources', *Economic Development and Cultural Change*, **31**, 1983, pp. 149–69; B. L. C. Johnson, *Bangladesh*, London, 1975, p. 71; Iftikhar Ahmed, *Technological Change and Agrarian Structure: A Study of Bangladesh*, Geneva, 1981, p. 29; S. de Vylder, *Agriculture in Chains. Bangladesh: A Case Study in Contradictions and Constraints*, London, 1982; B. D. Mabry, 'Peasant economic behaviour in Thailand', *Journal of South East Asian Studies*, **10**, 1979, pp. 400-19; Asian Development Bank, *Rural Asia: Challenge and Opportunity*, New York, 1977, p. 55; *Economic Bulletin for Asia and the Pacific*, **31**, 1980, p. 102; R. Dernberger, 'Agriculture in Communist development strategy', in R. Barker and R. Sinha (eds), *The Chinese Agricultural Economy*, London, 1982, pp. 65-83; R. Montgomery and Toto Sugito, 'Changes in the structure of farms and farming in Indonesia between censuses, 1963-1973', *Journal of South East Asia Studies*, **11**, 1980, pp. 348-65

One consequence of the growth of the agricultural population – both of farm families and wage labourers – has been that a significant proportion of the population is surplus to requirements on the farm. Thus in the late 1970s 35 per cent of the population of Bangladesh was unemployed or underemployed, and in Thailand in 1973 only 38 per cent of the available man-hours in agriculture were used. However, some of the underemployment so measured in Thailand reflects the lack of work carried out in the dry season. This is traditionally the period for work off the farm, and also for maintaining or improving irrigation works or clearing land for cultivation. In China the commune system has allowed a massive mobilization of labour in the slack season. In 1957–8 some 100 million peasants were working in the winter on water control projects; in the 1970s this figure may have reached 150 million. The rapid expansion of tube wells in the north was due to this type of labour.[41]

But the utilization of labour in this way does not conceal the fact that China's rural population greatly exceeds the requirements of even the very labour intensive agriculture of that country. Chinese sources estimate that 10–20 per cent of rural labour was surplus in 1958 and about 30 per cent in the late 1970s. Indeed Chinese authorities fear that if the production responsibility system becomes established (a system which provides incentives at the household and individual level), some 50 per cent of the Chinese labour force in agriculture will be superfluous.[42]

One consequence of the increase in the labour force, and particularly the growth of landlessness, has been a fall or stagnation in real wages in agriculture; this occurred in most Asian states in the 1970s, except in Taiwan and Korea where the labour force was in decline. Under these circumstances there seems little sense in pressing policies of mechanization in Asia, for this may further compound the problem. In northern China a farm was equipped for experimental purposes with American farm machinery, herbicides and pesticides; 20 workers replaced 300 peasants. In the very different conditions of central Thailand one tractor can cultivate 20–24 hectares; without the tractor it would need a buffalo and 20–30 men. Even very simple changes can have disastrous consequences. In Java the landless population depend upon harvesting for much of their income. When the ani-ani (a hand knife) is used, harvesting rice needs 150 men per hectare; when the sickle is used, only 55.[43]

There are of course cases for the use of machinery. Where double cropping is introduced it may be essential to use a tractor, for the time between harvesting and sowing the second crop is so short; similarly, some very heavy soils can only be cultivated mechanically. In parts of Malaya, which has not mechanized even though there have been rapid increases in irrigation, double cropping and the use of chemical fertilizers, the introduction of a second rice crop has prevented the use of straw as a bullock feed and encouraged some farmers to use tractors. There

[41] J. E. Nicklum, 'Labour accumulation in rural China and its role since the cultural revolution', *Cambridge Journal of Economics*, 2, 1978, pp. 273–86; S. de Vylder, *Agriculture in Chains: Bangladesh, A study in Contradictions and Constraints*, London, 1982, p. 11; C. F. Framingham, Sommuk Sriplung and E. O. Heady, 'Agricultural situation and policy issues', in K. J. Nicol, S. Sriplung and O. Heady (eds), *Agricultural Development in Thailand*, Ames, Iowa, 1982.

[42] Hsu, *op. cit.*, pp. 33, 78, 130; E. B. Vermeer, 'Income differentials in rural China', *China Quarterly*, no. 89, 1982, pp. 1–33.

[43] Asian Development Bank, *Rural Asia: Challenge and Opportunity*, New York, 1977, p. 53; Wiens, *op. cit.*, 1981; R. C. Y. Ng, *op. cit.*; Krinks, *op. cit.*

is also a case for the use of machinery in the few sparsely populated areas, such as Manchuria.[44]

But the decision to adopt tractors and other implements is not taken on the national level, except in China. It is thus on larger farms, particularly in the Indian and Pakistan Punjab, that the use of machinery has proceeded most rapidly, and indeed where tractors were increasing before the introduction of new high yielding varieties. Thus in India there has been a dramatic increase in the number of tractors in use, from 8500 in 1951 to 418,000 in 1981. But the impact of this has been limited. In 1974 half the tractors in India were in Punjab, Haryana and western Uttar Pradesh, and of the 141 million hectares cultivated in India in that year, only 2 million were ploughed with tractors. Indeed in most of Asia outside China human and animal power provides all but 3 per cent of the energy used on the farm; only in South West Asia does the proportion approach that of Latin America (table 10.20).[45]

Table 10.20   Sources of power on farms

	Africa	Far East[a]	Near East	Latin America
Tractors	3	3	20	25
Animals	9	23	15	13
Human labour	86	72	65	62

[a] Excluding China.
Source: FAO, *The State of Food and Agriculture 1982*, Rome, 1983, p. 63

In China little attention was paid to mechanization in the 1950s, although at times the Soviet model of collectivization and large scale mechanization was urged. Since the mid 1960s, however, the use of machinery has increased. China appears to have more tractors per hectare of cultivated land than any major region in the developing world (table 10.21). Nor do these figures include the 'walking tractors', an adaptation of the Japanese rotary tiller, which have greatly increased in number since 1965.[46] By 1981 it was estimated that 46 per cent of China's sown area was tractor ploughed at least once (compared with 1.6 per cent in 1960). A mechanical rice transplanter was introduced in 1958 but is used on only 0.7 per cent of the rice area, and only 2.6 per cent of the grain area is harvested by machine, mainly in the state farms of the north east. Less emphasis has been placed upon mechanization since 1978,

[44] R. D. Hill, *Agriculture in the Malaysian Region*, Budapest, 1982, p. 100.
[45] Dasgupta, *op. cit.*; FAO, *Production Yearbook 1981*, vol. 35, Rome 1982, p. 274.
[46] Stone, *op. cit.*, p. 240.

Table 10.21   Use of tractors and harvesters, major regions (per 1000 hectares of arable)

	Tractors		Harvesters	
	1961–5	*1980*	*1961–5*	*1980*
Africa	1.2	2.4	0.12	0.2
Latin America	3.2	5.4	0.5	0.79
China	0.6	7.5	—	0.26
Rest of Asia	0.45	6.6	0.05	2.67

Sources: FAO, *Production Yearbook 1981*, vol. 35, Rome, 1982; *Production Yearbook 1976*, vol. 29, Rome, 1977

because of the fear of unemployment. Indeed foreign visitors have noted that tractors are used more for transport than in the fields.[47]

Thus although much attention has been paid to the progress of mechanization in Asia, and particularly to its adverse consequences in Pakistan and the Indian Punjab, as yet only a small part of Asia's land is farmed with machines (table 10.20). However, FAO estimates suggest that more tractors are used per hectare than in Africa or, surprisingly, Latin America (table 10.21).

CONCLUSIONS

The increased output of Asian agriculture has matched that of Latin America since 1950, and in all but a few countries has kept up with population growth, though a significant surplus has been obtained in only a few countries. But the increase in output has been obtained in a very different way to that of Latin America, or the more modest increases in Africa. Colonization of new land has been important in only a few areas, and the reduction of fallow has been confined to a few countries. Instead Asian farming has increased output by traditional means – more irrigation, more intensive cultivation, more multiple cropping, and by the use of new technologies, improved seed and chemical fertilizer. For all the growth, neither poverty nor hunger have been banished. It is likely that in the future Asia's major problem will be to absorb its growing numbers rather than simply to raise food output, although that of course will continue to be necessary.

[47] Wiens, *op. cit.*, 1982; Hsu, *op. cit.*, p. 80.

11

Trade and Aid

Although food production has grown more rapidly than population in the world as a whole and in all the major regions except Africa, in many individual countries food production per caput has fallen in the last 20 years (see p. 84). Yet in all but a few countries available national supplies per caput are above the level of the 1950s (see p. 48). This is of course because home production has been supplemented by imports of food; this trade is now considered.

THE DEVELOPMENT OF TRADE IN FOODSTUFFS

Until the middle of the nineteenth century the high cost of transport and the impossibility of preserving many foods for long periods meant that there was little international trade in foodstuffs. In Western Europe before the eighteenth century only 1 per cent of cereal output crossed national boundaries. That proportion is now higher, but the great bulk of all foodstuffs are still consumed in the country of origin; less than one-tenth currently enter international trade. In the middle of the nineteenth century there was little long distance movement of foodstuffs (figure 11.1) and much of this was from Eastern to Western Europe, where the Low Countries had long imported grain and Britain had been a net importer since the late eighteenth century.[1]

After 1850 there was a dramatic increase in the trade in foodstuffs (figure 11.1). The export of people and capital from Europe to North America, Australasia and South America, the rising populations and

[1] P. Bairoch, 'Agriculture and the industrial revolution', in C. M. Cipolla (ed.), *The Industrial Revolution*, London, 1973, pp. 452–506; K. Campbell, *Food for the Future: How Agriculture can Meet the Challenge*, London, 1979, p. 123.

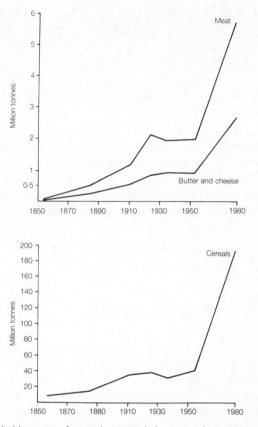

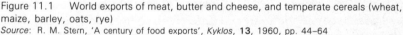

Figure 11.1   World exports of meat, butter and cheese, and temperate cereals (wheat, maize, barley, oats, rye)
Source: R. M. Stern, 'A century of food exports', *Kyklos*, **13**, 1960, pp. 44–64

incomes of Western Europe, and the abundant land of the European settlements overseas combined to produce a flow of cheap cereals, meat and dairy products to Western Europe and in particular to Britain. This was made possible by marked falls in oceanic and overland freight rates in the late nineteenth century and the introduction of refrigeration, which allowed frozen meat and dairy products to be moved. The exports of cereals, which in volume greatly outweighed that in other foodstuffs (figure 11.1), was dominated initially by the United States, Russia and Eastern Europe (the Danube countries), but later they were joined by Canada, Argentina and Australia. India was also a major exporter, with 10 per cent of world exports of grain in the 1880s. The trade in grain increased ninefold between the 1850s and the eve of the First World War.[2]

[2] R. M. Stern, 'A century of food exports', *Kyklos*, **13**, 1960, pp. 44–57.

Between the two World Wars the trade in foodstuffs stagnated or even declined (figure 11.1). However notable gains were made by some products, such as coffee. Most of the trade in meat, dairy products and cereals moved from the temperate regions of European settlements overseas to temperate Western Europe. But in the later nineteenth century there had been a substantial increase in the flow of tropical and subtropical foods to Western Europe and the United States. These included tea, coffee, cocoa and sugar; bananas and other fruits increased in the very late nineteenth century.

Since the end of the Second World War the trade in foodstuffs has increased at an unprecedented rate, and much faster than food output or population. In the 1950s world exports of temperate grains (figure 11.1) were little above the level of 1909–13. Between the 1950s and 1979–80 the volume rose nearly fivefold, and the meat trade, which in the early 1950s was *below* that of 1909–13, had tripled by 1979–80.[3]

THE DIRECTION OF THE FOOD TRADE

In 1980 (table 11.1) the developed countries – particularly Europe, the USSR and Japan – took over 70 per cent of value of all food imports, the developing countries just over one-quarter; the pattern established in the late nineteenth century still survives. The most important imports are the tropical beverages, closely followed by cereals, livestock products, oilseeds and vegetable oils. The imports of the developing countries are smaller in volume and value and different in composition. Cereals make up nearly three-quarters of the volume of imports, nearly half the value; oilseeds and tropical beverages, products of the developing countries themselves, are not important, but 15 per cent of the imports are of meat, butter or cheese.

Cereals are by far the most important item in world agricultural trade – indeed they are only exceeded in value by petroleum. They need some comment. Wheat, maize, rice, millet, sorghum, barley, oats and rye are all consumed as food by man in some part of the world, but the coarse grains – those other than wheat, rye or rice – which enter international trade are used as livestock feed. Wheat and rice, however, although generally used as human foods can be used to feed livestock, although it is only in Eastern Europe and the USSR that a high

[3] Stern, *op. cit.*; FAO, *Trade Yearbook 1981*, vol. 35, Rome, 1982.

Table 11.1   The structure of food imports, 1980

	Developed countries				Developing countries			
	Weight (million tonnes)	%	Value (US $ million)	%	Weight (million tonnes)	%	Value (US $ million)	%
Cereals	122.6	50.2	23,322	18.8	97.7	73.0	21,420	44.8
Meat	6.1	2.5	15,079	12.2	1.7	1.2	2,978	6.3
Dairy and eggs	2.5	1.0	9,249	7.4	1.0	0.7	4,303	9.1
Fruit and veg.	25.4	10.4	11,927	9.6	6.7	5.0	2,848	5.9
Sugar	16.2	6.6	9,854	7.9	10.9	8.1	5,996	12.5
Coffee, cocoa, tea	5.6	2.3	34,154	20.6	0.6	0.35	1,951	4.3
Oilseeds and cake	51.6	21.1	14,683	11.8	7.1	5.2	2,827	3.8
Wine, beer, tobacco	7.5	3.1	9,372	7.6	0.8	0.5	1,239	2.6
Animal and veg. oils	6.7	2.7	4,964	4.1	7.1	5.2	5,079	10.7
Total	244.2	100.0	123,804	100.0	133.81	100.0	47,641	100.0

Source: FAO, Trade Yearbook 1981, vol. 35, Rome, 1982

proportion of wheat is used as feed.[4] Trade statistics do not reveal the use of the cereals. However, the proportion of all cereal imports that is coarse grains is generally inversely related to income. The lower the income, the higher the percentage of imports that is in food grains (table 11.2). Thus the developing regions (except Latin America, the most prosperous) import mainly food grains, the developed regions feed grains. Of all grain consumed in the developed countries 60 per cent is fed to livestock, in the developing countries only 13 per cent.[5]

Table 11.2   Rice and wheat as a percentage of all cereals (volume), 1980

Africa	79.6	Latin America	51.2
Far East	76.4	Eastern Europe and USSR	45.8
Asian CPE[a]	73.5	Western Europe	32.5
Near East	71.0	Japan	23.9

[a] CPE: centrally planned economies.
Source: FAO, *Trade Yearbook 1981*, vol. 35, Rome, 1982

The volume of agricultural trade has greatly increased since 1950, and indeed has increased more rapidly than either population or food production. There have also been major changes in the direction of trade, particularly in that of cereals. In the 1930s Western Europe took nearly all the imports and the export trade was shared by North America, Eastern Europe, the Soviet Union, Australasia and temperate Latin America (table 11.3). But since 1950 Eastern Europe, the USSR and Latin America have ceased to be *net* exporters of grain and have become importers. The export of grain is shared by North America and Australasia, with the former providing 85 per cent of all net exports in 1980. The United States alone provided two-thirds of all cereal exports.

There have been equally striking changes in the major markets for cereals. Western Europe's imports – mainly of feed – rose until 1970 but the EEC policy of providing high prices for cereals has led since to a decline in imports. Japan however has greatly increased her imports, owing partly to rising population but mainly to greater prosperity. Between 1960 and 1975 meat consumption per caput tripled, and this could only be achieved by importing feed grains. Japan's self-sufficiency

---

[4] G. Bastin and J. Ellis, *International Trade in Grain and the World Food Economy*, The Economist Intelligence Unit, Special Report no. 83, London, 1980, p. 93.
[5] FAO, *The State of Food and Agriculture 1982*, Rome, 1983, p. 82.

Table 11.3   World grain trade, 1934–80 (million tonnes: positive values net exports, negative net imports)

	1934–8	1948–52	1960	1970	1979–80
North America	5	23	39	56	127
Western Europe	− 24	− 22	− 25	− 30	− 13
Eastern Europe and USSR	5	n.a.	0	0	− 40
Australasia and New Zealand	3	3	6	12	15
Japan	− 2	− 3	− 4	− 14	− 23
Latin America	9	1	0	4	− 9
Africa	1	0	− 2	− 5	− 13
Asia[a]	0	− 3	− 13	− 23	− 39

[a] Excluding Japan but including China.
Source: R. F. Hopkins and D. J. Puchala, 'Perspectives on the international relations of food', in R. F. Hopkins and D. J. Puchala (eds), *The Global Political Economy of Food*, Madison, Wisconsin, 1978, p. 7; FAO, *Trade Yearbook 1981*, vol. 35, Rome, 1982; *Trade Yearbook 1971*, vol. 25, Rome, 1972; *Trade Yearbook 1966*, vol. 20, Rome, 1967

ratio fell from 90 to 73 per cent in this period.[6] More dramatic has been the emergence of the Soviet Union as an importer, after a long history of exports. In 1950 Soviet agricultural output was little higher than in 1913. Output has increased very rapidly since then, but the USSR has two problems. First, much of the grain output is east of the Urals in very dry areas. There are thus marked year to year fluctuations in the harvest. Second, this output is insufficient, even in good years, to provide both bread and feed for livestock. Russian demand for meat has risen, and grain imports have become necessary. These imports began with large purchases from the United States in 1972 and, with various vicissitudes such as the embargo after the Russian invasion of Afghanistan, have risen to over 40 million tonnes in 1980, so that Russia is now the world's largest single purchaser of cereals (table 11.3).

FOOD IMPORTS OF THE DEVELOPING COUNTRIES

Although the developed countries still take a greater part of world trade in agricultural products (table 11.1) a noticeable feature of the last 30 years, and in particular the last 20, has been the remarkable increase of food imports, particularly of cereals, into the developing countries. In the 1930s neither Asia, Latin America nor Africa were net importers of grain (table 11.3), although of course some individual countries were.

[6] R. L. Paarlberg, 'Shifting and sharing adjustment burdens: the role of the industrial food importing nations', in R. F. Hopkins and D. J. Puchala (eds), *The Global Political Economy of Food*, Madison, Wisconsin, 1978, pp. 79–101.

It should be noted however that consumption levels were lower than they are now. By the 1950s imports into Africa and Asia were growing slowly; they accelerated in the 1960s and 1970s.

This change in the direction of trade can be variously illustrated. Thus the developing countries – including China – took 1.5 per cent of world cereal imports in the 1930s, 20 per cent in the 1950s but 44 per cent in 1980. The volume of these imports increased more than sixfold between the 1950s and the late 1970s. The developing countries' imports of wheat have increased rather more rapidly than the other grains; in the 1950s the developing countries accounted for 10 per cent of all wheat imports, by 1980 57 per cent.[7]

The reason for these imports would appear to be simple. In much of Africa population growth has outpaced food production and imports have been necessary simply to maintain consumption levels. In other countries they have been needed to try and raise the very low per caput supplies. But this assumes that population growth alone accounts for the rise in food imports. This is far from being so, for in many developing countries incomes have risen substantially in the last 20 years; this is most noticeable in the oil exporters, but also in several countries in the Far East. This has led not only to increases in wheat and rice imports but also to cereal imports to feed livestock. Those developing countries which the World Bank describes as middle income not only accounted for 80 per cent of the increases in developing countries' cereal imports between 1960 and 1979, but also fed one-third of their domestic grain production to livestock and half their cereal imports.[8] In short cereal imports to the developing countries are not directly related to population growth or to need. This is further illustrated in figure 11.2, which shows net cereal imports per thousand of the total population in 1980. A few countries – very few – had a grain balance in surplus. These included, as might be expected, the grain exporters of North America, Australasia, Burma, Thailand, Argentina and France, but also India and Pakistan. Those developing countries with imports of 100 tonnes per thousand or over include only the more prosperous countries – oil exporters such as Venezuela, Libya and Saudi Arabia, or countries which have achieved some degree of industrialization such as South Korea and Mexico.

[7] Bastin and Ellis, *op. cit.*, p. 88; H. Wagstaff, 'Food imports of developing countries', *Food Policy*, 7, 1982, pp. 57–68; FAO, *Trade Yearbook 1981*, vol. 35, Rome, 1982.

[8] Wagstaff, *op. cit.*; World Bank, *World Bank Development Report 1981*, Washington DC, 1981, p. 102; J. W. Mellor, 'Third World development: food, employment and growth interactions', *American Journal of Agricultural Economics*, **64**, 1982, pp. 304–11.

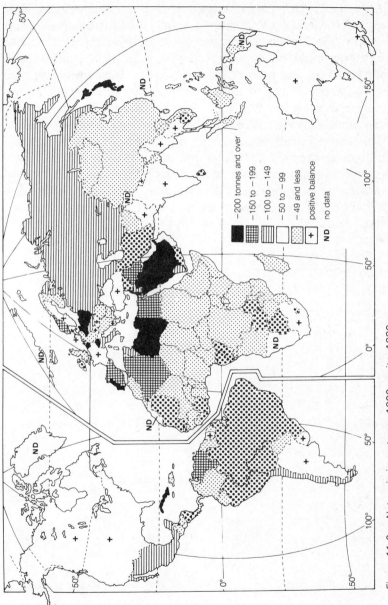

−200 tonnes and over
−150 to −199
−100 to −149
−50 to −99
−49 and less
positive balance
ND no data

Figure 11.2   Net grain imports per 1000 capita, 1980
Source: FAO, *Trade Yearbook 1981*, vol. 35, 1982

Although all the major developing regions have experienced substantial increases in their grain imports since 1960, the experience of individual countries has differed considerably (figure 11.3). In Pakistan and India imports in 1980 were no greater than in 1960, although population had increased by 88 and 58 per cent respectively. In both countries grain output per caput had been maintained, and both countries were net exporters, although only of small quantities. In China in contrast imports were very low in 1960, rose steeply to 1964 and then fell slowly, to rise dramatically after 1976 with the change of government; even so, imports remain a small proportion of consumption. The Near East and Africa both showed slow increases until the late 1960s but have since moved steadily upwards. But whereas four-fifths of Africa's cereal imports are of wheat and rice for direct consumption, much of the cereal imports in the Near East, with its numerous oil rich states, are for livestock feed.

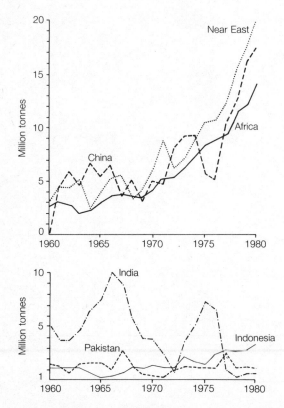

Figure 11.3   Gross cereal imports, 1960–80
Source: FAO, *Trade Yearbook 1976*, vol. 30, Rome, 1977; *Trade Yearbook 1981*, vol. 35, Rome, 1982

SELF-SUFFICIENCY AND DEPENDENCY

In the 1950s and early 1960s there was much discussion of the ability of the developing countries to increase output, and of the low level of national food supplies per caput; food imports were comparatively small and received little attention. The failure of the monsoon in India in 1964–6 and the steep rise in imports drew attention to the vulnerable situation of countries that relied upon imports. The great rise in grain prices in 1972–4 and the increase in imports led many to argue that developing countries should attempt to obtain self-sufficiency in food supplies.

FAO surveyed the degree of self-sufficiency in 103 countries in 1970–2 and concluded that 3000 million people of the total 3700 million in the survey lived in countries where home production was at least 95 per cent of consumption. Only 19 per cent of the population of developing countries lived in countries with a self-sufficiency ratio less than 95 per cent, but 29 per cent of the population of the developed world. Subsequent studies by FAO showed that the self-sufficiency ratio declined 1961–75 in all the major developing regions except the Asian centrally planned economies, and was below 100 in all but Latin America (figure 11.4).[9]

But both the methods of calculating self-sufficiency and its economic rationale are subjects of much debate. Many estimates of self-sufficiency have been made upon the basis of the *value* of food produced at home and imported. Clearly the FAO attempt to measure the calorific value of output and trade is preferable. But there are difficulties in estimating the proportion of crops used for feed, and doubt as to whether imported feed should be included. Furthermore a full account of self-sufficiency would require the inclusion of inputs – such as oil and fertilizer – purchased abroad. To all this it must be added that both production and trade figures are often of dubious accuracy.[10]

Some estimates of calorific self-sufficiency in the mid 1970s are shown in table 11.4, column 6. At that time Latin America was self-sufficient and South East and East Asia virtually so, whereas Africa and the Near East had to import 4 and 9 per cent respectively of their calorie consumption. Of the developed regions Japan was most dependent upon imported food, followed by Western Europe.

[9] J. P. O'Hagan, 'National self sufficiency in food', *Food Policy*, 1, 1976, pp. 355–66; 'Self-sufficiency: facts and figures', *Ceres*, 12, 1979, pp. 19–21.
[10] O'Hagan, *op. cit.*; S. F. Fallows and J. V. Wheelcock, 'Self sufficiency and United Kingdom food policy', *Agricultural Aministration*, 11, 1982, pp. 107–25.

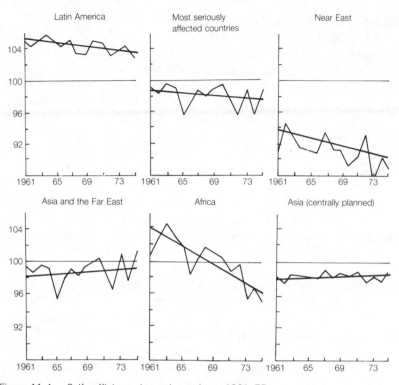

Figure 11.4   Self-sufficiency by major regions, 1961–75
Source: 'Self sufficiency; the facts and figures', Ceres, **12**, 1979, pp. 19–21

More recent data, but based upon cereal production and trade alone, are shown in table 11.4 and figure 11.5. Two points can be made. First, as noted earlier, of *all* the major regions only North America and Australasia are self-sufficient. Second, Africa and the Near East are the least self-sufficient regions in cereals, together with Japan. But this overstates Africa's position, for in West and central Africa root crops form a significant part of home food production.

Figure 11.5 demonstrates what is clear in table 11.4, that cereal imports make a small contribution to consumption in Asia, except South Korea, Malaysia and Japan, countries where rising incomes rather than merely rising populations account for sizeable grain imports. Lack of self-sufficiency in grain is most marked in North Africa and the Middle East, where however oil exports can finance imports: Nigeria and Venezuela also have this advantage. More serious however is the high dependency on imports in the Andean republics and Chile, and much of Africa. The high reliance upon imported cereals does not necessarily indicate such

Table 11.4 Grain and total calorific self-sufficiency 1979–80

	1 Home production (million tonnes)	2 Exports (million tonnes)	3 Import (million tonnes)	4 Consumption (million tonnes)	5 Home production as % of consumption	6 Total calorific self-sufficiency % 1973–4 to 1975–6	6 Total calorific self-sufficiency % 1975
Developing							
Africa	45.3	0.35	13.1	58.1	78	—	96
Near East	55.4	1.49	18.7	72.6	76	—	91
Far East	262.4	8.4	17.3	271.3	97	99	99
Asian CPE[a]	307.3	1.9	19.3	324.7	95	99	99
Latin America	86.4	12.8	22.0	99.2	87	—	103
Total developing	756.8	24.94	90.4	825.9	92	95	—
Developed							
USSR & E. Europe	257.4	6.0	46.0	297.4	87.6	97[b]	—
North America	324.9	127.2	1.37	199.1	163	127[c]	—
Western Europe	170.3	33.3	46.5	183.5	93	91	—
Australasia	20.6	14.7	0.05	5.95	346	—	—
Other developed[e]	26.8	3.9	26.4	49.3	54	55[d]	—
Total developed	800.0	185.1	120.9	735.3	108	110	—
Importers only	454.5	43.2	118.9	530.2	85	—	—

[a] CPE = centrally planned economies.
[b] USSR only.
[c] USA only.
[d] Japan only.
[e] Japan, South, Africa, Israel.

Sources: FAO, Production Yearbook 1981, vol. 35, Rome, 1982; FAO, Trade Yearbook 1981, vol. 35, Rome, 1982; G. L. Seevers, 'Food markets and their regulation', in R. F. Hopkins and D. J. Puchala (eds), The Global Political Economy of Food, Madison, Wisconsin, 1978, pp. 147–69; 'Self-sufficiency: facts and figures', Ceres, **12**, 1979, pp. 19–21

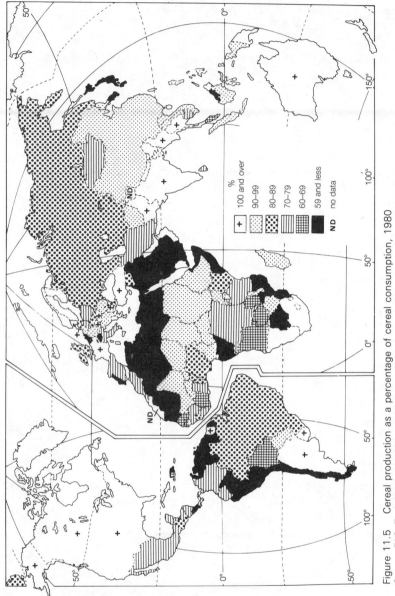

Figure 11.5 Cereal production as a percentage of cereal consumption, 1980
Source: FAO, *Trade Yearbook 1981*, vol. 35, Rome, 1982; *Production Yearbook 1981*, vol. 35, Rome, 1982

a reliance on overseas food supplies, for potatoes in the Andes and manioc and yams in Africa are an important source of food in these countries.

It is clearly difficult if not impossible to measure self-sufficiency with any accuracy; but the data suggest that the Middle East, much of Africa and western Latin America are the regions least self-sufficient. But even if the degree of self-sufficiency could be accurately measured, two points remain at issue. First, it is debatable if a country which is self-sufficient but has a low level of consumption is less precariously placed than one with a higher consumption level but not self-sufficient. Perhaps self-sufficiency should be measured against national minimum requirements (see pp. 22–3) rather than consumption alone. Second, it is debatable that self-sufficiency is a desirable aim if food can be imported more cheaply than that produced at home, always provided it can be paid for in some way. This point is returned to later.

FOOD AID AND FOOD STOCKS

The rising price of food grains has been one reason why many developing countries have sought to maintain self-sufficiency. But not all the cereal imports of the developing countries have to be paid for at the market price. Since 1954 substantial amounts of food – mainly cereals and milk products – have been sent to developing countries, primarily from North America either at reduced prices or as grants. Such apparently generous behaviour has received much criticism.[11]

Food aid began after the end of the Second World War when half the United States economic assistance to Europe's recovery was in the form of food. It became more formal in 1954 when a law passed through Congress – PL 480 – permitted the sale of United States grain on various concessionary terms to friendly and needy countries. This law was one response to the huge surpluses of grain accumulating in the United States, surpluses which were in turn a result of United States government policies first introduced in 1933 and variously modified since. In the late 1920s and the 1930s world recession reduced US farmers' exports and led to very low prices and much poverty. In 1933 the United States government introduced legislation that paid farmers to withdraw land from cultivation and grow legumes or adopt soil conservation policies, and in the case of cotton introduced an area quota. But the government was also prepared to buy all cereals which could not be sold

[11] Tony Jackson and Deborah Eade, *Against the Grain*, Oxford, 1982; J. Cathie, *The Political Economy of Food Aid*, Aldershot, 1982.

above a given price on the open market, and stored these surpluses. In the Second World War and its immediate aftermath there was no problem in disposing of surpluses. The adoption of new technologies led to great increases in output in the 1940s, but the rapid recovery of European agriculture reduced the overseas markets for US exporters, and PL 480 was one means of reducing the surpluses. Throughout the 1950s and 1960s stocks in the United States – and to a lesser extent Canada – were high, and acted as a world reserve that maintained price stability in the world cereal market. In the 1950s and 1960s approximately half all cereal imports into the developing countries were in the form of food aid (figure 11.6). [12]

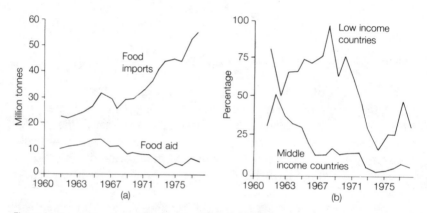

Figure 11.6   (a) imports of food and food aid; (b) Food aid as percentage of food imports
Source: World Bank, *World Development Report 1981*, Washington DC, 1981

In the late 1960s, however, successive United States administrations attempted to reduce the burden of agricultural support, and land was withdrawn from cultivation. In 1972 and 1973 this, combined with unexpectedly large Russian purchases of United States grain and droughts in parts of Africa and South Asia, led to a rapid rise in cereal prices and, because of the shortage in many developing countries, to increased imports. When by 1976 the period of high prices was over and world food output up again, the imports did not decline, because demand continued from the better off developing countries, particularly the oil exporters, who had benefited from their raising of oil prices. After the devaluation of the American dollar in 1971 and the increased cost of

[12] FAO, *The State of Food and Agriculture 1977*, Rome, 1978, p. 1–37.

US oil imports, the United States government determined to compensate by promoting United States food exports. For all these reasons food aid as a proportion of all developing countries' imports has fallen. It was 57 per cent in 1961–2, 38 per cent in 1970 and 18 per cent in 1977; by 1982 food aid was only 5 per cent of the international trade in cereals.[13] However, food aid to the low income countries remains a high if declining proportion of their total food imports (figure 11.6).

In the 1950s and 1960s the United States was the major supplier of food aid. In 1965, for example, it provided 94 per cent of all food aid. But from 1968 EEC policies of price support were also creating surpluses, particularly of dairy goods; the EEC began to provide aid, notably of milk products but by the late 1970s of cereals as well, so that by 1976 the United States share of all food aid had fallen to 68 per cent. In the late 1970s the United States, Canada and the EEC provided four-fifths of all food aid.[14]

Over the last 30 years more than 90 countries have received some form of food aid; between 1945 and 1980 $30 billion of aid has been distributed. There has been much criticism of the direction and consequences of aid. In the 1950s and early 1960s most aid was in the form of bilateral arrangements between the United States and recipient countries. It has been argued that much of this aid did not go to those countries most in need, but to those with which the United States had close military or political relationships, or to those countries which already traded with the United States.[15]

Since the mid 1960s an increasing proportion of food aid has gone through the agency of the World Food Programme, run by FAO, which receives food from donor countries but decides its destination. Since 1975 the US Congress has required that 70 per cent of United States food aid should go to the poorer states – in 1981 those states with a gross domestic product per caput below $795. These countries received four-fifths of all food aid in 1981. But there have been numerous other criticisms of food aid. It has been argued that imports of concessionary

[13] J. R. Tarrant, 'The geography of food aid', *Transactions of the Institute of British Geographers*, 5, 1980, pp. 125–40; E. J. Clay, 'Is European Community food aid reformable?', *Food Policy*, 8, 1983, pp. 174–7; FAO, *The State of Food and Agriculture 1981*, Rome, 1982, p. 1–27.

[14] S. J. Maxwell and H. W. Singer, 'Food aid to developing countries: a survey', *World Development*, 7, 1979, pp. 225–46; J. R. Tarrant, 'EEC food aid', *Applied Geography*, 2, 1982, pp. 127–41; FAO, *The State of Food and Agriculture 1982*, Rome, 1983, p. 41.

[15] Cathie, *op. cit.*, p. 9; R. Vengroff, 'Food aid dependency: PL 480 aid to Black Africa', *Journal of Modern African Studies*, 20, 1982, pp. 17–43.

grains have in some cases reduced the price of local products and hence been a disincentive to the increase of domestic food output. The fall in the wheat area in Columbia in 1960s is a much quoted instance of this, although a study of India, a major recipient of food aid, suggests that adverse effects on prices only operated over very short periods. [16] Approximately 70 per cent of food aid is sold at market prices to importing governments and the proceeds used to finance development projects. The remainder, described as project food aid, is supplied free and distributed in various ways – as free school meals, in health centres for mothers and young children, and as food for labourers on land improvement schemes. This aid does not always benefit the recipients. Thus supplementary feeding to children and infants is balanced by their receiving less food at home. Some foods sent as aid are inappropriate – such as Swiss cheese to Biafra. Further, the cost of transporting food aid to the developing countries uses up a formidable proportion of total aid. Current opinion appears to be that, except for emergency relief, food aid would be more beneficial in terms of untied financial grants or loans. [17]

In the 1950s and 1960s the price of wheat and other cereals was rising but did not fluctuate greatly from year to year, for the United States reserves could be fed into the system in times of shortage. With the rundown of these stocks and the growing proportion of commercial exports in total trade, there has been a renewal of a need for a central world food agency to maintain reserves. Although FAO now supports a small emergency fund there has been no success in forming a world food reserve, because of the conflicting interests of the developed exporters and the developing importers. However, world food reserves have recently returned to the high levels attained in the 1950s and 1960s, although they are mainly in the developed countries rather than in a world store (table 11.5).

AGRICULTURAL EXPORTS FROM THE DEVELOPING COUNTRIES

In 1950 agricultural produce accounted for much of the export earnings of the developing countries. This proportion has greatly declined with

[16] FAO, *The State of Food and Agriculture 1982*, Rome, 1983, p. 41; Maxwell and Singer, *op. cit.*; P. J. Isenman and H. W. Singer, 'Food aid disincentive effects and their policy implications', *Economic Development and Cultural Change*, 25, 1977, pp. 205-37; L. Dudley and R. J. Sandilands, 'The side effects of foreign aid: the case of Public Law 480 wheat in Colombia', *Economic Development and Cultural Change*, 23, 1975, pp. 325-36.
[17] Jackson and Eade, *op. cit.*

Table 11.5   Carry over cereal stocks

	Million tonnes	% of world consumption		Million tonnes	% of world consumption
1969–70	179	23	1976–7	166	18
1970–1	144	17	1977–8	177	19
1971–2	168	19	1978–9	200	21
1972–3	119	14	1980	256	18
1973–4	100	13	1981	252	16
1974–5	108	12	1982	275	18
1975–6	124	14			

Sources: FAO, *The State of Food and Agriculture 1978*, Rome, 1979, pp. 1–17; *The State of Food and Agriculture 1982*, Rome, 1983; *The State of Food and Agriculture 1975*, Rome, 1976, p. 74

the rise of oil exports and also, from a number of countries, of manufactured goods; thus agricultural exports accounted for 50 per cent of all export earnings in 1965, but only 23 per cent in 1980. None the less agricultural products still account for 38 per cent of all Africa's exports, 22 per cent of the Far East's and 45 per cent of Latin America's, and in many countries the dependence is far greater (figure 11.7). But the agricultural exports of the developing countries, although increasing substantially in volume and value, have declined as a proportion of world agricultural trade. In 1948–52 the developing countries accounted for about 53 per cent of all agricultural exports, in 1961–3 44 per cent (table 11.6) and by 1980 only 31 per cent. One ominous consequence of this, combined with the steep rise in food imports, has been the decline of the developing countries' ability to pay for food imports with agricultural exports.[18] Indeed by 1980 the value of imports had virtually equalled that of exports and only Latin America had a sizeable surplus. Of course other products are exported, but the dependence of many developing countries upon agricultural exports makes it increasingly difficult to finance food imports (table 11.7).

Many developing countries are vulnerable because of their dependence upon one or two products. Thus tropical beverages, which are largely luxury items, make up 25 per cent of all developing countries' agricultural exports; of 87 developing countries in 1980 half depended upon cocoa, coffee and tea for at least 30 per cent of their agricultural earnings. But concentration is not confined to these crops. Burma and North Korea derive over 70 per cent of their agricultural exports from rice alone,

[18] R. Duncan and E. Lutz, 'Penetration of industrial country markets by agricultural products from developing countries', *World Development*, **11**, 1983, pp. 771–86; FAO, *op. cit.*, 1983, p. 18; FAO, *The State of Food and Agriculture 1960*, Rome, 1960, p. 44.

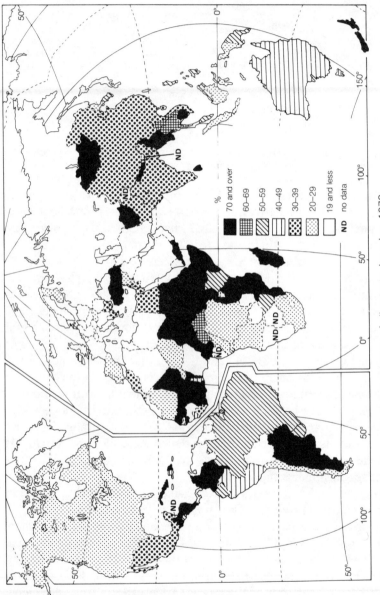

Figure 11.7 Agricultural exports as a percentage of all exports, by value, 1978
Source: World Bank, *World Development Report 1981*, Washington DC, 1981

Table 11.6   Share of world agricultural exports by value, 1961–3 to 1980

	% 1961–3	% 1972–4	% 1980
Developed			
North America	19.7	23.1	21.4
Western Europe	17.6	26.1	36.2
Oceania	8.2	7.1	5.4
East Europe and USSR	7.9	6.0	4.2
Other developed	2.1	1.6	1.8
Total developed	55.5	63.9	69.0
Developing			
Africa	9.1	6.5	4.5
Far East	12.5	8.3	8.5
Latin America	17.1	15.4	13.8
Near East	3.7	3.2	2.2
Asia CPE[a]	1.8	2.4	1.8
Other developing	0.3	0.3	0.2
Total developing	44.5	36.1	31.0

[a] CPE: centrally planned economies.
Sources: FAO, *The State of Food and Agriculture 1975*, Rome, 1976, p. 68; FAO, *Trade Yearbook 1981*, vol. 39, Rome, 1982

Table 11.7   Developing countries: agricultural imports as a percentage of agricultural exports by value, 1970–2 and 1980

	1970–2	1980
Africa	44	97
Far East	86	82
Latin America	32	44
Near East	97	363
Asian CPE[a]	105	215
All developing countries	60	95

[a] CPE: centrally planned economies.
Source: FAO, *The State of Food and Agriculture 1982*, Rome, 1983, p. 19

Bangladesh from jute, and Senegal and Gambia from groundnuts; over 90 per cent of Cuba's exports still come from sugar. Some countries have successfully diversified; thus Malaysia has added oil palm to rubber – albeit at the expense of several West African states – and Thailand has reduced its dependence upon rice, and Brazil has become the world's second soybean exporter. But it is the countries with either minerals or manufactures to export which have been able to finance food imports most easily. Hence in the Far East, where grain imports are admittedly not a major item, Korea, Hong Kong and Singapore take nearly half all the cereal imports, and in Africa, Algeria, Morocco and Nigeria a similar proportion; the Near East has dramatically increased its imports since the 1960s.[19]

The concentration upon relatively few exports is repeated when the major regions are considered. Some 60 per cent of Africa's exports are coffee and cocoa, 70 per cent of Latin America's are sugar, coffee and soybeans, 60 per cent of the Near East's are fruit, vegetables and cotton, and 60 per cent of the Far East's exports consist of rubber, rice and vegetable oils. The exports of the developing countries face a number of difficulties. First, those which are raw materials for manufacturing industry have been liable to be displaced by alternatives. Thus the rise of bulk carriers on land and sea has reduced the demand for jute sacks, and cotton, sisal and wool have been challenged by a variety of synthetic fibres. Although natural rubber remains a buoyant export, synthetic rubber manufacture has limited its rate of expansion. Second, much of the exports are commodities for which there is inelastic demand in the developed countries. During the economic expansion of the 1950s and 1960s in Europe and the United States, there was a continuing increase in demand for luxury commodities such as coffee, cocoa, bananas and tea, but by the early 1970s some argued that the market for these products was saturated. Third, output of many of the developing countries' agricultural exports fluctuate owing to variations in climate; thus prices oscillate violently. This is true of all agricultural products, but the impact is far greater when a country earns much of its export earnings from one or two products. Thus in the 1970s there have been numerous demands for the control of commodity prices. Fourth, about four-fifths of the agricultural products entering international trade are grown in both the developed and the developing countries. Only the products of the humid tropics are a monopoly of the developing countries. But in both North America and Europe a combination of price supports, tariffs and import levies make it difficult for developing countries to compete.[20]

For these and other reasons the terms of trade – the price of the developing countries' exports divided by the price of the manufactures

[19] FAO, *The State of Food and Agriculture 1981*, Rome, 1982, pp. 61–6.
[20] C. Mackel, J. Marsh and B. Revell, 'Western Europe and the South: the Common Agricultural Policy', *Third World Quarterly*, 6, 1984, pp. 131–44; M. E. Abel, 'The impact of US agricultural policies on the trade of developing countries', F. S. Tolley and P. A. Zadrozny (eds), *Trade, Agriculture and Development*, Cambridge, Mass., 1975, pp. 21–56; FAO, *The State of Food and Agriculture 1973*, Rome, 1973, p. 13.

they import – have been unfavourable for much of the post-war period, notably in the late 1950s and much of the 1960s, although they were strongly in their favour in the early 1950s and much of the 1970s. [21]

CONCLUSIONS

The period since the end of the Second World War has seen a great boom in agricultural trade and marked alterations in its direction. Since the early 1960s there has been a great increase in food imports by the developing countries. This has been due first to the rapid population growth and the inability of some countries, particularly in Africa, to maintain per caput food supplies from home production, and second to the imports of wheat, livestock products and livestock feeds into the richer developing countries. The latter has been possible only where there have been oil or manufactures exports. The poorer developing countries, often dependent upon one or two crops for much of their exports, have found it increasingly difficult to pay for food imports.

[21] FAO, *The State of Food and Agriculture 1976*, Rome, 1977, p. 1–40; FAO, *The State of Food and Agriculture 1960*, Rome, 1960, pp. 46–7.

12

Conclusions

The 40 years since the end of the Second World War have seen quite remarkable advances in the agriculture of both the developed and the developing countries, and, sadly, less dramatic changes in consumption levels. In the developed countries the rapid increase in output, and the comparatively modest increases in population, have provided a diet with a much higher livestock content, and also embarrassing surpluses of many products. More important, post-war economic growth has lifted the incomes of the poorest in developed countries so that malnutrition is no longer the problem it was even in the 1930s, and even more markedly in the nineteenth century and before. The history of the developed countries shows what many argue is true for the developing countries today – that the persistence of hunger is sometimes as much a matter of income as of food production. At the beginning of the nineteenth century malnutrition was probably widespread in Western Europe, for available food supplies were no higher than in much of tropical Africa and South Asia today. Technological advance in agriculture ensured that by the second half of the nineteenth century most West European countries had food supplies which were sufficient to provide an adequate diet for all if distributed according to need. But this did not eliminate malnutrition: the persistence of a substantial proportion of the population with very low incomes ensured that malnutrition if not undernutrition remained a major problem until the 1930s.

It is worth noting that factors other than production capacity and income were important in eliminating malnutrition in the developed countries. These factors included advances in refrigeration and in the processing of foods, and legislation that prevented the adulteration of food and ensured good standards of hygiene. Important too was the decline of the incidence of contagious disease among infants and young children. Until the beginning of this century there was little knowledge of the fundamentals of nutritional science; indeed the debate over the role of animal protein and the significance of infectious diseases suggests that there is still much to be learned about this subject.

In the 1950s, at the time that malnutrition was becoming a minor issue in the developed countries, the problems of hunger in Africa, Asia and Latin America were receiving a great deal of attention; the rapid growth of population led to fears of catastrophe. In the event, the world as a whole has increased its food output faster than population since 1950, as have all the major developing regions except Africa. But the record is not as satisfactory as this might suggest. First, it must be reiterated that there are countries – mainly in Africa but also in Latin America and parts of South Asia – where food output per caput has been in decline since the early 1960s. Second, in spite of the remarkable growth of food output, one-third of the population of the developing world live in countries where in 1977–80 available food supplies – output, stocks and imports – were insufficient to provide the population with an adequate diet even if it were distributed according to need rather than purchasing power. Third, even among those countries which had supplies in excess of national requirements, many were perilously balanced a percentage point or two above the minimum needs, and any major crises – such as the disruption in China during the Great Leap Forward or the failure of the Indian monsoon in 1964–6 – can lead to acute difficulties in feeding the population. Thus whereas it is unquestionably true that poverty is the principal cause of undernutrition and malnutrition, it does not follow that food production can be neglected. It is not only that in many countries food output is still insufficient to provide the minimum national diet; although there has been some slight decline in the rate of population growth in the last decade, rates of increase will remain high well into the next century in most countries in Africa, Asia and Latin America.

Between 1950 and 1980 the population of the developing countries approximately doubled. Those who predicted such rapid growth in 1950 doubted if food output could be increased as rapidly, and feared an increase in the numbers and proportion of the population undernourished. As has been shown, it is difficult to measure the extent of hunger, and even more difficult to measure changes in the extent of hunger. However, whatever measures are used – available food supply per head, the numbers living in countries with available food supplies less than 2200 calories per head, or the numbers receiving less than 1.2 basal metabolic rate (see pp. 49–50) – the *proportion* of the population suffering from hunger has declined, and the absolute numbers have not increased very greatly and indeed may have declined. This view is supported by the universally downward trend not only of the crude death rate but also, where data are available, of the infant and child death rates. By 1980 only 17 per cent of the population of the developing countries were undernourished, compared with 34 per cent in 1950, and 421 of the 534 million were to be found in Asia.

In 1950 a great many authorities doubted whether food production could be substantially increased: the supplies of cultivable land were held to be exhausted, the crop yields of Western Europe felt to be high and unlikely to be greatly increased, and the farmers of the developing countries thought to be bound by tradition, unresponsive to price changes, and too deeply committed to subsistence to experiment with new methods. All three observations have been proved to be wrong. In Western Europe and North America technological change has greatly increased crop yields and livestock productivity. The problems of Western agriculture are now those of surplus not shortage.

There have also been substantial additions to the arable area in the developing countries. This has been most notable in Africa and Latin America. In Latin America two-thirds of the increased food output since 1950 has come from extra cropland, and much of this is a result of colonizing new land; by contrast, in tropical Africa the reduction of fallow has been the major source of increased output. In most parts of Asia new land has been far less important, except in parts of Thailand, Sumatra and the Philippines, because Asia was already densely populated in 1950. Hence increasing crop yields, extending multiple cropping and improving irrigation systems have been the major sources of increased food output. Indeed in China 90 per cent of the increase in output since 1950 has been due to higher crop yields. Until the middle 1960s yields increased slowly, mainly by the use of traditional practices that required extra labour. However, since the 1960s the methods pioneered in Japan, Korea and Taiwan before 1950 were extended to other parts of Asia, notably India and Pakistan. The rapid spread of high yielding varieties in conjunction with better water control, and of pesticides and chemical fertilizers, has transformed regions such as the Indian Punjab and, although not resolving the problems of hunger, has certainly prevented them increasing.

Of the major developing regions, Africa has seen least agricultural progress since 1950 and food output has risen less than in Latin America or Asia. But population has grown more rapidly than elsewhere. This has put great pressure upon the traditional farming systems, which relied upon a long natural fallow to maintain soil fertility. Indeed much of the increased food output has come not from colonizing new land but by reducing the fallow. Alternative means of maintaining soil fertility have yet to be found. Africa still uses very few modern inputs – machines, fertilizers or improved crop varieties – and its capacity to increase output has not been helped by government policies that have favoured urban consumers at the expense of the farmer. Nor has disruption from civil and other wars provided conditions suitable for agricultural advance. Moreover, much of the African environment presents unresolved problems both for cultivation and, in the case of the tsetse fly, for livestock production. African agricultural difficulties are compounded by the lack of research on food crops or skilled extension workers; some would argue that an excessive proportion of Africa's cropland is devoted to export crops, land that could be used for growing food. As African food output per caput has declined, so there has been a growing dependence upon food imports. Whereas agricultural exports once paid for all these with ease, by 1980 the cost of tropical Africa's food imports nearly equalled earnings from agricultural exports.

In Africa not only has output per caput been declining for two decades, but in a majority of countries available food supplies are less than the minimum national requirements. In terms of food supplies Latin America has far less serious problems, few states having either declining food output per caput or less than minimum requirements. Much of Latin America's increased food output has come from colonizing new land; the arable area has doubled in the last 30 years, and yield increases account for only one third of extra output. The problems of Latin America are closely related to the distribution of land; in spite of land reforms, the bulk of the continent's land is still owned by a small proportion of the population, and the great majority are either landless or have very small farms. Hence, it has been argued, the dynamic sector has been the reformed latifundia; they have adopted new inputs such as machinery, often at the expense of their labourers. In contrast the peasant sector has lacked the resources to improve farming methods and has grown in the numbers it has to support. Thus in Latin America, in contrast to Africa, the problems of reducing malnutrition are mainly a matter of income distribution rather than of simply increasing the productive capacity of agriculture. As in other continents the poor are primarily in the rural areas; in Latin America land reform must play a role in any future improvement of their lot.

Although Asia has many tenant farmers, there is a world of difference between conditions there and in Latin America. Although the abolition of tenancy might improve farming efficiency, it would not release a fund of unused land. In most of Asia the landlord class owns small amounts of land and big farms are a matter of 10 hectares, not 100 or

1000. Yet the record of Japan, Taiwan, Korea and Malaya shows that a predominance of small farms is no impediment to rapid growth of food output, provided that support in the form of research, extension and marketing services is offered by the state or by co-operative organizations. Indeed the problems of East Asia – including, to some extent Japan – are a matter not of increasing efficiency of growth rates but of providing alternative jobs in industry as agricultural densities mount higher and higher and underemployment becomes greater. In Japan industry has attracted labour off the land for the last 30 years, and Taiwan and Korea are at the beginning of this major turning point in economic development.

Elsewhere in Asia agricultural population densities are far lower than in East Asia, but the prospects of reducing the agricultural population are limited in the foreseeable future, even if dramatic attempts to reduce population growth, such as those adopted in China, were pursued. However, over the last 30 years there have been major contrasts in the rate at which new inputs have been adopted. However halting the progress in much of South and South East Asia, it can be argued that higher yields and incomes are possible, for they have already been achieved in parts of East Asia.

Looking back over the period 1950–80 it can be argued that too many of the world's population remain impoverished and undernourished, and that too many farmers remain inefficient and unproductive, too many have too little land and unjust land tenure systems, and too many are subject to the depredations of their own governments or foreign capital. But it is as well to remember that the catastrophies predicted in the 1940s and 1950s have not occurred, however horrifying local famines have been. In an age of unprecedented population growth food output has also increased at hitherto unknown rates, and the proportion of those undernourished has declined. This may not be good enough, but it is a considerable achievement.

Index

In Search
of Your
Family Tree

In Search of Your Family Tree

HAROLD H. KELLEY

St. Martin's Press
New York

Library of Congress Cataloging in Publication Data

Kelley, Harold Howard, 1926-
    In search of your family tree.

    1. Genealogy. 2. United States—Genealogy—
Handbooks, manuals, etc. I. Title.
CS16.K43   929′.1   75-9486

ISBN 0-312-41160-X

Dedication

I wish to dedicate this book first to my deceased parents, Shelby and Gladys Millspaugh Kelley, for they are my family tree. Secondly, I want to dedicate it to my brothers and sisters, whom I love deeply; they broadened the family tree. I must also make a last dedication to my relatives and correspondents, the personnel of the courthouses, libraries, state libraries and other institutions in Indiana and other states; they have helped me greatly in my search for data to compile my family lines.

Table of Contents

In Search
of Your
Family Tree

1

An Introduction and General Outline

Let me begin this book by sharing my feelings about genealogy with you. As you will learn, accuracy is extremely important in research, but unshakeable proof is not always possible, and to be obsessed with it is to miss the spirit of our quest. You and I are in search of our ancestral roots, documenting our discoveries for future generations where we can, but seeking above all to know our ancestors, to find through them a richer sense of history and of ourselves.

Before you decide irrevocably to get involved with genealogy, let's discuss the kinds of commitments you will have to make, and the tools you will need for tracking down your ancestors.

The first thing you'll need is plenty of time.

Researching, traveling, organizing, planning and writing, all of these will require a sizeable time investment. However, it is one of my aims in this book to show you how to avoid the common pitfalls that waste precious hours, or even days, in your search.

Time is only one important investment you must be willing to make. Money is another. Most people are interested in the lives of their grandparents and great-grandparents, but many take the attitude that it wouldn't be profitable to get involved in research. Financially, they are right. If you do your own research, it will take you a number of years of running here and there for facts, which will cost money, not to mention the additional cost of having your findings published or printed. When all is said and done, you will have invested much more than you could possibly get out of your finished volume. However, if you want to bring together scattered bits of information on your predecessors, and pass this information on to your children and your relatives, you will get more than your money's worth in personal satisfaction.

In addition to time and money, you will need transportation, either a car of your own, or a friend who will take you in his or her vehicle to the many spots where you will want to dig for facts. Using a bus or other public transportation is ideal for some outings, but in most cases buses won't take you to a country graveyard or to the home of a fourth cousin or a great aunt.

What kind of person should you be to take up genealogy? Well, you'll find the job requires average intelligence as well as such personal qualities as perseverance and the ability to be meticulous about copying information. For instance, you should number each page of your notes, and you should start each new day that you do research by heading your page or portion thereof with the day's date. If you use shorthand or your own abbreviated form of writing, you must remember that later on you will have to reconstruct from your notes the same words as those in your original book or source of information. You needn't write in fancy script, but from the beginning use clear, legible handwriting.

You should get used to taking your notes in pencil, since many offices and archives will not allow you to use a pen. The necessity for this rule will become clear after you have come across a note in one of the deed records or other volumes, and are unable to determine whether it was written by the original writer or by some unthinking person years later. If the latter is true, is the information in the note to be trusted or was it just a guess on the part of the writer? This is a good time to ask you never to add your notes, comments or markings to public records. It takes only a few seconds to jot down the page number and volume title in your notes for future reference.

Up until now I've been giving you a general introduction to genealogy and its requirements, but I also wish to cover briefly some of the techniques you'll be using.

The first place to start digging is close to home. Interview the oldest members of your family, taking notes the whole time. Start with your parents, then interview their brothers and sisters. If your family lived in the same county where you now live, go to the county courthouse there. Be prepared to spend many days checking these local records. Check the county histories at the public library as well as the old county atlas, graveyard listings and any other county data there. Once you know approximately when an ancestor died, use your library's file of old newspapers to find death notices and obituaries. If there are no birth and death records in the county courthouse, they are probably stored in the county health department. Sites for these documents do vary from state to state.

State capitols have their own county courthouses and public libraries, as well as a state library and repositories for state documents and legal proceedings. Be prepared to take a trip to your state library and spend several days digging. There is a great deal of information stored there, and most of it is available for your use. In the state library you'll find the following sources of information: county histories, birth and death listings, graveyard listings, marriage records, census reports (very useful), Civil War archives, newspaper files for towns of any size, and histories of counties and settlements in other states, particularly the eastern (early) ones. Some records are mimeographed, some are in books, and some are on microfilm. Some are just indices to county records, so to get the complete picture, a further trip to the appropriate county or counties will sometimes be necessary. While at the state library, don't be surprised if you find material missing for some counties. This is partly due to the fact that much of the original compilation was done by the Works Progress Administration (WPA) during the thirties, a work force that went out of existence before the project was completed. Courthouse fires, floods, wars and other destructive forces have also taken their toll of valuable records.

When you have exhausted the sources within your state, you will have to follow your leads back to other states, and sooner or later, across the ocean, if a complete family history is to be compiled. You'll find in the other states much the same sources as in your own, with some variations. The eastern coastal states have passenger lists of ships coming into the main ports; this is particularly helpful after you have gathered information on you ancestor back to this point of entry.

Whenever possible, attend genealogy workshops or take related courses at state libraries, colleges and high schools. These are advertised from time to time in genealogical columns and sometimes in your local newspaper. You should also become a regular reader of genealogy columns.

Don't discount any source. All are subject to error, but often, different sources prove each other out. County histories are full of errors, but the dates and facts contained therein are often verified by deed records, will books or probate court records—all of which can also be found in the county courthouse.

Remember, if you copy from a county history or any other copyrighted volume, you cannot use this information word-for-word in your completed family history. I always copy material word-for-word into my notes, but only use the actual facts and dates in my final write-ups.

You'll get acquainted with a number of distant relatives during your data collecting, some of whom you won't have met before. They may own old photographs you'll want copies of or Bible records you'll want to copy. In the same way, you will get pleasure out of helping some of your contacts. You can't be stingy with the information you compile; don't write to strangers expecting to drain them of information, and tell them nothing. After one or two letters, they will see through you, and that will end your correspondence. If you don't intend to have your works published, share your information with the correspondents from whom you will be getting information in return. Make sure to give them data on their particular lines of the family. If you do intend to publish, then share only what pertains to their direct line. Without taking a selfish attitude, don't give all the information away that you have painstakingly collected, or you will detract from the value of the finished volumes of your family history.

If, during your research, you uncover facts that cast a blight on your family, you must use your own good judgment as to whether these should be included in your finished work. Some things you might include and laugh off as a family joke; other dark truths might bring a lawsuit from a distant cousin resenting your disclosure of a family skeleton.

Some time ago, during my own research, I was talking to a factory worker in Indianapolis who had been telling me of his extensive travels as a young man. When I asked him if he had been to Bristol or Bucks County in Pennsylvania he said yes, so I asked if he had run into one of my ancestral family lines, which I named. He looked at me for a little while before answering, "I wouldn't tell you, if I had." I was stunned, but I got the hint; he didn't want to destroy the pleasant image I had of my family by giving me the shady truth about characters he had known. Discretion is sometimes the best policy all around.

You can spend a lot of money on genealogy or spend modestly, depending on how you go about it and how severely you limit yourself. Remember, a lot of your research can be done through letters to appropriate people and places. Be prepared to spend some money on stamps; it's less expensive than unnecessary trips! Take advantage of the various newspapers' genealogical columns. The Sunday editions of most capital cities will usually have such a column, to which you may send your queries for information. If you are on a limited budget, don't buy an expensive county history reprint just because an ancestor might be mentioned in it; use the one at the state library or the local library at that particular county seat if it is nearby.

If you have a typewriter and can type, it will be very helpful. A camera will be useful for taking pictures in graveyards and of the cousins you become acquainted with. If you wish to do any copying of the records with your camera, you should probably have a thirty-five millimeter that will accept supplementary lenses for close-up work. Always take a piece of chalk and a bit of charcoal or a soft leaded pencil with you when you go to the graveyards. You can use these to make the letters stand out on the old grave stones when you photograph them.

Elderly people and retired persons get as much enjoyment from collecting data as young people do, maybe even more. They usually have more of the most important prerequisite for this hobby—time. In fact, maybe genealogy today should be called "the sport of the elderly," since so many retired people are enriching their twilight years by working at it. It's natural for older people to be interested in family, since it seems to have more meaning as one ages.

In the chapters that follow, I will take the important points that I have covered only briefly in this chapter and explain in detail the how, where and why of them.

So, without further ado, let's begin.

2

Word of Mouth

Word of mouth is the way family histories were originally preserved. In ancient times, before there were written languages, the tribal elder would recount the stories told to him in his youth. (It is said that the Book of Genesis was originally composed from stories handed down by the inhabitants of the Holy Land, people who believed in only one god.) But something always happens to a story that is preserved by word of mouth. The heroes are rendered more glorious with each telling, the villains blacker and more evil; the facts are changed with each teller, the stores are mixed with one another, and myth is interwoven or confused with fact. Yet in the beginning, stories were all the history that people had.

11

Today, for all our fantastic technological strides, the nature of genealogy hasn't changed all that much. Word of mouth is still a major source of information—it's definitely the best place to start!

Ask your parents what they remember of their parents, particularly any stories of early ancestors. If your parents are dead, ask your aunts and uncles, blood relations. Contact the oldest living members of the family line or lines on which you begin work and write down all the important facts they reveal (date your notes). To get the most complete story, you must learn to ask the right questions. Ask about marriages, burial places and the names of spouses and children. Get what dates you can, even estimated dates; these can be verified by courthouse and other records of the areas you will search in. If possible, use a small tape recorder during these interviews—an inconspicuous miniature would be less likely to make the person being interviewed ill at ease.

The family reunion is a good place to find out who knows what, but don't spend the few hours of that event gathering information. By asking a few well-chosen questions of the older family members, you will be able to find out which ones have the best memories and received the most information at home as children. Be sure to take down the names and addresses of the relatives you will want to contact later. Normally, the ladies will have been at home more and are therefore more likely to have been told the family stories, especially by their mothers. The men, on the other hand, usually won't worry their heads about family history until years later. By that time, most of the relatives who could have flooded them with stories and details will have passed away. It's unfortunate, but this is often the case.

I would have followed the same path as other men, but during high school my life was altered. A distant cousin of my mother—Bessie Thurston was her name—came to town seeking information on a family with my mother's maiden name, Millspaugh. During her stay, Bessie compiled, and had mimeographed, a Millspaugh family history. (This collection of data was incorporated into a more complete history compiled later by Francis C. Millspaugh of Massachusetts.) During her visit, Bessie gave me many valuable tips on how to research my family tree. I was also able to help her with bits of information, most of which I copied from records at the state library in Indianapolis. Like most beginners, I could only think of working on my father's lines, because I carried his name. I later saw that I was limiting myself by not pursuing my mother's lines as well. If she is still living, Bessie resides in Gary, Indiana, and is a sweel soul, a poet. I am proud to be even remotely related to her.

Taking Bessie's advice, I pinned down my father one day and asked him to tell me all he knew about his family lines. I was amazed at how much information he had stored in his mind. I took notes on all he told me, and that was really the start of the search for my family's roots. Some children's names that he could not remember or had mistaken were later added to or corrected by his two sisters, whom I also interviewed. By checking various county records, I was later able to fill in marriage dates as well as some birth and death dates. I took my family outlines with me to the Kelley family reunion and made further corrections and additions. I also had my mother tell me about her lines, but she, alas, knew little of her mother's history.

I have mentioned family reunions several times in this chapter. If your family schedules regular reunions, you should attend them, since, as I have mentioned, these are great places for scouting out subjects for interviews. If your family has no regular reunions, take the initiative for starting them yourself. This may involve regular responsibilities, but you'll find that these will be offset by a treasure of new information. The word will get around that you are the family historian, and soon you will have relatives seeking you out with bits of fact and family history.

Just as in the days of early man, stories handed down in the family are transformed by time, distance and the storyteller; you must expect this. Write these family tales down anyway, for they are a good place to start establishing your ancestors as real individuals, each with a unique personality and life-style. Also, you'll be surprised how many stories are proven out by the volumes at the courthouse or the library. Some are proven wrong by the same sources, and some will never be proven one way or the other but will haunt you as you try to substantiate them.

One such story comes to mind; it concerns my mother's grandmother, Rebecca. Most of the relatives who gave me details of Rebecca's life told me pretty much the same stories. But one of Mother's cousins, Rachel, had a variation that still lingers in my memory. Rachel said, as did my other relatives, that my great-grandmother's parents died when she was small, leaving three brothers, a sister, and a half sister behind. But Rachel added other details—which none of the others had told me—details that another of Mother's cousins, Pearle, had never heard before. Rachel told me that Rebecca's parents lived in Franklin county on a farm, not far from a stockade. One day, while her father was clearing land, an Indian, who had been hiding and watching the settler work, suddenly ran out, grabbed the rifle that Rebecca's father had propped up against a nearby tree, and shot him with it. When Rebecca's mother heard the commotion and saw what had happened, she snatched up the youngest child, took the others by the hand, and ran to the stockade. As they came in sight of the fort, her mother looked back and saw trails of blood made by the children's torn bare feet in the snow.

Chances are I'll never be able to verify this story. It may be completely factual; yet why did only Rachel know these details? Could she have unknowingly mixed in some details of a story from another line of her family? Rebecca's obituary does say she was born in Franklin county. The obituary of her sister, Bediah, states that she was born in Metamora, also in Franklin county. Yet, their father would have died in the 1840s, and I think the Indians had been removed from Indiana by that time, though I could be wrong. I'm still working with Franklin county records, but so far, no luck.

But I've gotten off the track. Remember, contact the older members of the clan as soon as possible. If you put off making contact too long, you'll be reading their death notices in the paper, and good prospects for vital information will have been lost forever. Don't be shy. Many of these older relatives are lonely and would be thrilled at the chance to meet you and show you the family's relics. If they are physically able to travel, and you are thoughtful enough to take them to the graveyards, they may show you where many of your ancestors are buried.

If you don't have a car, you're at a disadvantage, since so much of your research will consist of little trips here and there: to cemeteries, to various county seat libraries, and to the many courthouses. Without

a car, you will have to write much more correspondence. Writing letters isn't the very best way to gather
facts, but a reasonably good job can be done this way
if that's your only recourse.

In many county seats there lives one elderly
person whom the local inhabitants consider the
"county historian." This person is usually a very
alert oldster who either knows and remembers many
early residents or is a collector of county historical
facts. The one that comes to my mind, Virgil Davis,
lived in Brookville, Indiana. When he died, he was in
the process of making indices for the volumes of early
newspapers printed in that county seat over many
years. How valuable his information would have
been! I deeply regret the recent death of this
knowledgeable gentleman, though I met him only
once. He showed me where to find my great-
grandmother's death notice in the newspaper files at
the courthouse, and he helped me greatly in other
ways.

Make contact with this local wise man or
woman; you may be astounded by what he or she is
able to dig up on your ancestors. If there is such a
person in the community, the personnel in the offices
of the courthouse or public library will usually
know; he or she probably spends a good deal of time
in these public buildings gathering data and
compiling historical articles.

3

Public Libraries
and Cemeteries

Although I am a firm believer in thrift, I did not combine these two subjects into one chapter simply to save paper. The fact is that cemetery listings are usually found at the library. But not just any library. The best place to begin your research is the public library in the county seat. You will find all the library's material on county origins, early inhabitants and local history in one section of this library. Early newspapers are usually stored in another section if the library has such a collection. These newspapers are somewhat fragile because of their age, so you'll probably have to ask the librarian in order even to see them.

The special historical department of the library may be called the Genealogical Section, the County

Historical Department or some other departmental name. This section may contain a few family histories, but there is sure to be at least one county history, an early atlas, perhaps a graveyard listing (compiled by the local chapter of the DAR or some other organization), and various other volumes about the county in earlier times. The three most important volumes for our purposes are the *county history* or histories, *the atlas* and the *cemetery listing*. There may be a general index that covers two or more of these sources; use it first. Keep in mind that the county history volume may cover more than one county; a few include three or four. And be sure to bring along a list of names of the ancestors you expect or hope to find.

Now that I've covered what you are likely to find in the county seat public library, let me qualify this somewhat. A few counties have little to offer the genealogist in their libraries. One that comes to mind is the county seat of Liberty, in Union County, Indiana. Formed from sections taken from established surrounding counties, Union County got a late start. It never had much industrial growth and remained mostly agricultural. The newspapers throughout the years have tended to be weeklies. The public library is a small one and has no county historical volumes to speak of. However, few counties fit this description, so let's get back to the more common ones.

COUNTY HISTORIES

Most county histories were printed by subscription. What does this mean? Well, if your ancestor or one of his kin (or in-laws) paid the going price, a sketch of his life was included in the county history. If he and his kin were poor, or thought the price too great for the benefit, you won't find a sketch of his life in the county history. In this case, he or his predecessors may be casually mentioned as members of a certain church, as residents of a named village, or as neighbors of some person in a sketch of that person. The sketches contain various facts on the life of the person being covered, such as birth dates, who a man married and when, a list of children, and possibly their birth dates or other data. It may even list the person's parents and in-laws, with details for them, or it may tell which state in the East the families originally came from. Very rarely a photograph of the subject will be included.

As you may have noticed, I have consistently referred to the subjects of county history sketches as "he." The reason for this is that men, as property owners, were usually the ones subscribing to those histories.

The front section of the county history will usually break the county down into various townships and give historical facts on villages, agriculture, churches, fraternal organizations, and so on. You may find your ancestors mentioned under any of these topics.

County histories usually contain a small index, either in the front or back of the volume or set. Use it but don't depend entirely on it, for it usually contains only the names of the subjects of the sketches, topical headings, and chapter titles. A good many names found within a sketch are not included in the index. The wife (or wives), her parents, the daughter's husband, and many others may not be named in the index. Also, the names scattered through the front portion of the history—the part containing the history of the towns, churches, lodges, and the elected officials—may not appear in the index. After comparing the index against your own list of names, go through the volume, not reading it, but scanning it for names.

County histories are notorious for their mistakes, but just because these volumes contain errors is no reason to eliminate them as valuable sources of information. Tombstones, deed records, wills and other sources can later be used to correct mistakes. Some people say things like "I don't bother with the county histories, they're a bunch of bunk," and "I can't believe anything I find in the deed records, so I never use them." However, once you are aware of the county history's deficiencies, you can use it as a guide to steer you in the right direction. Then use other sources to correct for the errors you may find.

COUNTY ATLAS

The old atlas resembles a condensed version of the front section of the county history and will probably not name your ancestor directly. Check through it anyway, as it does include names of village inhabitants. The most valuable parts of the atlas, in my estimation, are the township maps. These show who the owners of the sections of land within the township were at the time the atlas was published. Using these township maps you can locate land owned by your ancestor at any given time and look it up in the deed records when you go to the courthouse (Chapter 4).

If you find your ancestor in one of these townships, you may want a copy of that particular map. Many libraries now have a copier of some sort and will make a copy for you at a reasonable cost. If, however, the original is in color, the colors sometimes confuse the copy machine and do not reproduce clearly. Then you'll have to go over parts of the copy with a black ink ballpoint pen. If you have a camera, copy equipment and color film, you can make your own copies.

CEMETERY LISTINGS

Check through the cemetery listings, using your previously compiled list of family names. The information contained in most listings is taken directly from the tombstones and omits both unmarked graves and graves where markers were put in place after the listing was made. There is not much to say about this source; you will either find your ancestor listed or you will not.

If your ancestor is not listed, there is some further digging you can do. Small cemeteries usually come under the supervision of some nearby large cemetery, but family graveyards on farms are only included in the listings when the compilers know of their existence. If you are fairly certain your ancestor is buried in a certain cemetery, you can find the exact lot if the ancestor was buried there after that cemetery started keeping books on grave locations. The caretaker will probably have to assist you in the search, since he will be familiar with the layout of the cemetery. For very old unmarked graves, the caretaker and his records will probably not be able to help you much. Most graveyards kept no books in the early days.

Once you have found some ancestors in the county seat library's cemetery listings, you'll probably want to go to the cemeteries to see the graves, record their inscriptions, and take pictures. If you are going to photograph grave stones, be sure to bring along a piece of chalk, and maybe a bit of charcoal, to make the engraving on the old stones stand out. Should the sun be wrong for snapping some of the stones, you may have to make a second trip.

Fig. 1 In this photograph of a tombstone, both chalk and soft-leaded pencil were needed to make the letters stand out.

Some of the other volumes included in this section of the library cover only important events in the history of the county and mention only such prominent citizens as mayors and lawyers. Leaf through them anyway, just to be on the safe side.

BOOKS ON GENEALOGY

Books on the subject of genealogy itself will probably not be kept in the same section of the library as the local genealogies and county historical volumes. It is more likely that a separate location will be set aside for books containing general directions for researching the family tree. Along with such books you will find volumes listing family names for which genealogies have been compiled. I will give you a rundown on the more important general genealogy titles in my library. Your library may not have all the volumes, but it should have most of them.

The Abridged Compendium of American Genealogy First Families of America, is edited by Frederick A. Virkus and published by F. A. Virkus & Company, Genealogical Publishers, Chicago, Illinois. We have a series of volumes of *The Abridged Compendium* at our local library, each volume covering a certain year and indexed separately. The numbering system within each volume uses number 1 to represent the subject of the record and number 2 to indicate his parents. The grandparents of the subject in both lines of descent are numbered 3, his great-grandparents in all lines of descent numbered 4, and so on.

You will find the *Lineage Book—National Society Of The Daughters Of The American Colonists* in volumes published by various printers over the years. Each volume covered more than one year. Also through the years various persons have been compilers; the latest volumes were compiled by Josephine W. Vincent of Annandale, Virginia. My local library has a long series of them, with a few volumes missing here and there. Members of the society are entered with an individual number, and his or her lineage is traced.

The Year Book Of The Society of Indiana Pioneers is in soft cover volumes and contains historical articles, a roster of members with their ancestral list, and a listing of deceased members. It is printed by order of the Board of Governors of that society.

The Hoosier Genealogist is published quarterly by the Genealogical Section of the Indiana Historical Society, 140 North Senate Avenue, Indianapolis, Indiana 46204. You must be a member to receive it, but local libraries of county seats usually have copies as does the state library in Indianapolis. Members also receive the *Indiana Historical Bulletin*, the quarterly *Indiana Magazine of History* and other publications of the society. The annual membership fee is ten dollars per calendar year. Other items for sale by the society are listed in the back inside cover of *The Hoosier Genealogist* and include federal census listings, early marriage listings for certain Indiana counties, early wills and executor's records, early county maps, and other listings and abstracts.

Thirty Thousand Names of Immigrants (In Pennsylvania from 1727 to 1776) was compiled by I. Daniel Rupp and published by the Genealogical Publishing Company of Baltimore, Maryland in 1965. It contains names of German, Swiss, Dutch and French immigrants from the towns, counties and settlements in Pennsylvania. It also contains: church lists, an interpretation of names, an index of the names found throughout the volume and an index to ships arriving at Philadelphia.

OLD NEWSPAPER FILES

At the public library of most larger county seats, usually hidden away from the main flow of traffic, you will find a file of old newspapers. Because they are old, it is not desirable to have them out where everyone, including children, will handle them. Don't use this file when you first start out researching; wait until you have collected enough dates and estimated dates to make the search fruitful. Otherwise, you will be coming back to this same source again and again as you gain new names to look for and new dates to check. The papers shouldn't be handled that much.

Some of these old newspapers may be bound together into volumes, taking in a year or two of issues. These are easier to handle without too much danger of damage to the fragile sheets. In many instances, old papers were made with a paper of better quality than they are now, and it's only their age that makes them fragile. When today's newspapers get that old, they'll crumble at the touch.

State libraries sometimes have files of early newspapers also; this source and the National Archives in Washington, D.C., will be covered in Chapters 6 and 9 respectively. Some of the materials in both places are available on microfilm—a great protection for the actual documents. My own local library has recently discussed the microfilming of the old newspapers of their collection. At present, they are proposing to put only the later issues on film. I hope that all the old issues will be placed on microfilm before the project is ended.

DEATH NOTICES AND OBITUARIES

In the older newspapers, say from 1850 to 1900, the most important thing you'll be after are the obituaries and death notices. Usually births were not recorded in a special column, as they are today. Some births did get into the paper through the various other columns, such as local blurbs from the smaller villages of the county. They usually revealed very little, except that John Bumpkin became a father again—information hardly worth searching for. If you are like me it will be awfully easy to get sidetracked in these columns and national news items and to loose too much valuable time just reading. Go through each paper quickly, scanning for death notices and obituaries, which may be on any page including the front page; that's if you have a great deal of time. Should you be limited to a one-day stay at the library, have a list of events and persons made up beforehand, with their dates or probable dates. Seek out only those issues dated within a week after the event.

If you are lucky enough, the library will have its file of papers indexed. If you are still luckier, they will be on microfilm, thus providing you the same material but without risk of damage to the actual papers. Constantly remember that thief of valuable time—reading of columns and articles not pertinent to your search for family facts. You'll be tempted; you may even suddenly become aware that you have been reading waste material for an hour or so. Get back to the right method of research immediately.

Death notices give the important facts concerning the person involved: the day of death, sometimes the wife's maiden name, the day of the funeral, the place of burial, and a list of those left to mourn. Other details may be included that will prove useful to you.

Obituaries are put in the paper after the burial, sometimes a year later. They contain a bit more information for your purposes, usually a brief life sketch. You are more apt to find the parents' names and the place of birth in the obituary, as well as more exact data on the children of the deceased. Obituaries also contain a good deal of flattery and praise for the individual. Reading obituaries, one gets the impression that no sinner ever died, only the righteous. So don't forget to read them with a grain of salt.

4

The County Courthouse

The county courthouse is probably your most valuable source of information. This includes the county courthouse where your family first settled upon entering the country, the various courthouses where the family spread out, and the courthouse where your family first settled in your state.

The information found in a county courthouse contains dates, is fairly accurate and in many instances is very detailed. Let's discuss exactly what we can expect to find in this vault of historical data. Although from county to county and state to state the requirements for recordkeeping may vary, the different offices within a courthouse remain pretty much the same.

THE RECORDER'S OFFICE

The county recorder's office keeps information on deeds, mortgages, discharges, plotting of cities and towns, sometimes adoptions, sometimes divorces and possibly wills. The reason I say "sometimes," is that there are certain records that may be found in either the recorder's or the clerk's offices.

The deed records are probably the most informative of the collection, so we'll take them first. In the county where I reside, the recorder has them broken down into three main divisions: Deed Records, Deed Record Town Lots and Deed Record Miscellaneous. There is also a volume of Deed Record Partitions. The Deed Records in my county started by encompassing all land transactions; later on (around the 1860s) the transactions of lots within a village or town were recorded in the Deed Record Town Lots volumes.

An entry in one of these books may be short and offer very little information, or it may cover several pages and be loaded with goodies that will keep you scribbling notes for a long while. Normally they provide dates as well as any or all of the following information on a given piece of property: who owned it and is giving up his or her right to it (grantor); who purchased it and is gaining the right to it (grantee); the person whose land it originally was a part of; in what county and state the giver and receiver reside; the names of parents, children or spouses; the location of the land within the county in directional parts, quarters, sections, and township number; and the number of acres. Sometimes it will give the date of death of the original owner; occasionally it will quote a Probate Court Order Book, giving you the book number and page. When heirs are listed, the children are named; and when an heir has died, the children of that heir may be named. The purchase price of the land is normally included, and it may run from one dollar and services rendered to thousands of dollars. There is no end to the variety of these recordings.

The Deed Record Town Lots volumes cover the same kinds of transactions, but they are usually confined to towns or cities and deal with numbered lots of designated additions or plots within that town.

Deed Record Partitions deal with the division of an estate among the heirs, and designate who gets how much and where it is located. The entries will be dated and usually start out: Mary Bumpkin versus John Bumpkin, Elvira Bumpkin, Lucinda Bumpkin, Ezra Anyname, and so on.

The Deed Record Miscellaneous volumes contain agreements between individuals, or partnerships or both, such as the release of mineral rights or rights to drill, rights given to a certain railroad, and countless odd items you couldn't imagine.

Normally each of the various deed volumes will

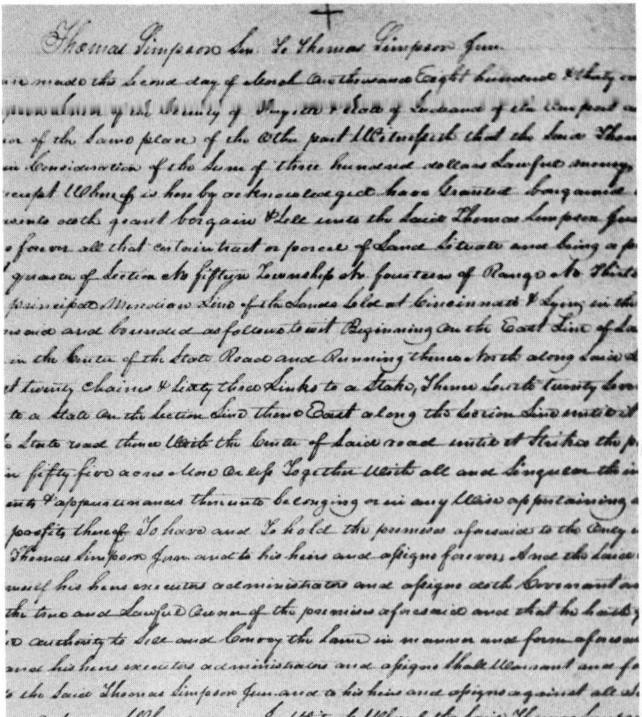

Fig. 2 A photograph of an early deed record entry, 1831.

be indexed. The indices are not too accurate, and names are often misspelled; be meticulous and keep a sharp eye out for similar-sounding names. Fortunately there is generally a series of volumes that provide an index to all the deed records I have mentioned. This also has its inaccuracies, but allows you to cover the whole group of records in somewhat chronological order. This set of indices is divided into two categories: grantor, the one who sells or relinquishes his right; and grantee, the receiver or gainer of the granted right.

The Mortgage Records will seem like a vast set of volumes, but if you have my luck, you won't find very many entries involving your kin. This will depend on whether your ancestors frequently got themselves too deeply into debt. A pertinent entry may provide valuable information as to heirs and so on.

I'll discuss wills when I get to the county clerk.

The recording of discharges doesn't carry too far back and depended on the individual to bring his discharge in to be recorded. The records of adoptions and divorces need little explanation; they can be a source of information when such situations developed in your family lines.

Let's backtrack to the time when your state was just a territory. When the lands were opened up, the settlers received grants for pieces of land (about 160 acres in my area). These original land grants are recorded in my courthouse in two volumes: the Deed

Book, Prior To; and the Tract Book, Fayette County, #1. After statehood, the transactions were recorded in the deed books previously mentioned.

THE CLERK'S OFFICE

Now let's walk over to the county clerk's office. Here we find the following: probate court order books, civil court order books, marriage books, marriage application books, the book of wills or record of wills, and boxes of receipts from the settlement of estates; this is how things are arranged in my state and locality. There may also be, as is the case in my courthouse, another set of volumes called Probate Court Order Books, Complete.

In the general court order books, the information you'll find will consist of cases where the estate of a deceased is ordered to be sold or divided up amongst the heirs. There may be a reference to a certain deed record book, giving page number. Occasionally, the date of death for the deceased is given; heirs are usually named or indicated. The entries are usually dated, and an administrator is usually named. Sometimes the ages of any minors concerned are also given. There may be from two to ten or more entries on the same case, before it is finally settled; it may cover several years.

The civil court order books are not as useful for your purposes, but they do establish a person within a locality if you can find the infomation. These books cover civil suits and legal actions. I corresponded with one lady, who found the most accurate, and indeed, the most flavorful material on her grandfather in the civil court order books. She said she found her ancestor to be a liar and a troublemaker. Of course there are two parties involved in a lawsuit; your ancestor may be suing. In such cases you may discover injustices suffered by your ancestors and find out how they were legally resolved.

There is generally a set of indices which covers both parties in the probate court order series, as well as an index within each volume.

The marriage books are self-explanatory; they are indexed and give the names of the two people involved, the date of the entry, the date of the marriage, who conducted the marriage, the county official's name, and sometimes the counties in which each of the two people lived. The marriage application books also give the names of parents (and sometimes more information), but they do not go back as far as the marriage books; such information wasn't required in the early days.

The book of wills or will record is very useful; but as you know, many people live, accumulate wealth and die without ever making a will. Also, old wills read very differently from each other, offering widely varying amounts of information. Some of them just say "I leave everything to my beloved wife" and do not name her or any of the children; others

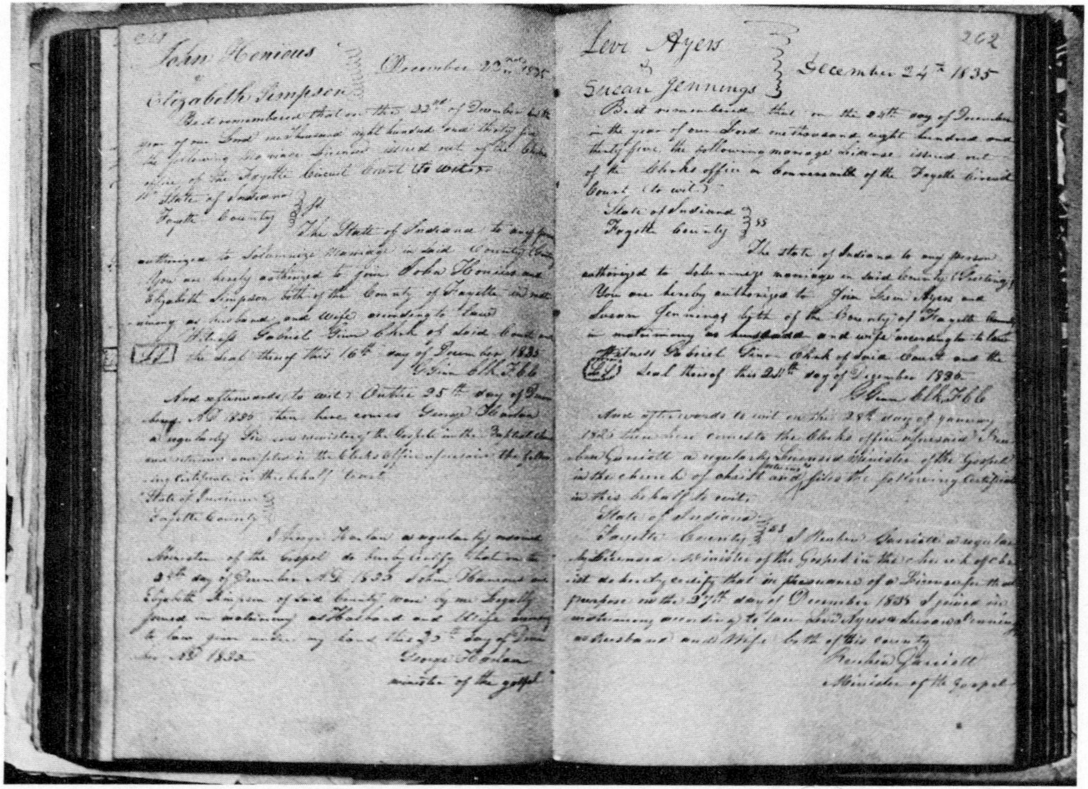

Fig. 3 A photograph of pages from an early marriage book dated 1835

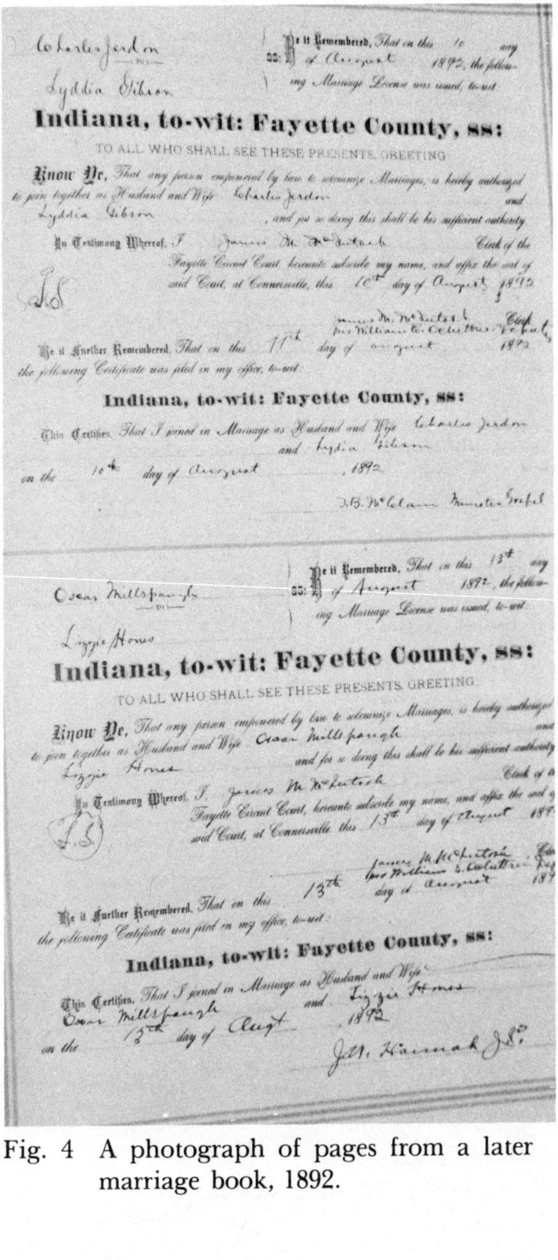

Charles Jerdon
—to—
Lydia Gibson

ss: Be it Remembered, That on this 10 day of August 1892, the following Marriage License was issued, to-wit:

Indiana, to-wit: Fayette County, ss:

TO ALL WHO SHALL SEE THESE PRESENTS, GREETING:

Know Ye, That any person empowered by law to solemnize Marriages, is hereby authorized to join together as Husband and Wife Charles Jerdon and Lydia Gibson, and for so doing this shall be his sufficient authority.

In Testimony Whereof, I, James M. McIntosh Clerk of the Fayette Circuit Court, hereunto subscribe my name, and affix the seal of said Court, at Connersville, this 10th day of August 1892

L.S.

James M. McIntosh Clerk
per William E. Ochiltree Deputy

Be it Further Remembered, That on this 11th day of August 1892 the following Certificate was filed in my office, to-wit:

Indiana, to-wit: Fayette County, ss:

This Certifies, That I joined in Marriage as Husband and Wife Charles Jerdon and Lydia Gibson on the 10th day of August, 1892

J.B. McClain Minister Gospel

Oscar Millspaugh
—to—
Lizzie Howe

ss: Be it Remembered, That on this 13th day of August 1892, the following Marriage License was issued, to-wit:

Indiana, to-wit: Fayette County, ss:

TO ALL WHO SHALL SEE THESE PRESENTS, GREETING:

Know Ye, That any person empowered by law to solemnize Marriages, is hereby authorized to join together as Husband and Wife Oscar Millspaugh and Lizzie Howe and for so doing this shall be his sufficient authority.

In Testimony Whereof, I, James M. McIntosh Clerk of the Fayette Circuit Court, hereunto subscribe my name, and affix the seal of said Court, at Connersville, this 13th day of August 18[illegible]

L.S.

James M. McIntosh Clerk
per William E. Ochiltree Deputy

Be it Further Remembered, That on this 13th day of August 18[illegible] the following Certificate was filed in my office, to-wit:

Indiana, to-wit: Fayette County, ss:

This Certifies, That I joined in Marriage as Husband and Wife Oscar Millspaugh and Lizzie Howe on the 13th day of Aug 1892

J.H. Hannah J.P.

Fig. 4 A photograph of pages from a later marriage book, 1892.

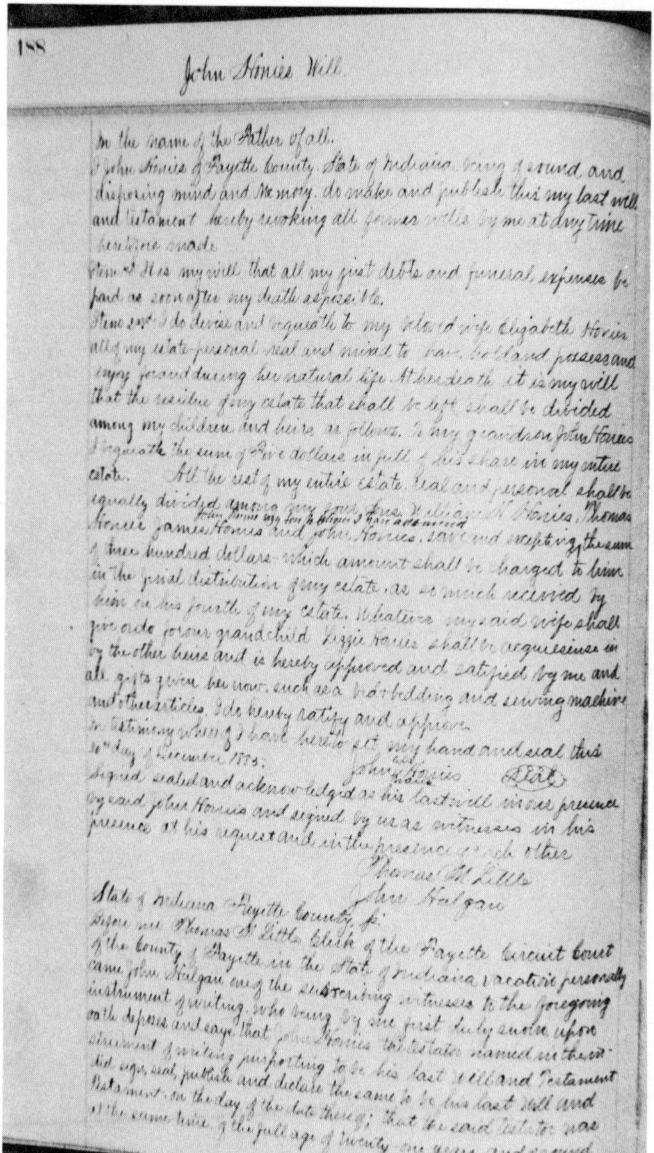

188

John Honies Will

In the name of the Father of all.
I John Honies of Fayette County State of Indiana being of sound and disposing mind and memory do make and publish this my last will and testament hereby revoking all former wills by me at any time heretofore made
Item 1st It is my will that all my just debts and funeral expenses be paid as soon after my death as possible.
Item 2nd I do devise and bequeath to my beloved wife Elizabeth Honies all of my estate personal real and mixed to have hold and possess and enjoy for and during her natural life. At her death it is my will that the residue of my estate that shall be left shall be divided among my children and heirs as follows. To my grandson John Honies I bequeath the sum of Five dollars in full of his share in my entire estate. All the rest of my entire estate real and personal shall be equally divided among my four sons William H. Honies, Thomas Honies James Honies and John Honies, save and excepting the sum of three hundred dollars (John Honies my son to whom I have advanced) which amount shall be charged to him in the final distribution of my estate, as so much received by him on his fourth of my estate. Whatever my said wife shall provide for our grandchild Lizzie Honies shall be acquiesced in by the other heirs and is hereby approved and satisfied by me and all gifts given her now, such as a bed & bedding and sewing machine and other articles. I do hereby ratify and approve.
In testimony whereof I have hereto set my hand and seal this 10th day of December 1873.
John his mark Honies (Seal)
Signed sealed and acknowledged as his last will in our presence by said John Honies and signed by us as witnesses in his presence at his request and in the presence of each other
Thomas H. Little
John Halgan
State of Indiana Fayette County, ss:
Before me Thomas H. Little Clerk of the Fayette Circuit Court of the County of Fayette in the State of Indiana vacation personally came John Halgan one of the subscribing witnesses to the foregoing instrument of writing who being by me first duly sworn upon oath deposes and says that John Honies the testator named in the instrument of writing purporting to be his last Will and Testament did sign, seal, publish and declare the same to be his last Will and Testament on the day of the date thereof; that the said testator was at the same time of the full age of twenty one years and of sound

Fig. 5 A photograph of a page from a will book, 1875.

name each individual and specify what he or she is to inherit.

In most cases, the steel cases that contain such items as receipts and bills paid are of no value to you. Usually they are all mixed up, and the dating of the drawer labels is inaccurate. You should be able to go from the settlement of an estate in the probate court order book to an indicated drawer and find the receipts concerning that settlement; often you won't be able to.

There are other volumes in the clerk's office, such as the license fee book, but you will probably find little to aid your cause in these. However, while you're at the courthouse, check to be sure that an additional file of old newspapers is not being stored here. Sometimes these are kept at the courthouse as well as the public library.

As for the other offices in the courthouse, I wouldn't bother with them unless you are led there by one of the probate court order books or other volumes I have mentioned.

Remember: don't make notes, add your written comments, or dog-ear the pages of the volumes at the courthouse; you would be doing a disservice to authentic historical documents. Maybe someday the material in all county courthouses will be on microfilm; then, finally, the documents will be in no danger from everyday use.

5

Correspondence and Genealogical Columns

GENEALOGICAL COLUMNS

Most large newspapers, such as those in state capitals, have a genealogical column of one kind or another. It is usually, but not always, carried in the Sunday edition. Some larger cities also carry a similar column in the local paper. As they are generally reliable, I'll deal mostly with these sources, even though there are sheets, newsletters and papers put out by individuals that print similar information for a specific area or family.

In using newspaper columns one should follow certain guidelines. In the first place, don't clutch at straws by writing to every newspaper on the hope that some of your ancestors traveled through that area. If, however, you found a lead in a deed record book that placed a line of the clan in a certain county in, say, Oregon, then a query to a column printed in that state's paper might get you some valuable replies.

So that we don't lose sight of our objective, let me remind you that the reason for sending a query to one of these columns is to get in touch with descendants of the people mentioned in your query, or a person who knows that a line of that family existed there. Unrelated persons will sometimes do a favor and find information or contacts for you. I have been helped this way in the past and I have aided others in a like manner.

When you send an inquiry to one of these columns, don't send it without any details: you'll probably get no answer. You should also acquire, if possible, a copy of the paper and column before sending out an inquiry. You should be familiar with the requirements of that particular column's editor before contacting the newspaper.

An example of a misguided inquiry is one saying "I am collecting data on the Jones and Dogwood families." Let's say Bernard Smith takes the Sunday paper and lives next door to Abraham Jones who doesn't take a Sunday paper. If Smith read the above query, he probably wouldn't feel it worth mentioning to Jones; and if he should, Jones would more than likely answer that there are a lot of Jones families, unrelated. You just might get a nibble on the Dogwood line, since the name is unusual enough so that there shouldn't be too many unrelated lines of that family name. Whenever you send an inquiry, *you must include enough information so that a descendant will recognize his ancestor.* For example: "I am seeking information and contact with descendants of George X. Jones, born about 1839, died January 2, 1911, married June 3, 1860, in Clackamus County, Oregon, to Lucinda Dogwood, born December 9, 1843, in Jackson County, Kentucky, died May 8, 1891. Children: George Jr., born September 11, 1863, died December 4, 1864; Amanda, born September 9, 1865, died July 4, 1890, married July 4, 1885, to Robert Q. Quick."

This gives readers the kind of specific data that will ring a bell when a Jones descendant or a Dogwood distant relative reads the column. Let me caution you, however, against sending too much information. If you send a three-page letter, printed, it will be broken up into several segments by the person who writes the column and be printed on separate dates. Due to an uneven volume of inquiries, which sometimes results in a great quantity at one time, genealogy columns are occasionally months behind. Your three or more pages of questions complicates the procedure of the editor tremendously. Furthermore, you will have sent along with your letter only one stamped, self-addressed envelope for notification of your inquiry's publication date, but the inquiry will be printed on more than one date.

When writing to various newspapers, don't worry about abbreviations, for the column editor will abbreviate the inquiry to keep the column condensed but understandable. If you have estimated the date of birth or some other dates, make that plain.

You may get no answers from a given query; you may get two or three letters that are of little or no help to your line of the family name; you may get many letters, some of which will be of great help. Answer them all. Postage may be going up, but you owe an answer to anyone thoughtful enough to write. Don't be too surprised if you get an answer to a query of yours that appeared two or three years earlier. The correspondent may have been sent an old column by a friend or relative who saved it. Also, the person could have found your query in a column pasted in a scrapbook or collection of queries in a public or state library.

Sometimes your previous hunches, or even data from a county history, will be either verified or proven wrong by one of your correspondents. Much of your researching can be accomplished with the help of information obtained in correspondence. So by all means use this method.

When sending an inquiry to a column, or when contacting any person for the first time by mail, enclose a stamped, self-addressed return envelope. You will want to be notified by the column editor as to when your query will appear, and you will definitely want an answer from whatever individual you are contacting about the ancestors. Some people always enclose a self-addressed evelope, no matter how long they have corresponded with a party. It shouldn't be necessary after you and your correspondent have established a reasonably close acquaintance, but it generally helps to make sure of a reply.

Don't be a selfish collector of data; give as well as take. You must reveal details in order to get information from most people. The quickest way to turn a correspondent off is to let him think you are going to drain him of information while telling him nothing. I touched on this problem briefly in the first chapter, but it bears repeating. It doesn't hurt your cause any to give a person some vital details on his line of the family, and it may get you considerable information from him on various lines of your clan. Being congenial forms a bond between you and your newly acquired cousins as well as friendships with unrelated persons with whom you correspond.

Genealogical newsletters, genealogical news-papers, and other specialized sources are often of little help to you unless your ancestors lived in the area that is covered by the bulletin. Many of these papers are concerned mostly with a certain clan or family group. The price for subscribing to them is often quite high. It makes one wonder whether some of the writers of the bulletins aren't more interested in making money than in sharing information.

There are some rental libraries in certain areas, such as Preble County, Ohio, that can aid you greatly if you know that a certain ancestor of yours spent a number of years in that area. Naturally, there is a fee for using their materials, but if you can't possibly travel to that area to research the actual records, joining a rental library would be next best. Don't join one of these library clubs in an area where your predecessors never lived; you'd be clutching at straws again. In Chapter 8 I'll cover some of these areas that were collecting points for people on their way west.

There was a time when you could write to the postmaster of a town or city, enclose a stamped return envelope, and that postmaster would send you a list of residents from the telephone book or city directory for a given family name. That time is no more. The volume of mail is too great these days and the cost of operating mail service has skyrocketed. They were not required to do it then; it was just a courteous gesture on their part. Now they have little time for such courtesies.

CORRESPONDENCE AND RECORD KEEPING

In another chapter I mentioned that letters from correspondents are a valuable source of information and that a file should be created for them. Each letter should have a date on it, and the file should be arranged according to these dates. The most recent dates first; the oldest dates last. Since your correspondents will very often pass on the family stories that have been handed down to them, this file will contain the human side of your ancestors, the living moments that county histories and public records from the courthouses seldom show.

In my own case, my mother's cousins once told me about their grandmother, who was also my mother's grandmother. Grandmother Rebecca was orphaned at an early age and raised by her Aunt Mary—they called her Aunt Mary though she may not have been a blood relative. Rebecca's expenses were paid for by her brother, a riverboat captain working out of Evansville, Indiana. One day one of Rebecca's friends talked her into charging some ribbons and material at the local store to make doll dresses. The storekeeper thought that the child's aunt knew of the transaction, since there was an agreement between the storekeeper and Aunt Mary that the items she bought for Rebecca were to be written up and paid for by Captain Richard on his frequent visits. However, this did not include frivolous items such as materials for doll clothes. When Aunt Mary found out, she scolded Rebecca and told her, "We'll keep the materials until your brother comes, and he will decide whether to return them or not. But in any case, they will certainly not be used for making doll clothes."

Life is made up of the endless procession of

51

trivial happenings, punctuated by important facts. You won't find many such glimpses of actual living in the records. The county histories have a few little human interest touches, but most other records show just legal or statistical details. One of the census reports listed Rebecca's brother and sister living in the household of John and Mary _____, so it's logical to suppose that at another time Rebecca probably lived with them. I think you'll agree that it's these little unimportant stories that bring you closer to your ancestor.

CARBON COPIES OF YOUR OUTGOING LETTERS

Why make and keep carbon copies of your outgoing letters? From my own experience, many times I've been writing to someone about the family lines and suddenly been confronted with "Have I said that once before?" or "Did I ask that question in another previous letter?" If your correspondent's letters and the carbon copy replies are filed and in order, a short hunt through that particular folder or section of the file will reveal the answer. It saves repeating yourself time and again, and it helps prevent your omitting from your correspondence a bit of data that you mistakenly thought you had already sent.

I keep my letters in manila folders, with the family name that the letters deal with marked at the

top left and the name and address of my correspondent at the top right. (See Figures 8 and 9.) The letters
are kept in a neat, easily-used stack, with a two-
pronged paper clasp at the top affixing the stack to
the folder. A hole puncher is necessary for a neat job
of making the required holes in the tops of the sheets
of paper and the folder.

If your correspondent writes you a letter on
smaller lined stationery or scraps of paper, as some of
mine have, just staple or scotch tape them and the
envelope to a sheet of typing paper for uniformity in
your file; it keeps your folder more usable. You don't
have to use this particular system for filing your
letters, but you should definitely employ some
system. A box or pile of letters in their envelopes is
not satisfactory, to say nothing of the possibility of
misplacing some of your letters that may contain
valuable data.

In corresponding, beware of the salesmen. Some
people just naturally get dollar signs in their eyes if
they think they have something you want. They may
have old letters written by a cousin or a photograph,
Bible or some other article belonging to your
ancestor or his or her kinsman. Money may not even
be mentioned directly, but it's there between the
lines. It makes no difference that the article is of no
use to them. It may have come into the possession of
their family by a second or third marriage of their
ancestor. I'm not saying not to purchase such an

article, for there may be information contained in the letters or Bible that you will want. If you think you should have the data or object, ask the correspondent whether it's for sale and for what price. But for the most part, try not to cater to greed if you run into it. Just try to get the information you want. If someone has some old letters, ask the person to have them xeroxed, and pay him or her something extra for their trouble, but don't buy the material or article at an exorbitant price. Also, don't borrow old, priceless photographs and the like through the mail. When I say priceless, I mean irreplaceable. Believe me, things do get lost in the mail. Wait until you can visit the person and take along your camera and copy equipment. If you do borrow photographs or negatives, have the copying or printing done at an early date in your home town and return the originals as soon as possible. The longer you retain them, the greater the chance of something happening to them.

Go through your correspondence folders and reread the letters once in a while; I do. I have found several answers to questions on my ancestors that puzzled me, even some unexpected marriage dates, by rereading old letters. Sometimes I had missed or forgotten something, or hadn't recognized the information as pertinent at the time I received the letter. Later, after I had done additional research and uncovered new names, the bits of information contained in the old letters took on new significance.

6

State Libraries

After you have visited the county libraries within striking distance of your home, the next stop will be determined by geography and common sense. If your state library is nearby, or closer than some of the counties you would like to search in, this is the place to go. If it is very far away, travel to your surrounding counties first. Remember, the county courthouse is your primary source of information. The state library comes next.

The state library, in most states, will be located downtown in the capital city of the state and not very far from the other government buildings. If your family lived in that state for several generations, be prepared to spend a week or two in the library gathering data. No doubt, if you know that the family lived in the state, you will also know which counties to check. Unless they are prohibitively distant, you should have already gone to the pertinent counties and checked the sources there prior to visiting the state library. If you do not know which counties to check, try the Civil War archives in the state library to see whether one of your ancestors was in service during that war. If so, his card will usually tell from which county or town he came.

This source of information is to me the second most important one, the county courthouses being first. You will be astonished at the vast quantity of material within this storehouse of recorded state history, but you won't be interested in every department in the building: just those relating to genealogy. In describing what you'll find there, I'll be constantly thinking in terms of the one I know best in Indianapolis. The address of that one is:

> The Indiana State Library
> Genealogy Division
> 140 North Senate Avenue
> Indianapolis, Indiana 46204

In some state libraries, you aren't at liberty to handle the volumes and material yourself, so you really can't become familiar with the actual documents in the library. I visited one state library where I had to furnish details to a librarian, who went back to the files or indices and did the checking for me on one of my ancestors. She came back soon and said she could find nothing on the person. I was sure only a feeble attempt had been made and found the incident very frustrating. It may have been one of the librarian's bad days, or she just may have been the kind of person who didn't care to put forth the effort to find the desired information. When I go to a state library or other source, I want very much to search for data myself. But this is just a matter of luck; some places you can, some places you can't.

When you enter the genealogy department of the state library, there will be a sign-in sheet for your name, address and the family names you will be researching. It's one of their requirements and can be helpful to you at times. I know I'm not the only one who checks back through those sheets to see who is looking for data on what family name. Also, someone else may be looking for information on the same family you are, see your name on one of those sign-in sheets, and contact you with some valuable data on your kin.

Normally, you'll find the following sources in the state library: county histories; old county atlases; volumes of compiled family histories; listings of marriages, births and deaths taken from county records; city, county and other area histories from other states; census reports; passenger lists of the ports of entry (within volumes on those states);

volumes on church and cultural settlements; Civil War archives; and collections of vintage newspapers from cities all over the state. I will briefly cover each of these, but the most important for our purposes will be the census reports, the Civil War archives, and the newspaper collections.

Fortunately, there are indices covering this multitude of material. Generally one index card file covers the census reports prior to 1850. It is set up alphabetically by head of household and gives the census year and county. The next index set covers the census of 1850 and is set up similarly. The more recent census reports run up to and including the one for 1890. There is also an index for heads of households who died within the census year. There is a further index file for books and listings found on the library's shelves. This is set up alphabetically by the names of people found within those volumes and contains symbols telling the librarian where to locate it. When you find what you need, there are small printed sheets that you must fill out with the symbols of the index card (and your name); then the librarian will bring the material to you.

The county histories represent most of the counties throughout the state, though there will be some counties for which they do not have the histories. In the state library they are collected together; this can save you some needless trips to the several counties you are researching. The same applies to old county atlases. When there is more than one history on a given county, a special index volume will generally cover the histories and the atlas.

As I have stated, the listings of marriages, births and deaths are generally merely the indices from the many county courthouses and county health departments. Thus a trip may be necessary to the relevant county for complete data—a trip you would more than likely end up making anyway. These listings may be mimeographed, or they may be microfilms of the actual county indices or records. Some counties will be missing. As I explained in the first chapter, the compilation of these listings was being done by the WPA, and the project was never completed. Fire and other disasters have also ravaged courthouses and other depositories of historical data.

CENSUS REPORTS

The census reports of 1850, 1860, 1870 and 1880 are the most informative census reports available, and they are the easiest to read. The 1790 report may be in book form, but most of reports are on microfilm. Ohio, Indiana, and the other midwestern states are not included until the 1820 census. The early reports are often confusing because of their lack of details. Only the head of the family is named, the wife and children merely tallied as male or female, according to age groups. If your ancestor was named

John X. Dingbat and you find three John Dingbats listed in the pertinent county, how can you tell which Dingbat is yours? You can't tell by the other family members, since most of the time they are not named.

In the state library at Indianapolis the census reports of 1850 through 1880 are on microfilm. Being later reports, these name each member of the family living in the household as well as anyone else living in the home (housemaids, farm help, and so on). Statistics on listed individuals may include the following: sex, color and age, occupation, land value, place of birth, and information on education. The 1860 census begins providing the personal property value, while the 1880 census also records the relationship of each individual to the head of the household as well as the birthplaces of the parents of each person.

These reports go county by county, listing each township and the families contained therein. They also have an incomplete listing for 1890, a re-tally after a fire destroyed the original census. It's less readable than the four decade reports prior to it.

The city, county and area histories of other states may not list your family name, but you can often get an idea of an approximate locality for your ancestors by checking for area settlements by culture, religion and nationality.

The volumes containing passenger lists of ships at the ports of entry into the country can also be helpful, but as with other early recordings, you should have your ancestors traced and documented back to this era and point; a big handicap of these volumes is the inadequacies of the indices. Some passenger lists are also available on microfilm at the Indiana State Library. This library has, in addition, incomplete county records for some of the other states.

CIVIL WAR ARCHIVES

The Civil War archives and the newspaper archives have until recently been kept together in an area of the basement of the state library. The genealogy department is to be moved very soon into a new annex. I have not heard as yet whether the Civil War archives or the newspaper archives will also move. Within the Civil War archives is a card file of the residents who served in the Civil War. The card file of the Indiana Volunteer Units is arranged alphabetically, taken from the original muster rolls. The following information may be included: the soldier's name, rank, company and regiment, period of original enlistment, place and date of enrollment, place and date sworn into service, age, physical description, birth date and occupation. The date, place and manner of leaving the service is given. Other notations (wounds received, decorations, and so on) may also be entered.

There is a card file (arranged alphabetically) on

the Indiana Legion. This was the state militia or home guards. It too was compiled from the original muster rolls. In addition to the name of the person, it gives the legion company, periods of active duty, and age.

There is also a card file of Indiana citizens who hired substitutes. During the Civil War, if you had money you could pay someone else to go into the service in your place. The card in the file would give the name of the individual, the name of the substitute, and the unit to which he was assigned.

The archives also have the Veterans Grave Registration File for fifty-one of the ninety-two counties of Indiana. These give the name of the veteran, the war in which he served, his unit and the cemetery location. You will also find other materials on soldiers and veterans of the Civil War, and other wars, in the archives of the Indiana State Library. Two items of information that you may not find anywhere else are listed on the card of the Indiana Volunteer Units file: color of hair and color of eyes. Don't be surprised if the company and regiment given are different from what the ancestor's obituary, his tombstone or the county history said: he could have been in two or more outfits. He may have transferred from one unit to another, or he may have been in the army for more than one hitch. You probably won't come across this next situation often, but you may have heard about men who joined in one area, went AWOL, then joined up again in another town or recruiting area during the Civil War. They did this for the bonuses, which in some places were quite high. To fill their quotas, recruiting areas paid up to a thousand dollars as a bonus to entice men to join up in their area, which also enticed men to desert and reenlist elsewhere. Of course, neither your ancestor nor mine would have been so low as that!

NEWSPAPER ARCHIVES

The newspaper archives may be of great assistance to you, if you know when and where your ancestors died. State archives have some collections of old papers from various counties and some on microfilm. Very few are complete: issues are missing here and there throughout. I have already discussed the values and pitfalls of newspaper researching, so I'll not go over that again. You simply have more area than just one county at your disposal at the state library. Newspaper collections kept in the county libraries are more likely to be complete than those at the state library, except some smaller county seat libraries.

State libraries, like other sources, vary from state to state in what they have to offer and in the form in which the newspapers are preserved. They also differ in the extent of their services. One eastern state, to which I sent a request concerning an ancestor who had lived there, must have checked out their card system and sent the card information on to the hall of records of their state government. I received a letter from that office telling me what was available on my ancestor and the price for a copy of that information.

At this time there is a project under way by the Indiana State Library to microfilm old documents, publications and any written materials concerning the history of Indiana. The library is urging citizens of the state who have such papers and documents to participate in the program. The owners of the materials may choose either to keep the documents after the microfilming or to accept copies of the materials instead (the state library would then retain and preserve the originals). Almost any historical photographs, family histories, records of organizations, Bibles, letters and diaries qualify under the project.

Let me now specifically discuss a state library other than my own. I have used the service (by mail) of the Pennsylvania State Library of Harrisburg, Pennsylvania, so I shall use this one. I visited there when I was in the service, but I was en route to my next duty station at the time and could only spare a few hours. I do remember, however, that it was somewhat restricted; they did their own researching from the facts and dates I gave them. That kind of system always leaves me with a bad impression, as I've told you. Of course, I would imagine this restriction is placed on them by the state government.

Don't misunderstand my feelings on this subject. There is much to be said for the preservation of the various state, county and city volumes and document records. The issue has two sides: on the one hand, people should have the right to see and use the information of the records; and on the other, records and documents should be safeguarded from careless handlers. Both needs can be satisfied if the materials are reprinted or microfilmed. Unfortunately this means spending money. These expenditures must first be approved and the money allocated (which may take quite some time). I do believe this is the solution to the problem, and I feel certain it will eventually be done all over the nation.

The Pennsylvania State Library book collection includes major bibliographies, indices and collected genealogies, such as the *American Genealogical Index*, the *Catalog of the Newberry Library of Chicago*, Lencour's *Bibliography of Ship's Passenger Lists*, Strassburger and Hinke's *Pennsylvania German Pioneers*, Jordan's *Colonial and Revolutionary Families of Pennsylvania* and Egle's *Notes and Queries*.

Their microfilm collection includes microfilms and microcards. They have the genealogical column of the *Boston Transcript* and the American and English Genealogies in the Library of Congress on microcards; on microfilm: the United States Census of Pennsylvania (1800–1880), the 1790 census indexed and in book form, and a printed index to the 1810 census. Also on microfilm: the 1800 Special Census of Union Veterans and Widows and United States Mortality Schedules, 1850–1880, for Pennsylvania; the Maryland Census reports of 1790 to 1820; Index to Passenger Arrivals, Port of Philadelphia, 1800 to 1906; and several genealogies of Bucks County families.

Selections from the abundance of periodicals available there include: the *Pennsylvania Genealogical Magazine*, the *National Genealogical Society Magazine*, the *New England Historical and Genealogical Register* and the *DAR Magazine*.

The Pennsylvania State Library does not conduct research in response to letter inquiries and does not compile genealogies. They will search the genealogical card index for materials by surname only. Their literature refers you to the proper place for records that the library does not carry, such as births and deaths, marriage records, divorce and adoption records, naturalization records, U.S. census records for 1900 to 1960, wills, administrations, orphans court records, grantee-grantor deeds, and tax records.

The state library in Harrisburg, Pennsylvania, also includes a listing of counties of that state, giving the county seat, the date formed, the 1960 population, the census reports available on it and the county or counties from which it was formed.

This rundown on the materials of one specific state library, plus the information on the Indiana State Library, should give you a pretty good idea of what you'll find in all state libraries. As you can see, some state libraries send information by mail and some don't. It is certainly worth thirteen cents and an envelope to find out. It can save you miles of unnecessary travel.

7

Odds and Ends

Some subjects that fall outside any main topic must be discussed at some point, so I have combined them into this separate chapter.

HANDWRITING

First, let's take a look at old handwriting. You'll be running into it at the courthouse, the state library, and other research spots. Leafing through a given set of volumes at the courthouse and through documents and materials on microfilm at the state library, you see the styles of handwriting change and change again. Some of this can be attributed to the peculiarities of the individuals who made the entries over the decades in the record volumes, but we should also remember that at one period of our country's history penmanship evolved into a work of art.

The handwriting was lovely, I think you'll agree; but to those of us who did not grow up with it, it is almost unreadable. Some of the more confusing aspects of it are the double *s*, the first of which appears to be an *f*, as in the name Ross (both may have been written as modified *f*'s); the capital *J* that looks like a capital *Y*, as in Jane; the *d* that may fool you into thinking it is *el*; or the *n* that you see as a *v*. When the name Jesse appears in a document, you may think it to be Yefse, and the names Daniel and David may seem identical. The capital *S* and the capital *L*, as well as the capital *D*, are not dissimilar in appearance—fancy curls, squiggles and lines that embellish the beginning and ending of written material. (See the examples in Figure 6.)

Penmanship seemed to reach a peak of elaborateness about 1860 to 1870. When one of the older employees of the courthouse retained his job past that period, the fancy writing continues until much later. When reading old handwriting, compare a doubtful word with the writing of the surrounding pages. Soon you will become more adept at reading old handwriting. You may even come to enjoy the challenge!

YOUR FAMILY LINES

Next, I think it wise to correct a misconception

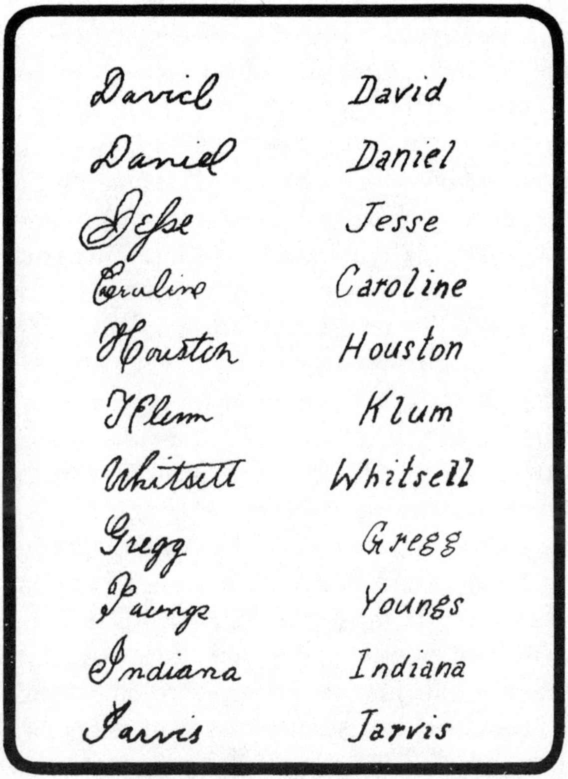

David	David
Daniel	Daniel
Jesse	Jesse
Caroline	Caroline
Houston	Houston
Klum	Klum
Whitsell	Whitsell
Gregg	Gregg
Youngs	Youngs
Indiana	Indiana
Jarvis	Jarvis

Fig. 6 Examples of the archaic writing styles found in early records and their modern equivalents.

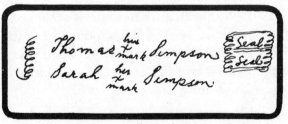

Fig. 7 A representation of "his mark" and "her mark" typical of early deed records.

about the relative importance of mother's and father's lines. Most people when they ponder checking out the family history think in terms of their father's line. It's a natural emphasis, since in our society one carries his father's name. But when you stop and analyze it no one line of your family is more important than another. Your mother's mother is just as related to you as your father's father, and, I can't resist the temptation to add, *more certain*. Remember the old adage "You may not be sure who your father was, but you know for certain who your mother was." Of course, even that statement is not entirely infallible. Some people grow up with a set of parents and find out they were adopted as babies. Now don't start to feel that since nothing is completely certain, it's no use to research your family background. We must take certain things for granted and depend on them; it's very important for our peace of mind. Just keep an open mind—things are not always as they seem to be. And remember the importance of all lines of your family when considering your genealogy.

MIXED BLOOD

In the Midwest, as in most parts of the country, those of us who work at tracing our lines back are surprised at how many nationalities we encounter in our family backgrounds. In fact, only in larger cities do you find long lines consisting of only one nationality.

Many families have passed down stories of Indian blood in their lineage. One claim may say an ancestor married a full-blooded Cherokee maiden; another may not even be that specific. However, unless the ancestor is named in a family tale, you will have a hard time proving it. As you know, each step back in search of your ancestors doubles the number of ancestral lines. Just as you have two parents, each of those parents had two—that's four; each of your grandparents had two—that's eight. You wouldn't have to go back too many generations to count hundreds of family lines. Just going back to the revolutionary war, you could easily have six to ten generations, which could mean up to a thousand or more direct ancestors and several hundred family names to be researched. So you can see how complicated it would be to track down a full-blooded Indian ancestor.

There's another hindrance to finding an Indian ancestor; there were times when it wasn't prudent to brag about having Indian blood. Too many people had lost parents or brothers and sisters from Indian raids. It certainly wasn't considered a compliment then to be known as a half-breed. These days it's a proud person who can say his great-grandmother was a full-blooded Indian, and name her tribe. I must point out here that undue pride in one's ancestors has always puzzled me, since one does not choose them.

The "Indian blood" in the family could also be a mistake. Great-grandfather may have referred to his wife as "my squaw" or "my little Indian maid" because she was dark-skinned, dark-eyed and had straight black hair. His grandchildren may have been misled into believing something that wasn't really so.

NAMES AND NICKNAMES

Some of the names people are given at birth these days were considered nicknames in earlier years. Such names as Polly, Peggy, Lizzie, Fanny, Sallie, Jennie, Nat, Jack and Johnny were seldom given names, but the persons nicknamed thus carried that label all their lives, even into their courthouse documents and onto their tombstones. Elizabeth became Liz, Lizzie, Lib, Beth, Bett or Betty; Frances became Fran, Fannie or Fanny; both Francis and Franklin became Frank; and Jane became Jenny or Jennie. Sarah was called Sallie. Nathaniel was tagged Nat, Nate or Nathan; Jonathan was shortened to John and Johnnie; and both John and Jackson became Jack. These are just a few examples. Books have been written on nicknames and on the original meanings of both family and given names.

You are probably aware that several centuries ago and before, people had no family name as such. They were given a name at birth or later, and referred to as of the tribe of so-and-so or the son of whatever their father's name was. They may even have been tagged with "from near the mill" or "made wagon-wheels" or some other identification. The name of the nearest settlement may also have been used to indicate a given person. As time went by, John's son became Johnson and Waggoner, Carter, Wheeler and Cartright became family names of those in the wagon- or coach-making trade. Remember that a son was, in most cases, trained by his father to follow his trade; this made descriptive titles or phrases (family names) stick even tighter.

Of course, many variations in names were the result of various writers within the courthouse. If your ancestors were farmers or immigrants, chances are they couldn't read or write English, possibly not even their names. Farm folk in those days thought education unnecessary to their occupation. As indeed it was. The son was needed to help with the farming, and besides, little Nellie would grow up and marry a farmer anyway. The effect of this attitude shows up in the pages at the courthouse. The signatures at the bottom of a document will show X's where it says "his mark" or "her mark." Often someone else was responsible for the spelling of their names, so you'll see all kinds of spelling variations, even in family or last names. (See Figure 7.)

POLITICS AND RELIGION

Politics was a strong force within the family. If you were born into a Republican home, you were raised a Republican. My grandfather took his sons to the polls to vote Republican. If yours was a Democratic family, you were expected to vote Democratic. Generally, the county seat newspaper sided with either one party or the other, so if your relatives agreed with the local newspaper's politics, you are much more likely to find them in the news.

Politics and religion moved, controlled and often divided the people within a community and within a family. Where two different churches were located in the same town, you will find two groups of inhabitants living, marrying and dying within their own group. Woe to the young person who fell in love and married someone outside his parents' religion. If the churches were Protestant and Catholic, there was even less association between the two groups. Usually, Catholics and Protestants traded and bought their provisions at separate stores. Today when we use words like *love, peace* or *tolerance,* we often think of church and religion. In the past, however, the divisions in the Christian religion, and between Christians and other faiths, have fomented considerable hatred.

Religion has its bright side, however. Religious groups made and kept records. If you know that your ancestor was a member of a certain church, and it is still in existence, this can be of considerable help in your research on that ancestor and his family. When a church is disbanded, one of the members of the church board of trustees (or deacons) is sometimes entrusted with keeping the old records. (I'm talking about Protestant denominations now.) Sometimes these records end up in a public library, and sometimes a fire destroys them along with their keeper's home.

The Roman Catholic Church keeps records of baptisms, marriages, communions and other ceremonies, both here in the United States and in Europe. In the United States, an abandoned Catholic mission's records may be placed in the hands of the state historical society. In the case of the Episcopal Church, the diocesan offices would retain such records.

Some other church bodies also keep records for their churches. The trouble here is that many splinter groups carried the Methodist or Baptist name, but didn't belong to the main church body. Mary K. Meyer, in her book *Genealogical Research In Maryland, A Guide*, lists this address for the Southern Baptist denomination:

> The Historical Commission of the
>   Southern Baptist Convention
> 127 9th Avenue, North
> Nashville, Tennessee 37002

The Commission has microfilmed Baptist records from every state and puts out a catalog. Mary Meyer's book on research is a good one, so if you are in search

of data on your Maryland ancestors, her book would
be a wise purchase. It is printed by:

The Maryland Historical Society
201 West Monument Street
Baltimore, Maryland 21201

There are many such books available on the market
for guiding you in your research of specific states and
areas. Some of them can be found in state libraries
and other places for your free use, but a few of them
are of sufficient value that you should purchase them
and keep them for reference. I can't be specific on
every state, but I would like to tell those of you
having ancestors in Utah that you will want to buy,
or at least see, *Genealogical Records of Utah* by
Laureen R. Jausci and Gloria D. Chaston (1974). It is
published by:

Deseret Book Company
Salt Lake City, Utah 84150

THE PHONE BOOK

When you are researching in a town or county
where some of your ancestors once lived, the local
telephone book or city directory or both may be an
ideal source for locating the descendants of the ones
who remained in that area. That isn't to say you
should check in every town you happen to visit or be

traveling through. Unless the family name is rare and unusual enough that only related persons would be carrying it, don't clutch at straws. For common names like Smith, Jones and McCarthy, you would only check the telephone book if an ancestor of one of those names once resided in that area. For unique names, including those not in their original form but changed or Americanized upon entry into the country, only related persons would be likely to be carrying it or spelling the name the same way as your ancestors. Use any and all telephone books on those family names.

FAMILY RESEMBLANCES

As you make contacts with distant cousins to acquire family data, you'll often be shown old photos and snapshots of their parents, grandparents, and other relatives. The first thing one does when examining an old photograph of a relative, is to look for a "family resemblance." This can be deceptive when you stop to think about it. One can get one's looks from either side of the family, and because a person may or may not look like the photograph of great-grandfather doesn't modify his lineage. Likewise, because he looks like his second cousin doesn't mean they both got their looks from their common ancestors. Also, a photograph of someone may not favor him or her. It is merely a glimpse of that person from one angle, at one instant on a good or bad day of his or her life. I say these things not to unsettle you about your particular family likeness but to make you consider the question awhile and be more broadminded in your consideration of family resemblances.

You mustn't waste your time fearing the shameful or terrifying unknown that your research may uncover. The past is past, and your knowledge of it will not modify it. When you shake an apple tree, you expect apples to fall. If there are a few rotten apples on the tree, you will get those along with the good ones. When you shake the family tree, you encounter a similar situation: a few bad ancestors fall along with the more abundant good ones. Horse thieves and murderers are uncommon in most people's lines, but they did live and there is no changing their actions. In the same way the family history you publish will not alter their lives nor change the past. There is no need to lie. Record what you find in your notes and leave out of your finished volume any shameful or unmentionable details. Even the worst criminal that ever lived did some good in his lifetime.

Of course, some of our ancestors' deeds, though not really criminal, did place a stigma on them and their families. Our civilized society has some strange and unfair rules. In many cases if we break those rules not only do we pay a price, but our offspring also pay dearly.

Be judicious in your final write-ups of sensitive data. If someone back in the 1830s was fatherless, no one living should be hurt by your recording the facts of that person. If your grandmother or your father's half-brother were fatherless, you wouldn't want to tell the world about it. It is not necessary in every case to tell all. The way in which you write up the facts will tell the reader of your history all he or she needs to know. Leaving out a marriage or birth date will often satisfy without lying.

PLAYING A HUNCH

At this point I want to discuss one of my favorite researching tools: the hunch. I often employ it, and sometimes I'm rewarded handsomely. It's an implement with two sharp edges, however, so be wary of it. A hunch is, in some cases, pure speculation; yet not always. It may be produced by a faint memory of something you've read or heard somewhere, though you can't quite recall where. Follow the hunch if it is strong enough, but beware of falling into the trap of wasting time. If you work on your hunch for fifteen minutes to a half hour, don't keep on wasting time; jot the thought down on a piece of scrap paper for follow-up later. Be sure to mark it with a question mark to identify it as speculation. This will keep you from thinking it a fact when you run across it again.

COMPETITION

Let me begin my next topic with a question: what if you have researched one of your family lines for a year or more, then discover someone else is also collecting data on the same family line? Should this happen to you—and it might—you can't ignore the situation and keep on working on that line. Such a course would be little more than a waste of valuable time. Get together with this person and discuss the situation. If both of you had intended to publish, whoever has the most material collected should get all of it. If only one of you is going to publish, that person should get all the information, while the other should keep an eye out for more information. The contributor should be sent a complimentary copy of the finished volume at publication, or given credit in a gracious acknowledgement in the book. If neither of you are intending to publish, share all your information with each other.

At times, you may want to help others by doing a little free research for them. When you are contacted by someone seeking help in digging from your county records, it won't hurt you to comply. Bonds of friendship are very often established by amateur researchers helping each other. I must warn you, however, not everyone who asks for your help will show appreciation. There are half-hearted data collectors and on-again, off-again researchers who will ask for your aid, and when you have given it, will either never write again or let you know that they didn't really want it in the first place. I have had that experience several times. One person wrote asking for help, and gave me a family outline of names that information was needed on. I worked for days at the courthouse, library, and other places, gathering and sending data. I even gathered material for that person by telephone. Suddenly I realized I wasn't receiving any letters from this individual. I wrote asking whether the information was still needed and explained that I was putting forth time and effort to obtain that data. The reply I received stunned me: "Don't bother getting any more information, I won't be collecting data anymore on any but my direct lines." The moral of the story is to make sure the person does want the material you'll use your valuable time gathering.

What can you do when you have difficulty getting cooperation from the source that you contact by mail? Your letters to various pertinent areas for material may sometimes get you the required details on your ancestors, but sometimes not. You may have clues indicating that your ancestor came from a certain county in a given state, but when you write to the county courthouse you receive no reply or a reply of "no information" on your ancestor. Naturally this will discourage you. Considering the situation, we must realize that the people working in a courthouse are residents of that state and county and are paid by the people of that same state or county. Their first allegiance will therefore be to their own. If the clerks have no sense of duty to the public outside that area, your letter will go into the waste basket. It may simply boil down to the question of what type of individual has received your letter. Of course, if you are there in person with your request for material, this applies a little more pressure on most individuals. Some people, when requesting information or photocopies by mail, enclose a small check of about a dollar or so with the instructions, "Here is a deposit of $ ____ ; let me know the balance, so that I can cover any additional costs incurred" (or something to that effect). This would act as a stimulus to the clerk at the other end.

When you get an answer to an inquiry that says in essence "no data on the named ancestor" you will probably wonder if any kind of search was indeed made. You must either (1) resign yourself to the supposition that a thorough search was made or (2) go there in person or (3) contact a professional genealogist in that area to do the necessary research for you. In the meantime, you should write to other sources within that state and county, for example, the state historical society, county historical society, state library or state hall of records. Be sure you give all the necessary information to help them find the pertinent data: dates or estimated dates, details known about the ancestor's life in that region, brothers' and sisters' names, birthplaces if known, and so on.

OLD BOOKS AND PAPERS

I have repeatedly given you advice on careful treatment of books and documents. Normal wear and tear on courthouse volumes and library books is to be expected. Even when handled with care, the handling itself causes wear. The inside pages of these courthouse documents cannot be replaced. They could be rewritten, typed or printed, but that would only produce duplicates. The outside cover of those volumes can be repaired or replaced as they show extreme wear. Originally they consisted of a hard core, covered with leather. Some are still made that way.

If you have old and valuable books in your possession that need repair, by all means have a professional bookbinder do the job. Most reputable book stores can give you the name of a good repair firm. For books of lesser value needing repair, you may wish to do the repair work yourself. When I was a child, I remember reading the fundamentals of bookbinding in one of the handicraft-type magazines (*Popular Mechanics*, I think). There are still books available on the subject. One such volume is *Cleaning and Preserving Bindings and Related Materials* by Carolyn Horton. It is published by the American Library Association and can be found at the public library. The paperback edition can be ordered from:

> The American Library Association
> 50 Huron Street
> Chicago, Illinois 60611

As you continue your research, you will find that the use of microfilm and microfilm viewers is becoming very popular. The Indiana State Library has two kinds of viewers. One of them displays the image on a frosted glass vertically in front of the user. The other shows the image more or less horizontally on a white painted surface. Some people prefer one kind and some the other. My eyes read the image better on the frosted glass variation. The outside casing or cabinet of both machines is very similar. There are controls to enlarge and diminish the image, to move the image in any direction, and to roll the film frame by frame or to speed roll it. These viewers, of course, are nothing more than modified slide projectors. The availability of these machines will continue to expand as libraries and courthouses are authorized to make the purchases.

8

Other States
and Overseas

In some respects this chapter is more difficult to write than the previous chapters. Tracing footsteps or wagon tracks back east seems nearly an impossible task. It would be entirely impossible except for the recorded bits of historical data that may have been left along the trail. If your ancestor was a highly educated man and held public office in the larger communities as he (and his family) slowly made their way westward, you'll be able to trace him more easily. If he was a farmer and relatively uneducated, your search will be a difficult one.

How can you discover your ancestor's occupation and his education level? If he made the trip west prior to 1850—and was settled in a western or midwestern area between 1850 and 1880—the census reports will tell you his occupation and sometimes give you the number of years of schooling. He may have had other employments from time to time, which may be listed in the county histories or other sources. For instance, my mother's great-grandfather ran a small farm, his wife's inheritance from her father. In most accounts, however, he is listed as a teamster. He evidently handled a team of horses well enough to make a living hauling materials. Another ancestor of mine was listed as a mechanic, a wagonmaker, as well as postmaster of the village where he operated his business.

The clues are generally found in the records and county histories. Sometimes these will tell where a family originated, the exact location in a given state. Of course, this usually isn't the end of the line (or beginning, I should say). This person's parents may have been born in another state, and so on.

If you find an area where your family spent several generations, perhaps you should place an ad in the classified section of the county seat newspaper (which you can do by mail). Many descendants may still reside there and would probably be happy to give you details on their particular line of the family. Afterward, you may wish to visit this area, check out the county records, and meet your newly found kinfolk.

Each state originally had trails that were trod by the pioneers entering and crossing that state on their way west. We must remember that the whole country was once a wilderness, mostly woods and prairie. The two main routes from the midwest onward were the Santa Fe Trail and the Oregon Trail. If your ancestors were part of a wagon train of any size, the wagon master probably kept a journal or record of births, marriages, deaths and other happenings. In most cases, these facts were registered somewhere toward the end of the trek, in one of the larger organized settlements or an army post. The most likely spots to find these recorded facts would probably be California, Washington and Oregon, at the western ends of the trails, and Independence, Missouri, at the eastern end.

When looking for ancestors who died along the western trails, don't be so foolish as to try to visit all the cities and county seats along each trail, for few of them existed at that early period. Confine your search to the state libraries and other larger repositories of data. Of course, wherever you are, whichever county library or state library you may be researching, always check through the volumes and collected data from other states and areas.

If your ancestors were Mormons or traveled westward with them, the Utah records will help you considerably. The Mormon historian is located in Salt Lake City, Utah, but normally you should not contact him with queries. In chapter 7, I gave you reference to a book that covers Utah sources, but you may come across other pamphlets or books on that state that you prefer to use.

In discussing travels westward by the pioneers, we must keep one other thought in mind: if your ancestor was an explorer, fur trapper or Indian trader, he probably traveled a path of his own through the woods, not following any main trail. He may have been accompanied by an Indian wife or companion and would then have been on foot or on horseback. He wouldn't have been burdened with a heavily loaded wagon, and family. It's almost useless to track this person, unless he made a big name for himself, and his story earned a place in state or county histories.

No doubt a few families, regardless of the extreme danger, didn't follow the regular trails or go with any group. When a member of that family died along the way, his or her grave was not marked in any permanent manner, and probably no record was made until they reached the midwest settlement.

Now consider the pioneers who came from the original thirteen states, with families and possessions. The Appalachian chain of mountains posed a considerable barrier to these pioneers with their loaded wagons. Families from New York and the New England states could travel the northern route through Pennsylvania, Ohio, Indiana and Illinois. Pioneers from Virginia, Maryland, New Jersey and Delaware were more apt to take a southern route through North or South Carolina, Tennessee, Kentucky, Ohio and/or Indiana. Some, of course, spread into the southern states and settled.

That was before the Cumberland Gap was discovered. In 1750, Dr. Thomas Walker found this natural break in the Appalachian mountains. Today the states of Kentucky, Tennessee and Virginia touch on this spot. This provided an easy alternate route that greatly facilitated movement to the West.

Certainly your best bet in tracing the steps of your ancestors, would be to follow the clues in the county histories, courthouse volumes and other data sources in your area and on the route traveled by your kinsmen. But this is not always possible. You must consider every navigable river as a trail; all the major towns and cities along it as collecting points of information for travel on that river. Keep in mind that robbers and murderers waited in many places along the Ohio River and other streams that were used for transportation. Better and longer roads provided access to vast areas of new land for eager settlers. Two of these important roads were the Pennsylvania Turnpike, later designated U.S. Route 40, and the Knoxville Road.

There are some key localities in Ohio and Kentucky that may also be checked for clues. People came into Ohio mostly from two directions: the Steubenville area of Ohio, including Zanesville, Columbus, Springfield, Dayton and on westward; or

Steubenville, Wheeling, West Virginia, and on down the Ohio River, stopping either at Marietta or Portsmouth, then either into Kentucky or up into Clermont, Hamilton, Butler and Preble Counties, Ohio. Cincinnati and the counties surrounding Hamilton County became gathering points as new lands were opened up in Indiana.

Those pioneers taking the southern route usually went through North Carolina. There are numerous possibilities for trails out of this state, so a search through the index files and records in the state library at Raleigh should be made. The same goes for Tennessee and Kentucky. Those families that went into Indiana, however, usually came in from three points: Hamilton, Butler and Preble Counties, Ohio; Clermont, Warren, Montgomery, Miami or Preble Counties, Ohio; or the Kentucky counties of Jefferson, Daviess or Henderson. The Kentucky counties to check for ancestors taking the Cincinnati route would be Boone, Kenton, Bracken, Bourbon, Franklin, Mason and Boyd. Perhaps a trip or a letter to the state archives in Frankfort, Kentucky, (the address is listed at the end of this chapter) would be helpful.

Those pioneers who traveled the southern route through North Carolina or South Carolina and then settled in the southern states may have gone through Tennessee and down or through Georgia. You had better start with letters or trips to the state libraries in the capitals of those states. If these bring you results in one county or locality, check out the county records and histories there. Letters, however, should be your first probes for information.

Trying to discover the route taken by an ancestor is difficult. Always use the clues of the county histories. You may know the church affiliation of your forefathers; other members of that church probably travelled westward with your ancestors. Check any sketches on church or locality members in the county history, and also check the front portion of the county history where it tells who came into the area and bought land and where they came from.

In Texas, the men who fought and died at the Alamo are written into our nation's history. With few exceptions, however, these were not settlers. There were some settlers in Texas then, and they had come from all over the union. There were also original settlers, who claimed Mexican heritage and citizenship. After the Alamo episode, the influx of settlers increased tremendously, again from all the formally recognized states. In order to find exactly which states they came from, you'll have to research the county records and histories where they settled in Texas and utilize those clues.

In naming counties in this chapter, I haven't intended to rule out others. The ones I named were just some of the more likely ones along the westward routes. Your ancestors may have stopped in one of them and spent a generation or two.

If you have found some leads that point back to a certain county in an eastern state and decide to go there to check the various records, don't forget to look for wills. A will dated as far back as the 1700s may not name your ancestor unless he is an eldest son, but contemporary records may support you in attributing that will to his father or mother, especially if the inheritance is a large piece of land. I've already mentioned that the wills of that era seldom listed more than the wife or the oldest son. The latter usually received the entire inheritance and was to care for the needs of the younger children. This is one of the chief reasons that female members of the clan (wives and daughters) are less likely to be named. You can, therefore, often come up with the names of males in your lines, while the wives' names remain a mystery.

Minority groups prior to the Civil War are difficult (sometimes impossible) to trace. Black people can sometimes find the pertinent data back to their freed ancestor, but prior to this, records only gave the number of slaves. Some blacks in the North, who were free persons and had family names, will be found in such lists as the census records. The 1850 census and later ones had a column to show *B* or *W*, the color of each individual listed. If one should trace his ancestry back as far as tribal Africa, he or she would then run out of written family information anyway. Alex Haley proved that it is sometimes possible to trace one's ancestry to Africa. Of course, he had an edge on other black researchers. Armed with family stories and words of an African language that was passed down in his family, he was able to find the place and people that were his "roots." When he found the tribe of his ancestor, he obtained his history from the "historian" of that people. The tribal history was carried in this man's head, not in written records.

Indians were on the move, keeping just ahead of the waves of white settlers. Their language—symbolic drawings and word of mouth—was not suited to the keeping of accurate records. When the white man's records listed them at all, it was merely as members of tribes. Much of the time the chief would be named and the number of persons in his tribe would be given. Mexican Americans and certain Indian tribes of Texas, New Mexico, Arizona and California can best find their ancestors through church records. People of French extraction whose ancestors lived in French settlements can use both the church records and county or parish public records for their research.

You will probably want to write to the state library or the county clerk or recorder of an area to which you have found a lead. I am giving you a sprinkling of addresses in this volume, but you will understand that I can't conceivably provide you with a complete list of all state library addresses, much less those of public libraries and courthouses in the counties of all states. What will you do when you can't find an address for a source you wish to write? You can use my system on these addresses that you do not know. From a map of that state, find the county seat of the particular county; write to: County Clerk, _____ County Courthouse, name of county seat and state, and zip code. Get the zip code from the post office; I'll talk about this again after a few more paragraphs. Here are two examples employing my method:

> County Clerk
> Guilford County Courthouse
> Greensboro, North Carlonia
> zip code

> or

> Archivist
> Maryland State Library
> Annapolis, Maryland
> zip code

State libraries have many employees, and any one of them may be designated to answer your letter. It is best, however, to address your first letter to either "the Archivist" or "Library Director." To the public libraries, address your message to "Head Librarian." Letters to the courthouses should be addressed to the person responsible in the particular office, as: "County Clerk" or "Recorder." Enclose a stamped, self-addressed envelope. If the librarian or clerk has any sense of being a public servant, you should get an answer. Some won't; your letter will be just another bother as they go about the daily chores. You'll find this kind of individual in every occupation—one who becomes lost in the numbers of workers and never makes waves so as not to be noticed. Fortunately, the scale is balanced by energetic, responsible people who care whether things get done.

If you get an answer from the state library, the data will probably be from its index card file, and they may quote you a reasonable price for copies of the material indicated by the index card. You may not be sure it is your ancestor, but you will have to decide whether or not to pay the fee and get the material. If you get a positive response from a county clerk or recorder, the source of that data will be the volume index or one of the indices that cover more than one set of volumes. If the office has a copy machine, they will probably quote a fee for copying and mailing those copies. If you can afford to travel to the east, you have an advantage; but it still makes sense to contact them by mail first to find out who has the information.

There are too many states and far too many good

books and booklets that apply to specific areas; it is impossible to give you a complete list of them. Of necessity, this book is general. There are an abundance of "helper" books for the various places, particularly the original thirteen states. Though I don't wish to start naming books, I have already given a few examples. One prime example was *Genealogical Research In Maryland, A Guide,* by Mary K. Meyer, a guide book that covers the various records and sources of that state. I mentioned it in chapter 7, giving you the publisher's address. Similar guide books for many of the other states are readily available for your use in their state libraries. Unless you feel a definite need for the booklet, use it in the library and copy the information and addresses from it into your notes.

How can one trace his ancestors to their origins overseas? By the time you finish working on sources in the United States, you will probably have found out from where over the ocean your ancestors came. This information may have come from county histories, various county records, or from hand-me-down information. The 1850 through 1880 census reports will yield the information, if the ancestor listed was born outside of the United States.

Your surname itself may provide a clue. I say "may," because names have been changed, misspelled and doctored by time and people. Your name may not be what your ancestor's name was, though you supposedly carry his name. Many people, upon entering the country, have had their name changed by law, because it is either odd sounding or difficult to pronounce by Americans. In the not-so-distant past, some immigrants Americanized their names without even bothering with the legal procedure. Those who were semiliterate in English often allowed others to write their names for them into the records. You will see the variations as you continue your research, but until you come to a legal name change, you must assume that the name in some variation goes back to a certain country overseas.

State libraries and main public libraries in larger cities have volumes on settlements and name origins. Some family names can be pinpointed to a region of a country; this usually points to the place the name originated, not necessarily the place where your ancestors last lived in that country. It does help though. Also, don't forget to check out the passenger lists of ships that came in to the main ports at the time you think your ancestor entered the country.

Once you have located the region in a country, where your ancestor(s) lived, you'll wish to contact the city or prefecture government for a check of the records. Depending on the country, you must acquire the title of the local head of government and the name of the district. The personnel of one of the larger libraries should be able to help you formulate an adequate address.

For Catholics, church records can be helpful once you have narrowed the search down to a certain region. In the case of Protestant ancestors, churches in foreign countries also may be of help. Normally, baptisms rather than births were recorded by these churches. Also, the district or town records may reveal some desired data.

Let me remind you that Mormons have collected data and records from all over, including European countries. The Mormon library is reputed to be especially good for the researching genealogist, and you need not be a Mormon to use it and its services. Mormons have been collecting information for quite some time, so they may now even have records whose originals have been destroyed by such misfortunes as war, riot or fire. Write to:

Manager of L.D.S. Genealogical
    Society Library
50 East North Temple Street
Salt Lake City, Utah 84150

One book which does a fine job of describing the materials at the Mormon library is *Handy Index To The Holdings of The Genealogical Society Of Utah,* by Mary J. Brown, published in 1971 by:

The Everton Publishers, Inc.
P.O. Box 368
Logan, Utah 84321

This book covers information (for the United States), state by state, with a breakdown of county sources.

Here are a few addresses of places in Indiana and other states you may at some phase of your research want to contact; I have used some of them, but I don't pretend to guarantee you'll get an answer on every inquiry you send out to them.

For war records in Indiana:

> Indiana Adjutant General's Office
> Records Division
> Stout Field
> Indianapolis, Indiana 46241

For birth and death records in Indiana:

> Indiana Records of Public Health
> State Health Department
> 1330 West Michigan
> Indianapolis, Indiana 46202

Many universities have microfilmed and other state records; in Indiana:

> Indiana University Library
> Indiana University
> Bloomington, Indiana 47401

Addresses from other states:

New Jersey State Library
Archives and History Bureau
185 West State Street
Trenton, New Jersey 08625

The New York State Library
Associate Librarian
Albany, New York 12224

State of Delaware Division
    Archives and Cultural Affairs
Hall of Records
Dover, Delaware 19901

Pennsylvania State Library
Box 1601
Harrisburg, Pennsylvania 17126

State Librarian
North Carolina State Library
Box 27727
Raleigh, North Carolina 27611

The Newberry Library in Chicago is similar to a state library, yet more of a national library; write to

The Newberry Library
60 West Walton
Chicago, Illinois 60610

You'll have to decide whether either of these rental libraries is suited to your needs. A rental library that publishes *The Ozark Quarterly:*

> Pioneer Enterprises
> R.R. 1, P.O. Box 195
> Billings, Missouri 65610

One place that advertises "complete Ohio records" is:

> "Gateway To the West"
> Ruth Bowers
> R.R. 3, Box 95
> Union City, Indiana 47390

A society in Connecticut that publishes a quarterly and supplies you with genealogical forms (free query service), for five dollars yearly dues:

> The Secretary
> Connecticut Society of Genealogists
> 16 Royal Oak Drive
> West Hartford, Connecticut 06107

A quarterly is also published in New York, costing ten dollars a year, with a library that belongs to the society. Write to:

New York Genealogical
& Biographical Society
122 East Fifty-eighth Street
New York, New York 10022

Many of the pioneers who settled Ohio, Indiana, Illinois and on across the prairie first came through Kentucky. Some of them stayed a few generations there and left their marks in the public records. The repository in Kentucky, which holds many of these records is:

Kentucky Reference Service
State Archives and Record Center
851 East Main, Box 537
Frankfort, Kentucky 40601

The addresses that I have given are just a sampling of the many that you will obtain in your research, and some of these places can be of great help to you, especially if travel is not possible. If you come upon an address with no zip code, you can find the appropriate zip code at the local post office. When you cannot acquire the zip code for a particular state library, find the zip code of the other government buildings; they are usually located in the same vicinity downtown. For public libraries in large cities, use the common numbers of all the zips listed for the city and complete it with blanks, as 4 6 9 __. Though not exact, this will help the post office to send the mail to the right area.

9

National Archives

The National Archives in Washington, D.C., contain the census returns for most states from 1790 on, as well as data compiled on veterans' affairs, immigration passenger lists and records for many Indian tribes. Records for most land grants are also stored here. Microfilm and other copies of some of the national documents and volumes are purchased from the National Archives by individual states, and some of the data compiled and kept by many states is either copied or the originals have been sent to the National Archives.

I will give you a breakdown on the materials stored in the National Archives in condensed form, but complete coverage is available in the booklet *Guide to Genealogical Records in the National*

Archives. The cost of this booklet is fifty cents. To order one, write to this address:

> Superintendent of Documents
> U.S. Government Printing Office
> Washington, D.C. 20402

Ask for form 7029 and fill it out as completely as possible when requesting a search. You may ask "If I have all that data to put on the form, why am I bothering with it?" When you think about it a bit, the answer becomes obvious: (1) your information may be only approximate and inaccurate, (2) you desire copies of the actual documents from the National Archives, and (3) the more closely you can pinpoint the time and area, the better chance the National Archives has of finding documented information and specific volumes. A free brochure *National Archives Publication No. 67-7* is also available. It is mostly a condensation of the *Guide to Genealogical Records in the National Archives*, however, so you won't need it if you send for the larger booklet.

A census of the population of the United States has been taken every ten years since 1790. The National Archives has the 1790 to 1870 returns, a microfilm copy of the 1880 census, and what's left of the 1890 returns, which were mostly destroyed by a 1921 fire; a few counties or townships in ten states remain. Naturally, the 1790 census includes only the states that existed at the time, and the returns for Delaware, Georgia, Kentucky, New Jersey, Tennessee and Virginia were destroyed during the War of 1812. As I explained in the chapter on state libraries, the 1850 through 1880 census reports are the most detailed.

The National Archives contain a card index for the 1810 census of Virginia, a microfilm copy of a card index to members of households (a separate cross-reference index lists each child aged ten or under whose surname differs from the head of the household), and a card index of the 1890 listing. The Archives also have special census returns from Union veterans and widows of veterans for part of Kentucky and for states alphabetically listed, from Louisiana through Wyoming. The Archives are now compiling microfilm copies of mortality returns of the 1850 through 1880 censuses, acquiring them from the various storage deposits.

A search will be made for you, free of charge, for a specific name in any of the National Archives's indices. A limited search for a name in the returns not indexed will be made, but you must provide the state and county of the individual's residence. For high population areas, they wish to be provided with the town or township; for large cities provide them with the street address or ward as well. When a requested entry is found, you will be told the price for a photocopy of the census page on which it appears.

If you wish, for a moderate price you may purchase from the Archives positive microfilm copy rolls of the censuses. They are alphabetically arranged by state, each state alphabetically by county. If you want these, request the publication *Federal Population Censuses, 1790–1890*; it contains a roll listing and prices per roll.

The National Archives contain bounty land and pension claims made for military service from 1775 on. A veteran's claim gives certain details that the genealogist desires: place and date of birth, place of residence and details of military service. A widow's application gives much the same information but may contain her maiden name, date of marriage to the veteran and the names of their children. When inquiring about a veteran, use Form GSA 6751, Order For Copies—Veteran's Records. Do not send any money; you will be billed two dollars for each file reproduced. You will find the address to mail it to on the form.

The above-mentioned form can be used for material on veterans of the American Revolution and the post-Revolutionary period, the War of 1812, the Mexican War, the Civil War, the Spanish-American War, and any other extended periods of military service. You would not use the form for copies of veterans of World War I, World War II, or subsequent service. For these, write to:

National Personnel Records Center
GSA (Military Personnel Records)
9700 Page Boulevard
St. Louis, Missouri 63132

Pension or bounty-land warrant application files will normally contain an official statement of the veteran's military service; this usually contains information of a personal or genealogical nature. Military service records seldom contain family data.

The Archives also contain the registers of enlistment in the U.S. Army from 1798 through 1914 and compiled military service records of volunteers from 1775 through 1903, which includes records of service in the Confederate Army. Many details about the enlistee are given, and this is a good source of data for you family researchers. Again, when placing a request for information, always include on the form as much information as you can about the individual. Naval and marine service records for early periods are also on file.

Passenger lists and immigration passenger lists of ships arriving from abroad at Atlantic Ocean and Gulf of Mexico ports are incomplete but are available at the National Archives microfilm reading room.

Records on Indians, arranged by tribes, are mostly dated from 1830 through 1940 and include Cherokee, Chickasaw, Choctaw and Creek, who moved west between 1830 and 1846. The record usually names the head of the family, and the number of persons in the family by age and sex.

The Archives also has various records concerning the District of Columbia and the naturalization records. Land records in the National Archives include donation land entry files, homestead application files and private land claims of individual settlers on land in the public land states. Certain states, including the original thirteen, retain their own records on these transactions, and the National Archives does not have these. A search will be made on request of land records for Alabama, Alaska, Arizona, Florida, Louisiana, Nevada or Utah for the period 1800 through 1908 if the applicant gives the full name of an ancestor and the name of the state or territory; for other states, more information is demanded.

When you have progressed in your researching to the point of needing information from the National Archives, be ready. Before you make any trip, send for the *Guide to Genealogical Records in the National Archives.*

10

Taking Notes
and Keeping Files

In this chapter two highly important techniques are considered, which, if performed properly, will facilitate the progress and accuracy of your research. First I'll discuss the best ways of taking notes; then I'll follow up with the most efficient systems of filing.

Let's be perfectly honest. Anyone who can read and write can copy passages from a book or a document. It wouldn't even be necessary to understand the words or sentences being copied, but the better researcher must perform the copying act in a particular way. Effective use of your time, and accuracy, are of great importance. Here are some tips:

1. It's better to use lined writing paper for notes, and it is a good idea to use the same size sheets

for all your notes; uniformity reduces the chance of losing smaller papers from your file. I personally prefer narrow ruled loose-leaf paper, because I can get more notes on each sheet. If writing small characters tends to give you hand cramps, then use the wide-lined paper.

2. Start the first page of your notes by numbering it "1," and then place the day's date at the top; the second page for that day will be numbered "2," and so on. If you use both sides of a sheet as I do, the reverse of page 1 would be numbered "2." If your researching lasts more than one day, on the second you have a choice: you can start where you left off, by putting that day's date and continuing on, or you can start another batch of notes with page 1 and the day's date at the top. Either way is fine, but if you use the latter procedure you had better keep each day's pages of notes clipped together separately. I usually use the continuation method.

3. Your writing must be completely legible, and if you abbreviate, do it in a consistent manner that will prevent guesswork at a later date.

4. Always identify the sources of your notes. If copying from a book, start by writing the name of the volume, the publisher, the place and date of publication and each page number.

5. When copying from a county history, atlas or other published volume, it's best to copy into your notes word-for-word. Set this segment of your notes

off with quotation marks. If you're extracting information concerning your ancestor from a sketch on some other person, use dashes to indicate where you have left out unwanted words, phrases or lengthy passages of the text. Get permission from the publisher if you plan to use large portions of a copyrighted text word-for-word in your family history.

6. When copying from a courthouse volume, don't bother copying the entire entry; just take what's important. Start with the volume's name and page number, as in "*Deed Record Town Lots 4*, page 188". At the beginning or ending of the entry, put the date of that entry. If you are at a state library researching this county information, you'll probably be jumping from one county to another, so identify the county with each entry or grouping of entries. If you are at a county courthouse, identify the county once at the start of your notes.

7. When copying the census reports into your notes, you can write instead of print, but try to make it as nearly the same format as you see on the microfilm viewer. Start by putting the names of the headings over the columns: name, age, sex, occupation, years of schooling, birthplace and so on. Leave a space between each household in the same way as the actual census. Be sure to identify the county, state, township and/or city of your census.

8. When typing up or recopying notes into

your file, separate them according to your file setup; if it is organized by family names or by individual ancestors, take the data from your original notes and place it within its appropriate file section, keeping the entries identified as to sources and dates. Don't throw away your original notes; keep them for future reference on items you may later question.

To organize your collection of data, you could use forms that you can buy to keep important facts together on each ancestor. I have never felt the need to use them, but these forms do make your file neater and more usable. Two such forms are the Pedigree Chart and the Family Group Sheet; I don't have an address for you to write for the Pedigree Chart, but the Family Group Sheet is printed by the Everton Publishers, Inc., P.O. Box 368, Logan, Utah 84321. They have a free catalog of genealogical aids. That Family Group Sheet is especially good to use when interviewing one of your relatives, and would be a time-saver in obtaining information at family reunions: pass out one sheet to each head of household and let him fill it out.

In my researching, I sometimes draw up my own family group sheet. It makes clear the members of that family at a glance. Otherwise the many Johns, Marys and Williams merge in my mind. To set up a family group sheet, follow this example:

John X. Jones ———┬——— Mary Lou Smith
  b. 1 Jan. 1800   b. 10 Dec. 1802
  d. 2 Feb. 1870   d. 11 Nov. 1880

┌——— married 3 Mar. 1820 ┘
  in Union Co., Ind.

├— Wm. Edward, b. 12 Oct. 1822, d. 6 Jan. 1825

├— Eliza June, b. 7 Jul. 1824, d. 8 Aug. 1850, m. 9
     Sep. 1843 to Elijah McGee, b. 1 Oct. 1822, d.
     2 Dec. 1845,
        3 children: Samuel, Ella and Ralph.

├— Michael P., b. 3 Jan. 1826, d. 4 Feb. 1890, m. 5
     Mar. 1847 to Lucinda May Griper, b. 6 Apr.
     1828, d. 7 Mar. 1850,
        2 children: Elmer and Zula.

├— Martha Marie, b. 8 Apr. 1828, d. 9 Mar. 1831.

└— John X., jr., b. 1 Jun. 1830, d. 2 July 1900, m. 3
     Aug. 1848 to Sarah Jane Backwoods, b. 4
     Sep. 1827, d. 5 Oct. 1882,
        1 child: John X. III.

117

Since you are building this chart to suit your own needs, you can put in as little (or as much) information as you see fit. My advice is to keep it relatively simple, since it is meant as a chart of family information and a visual aid, not a complete record of those included in it.

Filing, of course, goes hand in hand with keeping accurate records. I can't place too much emphasis on the importance of good filing habits, nor could I overrate the value of good filing systems. If you keep your notes and collected data in a pile with no sequence or order, you have nothing but chaos. It'll be a mess, and you won't be able to find any one piece of information without going through your entire pile. Many times you'll come up with new data and will say to yourself, "I've got some more facts on this person or event, now where are they?" If you have your notes in order, it will take just a short time to find the filed information that supports or elaborates on your newly acquired data.

Speaking from my own experience, I'd say you will require more than one file, and maybe more than one system of filing. Let's take your notes or collected data; there are many ways that you could keep these filed in good order.

One completely adequate system of filing involves the use of portable filing cabinets, which accommodate standard (8½″ × 11″) sheets of paper. Use dividers (cardboard or other) to section off this storage space into compartments. You may want to set up a section for each different ancestor and his family. If so, take any collected data you have found from your handwritten notes, type it on a regular-sized sheet of typing paper and insert it into the desired section of your file. Of course, when I keep mentioning typing and typing paper, I am assuming a situation that may not exist. If you have no typewriter or don't type, then use lined paper and write—or print very neatly and legibly—a copy for your file. Always use paper of the same dimensions for your file copies.

Another good filing system requires manila folders. Each folder may contain your collected notes on a particular person, and his or her family, or a particular source, such as "Deed Records." The advantage of manila folders is that they enable you to travel with your files when you need to. Just be sure to cover them with plastic for protection from rain and damp weather. It is generally a good idea to take your files with you on your searches, as you will be checking through them occasionally to make comparisons to new materials.

Don't destroy your handwritten notes after rewriting or typing copies. At home, keep your old notes in a large envelope or box so that you can always check back should you have doubts about the information in your typed file. Remember, the notes you take at the source are second-hand, (the original source we'll call first-hand) and the typed or handwritten copies stored in your file are third-hand information. It's always useful to be able to check yourself against your second-hand source.

If you set up your file case or folders by kinds of data (sources), you would have a section for each of the following: marriages, births, deaths, county histories, deed records, probate court order books, and so on. This is the easiest system to organize, but it necessitates a bit of a search to bring all the data on a particular person together. However, it might well serve as a good temporary system until you are ready to put together your data in its final form.

You should also have a correspondence file. I use manila folders for letters from my correspondents. In the chapter dealing with correspondence, I discussed the importance of keeping your letters filed and the best methods for doing so. These letters, as a source of information, are of great importance. They are not quite as trustworthy as Bible records, in most cases, because they are farther removed from the common ancestor or ancestors with whom they deal. However, the information and family stories they contain are sometimes verified by the legal records. Even if they are not, these letters will be valuable to you in a different way, as they begin to breathe life into people you know only as names and dates.

Each manila folder, then, would contain letters from a given relative and carbon copies of your letters

Fig. 8 A manila correspondence folder marked with the appropriate information.

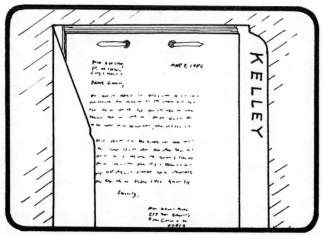

Fig. 9 A correspondence folder opened to show the letters in a neat, accessible stack, with a two-pronged paper clasp at the top affixing the stack to the folder. A hole puncher is required for a neat job.

to that relative. When you close the folder, the back side will protrude above the front, and on this extended space you can write the pertinent family name on the left side. On the right side, place the name and address of your correspondent. This can be a time-saver when addressing a letter envelope to this person.

11

Your Camera

If you don't have a camera and feel no need of one, you may skip this chapter. The fact is, you don't have to own a camera to enjoy collecting genealogical data. Photography is a hobby in itself. But if you do have an interest in photography, you'll find that photography and genealogy can work happily hand in hand.

Your camera: what kind should you have? How deeply should you go into photography? Should you try copywork with a camera? Would it be wise to purchase an enlarger and build a darkroom in your home? These are valid questions that the amateur researcher may ask. In this chapter I'll try to give you enough basic information to help you reach your own conclusions.

Photography can be as inexpensive as owning a Brownie, an Instamatic or a Polaroid camera. These come in a wide range of prices, which run as low as ten or twenty dollars. If all you want from your camera is to photograph gravestones, any one of these three will be a good buy. With the Polaroid camera, you will probably be using film that won't give you a negative, so for each print you must take a photograph; but it does have the advantage of providing an immediate picture.

For copying documents and old photographs you'll need a better—and therefore a more expensive—camera. For this work, you'll need a sixteen-millimeter or thirty-five millimeter camera; the thirty-five millimeter camera, I would say, would be a better buy. A suitable thirty-five millimeter camera will cost you from fifty dollars to many hundreds of dollars. You might be able to buy a good second-hand one at a loan shop, but if you do, bring along a friend who knows a good deal about cameras. Be sure to look at the lens to see that it is not damaged or covered with fingerprints and scratches. Check the shutter and see that it opens and closes freely.

Use your good common sense to determine how involved you want to get with photography. Buy yourself the kind of camera that suits your needs and let your pocketbook be your guide.

The reason for using photographic copywork in your research is to make yourself a record of pertinent entries of deed records, marriage books, old photographs and vintage newspapers you come across. To copy documents with your camera you will need supplementary lenses. Depending on the size of the material to be copied, the distance between the camera, and the material being copied, you can select the correct strength close-up lens. These are also called positive lenses; they run from plus 1 to plus 10. For small photographs and little areas of copy, you will use an extreme close-up lens of plus 4 through plus 10; for large volume pages and newspaper pages, you'll use the portrait close-up lenses of plus 1, 2 and 3. To give you the extremes as examples: with a plus 1 lens, at a distance of 38¾ inches, you can copy an area of 18⅝ inches by 28 inches with your camera set on infinity; this is for a camera with a 50-millimeter lens, which takes a 24 by 36-millimeter-size negative.

The little booklet that comes with your camera will tell you the size of your camera's lens. This is normally marked around the circle of metal or plastic that holds the camera's lens to the camera itself. The Kodak booklet on copying gives you invaluable tables that tell you for a given lens, camera setting and distance, what size area you can expect to copy.

If your camera is a single lens reflex type, you will be able to use the view screen to check whether you are in focus or not; this way you can adjust the focus on your camera, or the distance from camera to subject, without relying on the tables entirely. This, of course, makes the procedure much less complicated. Needless to say, the single lens reflex (SLR) cameras are generally higher in price than cameras without through-the-lens focusing.

The reflex-type camera, which does not view through the same lens that takes the picture, can also be used for copying, but then you will have the problem of paralax and must adjust the position of the copy or camera to compensate. The Rolleiflex is the old standard of this type and requires an additional supplementary lens for its viewing lens opening.

The regular thirty-five-millimeter camera without reflex or single lens reflex can be used also, but it is not quite as accurate in reproducing a sharp negative. One way of using this camera is to rely entirely on the information in the tables and to shoot a roll of test film to find the sharpest images at various camera-focus settings. Make notes on the settings used for the series of exposures and make your own tables from these using the prints as your guide.

I once ordered a supplementary lens from a photographic equipment dealer by mail and at the same time asked a few questions concerning its use with my camera. The reply I received from them informed me that I could not do copywork with my camera since it wasn't a reflex type and I'd have no way to accurately focus it. I have never owned a reflex-type camera, much less a single lens reflex, but I have made perfectly adequate copy negatives with several 35-millimeter cameras I've owned, and so can you. It is more trouble, but it's not impossible.

Of course, the better the camera, supplementary lens and other equipment, the sharper and more accurate the copy negative. For this reason, if you have a very small photo or a not very clear one, a professional will give you the best copy negative. There's nothing wrong with hiring a job out when you need extremely accurate work. If you intend to send old photographs through the mail to get professional copy negatives, you should first make a copy of each one with your camera and copy lens. This insures you of retaining a copy in case the mail service or the photo lab loses the original photographs. And don't forget to buy insurance for your package. Insurance won't bring back the lost photo, but buy it for the extra handling care it may mean for your package.

If money is no object, and you want excellent quality, get yourself an Exa, Exakta, Pentax, Minolta or another high-quality camera that can be matched with copying equipment made specifically for them. With this equipment you can produce exceptional copy negatives.

The use of a filter is sometimes necessary when copying old photographs and documents. If the image is black but the paper or page of copy matter is stained, use a filter similar to, but deeper in color than, the stains—a yellow or orange filter will often come in handy. If, however, the image or lettering is brownish and the photograph background or page of copy matter is also brown with age, then a yellow or orange filter would not do you much good. A filter of a contrasting color, perhaps blue, might help, if you compensate by using a high contrast paper to make your prints. Other techniques explained in the Kodak booklet on copying may be useful. If you use a sheet of glass to hold your copy matter in place, a polarizing filter should be used to eliminate reflections.

If you ever use the sun as your light source for copywork, you'll need some kind of light meter. (My greatest problem in using the sun is that I often create shadows on the copy matter with my hands and don't realize it until I have my negatives developed. This may sound silly, but be very careful or you'll find the same mysterious shadows appearing on your photographs.) If your camera has a built-in light meter, you can use that in some cases. A built-in light meter is not as handy as a separate one, and some of this type do not register reliably at the extremes of the meter range, in low light or very bright light. Therefore, a built-in light meter may or may not suffice for copy work. Before I acquired my first light meter I believed it was a mysterious, complicated instrument. It isn't. Learn the rules for using it, take your readings from light reflected from the matter being copied, and set your camera's f-stop to the correct number. Light meters come in a wide range of prices, but an expensive one is unnecessary unless you are going into photography and copying professionally.

You'll need to buy or build a copy stand and lights if you wish to copy at the courthouse, library or any other place outside your home. This will cost from twenty to fifty dollars if you buy an assembled copy stand. If you are a handy type and construct your own, you can save money. The copy stand adjusts the distance from camera to copy matter and locks in place, holding the camera firmly. If you make it yourself, it must not be a shaky affair.

For small areas and snapshot photos, small, handy close-ups stands complete with lenses are available. The one I own is called a Reprox 12. To use it, I clamp my camera at the lens mount, on top of the platform, with the camera's lens viewing down through the stand's lens and onto the material below. In the summer, I use the sun as my light source and do copying out-of-doors. With the Reprox 12, the camera's focus is set on infinity, which permits you to copy an area of approximately two by two inches. There is a little blurring at the corners, due to the lens properties, but the perimeter of the negative area can be cropped out when printed on the enlarger. I

129

Fig. 10   A photographic copy of a *Tintype,* showing the
black art paper masking and the perimeter
distortion of the copy lens.

usually make masks of black art paper and place one of these over the small picture that I'm copying. This also helps crop out the distorted areas. The Reprox 12 can be used with practically all cameras, and it disassembles to form a pocket-sized package. This particular copying device is also used for photographing coins, stamps, insects and other small items.

On my first attempt at copying photographs I used a Bolsey thirty-five-millimeter camera. That was the first good camera I owned, bought second-hand from a friend in the army. At the same time I purchased the Reprox 12 copy stand, and I was more than pleased with most of my efforts and experiments. Of course, I was limited to a copy area of about two by two inches, so later I built a focal frame for myself from plans in a *Popular Mechanics* magazine (or other magazine of that type). With this home-made frame, I could copy an area of about nine inches by seven inches. I purchased the proper supplementary lens to accompany the focal frame and used it for larger photographs.

Copy stands and focal frames are actually variations of the same thing, the difference being that the copy stand is adjustable (varies the subject to lens distance) and can accommodate more than one strength supplementary lens. Affixing lights to it is also commonly done. Either can be constructed by a handy person. In the case of the focal frame, one focal

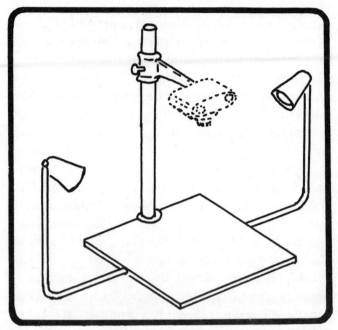

Fig. 11 A drawing of a simple copy stand and lights.

(BLACK ART PAPER)

Fig. 12   A drawing of a miniature copy stand with lens device.

frame is suited for one strength supplementary lens. The critical factor is the distance between lens and copy, and even this need not be too close: depth of field allows for some play in distance.

There are many good films for copying; Plus-X is what I frequently use. There are also some special films available for copying, such as reversal type film for making slides (positives) and Micro-file or Kodak High Contrast Copy film, for printed matter. Don't use foreign or special process films if you send your film out for developing.

If you have never developed your own film and you've never used an enlarger, it may seem like the magic of a witch doctor or alchemist, but it is actually not beyond the abilities of the average person. Developing film into negatives is a simple process for which you must follow simple rules. You load the film into a developing tank in a closet or other dark place, and then, out in the light, treat the film with three separate processes of chemicals: developer, stop bath and fixer. These processes are timed, and the water temperature is controlled; later you will wash the negatives, and dry them. For developing your own film you will need a closet or light-tight area, but not a complete darkroom. For printing or enlarging, however, a darkroom will be necessary. All Kodak film comes with a sheet of data, which includes suggestions on which developers to use. If and when you decide to develop and/or print your own copies, you can use any type of film whose processing you think you're able to handle. If you use Plus-X and other popular types of film, a photo lab can handle the processing and printing for you; just drop it off at the drug store, and expect to wait a week or so.

If you have copied newspapers or the large volumes of deed and other records, you won't be able to use the regular-sized prints from the local photo-developing service; you will probably want enlargements. It would be too costly to have these enlargements made by the professional labs, so you will need an enlarger and some kind of darkroom. Bathrooms make good darkrooms, but must be rendered light-tight by thoroughly covering the windows, door cracks and any other places where light might come in. Enlargers start at about forty-five dollars and go on up as high as you'll want to go. A seventy- or eighty-dollar enlarger will be about the right quality for your work. Let me warn you, if you do invest in this equipment, you'll get so much enjoyment working with it that you'll be using it for much more than to complement your genealogy work.

One aspect of photography may interest you, as well as help you in your search. You can send your thirty-five-millimeter negatives to one of the labs that advertise in photography magazines and have positives made from them. These can be viewed with a small slide viewer or shown enlarged with a slide projector. What you have done is make your own microfilm. If all you want are these positives, you can use Kodak Grain Positive or some other film of that type. The manufacturers of film are like soap manufacturers: they keep coming out with "new and improved" products. It's hard to keep up with their latest improvements.

For me, copying photos of ancestors and keeping these in a collection is almost as important as gathering data. In a way, it's easier to relate to pictures of individuals than to a paragraph about them. Of course, neither the photo nor the paragraph is completely accurate; both just provide glimpses into the life of that person. Nevertheless, these are the best efforts we can make toward discovering what our ancestors were like.

When my father's sister, Aunt Florence, was still living, she let me borrow two old family Bibles that were in her possession. One belonged to my grandmother Kelley, and the other to Grandmother Kelley's mother. The family record pages of both were rich with births, deaths, marriages and other family facts. There was little chance that either Bible would ever belong to me, so I chose the next best solution. I photographed both books. I took shots of their exteriors and of the family register pages inside. It isn't the same as owning the precious volumes, but it gives me something to keep and to look over every now and then. You may find it useful to photograph Bibles, diaries, old school books and other belongings that you feel played an important part in your ancestors' lives.

As you borrow and exchange old articles and photographs, remember one thing: do not attempt to clean up somebody else's old photographs, you could ruin them forever. About the safest method, which may only be slightly effective, is to rub them gently with a slice of fresh white bread to remove dirt. A soft gum rubber eraser (nonabrasive) may also be used lightly but *don't use chemicals*. For your own photographs, there are methods of cleaning with chemical substances, but don't take a chance with someone else's pictures. The Kodak booklet *Copying* gives some fairly safe cleaning instructions for various kinds of photographs.

I have just covered the camera, copying devices and procedures, and other pertinent photographic data. I have given you the high points to familiarize you with the main processes. Even if you have no inclination toward this phase of data gathering, you will still appreciate the knowledge of the various steps necessary to this broad art. Should you wish to do some copywork along with your researching, you must now purchase one of the booklets on copying at your local photography shop or write to one of the advertisers in the monthly photography magazines that carry close-up lenses and devices.

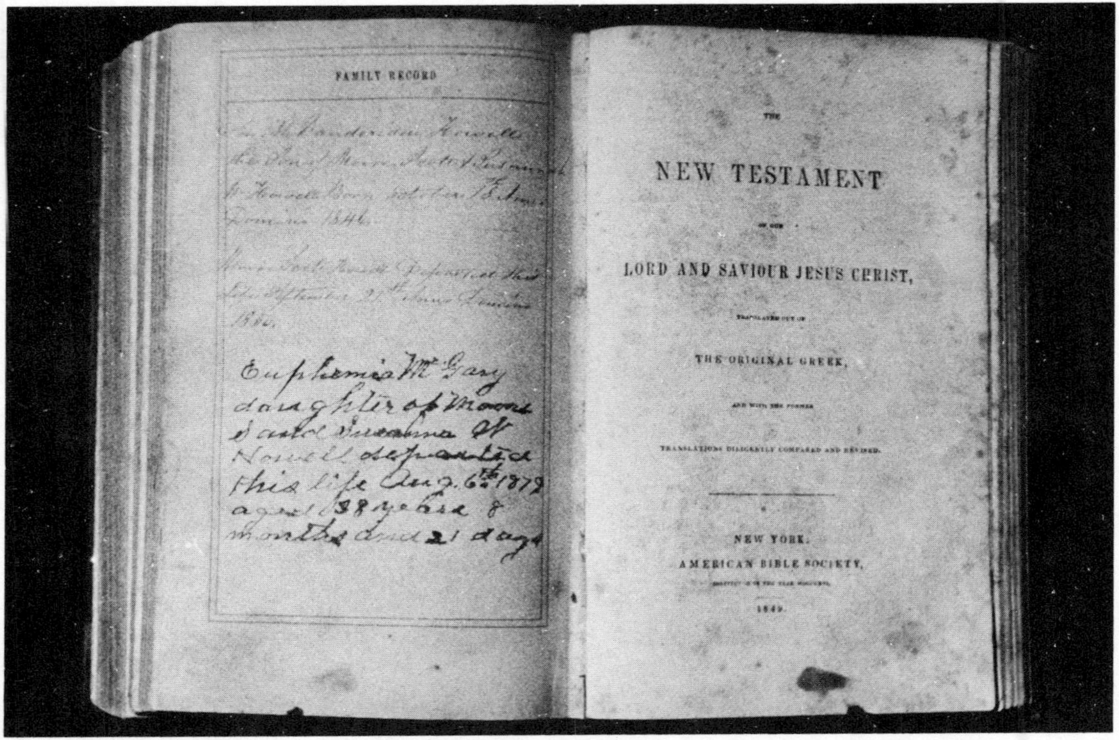

Fig. 13   A photograph of my great grandmother's Bible opened to the family record page.

As you first get into genealogy, probably the only use you'll have for a camera will be for prints of old gravestones and snapshots of your newly discovered kin. As you progress with your researching, however, you may feel a need for more of this chapter's content. After you learn to use the principles of photographic processing, don't be too surprised if you should temporarily be possessed by a feeling of euphoria. It may seem that you have unlocked some of the secrets of life.

12

Should You Publish?

From the beginning you may never have intended to have your family history printed. If you haven't changed your mind by the time you have finished your work, fine. Nevertheless, you should complete your history as nearly as you can; your children may some day want to have it printed, or your grandchildren may want to bring the collection of facts up to date and have it published. And there is always the possibility of a fire or other disaster destroying your only copies of collected information; your precious work would be gone, gone, gone! You'd better plan to make at least two copies of your work, and keep them in two separate places.

After you have collected all the pertinent information on one of your family lines and have it in good order, you may desire to have it printed. Are your contents complete enough to call it finished? I know that you could never find out everything about everyone belonging to your clan; the records and volumes across the nation are not totally complete themselves. There are bound to be brothers or sisters of ancestors back in the sixteen and seventeen hundreds, who are named but about whom you can find no other information. You may think you have found tie-ins, but you can't prove them using existing records, and you realize that speculation cannot be considered fact. How many babies and older children died and left no written record, we will never know.

As you must be starting to realize, your family history will *never* be complete. Your kin are marrying, having children, having grandchildren and dying; the process goes on and on, and new data are being written into the records, ad infinitum. For a "complete" history, this process would have to stop, and all the persons who are even remotely related to you would have to die. That's a horrifying thought; not to mention that as long as you live the work would not be complete, and after you died, who would conclude it? All you can do is make sure you have done everything possible to tie up loose ends before you consider "publishing."

And be aware that some day there will be a need for a revised edition, later another revision. After you have long been gone, someone else, possibly one of your direct line, may bring the work up to date and put out further editions.

What form should you put your work into in order to make it completely understandable and pleasantly readable? There are numerous ways that the finished history can be arranged. The first thing to do is visit your local public library and glance through the completed volumes of genealogies there, noting how they are arranged. Then look at your own personal needs. If you are satisfied that a finished work of only twenty-five or so pages is as much as you wish to compile and have printed, a simple narrative or story form will make a nice little booklet. Start with the earliest known ancestor and carry it through to the latest or newest members of the clan, allowing a paragraph for each member, his wife and children. Each child—with his or her spouse and children—will occupy a separate paragraph. Keep them in sections or chapters of family lines to make certain that someone else reading your volume will understand it and know which line everyone belongs to.

Normally, if you've been thorough and compiled data over a long period of time, you will have a considerably longer finished volume of one hundred to five hundred or more pages. You must use a numbering system of one kind or another to keep the many Johns, Sarahs and Williams identifiable.

Either go to your library and check over some of the published genealogies for numbering systems or devise one of your own.

One commonly used system begins with the earliest ancestor to whom you can prove a direct line; he is numbered 1. If you know that he or she had brothers or sisters, you can just name them. However, if you are going to carry the information of the lines down from these brothers and sisters, then you will have to give them numbers. In that case, your direct ancestor would not carry the number 1 unless he were the oldest of the family. From the oldest to the youngest the brothers and sisters would be designated 1, 2, 3, and so on.

If your direct ancestor were numbered 1, then his or her children would be numbered 11, 12, 13, and so on. Spouses of a numbered clan member are not numbered. If your ancestor married a cousin, then the spouse may carry a number from another line of the clan. The children of this marriage should be numbered from the husband's number: Harry Smith, number 13, married Ima Jones, number 51, and their children would be assigned numbers 131, 132, 133, and on. At the place in your history where the spouse is brought down from her parents, you would inform the reader that the children of that marriage are enumerated under Harry Smith, number 13, and refer to the page number where the family can be found.

For the usual marriages of unrelated couples, the children of clan member 11 would be 111, 112, 113, and so on, and the offspring of 12 would be 121, 122, 123, and so on. Realizing, of course, that many families in the early days were very large, you can only number the children through 9, and then you must substitute the alphabet for numbers; for instance, if ancestor 1 had twelve children, you would have children 11, 12, and on through 19, then 1A, 1B, and 1C. If clan member 136 had thirteen children, you would designate them 1361, 1362, and on through 1369, then 136A, 136B, 136C and 136D.

This is only one of the enumerating systems. This system is especially good in that if you later come up with a child you had not known about before, you will have no difficulty assigning a number. If after you have published your history, you come up with kinfolk that should be included, it would probably be better to assign unused numbers to the newly found kin than to reshuffle the numbers to accommodate the new ones. For example, let's assume that at the time of your first printing, you knew of only twelve children of Harry and Ima Smith and listed them as 131, 132, 133 and on to 13C. In ten years time, enough births and deaths of clan descendants had taken place to require another printing. Meanwhile, you learned that John and Ima had two children you knew nothing about. One, their second child, died at age three, and another, their fifth child, lived to marry and have three children. It probably wouldn't be advisable to revise all the Smith children to place the two previously unknown Smiths in their proper place. It would be less confusing to assign them numbers 13D and 13E. The children of 13E would then be given the numbers 13E1, 13E2, and 13E3.

Whether or not you will ever have your family history printed in a finished book or booklet form depends on many things. One essential factor is money. Can you afford to publish several hundred copies? You'll have to decide that, of course. But weigh it well: with luck, you may just about break even on the printing costs. This wouldn't include prior investments of time and money while gathering material.

Fortunately, there are many ways of "printing" your volume. You could simply type it up and have it run off on a duplicator or mimeograph machine by someone who has this equipment or you could purchase the machine and materials and do the job yourself—an impractical approach for all but the most wealthy. You would then have the necessary equipment in case more volumes were needed, but these materials might be old and outdated by the time you were ready to put out a revised edition (about ten years).

To have it done by a printer, who either uses old presses or newer offset method, would cost more but result in a beautifully finished product that would last for years. Perhaps if you are having three hundred to five hundred or more copies made, a printer would be your best bet.

Money is just one consideration when contemplating whether you should publish; I use the word "publish" loosely here, inclusive of all methods of printing or reproduction.

However, money is an important factor in the search for your ancestry. Like all the many extra aspects of researching that I have included in this book, the possibility of publishing your work depends on your finances and desires. If you are retired, or your income is small (regardless of your age), you must know your limitations and stay within them. Don't eschew sound judgment, and don't go in over your head. Enjoy this research work—any part of it—and don't get hurt. I have frequently mentioned finances, because this book will be read by a variety of people, whose incomes will vary widely. In this volume, I have tried to cover as many of the possibilities as I could, but you are best able to determine how deeply you can afford to go into it.

Now let me reverse my cautionary theme and talk about giving away your published works. Does that startle you? Many copies of your "published" works must be given away as complimentary copies; this should always be done. Who gets them? Your local library should get one, your state library should also, and probably the state library in the state where your clan first settled in this country. Certainly, any one of your kin who has done any amount of research for you should receive one as well. I don't mean the people you talked to or wrote to, and who replied with family stories and details on their line of the clan. They should feel rewarded by having their information entered into the volume. I am referring to any of your relatives who, without payment, went to their local library, courthouse or state library and dug out material for you. You are rewarding them for their efforts with a complimentary copy. Your immediate family you'll have to decide on, keeping in mind the large cost of printing and the desire to keep the purchase price of the volumes low enough to be salable.

That's it; you're on your own now. Get out there and dig!